C000143455

THE
CULTURE OF
ENGLISH
PEOPLE

Iron Age to the Industrial Revolution

N. J. G. POUNDS

CAMBRIDGE
UNIVERSITY PRESS

Published by the Press Syndicate of the University of Cambridge
The Pitt Building, Trumpington Street, Cambridge CB2 1RP
40 West 20th Street, New York, NY 10011-4211, USA
10 Stamford Road, Oakleigh, Melbourne, 3166, Australia

© Cambridge University Press 1994

First published 1994

Printed in Great Britain at the University Press, Cambridge

A catalogue record for this book is available from the British Library

Library of Congress cataloguing in publication data

Pounds, Norman John Greville.
The culture of the English people:
Iron Age to the Industrial Revolution / N. J. G. Pounds.
p.   cm.
ISBN 0 521 45099 3 (hc)
1. England – Popular culture – History   1. Title.
DA 110.P683   1994
942 – dc20   93-17826   CIP

ISBN 0 521 45099 3 hardback

For Liz and
her friends

CONTENTS

vii

ILLUSTRATIONS

TABLES

PREFACE

The author wishes to express his thanks to the many friends who have assisted him in the preparation of this book. In particular he is indebted to Dr Martin Millett of the University of Durham for his critical reading of the first three chapters; to Mrs E. L. Wetton for much sound advice, and to Mrs Christine North, Cornwall County Archivist, for her help with documentary sources. But errors and prejudices are all his own.

The colophons at the head of each of the twelve substantive chapters represent the 'labours of the months', in order, beginning with January at the head of chapter 1. They have been drawn from the late Anglo-Saxon manuscript British Library Cott. Jul. A. vi.

ABBREVIATIONS

AAG Bijd	*Afdeling Agrarische Geschiedenis Bijdragen*
Abh Preuss Akad Wiss	*Abhandlungen der Preussischen Akademie der Wissenschaften*
Actes Coll Int Dem Hist	*Actes du Colloquium International de Demographie Historique*
Agr Hist Rv	*Agricultural History Review*
Alc Club Collns	*Alcuin Club Collections*
Am Jl Leg Hist	*American Journal of Legal History*
Am Jl Soc	*American Journal of Sociology*
Am Mus Nat Hist	American Museum of Natural History
Ann Ass Am Geog	*Annals of the Association of American Geographers*
Ann Bret	*Annales de Bretagne*
Ann ESC	*Annales: Economies, Sociétés, Civilisations*
Ant	*Antiquity*
Ant Jl	*Antiquaries' Journal*
Arch	*Archaeologia*
Arch Ael	*Archaeologia Aeliana*
Arch Camb	*Archaeologia Cambrensis*
Arch Cant	*Archaeologia Cantiana*
Arch Jl	*Archaeological Journal*
Archt Hist	*Architectural History*
Ass Arch Soc, Repts Pap	Association of Architectural Societies: Reports and the Papers
Banb Hist Soc	Banbury Historical Society
BAR	British Archaeological Reports, Oxford
Beds Hist Rec Soc	Bedfordshire Historical Record Society
Berich Rijks Oud Bod	*Berichten van de Rijksdienst voor Oudheidkundig Bodemnonderzœk*
Berks Arch Jl	*Berkshire Archaeological Journal*
Brist Rec Soc	Bristol Record Society
Brit	*Britannia*
Brit Mus	British Museum
Brit Rec Assn	British Records Association
Bucks Rec	Records of Buckinghamshire
Bul Roy Soc Lund	*Bulletin of the Royal Society of Lund*
CBA Res Rept	Council for British Archaeology, Research Report
Cal Letter Books	*Calendar of the Letter Books of the City of London*, ed. R. Sharpe, London, 1899–1912

Cal Close R	*Calendar of Close Rolls*
Cal Pat R	*Calendar of Patent Rolls*
Cam Ant Soc	Cambridge Antiquarian Society
Camb Econ Hist Eur	*Cambridge Economic History of Europe*
Camd Misc	*Camden Miscellany*
Camd Soc	Camden Society
Cheth Soc	Chetham Society
Class Rv	*Classical Review*
Col Docts Inéd	Collection de Documents Inédits pour l'Histoire de France
Collns Hist Staffs	Collections for the History of Staffordshire
Cornw Rec Off	Cornwall County Record Office
Cur Arch	*Current Archaeology*
Cym Red Soc	Cymrodorion Record Society
Dev & C Rec Soc	Devon and Cornwall Record Society
Daed	*Daedalus*
Derb Arch Jl	*Derbyshire Archaeological Journal*
Deutsch Akad Wiss	Deutsche Akademie der Wissenschaften
Dev Arch Soc	Devon Archaeological Society
Dev Hist	*Devon Historian*
EcHR	*Economic History Review*
Ec Jl	*Economic Journal*
Ec Prat Ht Et, Civ et Soc	Ecole pratique des Hautes Etudes: Civilisations et Sociétés
Econ	*Economica*
Econ Geog	*Economic Geography*
EETS	Early English Text Society
EHR	*English Historical Review*
Encycl Brit	*Encyclopaedia Britannica*
Eng Dial Soc	English Dialect Society
Eng P-N Soc	English Place-Name Society
Ess Rec Off Pubns	Essex Record Office Publications
Ess Rv	*Essex Review*
Eth Slav	*Ethnographia Slavica*
Ex Pap Econ Hist	Exeter Papers in Economic History
Fed Fam Hist Soc	Federation of Family History Societies
Folk-L	*Folk-Life*
Folk Soc	Folklore Society
Gdn Hist	*Garden History*
Harv Theol Rv	*Harvard Theological Review*
Herts Rec Soc	Hertfordshire Record Society
Hist	*History*
Hist Childh Qu	*History of Childhood Quarterly*
Hist MSS Com	Historical Manuscripts Commission
Hist Techn	*A History of Technology*
Hist Wkshp	*History Workshop*
HMC	Historical Manuscripts Commission
HMSO	Her (His) Majesty's Stationery Office
JBAA	*Journal of the British Archaeological Association*
Jew Soc St	*Jewish Social Studies*
Jl Derb Arch Soc	*Journal of the Derbyshire Archaeological Society*
Jl Eccles Hist	*Journal of Ecclesiastical History*
Jl Ec Hist	*Journal of Economic History*

Jl Fam Hist	*Journal of Family History*
Jl Interdisc Hist	*Journal of Interdiscipinary History*
Jl Peas St	*Journal of Peasant Studies*
Jl Rom St	*Journal of Roman Studies*
Jl Roy Anthr Inst	*Journal of the Royal Anthropological Institute*
Jl Roy Inst Cornw	*Journal of the Royal Institute of Cornwall*
Jl Soc Arch Hist	*Journal of the Society of Architectural Historians*
Jl Soc Hist	*Journal of Social History*
Jl Wbg/Court Inst	*Journal of the Warburg and Courtauld Institutes*
Kent Rec Soc	Kent Record Society
King's Works	*The History of the King's Works*
Lancs Chesh Rec Soc	Lancashire and Cheshire Record Society
Lincs Rec Soc	Lincolnshire Record Society
Loc Pop St	*Local Population Studies*
Lond Rec Soc	London Record Society
LSE Mon Soc Anthr	London School of Economics Monographs on Social Anthropology
Med Acad Am	Medieval Academy of America
Med Arch	*Medieval Archaeology*
Med Arch Mon Ser	Medieval Archaeology Monograph Series
Med Hist	*Medical History*
Med St	*Medieval Studies*
Met Mag	*Meteorological Magazine*
Midl Hist	*Midland History*
Montg Collns	*Montgomery Collections*
Nat Mus Wales	National Museum of Wales
Nat Trust	National Trust
New Eng Hist Gen Soc	New England Historical and Genealogical Society
Norf Arch	*Norfolk Archaeology*
Norf Rec Soc	Norfolk Record Society
Northants Rec Soc	Northamptonshire Record Society
Notts Med St	*Nottingham Medieval Studies*
Occ Pap Loc Hist	Occasional Papers, Department of Local History, University of Leicester
Oxf Jl Arch	*Oxford Journal of Archaeology*
Oxf Rec Soc	Oxfordshire Record Society
Parl Pap	Parliamentary Papers
P & P	*Past and Present*
Pont Inst Med St	Pontifical Institute of Medieval Studies, University of Toronto
Pop St	*Population Studies*
Proc Brit Acad	*Proceedings of the British Academy*
Proc Dors NHAS	*Proceedings of the Dorset Natural History and Architectural Society*
Proc Prehist Soc	*Proceedings of the Prehistoric Society*
Proc Soc Ant Scot	*Proceedings of the Society of Antiquaries of Scotland*
Proc Suff Instd Arch	*Proceedings of the Suffolk Institute of Archaeology*
Pub Dugd Soc	*Publication of the Dugdale Society*
Qu Jl Roy Met Soc	*Quarterly Journal of the Royal Meteorological Society*
RAI	Royal Archaeological Institute
RCAHMW	Royal Commission on Ancient and Historic Monuments (Wales)

RCHM	Royal Commission on Historic Monuments (England)
Rec Bucks	Records of Buckinghamshire
Rec Econ Soc Hist	Records of Economic and Social History (British Academy)
Rep Res Com Soc Ant	Reports of the Research Committee of the Society of Antiquaries
Roxb Club	Roxburgh Club
RS	*Rolls Series*
Rv Nord	*Revue du Nord*
Sci Am	*Scientific American*
Seld Soc	Selden Society
Soc Geneal	Society of Genealogists
Soc Hist	*Social History*
Soc Med Arch Mon Ser	The Society for Medieval Archaeology Monograph Series
Som Arch	*Somerset Archaeology*
Som Lev Proj	Somerset Levels Project
Som Rec Soc	Somerset Record Society
Spec	*Speculum*
St Ch Hist	*Studies in Church History*
Suff Rec Soc	Suffolk Record Society
Sur Rec Soc	Surrey Record Society
Surt Soc	Surtees Society
Suss Rec Soc	Sussex Record Society
Tech & Cult	*Technology and Culture*
Thor Soc	Thoroton Society
Thor Soc Rec Ser	Thoroton Society Record Series
TLS	*Times Literary Supplement*
Trav Mém Inst Eth	*Travaux et Mémoires de l'Institut d'Ethnologie*
Tr B & G Arch Soc	*Transactions of the Bristol and Gloucester Archaeological Society*
Tr Birm Arch Soc	*Transactions of the Birmingham Archaeological Society*
Tr Cumb Westm AAs	*Transactions of the Cumberland and Westmorland Antiquarian and Archaeological Society*
Tr Cymm	*Transactions of the Honourable Society of Cymmrodorion*
Tr Ess Arch Soc	*Transactions of the Essex Archaeological Society*
Tr Hist Soc Lancs Chesh	*Transactions of the Historical Society of Lancashire and Cheshire*
Tr L & M Arch Soc	*Transactions of the London and Middlesex Archaeological Society*
Tr Newc Soc	*Transactions of the Newcomen Society*
Tr RHS	*Transactions of the Royal Historical Society*
Tr Roy Soc Trop Med	*Transactions of the Royal Society for Tropical Medicine*
Tr Worcs Arch Soc	*Transactions of the Worcestershire Archaeological Society*
Trav Mém Inst Eth	*Travaux et Mémoires de l'Institut d'Ethnographie*, Paris 1969
Urb Hist Ybk	*Urban History Yearbook*
VCH	*Victoria County History*
Wilts Arch Soc Rec Br	Wiltshire Archaeological and Natural History Society: Records Branch
Winch St	Winchester Studies, ed. Martin Biddle, Oxford
Yks Arch Jl	*Yorkshire Archaeological Journal*
Yks Arch Soc Rec Ser	Yorkshire Archaeological Society Record Series

Map of traditional counties, with abbreviations, as used in this book.

INTRODUCTION

Operationally defined, a culture is a constantly recurring assemblage of artefacts. To present the culture as a system, it is useful to consider not only the preserved artefacts, but the members of the society that produced them, the natural environment they inhabited and other artefacts (including the non-material ones such as language and projective systems) which they made or used.   Colin Renfrew

Every culture, every era exploits some few out of a great number of possibilities. Changes may be very disquieting, and involve great losses, but this is due to the difficulty of change itself, not to the fact that our age and country has hit upon the one possible motivation under which human life can be conducted.   Ruth Benedict

'Culture' is a word with many shades of meaning, all of them deriving in some way from its Latin root, *cultus*. Whether as a noun or as an adjective, *cultus* implied cultivation and a sense of growth, and, however used, 'culture' has always suggested a degree of sophistication and refinement. Today it can be taken to indicate people of education and taste as well as an assemblage of pots and artefacts from a prehistoric site. In the context of this book it is used to denote *the body of ideas which a people holds about itself and its environment, together with the tools and artefacts by means of which its members relate to one another and to the world which they inhabit.*

'Material culture', which was the subject of an earlier book,[1] denotes only the latter aspect, but it is a mistake, though one that is frequently made, to draw a distinction between them. It is impossible to separate a people's world, its *mentalité*, from the houses it built, the fields it cultivated and the rites it practised to ensure both that crops matured and the house remained secure. Culture denotes a spectrum of objects, artefacts, customs, rituals and beliefs, all interconnected, but in ways not always apparent either to the observer today or to those who lived their lives in the midst of that culture.

This book is concerned almost exclusively with traditional culture. This seems to be a convenient term for those cultures which prevailed in these islands before that sequence of events which is conventionally known as the Industrial Revolution. One cannot easily date the transition from pre-industrial cultures to post-industrial. That it began in the eighteenth century is probable, and most students would claim

Table I.1   *A schema of popular culture*

The imperatives of nature	Cultural response
1 Eating and drinking	a Types of food b methods of preparation c Rituals of eating d Forbidden foods
2 Shelter and relaxation	a Types of shelter b Domestic furnishing c Festivals and holidays
3 Communication	a Spoken language, dialect b Signs and gestures c Dress and costume d Story-telling, myth e Ritual
4 Sexual behaviour	a Courtship and marriage b Relations with family and kin
5 Birth and death	a Birth and child-rearing b Education, formal and informal c Treatment of sick and aged d Death and burial rites
6 Social and anti-social instincts	a Mutual assistance b Carnival and celebration c Aggression and modes of curbing it d Crime and punishment
7 Sickness and disease	a Folk medicine b Care of the sick
8 Religion and world view	a Animism and attitudes to the supernatural b Ritual and magic

that over much of this country traditional culture had either disappeared or was in retreat by the mid-nineteenth. All peoples share fundamental physical and emotional needs, and have broadly similar ways of satisfying them. We all, whatever our colour or creed and however far back in time we go, feel the need to eat, to sleep, to communicate, to defecate, to seek shelter from the elements. We all have sexual urges and aggressive instincts, and we feel the need for some 'rational' explanation of the world around us. This is part of our 'natural' behaviour. But the ways in which we satisfy these needs and compulsions differ from one society to another, and are part of our 'culture'. This relationship of 'nature' to 'culture' can be represented by a diagram (Table I.1).

This book is not concerned, except marginally, with the *natural* aspects of culture. They are not peculiar to any one people or society; they are common to humanity. It is the non-natural aspects of behaviour which distinguish one people, one culture from another. These are social in origin, and they are transmitted and perpetuated socially, and, like all social institutions, they can change both spatially and through time. The list of aspects of non-natural or cultural behaviour given above is not thought of as exhaustive, and each group is capable of endless extension, subdivision and refinement, but in a rough way it defines the scope of popular culture as conceived within the context of this book. Nor must the categories of cultural behaviour as listed here be seen as independent and mutually exclusive. They overlap, and, by and large, they constitute an interlinked whole, a rudimentary system. One communicates, not only in the modes listed in 3a–d, but also in the style of one's house, in the food one is seen to eat, the books one reads, and in one's familial behaviour. Sexual behaviour involves spoken language, gesture and dress and, to some extent, aggression. Sickness brings with it a multitude of folk-remedies, charms and magical rites, and the rituals once performed to ensure a bountiful harvest are interwoven with the physical need for relaxation and the urge to eat and drink more than the community could afford or the body needs.

Even within a culture not all individuals will be found to react in precisely the same way to any of the 'natural' urges, though intra-cultural differences will be slight compared with those between one culture and another. Members of a single family or of a particular community will be found to have more in common with one another than with members of different families and other communities. To some extent these similarities result from imitation, deliberate or otherwise. To a large extent they form part of the social inheritance which occurs within the home, the mother being most often the chief vehicle for the transmission of minor cultural idiosyncrasies. We can recognise localised cultural traits in styles of building and decoration, in costume and in dialect. Bernard Shaw's Professor Higgins was able to ascribe a certain speech pattern to Lissom Grove.[2] Few linguists, however, would claim such expertise, nor, indeed, would Shaw have expected it of them; he was only demonstrating with Shavian exaggeration how narrowly circumscribed, both socially and spatially, are cultural traits.

For convenience of exposition, culture is here divided into the material and the non-material. The division is, as has been suggested, arbitrary and unrealistic. There is a grey area within which objects were created – sculptures, standing stones, graffiti, even churches – as symbols of emotions and intellectual concepts. Figure 11.4 shows a sculptured boss found in an English parish church. What does it signify? Of course, it served as a keystone in a vault, but this purpose could have been served no less well if it had been left as a plain piece of stone. Clearly its sculpture was not functional; it was not used in the course of everyday life. But was it something more than the product of an artist who allowed free play to his imagination? Was it a symbol of some influence, benevolent or malign, or was it placed in the church for protection, just as a skull was set at the entrance to an Iron Age fort? Or did it represent the powers of evil which the church was called upon to resist and to overcome? Twentieth-century rational man, brought up on the concept that nothing should be accepted unless it can be verified, finds it difficult to adjust to traditional modes of reasoning.[3] The latter invents explanations and causes for phenomena, which thus become intelligible only as the consequences of its own a priori assumptions. We are continually meeting in traditional culture with modes of thought different from and often contrary to our own, but each having its own internal logic.[4] In no field is this more apparent than in medicine, for which a coherent system was devised with its own internal logic, but predicated on entirely erroneous premises. It is this which makes traditional patterns of thought so difficult for people of today to understand. Nevertheless, an attempt has to be made to get inside these earlier thought patterns, because, whatever we in this modern, scientific age may think, we have not entirely outgrown them. The debris of past systems of thought still lie strewn like archaisms through our patterns of thought and behaviour today.

Traditional cultures were always in process of change. They were transmitted orally or by physical exemplars. But what has been learned verbally is readily forgotten or remembered only in part. Physical goods decay, perish and have to be replaced. At each retelling and at every rebuilding, modifications, sometimes deliberate, more often unconscious, creep in, and the folktale, the myth, the ceremony, the artefact is slowly changed over the centuries. Distinct from such internal modifications of culture are the more radical and at times more revolutionary changes which arise from the impact of another culture. Changes may be imposed; old practices may be banned and new introduced as a result of cultural conquest. One thinks of the ways in which certain aspects of Indian or African cultures were banished at the will of their western conquerors. More often the impact of other cultures is slower and more subtle. Trade and travel make people aware of other ways of doing things and of different beliefs and customs. But rarely, perhaps never, does a society abandon one set of assumptions or one pattern of living for another. The human mind does not readily make such transitions.[5] More often the new is superimposed on the old; sometimes it is accepted only by one segment or 'class' of the society, and where the 'fit' is less than satisfactory, one is tailored to adjust it more or less to the other. This is the process of acculturation, which has been practised throughout history and never more so than today. The best example in the cultural history of Britain and, indeed, of most of western Europe, is the way in which Christianity adapted to, assimilated, or was absorbed by pagan Celtic beliefs and practices. Celtic spirits became or were assimilated to the saintly patrons of Christianity; pagan sites were adopted for churches; calendar rites, like the rituals of midsummer and midwinter, were given a Christian veneer, and continued to be celebrated in much the same way.[6]

Even in physical artefacts and structures, such as the house and its furnishings, there has always been change and development as need or opportunity arose. There was a random element, the consequence of some unforeseen happening or the free play of a craftsman as he worked with his materials. The grotesque may have no meaning beyond the expression of what went through the mind of an individual as he worked. What relationship his mental images bore to the culture within which he lived probably not even the craftsman himself knew. It is a mistake to read too much into the imagery and motifs employed, for example, by a medieval sculptor or artist. The erotic imagery which is frequently found in medieval churches and church furnishings must not too readily be accepted as 'fertility symbols', and accommodated to our own contemporary thought patterns as if this gave a kind of retrospective respectability to it. It may be no more than the simple result of a young man allowing his too fertile imagination to dwell on sexual fantasies.

But at the same time it would be wrong to deny that such imagery, whether carved, sculpted or painted, is devoid of meaning. It is a form of language, and the craftsman was attempting to communicate. He doubtless assumed that whoever looked at his handiwork received some kind of a message. Much of what he attempted to show diverged from the accepted or normative. It was intended to shock or to produce some kind of – perhaps pleasurable – excitement. The urge to shock or to send a frisson of excitement through the minds of others is part of our mental composition; it springs from our aggressive tendencies, which continue to find expression today. No longer can corbels, gargoyles and misericords be used to thumb the nose at society. Instead, the urge finds outlets on the inner sides of toilet doors, on blank walls, or in the London Underground. All cultures have, almost by definition, a very long history. they derive, changed though they may have been by internal mutations and by external acculturation, from their medieval and prehistoric past. Any culture can best be seen as consisting of superimposed cultural levels, a kind of 'layer-cake' in which the oldest cultural strata are also the lowest, surviving, disguised if not almost obliterated, in material structures or in the depths of the 'collective unconscious', as Jung termed it.[7] Here and there some element of the oldest cultural stratum rises to the surface and becomes visible, like a maypole raised in spring surrounded by the culture of modern suburbia, or the fires lighted in early November or on the eve of St John the Baptist, the longest day of the year.

Some fifty years ago Sir Cyril Fox published one of the most seminal books in the history of British archaeology and culture, *The Personality of Britain*.[8] In it he distinguished two parts of these islands, a 'highland' zone and a 'lowland' sone, with a boundary between them which ran from County Durham to Lyme Bay on the south coast (Fig. I.1). This line separated a predominantly hilly region of Palaeozoic rocks from a gentler region of Secondary and later rocks. These two regions, he argued, corresponded with two differing modes of cultural evolution. Simply expressed, his argument was that the bearers of outside cultural influences reached the Highland Zone often by sea and almost always in small numbers. Their impact was never sufficient to blanket or submerge the indigenous cultures. Instead they became assimilated. Elements of older cultures are today not only present, but conspicuously so in Highland Britain. Lowland Britain, by contrast, lay at the receiving end of a long series of invasions, from those who walked across the land-bridge which once existed with Europe to the more recent invasions of Anglo-Saxons, Vikings and Normans. Each wave was powerful enough to impress its own

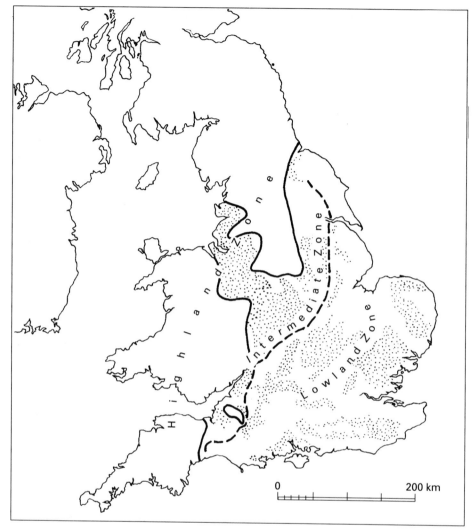

I.I Highland and Lowland Britain, as defined by Sir Cyril Fox, with intermediate Midland Zone added. Stippled areas were heavily wooded.

culture, and thus to mask or to destroy pre-existing cultures. Fox commented on the relative ease with which new civilizations are established in the Lowland Zone, repressing without necessarily obliterating those which had prevailed before. 'There is [thus] greater unity of culture in the Lowland Zone, but greater continuity in the Highland Zone.'[9]

The Fox model has not been without its critics. Some, including the present writer, would interpose a third zone covering the basically claylands of the English Midlands, between the Highland and the Lowland, with its own distinctive cultural history. But, however modified, the Fox model has been of incalculable importance to a cultural history of these islands. It gives a rational explanation for a phenomenon which will recur in the pages of this book, namely the persistence of early cultural traits in the Celtic west and north, and the greater degree of cultural homogeneity in the lowlands of the south and east.

Categories of material culture

The preconditions of human existence are, apart from procreation, a supply of food and the availability of shelter, and it is around these imperatives that much of popular culture has been shaped. In both there has been change and, one assumes, development. But change has not always been linear. There have been periods when culture lost something of its fine edge and sank back – during the late Roman and post-Roman periods, for example – only to make advances later and to regain the ground it had lost. But overall, there has been progress on a monumental scale during the past 2500 years. This is implicit in a comparison of the first and the last chapters of this book. But in traditional society there was little or no concept of progress as such; material things, it was supposed, were as they had always been and would continue to be (p. 408). The concept of progress was probably never entertained at a philosophical level before the time of Descartes or even of Condorcet, and it could not have reached ordinary people before it was thrust upon them by the rapid and fundamental changes of the nineteenth century.[10] Change, of course, they knew, but they probably conceived of it, if they paused to think at all, as fluctuations on one side or the other of a vaguely sensed norm, just as the harvest varied from good to indifferent to bad. The addition of a room to a cottage or the removal of the fire from the middle of the hall to a fireplace with a chimney built against the wall, a change of fundamental social importance, was not seen as progress; it was a simple alteration in domestic arrangements, necessitated by, perhaps, a growing family or a feeling that the central hearth was unsafe. It was progress because the change proved irreversible. But the peasant lacked any historical perspective that would have allowed him to perceive how different was his present from the past, and to project this change into the future.

The categories of material culture into which much of this book will be fitted can be summarised as:

1   *Food production*
Anthropologists distinguish three phases in the development of food production: primitive hunting and collecting, pastoralism, and arable husbandry. The first was without question the oldest, but the others should not be regarded as sequential forms. Though some societies in the past and even today pursued only one, most have practised all three in varying combinations. In Britain collecting survived into modern times, institutionalised as gleaning after harvest, and hunting, from being a fundamental form of food production, has survived only as a number of atavistic pastimes of negligible economic importance.

7

All societies have their traditional combinations both of foodstuffs and of the methods of preserving and preparing them. These may bear absolutely no relationship to food values and, often enough, little to the economy of labour. The long survival in England of the open-field system exemplifies this conservatism in traditional societies. This unwillingness to make changes may be due to an innate inability to make the mental adjustments that would be required, but it also springs from the fact that each aspect of food production was so integrated with other aspects of culture that change could not be accomplished without knock-on effects which society could not tolerate. There was, for example, resistance to new crops, like the potato, primarily because it could not be accommodated within existing agricultural systems.

2 Food preservation and consumption

Few foodstuffs, apart from fresh fruit, can be consumed in their natural state, and most occur seasonally and have to be preserved to supply out-of-season needs, just as a dog buries a bone and a squirrel accumulates nuts against the hardships of winter. Foodstuffs and the ways of conserving them are legion, and many were maintained even though agricultural and technical advances had made them superfluous. In no aspect of popular culture is conservatism more strongly marked than in the taste for food. The large number of regional and calendar foods still popular today is evidence of this.

3 Shelter

No climate is so benign that shelter from the elements is unnecessary. How protection was constructed must in the first instance have been constrained by the local availability of materials. The earliest forms of shelter in Britain must have been mainly of wood, since this was the most abundant and in some areas the only material available. Stone and brick then began to supplement and locally to replace timber. This may have been due in part to a growing shortage of timber, but in one of those developments without any firm basis in logic or economy, masonry came to have a prestige value, so that the more visible parts of a building might be in masonry and the rest timber-framed (p. 101).

The form or ground plan of a house was determined by social requirements, but once a satisfactory house-plan had been arrived at, it tended to be repeated on larger or smaller scale and with little functional change for up to a thousand years. In the eighteenth century the 'hall' house was gradually replaced by the symmetrical corridor plan, more suited to new aesthetic standards and social requirements (p. 107). The changes made in the traditional house were in the direction of greater comfort and privacy, and they reflected, by and large, an increasing level of real wealth and improving material standards. In the history of the vernacular house we can trace a kind of conflict between the desire to introduce new amenities without at the same time modifying its traditional plan.

4 *Domestic furnishings*

Even the most primitive forms of shelter required some kind of furnishing. At the least there had to be bedding, and by the end of the Middle Ages, when evidence first becomes fairly abundant, the equipment of an ordinary house included a bed, a table and some form of stool or seat. In the course of nearly a thousand years the whole pattern of domestic furnishing developed in line with the increase in wealth and the growing demand for comfort and privacy. But the forms assumed by furniture had been established at an early date, and, despite great improvements in quality and an increase it its volume and range, we have never wholly abandoned those adopted during the early Middle Ages. This persistence of form, despite changing material and an increasing elaboration of detail, is characteristic not only of furnishings but of many other aspects of material culture.

At the same time the appointments of the house – from cutlery to cushions – improved in line with the growing refinement of society. Glass supplemented or replaced window shutters; floor carpets were spread instead of straw, itself bringing about a change in manners, unless the carpet was to be fouled beyond use. The rough walls were hung with tapestries at the higher social levels and with painted cloths at the lower, until these were in turn replaced with wallpaper. In both plan and furnishings the house was, over the centuries, made into a home, a place where the family would desire to sit, to eat, to converse, not merely a place which offered a brief respite from work in the field or factory.

5 *Tools of the trades*

An ability to make tools in order to ease the tasks of producing food and building and furnishing homes had been demonstrated during the earliest phases of human existence. Man is a tool-using animal, and in this differs from the rest of the animal world. Indeed, the broad lines of human history can be traced only by the tools that were devised and used. The use of stone – in Britain chiefly flint and chert – was replaced, if only to a limited degree, by that of copper, then by bronze, and subsequently by soft or malleable iron and steel. A narrow range of tools, suited for working in wood and stone, had been invented by the late pre-Roman Iron Age, and remained in use with little modification until the Industrial Revolution. Figure 2.6 shows a number of tools in used in Roman Britain. One has no difficulty in recognising their shapes in the ironmonger's shop at the present day. The modern handtool differs from that of two thousand years ago chiefly in the material from which it is made. The replacement of soft iron by steel, and of carbon steel by alloy steels has created a revolution in the effectiveness of tools. But this revolution, if so slow a process can be so called, began early. Steel must have been an accidental product as a smith manipulated a bloom of soft iron on his hearth, alternately exposing it to a blast of air from his bellows and covering it with glowing charcoal. The act of discovery was the recognition that he had achieved something new and of value, and its repetition under what may be termed controlled conditions. An innovation of this kind might become widely adopted, or, on the other hand it might be ignored and its significance might go unrecognised, only to be rediscovered at a later date. 'Innovation remains', wrote Colin Renfrew, 'the least understood phenomenon in European prehistory, perhaps in culture history in general.'[11] Traditional society was not, in general, receptive to innovation, because it was so structured that it could not adapt to the social changes that would result.

Categories of non-material culture

Non-material culture consists of a body of belief, of attitudes to society and to the world, and of customs and practices which may have taken place at fixed intervals or at certain times of the year or even spontaneously. They were interrelated in so far as calendar customs were linked with religious belief, and social institutions like the family and the kindred were underpinned by practices which were overtly religious. Furthermore, as has already been pointed out, much of this non-material culture found symbolic expression in material objects. The symbolism met with in church planning and decoration and, to a lesser extent, in domestic, bridge the gap between the two aspects of non-material culture.

Non-material culture is an obscure area in so far as much of it never received any literary expression or explanation. In consequence its meaning has to be inferred from sculptured imagery or behavioural patterns, and much of it still remains obscure. This aspect of popular culture first gained widespread recognition in the sixteenth and seventeenth centuries, when it received extravagant attention from the reformers and Puritans. In their hostility they misunderstood and distorted the culture of the populace, effacing much of its visual representation. Elements of this can be projected back to the Middle Ages and even earlier, but the tendency was always to simplify and to conflate the elements of folk culture, so that a folk custom of early modern times may represent only a *Gleichschaltung* of rites which were at one time very much more complex:

> One cannot speak of the origin of popular culture any more than one can of the origin of *Homo sapiens*. There was no point of origin; no time at which they sprang into existence, fully formed like Athene from the head of Zeus.[12]

In looking at the evidences of past cultures one is apt to interpret them in the light of both modern stereotypes and of a modern *Weltanschauung*. The *sheela-na-gig* carved on a corbel in the parish church of Kilpeck (Hereford.) has been described as a 'fertility symbol'. By ascribing to it this more or less respectable function, Victorian prudery was able to gloss over the pure eroticism present in the sculpture itself (p. 391). It is highly unlikely that this was its connotation to those who created it in the twelfth century, but what it and others like it meant to their creators and to the people who used the church we have no clue. Whatever interpretations we may choose to give them, the manifestations of non-material culture may be grouped, if only for the convenience of discussion, under five heads.

Attitudes to the supernatural

All primitive peoples were in some degree animist. Their world was peopled with spirits, both benevolent and malevolent. The changes in nature, the growth and maturing of crops, life and death, all called for explanation, and this could be found only in the operation of a spirit world. The primitive mind cannot remain agnostic. Spirits were identified with natural objects like trees, springs of fresh water and rivers. If spirits were sensate beings, then they could be placated or cajoled into acting as people wanted them to do. It was but a short step from this to building shrines, temples and churches dedicated in some way to them, and also to the recognition that some people – priests, witches, 'cunning' men – had special powers to influence the spirits and thus to bring about miracles or acts of magic.

Such beliefs were both imprecise and localised. The primitive mind did not generalise. Deities were not universal; they were local, and each had its 'patch' and its specifically 'chosen' people. The biblical contest between the Israelites and the Philistines to determine which of their respective gods was the more powerful would not have seemed unusual; it could have been matched by arguments between neighbouring communities in the Middle Ages.

Spirits were imprecise in the sense that they could assume different forms as long as their attributes remained more or less constant. A well might have its 'spirit'; the well might be christianised and the spirit replaced with a compatible saint – and no one would notice the difference. Such continuities were common in popular culture. There was no limit to the shapes assumed by the spirit world in the popular imagination. There was an intense belief in it down to the seventeenth century. This belief was dented during the 'Enlightenment', but survived and, some would claim, is with us still in the fairies, the 'little people' and other such figures from the past.

Calendar customs

Closely related to a belief in the spirit world were calendar and related customs (p. 384). Their purpose was to propitiate the spirits which drove the seasons and brought about seedtime and harvest. It was not difficult for a propitiatory rite to turn into a kind of celebration and thus into an occasion for feasting and unrestricted jubilation. In this way calendar customs came to be cut off from their roots and to survive as independent celebratory occasions, as has happened with Mayday, Thanksgiving and Christmas rites today. At a less general level there were parochial and other local occasions which arose from the propitiary rites initiated in the first instance for local spirits and saints.

Psychological needs and their satisfaction

It is recognised in modern society that some intermission is necessary in the round of daily labour. Even God himself was conceived as tiring after six days of arduous and creative work. This need was recognised in earlier times by celebrations of saints' days, which became too frequent and numerous in the end to be economically sustainable. Sundays have, at least in Christian societies, been recognised as sacrosanct, and from the middle years of the nineteenth century part or all of Saturday has been added to Sunday to make a prolonged interruption of normal work. Such regular but short-lived breaks have, however, never been seen as adequate, and from early times there have been other occasions, more or less regular, when people attempted to escape from their lives of hardship and drudgery into a kind of fantasy world. This was 'carnival', a rite which neither the hostility of the church nor the misgivings of the state had been able effectively to end. It was a way in which the lower classes and the oppressed could openly flout and express their contempt for authority; it was an occasion for licence, for coarseness and vulgarity, for a 'world turned upside-down'. The psychological need for 'escape' is ever present, and for certain classes, then as now, this need is most readily met by vulgarity and vandalism, because these are the easiest ways of expressing defiance towards authority.

Social organisation

The family has, throughout most of history, been the essential building-block of society, and attempts to eliminate its role, as in classical Sparta or among the American Shakers, have always in the long run failed. Of the early organisation of the family, whether nuclear or extended, whether autonomous or absorbed within a kinship, little can be known with any degree of certainty. One assumes that it was in some way related to the economy, to the methods of creating and distributing goods. Within the historical period the role of the family has varied greatly. In the Middle Ages emphasis was rather on community and kinship than on the family, as, for example, in the method of law enforcement known as frankpledge. In modern times the role of the kin has disappeared, but not without leaving certain markers in institutional arrangements, and a sense of community has long been in decline. The nuclear family has thus come to the fore as the primary unit of human organisation.

The family was hedged around by restrictions and taboos. Rituals marked the successive stages in family life from baptism, through marriage, to death and burial. These have changed comparatively little during the Christian period. Within the family, however, there have been changes in its cohesiveness, in relations between parents and children and between the nuclear family and the kin and community in which it found itself. Very broadly, one might say that the cohesiveness of the family varied inversely with the strength of the community and the power of the state.

Population, health and physical well-being

Lastly, related in some way to almost all categories of popular culture, both material and non-material, are attitudes to population, health and hygiene. The necessity of marriage and the desire for children are basic features of all traditional societies. The biblical injunction to 'be fruitful and multiply' was one which they could wholeheartedly accept. The need for large families was brought home to them by the high mortality levels among the young. Ritual and magic were used to achieve fertility and to protect the young. Yet there was a kind of ambivalence towards children. Their vulnerability was a fact of life; no one was surprised at the death of children, and, it would seem, few felt any deep grief. The family meant so much more than any individual within it.

Until the medical revolution of the later years of the nineteenth century people could do little either to promote or to preserve life. The symptoms of some diseases were readily recognisable: plague in the later Middle Ages and early modern times, smallpox, typhus and venereal diseases in the seventeenth and eighteenth centuries, and cholera and consumption in the nineteenth. But their etiology was unknown, and without any theory of pathogens there could not be even the beginnings of an effective medical science. Practitioners had been trained in the doctrines of Hippocrates and Galen, as mediated through medieval writers like Avicenna. The whole system of medical thought was logical within itself, but was based on false postulates and was totally wrong and ineffective.

Beside the official medicine of the universities was the folk medicine of the herbalists and 'cunning' men, some of whom, in their own empirical way, had stumbled upon remedies of some significance, and the far more extensive world of magic. The latter ranged from incantations and charms to pilgrimage and prayer. Unless one believes in the power of auto-suggestion and self-fulfilment, these remedies must seem to us to be totally ineffective. Society strove hard to find cures for its afflictions, but only to a very limited degree in folk medicine did it achieve any success at all. Traditional societies compounded their problems by their ignorance of the nature of infection. In their casual attitude to personal hygiene, their failure to establish any adequate sanitary system, and their tolerance of vermin and bodily infestation, they went far towards creating the high mortality against which they tried to protect themselves. The end of traditional medicine, if indeed it has ended even now, came later than that of most other aspects of traditional culture, because it was more dependent than the rest on experiment and a scientific attitude to the natural world.

These, then, are the structural categories of the material and intellectual culture of traditional societies, as described in this book. The diagrammatic model on page 2 attempts to show them and their interrelationships. Many aspects of popular culture are either omitted from this book or are given scant attention. There is, for example, little reference to clothing and fashion, important though the latter was to some levels of society. Nor is there any discussion of traditional music and dance, significant though they were in popular rituals and entertainment. The reason lies, in part, in the lack of space, but more in the inability of the author to cope with materials so far removed from his central interest. More serious is the omission of any discussion of language and dialect. To any linguist speech is an important, perhaps the basic aspect of culture. In any form of communication the medium is an essential part of the message that is transmitted. In this, too, the author must plead lack of both space and competence.

Culture, popular and élite[13]

Certain observations of a general nature are called for. This book is specifically about popular culture. A distinction should be drawn, in theory at least, between élite culture and popular, between that of the aristocratic and wealthy classes on the one hand, and that of the masses on the other. There was never any clear-cut line of demarcation between them. They were parts of a spectrum, across which individuals moved and ideas and practices flowed. The upper classes had, by definition, wealth and leisure; they were under no obligation to work continuously in order to live, and they had freedom to indulge themselves, to travel and to assimilate new ideas and elements of other cultures.[14] Social innovation, as distinct from mechanical innovation and invention, originated as a general rule among the upper classes. From there it percolated downwards to the gentry, the yeomen, the husbandmen and craftsmen. The reasons were, on the one hand, the increasing real wealth of the middle and lower classes during the later Middle Ages and following centuries and their desire for greater comfort and convenience, and, on the other, the social emulation that arose among them. Cultural goods drifted slowly down the social scale, becoming in some instances trivialised in the process, as imitations and surrogates began to be mass-produced to satisfy the demand of those who could not afford the real thing.

Was there, one may ask, any corresponding upward movement of cultural 'goods'? In modern society, of course, there is. 'Pop' music and 'pop' art have all climbed socially from the cultural basement. But it is difficult to point to any such development in traditional society, other than, perhaps, the refinement of traditional popular songs and dances. The waltz, it should be remembered, derived from a peasant dance, the Ländler. The movement of culture, in the sense of refined or sophisticated living, was almost always downwards.

The same can be said of manners. One has only to read such manuals as those written in the later Middle Ages to instruct young aristocrats in how to conduct themselves at table and in the presence of their elders to appreciate the coarseness of the times and the attempts made at the higher social levels to introduce a degree of refinement[15]. In the seventeenth and eighteenth centuries, foreign and especially French influence became marked, largely, it would appear, through travel, and again it was the upper classes which first experienced this influence.

Lastly, cultural traits were spread spatially as well as socially. Repeatedly we find that a particular characteristic of vernacular architecture or of church decoration or a particular food or folk custom has a narrow geographical distribution. This may have been due to adaptation to the physical conditions of the local environment, such as climate, terrain or building materials. Or it may be due to that streak of human irrationality which makes some people imitate their neighbours and leads others to be assertively different. There is little logic in the growth of popular culture. It stems from millions of decisions made by millions of people over thousands of years, not all of which might seem in retrospect to have been either sensible or desirable.[16] Ideas were conflated, customs confused, symbols rationalised. It might seem that each generation imposed its own interpretation on the culture it had inherited, and in doing so removed it yet further from its primitive roots. How far back can these roots be traced? The answer must be to the earliest recorded phases in human history. But a line has to be drawn, and in this book we begin with one of the earliest societies whose culture is known to us in any detail, that of the pre-Roman Iron Age. And within the disparate cultures of Iron Age Britain we turn to one particular society which lived on the chalk downland of northern Hampshire between the sixth century BC and the second.

CHAPTER 1

THE VIEW FROM DANEBURY

... The true centre of a people's interest and passion can be judged by the nature of the buildings to which they will devote most labour and most material. With these Iron Age tribesmen it was not ancestral tombs, not temples, to which they showed this passion but military fortifications.   Jacquetta Hawkes

Danebury is a hilltop amid the rolling chalk downland of northern Hampshire, and, like many such hills in Wessex, it is crowned by the banks and ditches of a prehistoric settlement. Danebury is no larger, no better preserved than dozens of such hillforts in southern Britain (Fig. 1.1). What makes it different from others is that it has been excavated, thoroughly if not completely, using the most up-to-date archaeological techniques.[1] The result is that we know a very great deal about the people who cut the ditches, built the ramparts, and erected their huts within the security which they offered. We can handle the tools they used; we can walk the fields they cultivated; we can, up to a point, understand how they tilled the land and evaluate their food supply. In short, archaeology reveals much of the material culture of these distant people.

But there is much that the excavation of Danebury does not tell us, and there are many subjects that are only faintly illuminated. We know little of the social structure of its inhabitants, and almost nothing of their customs, cults and religious beliefs. On the lower ground below the hillfort there lay a series of small settlements, some of them in isolation; others in groups; many protected by a bank and ditch (Fig. 1.2). These were farms, and each in all probability represented a large or extended family. How did the farmsteads relate to the fort? Did their inhabitants keep some part of their possessions in it and resort to it in emergency? Was the hillfort the focus of religious observance, a cult centre, and the seat of political power for an extensive area, including the scattered settlements in its vicinity? Was it, in short, the 'central place' for this area of downland? The answer to these questions must be a qualified 'yes', but this is only implicit in the archaeological record; there are no specific answers. On the less tangible aspects of culture our knowledge is even less adequate, and many of our assumptions arise from the practice of projecting back into this pre-literate age the institutions and beliefs of a later and better documented period.

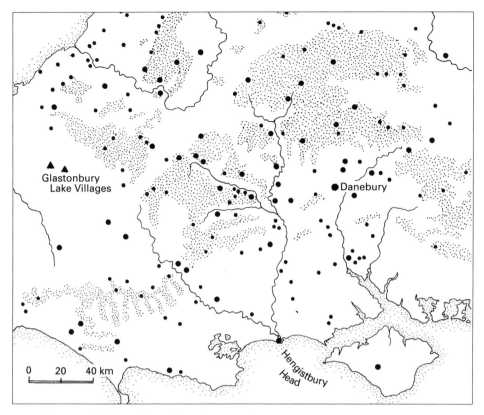

Glastonbury
Lake Villages

Danebury

0 20 40 km

Hengistbury
Head

1.1 Iron Age hillforts of central Southern England. Based on *Map of Southern Britain in the Iron Age*, Ordnance Survey, 1976. Stippled area is above 500 feet (152m).

The age of Danebury has been assessed with a fair degree of certainty. The site was settled and the first ramparts built in the middle of the sixth century BC, and was continuously occupied until about 100 BC. During this period buildings were erected, decayed and were renewed. The ramparts and ditches were enlarged and strengthened, until, for reasons which we can only surmise, Danebury was abandoned (Fig. 1.3).

People lived within the ramparts of Danebury in round huts, their vertical sides made either of woven hazel wattle or of strips of oakwood set vertically in the ground. This we know because their imprint in the soil has survived. Roofs, however, have vanished without trace, and one can only assume that they were conical in form, supported by posts, because this is almost the only way to roof a circular space, and thatched with reed or straw. They varied in size, but most were from 5 to 10 metres in diameter, rather like the bell-tents, once favoured by the British army. How these huts were used is more obscure. Were they only for sleeping and cooking, as shown by their charred surfaces, or were specialised activities carried on in them? This again the material record does not say, but an

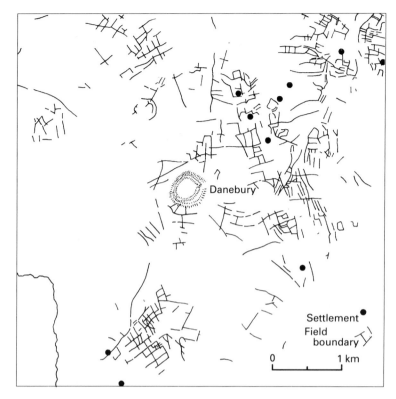

1.2 Farm settlements on the slopes below Danebury hillfort. After B. Cunliffe, *Danebury*.

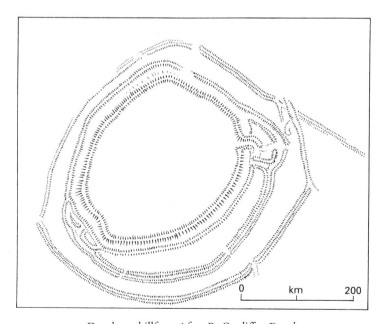

1.3 Danebury hillfort. After B. Cunliffe, *Danebury*.

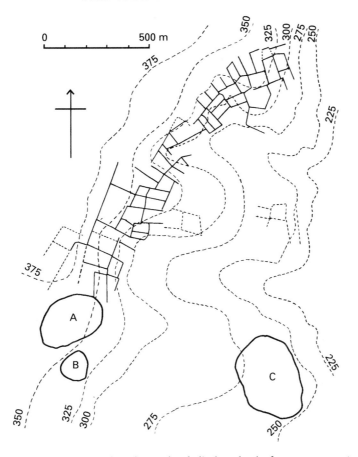

1.4 Iron Age field-systems. These lie on the chalk downland of Dorset, near Pimperne.

answer is important, because only in this way can an estimate be formed of the size of the community which lived here.

The inhabitants of Danebury practised agriculture. Their small, squarish fields lay over the slopes below the fort (Fig. 1.4), and were tilled with wooden ploughs drawn by cattle, of the kind commonly known as ards (Fig. 1.5). These did little more than scratch the surface, but the light downland soil lent itself to this form of cultivation. Their crops consisted of wheat and barley, which must have made up the greater part of their food supply, together with some animal products. The corn was ground in hand-querns, consisting of a round base with a flattened, cone-shaped surface, and a 'runner' which turned over it and pulverised the grain (Fig. 1.6). The material of which the querns were made had to be slightly rough or porous, and there were few sources of stone in southern Britain, and none near Danebury which had these qualities. Quern fragments excavated at Danebury were found to be of Greensand, probably brought from the Weald. Indeed, quernstones were among the few commodities which had to be imported into this area.

19

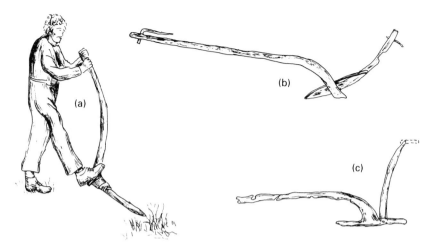

1.5 Ards: (a) spade-ard; (b) crook-ard. These were found in Danish bogs, but those used in southern Britain would have been broadly similar. For comparison (c) shows a caschrom or 'foot-plough', as used in remote areas of Scotland in modern times.

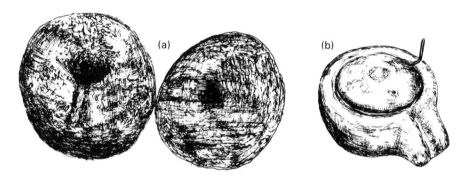

1.6 Quernstones from Danebury. (a) The stone on the right is the 'runner', with a hole for the corn. The groove in the left-hand stone is for the discharge of the pulverised grain. (b) A hand-quern seen by the author in the Auvergne.

Meat was eaten, and probably also dairy products of one kind or another. Sheep were the most numerous of domesticated animals, to judge from the frequency of their bones, and they may have been grazed over the stubble of the cornfields, where their droppings would have contributed what little nutrients these thin soils ever received.

Cattle were reared, and were used for drawing the plough and doubtless also for dragging timber from the valley woodlands for the construction of huts and ramparts. Their bones show signs of butchering, so it can be assumed that their meat was eaten, and it is likely that their milk was consumed, but in what form we do not know. Running eastwards from Danebury is a long, sinuous earthwork, too slight to have had any military value, and similar banks have been found at other

1.7 A grain-storage pit: after S. Piggott in *Roman and Native in Roman Britain*. Such pits were largely confined to the chalk and other areas of well-drained soil.

settlements in the region. These were probably built as a means of restraining or coralling animals and of so guiding them towards the fort.

In all societies and at all times the storage and preservation of foodstuffs has presented difficulties. Grain in an agricultural society had to be kept from one harvest to the next, and it was doubtless desirable also to keep other commodities, such as milk, which are seasonal. The archaeological record does not say whether the Danebury people made cheese, which has a much longer 'life' than milk, but we know how they stored their grain. The ground within the ramparts is pock-marked with pits, cut into the chalk. Some have vertical sides and flat floors; others broaden as they become deeper. Whatever uses the former were put to, the latter were without question used for storing grain. Such pits, if well sealed to exclude the air, could hold grain in an eatable and germinable condition for a very long time (Fig. 1.7). They were found to contain human and animal remains, which appear to have been placed there in some ritual fashion. Cunliffe relates this to the need felt by the Danebury people – and others – to ensure that the seed (for the stored corn would have included seed) would germinate and give a productive harvest.

It was a self-sufficient society that lived at Danebury. It produced its own food, with the exception of salt, and most of the tools which it used were made locally. Crafts were well developed and enough products have survived to give some insight into the material culture. Most abundant, as on prehistoric sites generally, are broken pottery sherds. Ceramic ware is eminently breakable, but almost indestructible. Over a period of five centuries vast quantities of broken pots were accumulated, disposed of in ditches or abandoned storage pits, or just thrown out to be gathered by today's field-walker. Most had been made locally from clay and brickearth, taken

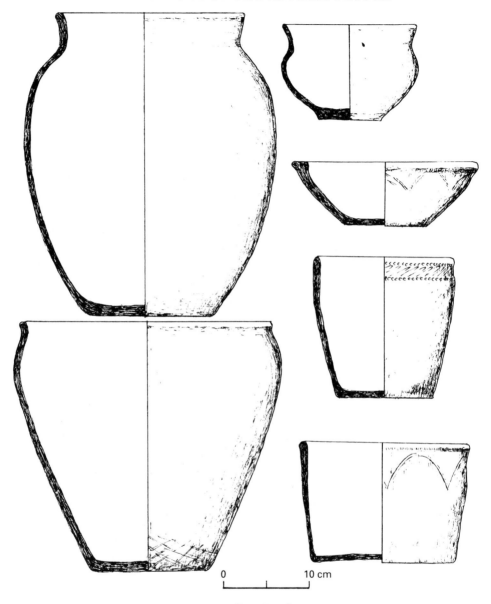

0   10 cm

1.8 Pottery from Danebury.

from the nearby valleys and 'tempered' with sand or finely ground flint. The pots had been shaped by hand; there is no evidence for wheel-thrown pottery before the last stages of the occupation of Danebury. Usually a pot was built up by coiling a long strip of clay into the required shape. It was then smoothed by hand, wiped clean with a piece of leather or a bunch of grass, and left to dry. Pots were then arranged in piles and covered with fuel, which was ignited and the pots left until they had become hard and brittle (Fig. 1.8).

22

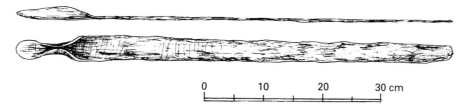

0   10   20   30 cm

1.9 A currency bar: after Sir Cyril Fox, *The Personality of Britain*.

Some form of decoration was frequently added before burning in the form either of thumb-prints around the rim or of shallow scratches on the body of the pot. These contributed nothing to its functional value. They were wholly decorative, and are an early example of the human tendency to elaborate, to turn a functional object into an aesthetic experience. Decorative motifs tended to become traditional within a society and were modified only slowly. Some such motifs display a regional character, and their distribution helps to define a 'culture area'.

Most of the pots conform to one of two simple patterns. They were either shallow bowls, probably used for holding food or for drinking, or larger vessels with wide open and sometimes everted rims. The latter were used for storing food such as cereals and perhaps nuts and berries. In each inhabited hut there must have been two or three such pots, whose broken sherds were in the end added to the mounting pile around the site.

Pottery may be to us the most conspicuous of the crafts practised at Danebury, but it was very far from being the only one. Metals were worked, wool was spun and woven, leather was tanned, and wood was worked with the help of tools which have a surprisingly modern look. In the conventional chronology of prehistory Danebury belonged to the middle and later phases of the Iron Age. The practice of smelting iron-ores and making tools, weapons and ornaments had first appeared in Britain some two centuries before the earliest constructions at Danebury. Ores of iron were widely diffused, but were small in quantity and poor in quality. They were extracted from small bell-pits, smelted with charcoal on a hearth, and thus reduced to a 'bloom' of soft iron. Hammering reduced the bloom to manageable shape, and, in the process, expelled some of the slag which it contained. In the end, the blooms were reduced to long strips, with 'handles' forged at one end, presumably for convenience of carrying (Fig. 1.9). These have come to be known as 'currency bars' in the mistaken view that they were used as a medium of exchange or a means of storing wealth. A hoard of such bars was found buried beneath the floor of one of the Danebury huts. Where they had been made we cannot tell; perhaps in the Weald of Sussex or of Kent, where an iron industry remained active into the eighteenth century. Blooms or bars of iron were worked up within Danebury itself into tools, weapons and decorative goods. The output of iron ware increased during the period when Danebury was occupied, and with it the skill of the smiths and the quality of their products.

23

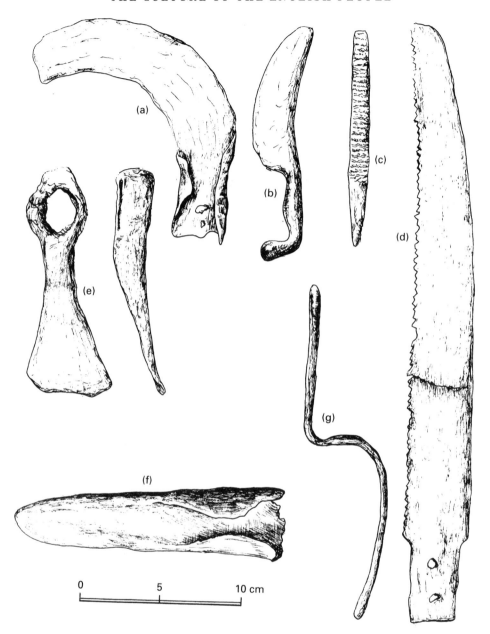

1.10 Tools from Danebury; these were of soft iron: (a) reaping hook, (b) chopper, (c) file, (d) saw, (e) adze, (f) tip for plough-share, (g) latch-lifter.

The soft iron that came from the bloomery could be forged with relative ease, but its softness meant that it did not easily take or hold a cutting edge. The addition of a small proportion of carbon – carburising, as the process is called – had the effect of making the iron harder and nearer to steel in its chemical and physical properties.

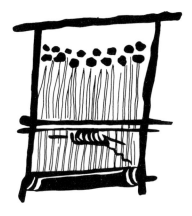

1.11   Warp-weighted loom; after a classical Greek painted pot.

Iron Age peoples discovered, entirely empirically and without any concept of the metallurgical processes involved, how to carburise soft iron and even to temper the steel produced. The result was the production of very effective cutting tools: sickles and knives, made to be fastened on to wooden hafts; tips to plough shares; woodworking tools like saws, chisels, gouges and the adzes used to dress massive timbers (Fig. 1.10 b, d, e). Handtools are today sharper and more refined than those of 2500 years ago, but the *forms* they assume and the uses to which they are put show little change.

By the time that Danebury had come to be occupied iron had for many purposes replaced bronze which had hitherto served for tools and weapons. It was harder and, if properly carburised, could take an edge far sharper than any bronze tool. But bronze was more easily made than 'steeled' iron. It was an alloy of copper and tin, though other elements were usually present. These metals could be obtained from south-western Britain, and smelting them called for temperatures considerably lower than those necessary for smelting and refining iron. Bronze, furthermore, could be melted and run into moulds; it was to be another 2000 years before temperatures were reached that were high enough to do the same with iron. So bronze continued in use, though not for weapons and cutting tools, in the decorative metalwork for which the later Iron Age was noted.

The large numbers of sheep which grazed over the downs provided milk and meat, but were especially important for their wool. Spinning and weaving were practised but the perishable nature of both tools and products means that they are far from prominent in the archaeological record. Sheep at this early date had not been bred for their wool, which was, in fact, more like hair. It was, nevertheless, combed and spun on a spindle and was then woven on a simple warp-weighted loom (Fig. 1.11). The cloth may then have been dyed with vegetable dyestuffs. But only spindle-whorls, loom-weights and weaving-combs, used to press the weft into place, survive to give some measure of the scale of the prehistoric cloth industry (Fig. 1.12).

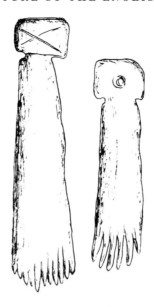

1.12 Bone weaving-combs from Danebury.

Skins and hides were also products of animal rearing. It must be presumed that they were tanned, perhaps with oak bark, and made into utensils and articles of clothing. Leather is preserved in the wet environment of a bog, but in the dry soil of the Hampshire chalk it perished rapidly, and the extent of the use of leather constitutes one of the gaps in our knowledge of the material culture of Danebury.

Animal bones were also used as tools. Slivers of bone served as awls; they were pierced with an 'eye' and used as needles, evidence, if any were needed, that cloth was sewn to make clothing. Flatter pieces of bone were cut to make the combs used in weaving, though their use for combing the hair – the Celts were notoriously vain – cannot be excluded.

The Celts were accustomed to adorn themselves with dyestuffs and to wear jewellery on a scale not met with again for many centuries. Among the finds at Danebury were bracelets and beads of bone, glass and Kimmeridge shale, a black rock from the Dorset coast which lent itself to carving and polishing. There were torques to be worn around the neck and rings of copper and bronze for the fingers, many of them engraved with the spiral motifs which were characteristic of Celtic art.

Archaeology is concerned mainly with material culture. It can tell us directly very little about how these people organised their lives and viewed the world. The existence of large earthwork forts implies some controlling hand, some hierarchical organisation of society and of labour. Were these constructions the product of forced or slave labour? Did the local chiefs live in them? Did they serve as refuges in time of danger for the people of the region? And did the immense number of storage pits represent the accumulation of food for use in emergency? To none of these questions are there certain answers. Nor can we know and understand the cults that may have been practised here. The claim that one set of post-holes represents a temple may be likely but it is not certain. There are no written sources, and it is only through the physical objects that they have left that we can penetrate the minds of earlier peoples. Julius Caesar wrote an account of the religion and religious practices of the Gauls, but these were seen through Roman eyes, and his account may have borne little relationship to those of the Iron Age Celts of Wessex.[3] One assumes that the gods of the Celts were local spirits, inhabiting woods and springs and representing some form of life-giving force. They were to be revered, placated, appeased, called upon for help. Caesar ascribed some sacerdotal role to the druids, who appear to have been a caste of 'cunning' men, supposed to have a powerful influence with the deities. But the concept of white-robed elders, executing elaborate and mystical rituals around oak trees, like some prehistoric freemasonry, must be dismissed as the product of modern romanticism. Yet there were, in all probability, shrines, sanctuaries, holy places, for these are the paraphernalia of animism. But what form they took we just do not know.[4]

One widespread practice of the Iron Age Celts, though not actually identified at Danebury, was the cult of the human head. Celtic warriors removed the heads of their victims, just as North American Indians took their scalps, and carried them back to their fortress homes. There is good evidence that they were often exhibited, but whether as a mark of prowess, threatening symbols to their enemies, or as some subtle way of assimilating the strength of the enemy to themselves, we cannot possibly tell.[5] But the cult of the head survived in much of Europe that had once been subject to the Celts. One is even tempted to suppose that this element in their culture lasted into the Middle Ages, deprived of its more violent aspects and in some way assimilated to Christianity (p. 395).

Cult practices were immensely complex, and the fact that they were probably individual to each tribe or region makes their interpretation especially difficult. Burial practices often shed light on cults and ceremonies, but at Danebury there is all too little evidence of human burials: little more than a few skeletons, some of them dismembered, tossed into disused storage pits. Some animals, notably the horse and the dog, had been buried with some ceremony, but whether these were propitiatory offerings or creatures sent to accompany the deceased to another world we have no means of knowing. Not until the early Middle Ages is it possible to study human inhumation practices, and it would be rash indeed to think that what happened then bore any close relationship to burial practices in the Iron Age.

Danebury and its neighbours

Danebury was but one of many such hillforts to be found on the hills of southern Britain. Most were roughly contemporary with Danebury itself, and probably had a broadly similar culture.[6] Indeed, it is possible that each was the focal point, the central place for some kind of tribal territory. If, then, we have a network of such strong points, each a local centre of power, we may ask what were the relations between them. The strong defences suggest that the Danebury people lived in some danger. The ramparts were renovated and strengthened at intervals. At one stage the east gate appears to have been burned, and stores of slingstones, ready apparently for the defence of the fort, have been found. This condition of imminent hostility is confirmed by Roman writers, who described a state of almost constant warfare among the Celts. These reports may have been exaggerated, but the multiplicity of hillforts points without question to a sense of insecurity.

What, then, could have been the motives for inter-tribal warfare? The land was not too densely populated; there was, on the fringes of the chalklands, abundant heath and forested land, and with their iron tools the Celts could, if need be, have cleared it for settlement and cultivation. It appears, rather, that warfare was part of their culture, of their world-view. The Aztecs of Central America, when conquered by the Spaniards in the early sixteenth century, were continuously at war with their neighbours, but not for land or resources; their warfare had no economic motivation. It was for victims to sacrifice to their tribal gods on the pyramid altars of Tenochtitlan. Could the Iron Age Celts have fought their wars just to acquire heads to adorn their gates and homes, to add the vital spark of other peoples to their own?

Yet the Danebury people must at times have lived at peace with their neighbours. They traded with them, and thus acquired the quernstones, the currency bars and the Kimmeridge shale, which they could not have produced within their own tribal area. But their trade may not have been commercially based. Their frequent raids and skirmishes are not incompatible with 'gift-exchanges' – a kind of primitive diplomacy such as Malinowski found among the Trobriand islanders earlier in this century.

In the Wessex region there were also communities which do not appear to have been organised for war. Not far from Danebury, on the downs to the south-west of Salisbury, an excavation scarcely less important than that of Danebury itself, was carried out just before the Second World War by Gerhard Bersu.[7] He had identified a prehistoric settlement site from aerial photographs, and on digging it, found evidence for a large, round hut, its roof doubtless conical in shape, supported near the centre by four massive posts as well as by a double ring of more slender posts. The whole was set in an enclosure with a palisade adequate to restrain animals (Fig. 1.13). Stretching away over the downs were sinuous linear earthworks, similar to that found near Danebury and probably serving a similar purpose. There are many such settlements scattered over the Wessex downland, apparently isolated and unprotected. Nor do they appear to have been dependent on any particular hillfort or to have felt as insecure as the hillfort people appear to have done.[8]

Other societies met with on the Wessex downs probably had a social structure and a material equipment and economy broadly similar to those of Danebury itself. But if we could travel west and north from Wessex, subtle differences would begin to appear. Cultural innovations at this time originated, by and large, outside Britain, and were brought here by immigrants from continental Europe, or were conveyed here by trade or gift-exchange. From south-east Britain they were diffused towards

28

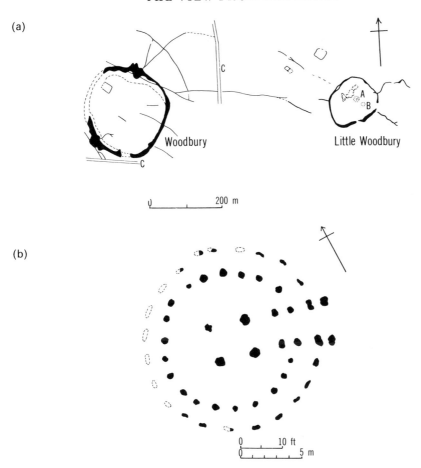

1.13 Little Woodbury: (a) plan of settlement, (b) plan of hut; its conical roof would have been supported by four massive posts and a double ring of smaller posts. After Gerhard Bersu.

the west and north. At any one time the south-east would have appeared more developed in material terms than the rest of the country. At the same time, however, the acceptance and deployment of an innovation were conditioned by environmental and social constraints. Climate, soil and vegetation set limits within which human societies existed. These constraints operated more powerfully on prehistoric peoples than on those of today, since the course of human development has been marked by an increasing ability to manipulate nature and to extract a livelihood from environments which would to an earlier generation have seemed difficult or even intractable. Tilling the clay soils of the Midlands was a very different matter from scratching the light soils of the chalk. It called for a heavier and more strongly built plough and a larger team to pull it. Animals could not be grazed in a wooded area in the same way as on the downland, a distinction which became apparent at a later date when half-wild pigs, instead of sheep, were kept on the claylands.

Above all, woodland had to be cleared of trees and heathland of its scrub before they could be cultivated. While Iron Age peoples were quite capable of felling a tree or of burning off the vegetation, there was no incentive to do so except on a small and local scale. These lands remained marginal until increasing population made their settlement necessary and improved tools made it possible on a large scale.

Small environmental differences brought about sharp changes in material culture. The balance between arable husbandry and pastoral shifted. Diet might become more farinaceous or less so. Meat, fish and milk products might assume a greater or a lesser role in diet. Material aspects of culture also underwent subtle changes. Stone might in some areas replace the wood and wattle of the Wessex downland. The size of settlements might become smaller, until we find the dominant form not the large community within a ramparted fort, but the isolated steading of an extended family alone on the moors.

The fact that Iron Age peoples moved into the woodlands, wetlands and moorlands, on however small a scale, suggests that they had in some way been squeezed out of the more tractable lands of the south-east. Population on the chalk downland *may* have reached an optimum density, though of this there is no evidence, driving any surplus population to look for new lands. The interminable warfare may have led some to migrate. Environmental change, slight fluctuations in rainfall or in winter temperature would have rendered some settlements uninhabitable. At the same time, improving technology and better tools might have brought marginal lands within the limits of profitable use. Lastly, fresh peoples, each group perhaps better armed and equipped than those already here, were filtering into Britain, sometimes assimilated by the indigenous people, sometimes driving the latter before them. All these factors must have been present in some degree in the long, slow and uneven peopling of this country.

It is impossible, within the scope of a very short chapter, to discuss the totality of Iron Age cultures of Britain. That has been done more than adequately by specialists in the field.[9] It must suffice to mention only one culture, contemporary with Danebury but adapted to radically different environmental conditions. Only 90 km to the west of Danebury, the chalk and limestone hills of the Lowland Zone (p. 6) end abruptly against the Plain of Somerset. Here a rise in sea-level had produced a drowned landscape which, as the waters receded, had slowly silted and formed shallow lagoons. These in their turn had yielded a growth of *Phragmites*, or reeds, and of other marsh plants, which died and were compacted into peat. The surface of the marsh became, with the growth of vegetation, slightly elevated above the water-level, enough for birch and alder to become established. Low 'islands' were thus formed in the marsh, and from an early date had attracted settlers. We cannot know what drove people to this unpropitious environment, though it must have provided a refuge from the interminable warfare of Celtic society. Certainly, few aspects of the downland culture could have been practised here. Even settlement sites had to be created from the bog. Near Glastonbury and Meare (Som.) felled trees and brushwood were laid on the peat for form 'crannogs', high and dry enough to form

1.14 Crannog in a Somerset lake-village. After A. Bullied.

sites for round huts, not unlike those of Wessex (Fig. 1.14). Some of these settlements became quite large; that excavated by Bullied near Glastonbury had some eighty separate hut sites,[10] though not all are likely to have been occupied at the same time. The huts were of osier, plentiful in this marshy region, daubed with clay, and thatched in all probability with reed. In the centre of each hut a low mound of ash showed where a fire was kept burning both for cooking and warmth.

The material culture of the 'lake-dwellers' differed radically from that of the Danebury people. Settlements were linked with one another and with the *terra firma*, which lay around the margin of the marsh, by tracks built of split logs, laid directly on the peat.[11] Both trackways and wooden artefacts have survived because they were buried in the peat, which excluded oxygen and protected them. Wooden tubs and ladles were used; wood was employed for the handles of tools, and wickerwork baskets of strikingly modern appearance have been recovered. Fish must have been a prominent part of the diet of the lake-dwellers, but in all probability they also cultivated patches of arable around the margins of the fen in summer and they may have grazed sheep over the more distant hills. They made pottery, which they decorated with characteristic Celtic motifs. They belonged to the broad Celtic culture of southern Britain, but within it had created a subculture closely adjusted to their physical environment and its resources.

The marsh settlements of the Somerset Levels are by no means the only such wetland sites. In recent years the crannog and village of Flag Fen has been discovered on the western edge of the Cambridgeshire Fenland. Others have been found in northern England and in Scotland, and doubtless yet more await discovery and excavation.

To go northwards and north-westwards from Danebury was to go backwards in time. Not so very far out into the Midlands and north-eastern Britain lay the frontier of Iron Age Britain at this time. Beyond it iron may have been known but was not in common use. These were Bronze Age cultures; yet further north tools were of stone and society was aceramic, without pottery. Jacquetta Hawkes tells, on the basis of archaeological finds, of the bronze-worker, unable to face the competition of the new race of iron-working smiths of southern Britain, who had escaped into this northern cultural wilderness, bringing with him his skills and the tools of his craft.

Hawkes describes in vivid, if somewhat imaginative, terms how this immigrant from the south opened the eyes of the backward northerners to the wonders of metal.[12]

Enough has been written to show that, during the centuries when Danebury was inhabited, Britain was a land of many contrasted material cultures. This pattern was continuously changing, as new elements were introduced from continental Europe and the older were diffused more widely. And as they spread, so they became modified and adapted to differing environments. There were contrasts far greater than that between Danebury and the Somerset lake-villages within the cultures of the Iron Age. These were, when all is said, settlements of Celtic agriculturalists, who ploughed the soil and grew crops. On the moorlands of the far south-west and on the hills of Wales and the north crop-farming was of little or no importance. Society was, in the main, pastoral, dependent on its flocks and herds and subsisting mainly on meat and milk products. The Welsh hill-farmer is the successor, if not also the descendant, of those whose flocks grazed these hills in the Iron Age. The names which were given to settlements and natural features and which remain in use today hark back to a phase in their history when people practised a primitive pastoralism and lived in small, scattered trevs.

The cultural history of this land is one of simplification, of the smoothing out of this regional patten of cultures, of the strengthening of their common features and of the weakening and disappearance of local subcultures. This process moved more quickly in the Lowland Zone, while localisms have survived longer and more vigorously in the Highland. The progression from local cultures to a national culture has been a very slow process, and is still far from complete. New cultural elements have continued to enter this country, and their assimilation has presented problems not unlike those that must have faced Iron Age peoples. The process of acculturation has moved faster in modern times, with the appearance of nationwide markets and media and the development of modern means of transport and communication. The basis of local and traditional cultures has been undermined just at a time when extraneous and less assimilable cultures are beginning to impinge on British society.

❖ CHAPTER 2 ❖

ROMAN INTERLUDE

The civilization of Roman Britain was neither merely provincial nor merely
cosmopolitan, neither Celtic nor Roman simply, but a fusion of the two, though an
imperfect and unstable fusion, whose elements were mixed in varying proportions in
different social strata and in different parts of the country.   R. G. Collingwood

The Roman invasion of AD 43 had been presaged, not only by Julius Caesar's forays
a century earlier, but also by the growing commercial and cultural ties between
Britain and the nearby continent. It was, indeed, the closeness of these ties and the
fear that an independent Britain might stimulate rebellion in Gaul that led to the
Claudian invasion. The course of the conquest of much of Britain which followed
gave further emphasis to that threefold division of the island that has already been
mentioned (p. 6). By AD 47–8 the Romans had overrun south-eastern Britain and
had established a military base near the present town of Colchester as well as forts
elsewhere to hold the conquered territory. Their advance was halted, if only
momentarily, along the line of the Jurassic escarpment. From its edge they could,
metaphorically at least, look down on to the clay-floored and forested Midlands.
Along this line they built a series of segments of roads, later linked to form the Fosse
Way. It became a military road from Lindum (Lincoln) to its original south-western
termination on Lyme Bay, later moved to Isca Dumnoniorum (Exeter). They were
thus enabled to move troops along the frontier to any point that might be threatened
(Fig. 2.1).[1]

Celtic hostility, and notably the 'revolt' of Caratacus, showed that this was no
place to halt the Roman advance, and that there was danger as long as unsubdued
territory lay beyond.[2] In the 50s the Midlands were overrun and forts established
against the Welsh from Caerleon and Usk in the south to Chester in the north. Not
until the 70s did similar circumstances necessitate an advance beyond the Trent and
the Humber. Eventually the Romans reached the borders of the Pictish lands in the
north, where they eventually stabilised their frontier between the Solway Firth and
the river Tyne. An advance into central Scotland was short-lived, and the Romans
withdrew to the line which the Emperor Hadrian had demarcated and, in a sense,
fortified in 122 and the following years. This became a physical reminder to the

33

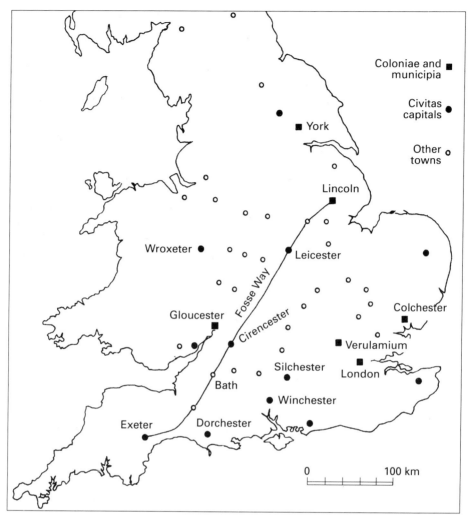

2.1 Urban settlements in Roman Britain.

barbarian peoples who lived beyond that thus far only could they come; beyond it lay the sphere of Rome.

The fundamental question to be addressed in this chapter is what the nature of the process of romanisation was and the extent to which the native peoples were assimilated to the culture of Rome. Roman civilisation had cast a long shadow before it. Native Britons had picked up many of the ways, not to mention the artefacts, of Rome even before the conquest. They struck coins on the Roman model, made pots like those of Rome, and drank wine from the Mediterranean. British society was already highly structured. An élite class created a demand for 'foreign' goods for both consumption and display. Long before the Claudian conquest the Britons, at least those living in the south-east, were predisposed to welcome the good things of life that Roman civilisation offered. This helps to explain the ease and the speed with which the Romans overran the south-east and the relative weakness of British resistance. The conquest itself was followed by an inflow of Roman pottery and of amphorae containing wine and oil, together with other exotic artefacts and foodstuffs on a scale not known before. At the same time Roman styles of living were adopted by the native élite and imitated by the humbler members of their tribes and clans.

Roman culture, as it spread through southern Europe, was essentially urban, and it was an urban culture that the Romans strove to impose on their conquered province of Britain. The Roman governor, Gnaeus Julius Agricola (d. AD 93), was credited by his son-in-law and biographer, Tacitus, with giving 'private encouragement and public assistance to the building of temples, public squares and private mansions',[3] the hallmarks of the Roman city. It is more than doubtful whether the development of towns in Britain owed as much as Tacitus liked to suppose to the activities of Agricola. More likely, 'the establishment of towns was largely a result of the native élite's desire to participate in a Roman style of life'.[4]

The principal instruments of romanisation were, first and foremost, the development of town life, then the establishment of villas, most of the *villae rusticae*, or elegant farms, which served as centres for cultural assimilation throughout the countryside. Lastly, the use of the Roman currency, with the head of the emperor and, on the reverse, the insignia of empire, helped to impart some concept of its majesty and power. The urban concept was not entirely new. If it has been, it might not have been accepted with such alacrity by the local population. There were already central places, some of them with urban pretensions, within the territory of each tribe. These were the *oppida*, of which Danebury is an example. But *oppida* were, broadly speaking, of two kinds: those, like Danebury, which were perched upon hilltops and could be defended with relative ease, and those, like Colchester and Stanwick (p. 47) which had been established on low-lying ground. They were cult centres and within them were to be found houses, storage places for food, and evidence for the practice of crafts such as metal-working, as well as for the pursuit of trade.[5] There appears to have been a hierarchy of such defended sites within any particular tribal area. The Romans, almost inevitably, sited a military settlement in the close proximity of the more important of them. The fact that the Roman settlement grew into a town, whereas the *oppidum* was abandoned, need not have been the consequence of any deliberate policy of compulsion on the part of the Romans, The security, comfort and convenience offered by the Roman town might alone have been enough to tempt the local population to leave their *oppidum* and to become citizens of the new foundation. Most of the more important towns of Roman Britain were heirs to Celtic *oppida*. They became the central places, the *civitas-*capitals, of the former tribal territories (*civitates*), often even succeeding to the tribal names: Venta Belgarum, Isca Dumnoniorum, Corinium Dubunnorum, Venta Icenorum, and so on.[6]

Not all towns in Roman Britain derived their function and their population from pre-existing Celtic *oppida*. There were also legionary forts. Some of them were short-lived, but many attracted a civil population and grew into permanent settlements. Then there were *coloniae*, the highest ranking of Roman settlements, like Gloucester, Lincoln and Colchester. In origin they were settlements of superannuated legionaries, each given a tract of land to occupy his old age. A generation or two hence these had come to be settled as much by the native people as by the retired soldiers of Rome. But the town which was to become the largest and economically the most important of all was none of these. London grew up at a crossing-point of the Thames and near the meeting-point of three tribal territories. It was a port, and it became the focus of the road system which the Romans developed in Britain.

Towns in Roman Britain, and also in much of the western Empire, derived from the marriage of Roman leadership and technology, on the one hand, with the aspirations of the native population on the other. In all the towns of Roman Britain the population must within a generation or even less of their foundation have come to be largely made up of the native Celtic people. Indeed, there were no others, for the Romans did not readily migrate from other parts of the Empire to this province on its far frontier, with its vile climate and only slowly developing amenities.

The process of acculturation gained momentum from the early days of the conquest. Despite the occasional revolts against Roman rule, notably that of Boudicca amongst the Iceni (AD 60–1) and the campaigns of Caratacus on the Welsh Border, the principal elements of Roman culture were accepted by the Celtic élite with willingness, even alacrity. After all, it was a guarantee of the continued supply of those luxuries, from pottery and jewellery to wine and oil, for which they had already acquired a taste. The scale of these imports increased, and as the needs of the élite became satiated, they found a market among the humbler levels of society.

The areas where this process of acculturation was most successful and far-reaching were those where a harmonious relationship had been established between the small population of Roman soldiers and administrators, on the one hand, and the native élite, and this was, by and large, the south-east of the country. It was something more than the accident of conquest that gave to south-eastern Britain – the area lying south and east very approximately of the Jurassic escarpment – a far more settled and cultivated look than the rest of the country. This had also been the most populous and developed area of pre-Roman Britain, and it was here that towns were most numerous and that villas lay thickest on the ground. By contrast, the Midlands were relatively thinly populated, and were to remain so until the later Middle Ages, while the north remained on the whole an area of military occupation. This threefold division of the country, anticipated in the pre-Roman Iron Age, was to remain a powerful influence on the country's social and cultural development, and not until the time of the Industrial Revolution were their roles to be reversed.

In this chapter the process of acculturation, of the romanisation of the native population, is discussed under three principal heads: (1) rural settlement and agriculture and, in particular, the villa; (2) the foundation of towns and the creation of an urban society; and (3) the changes that took place in what may be termed the 'lesser arts of life', the refinements in daily living that helped to transform barbarism into civilisation.

The villa society

It would be a mistake to think of villas as created by Romans for Roman settlers. No doubt there were some which owed their origin to an enterprising legionary or retired official, but Britain was never colonised in the modern sense of that term. It was the Britons themselves who picked up elements of Roman culture, either because these flattered their self-esteem or because they enjoyed the greater comfort which they offered. The Romans brought no technological revolution with them; indeed, they were not an inventive people. Their strength lay in their ability to organise and to maintain a kind of order. If the majority of the population was better off in material terms than they had been during the pre-Roman Iron Age, this was not because available resources were any greater or because new techniques had come into use for their exploitation. It was because a more disciplined and more carefully planned use was made of them. Far more has been achieved in the course of human progress by management than by innovation.

Pre-Roman rural settlements had consisted, by and large, of small clusters and isolated farmsteads, most of them subordinated in some way to *oppida* which served as political and cult centres. The process by which the élite of Celtic society turned their lands and farms into villas is far from clear. It began early; the most lavish of British villas, that built for the British tribal leader, Cogidubnus, at Fishbourne (Sussex), was begun before the end of the first century. Villas, furthermore, were most numerous in south-eastern Britain which was overrun in the first phase of the Roman conquest. By contrast, they were few in the Midlands, and they were rare throughout the Highland Zone.[7] Within the villa region of the south-east, they clustered around tribal capitals such as Corinium (Cirencester), Lindinis (Ilchester, Som.), Venta (Winchester) and other towns like Durobrivae (Rochester) and the other Durobrivae (Water Newton, Northants) (Fig. 2.2). They lay in the more fertile areas, and it has been argued that one of their purposes was to provide food for their neighbouring tribal towns. In fact, however, the significant growth of towns came later than the initial expansion of the villa economy. Whatever economic advantages may later have been derived from villa-farming, one must assume that its creation must, in general, have sprung from the pride of the local élite and from their desire to emulate the ways of the Romans. They must already have been broadly familiar with the concept of the villa as it had been developed in southern Europe, and they must have had at their disposal a not inconsiderable surplus of wealth generated by local agriculture and no longer consumed in tribal warfare. Villas thus represented a form of conspicuous consumption, not out of line with the resources of a society which could, centuries earlier, build the hillforts described in the previous chapter.

37

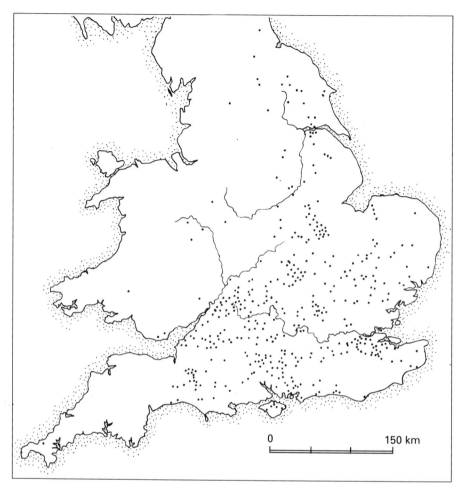

2.2 Distrbution of villas; after *Map of Roman Britain*, Ordnance Survey, 1978. The original map distinguishes between villa sites and probable sites.

A second wave of villa construction followed some two centuries later, when many simple farmsteads were enlarged and refined. This movement accompanied a relative decline in urban population and prosperity. It was as if the urban élite were abandoning the problems of urban life, of which high local taxation was far from being the least, for life in the countryside.

Villas, broadly speaking, were to be found only in the areas of most productive soil. By and large, they eschewed not only infertile areas like the Weald and the New Forest, but also such intrinsically fertile regions as the claylands of Essex and the Midlands, for which their agricultural technology was not yet suited. A villa, in Britain at least, was a working farm, the centre of an estate or *fundus*. It seems, furthermore, to have been regularly inhabited by its owner. Some villas have been shown to have occupied the sites of Iron Age settlements, and it must be assumed

38

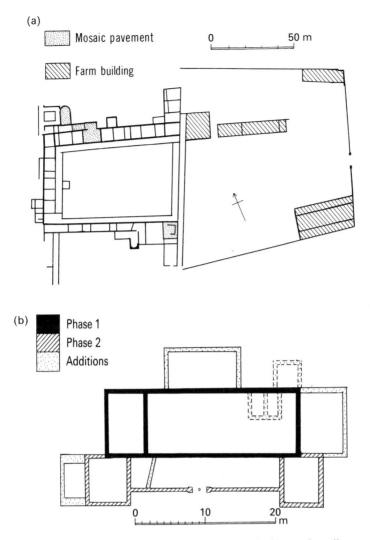

2.3 Plans of villas: (a) the elaborate villa at Bignor (Sussex), (b) simpler villa at Farmington (Glos.), which developed from a simple rectangular house in the fourth century.
(After Alan McWhirr.)

that it was the inhabitants of the latter who rebuilt them as villas. Villas represented 'the transformation of the existing system rather than the superimposition of something new'.[8] The villas themselves assumed a variety of forms, which must have reflected the wealth, the aspirations and the concepts of their builders. Some were remarkably simple, consisting of little more than two or three rooms separated by a cross-passage, or opening on to a corridor or verandah. But such a plan was capable of endless elaboration (Fig. 2.3). Wings could be added at the ends; a gallery or verandah could be built along the front; the wings could be extended to form a courtyard, and the latter might even be enclosed and some form of gatehouse constructed. The internal structure was also capable of endless refinement. The two or three simple rooms of the earliest villas might be extended to include a dining-room or *triclinium*. Private chambers might be added, opening off a corridor or walkway which gave access to all parts of the villa in all weathers.

The more elaborate villas, which in general were those built or extended in the later centuries of Roman rule, had bath suites, sequences of rooms with water temperatures graduated from that of the hot *caldarium* to the cold *frigidarium*, the heat being supplied from a hypocaust with radiating flues. Lastly, there would have been a plunge bath to bring the bathing ritual to an end. Such structures would have required frequent repairs and occasional rebuilding. It is in consequence extremely difficult to reconstruct the building history of bath suites, such as those at Chedworth (Glos.) or Bignor (Sussex).

Most, if not all, British villas were also farms. In some the court, formed by the projecting wings of the villa, was effectively a farmyard, though in the larger and more sumptuous villas farming activities were banished to an outer court. At Bignor and perhaps also at Chedworth and Woodchester (Glos.) the second court, in which the animals and equipment were kept, was separated from the first by a substantial dividing wall. Only occasionally was the principal court developed as an ornamental garden, as was commonly the case in the sophisticated, residential villas (*villae surburbanae*) of Italy. The foremost British example of this development was at Fishbourne (Sussex).

The Roman villa, as a structure, owed nothing beyond perhaps its site to the culture of the pre-Roman Iron Age. Its origins lie in southern Europe, where its form was most fully developed. There it remained the preserve of the social élite; in Britain it seems rather to have been built by those able to afford it. It was not essential to Roman agriculture, and in itself marked no revolution in the methods of farming practised in this country. If we can assume that the total number of villas in Roman Britain was of the order of 600 to 700, we can be sure that the number of small settlements of the Romano-British population was far greater. The villas themselves did not constitute a clearly defined category of broadly uniform character. They formed a spectrum, with, at one extreme, the elaboration of Fishbourne, and, at the other, simple structures like Magor (Corn.), which differed little from the hutted structures of the rest of the population.

It has, at least since Bersu's excavation of Little Woodbury (pp. 28–9), become part of our accepted wisdom that late Iron Age settlements consisted of large huts, circular in plan, set within fenced enclosures, and surrounded by small, square or lyncheted fields.[9] Too little is known of such settlements, because, in general, they have left so small an imprint on the land. Little Woodbury itself was found only through a crop-mark observed from the air. It is, for example, by no means certain that all huts in the pre-Roman Iron Age were round, and that under Roman influence the British began to build on a rectangular plan.[10] A small settlement of the early Roman period has been excavated at Catsgore (Som.), showing both round and rectangular hut plans.[11] But in general, huts which can be securely dated to the

Roman period seem to have been rectangular,[12] whereas those of the Iron Age were usually round.

There was a tendency, especially in the later centuries of the Roman occupation, for settlements to become more nucleated and for incipient villages to form. Farmsteads began to occur in small clusters – *vici* – rather than in isolation. There are even instances, Kenchester (Hereford.) for example, of defences constructed to protect such settlements, like village enclosures of the later Middle Ages. Their inhabitants must have benefited from the more abundant supply of consumer goods, and artefacts of continental and, indeed, of domestic origin seem to have become more diffused socially, as people lower in the social scale and situated further from urban centres began to acquire a taste for them. This process of acculturation has been summarised by Millett: 'the successful Romanized areas [were] those where the native élite benefited from an alliance with Roman power. In some of these areas Romanization was entirely indigenous; in others it was stimulated by passive encouragement. However, Romanization failed in those areas where, either through warfare or continued military occupation, the Roman presence was socially disruptive.'[13] It failed also, it might be added, in areas like the south-western peninsula, where a romanised élite was never present in sufficient numbers to serve as a model.

One should not be surprised that, at the end of more than three centuries of Roman rule, there remained pockets, not so much of barbarism, as of late Iron Age culture, on which Rome had made very little impact. In the south-western peninsula the Roman presence was inadequate and trade was insufficient to break down its cultural isolation. Settlements at Chysauster (Corn.) and elsewhere show no evidence of the impact of Rome. The Midlands, which contributed little to the economy of Roman Britain, were just a territory through which the Romans passed as they travelled to the northern or western frontiers, leaving little cultural evidence behind them. And in the north there was always a military presence, resented and its cultural impact probably resisted by the local Britons more strongly than would have been the case with a civil administration.

Agriculture and food supply

In the cultivation of the land and the production of food the impact of Rome was far from revolutionary. Those who tilled the fields of Roman Britain were the descendants of the cultivators of the late Iron Age, and one should not look for any fundamental change. The crops they grew were similar to those cultivated by the Iron Age Celts, though the balance between them may have tipped one way or another. Yet there was change and growth. A larger population, at least by the third century, coupled with the demands of taxation, the army and urban-dwellers, led to an increased output. Some land was reclaimed, as in the Fenland, and marginal land elsewhere was brought under cultivation. Villages increased in size, and a mechanism must have been devised for shipping surplus food around the country.

2.4 The Piercebridge ploughman: (a) bronze excavated in County Durham, (b) the kind of
plough which he is shown using.

The fields of the late Iron Age Britons had been small, forming a kind of
chequerwork around every rural settlement. While such fields must have continued
under the Romans to provide the larger part of the cereal output, two other kinds of
field-system may also have made their appearance. There is some slight evidence for
the cultivation of long, narrow strips, such as are associated with the open-fields of
the Middle Ages. At the same time, it is claimed, 'centuriated' fields, like those still
found around the former Roman *coloniae* in northern Italy,[14] were laid out in some
parts of Britain, though for this there is no convincing evidence. The problem is, of
course, that continued cultivation under different social and economic conditions
has led to the distortion and even the obliteration of traces of earlier systems.
Nevertheless, attempts continue to be made, by manipulating later boundary lines,
to recover some semblance of the earlier systems. But much of the evidence appears
on close examination to be nothing more than a fortuitous arrangement of modern
field boundaries.

The question of field shape is closely linked with that of the tools of agriculture.
There can be no question but that the plough used over most of Britain was the ard,
little different from that used in the pre-Roman Iron Age. Models of it have
survived, notably the Piercebridge ploughman (Fig. 2.4) from County Durham. It
was light and easily turned at the end of the furrow, and there is no reason to doubt

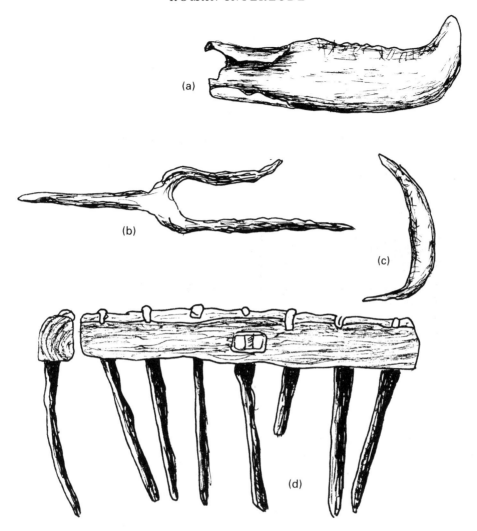

2.5 Roman agricultural tools: (a) billhook, (b) pitchfork, (c) unbalanced sickle, (d) rake, with metal teeth set in a wooden frame.

that the small square fields were ploughed in both directions with such an instrument. To this extent the design of the plough dictated the shape of the fields. But certain refinements appear to have been made to the ard. In the first place, a coulter was sometimes set vertically in the beam, thus making a cut through the soil in advance of the share. Iron coulters are not uncommon on Roman sites (Fig. 2.5a). At the same time, the iron tip to the plough was made asymmetrical, so that it turned the soil more to one side than to the other. The turning of the soil was further assisted by the addition of a 'wrest', or incipient mould-board, and of wooden 'ears' to the 'sole' or share. In such ways the light ard was beginning to approximate, if

43

ever so slightly, to the heavy, medieval mould-board plough. But there is no hard evidence that the latter, though perhaps known in continental Europe, had yet made its appearance in Britain.[15] The association of medieval strip cultivation with the heavy, mould-board plough cannot be disputed. It is possible that the incipient strip systems met with in Roman Britain may have been made possible by adaptations to the ard which had made cross-ploughing unnecessary.

While improvements to the ard, achieved mainly in south-eastern Britain, made it a more effective instrument, primitive tools of cultivation remained in use in the north. Here a stone share was sometimes fastened to a wooden sole, and the even simpler caschrom, a development of the digging-stick, must have been used, as, indeed, it continued to be into the present century.[16] For the rest, the Romano-Britons used hand tools of a kind that remained in use through the Middle Ages and in some instances into the present century. Hoes and rakes, spades and mattocks, excavated on Roman sites, have an uncannily modern appearance, and could today be used to cultivate the garden (Fig. 2.5).[17] The spade was of wood with an iron cutting edge, almost identical with those used throughout the Middle Ages, and the rake consisted of iron teeth mounted on a wooden bar. Reaping was with the sickle and the newly introduced scythe. The pre-Roman sickle was an unbalanced instrument (Fig. 2.5c), always tending to turn downwards as it moved through the crop. The Romans may themselves have introduced a balanced sickle, easier to swing in a horizontal plane. The two-handed scythe was also probably a Roman invention. It covered the ground faster than a sickle and cut close to the soil It was ideal for cutting hay, and this seems to have been, as it has since remained, its principal use. The small improvements made in agricultural tools may have led to a marginal improvement in productivity, but they fell far short of an agricultural revolution.

The chief bread-grains of Iron Age Britain had been spelt and emmer, primitive varieties of wheat, together with both naked and husked barley. Both rye and oats made their first appearance during the Roman period,[18] but this was less a conscious introduction than the recognition of grasses which had previously been known as weeds of the cornfield.[19] The spread of oats at this time and later, especially in northern Britain, suggests, however, that there was some conscious adaptation of crops to local conditions of soil and climate. There appears also to have been an attempt to plant wheat in the autumn, a practice which would have been familiar to immigrant farmers from southern Europe, and the balance of crops at some excavated sited suggests an alternation of winter- and spring-sown cereals, with, perhaps, an intervening fallow year. The medieval system of rotation may thus have been anticipated.

The cultivated grains of the pre-Roman Iron Age had been the primitive forms of wheat: spelt (*Triticum spelta*), einkorn (*Tr. monococcum*) and emmer (*Tr. dicoccum*) (Fig. 2.6). During the Roman period the last two declined in importance, and club wheat (*Tr. compactum*) became more important, but it was spelt which, together with barley, became dominant. Small changes in the varieties of grain cultivated

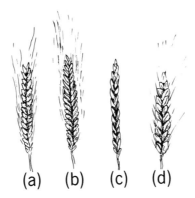

2.6 The breadgrains cultivated in Roman Britain: (a) einkorn, (b) emmer, (c) spelt, (d) common wheat.

could have had a significant influence on the material life of the population. The cultivation of oats assisted in the keeping of horses, and that of rye encouraged the use of marginal land. The increasing availability of wheat led to a greater consumption of bread, and the spread of the hulled varieties facilitated milling and improved the quality of the bread made from its flour.

The role of the Romans in introducing other food crops was more deliberate, though the evidence lies largely in the chance survival of their seeds. Vegetables and pot-herbs had not been conspicuous in the diet of pre-Roman peoples. Although we know little about the Roman kitchen garden, it is apparent that varieties of the pea and of *Brassica* were cultivated, and, amongst the root crops, the turnip and parsnip. To these should be added a wide range of herbs, including parsley, dill, fennel and coriander. Indeed, the kitchen garden in Roman Britain probably 'lacked little that the continent possessed, within the limits set by climate'.[20]

Greater uncertainty surrounds the question of fruit trees. The apple, pear, raspberry and blackcurrant were native species which appear to have been domesticated under the Romans. The cultivated cherry was introduced, together, in all probability, with the medlar, fig and mulberry, but the orchard had little importance compared with its role in later centuries.

It is, however, in the cultivation of the grape vine that posterity has shown the greatest interest. Wine had been a significant import into Britain during the Iron Age, and it might have been expected that the Romans would have tried to establish the grape vine which supplied it. We have both documentary and archaeological evidence for viticulture, chiefly in the south, but the experiment achieved little permanent success. Vineyards probably remained 'small affairs in walled gardens and the like, possibly only a few plants in any one location'.[21] It is apparent that neither fruit trees nor the vine can have added significantly to the amenities of life in Britain, and it is highly improbable that viticulture outlasted the Roman occupation.

Pastoral farming was of some importance in south-east Britain, but was dominant elsewhere. In the north arable was of little importance before the Roman occupation, and was significant thereafter chiefly as an adjunct to military occupation. Rye, oats and perhaps barley were grown, but wealth came largely from animal rearing.[22] Pigs were rare in areas of open moorland, but sheep were grazed and, as the archaeological record shows, wool was spun and cloth woven. That cattle were reared in considerable numbers is apparent from the fact that beef was supplied to the legions at least occasionally.

A problem of stock-rearing in a hilly or mountainous environment must have been the supply of winter fodder. The flocks and herds may have been largely transhumant, for transhumance is a common way of using marginal land. They would have spent the summers grazing on the uplands under the care of a shepherd or cowherd, while on lower ground a harvest of hay was being prepared. Such remained the pastoral pattern in much of Highland Britain until modern times.

In south-eastern Britain sheep, cattle, pigs and horses were reared. There is evidence that vetch and roots, as well as hay, were used for fodder; oats were grown for the horses, and pigs were allowed, as in the Middle Ages, to forage in the woodlands.

Diet was circumscribed by the narrow range of domestically produced foodstuffs. No doubt it consisted basically of cereals and vegetables, as, indeed, it continued to do well into modern times. Grain was generally reaped in August, and the crop had to last until the next harvest. Keeping the grain in an edible condition always presented a problem in a damp climate like that of Britain. The late Iron Age farmer had used sealed storage pits (p. 21). The Romano-Britons seem to have followed the continental practice of keeping their grain in granaries built above ground and often of masonry. But first it was threshed, perhaps by treading it with the hoofs of animals or by dragging a heavy wooden block, its lower surface studded with nails or flints, across it. It was then winnowed and the grain collected. The frequency with which corn-drying kilns have been found at villa sites suggests that all corn not destined for use as seed was dried or parched before storage. The evidence,[23] however, makes it probable that these kilns served many purposes, including the roasting of germinated seed for the production of malt. It may be that the use of the corn-drier for breadgrains was general only in the wetter parts of Britain. The kiln may have been a regular feature of the well-appointed villa. It cannot, however, be supposed that every peasant farmer had his corn-drier. He is more likely to have relied on some form of communal kiln, like that found at Hambledon (Bucks.), where 'a corn-drying factory [served] the farms which existed along the banks of the Thames'.[24]

Milled flour does not keep well, and it is likely that the corn was ground only when required for baking. Elaborate donkey-mills have been found at Pompeii, but it is unlikely that such mills were common in Britain, though a fragment of one has made its way into the London Museum. In most homes there would have been a hand-quern, its upper stone, or 'runner', rotated by means of a handle. The best quernstones were made from a vesicular igneous rock, and andesite from near

Mayen, in the Eifel, was imported for the purpose. In remote areas the simpler saddle-quern or even rubbing-stone remained in use.

Bread was cooked in an oven, masonry-built and dome-shaped. It did not have a continuous source of heat. Instead brushwood was burned inside it until the masonry had become hot. The ashes were then raked out and the loaves placed on its flat floor (p. 193). Meat was roasted and a vegetable stew was made over an open hearth on the floor. Three-legged trivets were used to support pots, and meat was probably turned on a spit above the hot ashes. To this extent the Roman kitchen can have differed very little from the better known facilities of the later Middle Ages.

Diet varied with social class in Roman times no less than in later. Classical writers, like Athenaeus, Petronius and Martial, described banquets of gargantuan proportions, but these must, even in Italy, have been eaten only on rare occasions and by very few of the population. There is no record of such luxury in Britain, but the owners of the grander villas unquestionably lived well. The leisured Roman took only two meals in the day after a very light breakfast. The first was *prandium*, or lunch, but the evening meal was often the more substantial. How the field-worker adapted to this regime can only be guessed.

Towns in Roman Britain

The development of towns and the encouragement of urban living were, if we follow Tacitus, amongst the objectives of Roman policy. If this was indeed the case it would have been wholly consistent with the expectations of the native élite. The *oppida* of the immediate pre-Roman period can be thought of as proto-cities. They already focused political and economic activities within their tribal areas; they probably also served as cult centres and contained the few manufacturing activities that were carried on at this time. Under Roman rule the functions of the tribal capitals were perpetuated in the '*civitas*-capitals' of the Romans. In a few instances the location of the *oppidum* was displaced by only a few miles, as when Maiden Castle was replaced by Durnovaria Durotrigum (Dorchester, Dorset), which thus perpetuated the name of the Celtic tribe whose central place it had become.[25] There was sometimes a shift from a defensible site on higher ground to one on lower ground, where, if we may transpose the words of Strabo, alluding to a similar shift amongst the Allobriges of Gaul, 'they now cultivate the plains . . . and live in villages, except that the most notable of them dwell in Vienna (Vienne, Isère), which they have built up into a city'.[26] Such was the process that led to the creation of Corinium Dubonnorum (Cirencester, Glos.), Venta Belgarum (Winchester), and Calleva Atrebatum (Silchester, Hants) and several others. The new towns, with their markets (*fora*), temples and basilicas, attracted the élite of the surrounding tribal areas. There they built town houses, and may even have severed all connection with their rural dwellings.

The town was, in the Roman view, 'the *sine qua non* of civilization',[27] but it grew and prospered only through 'the native élite's desire to participate in a Roman style of life'.[28] But the Romans did not apply their policy of urbanisation as rigorously as they might have done. There were only eleven indubitable *civitas*-capitals, with a further eight that might also qualify.[29] The tribal name was preserved in most of them, as it was in Gaul, but Roman policy was to replace tribal loyalty with dedication to the Empire and to the deified emperor, who was seen as its personification. But only in the case of Canterbury (Durovernum Cantiacorum) has the tribal name survived in the modern place-name.[30]

The *civitas*-capitals may as a group have been the most important product of Rome's policy of urbanisation. But there were also two other groups of towns: the *coloniae* and the *municipia*. The *coloniae* were deliberate creations for the purpose, in the first instance, of providing homes and agricultural holdings for legionaries whose term of service had ended. There were never more than four *coloniae*, and in size and function they came to differ little from the tribal capitals. Intermediate in status between the *coloniae* and the tribal capitals were the *municipia*. These were in general prosperous settlements which fell into neither of the other categories. Verulamium and perhaps London and York were *municipia*.

These titles were not merely honorific; they affected the legal rights and privileges of their inhabitants. The *civitas*-capitals were governed by decurions chosen from among the local inhabitants, who were saddled with numerous burdensome obligations, which included the collection of and accounting for taxes within their local areas. It was also expected of them that they would contribute to the amenities and entertainments of their cities. Being a member of the urban élite was an expensive honour, and its obligations, especially under the later Empire, drove many to withdraw from city life and to return to their rural estates.

Below the rank of the tribal capitals, which served as administrative centres for their tribal areas, were *vici*, a term variously translated as 'village' or 'small town'.[31] These were much less important than tribal capitals, and their functions were less diverse. In reality most of their inhabitants would have been engaged in agriculture. They have left few visible remains, and only a handful have been excavated, in part because their sites have been continuously occupied. In consequence, comparatively little is known of their functions and internal arrangements.[32] For this reason it is difficult to generalise, but it seems that in the early years of the Roman occupation they tended to be small. During the second century and later they appear to have grown in size, perhaps at the expense of the tribal capitals, many of whose citizens withdrew to the countryside.[33]

The Roman house

Villas and towns were but the media of acculturation, the means whereby the practices and the artefacts of Roman culture reached the mass of the Romano-British population. Most towns served as local markets, and were frequented by the local population intent on selling produce and acquiring goods that were not available in their local *vici*. Both villas and towns were centres of conspicuous consumption, showcases for the local population and objects of emulation to their neighbours.

The internal arrangements of both villas and the richer town houses, which in many respects resembled them, are fairly well known. Enough has survived for their plans to be established and their material equipment to be reconstructed. Their foundations and at least part of their walls were of masonry, and masons' tools that have been found have a strikingly modern appearance (Fig. 2.12). The villa itself was generally made up of a number of communicating rooms, often opening off a small court or atrium, or linked by an enclosed gallery or corridor (Fig. 2.3a). The more important rooms would have been fancifully decorated. About a quarter of known villa sites have been found to have mosaic floors. Woodchester and Fishbourne each had more than twenty such floors. They were costly to lay, and thus became a symbol of economic standing and social status. The majority appear to have been laid in the fourth century, which was a period of considerable rural prosperity. At this time schools of mosaicists emerged, each with its distinctive style and motifs.[34]

The rooms to be floored in this way were, as a rule, rectangular in plan. The floor area was first enclosed within a frame of regularly repeating motifs. The space within was then divided into a series of regular compartments, in each of which one of a series of related subjects was depicted by means of coloured tesserae. A few showed only geometrical patterns, but most had a story to tell. The mosaicist must have had some kind of pattern book, a repertory of set designs, but it is apparent that he was always ready to incorporate whatever motifs might be demanded by his clients. Most common were themes from Graeco-Roman mythology, in particular stories about Jupiter, Neptune, Orpheus and Bacchus, and some scenes were closely related to the writings of Virgil and Ovid.[35] It is doubtful whether these mosaics were any measure of the depth of classical culture among the romanised Britons, but the motifs clearly show the direction in which their aspirations lay. Next in popularity came scenes from nature, especially those representing the attributes of the months and seasons. Aquatic creatures, notably the dolphin, were common, and a few mosaics display sporting themes or events in the Roman circus. A few designs appear to have held a deeper philosophical or religious connotation, including the use of Christian symbolism and of imagery that can only have belonged to the Gnostics. If evidence were needed that the upper strata of Romano-British society had been to a considerable degree assimilated to classical, Mediterranean culture, it is to be found in the imagery and symbolism of domestic mosaics.

'The history of interior decoration in Britain', wrote Joan Liversidge, 'may, perhaps, be said to begin in the Roman period.'[36] The inside walls of every villa were plastered, usually with lime and sand, and were then coloured and decorated. Homes in the pre-Roman Iron Age had shown no such sophistication, and both the technique of mural decoration and the craftsmen who practised it must have derived from southern Europe. Mural decoration is more difficult to reconstruct than floor covering.[37] The walls have in large measure been destroyed, and their plastered rendering has survived, if at all, only as small fragments, the colours bleached and the design almost obliterated. Nevertheless, enough has been found to demonstrate in general terms the patterns and methods of the Roman plasterer. A pigment was applied to the damp plaster to give a basic colour. Decoration was then added *secco*, with paint bonded with gum or tempera. The pigments were mainly metallic oxides, with lampblack where needed. An attempt was often made to match both colour and design with those in the floors, but it seems that pastel shades were rare and that the overall impression was dark.

Ceiling heights were generally considerably higher than the standard 8 feet (2.5m) of contemporary homes. The walls were frequently divided into three parts. At the base was a dado, up to a metre in height, and close to the ceiling was a narrower cornice or frieze. Between the two a series of panels, outlined with bold strokes, occupied much of the wall. They might contain figures and scenes comparable with those represented in the mosaic floor, but more often the panels were filled with trailing leaf motifs or swags of vegetation.

Such was the interior decoration of most villas and of the larger and more sophisticated town houses, but how far down the social scale, it might be asked, were such refinements to be found? Any judgment is likely to be modified by future excavation and discovery, but we can be sure that mosaics were absent from the cottages which made up the *vici*. Their walls may have been rendered on the inside, but no evidence has been found for the kind of decoration met with in the villas. In terms of décor there was a social range not unlike that to be met with in England in the early or mid-nineteenth century.

Windows were fairly small, probably because large pieces of glass were not available. The manufacture of window-glass had been introduced by the Romans from continental Europe.[38] The glass itself was thin and of a greenish tint, and it seems to have been mounted in wooden window-frames. The rooms of a villa were usually intercommunicating, but were fitted with hinged doors to give some degree of privacy. In a few instances there is evidence for a hearth in the floor of some rooms, but generally heating was by ducts constructed beneath the floor from a conveniently located furnace room. After circulating between the *pilae* which supported the floor, the hot air was evacuated through flues of hollow tile built into the walls. No more effective system of domestic heating was devised before the present century.

The larger and more sumptuous villas also had a bath-house, usually built as an integral part of the house, but sometimes free-standing.[39] It usually consisted of three rooms, with their respective plunge-baths. Heat was supplied both for the water and for maintaining a proper temperature in each of the rooms, from hot gases which circulated beneath the floors.

Every villa had a kitchen, though the robbing of masonry often makes it difficult to discover where it was. A bas-relief on the Igel column, near Trier, Germany, shows an oven of a kind that remained in use until comparatively modern times, a large mixing bowl, and a bench on which food was prepared.

Villas were comfortably, though not elaborately, furnished.[40] Furnishings were in the main of wood, which has, of course, perished. More durable Kimmeridge shale was carved, especially for table legs, and has been found at several sites in the south-west. For the rest we are dependent very largely on the representation of household furnishings on funeral *stelae*. Most important was the couch, usually with both end- and back-rests, closely resembling a nineteenth-century settee. Its legs were turned and it was probably upholstered, and it may have had cushions. It was used both for sleeping (*lectus cubicularis*) and, as the *lectus tricliniarius*, for reclining at feasts. If there were structural or decorative differences between the two, these have been lost. In funerary sculpture a small, round, three-legged stool was almost always shown beside the couch. Sometimes small pottery vessels were set upon it. Such tables must generally have been made of wood, but a number of examples made of Kimmeridge shale have been found. The legs often appear to have been carefully carved and to have ended in claw-feet. Some specimens in shale incorporate carved animal heads. There would also have been benches and chairs, of which nothing is known to have survived. Amongst the latter were chairs with high, rounded backs, made of wickerwork. They are known only from their sculptured representations and a few literary allusions, but they give the appearance of extreme comfort. Shelves and chests would have been used for storage, and benches for preparing food.

But for its uncluttered look, the Roman upper-class home would have borne a close resemblance to a Victorian drawing-room. It represented a high level of comfort, if not also of taste. Collingwood condemned the 'dull, mechanical imitation . . . [the] ugliness which pervades the place like a London fog'.[41] Such a judgment is unduly harsh. Romano-British designs, motifs and techniques derived from the continental Empire, and were brought to Britain in the wake of the Roman army. Interpreted by native craftsmen, however, they became increasingly unclassical. Sculpture in particular assumed a 'stylised, linear and two-dimensional character',[42] and designs in mosaics were often crude and clumsy. Artistic creativity in Britain was not of a high order, but the local people lacked standards by which to judge it, and doubtless took much pride in whatever they happened to possess without any thought for the judgments of art historians.

Amenities like the household furnishings described here did not in all probability reach far down the social scale. If we look at the few *vici* and farmsteads that have been excavated, we find no evidence for the level of sophistication met with in even the humblest of villas, and in the primitive huts found in the south-west and in Wales there is no shred of evidence for such comforts.[43] Only the rectangular plan and the odd sherd of Samian or other ware betokens the proximity of the civilisation of Rome.[44] Whatever changes there may have been in the size and layout of rural settlements, one is left everywhere with the impression that outside the towns and villas, the culture of the pre-Roman Iron Ages continued little modified by that of Rome.

The lesser arts of life

The effect of the Roman subjugation of Britain was to widen the gulf which already existed between the native élite and their entourages, on the one hand, and the humbler members of society on the other. The former were able to adopt the amenities which Roman civilisation had made available. The latter lived, by and large, as they had done before the Romans came. At the periphery of Roman rule, in the north, in Wales and the far south-west lived a poor peasantry which may have lost rather than gained through the Roman conquest, since they had still to pay their *annona* for the support of the Roman armies.[45] But for those with the means and the social standing to profit from the material culture of Rome the quality of life must have been raised immeasurably by their comfortable and well-heated homes, by the quality and abundance of fittings and equipment, and by the abundant facilities for personal hygiene, clothing and adornment.

In no respect is the change in material standards more prominent than in pottery and in the means for preparing and serving food. Pottery in the pre-Roman Iron Age had, in the main, been coarse in texture and hand-made from local clays of whatever quality. Pottery imported by the Romans stood in marked contrast. It was wheel-thrown, made from clay of a more refined quality, and its decoration was often applied with ceramic moulds. Within a century of the Roman conquest domestic kilns had begun to imitate the wares imported from Gaul and Italy, and very passable imitations they produced. A large number of kilns was established, many of them short-lived, producing bowls, *mortaria* and cups in great profusion. The market for good, serviceable ware ceased to be restricted to the élite; the volume produced was too large for that. Pottery became an important industry,[46] and all classes must have come to enjoy in some measure the convenience of cheap table and cooking ware.

Glass for everyday use was probably made in Britain, but vessels of better quality were imported in some quantity from continental Europe. They would have been used, if Pompeian mural paintings are any guide, to contain fruit, wine or perfume.[47] Bottles of a surprisingly modern design have been found, as well as pitchers which were probably used for wine at the table. Pewter, probably of British manufacture, was used for bowls and dishes, and silver made a rare appearance in tableware, as in the well-known Mildenhall find, now in the British Museum. The well-appointed table lacked, however, the range of cutlery that has come to be expected in modern times. Diners carried their own knives with them, and, for the rest, used their fingers. A number of knives, made of iron and set in wooden or bone handles, have been found, and may have been used at the table. There were no forks in England before the seventeenth century (p. 164) but spoons were in common use for eating liquid dishes (Fig. 2.7). A type of spoon with a small bowl and a pointed end, seems to have been quite common. It may have been used for eating eggs and opening shellfish, and, it has been suggested, for picking the teeth. The dining-table of the well-to-do Romano-Briton cannot have differed significantly, apart from the

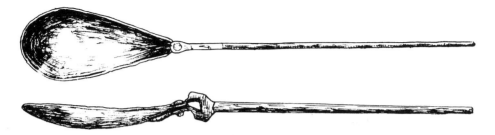

2.7 A Roman spoon; a large number of spoons of this and similar designs has been found at Roman sites.

presence of couches instead of chairs or benches, from that found in England a thousand years later.

Villas were, as a general rule, heated by means of hypocausts, but houses of lesser standing had hearths of tile or stone, placed either in the centre of the room or against a wall. There is little evidence for chimneys, apart from those which carried the fumes from the hypocaust, and smoke, in the words of Sidonius Apollinaris, 'curls upwards, then fades away and spreads a mitigated heat all over the roof'.[48] In some excavated sites the complete absence of any evidence for fireplaces suggests that movable braziers were used. Wood must have been the fuel in general use, perhaps carbonised to form charcoal, but fragments of coal have been found on villa sites, suggesting that hypocausts were sometimes heated in this way.[49] Burning coal on an open fireplace without a flue to carry away the fumes would have been intolerable. Some of the finds of coal can, no doubt, be associated with smithing or metal working. All were close to an outcrop of coal except those found in the Fenland. How these had been transported is still a moot question.

The Romans' skill as hydraulic engineers is well known, and the excellence of the aqueducts which brought water to Rome itself was not equalled before the nineteenth century. Works of such complexity were not needed in Britain, but every settlement of consequence had an assured supply of water, delivered by pipe or aqueduct from a river or distant spring.[50] Most elaborate, perhaps, was the system built at Lincoln, which was 32 km long and included a syphon to raise the water to the level of the upper city.[51] Military establishments were in general better provided than civil. Water was sometimes brought in open leats, sometimes by pipes of wood, clay tile, or lead. The generous water-supply to most towns was used, in the first instance, to supply the public bathing establishments, and the rest was distributed for domestic use. It cannot be assumed, however, that an exclusive dependence was placed on this public supply. There were also wells, many of them within the gardens of urban houses. Villas seem to have relied on wells, though cases are known of short aqueducts and pipelines constructed to supply their needs.[52]

Another innovation introduced by the Romans was the latrine. Though latrines in Britain seem never to have reached the level of sophistication met with around the Mediterranean, they were a great improvement on anything that could have existed

53

in the late pre-Roman Iron Age. At Silchester there was a public latrine in a freestanding building, the seats placed above a brick-lined drain through which a stream had been made to flow.[53] At Caerwent (Mon.) drainage from a roof was used to flush out the trench beneath the latrine. There is some slight evidence for sewer systems beneath several other Roman towns, but only at Lincoln and York have sewage disposal systems, integrated with a piped water supply, been found.[54] Public latrines are unlikely to have satisfied the needs of most towns. Roman towns, at least in Britain, were not closely built, and houses often had a generous space around them. There was scope, therefore, for digging cesspits, which drained naturally and could be abandoned as they filled up and be replaced by others.[55] The same must have been the case at villas, where remarkably little evidence has been found to suggest that there were properly built latrines.

Considerable advances were made during the Roman period in domestic lighting. Oil-burning lamps had been known at least from the later Stone Ages. Without them underground mining, such as that at Grimes Graves, would have been impossible.[56] They consisted in general of soft rock, hollowed out to contain oil, together with a wick made of rush or moss. In northern Europe oil for the lamps was obtained from animal fat. Lamps were no doubt supplemented by torches of resinous wood. With advances in potting, ceramic lamps with a spout to hold the wick were introduced, probably displacing the cruder forms of lamp.[57] They were mass-produced and were traded in large numbers. An unopened crate of such lamps was, for example, found at Pompeii. Usually the oil vessel was covered, and its lid was sometimes decorated with embossed figures and motifs. They were doubtless cheap, and one must visualise them as placed around the home on small shelves or suspended by chains. Finds of such lamps have, however, been strangely few in Britain. Bronze lamps, made as castings in a clay mould, were to be found in better-off homes.[58] Their mode of manufacture permitted a wide range of decoration. Some assumed the shape of a dolphin, with the wick protruding from its mouth; others incorporated a serpent shaped to form a hook for hanging.[59] There were lamps with multiple wicks and lamps with messages and good wishes moulded on to their rims.

An alternative form of lighting was the candle, but, to judge from the relative scarcity of candle-holders, it must have been used much less frequently than the lamp. The reason could have been the difficulty in obtaining a fat which would retain its rigidity. Early tallow candles not only gave off an offensive smell but often wilted in their own heat. For this reason an early papal injunction required candles for church use to be made of beeswax.[60] An iron candlestick of classical date, now in the Museum of Archaeology, Cambridge, has an iron tube to receive the end of the candle and tripod legs to achieve a degree of rigidity. A bronze candlestick of Roman date was found in London, and is now in the London Museum.[61] The candlesticks and, in particular the lamps, which proliferated during the Roman period, were of a style and pattern which, for ordinary use, underwent no significant change before modern times. The Roman lamps could readily be mistaken for those of the later Middle Ages.

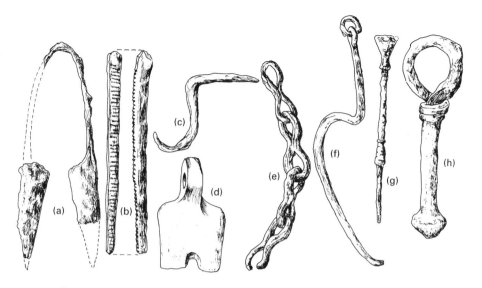

2.8 Miscellaneous Roman ironwork from the villa at Barnsley (Glos.): (a) shears, probably for sheep-shearing, (b) file, (c) wall-hook, (d) hinge, (e) chain, (f) latch-lifter, (g) stylus, (h) 'eye', probably mortared into a wall.

In other lesser arts the Romano-Britons achieved a standard and a style which survived little changed for more than a thousand years, and were not improved upon before modern times (Fig. 2.8). Sewing was carried on by means of bone needles, with a thimble to protect the fingers. Cloth was cut with small shears of the kind later used for shearing sheep. Scissors did not appear until very much later. Wool and flax were spun with distaff and bone spindle, its turning action assisted, as in the Iron Age, by a whorl, usually also of bone. Most homes would have contained a vertical loom, probably with a bottom beam or roller, as there is little evidence for warp weights (p. 25). The combs, commonly of bone, which served to press the weft into place, occasionally turn up at Roman sites.

The clothing worn by civilians was comparatively simple, and called for little sewing. The toga, commonly regarded as the pre-eminent Roman dress, is not met with on carved *stelae* in Britain. Instead, men are shown in short tunics, loosely gathered around the waist and reaching only to the knees. Underclothes may have consisted of nothing more than pants, but a cloak seems often to have been worn over the tunic and to have been held in place with a metal clasp or brooch. Such dress appears quite inadequate for a cold British winter, and it seems that for field work at least a form of loose-fitting trousers was worn. In addition there was a long tunic with a hood. This was the *byrrus*, and most people must have relied on it in cold and wet weather. A bas-relief at Housesteads, on the Roman Wall, shows three figures, each wearing a *byrrus* (Fig. 2.9).

The evidence for female dress is scanty. It appears to have consisted generally of an under-tunic, descending to the ankles, and, on top of it, a short over-tunic with

2.9 Bas-relief showing three persons wearing the *byrrus*; from Housesteads (Northbld.).

sleeves. Women left the home less frequently than men, but when they did so they probably used a cape similar to that worn by the men.

Footwear came in many styles and shapes. Most common was a sandal of leather, held in place by a thong which passed between the toes and around the ankle. But there were also shoes with leather uppers welted to the sole and intended for outdoor use; shoes with thick durable soles made by fastening together two or more thicknesses of leather with hobnails; and shoes, more akin to slippers, made of soft leather lined with wool.[62] In general Roman footwear had no pronounced heel and nothing to support the instep.

There is nothing to suggest that well-to-do Romans were particularly fashion-conscious. Ladies' shoes were sometimes brightly coloured, but their tunics were probably drab, and the only evidence of personal adornment lies in the brooches with which men held their capes in place and in the rings, bracelets and necklaces worn by the ladies. Strings of beads, made of glass, amber, jet or other such substance, and even chains of gold links were popular. Most of this jewellery was broadly classical in design, but the motifs with which it is embellished not infrequently reveal that underlying Celtic sub-culture which survived acculturation both by Roman and also by medieval civilisation.

The family

We can trace in not inconsiderable detail the planning of villa and urban house, but what we cannot penetrate is the domestic and family life that was lived in them.

There are no diaries, portraits or intimate records. We do not know how large were completed families, what was the expectation of life, and how land and chattels were passed from one generation to another. Least of all do we know how many of the customs practised by the romanised élite also prevailed amongst the Celtic masses. One small insight into the family life of at least the cultivated Roman-Britons can be gained through the funeral *stelae* which they sometimes erected. These occasionally represented scenes of domestic bliss, and showed family groups such as the Victorians loved to portray. The expressions of deep affection found in the inscriptions may, like the embraces of the parents, be little more than convention. But this was, nevertheless, the impression which they wished to leave for posterity.

At a more realistic level, we know that society was male-dominated; that in upper-class households the wife ran the home, entertained guests, but took no part in public life. On the other hand, both law and custom prescribed that a widow should have for the rest of her life a considerable share of her late husband's inheritance. Only then did she have the opportunity and the means to live a life of her own. But it would appear, from the totally inadequate evidence of funeral *stelae*, that the proportion of wives who outlived their husbands was relatively small. Women were at far greater risks from child-bearing than they are today, and infant and child mortality, on the basis of the same non-random evidence, was also high. The *stela* of Flavia Augustina, widow of a Roman soldier stationed at York (Fig. 2.10), shows a family with two children who both died before they had reached the age of two.[63]

The world-view

How did people in Roman Britain view the world in which they lived, and what did they perceive to be their place within it? Villas, with their tesselated floors and painted walls, suggest an urbane and sophisticated way of life, to which the gods of Greece and Rome and the legends of heroes provided only a colourful backdrop with which they interacted scarcely at all. On the other hand, they set up little altars to the guardian deities of the household, their particular *lares* and *penates*.[64] The origin of these deities is as uncertain as the degree of reverence with which they were regarded. They were venerated, perhaps in much the same way as the statuettes set in niches and corners of an Italian house today. Together they were seen to guard the home and to represent the spirits of the family's ancestors.[65]

At a more general level, the principal cult of the Empire was that of the emperor himself and of his deified ancestors. They were venerated as symbols of the might and majesty of the Empire itself. It is a mistake to suppose that citizens looked upon their emperors as omnipotent deities; the violent ends of many of them would serve to contradict this view. Most towns of any importance would have had a temple dedicated to the imperial cult, and Boudicca was at pains to destroy the temple dedicated to the Emperor Claudius at Colchester. Reverence for the traditional gods of Rome was often associated with the imperial cult, since they were regarded as

2.10 *Stela* of Flavia Augustina, York.

protectors of the emperor and Empire. One cannot assume that Romano-Britons had any deep regard for cults so foreign to their Celtic traditions. Liversidge has pointed out that dedications to the classical gods were most common at military establishments, suggesting that their cults had arrived with the soldiers from other parts of the empire.[66]

Dedicatory altars, *stelae* and temples suggest a superficial acceptance of the classical hierarchy of gods and goddesses, some of whom came to be identified with traditional Celtic deities. The temple at Bath (Aquae Sulis), for example, was dedicated to Sul Minerva, a hybrid Celtic-classical deity (Fig. 2.11),[67] and there are other instances of the conflation of Roman deities with those of the native Celts. The pediment of the Bath temple contained a depiction of the gorgon's head, which both conformed with the Celtic reverence for the human head and contained also an element of classical mythology. There were other cult sites within the city in

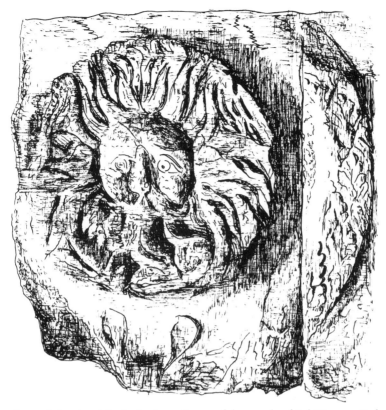

2.11 Gorgon's head, originally in the pediment of the temple of Sul Minerva, Bath. See I. A. Richmond and J. M. C. Toynbee, 'The temple of Sulis Minerva at Bath', *Jl Rom St*, 45 (1955), 97–105.

addition to the temple of Sul Minerva. Their dedicatees are unknown, except the one to the imperial divinity. Bath appears to have combined the roles of resort and spa with that of cult centre – a sort of classical Lourdes. Indeed, it would have been difficult to distinguish between these functions since a medical cure was attributed to the direct intervention of the gods. The power of the deities, both classical and Celtic, is demonstrated by the vast number of votive objects thrown into the reservoir of the hot springs. Some were curses which the deity was called upon to implement; others were coins and small metallic objects, evidently regarded in the popular mind as rewards for services rendered by the gods or as payments in anticipation. In essence this practice was no different from that of the tourist who today casts an odd coin into the Fountain of Trevi. We see the beliefs and practices of the Celts impinging here and there on the religious customs of Rome. One must, however, never lose sight of the fact that Britain was a land of two cultures: that of the romanised élite and that of the mass of the Celtic population, however frequently these cultures may seem to meet and commingle.[68]

Implicit in the religious practices of both the élite and the popular cultures is some kind of a belief in a future life. This is evident from both literary and archaeological sources. But it is less clear where the deceased were to spend their eternity. The belief that there existed a distant place beyond the Styx, where spirits would reside in perpetuity, was widely held, as was the view that rituals had to be performed in order to assist the passage of the spirit to this promised land. Burial ceremonies were thus of great importance. Cremation was practised throughout most of the Roman period. The prevailing view seems to have been that fire purged the soul of its earthly mantle, leaving it free to join the ethereal spirits in the Elysian Fields. In this regard the views held a thousand years later did not differ fundamentally from those accepted in Roman Britain.

An alternative view would have left the dead in the graves where their bodies or their ashes had been buried. There the spirits would continue to live, returning to help or to haunt the living as circumstances might dictate. This latter point of view might seem more consistent with the pantheistic world-view which was part of Celtic culture. The dualistic concept of a heaven separate from earth and of death as the passage from one to the other is classical in origin, and is likely to have held the greatest appeal to the more romanised élite of Romano-British society. It is against this background that we must set the arrival of cults, mainly of Middle Eastern origin, during the closing centuries of the Roman Empire.

These cults were, in the main, introduced by soldiers who had served in other parts of the Empire, and by traders whose business had taken them to southern Europe and the Levant.[69] Their appeal was mainly to soldiers and to a romanised upper class, and it was mainly in the town and military camps that their followers were to be found. The cult of Mithra was important enough for its followers to have built a large temple within the city of London. It was characterised by secret rituals, and, perhaps for this reason, had no lasting impact on popular culture.

Christianity reached Britain later than Mithraism, with which it had certain features in common, and appears to have been more widely accepted. A number of late Roman buildings have been identified, however tentatively, as Christian churches. Charles Thomas lists a dozen such sites.[70] Christianity differed from other cults of oriental origin by its more public nature and by its official recognition under Constantine, in AD 312, as the religion of the Empire. But it was in the main an urban cult and its impact on the Celtic culture of the countryside was probably slight; the people of the *pagi* remained predominantly *pagan*.

Whether Christianity disappeared from Britain with the collapse of Roman rule is a moot question. It had reached Ireland in the late fourth or early fifth centuries, and its development there was uninterrupted. But in Britain towns were by and large, abandoned, and the urban élites, who are most likely to have been converted, disappeared. The invading Anglo-Saxon and Jutish peoples of the later fifth and the sixth centuries, were pagan, and under their influence one might expect any surviving traces of Christianity to have been submerged. But the church may have survived in Wales,[71] and it was certainly active in Ireland throughout this period.[72] At the same time the church was making progress in Gaul and it would be surprising if Britain – now in process of transformation into England – remained immune to its influence through those centuries. When Augustine reached Canterbury in 597 he found a pagan chieftain with a wife who was at least a crypto-Christian. But the scale of any survival of Christianity into the early Anglo-Saxon period must have been insignificant. Not until the Middle Saxon period did Christianity begin to have a significant impact on the popular culture of this island. This influence was, however, a two-way process. The popular culture of the pagan population had an impact on Christianity which lasted through the Middle Ages and is in some respects present still.

Decline and fall

In the year 410 Rome was occupied by the Visigoths, and the Emperor Honorius left the provincials in Britain to look to their own defences. The popular imagination has long equated this event with the 'fall' of the Empire. But the Empire had always been more a federation of provinces than a unitary state, and the province of Britain was itself a grouping of quasi-independent *civitates*, without any powerful central authority. To this extent, the withdrawal of the legions, which occurred gradually through the previous century, increased the danger of Germanic invasion, which, nevertheless, did not come in any significant fashion for at least another half-century. The 'fall' consisted rather of the breakdown of social and economic institutions, a process which had its origins long before the Western Empire began to be seriously threatened by Germanic and barbarian tribes.

Roman Britain had been a land of two cultures, but the divide between them was far from unbridgeable and was nowhere clear-cut. The culture of the romanised minority flourished in the towns, with which the rural villas maintained close contacts. This group enjoyed the material comforts and the physical pleasures which the Empire had made possible. They probably spoke Latin, if only badly, and their cults and rituals, none of them very deeply felt, were those of Rome. They enjoyed the urbane, sophisticated pleasures of the forum and the baths. Many of them were, of course, soldiers and merchants, but most were in some measure *rentiers*, their comfortable way of life made possible by income from rural estates and urban property. And, like all *rentiers*, their way of life was predicated on economic stability. And this is what, in the closing centuries of the Empire, they did not have. High taxation, problems of urban government, the cost of maintaining public works, and the most severe inflation known before modern times all combined to weaken both their economic and their social position. Long before the end of the Western Empire they were beginning to desert the towns, where many of them could no longer afford to maintain their lifestyle, and to retreat to their villas and country estates. And with their departure urban trade and crafts became depressed and the local infrastructure decayed.

This is what was happening in the fourth and fifth centuries. It was a process of *deculturation*; of the gradual elimination of an élite or its transformation into a

61

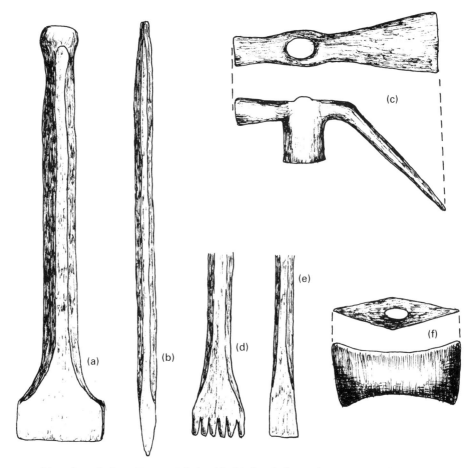

2.12 Mason's tools from Roman Britain: (a) chisel or bolster, (b) point, (c) adze, (d) claw-chisel, (e) chisel, (f) axe. This level of sophistication disappeared after the withdrawal of Roman control. After T. F. C. Blagg, 'Tools and techniques of the Roman stonemason in Britain', *Brit*, 7 (1976), 152–72.

germanised upper class. This process could only have been accelerated when a sense of impending disaster was sharpened by the departure of the legions. There is no record, other than archaeological, of these trends. But the course of events is clear. Towns were gradually depopulated; the line of their streets was lost beneath the rubble and 'black soil' of urban decay, and the handful of people who continued to live there were engaged only in rural pursuits.

What matters in the context of this book is the disappearance of an élite culture, with its veneer of classical learning, its urban infrastructure, its public buildings and its private comforts. With it went the popular use of the Latin language, for it is highly unlikely that it was, apart from a few words and phrases, in common use among the mass of the population. Their speech was almost certainly a form of Brythonic Celtic, such as survived in the South-west into modern times.

The culture of Britain thus became a *popular* culture, and this it remained until such time as an élite culture could again emerge. The forms that had been assumed by élite culture were generalised; they differed little from one part of the country to another because the bearers of that culture travelled and had frequent and regular contacts with one another. Popular culture, on the other hand, was locally based. It reflected physical conditions and personal idiosyncrasies. Custom and ritual, dialect and belief varied from one settlement to another. The bearers of popular culture did not see themselves as members of a countrywide society. Their mental horizon was narrow. Their spirits and saints were different from those of their neighbours. It is to this intense local culture, in part Celtic in origin, in part derived from immigrant Germanic peoples, with, over it all, a Christian veneer, that we now turn in the later chapters of this book.

❖ CHAPTER 3 ❖

HOUSE AND HOUSEHOLD

Methods of construction filtered down in the course of time from one stratum of society
to another.
C. F. Innocent

There can have been few occasions in the course of recorded history when physical standards of well-being fell as sharply and as profoundly as they did after the legions had been withdrawn from Britain. But it may be questioned whether this was equally true of all levels of society. It is possible that the end of Roman rule was as little marked on the western and northern fringes of Britain as its establishment had been some four centuries earlier. There is, indeed, good evidence to suppose that the material culture of the late pre-Roman Iron Age continued with little significant change, not only through the centuries of Roman rule but also into those of the Anglo-Saxon conquest which followed.[1] In cultural terms, the end of Roman rule was marked by the elimination of the upper strata of late Roman society. Villas were abandoned because the economic structure which had supported them had disintegrated. Towns ceased to be centres of urban life because their crafts and trade were no longer needed by a society increasingly rural and self-sufficient and because the machinery of government, which had centred in them, had disappeared. In Britain, there ceased, in any cultural sense, to be an élite. Material standards fell. It was not that villas and public buildings were no longer built; those that already existed were not even maintained in usable condition. Excavation shows that villas and towns were not, in general, destroyed, but that they were abandoned and allowed to fall into decay. The Empire in Britain ended, not in a blaze of warfare and destruction, but with scarcely a whimper.

Building, vernacular and élite

This chapter is concerned with the physical structures in which people lived during the centuries which stretched from the coming of the Anglo-Saxons to the eve of the Industrial Revolution in the eighteenth century. This society was far from egalitarian. There were extreme differences in wealth and status; there were thegns as

64

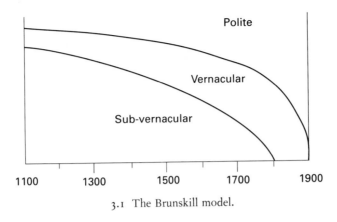

3.1 The Brunskill model.

well as ceorls in Anglo-Saxon England, and, after the Norman Conquest, lords as well as villeins. Status and wealth were reflected in the quality of diet and dress and, above all, in housing. An emerging élite class generated in the course of time an élite style of architecture. From the roughly built huts of the invasion period there emerged, slowly and hesitatingly, a more elaborate style of building, larger, more highly decorated and, above all, more comfortable and more durable.

Brunskill has offered us a model showing how the standards of the upper social strata were gradually diffused downwards towards the lowest levels of society. He distinguishes three classes of structure. Simplest would have been those of which no visible trace remains above ground, and usually only post-holes below, either because they were not sufficiently durable or because they had been torn down and replaced by others more commodious and comfortable. Such simple structures lay, in Brunskill's words, below the vernacular threshold. Above that line (Fig. 3.1) there evolved the immense range of vernacular building. This, as Brunskill has defined it, consisted of buildings whose designers 'have made some attempt, however untutored and however unsuccessful, to make the buildings pleasant to look upon . . . examples of architecture rather than building'.[2] Most domestic and farm buildings surviving from the pre-industrial age belong to this class.

At a higher social level there slowly emerged a style of building variously known as 'grand', 'élite' or 'polite'. It was distinguished by its greater size and the richer elaboration of its architectural and decorative detail. It was, to use an expression that came later to be applied to it, professionally designed and constructed. It was available only to a minority of the population because its costs of construction were high. Nevertheless, aspects of the 'grand' style came in time to be incorporated into the vernacular, as wealth increased and standards improved, so that the number of houses above the élite threshold increased markedly with time.[3]

At the same time sub-vernacular buildings became less numerous and important, as, with successive rebuilding, they came within the range of the vernacular. Vernacular building also tended to move upmarket, with the adoption of features — suites of chambers or withdrawing-rooms, large kitchens with separate buttery,

65

pantry and brewhouse, and very large halls – which had characterised the 'grand' style. It was this tendency for a building to transform itself and, in doing so, to move from one category to another, that makes the classification of domestic buildings so uncertain.

This change became especially marked in the sixteenth and seventeenth centuries, the period of the 'great rebuild'.[4] It was then, that the number of sub-vernacular buildings declined most sharply, though they had not completely disappeared even by the nineteenth. This change was not uniform throughout the country. It was later in some counties than in others, and there were places where it scarcely appeared at all. At the same time grand building became even grander, and the spectrum of domestic building was never broader – from the one-roomed hovel to Chatsworth and Stowe – than it was in the middle years of the eighteenth century. It was innovation in the division and specialisation of rooms, in the adoption of the fireplace instead of the central hearth, in the banishment of cooking from the living quarters to a kitchen, in the construction of solars and the insertion of upper floors, and, at a much later date, the introduction of bathrooms and toilets, that raised the sub-vernacular to the vernacular, and the latter to the grand. The comforts and conveniences which the rich had been able over the centuries to install in their houses, were imitated by those of smaller means and were adopted in their less pretentious houses. This was the path of progress, the rich blazing the way and the less rich following and imitating at their individual rates. In this way comfort and convenience slowly filtered down from precedent to imitation.

The villa of Roman Britain bore little or no relationship to the Iron Age huts that had preceded it. It was an imported concept, the product of a foreign culture of Mediterranean origin, and was in all probability built by those who had the means to do so as much as a status symbol as for the comforts it offered. It was, despite the variety of forms that it assumed, a form of 'grand' building, standing in the strongest contrast with the ordinary housing of the greater part of the population.

The 'grand' building of the Middle Ages, if we may exclude from this discussion the castle and the strongly fortified home, grew, by contrast, out of the prevailing folk culture. The 'grand' manor-house embraced the same elements as the simple cottage, often arranged in very much the same way, but it had become bigger in concept and scale. The manor-house was the cottage 'writ large', and the 'stately home' – the grandest of the grand – grew out of the manor-house and embraced the same features, though their relative scale and importance would have changed and ashlar masonry and decorative brickwork might have replaced timber-framing and wattle and daub. Though the concepts of sub-vernacular, vernacular and grand may be clear enough in theory, it is remarkably difficult to draw a line between them in the field, so readily does the one merge into the other.

Some idea of the type of housing that prevailed in the invasion period can be obtained from the few Anglo-Saxon sites that have been discovered and excavated. Domestic building before the Norman Conquest was almost exclusively in wood, and one looks in vain for structures comparable with the masonry-built churches of the period. Excavated Anglo-Saxon settlements have tended, by and large, to be those that were occupied for only a relatively short period before being abandoned.[5] Those which were continuously occupied are, in the main, little known, because their remains lie buried and inaccessible. Furthermore, most of the Anglo-Saxon sites that have been explored lay on the well-drained sand and gravel deposits of valley terraces, where the chances of survival of post-holes and other remains are greater than they would have been in clayland villages.

The majority of excavated structures of the early Anglo-Saxon period show sunken features. They are what have been termed 'pit-dwellings' or *Grubenhäuser*, the floor being sunk up to half a metre into the soil. Such dwellings were practicable only on a porous soil; elsewhere they would have filled with water after every storm. If a more random selection of Anglo-Saxon sites could have been excavated, 'pit-dwellings' might not have been as dominant as at present they seem. Sunken structures are more or less rectangular in plan, and range between 3 and 5 metres in both length and breadth.[6] It is very doubtful indeed whether they actually served as 'underground' dwellings. More likely the depression was boarded over, and the space beneath used for storage and for insulation. At Mucking (Essex) no less than 211 sunken huts have been excavated within an area of only 20 hectares. This denotes, 'not a single, sprawling village, but rather . . . a shifting hamlet', the huts undergoing a continuous process of building, decay and rebuilding.[7] New pits are found to cut into older pits that had been abandoned as they filled with rubbish or their sides collapsed.

At West Stowe (Suffolk) a small village of such huts has been excavated. The structures, of which only post-holes and a few artefacts have survived, were far from primitive. A framed building, with presumably a ridge roof of thatch and walls of split boards, was set over the sunken floor. The accommodation may well have seemed warm and comfortable.[8] That some huts served as spinning sheds or workshops is suggested by finds of loom-weights and weaving pins.

As at Mucking, there is evidence for a shift in the location of the huts, if not also of the whole settlement. But at any one time the huts seem to have been arranged irregularly around a building two or three times larger than any of them (Fig. 3.2). Its floor was not sunken and there were traces of a central hearth. Post-holes suggest that it was a strongly built structure, which could have served as a kind of hall.

Later in the Saxon period sunken huts seem to have been replaced with framed buildings set directly on the ground. Their vertical members were placed in post-holes, and rigidity was provided by wall-plates, braces and even wooden buttresses, all held together by tenon joints. Roofs consisted of rafters, securely fastened by means of pegs and held firm with purlins. The whole was probably covered with thatch. Such construction methods allowed buildings even larger than the halls which were the dominant feature at West Stowe to be erected. By the late Saxon period an élite style of building had begun to emerge from the general run of huts, whether sunken or not.[9]

The palace of the middle and late Saxon kings consisted of a great hall, together

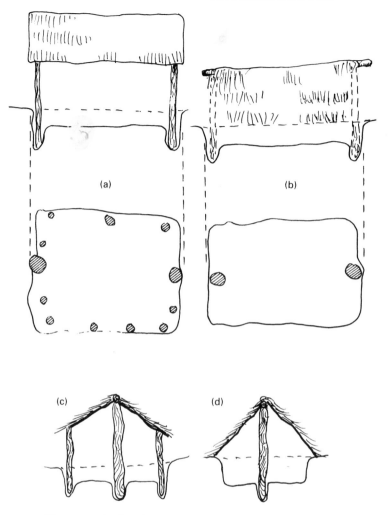

3.2 West Stow (Suff.): drawings showing the construction of huts.

with various ancillary buildings, which were later to be organised into a regular plan. Such halls have been excavated at Yeavering (Northbld.)[10] and at Cheddar (Som.).[11] The former was an aisled hall of five bays, its roof partly supported by a double row of massive wooden posts. Its dimensions, about 25m by 11m, were a measure of its importance. Its form derived from the Low Countries and north-west Germany, where aisled halls of considerable size had been built at least as early as the Roman period (Fig. 3.3).[12] In England it became the model from which were ultimately derived the great halls of the Middle Ages, such as those at Oakham (Rutland), Leicester and Winchester.

The other great house of Anglo-Saxon England excavated so far was at Cheddar. It was built in the late ninth or early tenth century, and consisted of a hall almost 25m

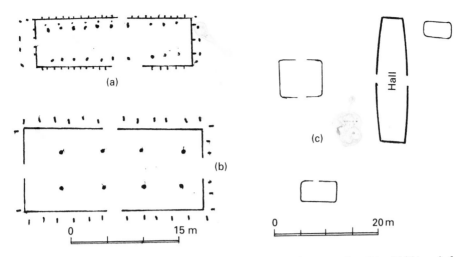

3.3 Aisled halls at (a) Fochtelo in Friesland, Netherlands; (b) Yeavering (Northbld.) and, for comparison, (c) the 'bowed' hall at Cheddar (Som.).

long, with at least three ancillary buildings. A feature of the Cheddar hall is that it almost certainly had an upper floor over at least part of it, thus making it, in later terminology, a 'first-floor hall'. The Anglo-Saxon Chronicle, under the year 978, tells how the upper floor of such a house, in which the king was present, collapsed, leaving the archbishop perched on a joist.[13] The earliest surviving illustration of an Anglo-Saxon house also shows it as a first-floor hall. It is the representation in the Bayeux Tapestry of King Harold feasting in his hall at Bosham (Sussex) before setting out on his ill-fated voyage to Normandy (Fig. 3.4). The upper floor is shown supported by what look like pillars, ostensibly of wood, and reached by an outside staircase.

The rectangular huts excavated at Mucking, West Stowe and elsewhere, were constructed exclusively of wood, but in parts of western Britain stone was also used. This was due in part to the lack of good timber, but also to the abundance of rough stone that rose naturally to the surface of the ground and could literally be gathered and used. In plan also the western house sometimes differed from that built in lowland Britain. It was often longer in proportion to its width and embraced beneath the same roof accommodation for both human beings and animals. The two compartments were separated by some form of cross-wall, with an opening to give access from the one to the other.[14] One cannot say how widespread was this so-called 'long-house'. It is sometimes said to have been characteristic of the Celtic west, largely because it is there that most surviving examples are to be found (p. 77). The plan was adopted and has survived probably because it 'provided shelter . . . for man and animal in conditions where easy access to the cattle in all weathers was a necessity'.[15] Such houses had been built in the Germanic homeland of the Saxon peoples, where stabling and barn are still to be found today beneath the same roof as

3.4 Harold feasting at Bosham (Sussex) prior to setting sail for Normandy: after the Bayeux Tapestry. This is the earliest known representation of an aisled hall.

living-rooms and kitchen but there is little or no surviving evidence for its existence in lowland England.

A generation ago such a house was excavated on the slopes above the cove of Mawgan Porth, on the north coast of Cornwall.[16] It was not particularly long in relation to its width, but it contained the essential feature of a long-house, a cattle byre at one end, directly accessible from the living quarters (Fig. 3.5). The settlement is difficult to date, but may have been of the late ninth century, and thus contemporary with the 'palace' at Cheddar. More recently other long-houses of early medieval date have been identified in the south-western peninsula, notably at Tresworn and Treworld in Cornwall and at Hound Tor on Dartmoor. They are all longer in relation to their width than that found at Mawgan Porth, and in each case the byre could be entered directly from the living area.[17]

(a)

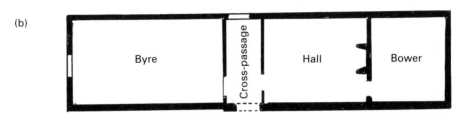

(b)

Byre

Cross-passage

Hall

Bower

3.5   A typical long-house: (a) elevation, (b) plan.

Norman Conquest and after

The conquest of much of Britain by the Normans during the years following 1066 intensified the rate of change in domestic housing. They brought new ideas, as well as craftsmen skilled in techniques that had already been developed on the continent. The familiarity with this country, which the Normans quickly gained, opened up for them a wide range of building resources, and the greater degree of unity which they imposed facilitated both the flow of ideas and the transport of materials.

The widening gulf between the halls and palaces of the Saxon aristocracy and the simple huts in which the majority of the population lived has already been demonstrated. At the bottom of the social scale there were still the huts of the ceorls, while at the top the Saxon thegn might have enjoyed the security of a fenced enclosure, with a hall and some kind of protected entrance. The effect of the Conquest was to widen the gulf which separated them. Yet there must have been some degree of social mobility. 'If a ceorl', in the words of the Anglo-Saxon *Rectitudines singularum personarum* 'throve so that he had fully five hides [of land] . . . a church and kitchen, bell-house and burh-gate, seat and special duty in the king's hall, then was he henceforth worthy of thegn-right.'[18] One can, with the help of recent excavations, visualise the thegn's hall, with its detached kitchen, its private church, destined before too long to become a parish church, bellcote and protected

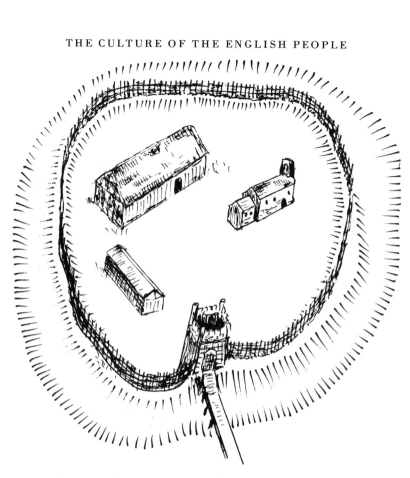

3.6 A late Anglo-Saxon thegn's house, showing hall, barn, church and protected entrance; based on G. Beresford, *The Medieval Clay-land Village*.

entrance (Fig. 3.6), far removed from the simplicity of a hut at Mucking or West Stowe.

The Normans who had inherited the land must also have taken over the halls of the Saxon thegns. In some instances these were replaced, *in situ* or elsewhere, by buildings of greater military significance. In others the earliest Norman manor-house can have differed little if at all from the thegn's lightly protected hall. Indeed, there might have been no change at all. The castles which began to proliferate during the closing decades of the eleventh century were essentially the fortified homes of the king and his barons. Minor barons and mere knights had to be content with less secure homes.[19] But there was a grey area, represented by ringworks and the smallest mottes, where the thegn's hall merged with the fortified home. It is with the unprotected home and its development within the limits of traditional society that we are largely concerned in this and the following chapters.

The cottages in which the mass of the population lived – sub-vernacular in Brunskill's terminology – must remain largely unknown. They were small and flimsily built, and can have lasted only a few years before being renewed on the same

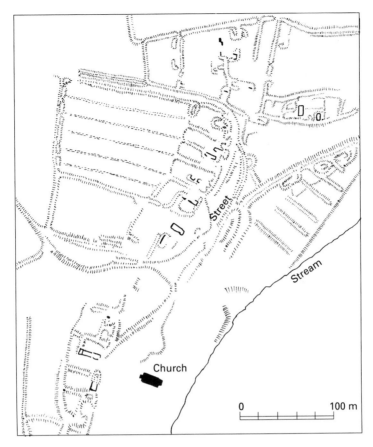

3.7 Wharram Percy (E. Yorks.), a deserted village abandoned in the later Middle Ages. After M. Beresford and J. G. Hurst, *Deserted Medieval Villages*, edn of 1989, Gloucester.

or an adjoining site. This constant building and rebuilding figures in the manorial court rolls, but has left little trace in the landscape. Only when a village was abandoned, as very many were during the later Middle Ages and the sixteenth century, can one obtain by excavation a picture of the medieval cottage and of the village of which it formed part.[20]

No drawings or literary descriptions help one to trace the slow elaboration of the simple one-roomed cottage. It can only be said that in the course of its continuing renewal, it grew larger, became divided into two cells, acquired windows and an extra door, and sometimes even a separate kitchen, like the thegn's hall. Such were the cottages that have been revealed in recent years by the excavation of deserted village sites. They are found ranged irregularly along the sides of a winding village street, each surrounded by its small toft, on which the cottager was free to grow what he chose and to keep a pig and a few hens (Fig. 3.7). The whole cluster was encapsulated, at least in Midland England, within its open-fields, each made up of

73

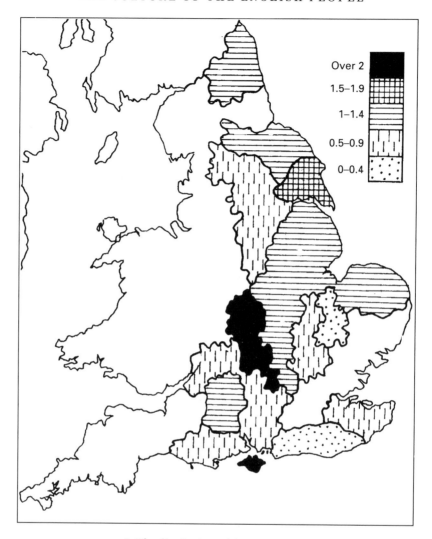

3.8 The distribution of deserted villages.

bundles of selions or strips, on which the peasant toiled for much of the year. In many deserted villages it is possible to locate one or more houses of greater size. These were in all probability manor-houses, seats of the local lord and more carefully crafted than the rest, models for the emulation of the rest of the local community. The manor-house might occasionally have been sufficiently large and elaborate to justify the term 'élite' or 'grand', but most belonged to the upper range of vernacular building. The date of foundation and even of abandonment of such villages can be known only approximately, but it is probable that most represent at least two centuries of growth beyond the late Saxon period. During this time there was development in three directions: in plan, in the mode of construction, and in the kinds of material used. Each of these aspects of vernacular architecture will be examined (Fig. 3.8).

The cottage plan

The cottage of the medieval peasant can at first have differed little from those of the early Saxon invaders, except that the floor was no longer hollowed out. It was rectangular in plan, with a single entrance and a hearth in the middle of the floor. There was no chimney, and the smoke was allowed to escape where it could. Such huts have continued into modern times to be inhabited in remote areas of the north and west, but over much of Britain cottage plans became much more complex than this long before the end of the Middle Ages. Chaucer's 'poor widow', who was certainly far from affluent, had

> a narwe cotage,
> Bisyde a grove, stonding in a dale.
>
> .   .   .   .   .   .
>
> Ful sooty was hir *bour*, and eke hir *halle*
> In which she eet ful many a sclendre meel.

Chaucer went on to describe her toft:

> A yerd she hadde, enclosed al aboute,

in which she kept her remarkably talented cock, as well as:

> Three large sowes . . .
> Three kyn [kine], and eek a sheep.[21]

The peasant cottage had by this time come to be divided by a cross-wall or partition into a hall, or living-room, and a bower, which may have served for storage and for sleeping during the warmer months. A hearth in the midst of the hall floor served for both heating and cooking, and its smoke was allowed to rise to the blackened rafters. Such a plan lent itself to a range of variations and additions. As well as the bower at one end of the hall, a kitchen and other domestic quarters might be added at the other. A second entrance might be opened opposite the first, thus creating the cross-passage, which was to become so dominant a feature of the later medieval and early modern house. The chamber block at one end of the hall as well as the kitchen block at the other might be built forwards to give greater space, so that the hall would appear to be recessed between them. These 'wings' might then be given upper floors, which might 'jetty' or project over the lower. The next stage in the evolution of the house might be to shift the hearth from its central position in the hall to a side wall, where a hood and chimney could be built to carry away the smoke. Lastly, the open hall itself might be divided horizontally, with joists and floorboards inserted to create an upper storey. These developments, spread over four or more centuries, are shown schematically in Figure 3.9.

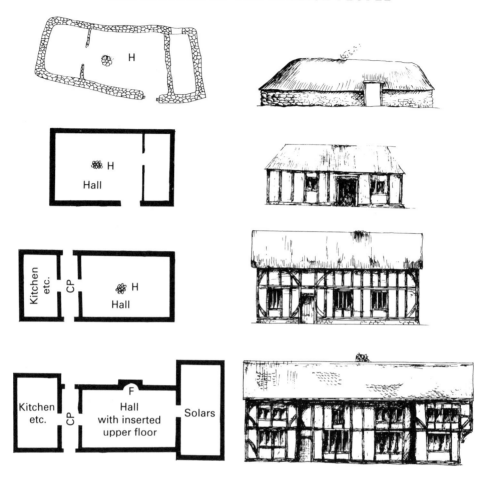

3.9 The pedigree of the traditional English house. It is not suggested that any single house ever evolved through these stages; only that these were sequential forms in house construction. This scheme applies to Midland and south-eastern England. The sequence would have been significantly different elsewhere.

One must, however, beware of thinking of this as an evolutionary process in which all houses participated. It was, in fact, highly selective. The houses of the richer members of a community might be expected to develop more or less along these lines, but those of the poorer did not. At any one time in the later Middle Ages or early modern times a community might exhibit houses of advanced plan and construction cheek by jowl with others which showed little improvement over the huts of the Anglo-Saxon period.

The size and especially the width of a cottage depended in part on the resources of the peasant who built it, and in part on the availability of timber of adequate length and girth. The peasant commonly enjoyed the right of 'husbote', of cutting and gathering timber for building and repairing his house from the lord's woodland, and sometimes one finds a record of a special dispensation to take sufficient timber for a specific purpose. But in the more densely settled parts of Britain an increasing shortage of suitable trees restricted building practice and led to the adoption of devices for using shorter and less massive timbers and for spacing them more widely in a framed building. There is evidence for more careful exploitation of the woodlands, if not also for deliberate conservation. Rafters and the studding of walls must often have been thinner and more widely spaced than was desirable to support a heavy roof. Cottages were, as a general rule, up to 10 m in length, but rarely more than 4 m wide. This was as much as the peasant was likely to have the timber to roof. But there were very great variations between one part of the country and another and between the rich peasant and the poor.

Only post-holes, the imprint of a wooden sill or stone footings can as a general rule be found today, and it is difficult to infer from these the construction of walls and roof. Our knowledge of building construction derives mainly from houses higher in the social scale and mainly of later date. Generally speaking, walls, whether timber-framed or partially of masonry, were low, and supported the roughest of rafters, secured by simple ties, collars and purlins. The roofs were commonly of thatch or turf. Such a cottage, found in mid-Wales and described at the end of the last century, must be regarded as a modern representative of the early medieval peasant house (Fig. 3.10).[22]

The long-house, already mentioned (p. 69) was a particular development of the simple one- or two-celled house.[23] Evidence for its continued use in modern times is almost exclusively from the western parts of the British Isles, where both climate and terrain made it desirable. The last long-house in Ireland is said to have passed out of use only in the middle of the present century.[24] This form of house was widely used in Wales in the seventeenth century, and there is evidence for it at a much earlier date in some parts of lowland England. Much of it comes from excavated house sites, but there is also corroborative evidence in court rolls and charters. There are references to *domus longa*, and one Worcestershire peasant had '*i domun pro aula sua et pro bovira*' (one house for his hall and for his cattle).[25] Excavations carried out by Musty and Algar at Gomeldon (Wilts.) demonstrated not only the development of a long-house settlement, but also the final abandonment of 'the classic function of the long-house towards the end of the 13th century' (Fig. 3.11).[26] The replacement of the long-house by a cottage with separate byre and barn was part of the general improvement in material standards of living which took place in the later Middle Ages.[27] Surviving long-houses became objects of contempt or ridicule, as William Moffet's lines show:

> A house well built and with much strength
> Almost two hundred feet in length.
>
> .   .   .   .
>
> At one of th'ends he kept his cowse.
> At t'other end he kept his spouse.

77

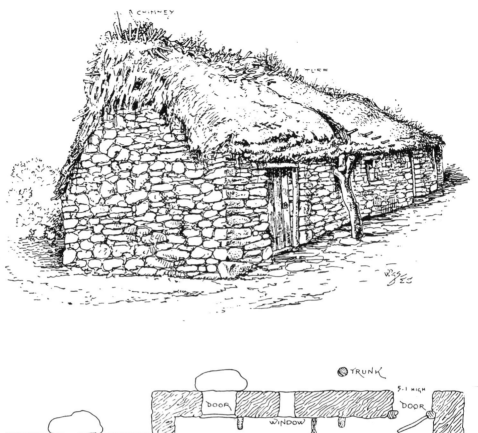

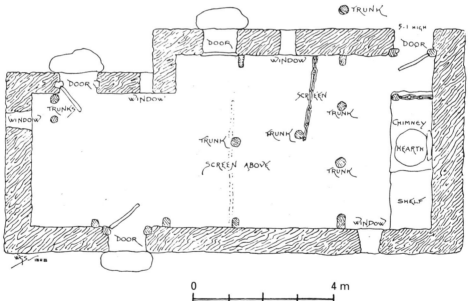

3.10 A Welsh peasant's cottage; from S. W. Williams, 'An ancient Welsh farmhouse, *Arch Camb*, 5th ser., 1899, 320–5; this was, in effect, a long-house.

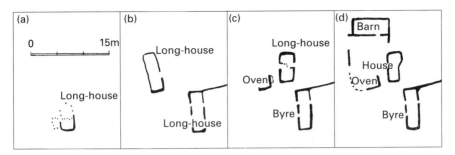

3.11 Gomeldon (Wilts.): the evolution of a farmstead from a long-house to a farm with detached stable and barn. The long-house was probably more widespread in Lowland England than present evidence might suggest.

But a dual-purpose house did not have to be long, with a cross-passage and direct communication between its two parts. It could, and often did, assume other forms. The bastle-house of northern England and adjoining parts of southern Scotland was a building of at least two storeys, with accommodation for the animals on the ground floor and for its human occupants above.[29] Bastle-houses were, by and large, of the sixteenth and seventeenth centuries. They were strongly built and were intended to give protection against cattle rustlers and feuding kinships (p. 255). Even later in date was the laithe-house of the northern counties. Here the barn and byre were set beside the house, but without cross-passage and, often enough, without communicating door.[30] Its upper floor, greater space and, frequently, its wagon-entry were marks of its higher economic status. The close juxtaposition of man and beast in all these types of building may have resulted from simple convenience, or it may have represented the local survival of an age-old building tradition.

The structure of the house

Early Saxon huts, if modern reconstructions at West Stowe are to be trusted, were built of a framework of posts, set in post-holes, and held rigid at the top by a wall-plate to which the rafters were affixed with pegs. The walls themselves were covered with either wattle and daub or with wooden boards. The most serious shortcoming of this mode of construction was that the posts rotted in the ground, leading to the collapse of the hut. A partial solution was to set the posts on a sill-plate or 'sleeper' which was placed directly on the ground. But the use of a stone footing or plinth for wooden or timber-framed walls was the only long-term solution.

In this, the commonest mode of construction, wall and roof were separate, the one resting on and supported by the other. An alternative method of construction was to make the wall and roof in one piece. Two 'blades' were set in the soil or on the ground opposite one another and meeting overhead to form a ridge roof (Fig. 3.12). This was 'cruck' construction.[31] It called for heavy timbers of a thickness not often

79

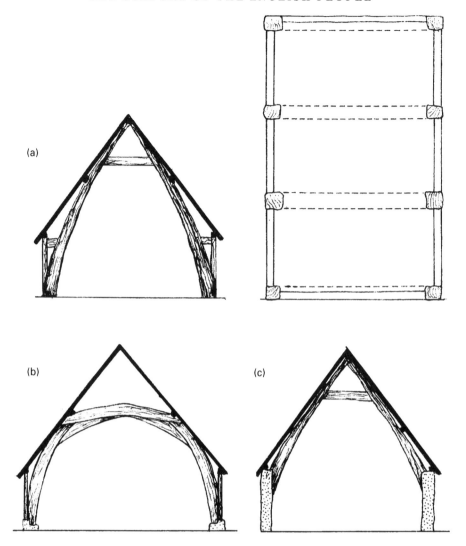

3.12 The principal types of cruck construction: (a) full cruck, (b) base cruck, with roofing truss scarfed to it, (c) raised cruck, supported by a base of wood or masonry. After N. W. Alcock, *Cruck Construction*, CBA, Res Rept 42, 1981.

found in the later Middle Ages. The two blades consisted essentially of a tree-trunk, split down the middle, and were held fast by means of a collar. At least two pairs of crucks were necessary for any structure, and the smallest cruck-built cottage usually had three or four pairs. Two pairs of crucks, their distance apart determined by a purlin, constituted a 'bay'. Inventories not infrequently mention cottages of two, three or even more 'bays'.

Few crucks extended all the way from the ridge of the root to the ground; suitable timber was rarely available. Instead, the cruck often sprang from a masonry base,

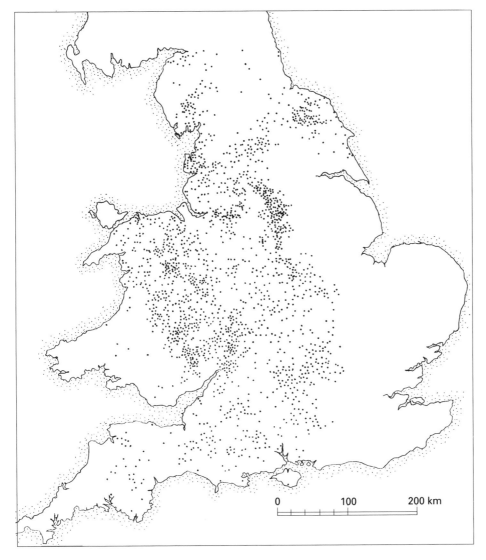

3.13 Distribution map of cruck buildings surviving today: based on a computer-generated map in N. W. Alcock, *Cruck Construction*.

which served in addition to protect it from the damp soil; or it was made from two pieces of timber scarfed together. Figure 3.12 shows the more significant forms assumed by the cruck. Although crucks are to be found in most parts of Britain except the east and south-east (Fig. 3.13), they were always most numerous and have survived in the greatest numbers in the western parts of Britain. The cruck was an essentially medieval mode of construction. The earliest surviving crucks are to be found in houses of superior status. But by the fifteenth century the cruck remained in vogue only amongst the more prosperous peasantry, and a century or two later it was employed only in the humblest homes. Thereafter it ceased to be used in newly built houses.

The cruck-built house had two major disadvantages. In the first place, it required heavier timbers than the standard timber-framed home, and these in the later Middle Ages were becoming increasingly scarce. Secondly, the task of working up a trunk into two blades was extremely laborious. 'Selecting the oak tree,' wrote Charles,[32] 'felling and cleaving . . . its huge trunk working the two halves into exact pairs of cruck blades must have required age-long experience and skill. There is evidence that oak was cultivated in order to produce crucks,' in just the same way that it was made to grow into the shapes needed for ships' timbers.[33]

The practice of timber-framing continued to develop during the later Middle Ages and sixteenth century. Post-holes and sill-plates generally ceased to be used, and the timber-framing was raised on a masonry plinth. The framing itself was strengthened; its vertical members were tenoned into a wall-plate attached to the masonry footing, and were as closely spaced as the supply of timber permitted. Braces were used to strengthen the corners, and transoms were introduced to give rigidity.[34] Carpenters, or at least the more skilled amongst them – those who would have been employed on the grander buildings – had developed a great range of skills. One constantly marvels at the complexity of some of the joints which they had developed in order to scarf or splice pieces of timber. Without this ability they could never have erected some of the more elaborate late medieval structures, especially their roof members.[35]

One of the features that advancing woodworking techniques had made possible was the insertion of an upper floor in the halls of both cottages and the larger houses. The hall, the central room of the house, had always been open to the roof, but the bower at one end might already have been given an upper storey of some kind. This might at first have been nothing more than a 'cragloft' or 'cockloft', a kind of wide shelf, reached by a ladder, on which someone might sleep or goods might be stored.[36] The floor might then be extended over the whole of the solar block, and even over the kitchen as well. Lastly, these blocks might be designed initially as structures of two or even more storeys.

An upper floor could not be inserted into the open-roofed hall as long as a fire burned on its central hearth. A fireplace had first to be constructed against a side wall, with a chimney to carry away the smoke. The development of the fireplace, as distinct from the hearth, is discussed in the next chapter. Like every other innovation which added to the comforts of the home, the fireplace appeared first in 'polite' houses, and only then did it spread down to the houses of the yeomen and lastly to the simple cottage. In the sixteenth century it was still to be found mainly in upper-class homes.

If the roof of the hall was high enough – and not all of them were – it might have been possible to insert a floor into an existing building. This was done even with cruck-built houses, though the upper floors, with their steeply sloping walls, must have been extremely awkward to use. If an upper floor had been planned from the beginning, an entirely different type of construction would probably have been employed. The joists which supported the upper floor might have been made to extend beyond the walls of the ground floor; in other words, it was 'jettied'. The advantages of a jetty were considerable. It gave added space to the upper floor; it obviated the need for timbers that ran the whole height of the building, and the downward pressure on the outer ends of the joists, may, it is claimed, have prevented the floor itself from sagging. Above all, the jettied house looked attractive, as, indeed, it still does, and it became a kind of status symbol.

A contract of 1491 for the building of a house in Great Chesterford (Essex) required the builder to 'jutty the seid chambres 18 inches thoroughley', that is on all sides.[37] On the other hand, it was recognised that a jetty added nothing to the stability of a structure, and in 1519 William Horman noted that a 'buyldynge chargydde with iotyes [jetties] is parellous when it is very olde'.[38] A 'thoroughly' jettied house (Fig. 3.14) called for very sophisticated craftsmanship. Its corners, with diagonal braces, or 'dragon-posts', were difficult to construct, but they were often highly decorated, as if to serve notice that its owner had the wealth to invest in such niceties (Fig. 3.15).

Often, however, it was only the apartments at the end of the hall that were given an upper floor, with the joists projecting forwards and sometimes also to the rear. Jettied and gabled wings, the open hall with its tall windows recessed between them, made not only a functionally convenient, but also an aesthetically attractive design, often called the 'Wealden' house, though it is very far from restricted to the south-east of England (Fig. 3.16). Most surviving examples appear to date from the sixteenth and early seventeenth centuries, the period marked by the 'great rebuilding', which marked the culmination in the growth of the medieval house. In the seventeenth century styles began to change, and the early modern house assumed a plan and elevation radically different from those that had been built in earlier centuries (p. 107).

The roof was the most important structural element in any traditional house, because it alone protected the body of the house from the weather. Roofs were invariably of timber, covered with thatch, slate, tile or even turf.

The chief constraint, as always in a timber-framed house, was the supply of timber of adequate scantling. Roofs were, as a general rule, steeply pitched, and were supported by rafters, mounted on wall-plates and held rigid with purlins which ran the length of the roof. Only 'principal' rafters, usually every fourth, fifth or sixth, had ties or collars. The others were generally of lighter construction, and were linked with the 'principal' by the purlins (Fig. 3.17). The principal rafters, together with their ties and collars, were known as 'trusses'. Trusses were usually assembled on the ground, as they continue to be today, and were then lifted into place.

A hall could be only as wide as the truss that was constructed to span it. But the late medieval joiner became adept not only at scarfing shorter pieces of timber, but also at giving the truss the greatest possible strength. At the same time great care was lavished on making the roof trusses, rafters and purlins not only severely functional,

3.14 A jettied house with dragon-post. This house stood in Exeter, but has now been demolished. After D. Portman, *Exeter Houses 1400–1700*, Exeter, 1966.

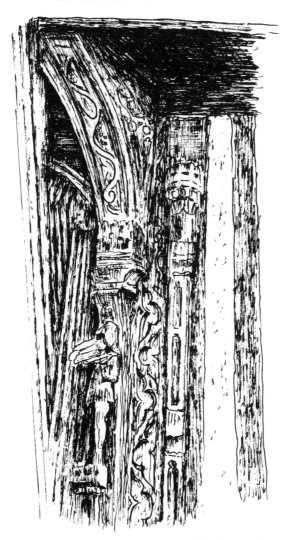

3.15 Highly decorated dragon-post in the Guildhall, Lavenham (Suff.).

but also attractive to look at. The medieval joiner also practised his craft on parish and other churches, and it is to these that one should turn for the finest surviving examples of his work. There are, however, many hall-houses of the more genteel kind which retain roofs almost as elaborate and decorative as the best to be found in churches.[39] This level of sophistication was, however, never to be found in the cottage; here the simplest and roughest of trusses were used.

The roof truss, the essential element in the rigidity of the roof, depended on the properties of the triangle. Figure 3.18 shows diagrammatically the increasing elaboration of roof design met with in both domestic and ecclesiastical construction. It can be seen that the longest pieces of timber used in any roof were likely to be the

85

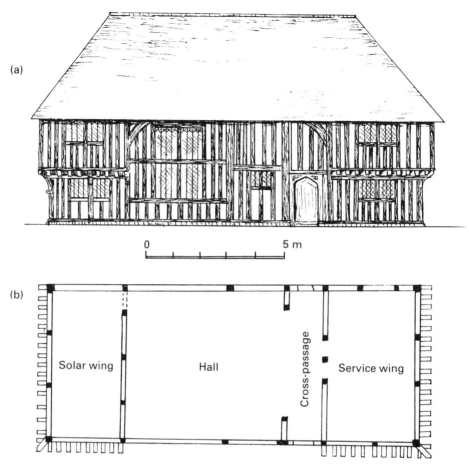

3.16 Typical Wealden house: (a) elevation, (b) plan. The absence of a chimney suggests that there was still an open fire in the hall, which is embayed between two jettied wings.

rafters and the main tie-beams. Others were relatively short, and their provision constituted less of a problem. The urgent need to reduce the dependence on long tie-beams, and to replace them with shorter collars without loss of rigidity taxed the ingenuity of carpenters and joiners. To some extent, this could be done by means of braces. One solution to the problem was the use of the so-called 'hammer-beam', the most evolved and potentially the most beautiful of medieval roof forms, though it is likely that its contribution was more to the beauty than to the rigidity of the roof structure. Instead of a tie-beam, two short hammer-beams were used, supported by braces, and supporting in their turn hammer-posts (Fig. 3.19). The collar might also be cut away to give another pair of hammer-beams, each with its hammer-post, which might support a further short collar close to the apex of the roof.

Such a roof called for a great deal of expert joinery, and most people who could

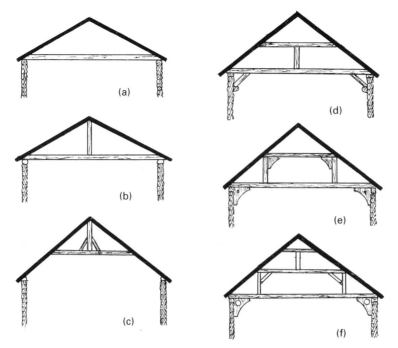

3.17 Sequential forms in the development of roofing trusses. Though most could have been found in domestic buildings, they are best seen today in churches.

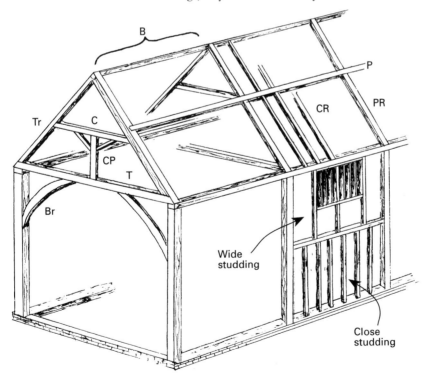

3.18 The nomenclature of vernacular architecture: B, bay; Br, brace; C, collar; CR, common rafter; CP, crownpost; P, purlin; PR, principal ratter; T, tie; Tr, truss.

3.19 A hammer-beam in Upwell parish church (Norf.). The beam and post are of little importance in supporting the roof. Their role is primarily decorative. After a photograph by Mrs E. L. Wetton.

afford this luxury usually had the means to embellish it as it deserved. Hammer-beams and posts, as well as braces, were often elaborately carved. In particular the projecting ends of the hammer-beam invited decoration. They were sometimes carved with heraldic symbols or with human heads, and in churches the human heads often grew into full-bodied angels. Then wings were added, either swept back along the beam or outstretched as if in flight (Fig. 3.20). The angels, more than a hundred of them, in the roof of the church of March (Cambs.), with outstretched wings, soaring tier above tier, are one of the most memorable creations of the medieval woodworker.

The great house

The methods of framing and roofing that have been described might, with the exception of the more refined developments of the truss, have been met with in the home of any well-to-do peasant or yeoman. There were, however, other types of construction which made their appearance only in the grandest structures.

The aisled hall derives from the type of hall that was excavated at Yeavering (p. 69). Its essential feature was the double arcade or, on rare occasions, a single arcade of wooden pillars which supported collars at their junction with the principal rafters (Fig. 3.21). Such a hall could he built larger and, in particular, wider than any structure roofed in the ways illustrated in Figure 3.18. It was suited to the grand

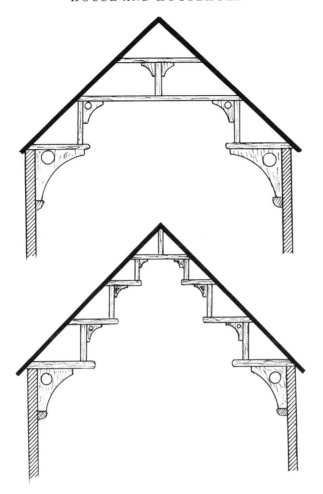

3.20 Structure of hammer-beam roofs.

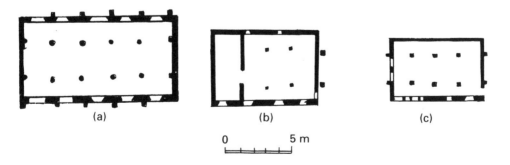

0   5 m

3.21 Aisled halls: (a) Winchester, (b) Oakham (Rutland), (c) Warnford (Hants).

3.22 Small aisled hall at Hafod Rhiwlas (Denbigh.); after *Arch Camb* , 5th ser., 15 (1898).

assemblies which met at the royal court and in the households of bishops and of the leading members of the lay aristocracy. Westminster Hall was in origin an aisled hall,[40] and the great hall of Winchester Castle was rebuilt in this way.[41] The surviving bishops' palaces at Hereford and Exeter encapsulate aisled halls, and it is still possible in both to see the massive oak piers of the original arcade.[42] The present courthouse in Leicester Castle has been developed around an aisled hall of great size, built in all probability by the Earl of Leicester in the twelfth century. The aisled hall was rarely found at lower social levels; it was too costly for a manorial lord of average means as well as far beyond his needs. Nevertheless, a few smaller examples have survived, notably at Warnford (Hants), Nursted (Kent),[43] and Oakham Castle (Rutland), and a little-known example at Hafod Rhiwlas (Denbigh) is illustrated in figure 3.22.[44] These must be regarded as the creations of aspiring members of the gentry.

Aisled halls were mostly built in twelfth and early thirteenth centuries. Thereafter, with developments in roof construction, they tended to he supplanted by ground-floor halls without either aisles or arcade. Westminster Hall, built as an aisled hall at the end of the eleventh century, was reroofed at the end of the fourteenth with the single-span roof which survives today.[45] The great halls built in the later Middle Ages were almost all designed as ground-floor halls, and their increasing width made possible by the employment of root trusses of increasing complexity. Many such halls have survived, with or without their original roofs, including those built within important castles, like Caerphilly, as well as those in the older colleges of Oxford and Cambridge.

The plan and style of the aisled hall moved down-market in the later Middle Ages. It ceased to be built by the upper ranks of society, and was adopted as the proper way to build a large barn. Barns were needed, especially by the great monastic houses, to store and thresh the vast quantities of grain which they received, mostly as tithe payments, after harvest.[46] Some of the finest monastic barns surviving today are aisled such as those of Great Coxwell (Oxon.), Tisbury (Wilts.), Bredon (Worcs.) and Abbotsbury (Dorset) (Fig. 3.23).

If the great aisled hall was the élite residence *par excellence* in the earlier Middle Ages, the first-floor hall often served the needs of an intermediate class of manorial lords. Like the aisled hall, the first-floor hall was also known to the Anglo-Saxons (p. 70). In the twelfth century it was generally masonry-built, with a hall raised above a vaulted undercroft. According to Margaret Wood, some fifty examples are known to survive. Many must have been destroyed and there are doubtless others awaiting discovery encapsulated within later building (Fig. 3.24). Apart from the hall of the future King Harold at Bosham, of which nothing survives, the oldest are probably those built in the bailey of Christchurch Castle (Hants)[47] and Scolland's Hall on the cliff-edge within the perimeter of Richmond Castle (N. Riding, Yorks.). Somewhat later, though broadly similar in plan and elevation, are the halls at Boothby Pagnell (Lincs.) (Fig. 3.25) and Hemingford Grey (Hunts.).[48] Elsewhere one finds a first-floor hall as part of a complex of buildings, most often monastic. The Prior's Hall at Ely,[49] and the dining-hall at Jesus College, Cambridge,[50] are outstanding examples. In a number of castles a first-floor hall was built against the encircling wall, as at Framlingham (Suffolk), Grosmont (Mon.), Ludlow (Shrops.) and several others.[51] The first-floor hall was, with very few exceptions, a monopoly of the upper classes: abbots and priors and lords of many manors. The cost of masonry construction and of vaulting the undercroft put such a hall beyond the means of all except the rich.

The floor-space within a first-floor hall was very much less than that of an aisled hall, and the absence from many of them of any evidence for a kitchen, as at Little Wenham (Essex), has suggested to some that, as we see them today, they are incomplete; that they are only an extravagant version of the solar block which may once have accompanied a vanished ground-floor or aisled hall. It can only be said in reply that there is no incontrovertible evidence for a lost hall, either attached to the raised hall or freestanding nearby. But it is not impossible that a timber-built hall and

91

3.23 Late medieval aisled barn at Harmondsworth (Middx.).

also a detached kitchen could have existed close to, if not contiguous with, a raised hall-block.

The types of hall just discussed were never numerous, and in the later Middle Ages they ceased to be built. They gave way to the open, ground-floor hall, with its ample fenestration and elaborate roofing trusses. These were, as a general rule, strongly built, and many survive to demonstrate the degree of comfort, even luxury, enjoyed by the upper classes in the later Middle Ages. They range from such great halls as Gainsborough Old Hall (Lincs.) and Eltham Palace (Kent) to smaller halls like those surviving at Stokesay (Shrops.), Great Chalfield (Wilts.) and Northborough (Northants.). Similar in plan and function, though smaller in scale, was the hall of a well-to-do peasant or yeoman.

3.24 An aisled hall near Colchester, modernised and now a dwelling-house.

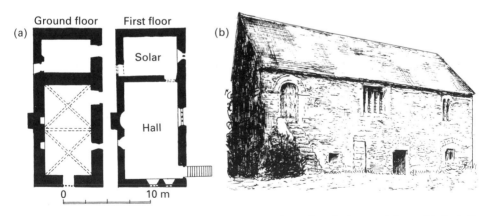

3.25 First-floor hall at Boothby Pagnell (Lincs.): (a) plans of vaulted ground-floor, (b) the hall from the south-east.

93

3.26 The highly ornamental jettied upper floor of a merchant's house – Paycockes, at Coggeshall (Essex).

In this very broad spectrum we see the universal tendency for innovation to occur at the top, in the halls of the aristocracy, and to spread downwards towards the halls of the peasantry. There was at the same time a universal urge to decorate and elaborate beyond the structural needs of the building itself. The ornamentation of roof trusses has already been mentioned. Door-frames, gable-ends, barge-boards, wall-plates, and, above all, the soffits of jettied upper floors all tended to be carved, sometimes with complex figures, more often with conventional trailing vinescrolls or simple, repeated motifs (Fig. 3.26).

Solar and crosswing

'The invariable, and, indeed, the only essential feature of the English medieval house was the great hall.'[52] But the hall rarely stood alone; the king's hall, like that of Chaucer's poor widow, had its ancillary buildings. She had her bower; the king, a complex of chambers and chapels which provided a refuge from the boisterous life of the hall, as well as kitchens to provide food for the royal table, and buttery and pantry from which to serve it. The private apartments were almost invariably reached from the upper end of the ball. At the lower, beyond the 'screens' passage, doors gave access to buttery, pantry and kitchen. In a vernacular house a single room served all these purposes, but there was a growing tendency in the later Middle Ages and early modern times to construct ever more specialised rooms, for example a brewhouse and a dairy. The buttery in any house above the vernacular level was the 'boterie' where bottles and casks were kept – the domain of the 'butler', while the pantry served for the storage of table equipment and 'dry goods' like bread.

The kitchen, which had replaced the all-purpose hearth in the great hall, usually

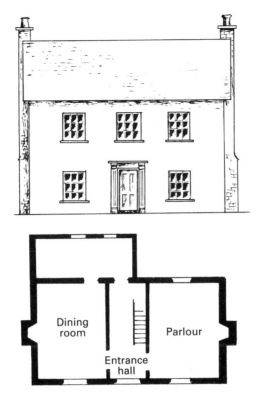

3.27 A symmetrically planned eighteenth-century house.

contained wide fireplaces, where pots could be hung and spits and other hearth gear
(p. 117) be deployed. There would also have been large tables for the preparation of
food. The danger of fire was considerable, and for this reason the kitchen was
sometimes a detached structure. Kitchens that survive from the Middle Ages are
large and generally rectangular in plan, sometimes with the fireplaces, each with its
own chimney, built across the corners (Fig. 3.27). The kitchen plan can be seen in all
its detail at monastic sites, like Glastonbury and Durham, in the Bishop's Palace at
Chichester, and in secular buildings such as Gainsborough Old Hall (Lincs.),
Dartington Hall (Devon) and Stanton Harcourt (Oxon.). Such kitchens were built
to serve very large communities, and were only to be found in monasteries, palaces
and houses of the highest standing. At the vernacular level the kitchen was at most a
small room at the lower end of the hall, where it also served a variety of other
domestic uses.

The oven always presented a difficult problem for those who designed and built
both vernacular and élite houses. It was a considerable fire hazard, since it was heated
by burning wood within it, and then raking out the smouldering ashes before
putting in the loaves of bread (Fig. 6.6). Many houses, including most at the

vernacular level, had no oven, and even in the grandest houses, it was often a free-standing structure erected in the courtyard. Most people were obliged to use a communal oven, often the property of the manorial lord, who exacted a fee for its use.

As and when additional space was required within a vernacular house it was usual to add a room, which might be as small as a lean-to, 'linhay' or 'outshut', or as large as a crosswing. Inventories of household possessions made frequent mention of such additions. In this way simple houses sometimes grew into large, rambling structures with many rooms in addition to the basic hall, chamber and kitchen. Probate inventories, which did not become common before the late sixteenth century, frequently listed the possessions of the deceased according to the rooms in which they were found. In this way one can determine the number of rooms and form some estimate of their probable use. Most, of course, were bedrooms, and their proliferation in the homes of the better-off is a measure, not only of increasing affluence, but also of a growing desire for privacy.

In the course of some five hundred years the village, at least in much of England, had grown from a cluster of huts into one of varied but not inelegant houses. Even the simple cottage had evolved beyond the furthest imaginings of anyone living in the twelfth century. It was usually of two rooms at least, with possibly a separate kitchen and a linhay for storage. It had windows, shuttered if not glazed, and often a fireplace with a chimney to carry away the smoke. Higher in the social scale, the yeoman's house had begun to assume many of the features that had previously belonged only to the manor-house. It retained its hall, but this was ceasing to be the focus of family life. Even before the end of the fourteenth century William Langland had complained that:

> Elenge is the hall   eche daye in the wike,
> Ther the lord ne the lady   liketh noghte to sitte.
> Now hath ech riche a rule   to eten by hymselve
> In a pryvee parlour   for povre mennes sake,
> Or in a chambre with a chymenee   and leve the chief hall
> That was mad for meles,   men to eten inne.[53]

He was, in the fourteenth century, thinking primarily of those lords of manors who would in an earlier generation have eaten with their servants and dependants in the great hall. By the sixteenth century the practice would have moved socially downwards to families of the yeoman class. It was increasingly common to have a set of chambers at one end of the hall, sometimes extending into a cross-wing, and providing privacy and quiet, as far removed as possible from the noises and smells of the kitchen and hall. It became increasingly common also to have a fireplace, not only in the solar, but also in the bedrooms.[54] These private chambers became more and more decorative and comfortable. Hangings reduced the draughts; the timber joists were carved and even gilded or painted, and the walls might be adorned with scenes drawn from hunting or from mythology or history or hung with 'painted' cloths, the poor man's form of tapestry (p. 154).

Such were the houses described or implied in countless wills and inventories of the sixteenth and seventeenth centuries. At its most ambitious the yeoman's house might assume the plan of the Wealden house, described earlier (p. 83). The entrance still occupied its traditional place, opposite the lower end of the hall, and led into a screens passage, partially cut off from the hall itself by the 'screens'. Before long, with the gradual abandonment of the hall as the principal living quarters, the screens passage would itself be eliminated; the entrance would be centrally placed into the hall; the hall itself reduced in size, and the main rooms grouped symmetrically on each side of it (Fig. 3.27). The kitchen might be set behind the chief rooms or even, as in many later instances, in a basement beneath.

The sixteenth and early seventeenth centuries formed a period of rapid change in domestic architecture. It was the time of the 'great rebuilding', the period from about 1570 to the beginning of the great Civil War,[55] but its timing varied from one part of the country to another. The change began earlier in the south-east than in the Midlands and west, and earlier there than in the north, for the urge to rebuild sprang from many factors. It was the product of human decisions, consciously made by people who had to balance their desires, ambitions, physical needs and resources. It has often been said that the 'great rebuilding' was the direct consequence of increasing wealth and of a larger disposable surplus in the hands of the growing middle class. Building had, of course, to be paid for, but the simple equation of greater monetary income with increased building activity is too simplistic.

The building of a timber-framed house was not, in relative terms, particularly expensive. One cannot be precise, since the cost of labour and materials varied greatly. Hoskins has quoted figures which may have been typical. At Oxford a cottage was built in 1516 for £29, the materials being provided from the estates of an Oxford college. A year or two earlier a very substantial house was built in Wiltshire for £10, and there are instances of small houses being built for less than this. Hoskins has estimated that about 1500 a farmer 'could have built himself an average-sized farmhouse for £6 to £15'. This is borne out by the building contracts published by Salzman.[56] It should, however, be noted that there was no compunction about reusing old materials, and that it was exceptional to go far afield in search of new.

Inflation greatly increased the cost of building during the sixteenth century, and before its end costs may have increased threefold. Nevertheless, building remained cheap in proportion to incomes. A craftsman might expect, early in the sixteenth century, to earn about 10s. a week, so that a modest home might represent less than six month's earnings. A house of some opulence was well within the reach of a yeoman who employed labour and sold his produce into the market. The movement of prices during the previous century had been strongly in favour of those who rented or leased land and produced for sale. Under the prevailing systems of tenure rents had remained stable and relatively low at a time when agricultural prices were

97

rising in response to the growing demand from an increasing population. It must, however, be remembered that those who built vernacular houses were unable to anticipate future income by any systematised way of borrowing.

The evidence of wills and inventories is highly selective. Those whose chattels were worth less than £5 were not required to make a will, and their goods need not have been inventoried. In a few instances one can match a particular will and inventory with a surviving house, though this is rare before the eighteenth century. More often the chattels were listed by room, thus providing some idea of the uses to which individual rooms were put. There was a lack of specialisation in the use of rooms: people slept beside the hearth in the hall, they stored farm goods in the solar, and practised crafts, especially spinning, in the bedrooms. Specialisation in the use of rooms first appeared in higher levels of society, and spread very slowly downwards until at the lowest level, that of the one-roomed cottage, no specialisation was possible.

A survey was made in 1631 of the Wiltshire lands of the Earl of Pembroke.[57] Seventeen separate manors or groups of manors were enumerated, containing in all 636 separate tenancies. These can be classified as:

Freehold	5
Tenements by indenture, usually long-term leases	156
Copyhold	475

A feature of the survey is the careful attention that was given to the house or cottage on each tenement. The number of rooms is given with great precision in the case of tenants by copyhold, but the homes of freeholders and leaseholders were less carefully defined. At Dinton, for example, 'a fair dwelling house with many roomes'; at Bulbridge 'twelve lower roomes and thirteene upper roomes'. The average number of rooms in houses of this standing, where they were stated, was $7\frac{1}{2}$. By contrast, the size of all copyhold houses is clearly stated: 'a dwelling house of 3 ground rooms, 2 of them lofted over' or 'of 2 ground rooms lofted over'; or 'of 3 ground rooms and a part of a kitchen lofted over'. The meaning is clear. In a majority of cases a first floor or 'loft' had been inserted above one or more of the ground-floor rooms. The size of the houses occupied by the copyholders of the manor of Broad Chalke, near Salisbury, turns out to be surprisingly large:

5	rooms, all lofted over				1
5	,,	, 3	,,	,,	1
4	,,	, all	,,	,,	8
4	,,	, 2	,,	,,	2
4	,,	, none	,,	,,	1
3	,,	, all	,,	,,	10
3	,,	, 2	,,	,,	6
3	,,	, 1	,,	,,	3
3	,,	, none	,,	,,	1
2	,,	, all	,,	,,	12
2	,,	, 1	,,	,,	6

2	”	, none	”	”	3[1]
I	”	, I	”	”	2[2]
I	”	, not	”	”	O

[1] one with a separate bakehouse
[2] one with part of a kitchen

The one-roomed cottage had in effect disappeared, at least from the copyholder class, though one cannot say to what extent it survived amongst the landless labourers.

Attempts have been made to relate the size of the house to the status of the builder, to the extent of the land which he held, and thus to his probable income. Chevenix Trench has analysed this relationship for a part of southern Buckinghamshire:[58]

Number of rooms

$$
\left.\begin{array}{l}
9 \\
8 \\
7 \\
6 \\
5
\end{array}\right\} \text{Gentleman}
$$

$$
\left.\begin{array}{l}
5 \\
4
\end{array}\right\} \text{Yeoman}
$$

$$
\left.\begin{array}{l}
3 \\
2 \\
1
\end{array}\right\} \text{Husbandman}
$$

Few have succeeded in establishing a relationship any closer than this. The problem is that houses were built over an indeterminate but often long period of time, and that tenancies and income were far from constant. That there was a positive correlation between wealth and status on the one hand and the quality of housing on the other must be accepted, but it is difficult to quantify, even to demonstrate, this relationship. It may not be too much to say that the great majority of the vernacular houses that survive must have been built by men of the class of yeomen and the better-off of the peasantry. One can point, at least in England, to very few surviving cottages that could have belonged unquestionably to the class of landless labourer or even to that of the husbandman who continued into the eighteenth century to cultivate his few acres.

Building materials

The plan and style of a traditional building have been influenced, not only by customary methods and ideas, but also by the materials available to the builder and the wealth that could be expended upon them (Figs. 3.28 and 3.29). William Harrison, writing towards the end of Elizabeth's reign, claimed 'the greatest part of our building . . . consisteth only of timber, for as yet few of the houses of the commonalty . . . are made of stone'.[59] There were, however, many exceptions to Harrison's generalisation. Masonry was widely used, not only in castles, but also in

99

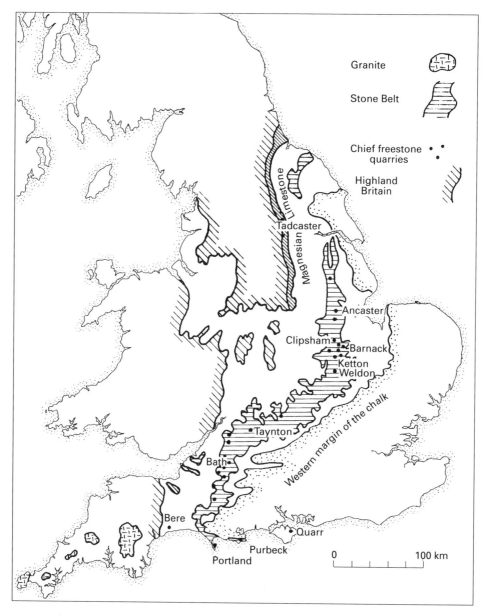

3.28 Geological map of England, showing the Jurassic 'Stone Belt' and the location of the more important quarries.

the homes of the aristocracy and of the better-off members of the gentry. Even at the peasant level stone was used, not only in the footings and plinths, but even in the walls, if it happened to be available locally and cheap. 'Building in Pembrokeshire', wrote George Owen of Henllys (Pemb.) 'is altogether of stone & not of Timber ... more for the comodiousness of the abondance of sondrye and severall sortes of

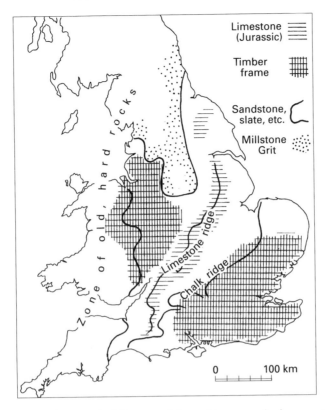

3.29 Map of predominant building materials used in vernacular houses: stone and timber-framing.

stones fitt for buildinges than for want of tymber.'[60] In the south-western peninsula the situation was similar,[61] with abundant and varied stone and a real shortage of good timber. Granite, or 'moorstone' proved 'very profitable for manie purposes . . . They make of them, instead of timber, mayne postes for their howses, dorepostes, chimny and wyndow peeces.'[62]

But the excellence of a particular building material did not in itself ensure that it would be used. The Cotswolds, especially in the vicinity of Burford, are unsurpassed in the quality and abundance of their building stone, and yet timber-framing was used in the Middle Ages for prestige construction. There is even evidence for building a town house of stone and for covering its street front with timber-framing.[63]

Materials used in vernacular building range from turf and cob, through timber, wattle and daub, to masonry in stone and brick, and roofing materials from straw and turf to slate, cleft stone and clay tile. Most primitive must have been the use of turf and clay. But turf, whatever its prehistoric importance, was little used for walling in medieval Britain, though it was sometimes employed over a framework of rafters for roofing (p. 106).[64]

IOI

Mud, cob, pisé, clay-lump and all forms of 'unbaked earth' were of not inconsiderable importance, not only during the Middle Ages, but in some areas also even in recent times. The clay was usually puddled, commonly with an admixture of straw, flakes of slate or shale and even pebbles, and was then poured between wooden shuttering. Sometimes the wall was reinforced with timbers, set horizontally or vertically within it.[65] Even imperfect timber, unsuitable for framing, could be used in this way. The result was a wall of considerable strength and durability. A cob wall was usually thick, up to a metre, and provided good insulation. But it had to be kept dry. There was a saying in Devon that a cob wall needed only 'a good hat and a strong pair of shoes'. These walls were often protected by wide, overhanging eaves and were erected on stone footings which served as a damp-course. Nevertheless, they were often short-lived, and after their decay they have commonly left only a shapeless heap of soil. For human habitation cob-walled houses were usually replaced at an early date by structures of more durable material,[67] but in secondary structures, like farmyard buildings and garden walls, clay in its various forms can still be found in quite widespread use. In fact, cob walling is still found very widely in Devon.

Over England and Wales as a whole timber-framing was by far the commonest mode of construction. The sill-plate came eventually to be set on masonry footings, and walls were built of vertical studding, with transoms, braces and wall-plates to give them rigidity (p. 87). Vertical studding remained the most popular, the spacing of the studs being determined largely by the availability of timber. 'In the more wooded areas,' wrote Harrison, 'there are not above four, six or nine inches between stud and stud,' whereas 'in the open and champagne countries they are enforced for want of stuff to use no studs at all', but only corner-posts, transoms and braces.[68] The great framed houses that survive in Lancashire and the Welsh Border display a lavish, even extravagant use of timber, whereas in the more populous south-east the studding, is generally more widely spaced and the studs themselves thinner.

The space between studs was usually filled in with wickerwork of osier and plastered with clay both inside and out. Wattle and daub was the most common accompaniment of timber-framing, but tended in many areas, especially eastern England, to be replaced with brick 'nogging'.[69] From the sixteenth century the growing scarcity of good timber – and it was almost exclusively oak that was used – rendered close studding impracticable in much of the country. Green timber had often to be used, leading to the distortion that has taken place in many timber-framed buildings. At the same time, however, brick nogging gave an added strength and rigidity to framed buildings. Timber-framing remained the preferred mode of building at the vernacular level – perhaps as much for aesthetic reasons as for practical – until the later seventeenth century.

The Roman tradition of masonry construction for domestic purposes was lost during the Dark Age which followed, and when it was revived it was used at first almost exclusively for church building. After the Norman Conquest it appeared in élite buildings, and from this level its use spread downwards socially, but remained significant only in those areas which had an abundant supply of good building stone. A problem with all masonry construction, except the crudest, was that its components had to be secured with mortar, and the rougher the building stone the greater was the consumption of mortar. Medieval mortar was a simple mixture of unslaked lime and sand. The provision of lime required a supply of limestone. It was usual in the later Middle Ages, when ashlar limestone was being used, to build a kiln and to use offcuts and waste from the mason's yard to make it. But in areas where limestone was not readily available, a supply of lime was a matter of some difficulty, and it had often to be imported at a considerable cost.[70] Scarcity of lime contributed in some areas, notably the south-western peninsula, to the use of well-puddled mud or clay for bonding, but, like cob walling, clay mortar required some protection from the elements.

Masonry construction was always more expensive than timber-framing, even if the transport of stone posed little problem, and for that reason spread only slowly down the social scale. On the other hand, it was more durable, more hygienic, and safer in an age when fire was a continuous threat. It assumed a great variety of forms, depending on the quality and characteristics of the stone being used and the amount of labour expended on it. Regional variations in timber construction were slight in comparison with the rich variety found in masonry building.

Britain is rich in stone of indifferent quality, but good building stone can be found only in restricted areas. The clay belts were, by definition, devoid of stone (Fig. 3.28), but the easily dug clay facilitated the making of bricks, which came into general use in the later Middle Ages. There is space here to note only the more important building stones, whose quality was held to justify long-distance and expensive transport to the site of a monastery or of an élite house. The chalk which underlay much of south-eastern England was too soft to be used as a building stone, but at the base of the chalk series lay a bed of hard chalk, variously known as 'clunch' or Totternhoe stone. It lends itself to delicate carving, and was often used for indoor decorative features. It weathered badly, however, and was rarely used for exterior work.

The 'stone belt' *par excellence* extended from the Dorset coast diagonally across England in a narrow strip to Lincolnshire. It is made up of beds of limestone, intercalated with clay. Much of the stone is friable and shelly, and is suited only for rough masonry, such as that employed in the drystone walls of the Cotswolds. It does, however, include stone of the highest quality, suitable for ashlar masonry, in parts of Lincolnshire, Northamptonshire, in the Cotswolds, near Bath and at several points in south Somerset and Dorset. Many of the cathedrals, monasteries and great houses used stone from these quarries, but it appeared only rarely in buildings at the vernacular level, unless they were located close to the quarries. This stone could be cut to smooth, regular blocks, which were often transported very widely, irrespective of transport costs. Small quarries, however, were opened almost anywhere within the stone belt, and a coarse 'ragstone' extracted for local use. In some parts of the Cotswolds the roads were bordered by such quarries, now largely filled in with local waste and lost, from which a poor quality stone had once been taken for local use.

Other building stones fell far short of the 'oolites' of the Stone Belt both in ease of working and durability and also in the aesthetic satisfaction which they gave. They include the Lias Limestone of Somerset, the Magnesian Limestone of Nottinghamshire and Yorkshire, the Millstone Grit of the Pennine uplands, and the red sandstones of the Welsh Border. Elsewhere, and especially in the south-west, shale and slate were used for rougher kinds of masonry. Throughout East Anglia and over much of south-eastern England there are no outstanding building stones and very few even of mediocre quality. One of the better is the so-called Kentish Rag, a sandstone taken from the Greensand beds and obtained from the area south of London. It was much used in the early building of the city. Alternative materials had therefore to be used, and the most conspicuous of these was without question flint. Flint occurs, as rounded nodules of highly irregular shape, in beds within the chalk. It has been quarried and used since the early Stone Age. In the Middle Ages, flints were shaped by chipping and flaking and made to resemble bricks (Fig. 3.30). This was a highly expensive process, justified only by the absence of any free-cutting stone. In their rough state they were used in walling, and, cut to shape, in the 'flushwork' met with in many East Anglian churches. Flint was rarely used in quoins, sills, lintels and tracery, and for these purposes stone, imported into the area, and brick were commonly used. Even lower in the scale of building stones were iron-pan and conglomerates, or 'pudding-stone', which occurred in the Tertiary beds of East Anglia. They could not be cut to regular shapes, and, used in rubble masonry, yielded one of the least attractive building materials ever to have been used in this country.

At the opposite end of the geological spectrum are the granites and other hard igneous and metamorphic rocks, chiefly met with in the west and north. They were very durable, but difficult to work with the chisel and costly to transport. They were, before modern times, used mainly in areas close to the quarries where they were obtained, but only in a few areas, such as the Lake District, parts of Wales and the south-western peninsula, did they enter into vernacular architecture.

By the sixteenth century the use of masonry was creeping down the social scale, and in grand building was being adopted almost to the exclusion of timber-framing. 'Amongst noblemen and gentlemen,' wrote Harrison, 'the timber frames are supposed to be not much better than paper work, of continuance [durability].'[71] The Dissolution of the monasteries and of other religious foundations (1536–40) and the resulting abundance of stone that could be retrieved from their ruins must have encouraged masonry construction, for the cost of quarrying and of working up new stone was high. At the same time, however, the movement towards masonry construction was undoubtedly hastened by the growing shortage of timber.

Brick construction was of increasing importance in the later Middle Ages. The Romans had used brick extensively, but after their withdrawal the craft of burning

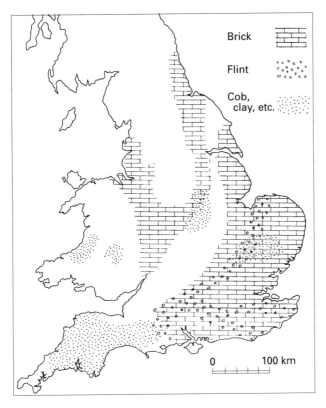

3.30 Map of predominant building materials used in vernacular construction: brick, flint and clay.

bricks appears to have been lost, and was not reintroduced until late in the twelfth century.[72] Brick-making called not only for a supply of suitable clay, but also for wood, for the brick-kiln was an extravagant consumer of fuel. Harrison, always perceptive in such matters, complained that 'in burning [bricks] a great part of the wood of this land is daily consumed and spent'.[73] Small kilns might serve for burning pots or tiles, but bricks were used in tens of thousands, and this called for very large kilns and an abundant supply of fuel.[74] The manufacture and use of brick was at first restricted to the eastern parts of this country, where the demand for an alternative to stone was greatest and clay was most readily available. Nevertheless, bricks were not greatly used before the later thirteenth century, but thereafter demand for them increased rapidly.[75] The size of bricks was more or less standardised, a necessary prelude to their more regular use, and the various types of bond gradually refined.[76] Brick came to be the chief material used in many late medieval grand buildings such as Tattershall (Lincs.), Caistor (Norf.) Herstmonceux (Sussex), and many others, and, early in the sixteenth century, Hampton Court.[77]

The sixteenth century was the golden age of brick construction. Most of the great houses built during this period made some use of brick. Moulded bricks were used in architraves, as coping on walls, and for a variety of decorative purposes. At the same time the use of brick began to move socially downwards, and to be used, often in only small quantities, in the homes of yeomen and even peasants. At this level, however, brick never really replaced traditional materials until the nineteenth century. This was due, not only to the higher cost of brick, but also to an innate conservatism. Nevertheless, bricks came to be used widely where their refractory qualities were of value, as in fireplaces and chimneys, where they did much to reduce the danger of fire, and also as 'nogging' in timber-framed buildings.

The growing use of brick at the vernacular level was made possible by the appearance in many parts of the country of small village brickworks, employing only two or three men and satisfying the needs only of their local areas.[78] But large brickyards were also to be found in the clay regions of the east Midlands and east. Clay was not a readily transportable commodity, and brick construction was little used where clay was not available nearby. In Midland England one can almost map the boundary between the clay and the limestone simply by observing the construction of traditional cottages.

Roofing materials

The rafters and the laths that were nailed to them together supported the roof. Roofing materials had to be both water- and weather-resistant, and at the same time light enough to be supported by the timber structure beneath. Thatch was at first by far the commonest material. Wheat or barley straw, cut close to the ground, was most often used, with reeds where they were available. Thatch had great advantages. It was light, gave good insulation, and, if well laid, was waterproof. Its grave disadvantage was that it was inflammable and was readily ignited by sparks from the hearth. More primitive than thatch, though less susceptible to fire, was turf. Rafters were first laid across the space to be covered and were then covered with a lattice of boughs and brushwood on which the turf was laid to form a rounded heap. Only small buildings could be roofed in this way, and turf seems to have been used mainly in ancillary buildings, 'a late survival at a low social level of a once common method of roofing'.[79]

Alternative roofing materials were slate, tile and lead. Thinly split 'blue' slate was probably the best, because it was relatively light, impervious, and, if well fitted, it provided a weather-proof roof.[80] On the other hand, slate was highly localised in its natural occurrence. Before the North Wales quarries were opened, most came from south-western England. Here the quarries near Delabole (Corn.) were in production long before the end of the Middle Ages.[81] Next came the coarser and heavier slates obtained by splitting certain fissile limestones that occur especially in the Cotswolds and in Northamptonshire, known respectively as Stonesfield and Collyweston slates. They were thicker than 'blue' slate; they did not fit tightly together, and their considerable weight called for heavier rafters. On the other hand, 'stone' slates, with their rough surface and varying shades of colour, provide one of the loveliest of roofing materials, seen to perfection in the villages of the limestone belt in central England.

Tiles of baked clay shared the advantages of 'blue' slate. The Romans had used S-shaped pantiles, introduced from southern Europe, but these later disappeared from the native building tradition. The practice of burning clay tiles was re-introduced several centuries later. In 1189 the citizens of London were required, after a very serious fire, to build in stone and to roof with 'slate or baked tile'.[82] But little use appears to have been made of clay tile at this time, and not until the thirteenth century is there widespread and unambiguous evidence for its widespread employment. Clay tiles first appeared in the grander building, and it is doubtful whether they were used generally in vernacular construction much before modern times. Amongst the burnt clay goods which came into use in the late Middle Ages were shaped tiles to be placed on the roof ridges – 'cresting', they were often called – and also louvred vents to be set above the open hearth in the midst of the hall (Fig. 4.2). The style of the latter has survived in the chimney-pot of modern times.

Lead, beaten or rolled into thin sheets, was one of the best roofing materials, but it was costly, and its great weight required heavy timbering to support it.[83] Its use was restricted to churches and a few grand buildings, but lead was also much used for guttering and for the 'flashing' which covered the junction of roof timbers and walls.

The eighteenth century

The concept of the traditional house underwent little change before the middle of the seventeenth century. It remained fundamentally a hall-house, with entrance and cross-passage at the lower end of the hall. In appearance it was asymmetrical. The wings were very rarely mirror images of one another, and the entrance, sometimes emphasised by the presence of a porch, was usually opposite the cross-passage. Some time in the seventeenth century this began to change at the vernacular level; it had already been greatly modified at higher levels of building. The detached house of the late seventeenth and eighteenth centuries was fundamentally different from that which had gone before. The essential developments were twofold: the total abandonment of the hall as the social and architectural focus of the house, and, an almost inevitable consequence of this, the introduction of an upper floor – sometimes more than one – over the whole span of the house. At the same time, the staircase, previously relegated to a corner of one of the wings, began to assume a central role in the house. In grander examples of domestic planning the staircase became the centrepiece of the entrance hall. Timber-framing was, by and large, abandoned, and houses came to be built of stone or brick or of a combination of the two.

The dominant features of this 'centrally planned house' have been summarised by Peter Smith as:[84]

(1) symmetrical main elevation, with central doorway and windows equally balanced on each side of it (Fig. 3.27);

107

(2) 'a centralized system of circulation' within, with a central passage, the front door at one end and, usually, a rear door at the other. A framed 'dog-legged' staircase opposite the main entrance rose within the passage to the upper floor. Fireplaces were generally placed at the gable-ends of the building, and were usually repeated, often sharing the same chimney stack, on the upper floors. There were commonly two main rooms, later to be designated 'dining' and 'sitting' or '(with)drawing', one on each side of the central passageway. The kitchen and other domestic offices were pushed to the rear of the house.

When the traditional hall-house was enlarged it was usually extended lengthwise. The new, centrally planned house could not be extended in this way without compromising its symmetrical character. Instead, a second set of rooms was often added to the rear, thus giving the 'two-pile' or two-deep house, more nearly square in plan than anything that had gone before, and more economical to build and heat than houses of the sprawling traditional plan.

There were also, as Peter Smith has pointed out, distinguishing features in the location of centrally planned houses. The house was often treated as an integral part of the landscape, and in this, as in so many other ways, it followed the example set by the grand house.[85] It was often sited away from other structures; it ceased to be enveloped by farm buildings, and was often made all the more impressive by a carefully planned and tree-lined driveway. In other words, the house of the yeoman and the farmer was coming to resemble a great house 'writ small'.

The earliest dated examples of a centrally planned house belong to the middle years of the seventeenth century. It was, in its beginnings, essentially an upper-class development. But by the end of the century it was gaining wide acceptance amongst the gentry, and was spreading to the more substantial of their tenants, and during the next century it became general in most newly built houses. 'As a design for rural living,' wrote Peter Smith, 'this plan is the most important contribution the seventeenth century had to make to the development of architecture.'[86] Such houses spread through the English countryside and, to some extent, also the Welsh, during the eighteenth and nineteenth centuries. One sees them in their hundreds, standing amid their fields, often with a windbreak of trees, or ranged along a village street, solidly built of masonry, with symmetrical facades and sash windows, centrally placed, classical doorways, and here and there just a suspicion of Palladian style or Adam decoration. They became the outward symbol of the prosperity of the class of tenant-farmers which was coming into being as the peasantry disappeared from rural society and their smallholdings were absorbed into large farms, held on long-term leases. They marked the triumph of classicism, of the architectural ideas which were spread through Europe during the Renaissance. Its inspiration derived from Italy, where classical styles could still be seen. It was first adopted in Britain by the court and nobility, many of whose members had travelled in Italy, and it spread 'from the nobility to the gentry, and finally from the gentry to the peasantry (an even slower process) . . . the role of the court and of the upper classes was vital'.[87]

CHAPTER 4

HEAT, LIGHT AND INSECURITY

Except in summer, the traditional house was cold and draughty, and at all times dark and gloomy. Its doors and windows admitted more air than light and gave little protection against the intruder. For most people their security lay in the paucity of goods worth stealing. People spent much of their time out of doors. Houses were for eating and sleeping, and only during the dark days of winter would people have spent much time within them. In the course of the later Middle Ages and early modern times, however, household furniture increased; domestic comforts, like cushions and curtains and decorated walls, became more common, and by small increments a house was slowly turned into a home.[1]

The central hearth

Before the sixteenth century most homes had only a single hearth, centrally placed within the hall.

> Amidde the halle flor
> A fier, stark and store
> Was light and brende bright.[2]

It was usually made of small stones set on edge, but sometimes of stone slabs, and occasionally of fire-hardened clay.[3] Here a fire smouldered and was rarely allowed to go out because there was no ready means of lighting it again. Should it be extinguished, it had generally to be relighted with embers carried from a neighbouring house. This was a hazardous undertaking, and the rolls of the coroners' courts occasionally contain references to the disastrous consequences of the careless handling of a burning brand.[4] The hearth was the only source of warmth and sometimes also of light (Fig. 4.1). In winter the family often slept on the floor around it, and only withdrew to the greater privacy of solar or chamber during warm summer nights. The hearth served also for cooking (p. 141), and its iron gear for suspending pots or roasting meat stood above the ashes as late as the nineteenth century. Smoke rose from the hearth and circulated between the blackened rafters.

4.1 From a series of the Labours of the Months: February. After a roundel, formerly in a Norwich church and now in the Burrell Collection, Glasgow.

In more sophisticated halls, a louvred cupola of wood or even of baked clay was set above the ridge of the roof to allow the smoke to escape (Fig. 4.2), but generally it found its way out through a simple hole in the thatch, by vents in the gable or by cracks and gaps wherever they might be.[5] There was always smoke in the house, despite the fact that wind blew through its shuttered windows and ill-fitting doors. Eyes were sore with smoke, and sparks that rose from the hearth not infrequently set light to the roof.

In many an excavated hut site within a deserted village the baked soil and traces of carbonised fuel show where the hearth had been, and, in cottages that have survived, the smoke-grimed rafters and roofing ties tell of the time when the smoke curled upwards and hams and sides of bacon were hung beneath the thatch to cure (Fig. 4.3).

The fuel in general use was wood or peat, though fragments of unburnt coal are occasionally found, showing that the peasant may at times have used it if it could be obtained nearby.[6] The sulphur content of coal must have made it acutely unpleasant to use, at least until a smoke-hood and a chimney had been built to carry away the

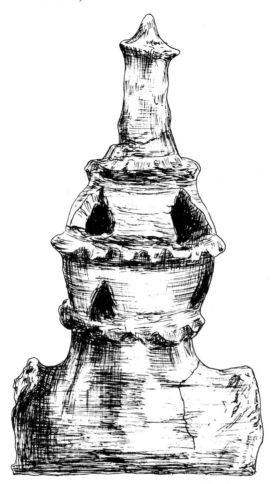

4.2 Louvred chimney-pot, to be set on the ridge of the roof over a domestic hall.

fumes. Fuel consumption was heavy, even in a small cottage, and gathering twigs and fallen boughs was a traditional occupation, especially for women. Trees were not, as a general rule, felled for fuel, though when they had been cut the branches and trimmings were without question burned on the domestic hearth. The peasant, on the other hand, commonly had the right to take 'firbote' from his lord's woodland, but this was often restricted to fallen branches and dead trees. The trunk was reserved for building construction. Peat was used only in areas where it was readily available, as in mid-Somerset, the Fenland, Norfolk and the Humberhead marshes. Many of the lakes that occur in these areas today were formed as a result of medieval peat-cutting. Wood was gathered at all times of the year, but especially in autumn, when a woodpile was accumulated in advance of winter. Where to place the fuel was often a problem, and there was a considerable inducement to place it against the house, where it had some protection from the rain. This was seen as a dangerous

4.3 Sides of bacon shown hanging in the roof space of a cottage. After a misericord.

practice because it added to the ever-present hazard of fire. The courts frowned upon
it and often required that a woodpile be relocated at a greater distance from the
cottage.[7]

The provision of enough fuel for the domestic hearth was always a serious
problem. According to calculations made by Bairoch, each urban-dweller required
from 1.0 to 1.6 tonnes of wood per year, and there is no reason to suppose that rural
inhabitants needed any less. This amount could have been supplied from 0.5 to 0.8
hectares of woodland if properly managed.[8] This estimate seems rather high, and it
may be that it was intended to represent the average consumption of a household.
Such an extent of woodland may have been available early in the Middle Ages; it was
not in later centuries. And this is the reason, on the one hand, for the careful
husbanding of forest resources by landowners, and, on the other, for the growing
exploitation of other fuels like peat and coal. It was inevitable that many people went
cold as well as hungry during much of the year throughout pre-industrial times. In
the Surrey Eyre of 1235 a very poor woman was found and arrested 'in the woods of
her lord stealing brushwood'.[9] One sometimes forgets that stealing fuel was no less
necessary than stealing food for the poorest members of society. The words of Piers
Plowman are an eloquent expression of the miseries of cold:

> And yet is wynter for hem worse,   for wet-shod they gone
> Afurste and afyngered   and foule rebuked
> Of this world rychemen,   that reuthe is to here.
> Now lord, sende hem somur somtyme   to solace and to ioye
> That at here lyf leden   in lownesse and in pouerte.[10]

Fireplace and chimney

One of the most far-reaching changes in domestic architecture was the removal of the hearth from its traditional place in the centre of the hall to a position against a wall. This was most often an outside wall, which would have been thicker and more suited to the construction of a chimney, but it was sometimes built in an internal wall or against the cross-passage.[11] It is generally supposed that an important factor in this change was the desire to insert an upper floor into the hall. But it is clear from surviving hall-houses which lack an inserted upper floor that this was not the only reason. Eradication of smoke from the hall must have been a powerful motive.[12]

Amongst the earliest fireplaces and chimneys in Britain may be those found on the first floor of the keep of Colchester Castle (Fig. 4.4). They are recessed in the very thick outer wall, and appear as round-headed openings with short flues which rise in the thickness of the wall to terminate in slits in its outer face.[13] These fireplaces must date from the original building of the keep in the last decades of the eleventh century. Comparable fireplaces have survived in the keeps of Rochester and Castle Hedingham (Essex),[14] in the hall at Hemingford Grey (Hunts.),[15] the so-called King John's House, Southampton,[16] and the freestanding hall within the bailey of Christchurch Castle (Hants).[17]

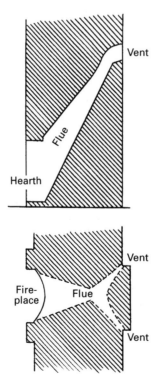

4.4 Plan and section of fireplace and flue, Colchester Castle; late eleventh century.

4.5 Twelfth-century smoke-hood, Conisborough Castle (W. Yorks.).

No one who has tried to manage a domestic fire will be unaware of the problems of a smoking chimney. Early attempts to control the smoke consisted of building a smoke-hood and raising the height of the chimney. The earliest smoke-hood to have survived may well be that at Boothby Pagnell (Lincs.) manor-house of about 1200.[18] The stone hood was corbelled out from the wall in order to trap the smoke more effectively, and, to judge from the number of such structures that have survived, it must have been moderately successful (Fig. 4.5).[19] The other method, to increase the draught by raising the height of the chimney, is less in evidence, because fewer medieval chimney-stacks have survived. Nevertheless, there are tall, slender chimneys in the twelfth-century hall of Christchurch and in the thirteenth-century castle at Grosmont (Mon.).[20] The chimney reached its highest development in the late sixteenth and seventeenth centuries, when it was often built of moulded brick and terracotta. These chimneys, 'extravagantly tall . . . informed the neighbours that one had arrived on the social scene'.[21] The chimney became an exterior status symbol, just as the fireplace was within the house. The moulded chimney-pot, often with louvres to assist the draught, has continued in use until the present day. The fireplace itself became the centrepiece of the room, as the open hearth had once been (Fig. 4.6).[22] Renaissance fireplaces sometimes reached extravagant proportions, rising in a rich array of carved and coloured stone right to the ceiling. This was encouraged by the practice of building the fireplace forward into the room, thus forming a chimney-breast. Early fireplaces were often very large in plan, and could accommodate not only the logs which were the chief fuel, but also the iron hearth gear, which continued to be used for the preparation of food. At the same time, however, the smoke-hood became less necessary as chimneys were built higher, and

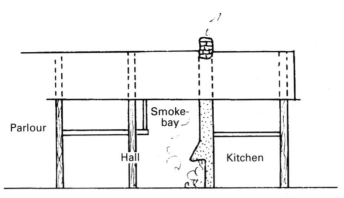

4.6 Section through a hall-house with partial upper floor, leaving a smoke-bay.

the face of the fireplace often constituted a rich pattern of panels and friezes above a straight lintel or four-centred arch. The hearth and back-wall of the fireplace were at first of stone, but they came increasingly to be built of refractory material such as brick. From early in the sixteenth century this began to be protected further from the heat of the fire by a cast-iron fireback, sometimes called a 'reredos' in the inventories.[23] Thousands of these have survived, either *in situ* or in collections, most of them decorated in relief with heraldic, domestic or religious symbols and images.

These developments in fireplace and chimney took place mainly in grand or élite houses. But there was a comparable evolution in the vernacular. Here too the insertion of an upper floor into an open hall necessitated the removal of the fire to the side of the room, but this change sometimes took place without the compulsion of an added floor. The nineteenth-century drawing of a primitive cottage at Strata Florida (Fig. 3.10) shows a simple way of achieving this. A fireplace against an end wall was covered with a smoke-hood, made, it would appear, of wickerwork, daubed with clay to give it some protection from the flames. There was little by way of a chimney: merely holes in the outer wall, by which much of the obnoxious smoke would probably have escaped. Such a fireplace and smoke-hood may not have been uncommon in the humblest cottages, but development at the vernacular level usually went far beyond this simple level.

The insertion of an upper floor into a hall was rarely the easy operation that it has been represented in this and the previous chapter, if only because the removal of the hearth to the side of the room called for important structural changes in the house itself. In some cottages a 'smoke-bay' was an intermediate stage (Fig. 4.7).[24] In a cottage of, say, three bays, two might be given an upper floor, leaving the third open to the rafters. The fireplace would be set at this end of the hall, so that the smoke would rise into the roof space at this point, leaving the rest of the hall relatively free. The former existence of such a smoke-bay can usually be demonstrated from the varying degree of smoke-blackening in the roof timbers.[25] In the course of time a masonry fireplace with chimney might be built, and at this stage the upper floor would be extended throughout the hall.

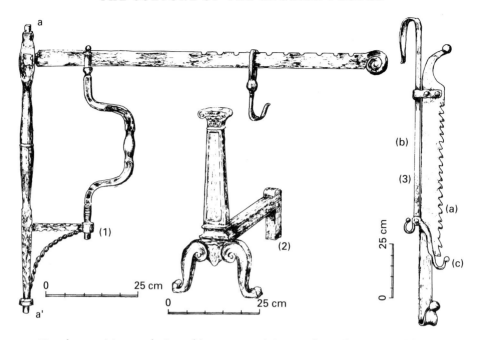

4.7 Hearth gear: (1) wrought-iron chimney crane; it was made to pivot on aa¹, (2) cast-iron andiron of late sixteenth century date, confirmed by the ER on the upright, (3) wrought-iron pot-hook: (a) slides up and down on (b), and is held at the required height by (c).

The position of the fireplace varied greatly, and to some extent accorded with local custom. It might be placed in a side wall or an end wall of the hall. Sometimes it was built into the cross-passage in order to avoid a loss of space within the hall. Sometimes it projected outwards, forming a large external chimney-breast; on the other hand, it might protrude deep into the hall.

The fireplace itself was often recessed between flanking walls. The latter supported a lintel, commonly a massive beam of oak. Such cavernous fireplaces survive in their hundreds, sometimes partially filled with masonry; sometimes occupied by a cast-iron grate or a wood-burning stove. There might even be room for seats within the fireplace – the inglenook, chimney-nook or chimney-corner – where one might sit, protected from draught and in the warmth of the fire. In such fireplaces there was abundant space for hearth gear, though at this stage in the development of the house much of the cooking would probably have been done in a separate kitchen.

The chimney was, as a general rule built of stone or brick but occasionally it was of wood, plastered to give it some protection from the heat and sparks. It rose through the rafters and thatch to terminate a foot or two above the roof-line. The construction of an upper floor meant that the joists supporting it were sometimes built into the stack, occasionally even extending into the chimney space. Cottage fires not infrequently originated when the unprotected end of a beam thus was ignited by sparks from the hearth.

The chronology of these developments is not easy to establish, partly because early examples have disappeared or have been drastically altered, partly because the rate of development varied from one part of the country to another. In this respect, as in so many others, innovation began in the south-east and spread slowly westwards and northwards, resisted in some areas, eagerly accepted in others. In south-eastern England upper floors began to be inserted into vernacular buildings early in the sixteenth century, though few examples can be dated earlier than the time of Elizabeth. In the north and west the upper floor remained a rarity even in the seventeenth century.[26]

Both hearth and fireplace had their appropriate furniture. Andirons or firedogs (Fig. 4.7), whose purpose it was to lift the burning logs above the surface of the hearth and thus to allow a draught to blow through them, were almost universal, though the highly decorated pieces of wrought-ironwork, met with in museums, may in fact have been uncommon.[27] If the hearth was to be used for cooking, as it had to be before a kitchen was built, there were also 'trivets' or tripods for supporting pots, 'gallows' from which pots were hung, and spits, usually turned by hand, for the purpose of roasting meat. Such 'hearth gear' is listed very frequently in probate inventories. As has been noted, the fire was rarely allowed to go out on the hearth, but it nevertheless required protection. At night it was the practice 'to rake the coals in the fireplace together and set over the pile the curfew', a rounded cover of coarse earthenware 'which preserved the fire till morning'.[28]

If the purpose of the curfew was to suppress the draught and to permit only a slow combustion, there was also an occasional use of draught stimulators, or 'hearth-blowers'. These were hollow vessels, often anthropomorphic, which were filled with water and set amid the ashes. As the water boiled, the escaping steam stimulated a draught within the fire.[29]

So far only the hearth and fireplace within the main hall have been mentioned, and until the later Middle Ages other fireplaces were few. The hall was, indeed, the 'fire house', as it was occasionally called.[30] But long before the end of the Middle Ages it became the practice to build fireplaces in solars and other private apartments. Tattershall Castle (Lincs.), built about 1434–45, had a large and ornamental fireplace on each of its four floors,[31] and they were installed in the royal apartments at Westminster and elsewhere at a much earlier date. In the early sixteenth century fireplaces began to be built in the private rooms of manor-houses and in the better urban houses. Andrew Boorde, a monk who turned to writing about health and domestic matters, advised his readers 'to have a fyre in your chambre and consume the euyll vapours within the chambre'.[32] The fire may have served to dry out the apartment, but possibly did little to moderate the chill, for he went on to recommend 'a good thycke quylt [a] couerynge of whyte fustyan', and a scarlet nightcap.

By the later seventeenth century fireplaces had become sufficiently numerous to provide a basis for national taxation — the Hearth Tax. In 1662 a survey was conducted on a parochial basis to show the number of hearths in each house, excepting only smiths' forges and bakers' ovens, and a tax of 1s. every half-year was levied on each. Paupers, that is those not assessed for poor or church rates, were exempt, and their houses were generally, but by no means always, omitted from the survey. The great majority even of those above the poverty level had only one hearth, at least in the parishes examined by this writer.[33] Many of those who were reported to have had more than one were found in the corrected survey of two years later to have 'blocked up one' in order, presumably, to reduce their tax liability. But what is remarkable in the tax records is the considerable number of houses with six or more fireplaces. One can distinguish the great houses of the period because they were often credited with as many as twenty or even more fireplaces.

Windows and lighting

Before modern times the windows in vernacular and sub-vernacular houses were small, and were shuttered rather than glazed. At the same time means of artificial lighting were few and very inefficient. The problem was, of course, that to increase the number and size of windows was to admit more air than was desirable. In Britain the outdoor temperature is for much of the year lower – often very much lower – than that deemed necessary indoors. Large glazed windows were prohibitively expensive before glass began to be mass-produced in modern times. Windows in a medieval cottage consisted of small rectangular openings, framed in wood, with vertical, closely spaced slats, which reduced the flow of air but also the passage of light (Fig. 4.8).

The use of glass in windows spread very slowly. There were no glaziers in early Anglo-Saxon England, and Benedict Biscop appealed to France for craftsmen to work on his church at Jarrow. After the Norman Conquest masonry-built churches became very much more numerous and the size of their windows greater, but there is no good evidence that windows in secular buildings were glazed until much later. After the twelfth century the increasing size and elaboration of church windows reflected the growing availability of glass as much as the greater skills of the mason. Elite domestic buildings, in particular great halls, began to be fenestrated and glazed like churches, but below the élite threshold one cannot look for glazed windows much before the end of the Middle Ages or even the later sixteenth century. Horn or oiled fabric were sometimes used to seal small windows, but could not be used to cover large openings. For most people the alternatives were draughty, unglazed openings or wooden shutters. Inventories made for probate purposes in the 1580s show that glazed windows, where they existed, were not regarded as fixtures and were devisible by will.[34] Earlier wills make no mention of glazed windows, and this can only mean that there were none in houses at this level. 'Wooden lattice-work, shutters and window (or "winnow") sheets . . . frequently mentioned [in inventories] were used to keep out the wind and rain . . . Ten of the eleven people [in

4.8 A slatted window of fifteenth or sixteenth century date in Linton (Cambs.).

Leicester] who had glass in their inventories were residents of towns, and it may be that glass had not yet been adopted in rural areas except among the wealthy.'[35]

At this time, however, there was a sharp increase in the production of glass. French and Italian methods of manufacture were adopted, and near the beginning of the seventeenth century coal began to be used in glass furnaces.[36] This was of great importance, because the industry had hitherto been inhibited by a shortage of fuel.[37] The greater abundance and lower price of glass were quickly reflected in building styles. One no longer finds evidence for windows that could be detached from the houses in which they had been fitted and transferred to others. Windows in vernacular houses were made larger and were treated as fixtures, and in élite houses an extravagant use was made of glass. The display of glass in the facades of, for example, Hardwick Hall (Derby.) and Barlborough Hall (Derby.) and in the Long Galleries of Montacute House (Som.) and Haddon Hall (Derby.), all built between the 1580s and the early seventeenth century, is unparalleled in any construction before the recent past. Large windows, like tall, moulded chimneys, became a matter of prestige, a visible symbol that their owners possessed the means to keep abreast of both technology and taste. A century later the use of glass, as, for example, at Chatsworth (Derby.), was very much more restrained; showmanship had by this date assumed a different form.

Early glazed windows were made up of small panes, most often diamond-shaped, leaded together and fastened into wooden frames. In the later seventeenth century these gave way to rectangular panels of somewhat greater size. At the same time windows were made to open. At first they were hinged at the side – casement windows – so that they could be made to swing open. From the closing years of the century these tended to be superseded, at least in the better buildings, by sash-windows, always mounted in pairs, which could be made to slide up and down within wooden grooves.[38] Weights were used as a counterpoise, so that each sash would remain carefully balanced at any level. It was the sash-window which provided both illumination and ventillation for the grand house of the eighteenth century.

Artificial lighting

Despite the increasing size of windows there were always times when artificial lighting became necessary, and this could be achieved only by combustion. The use of incandescence, whether of an electric filament or of a gas 'mantle' was not possible before the middle years of the nineteenth century. Apart from such illumination as derived from the domestic hearth, there were only two combustible materials that could be used: oil drawn up through a wick, and a wick impregnated with or enclosed in combustible fat. The former was the mode of lighting generally favoured in Mediterranean Europe; the latter in Britain and northern Europe. This difference is likely to reflect the fact that olive oil was relatively abundant in Mediterranean Europe, and tallow in northern. Torches, commonly used out of doors but dangerous within, belonged to the latter category, consisting, as they did, of wood impregnated with oil, fat or pitch.

The oil-burning lamp consisted of a shallow vessel to hold the oil, with a wick, most often of flax or hemp, which dipped into it and usually hung over the rim. Seashells were sometimes used, and the form of early lamps seems to have been derived from the conch. Roman lamps were most often of pottery, their bowl partially covered, with a small hole through which the wick could protrude. Such lamps could be placed on a shelf or suspended from the ceiling, and were, in fact, the precursors of the chancel lamps used in the later medieval church. Not dissimilar was the crusie lamp, also intended to hang from a chain, but having a shallow pan to catch any oil that might drip from it.[39]

Such lamps shed little light, and it was a frequent practice to group them to form a cresset.[40] This often consisted of a large stone in the upper surface of which were a number of holes for oil and a floating wick. Most surviving examples had been used in churches, but they were in all probability no less common at one time in domestic halls (Fig. 4.10).

Alternative sources of light were the candle and rushlight. The former consisted of a wick, most often of flax, cotton or even wood, which had been thickly coated with tallow or wax. It has always been of major importance and, overall, formed the most important mode of domestic lighting in Britain throughout medieval times and, indeed, until the nineteenth century. The candle was simple to make, and the

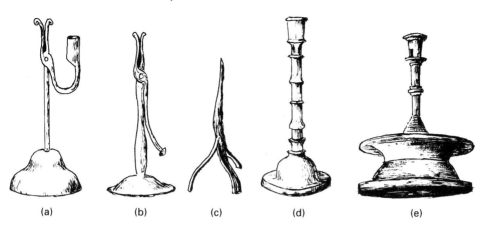

(a)   (b)   (c)   (d)   (e)

4.9 (a) Combined rushlight holder and candlestick, seventeenth to eighteenth century; (b) rushlight holder, eighteenth century; (c) pricket candlestick, late medieval; (d) brass candlestick, sixteenth century: this pattern continued little changed into recent times; (e) candlestick of the early sixteenth century, with pan to catch the grease; after a painting in the Uffizi Gallery, Florence.

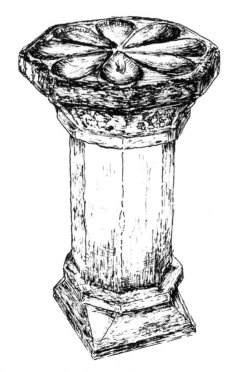

4.10 Cresset stone, Bodmin Priory church (Corn.). A separate wick would have been allowed to float in each of the eight receptacles.

tallow 'dip' remained a domestic craft into modern times. But tallow gave a smoky flame, and its smell was far from pleasant. During the nineteenth century it was replaced by both spermaceti and paraffin wax. Candles were, however also made from beeswax, much more expensive than tallow, but more pleasant and convenient to use, and wills which made provision for altar or rood lights in churches were often at pains to specify that they should be of wax.[41] Long candles, or tapers, were carried in procession and burned before the pyx. A well-made candle burned so evenly that it was sometimes used as a measure of time.

The rushlight was a simpler and cruder form of candle. It consisted, as its name implies, of a rush impregnated with oil, tar or other combustible substance. It was the commonest form of illumination amongst the poor, and William Cobbett wrote that 'I was bred and brought up mostly by rush-light', and that his grandmother 'never, I believe, burnt a candle in her house in her life'.[42] While the manufacture of candles became in some degree a professional occupation, rushlights continued to be made in the home by 'decayed labourers, women and children'.[43] The prepared rush was impregnated with any fat or grease that was available. It gave a flickering and uncertain light, but had the merit of being cheap and of consuming little by way of scarce materials. It thus recommended itself to the poor, and for this reason its manufacture was described in detail by Gilbert White: 'a poor family', he wrote, 'twill enjoy $5\frac{1}{2}$ hours of comfortable light for a farthing'.

Both candles and rushlights constituted a serious fire danger, and they had to be securely held. Candles were secured in two ways: in a socketed candlestick or impaled upon a metal or wooden pricket. Socketed candle-holders had been used by the Romans, and have remained in use until the present. The pricket became more common in churches because it was better suited to the large wax candle commonly used. The wrought-iron rail around some medieval tombs was sometimes surmounted by spikes on which were impaled the many candles customarily burned for the soul of the deceased. Iron-socketed candlesticks assumed many forms but all incorporated as their essential feature a loop of flattened metal within which the base of the candle was set. Most often they had three legs or feet to enable them to stand more securely on the rough surfaces on which they were often placed. Towards the end of the Middle Ages brass began to replace iron in candlesticks, and their bases became flat, round dishes, which caught the unburnt wax which dripped from the candle. This form of candlestick, in brass, pewter or chinaware, has continued in use until the present.[44]

Candlesticks were, and have remained, an essential part of the furnishings of church and home, and their elaboration and decoration became part of the 'superfluous behaviour' discussed later (p. 268). Indeed, the essentially decorative candlestick remains today an accessory of the dining-table, even though it has functionally been replaced by electricity. Church candlesticks sometimes reached great size and were elaborately decorated.[45] Nevertheless, the light shed by a single candle was small and came in fact to be the minimal unit in the measurement of illumination. It thus became a common practice to group several candles together,

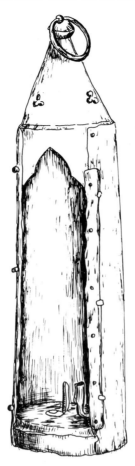

4.11 Portable lantern; London Museum.

rather like the cavities in a cresset stone. The result was the candelabrum, either suspended from the ceiling or supported on a pillar. In great houses the number of candlesticks was immense. The Shardeloes household in the late seventeenth century contained '12 large brass candlesticks, 10 "lesse[r] candlesticks", 6 lanthorne candlesticks and 5 handle candlesticks'. All were kept in the kitchen, which was itself lighted by a 'brass hanging candlestick'.[46]

The lantern was at first merely a portable candle-holder in which the flame was protected by a metal shield with a window of horn or glass. It was used within the home, but was intended primarily for outdoor use, and was often fitted with a ring for convenience in carrying or hanging (Fig. 4.11). Such lanterns figured not infrequently in the art of the later Middle Ages and Renaissance, and their form has continued to be used, little altered except that the candle has often been replaced by an oil-burning wick.

The last stage in the development of the lamp to be discussed here was the introduction of a central wick, which dipped into an oil bath and was moved by a simple screw mechanism. A glass funnel protected the flame and stimulated a draught. Its development from the simple oil-burning lamp was effected by a number of minor innovations, spread over a long period of time. It was generally of brass or pottery. The wick was wide and flat, and the fuel most often used was paraffin, which came into general use only in the nineteenth century. Late in the eighteenth century the French inventor, Aimé Argand, introduced the glass chimney, with holes pierced near its base, enclosing a *circular* wick. It was Argand's lamp that was first used to illuminate the streets of London.[47] Lamps, designed to be set on the table or desk, were made in a variety of sizes and patterns; many were highly decorated or painted, and were given shades to reflect the light downwards on to a desk or table.[48] The paraffin-burning lamp largely displaced the candle from the Victorian drawing-room, and its brighter and more even light revolutionised domestic living. The candlestick continued, however, to be used whenever a light had to be carried around the house. The use of the table-lamp progressed socially downwards, slowly displacing candle and rushlight, until it was itself replaced by gaslight and then electricity.

All forms of artificial heating and lighting called for some form of ignition. In most homes the fire supplied the flame when needed. But when it went out it was usual to take a burning brand from a neighbouring house at a not inconsiderable risk. Numerous house fires are recorded to have originated in this way. A jury at Salford (Lancs.), about 1600, recommended that 'there shall none carie ffyer openlie uncovered nor delyver ffyer out of his howse'.[49] If a brand was not available people had of necessity to turn to the primitive steel and flint. A spark produced by the friction of the one on the other was used to fire the flintlock gun, and the tinder box, kept in many homes as late as the nineteenth century, served the same purpose. But clearly a simpler means of producing a flame was desirable, especially with the increasing number of table-lamps, and experiments aimed at producing such a tool continued through much of the eighteenth century. The readiness of phosphorus to ignite when combined with oxygen or sulphur was already known, and this chemical reaction was used to produce a variety of what can only be termed expensive and dangerous toys. Matches whose heads contained phosphorus, which ignited when struck against a roughened surface – 'lucifers' they were called – began to be made in the 1830s. By the mid-century a 'safety match', which ignited only when struck on a prepared surface affixed to the box, was produced, and quickly drove both the tinder-box and the phosphorus match from even the poorest homes.[50]

Crime and security

The traditional home was insecure, as well as dark, cold and damp. Insecurity came in many forms. There was the danger of theft from ill-protected houses. Fire was an ever-present risk from the hearth, the oven and the naked flame of rushlight and candle. Then there were the countless causes of accidents – the brewers' vats and unmarked holes in the ground; insecure scaffolding and pots of boiling gruel set unsteadily amid the ashes on the hearth – all contributed to the toll of accidental deaths that were recorded in the rolls of the coroners' courts.

Pre-industrial Britain was a lawless land. 'Crimes of violence were common and . . . the criminal law was exceedingly inefficient . . . even in quiet times few out of many criminals came to their appointed end.'[51] Law enforcement was, by and large, the unpaid responsibility of all the inhabitants of every vill in the land. There was no privacy within the community. Almost every activity was communal, and this led inevitably to friction and dispute, to violence and homicide. But the very openness of society meant that every personal feud was known to all the neighbours, and, in the event of homicide, a suspect could usually be identified at once. And to be suspected was to be 'presented' to a court and found guilty. The discovery of a crime or, indeed, of any suspicious circumstance was followed immediately by the 'hue and cry'. This was 'raised by shouting, by blowing the horn . . . even by the ringing of church bells. It was a call to action and arms, which every man, woman and child must obey. Anything suspicious, any robbery, or house broken into, indeed any disturbance involving bloodshed, required the raising of the hue.'[52] Jurors at the manor court of Wakefield (W. Yorks.) stated that a certain house 'was burgled by thieves unknown and the aforesaid hamlet did not raise the hue nor prosecute [i.e. pursue] the thieves'. It was therefore 'in mercy', that is to say, it was fined for its failure to do its duty. The evidence of the same court rolls shows not only that burglary was very common but that 'most culprits were successful in escaping arrest'.[53]

The culprit would usually flee, pursued by a noisy and ineffective rabble. If he escaped beyond the community's – usually the parish's – boundary, he was safe, at least for a time. He might later be pursued by the sheriff, but the mechanism of the law was slow and cumbersome. His difficulty then was that no other community would welcome him because he would be a 'foreigner'. He would probably be declared an outlaw, 'reduced to the status of hunted vermin, liable to arrest when seen and execution when arrested'. The outlaw has tended to become a romantic figure, and to be glamorised like Robin Hood. There was indeed much waste land where he could find a refuge, but not a livelihood. He had necessarily to prey on settled communities, and many of the intruders who broke into homes and escaped with food must surely have been outlaws. The life of the outlaw was, indeed, far from 'merry'.

Another recourse of the escaping criminal was to find sanctuary within a church, in other words to seek the aid and protection of its dedicatory saint. But sanctuary was short-lived. The act of taking sanctuary was itself an admission of guilt, and the criminal who then surrendered was forced to abjure the realm before a coroner, and then given a specified period of time in which to make his way to a port and take ship for the continent. Many recognised sanctuaries were dissolved at the Reformation, and the right of sanctuary for felony was abolished in 1623.

Foremost amongst recorded crimes were larceny, burglary and robbery, all of which were frequent and together constituted nearly three-quarters of indictable offences in the early fourteenth century. Burglary, the forcible entry for the purpose of committing a felony, made up about a quarter of all crimes. At Wakefield on one occasion burglaries were so numerous that double juries had to be impanelled 'on account of common burglaries and the great number of thieves, as to which the truth cannot be ascertained'.[54] Most offences were committed by men rather than women, though women were often reduced to stealing food.

Homicide was common, but juries did not – perhaps could not – distinguish between premeditated murder and manslaughter, perpetrated in the heat of an argument or as the result of an accident. It can only be said that manslaughter in self-defence usually resulted in acquittal. Everything in the rolls of the courts indicates that most homicides 'resulted from disputes between peasants, from quarrels between labouring men'.[55] Homicide within the family or home was comparatively rare. Public opinion disapproved of violence within the family and had its own methods of stopping it and of exposing those responsible for it to ridicule (p. 338). A high value was placed on children and infanticide appears to have been exceptional.

A restriction on theft was the difficulty of disposing of stolen goods. Any sudden accession of wealth within a peasant society would arouse immediate suspicion. At Bradninch (Devon) in 1238 it was reported of John le Fatte that 'he eats well, drinks well and dresses himself well but they [the jurors] do not know where his money comes from'.[56] The suspicions of the jurors could not immediately be confirmed. They were, however, well founded, and John subsequently absconded under suspicion of stealing pigs. In Bracton's view anyone who lived above his station might be suspected of having discovered treasure which had not been disclosed to the coroner as 'treasure trove'.[57]

Burglary was assisted by the ease with which houses could be entered. Door fastenings remained flimsy in the extreme well into modern times, and could easily be forced. Wooden window-bars were usually placed close enough together to make entry between them difficult, but they rotted or were broken, and entry could be effected, at least by a child. The Norfolk assize rolls record the case of the young man who entered a house in this way, but found himself jammed between the window slats as he made his escape, and was arrested.[58] Court records tell of countless cases, amusing or tragic, which show how tempting it was to break into an ill-protected cottage and easy to escape with part of its slender contents. Indeed, the only protection against burglary was to have nothing worth stealing. How little things have changed since the Middle Ages!

Barbara Hanawalt has shown that burglary was most common in the winter months, when the harvest was in store and darkness facilitated escape.[59] The habits of most people were well known to their neighbours, and it was not difficult to choose a time when the occupants were working in the fields or at church, to enter the house. Sometimes a lath-and-plaster panel of a timber-framed house was beaten in; sometimes a window or a door was forced; occasionally a ladder was used to reach an upstairs window. Most burglars were opportunist and quite unsophisticated, and few would have been capable of picking a simple iron lock. Instead, like the common burglar today, they merely smashed whatever stood in their way.

For those arrested and convicted the penalties were harsh in the extreme throughout the pre-industrial period. The death penalty was commonly imposed for theft of goods to the value of more than a shilling, though this level was later raised in line with inflation, and in the eighteenth century deportation became an alternative sentence. Trial in all such cases was by jury. The original jury was a 'presenting jury' which judged from personal knowledge of the case and of the defendant. It was not a judge of evidence so much as a witness to what had taken place. The transition from the one form of jury to the other was one of the most important changes in the medieval legal system, though the tradition of the 'presenting' jury survived into the present century in the shape of the 'grand jury'. The reading of the rolls of assizes suggests that juries tended to be lenient, but whether this arose from any feeling that penalties were excessive, or from uncertainty regarding the evidence, we can never know. It would appear that more prisoners were acquitted than were convicted. Numerous cases in the Norfolk gaol delivery rolls record that the prisoner stole 'because he was hungry and destitute', or that 'he did this because of hunger and destitution' and was acquitted. Hanawalt has shown that the 'scarcity of goods due to crop failures and scarcity of land due to inheritance customs had a great influence on the volume and types of crime'. There can be little doubt that a high proportion of all crimes right down to the nineteenth century was due to poverty and destitution. It appears, furthermore, that an *un*successful attempt to commit a felony incurred no penalty. At Tunstead (Norfolk) 'the jurors say that S. A. broke a window in the partition of Robert of Beeston's house and wanted to enter . . . through it. The window was too small to enter or to use for carrying out goods.'[60] He was acquitted.

Most burglaries that came before the courts were by petty criminals and at the expense of humble cottagers. There are cases of a burglar, after a successful raid on a house, going straight to sell his loot in a nearby market where it was instantly recognised. But not all were as unprofessional as this. The not infrequent theft of a chalice or of other church vessels and goods must have been for melting down and sale at a distance. Burglaries were sometimes at the expense of great houses or castles, though these were less often left unguarded. In one recorded instance the intruders became so drunk at the expense of their unwitting host that they were unable to flee and were apprehended.[61]

Homicide was one of the commonest of crimes, second only to burglary and robbery. Indeed, it may at times have been more frequent. Of 110 criminal cases heard before the justices at Bedford in 1227, no less than 53 were for murder or manslaughter.[62] It was a violent age, when disputes of trifling importance often led to fighting and death. The blood-feud, it is true, had ceased to be of significance in England, but it continued in Wales and Scotland until late in the Middle Ages, and must have contributed to the death toll.[63] The violence which afflicted society was due in part to the slow, cumbersome and ineffective mechanisms of police and justice; in part to the greater aggressiveness that seems to have characterised human behaviour. Trials of strength and games of chance, however friendly they may have been to start with, readily led to violence and death.[64] Most men carried arms of some kind, if only the large sheath-knife which they used to cut their meat, and showed no reluctance to use them in their quarrels. At a time when ale or beer, albeit weak by modern standards, was the normal drink for all classes, drunkenness was rife and brawls frequent. The efforts made throughout the pre-industrial period to restrict drinking and drunkenness were due in the main to the violence which they generated.

The criminal caught *in flagrante delicto* and without extenuating circumstances might escape the death penalty by taking sanctuary.[65] In this case he was usually forced to abjure the realm and go into permanent exile. A further recourse for the small minority who were literate was to claim the privilege of clergy. Ordination called for little qualification, other than an ability to read, and it was assumed during the Middle Ages that anyone able to read a passage, generally from the Bible, was in orders, and thus was exempt from civil jurisdiction. This practice survived the Reformation. The Cornish diarist, William Carnsew, noted in 1576 that an alleged felon 'had his books' or, in other words, demanded to be allowed to demonstrate his ability to read, and was presumably allowed to go free.[66] The practice continued into the seventeenth century, when it is said to have been a minor inducement to people to learn to read.[67] It did not, however, outlast the Interregnum.

Lock and key

People of all classes did what they could to protect their homes and possessions, few though they may have been. Most efficacious were locked doors and chests, which the poorest classes could not afford. The earliest locks were little more than a device for keeping a door closed – a simple latch with a hooked piece of metal which could be inserted through a hole in order to lift it, no different from the Roman latch-lifter, shown in Figure 2.8f. A refinement, probably of Roman date, was to fit wards to the key and obstacles in the keyhole so that only the correctly shaped key could pass through and turn. This led on to the medieval lock and key with a complex system of wards, which prevailed until modern times when it began to be superseded by the tumbler and other more sophisticated forms (Fig. 4.12).[68] The medieval lock consisted essentially of a box into which the key was inserted through the keyhole. The appropriate key had grooves and slots so placed that they allowed it to turn through the wards of the lock. This in turn moved the bolt into and out of its 'receiver'. Usually the lock was affixed to the door, and the bolt was made to slide into a 'receiver' fitted into the door-frame. In the case of a chest, the lock was built into its side and a hooked bolt engaged the lid, holding it firm.

A good lock was a complex product of the smith's craft, which only the well-to-do could afford to use. It is doubtful whether the poorer homes had much more than a latch-lifter before modern times, and little strength or skill was required to break

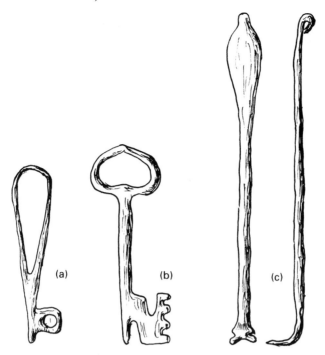

4.12 Early types of key: (a) twelfth century, (b) late medieval, (c) early padlock key.

in. Great houses, with very much more to attract the thief, were protected by more complex locks, as well as having locked chests strong enough to resist all except the most determined of intruders.[69] The wrought-iron key became a symbol of security, and the keys of the Kingdom of Heaven, held by St Peter, were identical with those that opened the great door of the manor-house or church. The word 'key' denoted a right of access. The victor in battle assumed metaphorically the keys of castle or city, though in reality no such things existed.

The chest provided the safest place of storage. It was usually of oak and bound with bands of iron (Fig. 4.13). Its lid was hinged and secured by one or more locks which were relatively difficult to pick. Indeed, the easiest way for an intruder to get into them was by cutting their wire hinges. Every well-to-do household had a chest, sometimes several, and from the Renaissance they tended to become highly decorative pieces of furniture. Chests were used for keeping plate, jewellery, coin, legal documents and other valuables. But most of the population had neither the means to acquire so bulky a piece of furniture nor possessions sufficiently valuable to deserve such protection. When necessary they were far more likely to use the communal chest, kept usually within the parish church. But even the parish chest was not immune to theft. In 1385 a thief broke into the 'locked common chest of the parishioners [of Ticehurst, Sussex] and took from it eight pounds of wax and other goods to the value of 20s'.[70] Goods of relatively small value were evidently placed in the chest for safe-keeping.

4.13 Medieval chest for storing valuables, and commonly placed at the foot of the bed. After *The Babees Book*, EETS.

The burglar hoped no doubt to find money, but the records show that he most often made away with bulky goods of little worth that could not easily have been kept in a chest, such as rolls of cloth or bags of unmilled grain.[71] Silver was sometimes taken from an unprotected church, but before modern times there was little by way of an organised market for such goods. A change took place in the eighteenth century when there was a conspicuous increase in the volume of goods, both decorative and useful, in the ordinary home. This tendency to accumulate the 'things' which turned a house into a home culminated in the cluttered interiors of the Victorian household.

The crime of burglary increased with the volume of goods worth stealing, and with it proliferated the means of disposing of stolen property. 'For this reason,' wrote Asa Briggs, 'locks were among the most important of Victorian things',[72] just as today the same might be said of the burglar-alarm system. The volume of goods to be protected was continually increasing, and corresponding improvements were made in the locks used to secure them. The ward lock had given an uncertain protection against the sophisticated burglar. In the 1780s types of locks were devised that used 'tumblers' – pins or rods which dropped into holes or slots in the bolt, and were lifted by means of a key. This line of development culminated in the Chubb lock, first made in the 1840s at Wolverhampton.[73] At about the same time Linus Yale, in the United States, began to make locks which combined the principle of pin-tumblers with a round barrel into which they dropped. The Yale lock, imported into Britain, became the chief rival of the Chubb and was advertised as 'impregnable against every practicable method of picking, fraud or violence'.[74] It was, of course, nothing of the kind, as many whose houses have been entered today can testify, but it was, nevertheless, a great improvement on the ward lock, and enabled property-owners to keep a very short distance ahead of at least the opportunist thief.

Fire hazard

After burglary the most serious threat to home and property was fire. Timber-framed cottages and thatched roofs were in any event very vulnerable, but the danger was increased immeasurably by the curious practices that prevailed. Fire was lighted beneath the inflammable roof; burning brands were carried from cottage to cottage; candles and lamps were propped up in odd corners, and flooring joists were sometimes built into the chimney-stack, and in extreme cases the chimney might itself be constructed of wood. Brewers and bakers often allowed fires within their congested homes to get out of control. Piers Plowman evidently thought brewers particularly culpable:

> Som tyme thorw a brewere
> Meny burgagys ben ybrent   and bodyes ther-ynne;
> And thorw a candel, clomyng   in a corsed place,
> Fel a-doun, and for brende,   forth al the rewe.[75]

It was taken for granted that in any community there might be several fires within a year. The gravest fear was that a fire might spread and engulf the village. Sparks from a burning thatch constituted the greatest danger, and it was customary to use rakes to tear the thatch from a burning cottage. At Acomb (E. Riding, Yorks.) two householders were fined in 1622 'for not removing their fiery thatch to the great terror of their neighbours'.[76] At Salford (Lancs.) 'bucketts and hookes' were acquired for this purpose at public expense,[77] and a similar provision was probably made in most communities in the country.

Parochial officers were always on the lookout for anything that could increase the fire risk to any cottage and thus to the whole village. At Acomb action was taken to prevent a parishioner from keeping dry flax and hemp within his 'fire-house', or hall, where it could easily catch fire.[78] At Salford it was reported to the Portmote that 'there hath beene layd great store of kydds [faggots] at the back of ther Backhouse [bakehouse] to the great danger of the Towne'. It was ordered that only a day's supply should be kept there.[79] There are other warnings of the danger of storing fuel against the walls of a house elsewhere in the court rolls.

Local regulations attempted to reduce the risk of fire. In the city of London, following a disastrous fire in 1189, it was ordained that all newly built houses should be roofed with stone or slate and that the party walls between contiguous houses should be of masonry.[80] The problem was to enforce such regulations, and about 1300 a citizen was made to replace his thatched roof with one of tiles in the city parish of St Lawrence Candlewick.[81] London was, on account of its great size and of the large number of crafts which used ovens and hearths, the most vulnerable of English cities. In each of its wards ladders and iron hooks were available for tearing down burning buildings, and, to prevent the spread of fire, 'every householder [was required] to have before his front a barrel of water'.[82] In 1446/7 the building of 'treene [wooden] chimneys' was forbidden,[83] though somewhat illogically smiths were allowed to continue to use them.[84] Other cities and towns were slow in following the example of London, but most attempted in a half-hearted fashion to regulate construction and to restrict the use of forges and ovens to specific areas. In 1599 the town of Abingdon (Oxon.) required thatch to be replaced with tile, and even authorised its officers to enter the roof space of any house in order to survey the risks it posed.[85] Later town regulations called upon the citizens to provide buckets, ladders and 'great hooks'. In rural areas the danger was reduced because buildings were usually more widely spaced and few rural crafts called for hearths and furnaces. Manorial courts, nevertheless, not infrequently made wise regulations regarding fire precautions, but rarely took steps to enforce them. No British town has been spared a major conflagration, and some have been devastated on more than one occasion. No village was without its cottage fires, many of them unchronicled or at most barely mentioned in the parish records. The terse entry in the churchwardens' accounts of the parish of Shillington (Beds.) in 1595 says it all: 'given to a poore woman that had great losses by fyer'.[86] She was probably travelling around the country, armed with a 'brief', a note from the justices of her home place, stating the cause of her distress and appealing for help. Sometimes a manor court acted when the cause of a fire could be precisely determined, as at Ruthin (Denbigh.), where a man was arrested 'because through his fire, not guarded, a conflagration commenced and burned the houses of his neighbours'.[87] The Great Fire of London began, not inappropriately, in a bakery in Pudding Lane, an alley which sloped down to the Thames in the east of the City. The flames, fanned by a north-east wind, spread westwards as far as the Temple, before the wider spacing of buildings set a limit to their progress. This, the greatest urban fire in English history before the Second World War, is reported to have consumed 89 churches and 13,200 houses.[88]

Apart from preventive measures, like building in masonry and using tile instead of thatch, there was little that could be done to prevent fires other than to maintain a perpetual watchfulness. The Statute of Winchester of 1285[89] required that both villages and cities be guarded by 'ward' during the day and by 'watch' at night.[90] This was aimed primarily to prevent burglary and the intrusion of outsiders into the community, but a secondary purpose was unquestionably to guard against fire. In some cities of continental Europe a watchman was appointed to maintain permanent

4.14 A Sun fire insurance disc of the early eighteenth century.

watch from some vantage-point for the curl of smoke that might indicate the beginning of a local conflagration.[91]

Until the later years of the seventeenth century there was no institutionalised aid for the victims of fire. Those who had lost all were dependent on the charity of their neighbours, as countless local records show. In the case of a severe fire it was a common practice in early modern times to circulate an appeal among neighbouring parishes. This was read out at church services, and the pence collected were remitted to the afflicted parish. Churchwardens' and vestry accounts for four parishes in County Durham give some idea of the frequency and seriousness of domestic fires and of the sums raised to repair the losses. In dozens of 'briefs' which were circulated between 1580 and 1700 the great majority related to domestic fires, one of them, at Haverhill (Essex) 330 km from the parish where it was recorded.[92] Fire insurance, in which a premium was paid in proportion to the estimated risk, was not instituted for private homes before the eighteenth century. Attempts had been made to establish some form of insurance along the lines of marine insurance even before the Great Fire of 1666.[93] Thereafter they became more frequent. In 1681 a speculative builder opened a 'fire office' in the City, and it is claimed, somewhat improbably, that he insured up to 10,000 houses. Other mutual projects followed, all of them concentrating on protecting private homes against fire. In the course of the eighteenth century the London insurance business became more diversified, and factory insurance assumed an important role. At the same time promoters extended their activities to other cities, but the business still remained predominantly urban.

4.15 A row of leather fire-buckets, probably of the late eighteenth century, in Haughley (Suff.) parish church.

The number of companies offering protection increased, and several, notably the Sun Insurance Company, even maintained fire-pumps with crews to man them.[94] Reports that such 'brigades' refused to extinguish fires unless the property was insured with their companies, are well authenticated. Small metal plaques, many of which have been preserved, indicated which buildings were insured and with what company (Fig. 4.14). Villages, meanwhile, were left to their own resources, and often acquired and operated a fire-pump for their own communal use.

Public authorities were reluctant to accept the view that their obligations extended to fire protection, but in the course of the eighteenth century they began to acquire fire-pumps, fire-buckets and reservoirs in which to hold a reserve of water (Fig. 4.15). Pumps were operated by hand and hosepipes were short. Water had often to be delivered to the pump by a 'bucket chain' of people who passed the containers from hand to hand. Not until the mid-nineteenth century was steam-power first used to pump water, and high-pressure water-mains and hydrants came a great deal later. Fire hazards could never be completely eliminated, but their drastic reduction must be regarded as one of the major achievements of the later eighteenth and nineteenth centuries.

Accident and Act of God

Fire and burglary were not the only hazards to which the pre-industrial household was exposed. There were dangers in almost every aspect of daily life, and accidental death, as recorded in the coroners' rolls, reached levels that would today be regarded as intolerable. There were risks in the open fireplace, in flimsy ladders and ill-constructed lofts. Holes dug in the roads were left unprotected. There were cesspits covered only with rotting boards., into which the unfortunate might fall and be drowned. Benjamin Rogers, rector of Carlton (Beds.) recorded in his diary in 1733 that his 'son . . . being about 5 years old fell backwards into the Pottage Pot just as it was taken boyling off the Fire for Dinner'. In this case tragedy was averted, and he 'was taken out immediately by the Maid'.[95] Women and children were most susceptible to accident in the home, where they spent much of their time. Large, unwieldy cooking-pots and deep, unprotected wells claimed many lives, both young and old.[96]

All such cases of sudden or unnatural death had, after the end of the twelfth century, to be referred to the coroner, whose duty it was to elicit the cause of death and, in the name of the Crown, to exact whatever penalty might be due.[97] If death was at human hands, this was murder or manslaughter, and the case was referred to the courts of criminal jurisdiction. In other cases the fault might lie with a broken ladder, a pot of boiling water, a broken cartwheel. It was then the primitive practice to punish the inanimate instrument of death. At one time it would have been destroyed. Later it became forfeit to the crown, since the crown was deemed to have suffered by the death of its victim. By the time that records began to be kept it had become customary to assess the value of the object and to levy this as a fine or *deodand*:

a little boy . . . fell into a pan of milk and was drowned . . . The pan is worth *6d*.[98]

a boy feeding maslin into a mill was caught by the 'cogges' and dragged into the mechanism . . . the wheel with 'cogges' worth 18*d* . . . the sails with cloth worth 2*s* . . . the mill with the millstone worth 10*s*, and the basket .. 1½*d*.[99]

Sarah lived in a frail and delapidated house [which] fell in upon her . . . and she died . . . The fallen wood and stones are appraised at 12*d*.[100]

The money thus collected was supposed to be distributed by the king's almoner to the poor. It is evident, however, that not all the money received in this way ever reached the royal officials. In 1422 an inquiry was ordered into 'deodands concealed'.[101] The law regarding deodands remained on the statute book until 1846, but the fines had long since ceased to be collected.

CHAPTER 5

THE HOUSE FURNISHED

I know not how it may be with others
    Who sit amid relics of householdry,
That date from the days of their mothers' mothers,
    But well I know how it is with me
        Continually

I see the hands of the generations
    That owned each shiny familiar thing
In play on its knobs and indentations,
    And with its ancient fashioning
        Still dallying.   Thomas Hardy

A comfortable and well-furnished home was for most classes of society a product of the nineteenth century. The history of the home, like that of the house, has been one of innovation at the higher and richer levels of society and of imitation at the lower. This downward spread of standards of comfort, if not always of good taste, was made possible by a rising level of real wealth, and in this there can be little doubt but that the fifteenth and sixteenth centuries marked a turning-point. It was then, for the first time at least since the beginning of the Middle Ages, that the real incomes of the rural classes – yeoman, copyholder, husbandman – showed any appreciable increase, giving them a disposable surplus and a discretionary power over its use.[1] It was during this period that the forms of domestic life which have remained with us ever since were first developed. Tables, benches and chairs, cupboards and sideboards began to assume their familiar shapes. The solar or parlour developed distinct from the hall. Beds became frames, lifted above the cold floor and fitted with mattresses of increasing softness and comfort, and covered with an array of blankets and coverlets. Armouries, closets and chests were adopted for the storage of an increasing volume of knick-knacks and personal goods. Cushions and upholstery began to soften the hard seats, and walls were covered with coloured cloths and, at least in upper- and middle-class homes, hung with portraits and pictures.

One can form some idea of the furnishings of grander houses, even in the Middle Ages, because so many were represented in illuminated manuscripts. But of the cottages of the peasantry little can be known until the later years of the sixteenth and the seventeenth centuries, their contents began to be recorded in probate inventories. By and large, there was little to record, and one can only assume that during the Middle Ages their furnishings amounted to little more than table and bench, a rough bed or even straw to lie on, and a simple pot for cooking.

Wills and inventories

The earliest firm evidence for the contents of a house, whether of the rich or of the poorer classes, comes from wills and probate inventories. Though wills survive from as early as the Anglo-Saxon period, they are few in number before the later Middle Ages.[2] The first wills are terse and are concerned more with the spiritual welfare of the deceased than with his or her personal effects. They became fuller, more informative and more numerous during the later years of the fifteenth century, but it is not until the Elizabethan period that wills can be said to give a cross-section through much of contemporary society. Even then the poorest members were sparsely represented because they were not required to make a will if the value of their chattels was thought to have been less than £5. That some in fact did so is probably to be attributed to the fear of disputes among heirs.[3]

Later wills tended to become an abbreviated list of what might be thought of as the more important of the testator's chattels, but the fullest of them fell considerably short of an inventory of the deceased's possessions. Though inventories of personal possessions had sometimes been made – most often in connection with lay subsidy assessments or debts[4] – it was not until the early sixteenth century that the law required the will to be accompanied, when it was presented for probate, by a list of the goods of the deceased.[5] The inventory was usually drawn up and the value of the goods assessed by local appraisers. It was sometimes prepared in a perfunctory fashion by men with a limited knowledge of the value of the goods they were appraising. They seem in general to have undervalued the goods, a practice not unknown today, and they tended unfortunately to lump together a wide assortment of goods under such uninformative labels as 'trash and trumpery' and 'stuff in the kitchen'.

To the student of the wealth and welfare of past generations inventories may offer the most widespread and accessible evidence, but they are not without their shortcomings.[6] They related, in the first place, only to the chattels and to the debts owing to the deceased. Even these are not always complete. There are instances of items specifically named in the will but omitted from the inventory. They had, presumably, been removed by a beneficiary before the inventory had been made. Then there is the matter of financial obligations. Debts owed by the deceased were not listed, even though these can sometimes be shown from other evidence to have been very large. Lastly, real estate was always omitted, though some indication of the size of the house was given when the chattels were listed room by room. The usual practice was to file the inventory along with the will, but in the course of time the two documents became separated and in many instances the probate inventory was lost. More importantly, while the bishop's registrar recorded the will, he showed no interest in the inventory. A problem in using inventories as a measure of wealth and status, apart from the unreliability of the valuations given and the haphazard way in which they have survived, is that they were not required of the poorest and probably the largest segment of society. Nevertheless, most collections of wills and inventories contain a few which indicate an estate of as little as £2 or even less. It is impossible to say how large was this excluded class, but comparison with other types of document, such as the Hearth Tax rolls, suggests that it was not inconsiderable. Havinden suggests that it may have made up from a quarter to a third of a rural community.[7] In a revealing will of 1593, the testator left £6. 13s. 4d. 'to my poor neighbours', and stipulated that

my executors shall take view of the poorest to go into their houses to see what lodging they have, and [if] you shall find it too bare for any Christian . . . you shall see [what] they have most need of and provide for them . . . as to have a bed to lie in and a blanket and a coverlet of shreds or what you think good.[8]

If a man worth less than £7 could afford to be so charitable, the recipients of his generosity must have been poor indeed.

A will of rather earlier date left '200 ells of cloth . . . to make thereof shirts and smocks' for the poor of three designated parishes.[9] Occasionally money was left to the poor – *claudos et debiles*[10] – often at the rate of a penny or a loaf of bread to each.

An analysis made by Havinden of Elizabethan wills from Oxfordshire shows the following breakdown of testators by social class:[11]

		%
Gentry and clergy	6	2.7
Yeomen and husbandmen	145	65.3
Craftsmen and tradesmen	61	27.5
Labourers and domestic servants	10	4.5
Total	222	100.0

Other evidence suggests that labourers and servants made up from a fifth to a quarter of the population, showing how under-represented they were in wills and inventories. Comparable figures were obtained by Lorna Weatherill from a sample of nearly 3000 inventories made between 1675 and 1725, the chief difference being the considerable number of craftsmen and tradesmen included:[12]

		%
Gentry	122	4.2
Tradesmen, craftsmen	987	34.0
Yeomen	952	32.8
Husbandmen	332	11.4

138

Labourers	28	1.0
Others	481	16.6
Total	2902	100.0

At the opposite end of the social spectrum were the aristocracy, the gentry and the wealthier members of the church and the merchant class. As a general rule, their wills and inventories are long and very detailed, but tend to focus more on silver, tapestries and the expensive adjuncts of gracious living than on household and kitchen furniture. Most inventories, except those of tradesmen and craftsmen, expand on the agricultural equipment owned by the deceased. In the aggregate this was usually many times more valuable than essentially domestic possessions.

The fifteenth and sixteenth centuries were a relatively good period for the yeoman and small farmer. His fixed outgoings remained low, while inflation raised the return he received for his marketable produce. There was a tendency to use part at least of this surplus income to make the house a larger and more comfortable place in which to live.[13] This expansion of the house and the increase in the volume and variety of its contents reached its apogee in the half-century from 1575 to 1625. 'At the gentry level,' wrote Lawrence Stone, 'there is some rough statistical evidence to suggest that these years . . . saw more country-house building than any other fifty-year period in our history.'[14] It must always be remembered, however, that the majority of wills and inventories were left by those classes which benefited most from changes in the level of prices. Wills occasionally make mention of structural changes in houses, of the insertion of upper floors, of the building of chimneys, of the addition of outhouses, and the replacement of ladders by fixed staircases.[15] Sometimes also a testator prescribed that his money should be used specifically for such a purpose, as if a more spacious and comfortable home was the most desirable legacy that he could leave to his heirs.[16]

A will of 1561 enjoined the testator's widow to 'plancher [add a ceiling to] the residue of the soler that is now undone over the hall within 4 years . . . [and] thatch the [out] houses that be now set up before Christmas next',[17] or again, 'I will that my executor shall set up the roof of my kitchen with such goods and timber as is mine, and then my wife to thatch and daub [render] it at her own costs.'[18]

In the matter of furnishings the change is yet more marked in the both quality and quantity. 'In the sixteenth century joiner's work was beginning to replace that of the carpenter. [Wills] make reference to "turned" chairs, that is chairs with lathe-turned legs, and "bake" chairs with backs for greater comfort.'[19] Chairs began to replace forms or benches in the hall; the number of 'ambreys' or small cupboards, chests and 'presses' increased, and open shelves for cups and other vessels were enclosed and fitted with doors to form what later generations were to call 'cupboards'. At the same time hangings of decorative or painted cloth were used increasingly to hide the roughness of the walls. A will of 1573 bequeathed 'all the pented clouthes that are within my house except the paynted cloth that hangeth' in the hall.[20] In a Bedfordshire house there were even 'paynted clothes in the loaft [loft]' presumably in store, worth 3s.[21] Hangings seem frequently to have been placed in bedrooms, in the 'chamber wher he laye',[22] probably in an attempt to take away the chill of an unheated room. A surviving example, now in the Luton Museum, shows biblical scenes, painted in tempera on canvas in bold, simple colours, with a border of formal, floral design. The painted cloths in one Bedfordshire house consisted of a 'back-piece and two side-pieces', showing the siege of Troy.[23] Painted cloths were the poor man's tapestries, though they were also to be met with in less important rooms in the homes of the rich. They brightened a room and had the further advantage of reducing the draught from the cold walls in winter. Wall hangings were also made from unpainted but relatively expensive cloth. The will of a King's Lynn merchant of 1536 mentions his 'hangings of red saye in the hall and the hanginges in the parlour of redde and yelowe saye'.[24] Inventories also mention the use of 'carpets'. These were not at this time floor-coverings – the latter were known as 'rugges' – but decorative cloths that were spread over tables and chests. Church inventories almost always refer to altar coverings as 'carpets'. Where interior walls were not covered with hangings, they were often plastered and painted, sometimes with mythical or rural scenes, sometimes with repeating geometrical patterns, but most often with a simple, plain colour. Inventories not infrequently define rooms as 'the red room' or the 'green room'.

The testament was concerned only with chattels or moveables, which the testator had complete freedom to devise, but there was a degree of uncertainty regarding the nature of 'moveables'. Of tables, chairs, benches and beds there could be little question, though there are some early wills in which they too seem to have been regarded as permanent features of the rooms in which they were found. But what of the panelling in the solar and the glazed windows in the hall? William Harrison noted in 1577 that glass was becoming more plentiful.[25] A glazed window in a private house not only made the interior lighter and more pleasant, but, since it could be seen from without, contributed to the prestige of its owner.[26] Perhaps for this reason glazed windows were often treated as moveables, devisable by will.[27] On the other hand, one Essex widow about 1570 thought it necessary to prohibit the removal of 'glazing in the windows' as well as lattices and doors of her house.[28] Wooden lattices had been the predecessors of glass in window-openings, and there are instances of the removal even of these items from a house on the death of its occupant. Within a short time, however, the greater abundance and lower price of window-glass made such provisions unnecessary, and windows and other such fittings ceased to be mentioned in wills after the early seventeenth century.

At an earlier date even furniture might be treated as a fixture. A Lincolnshire will of 1527 required that 'the paynted cloth, the tabull, the long settyll and the chare with the form, as they stand in the hall, do remane in the house . . . as hayre lomys [heirlooms]'.[29] And again, in 1571, a husbandman desired that 'my table in the hall with the form, benchboards, stained [painted] cloths and lattices in the hall' should 'remain with my house and not to be taken away'.[30] Even small items of household equipment could be treated in this way.[31] In 1530/1 a testator required that 'my mylne [quern or hand-mill] be as an hayr lumbe perteynyng to the hed mansion',[32] or again, 'I will that one cownter that standyth in my hall stande styll in my house.'[33] Such injunctions are found most often in the wills of the poorer members of society, of those least able to conceive of things ever being different from what they knew them to be.

The hall and its furnishings

The hall was the centrepiece, not only of the great house, but also of the smallest cottage. It was the focus of all social activity within the household. It was a 'front' area through which its members sought to present their own image of themselves to the world at large. Its gradual abandonment between the later Middle Ages and the eighteenth century marked one of the most important changes in domestic manners in this country. At the cottage level the hall was the living-room, the 'fire-house', where a fire burned constantly and much of the cooking was done, where the household lived when it was indoors and where some of its members slept at least during the coldest months of the year. It is paradoxical that the more varied were the uses to which the hall was put, the more scantily does it appear to have been furnished. It was as if space, above all, was needed for the activities that took place there. Even the table was sometimes of a kind that could be dismembered and hidden away. The lack of inventories makes it difficult to assess the equipment to be found in the homes of the poorest members of society. An inventory of 1545, with a total value of £1.5s.1d. must represent the possessions of one of the poorest of those who ever made a will.[34] They consisted of a table, a bench or form, bedding without bed-frame, chairs, a 'counter', hearth gear and sundry tools. At the highest social level the hall held little more, though the items were unquestionably larger, more stoutly constructed and better crafted.

In almost all halls of which we have documentary record there was a table, together with some form of seating.[35] The earliest tables mentioned in inventories were of two kinds: (1) the trestle-table, and (2) the so-called 'dormant' or 'joined' table. The former consisted merely of planks or boards supported at each end by a trestle. Such a table is shown in the feast in the Luttrell Psalter (Fig. 6.17). Trestle-tables are likely to have been taken apart after a meal and stowed away wherever possible within the house. They would have been a feature of cottages and smaller halls, where space was small and the means to acquire the heavier framed table limited. It is all the more surprising to find in a husbandman's cottage in 1573 'a pair of dormans standing in the hall'.[36] The 'dormant' table was of more solid construction, and was more likely to grace the halls of the better-off. Instead of trestles, it had four or more legs, joined together by stretchers set close to the floor, on which the table-top rested. Though the top could be taken off, the frame was too large and heavy to be conveniently stowed away. Nevertheless, the two parts were often listed separately in inventories, as, for example, in a list of 1597: '1 table boarde, one playne frame, 1 longe form to it'.[37] Chaucer's Franklin, fastidious in both diet and behaviour, always had abundant food on hand:

> His table dormant in his halle alway
> Stood redy covered al the longe day.[38]

Towards the end of the sixteenth century such tables began to acquire the bulbous and finely turned legs of the kind that are often termed 'Jacobean'. Later the decoration became plainer – the so-called 'Cromwellian' table – and the table itself longer, giving rise to the 'refectory' table of the antiques trade. In the course of the eighteenth century further refinements were made to the simple table. Legs at the corners might give way to centrally placed 'pedestals'; the 'drop' table, with hinged flap, supported by gate-legs, was introduced; there were 'drawing' tables, fitted with an extra leaf which could be drawn out for greater length. Small tables were made for card games, and round and oval tables for greater ease of conversation. By the eighteenth century the range in size and design had become immense, and there could have been few homes in which a 'joined' table was not to be found. The making of such tables, having long since passed from the carpenter to the technically more sophisticated joiner, was now being taken over by the cabinet-maker. At the same time, the pattern of tables, as of chairs and other furniture, was falling increasingly under the influence of the designer, whose pattern books were there to be copied.

The 'dormant' table was commonly covered by a 'carpet', the term used before the eighteenth century to denote a runner. It is probably in this sense that Chaucer's table 'stood redy covered'. In the halls of great houses a long 'dormant' table was likely to be set across the hall at its upper end, sometimes on a raised dais, and it is a table such as this that is often portrayed in medieval illustrations of banquets. Trestle-tables, however, long continued in use in the body of the hall for servants, retainers and others who were not admitted to the exclusive society of the 'high' table.

According to the earliest inventories, seating within the body of the hall consisted mainly of 'forms' or benches, without any form of support for the back, which could be drawn up to the table or piled elsewhere in the hall. There were also stools, three-legged rather than four-, in order to stand more securely on the uneven floor. Some inventories with a total value of less than £5 recorded only stools. James I's order 'to set stools for the ambassadors' was not the calculated insult that it has been represented by some historians. Chairs – the term is reserved for single seats with some form of a back-rest – began to appear in inventories during the sixteenth century, but they long remained few in number, and were reserved for the master of the house or for an honoured guest. The phrase 'to take the chair' has a respectable ancestry, though its meaning has undergone a subtle change. Chairs, with back-rests and arms, were known centuries before this date but seem generally to have been reserved for ceremonial occasions as, for example, the royal throne and the bishop's *cathedra*.

The earliest chairs were chests to which backs had been attached, and many formal chairs have since retained this box-like form, though their lower parts are no longer used for storage. By the sixteenth century most chairs consisted of a wooden seat, more or less square in plan, supported by four legs, which in turn held a back-rest. That the craftsmanship expended on such chairs became more and more sophisticated is indicated by the number of them that are described as decorated or 'turned' on the lathe. In the course of the seventeenth century the use of chairs moved socially downwards from the upper classes to the middle and lower, though forms or benches remained in common use in homes until the nineteenth century and in schools and institutions into the twentieth. At the same time, chairs, like tables, became more decorative. Their manufacture also passed from the carpenter to the joiner and cabinet-maker, who was often called upon to produce matching table and chairs, often in sets of six, ten or more.

At first a chair, placed at the end or 'head' of the table, was for the master of the house. But as others at the table acquired the greater comfort of chairs, so the head chair was itself further elaborated. It might be more intricately carved, and fitted with arms to serve as arm-rests. This first became common in the designs of the master-craftsmen of the eighteenth century, who established a style which has since been widely copied but never surpassed. The dealer who today advertises 'six dining-room chairs and a carver' is perpetuating a usage which developed in the later years of the seventeenth century.

In a small house or cottage there could not have been more than a single table, with trestles or frame, one or two forms and a chair. Sometimes an inventory contains no mention of a chair, and this must be taken as a measure of poverty. On the other hand, one of the gentry might have several tables with commensurate seating. In 1567 a well-appointed hall contained:

2 tabelles & 2 forms; a joined chaer; a torened
   [turned] chaer; a joined [i.e. dormant] table; a lettell table
     & 4 stolles [stools].[39]

How these would have been arranged within the hall and used at meal-times is far from clear. One table may have served as a 'head-table', the others being set in the body of the hall for the use of the less privileged members of the household. Alternatively, a table might have been placed against a wall and used as a sideboard for carving and serving.

Table and chairs were without question the most significant of the furnishings in the hall, but they were, in all except the poorest households, complemented by others variously known as cupboards, chests, 'arks' and 'hutches'. The cupboard was in origin, as its name implies, a shelf on which table-ware could be set when not in use. Eventually the shelf, or shelves, was enclosed and fitted with doors, without ever losing its original name. In the better homes the cupboard became a vehicle of display rather than of storage, and, from the eighteenth century, was not infrequently fitted with glass doors to show off the Royal Worcester or Crown

Derby inside. The chest was a box-like piece, with a hinged lid and frequently fitted with a lock. It was often highly decorated, and was clearly a valued piece of furniture. Chests were used throughout the Middle Ages, and a parish chest, kept at the west end of the local church, frequently served the needs of the local community (p. 129). Domestic chests became common in the sixteenth century and continued to be made throughout the seventeenth. During the eighteenth century, however, they tended to be replaced by cupboards of increasing size and by that piece of furniture generally known as a 'chest of drawers', one of the more significant products of the joiner's craft. At the same time these items were gradually banished from the hall, and in the later inventories are usually to be met with in bedrooms, where they served for the storage of the growing wardrobes of the middle and upper classes.

An 'ark' was mentioned not infrequently in earlier inventories. It was a form of chest, often simply constructed by a carpenter rather than a joiner, and was used for storage. The fact that its form is preserved in the corn-bins of farm buildings suggests that it was used mainly for storing goods of low value. The hutch, by contrast, was a form of cupboard, with a perforated front, in which food might be stored. Its name survives in the ventilated hutch in which small animals are sometimes kept. Both ark and hutch came in time to be banished to the kitchen and pantry, as the chest was to the bedroom or storeroom.

Solar and parlour

The variety of furnishings in the traditional hall reflected the many purposes to which it was put. It was the social centre of the household, from which the master and his family tended increasingly to withdraw to the quiet and privacy of their solar or parlour (p. 96). It is this which helps to explain the apparent bareness in the furnishings of the hall in later inventories. Items of furniture which would once have graced the hall had come to be placed in the parlour, kitchen or chamber. There was a growing specialisation in the use of individual rooms in all except the smallest houses. Nevertheless, the room which opened off the hall, the bower, solar or parlour, as it was most often called, also served a number of purposes, of which sleeping space was only one. If those inventories in which items are grouped by room can be trusted, it was also used for storage and even for the pursuit of a domestic craft. From the sixteenth century onwards further rooms were often added to a house, especially above or behind the solar and on an upper floor inserted into the hall. These were commonly designated 'chambers', and were clearly used primarily for sleeping. In the meanwhile, the original ground-floor room or solar, which began to go by the name of 'parlour', assumed some of the functions of the hall. If meals continued to be taken in the hall, it then became a kind of 'withdrawing-' or sitting-room, smaller and more cosy than the hall and more comfortably furnished, especially if a fireplace had been added. It might, alternatively, become a dining-room, with a table and 'set' of appropriate chairs permanently in position. The 'sideboard', on which meat was carved and dishes prepared, would have been transferred from the hall, as would the cupboards, now in process of being turned into display cases.

These changes in the functions and, in consequence, the furnishings of individual rooms began in the sixteenth century and continued into the nineteenth. In newly built houses, especially from the later years of the seventeenth century, the traditional hall was abandoned or was reduced to little more than an entrance passage (p. 107). At the same time, the rooms on each side shared between them the original functions of the hall. They became respectively the sitting-room or parlour and the dining-room, with a kitchen added at the side or more often behind the dining-room. The newly expressed desire for symmetry in the facade even of relatively simple houses encouraged this plan, with balanced drawing- and dining-rooms on either side of the entrance passage. At the same time, the development of the joiner's craft and the appearance of the yet more sophisticated craft of the cabinet-maker were leading to the production of furniture appropriate to each room. From quite early in the seventeenth century furniture became a status symbol, and the availability of good furniture contributed to the design of houses in which to show it off, as much as house design did to the evolution of its furnishings. In the later Middle Ages and even the sixteenth century, that very human love of conspicuous consumption tended to be lavished on the exterior of houses, and was demonstrated in carving and pargeting, in decorative studding and fanciful chimney-pots. A century or two later it was the interior which received the greater attention, with fine plasterwork, pictures, floor- and wall-coverings and, above all, good furniture.

Bedroom and chamber

Much of the time spent within the house was passed in bed, and the care and elaboration displayed in beds and bedding stand in marked contrast with the starkness which often characterised the hall. The bed itself was evolving during the later Middle Ages and early modern times. One must assume that in the humbler homes, for which no inventories survive, beds were at most simple wooden frames, across which were strung cords to support some kind of mattress. A 'berded' bed probably had boards or wooden slats instead of ropes, their hardness being compensated by the greater thickness of the mattress. The bed-frame itself began to be supported by taller legs, and the mattress often came to be so high above the floor that a 'fote payce' or 'foote paise [piece]' had to be provided in order to climb into bed. The purpose was primarily to give a greater protection from draughts. But even more important in this respect were the tester or canopy and the curtains which could be drawn around the bed. The 'great bed' was developed, to judge from probate inventories, in the sixteenth century, and the persistent legends that Queen Elizabeth slept in this great bed or that are at least correct in chronological terms.[40]

Beds and bedding often represented 'a high proportion of the total value of household furnishings . . . at least half is not an unusual proportion'.[41] There were more beds than chairs in Rufford Hall (Lancs.) in 1620. In such a household about a

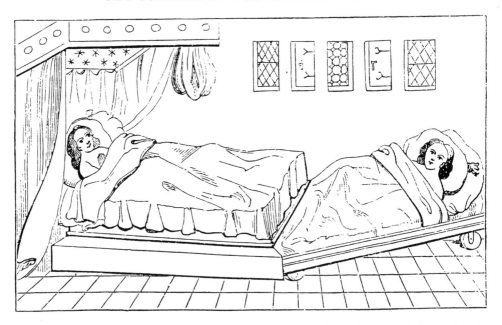

5.1 Truckle bed: the wife, in disguise, sleeps in the servant's bed in order to watch her husband.
From *The Babees Book*, EETS.

third of the beds would have been 'standing' beds, each with 'seller' or 'ceiling' (canopy) and curtains. The others would have been of two kinds. There would have been plain wooden beds or 'bedstocks' each consisting of a frame with ropes or slats; a will of 1572–3 bequeathed 'my bedstead with the boards belonging'.[42] The others would have been 'truckle' or 'trundle' beds. These rose to only a small height above the floor, and could be pushed under the great bed when not in use. A will of 1573–4 mentioned 'my feather bed lying on the trindle bedstead and my great standing bedstead'.[43] The truckle bed was sometimes fitted with wheels for ease of movement: a North Country will of 1587 recorded 'one standinge bedd and a *wheele*bed [my italics] in ye parlor where I was accustomed to lye with ffyve sylke curtaines to the same colors redd and grene'.[44] The provision of a bed that could be pushed out of the way during the daytime suggests that the room itself served other purposes. This is in line with the lack of specialisation, already commented upon, in the use of rooms before the seventeenth century or even later. It appears, however that the truckle bed was often used by a servant who slept in the same room as his master. This is apparent from the drawing (Fig. 5.1) which shows the jealous wife, disguised and occupying the servant's bed in order to watch on the amours of her husband. It was 'comparatively rare to find a [bed]room with only one bed in it'.[45]

The adoption of the massively built 'jointed' bed, with bedposts, tester or bedhead, and curtains, was one of the most conspicuous aspects of the rising material standards of the sixteenth century.[46] The design of the bed and the colour scheme of the curtains seem to have been no less important than the structure of the bed itself, and were not infrequently noted in inventories. That of Edward Cheyne of Bedford in the early fifteenth century noted 'the whole tester of the largest size, embroidered with the complete arms of Edward Cheyne on it on the one part, and the arms of John Cheyne on it on the other part, with three curtains of the same, two plain and the third striped with lead-grey ribbon'.[47] A couple of centuries later this heraldic extravagance had given place to carefully considered colour schemes in the furnishing of a bedroom. In 1617 Sir William Ingilby, a Yorkshire gentleman, bequeathed 'one hye cheare suttable [agreeing in style] to the bed' and also a 'tester of cloth of tissew and crimson wrought velvett with vallaines [vallances] answerable with gold and silke fringe'.[48]

It is quite clear that by the early seventeenth century it is no longer correct to refer to bedsteads as luxuries 'enjoyed mostly by the yeoman and higher classes . . . by 1600 cottagers, however poor, no longer slept on a straw pallet on the floor as . . . their grandparents [had] done.' A good bedstead was becoming a matter of personal pride, and a man was 'sometimes judged by the costliness of his bed, it being regarded as one of the most important features in a seventeenth century home'.[49] William Harrison wrote disparagingly in 1577 of the sleeping arrangements of the quite recent past: 'Our fathers, yea, and we ourselves have lien full oft upon straw pallets, on rough mats covered only with a sheet, under coverlets made of dagswain [a coarse woollen cloth] or hap-harlots [low-grade bedspread], and a good round log under their heads instead of a bolster or pillow.' He added that if 'the goodman of the house had within seven years after his marriage purchased a mattress or flock-bed, and there to a sack of chaff to rest his head upon', he thought himself well served.[50] Harrison's judgment on the lack of comforts of his forebears is not wholly borne out by the wills and inventories that they have left. Nevertheless, there had been conspicuous progress within the preceding period of only a few decades. By the early seventeenth century there were few inventories that did not list a collection of such luxuries as feather, down or flock beds, bolsters and 'pillowberes' (pillows), and sheets of linen, towen (an inferior linen), 'poldavy'[51] or canvas that might be the envy of many a housewife today. There were coverlets or blankets of broadcloth, kersey and 'dornix', a coarse cloth which took its name from the Flemish town of Tournai (Dornik).

The practice in many of the longer inventories of listing the contents of a house by the rooms in which they were found allows us to judge what other furniture there may have been in the bedroom. A well-furnished bedroom in the later sixteenth century might contain 'all my stuff in my grete chamber, as my bed complete, hanging, pillows, cussiouns, table, chayres, cofers at the beddis feet with all that is therin, with a coberd'.[52] In addition there might have been found, especially at a later date, a warming-pan of copper or brass in which hot coals could be placed in order to heat the bed, and a commode or, at the least, a chamber-pot.[53]

A journey into the cold, dark outdoors in order to attend the call of nature must have seemed a major affliction, and the provision of chamber-pots in the bedroom a minor blessing (Fig. 5.2). Indeed such vessels seem sometimes to have been so

 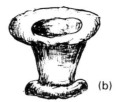 

(a)   (b)   (c)

5.2 Three drawings of about 1600, copied from BL Hanl. 2027, fo. 321v: (a) 'a chamber-pott: this is a thing much used in [obscured] and tipling houses & is usually termed by frequenters of such places, a looking glassse, a pise pott, a rogue with one dore & sev'all others like to it'; (b) 'a stoole pan, a close stoole pan'; (c) a bed pan.

numerous and scattered so widely through the house that resort to them is unlikely to have been confined to the night-time. An inventory of 1572 even noted a 'close chair' amongst the furnishings of the hall.[54] The coarse remarks of Andrew Boorde reveal all too clearly what customarily happened. 'Beware of pyssynge in drawghtes [corridors?],' he wrote, '& permyt no common pyssynge place be aboute the house or mansyon; . . . And beware of emptynge of pysse-pottes, and pyssing in chymnes, so that all euyll and contagyous ayrres may be expelled, and clene ayre kept unputryfyed.'[55] In one inventory no less than twelve chamber-pots were located in the kitchen. One can only assume that it was the custom in this ménage for each member of the household to collect a pot before retiring to bed.[56] No doubt they were gathered together the next morning and returned to the kitchen by a servant. A Yorkshire inventory of 1674 shows 'the old Gent's chamber' equipped with 'three chamberpotts . . . & a Close Stoole pann'.[57]

The close-stool or commode had made its appearance during the previous century. Its convenience was obvious. The earliest reference to this particular piece of furniture met with by this writer was the 'close chayer', recorded in a London inventory of about 1530.[58] It is not clear where it was kept in the house, but another inventory of 1572 makes it quite clear that the 'close chair' was amongst the furnishing of the hall! Thereafter commodes became increasingly common, usually as part of the bedroom furniture, as indeed they continued into the present century. It was by such small increments as these that the level of comfort was raised in early modern times.

The kitchen

A separate kitchen, no less than a well-appointed chamber, became in the sixteenth century a mark of the gentry and yeoman class, and even of the better-off husbandmen (p. 95). In the poorest cottages, with only two rooms and a central hearth in the more important of them, food was necessarily prepared where it was eaten. But in gentry houses from the thirteenth century, if not earlier, a separate kitchen, accessible from the hall, served for the preparation of most of the food.

Indeed, in a large and in the main self-sufficient household there might also be a separate pantry, buttery, dairy and brewhouse, closely grouped at the lower end of the hall (p. 94). During the following centuries these facilities continued their socially downward path, until in the nineteenth century they appear as kitchen, scullery and larder even in some working-class homes.

The separation of cooking from the fireplace in the hall was a gradual process, and, no doubt both hall and kitchen long continued to be used at the same time. Those who today make toast or roast chestnuts before the open fire in the living-room, while leaving more important cooking to the kitchen, are thus continuing a centuries-old tradition.

Few inventories fail to list in some detail the heavy iron gear associated with the hearth and cooking. At the least there were andirons to support the burning wood above the ash, as well as 'gallows', 'cobirons', gridirons and trivets, intended in their different ways to support a pot or hold a joint of meat while roasting. A Yorkshire hearth in 1570 was graced with 'one gallowe bawke of yron, 4 gallowe crukes, one patere [pair] of iron tonges, two brandrethes [gridirons to be set on the hearth], one yron colrake, a tostinge yron, 2 payre of potkilpes [pothooks]'.[59] The inventory of chattels in a simple two-roomed cottage of 1531 contained 'yn the Hall' a list of hearth gear that might well justify the description of 'culinary obstacle race':[60]

3 crokes [crocks] 5 pannys
3 pewter dyshe performyd [complete]
A peper corne & a salt & a chendel [candlestick]
3 treyng [treen, wooden] dyshes
On clome [earthenwarel vessell
On hoggehede & a trendell [iron ring to support pots] & a pype
Two coostes[61]
A mootocke [mattock] & adonge zvyll [shovel] & 2 hachettes & 3 wolde hockes
3 wayegs [wedges][62]

The total value of this assortment was given as 31s. 9d. In so small a cottage there can have been little room for the comforts of life. Another inventory of a half-century later dismisses the hearth gear as 'Iron stuffe belongyng to the chymley 4s'.[63] In this case, however, there may have been a separate kitchen, even though it is not mentioned in the document.

The kitchen itself usually had a fireplace built into a corner or against an outer wall. Sometimes the structure of the kitchen included that particularly dangerous piece of culinary equipment, a stone-built oven (p. 193). The latter, where present, was sometimes built as a free-standing structure in the yard. The fittings of the kitchen were otherwise very broadly the same as those found on the hearth in the hall:[64] pot-hangers, gallows, spit with a dripping-pan beneath it, together with such vessels as posnet [saucepan] and skillet [frying-pan], often fitted with three short-legs so that it could stand more securely amid the ashes. There would also have been a trivet, to support round-bottomed vessels of metal or earthenware. The kitchen

149

may also have had a table for the 'dressing' of meat and other items of food, which became known as a 'dresser': 'one deal dresser board with doors and drawers'.[65] The dresser subsequently lost this function and became a vehicle for storage and display. In origin it must have been not unlike the benches met with today in old-style butchers' shops.

Such a kitchen might, especially if it was free-standing, assume an immense size. The Abbot's Kitchen at Glastonbury, the kitchen at Stanton Harcourt (Oxon.), and those which served the great banqueting hall at Hampton Court[66] and the colleges at Oxford and Cambridge, each had two or three cavernous hearths with appropriate gear, as well as oven, working tables and a vast array of pots and pans. The inventory of an élite household at Wardley (Lancs.) in 1547/8 listed:

7 brasse potts
one caldroone of brasse
2 smale pannys
2 chafinge dishis
a morter and a pestell
one chawser [chaffer, heater] for water
2 frienge pannes
5 spitts
2 pair of yrne galberts [gallows]
one brendirne [gridiron]
2 cressetts and 2 grydirnes
4 paire of tongs
breede [bread] graters
2 yrnes for the oven mouthe and a firefork
a dressinge knyfe
2 backinge [baking] knyves
2 mynsinge knyves and three other smale knyves
one skymm[er]
one brasyn ladill
one fleshe axe and one flesshook
19 broode pewter dishis
18 narroo dishes
12 soosers [saucers] and 6 potingers
3 saltinge tubbes, 2 leeds, 2 stounds, one water tubbe
and one almere [aumbry, small cupboard][67]

In addition there were a well-equipped bakehouse and brewhouse. The volume of the tools and utensils in the Wardley kitchen cannot have fallen significantly short of that found in the nineteenth-century kitchens at such great houses as Saltram (Devon) and Erddig (Denbigh.) By contrast, a brass pan or an iron posnet might be a treasured possession of a cottage household. 'I will that my wife shall have and occupy my copper pan during her life,' ran a will of 1564, 'and after her decease I will

5.3 Washing dishes; from an East Anglian misericord.

that it shall remain unto the house I dwell in as a standard [fixture] of the same.'[68] So great a store was set by the poor on a simple article of kitchen gear.

In addition to the kitchen, the greater houses would have had pantry and buttery, as well as brewhouse and dairy and a place, later known as a scullery, where dishes could be washed and the more menial tasks accomplished (Fig. 5.3). In houses of lesser standing some of these functions would have been merged, and in the smallest of them, all, in so far as they were performed at all, would have been carried on in the kitchen. The pantry was a store-chamber, in which were kept bread and what are sometimes termed 'dry goods'.[69] At Bramall, only a 'coffre and a half of tallow candels redie made' were recorded in the pantry. The buttery was in origin the space where bottles and casks were kept. It became the domain of the butler and later was sometimes made into a secure room where silver was kept. The same Bramall inventory recorded the contents of the buttery as '17 silver spones and a silver salt wt [with] a cover, 18 chandlers [candlesticks?]'. Brewhouse and dairy were necessarily more fully furnished, since the purposes to which they were devoted required a great deal of equipment. The brewhouse always had a 'fornes' (furnace), whether recorded or not, consisting of a large vat in which the wort could be heated and allowed to ferment (p. 203). In addition there were various dishes. The brewhouse at Wardley contained: a furnace and various dishes, together with 'a drepinge panne, 2 goberds [gallows for suspending pots] and 4 broches' (spits), which, since their purpose had nothing to do with brewing, must have been put here because there was no more suitable place for them. The equipment of the dairy consisted of churns and pans whose purpose it was to make butter and cheese.

Floors and floor coverings

In few respects were the rising material standards of early modern times more apparent than in the flooring of houses and cottages. Upper floors had always to be floored, at first in oak or elm, but increasingly in deal,[70] except in the few cases where the ground floor was vaulted in masonry. Wooden floors were rare indeed in ground-floor rooms. Placed directly on the soil, they would have decayed quickly, and a 'suspended' floor above a crawl-space would have required more timber for joists than may have been available. In the better homes stone slabs were used, bedded in sand, but suitable stone was available in comparatively few areas. Some Jurassic and Liassic limestones were used since they could be split to suitable thickness. Sandstone was used, but generally called for an expensive process of cutting. In the south-west granite was often employed for flooring and especially for thresholds. In eastern England some use was made, especially in the seventeenth and eighteenth centuries, of bricks, often termed 'pamments' in the records. They were larger in surface area than ordinary building bricks and much thinner, approximating tiles in their proportions. All terracottas are fairly soft, and paving-bricks were sometimes hardened by the addition of sulphur to the clay. This gave the 'brimstone bricks' used especially in kitchens and stables.[71] Cottage floors were most often of beaten earth, sometimes with the addition of cinders or ash, and covered with straw to mop up some of the waste and spillage that fell from hearth and table.

Inventories tell us nothing about the floors and very little about floor coverings. The only evidence, apart from the odd remark in Boorde or Harrison, is the collection of Terriers in which church property was periodically surveyed for most dioceses in this country. Their dates vary from one diocese to another, but most are of the late seventeenth and the eighteenth centuries. Many began with a brief description of the parsonage house, the number of its rooms, some detail of the building materials and of internal decoration, and, not infrequently, of the nature of the flooring. The parsonage house at St Anthony-in-Meneage (Corn.) consisted of '5 under rooms all earth-floored', and at Marhamchurch (Corn.) the parlour was 'floored with lime ashes'.[72] In all, 58 out of the 98 parsonages in Cornwall for which this information was given in the period 1673–1735 had floors entirely of 'lime and ash', beaten earth or clay. One was described as having under foot 'no other Floor butt the country'. A further 25 were floored or 'planched' in part with wood or stone, and only 25 appear to have been wholly floored. Nevertheless, there was progress in these years. Altogether twelve houses showed improvements between successive surveys, and one was in 1727 about to be 'newfloored with boards'. Parsonages were, in secular terms, equivalent to those of the yeoman farmer and better-off husbandman. It can be assumed that in the late seventeenth and early eighteenth centuries, earth floors would have prevailed in the homes of labourers, husbandmen and the poorer yeomen.

Such floors must always have been cold and damp, and it would be surprising if no attempt had been made to cover them. The 'carpets' mentioned in inventories were, before the eighteenth century, coverings spread over furniture. There is little evidence for floor carpets before the late seventeenth century. In 1651 a Lancashire inventory mentioned a 'foote carpett',[73] but carpets, as understood today, became common in great houses only towards the middle of the eighteenth century, when they began to be imported from the Ottoman Empire and beyond.[74] The oriental carpet was hand-woven and was, by the time it reached Europe, very costly. Attempts to imitate the techniques of the oriental weaver had been made in Europe early in the seventeenth century, but the volume of production remained minute before a mechanical loom began to be used for the purpose in the eighteenth century. In England carpet-weaving on a larger scale was commenced in the middle of the century at Kidderminster (Worcs.) and Axminster (Dorset). Carpets then became cheaper and more abundant, though retaining something akin to the patterns of the imported oriental carpets. By the later eighteenth century they had become a normal feature of good houses. Such floor-coverings scarcely figure at all in probate inventories, since these were rarely compiled after about 1725.[75]

Wainscot and wall coverings

The interior walls of a house were usually rough, being made of rubble masonry or plastered wattle. In most instances they were left so, or were at most smoothed with a lime plaster. For this reason they were often covered with a painted or dyed cloth. Many of the curtains mentioned in inventories must have been wall-coverings. But the most refined way of covering a wall was with wooden panelling or wainscot. The use of such panelling became widespread in better houses during the sixteenth century, but it was not always regarded as a fixture. A will of 1607, for example, bequeathed 'the wooden furniture in the hall . . . to be removed, [such] as wainscott and panelled work, cupboards, long table with frame chayres'.[76] On the other hand, a will of 1597 from West Ham (Essex) prescribed that the wainscot and glazed windows should not be separated from the house.[77] It was evidently thought necessary to state formally that they were to remain in place. A comparable will from Colchester expressed a similar desire that no one should 'take away the wainscot but leave it with the glass windows about the house'.[78] There was clearly much uncertainty at the turn of the seventeenth century whether panelling was to be treated furniture and thus moveable, unmistakable evidence of its newness. Soon after this it became an established principle that wainscot, which was becoming increasingly common, especially in the familiar 'linen-fold' pattern, was part of the house and was not devisible by will. Henceforward we lose this valuable insight into the quality of housing.[79]

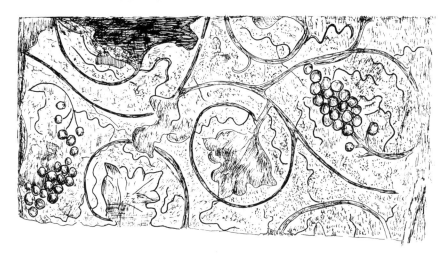

5.4 Domestic wall-painting of the early seventeenth century, from an Essex house, now demolished.

The use of hangings and painted cloths was not infrequently mentioned in inventories. In the homes of the well-to-do there was a wealth of curtains, usually of woollen cloth such as kersey or worsted. A merchant of Kings Lynn had in 1536 'hangings of red saye in the hall and . . . hanginges in the parlour of red and yelowe saye'.[80] It is difficult to be sure, but it seems that hangings of woollen cloth were considered to be more up-market than simple painted cloth, which was probably of linen.

The general tendency at this time to make the interior of the house more colourful and attractive was demonstrated also by the use of painted scenes and patterns on the walls, by pictures, and even by hanging mirrors. The Reformation put an end to the activities of those who travelled the countryside painting biblical and other scenes on the interior walls of churches. This was followed by an increase in the use of wall-paintings in domestic buildings.[81] Clive Rouse, who has catalogued domestic wall-paintings in parts of Buckinghamshire, Hertfordshire and elsewhere, has commented on 'the very widespread practice of mural decoration even in quite humble buildings'.[82] The themes were still, in many instances, biblical, though scenes from classical and English history became increasingly common.[83] In one house a bedroom was graced with a representation of David killing Goliath, together with the bloody scene of Judith with the head of Holofernes, hardly decoration calculated to induce an undisturbed night's sleep. Often, however, the paintings showed geometrical patterns and panels with guilloche borders (Fig. 5.4). In fact, these forms of mural design were the predecessors of Victorian wallpaper patterns, and one can sometimes recognise in floral designs and geometrical patterns a direct continuation from the one to the other. Rooms were often designated in inventories by their main colour. A will of 1647, for example, specified the contents of 'the Greane Chamber [and] the Read Chamber'.[84] Whether the walls were in these

5.5 A painted wall of the late sixteenth century at Thaxted (Essex). The design had been carried over the wooden studs.

instances of a uniform colour or relieved with foliage and geometrical patterns one cannot know.

In many surviving examples the plastered panels between the vertical studs had been painted in a neutral colour, while an arcade or frieze in stronger tints was added below the ceiling (Fig. 5.5) A feature of mural decoration in the later sixteenth and following century was the use of stencils either to create repeated background motifs or to establish a general pattern which could be elaborated by hand. It is difficult to see how the regularity of some patterns could otherwise have been obtained.

Painting was not only restricted to walls. It was often spread over ceilings, occupying the plastered surfaces between joists. Ceiling-painting, at least in this country, seems to have been restricted to regularly repeated geometrical patterns. In the course of time the design, painted on plaster, gave way to wallpaper, affixed to the wall with an adhesive. A prerequisite, as any amateur paperhanger today well knows, is a truly smooth surface, and wallpaper could be used only after the plasterer had learned to do a more perfect job than that which is apparent in many vernacular houses. The earliest wallpaper, of the late sixteenth century, was made in small

155

rectangular sheets which had to be assembled on the wall.[85] A width of about 22 inches (57 cm), established at this time, has since remained the standard width of a roll of wallpaper. The advantage of wallpaper was that the designs, whether applied with a stencil or 'printed' with wooden blocks, could be applied before the paper was hung, and were thus more regular. But designs and motifs were basically the same as those used in wall-painting, and one can readily recognise in mural decorations of the sixteenth and seventeenth centuries the designs which graced a Victorian bedroom. Wallpaper made in long rolls had to await the coming of a process of continuous paper manufacture in the early nineteenth century.

It became customary during the sixteenth century to hang pictures on the walls of grander houses. These seem at first to have been generally portraits, and this practice has continued until the present. The use of family portraits is part of that historical sense which was becoming apparent during the Renaissance as well as of the growing interest in family origins. A testator in 1742 left 'all the family pictures which are or were in the great parlour at Spurstow [Ches.], and mine and my late dear husband's picture to be kept and to remain in the great parlour . . . from generation to generation'.[86] In modern times the use of pictures spread socially downwards, and their subject matter was broadened with the inclusion of small but elegant engravings of important personalities. At the same time, maps, such as those of Bleau, Saxton and Speed, were turned out by cartographic engravers in great numbers and at a relatively modest price. They served not only to give some colour to domestic interiors, but they also helped to break down the parochialism of rural society. A Devon inventory of 1602/3 listed 'fowre greate mapps with frames of the fower partes of the world', and valued them at only £1.[87]

Taste in decoration underwent far-reaching changes. Family portraits continued to be the foremost examples of visual art, followed in the later seventeenth century by engravings of celebrities. At the same time there developed a vogue for landscapes. An inventory of 1674 recorded the presence of 'lanskips'.[88] Religious paintings, on the other hand, seem not to have been popular in puritanical Britain, and many of those which did appear on the walls of great houses had probably been acquired by their owners in the course of a 'grand tour'.

Clocks first appeared in religious communities which were obliged to perform the offices at prescribed times during the day and night. Not until the end of the Middle Ages does one find evidence for clocks in private homes. The clock preserved at Cotehele House (Corn.) had been made about 1485–9. It had no face, and instead activated a bell mechanism which struck the hours. Small domestic clocks – chamber clocks – became fairly common after the mid-sixteenth century. Earlier clocks had been the work of the blacksmith, who forged the parts from hot metal. The craft now passed to the locksmith, who was more accustomed to working in cold metal, brass as well as iron,[89] and was capable of making finer and more delicate parts than the smith. The result was both the pendulum clock, controlled by a verge and foliot mechanism, and also the smaller 'chamber' clock of the so-called 'lantern' pattern.[90] It was probably the latter which were mentioned in inventories more and more frequently during the seventeenth century. It appears that the clock was generally kept in the hall,[91] and by the end of the century it could probably have been found in the homes of most well-to-do yeomen.

Along with the clock, the wall- or hanging-mirror became popular in the better households in the later seventeenth century.[92] At a house in Doncaster (Yorks) in 1674 'there were in the dineing [sic] Roome and the Clossett . . . Two Seeing Glasses', as well as twelve pictures.[93] Mirrors seem to have been hung in chambers or parlour rather than in the hall. They were much more common than clocks, but are to be found in less than two-thirds of the inventories even of the better-off segments of society.

Domestic crafts

Inventories contain a rich variety of information on the tools and equipment of agriculture and on the crafts practised within the home. The former are discussed elsewhere (p. 43), but within the home the tools of the smith and the carpenter are sometimes mentioned and, less often, an inventory of the stock of a shopkeeper. Most common is evidence for the domestic pursuit of spinning. References to a 'wheel' are frequent, sometimes further defined as a 'flax-wheel' or a 'wool wheel'. Spinning was clearly the most widespread of domestic industries, but one cannot assume from the presence of a 'wheel' in a chamber or parlour that it was in regular use. It must, however, have been used at least intermittently. Emmison wrote of his Bedfordshire inventories that there was 'at least one spinning wheel in the majority of the cottages of Bedfordshire about 1600'.[94] Sometimes there was also a store of wool, flax or hemp, evidence that the wheel was being used. One will mentioned 'my spinners', together with the amounts of unspun wool that they had received of him and which were to be reckoned as part of the estate. The cottagers for whom spinning would have been a significant source of income were in all probability too poor to have left wills and inventories.

Relatively few wills and inventories relate to craftsmen and shopkeepers, but when they occur they often give a wealth of information regarding tools, materials, the volume of stock carried and the tastes and demands of their customers. Most of these inventories relate to townsmen. Rural craftsmen whose goods were listed and valued were primarily smiths, tanners and carpenters.

These pages have been based almost entirely on the evidence of wills and probate inventories. Unfortunately, the inventories themselves become fewer and more attenuated during the middle years of the eighteenth century, and cease to provide a sufficient sample for conclusions to be drawn. But for a period of some two hundred years their value cannot be questioned; no other source illuminates the domestic scene as thoroughly, and without them the history of vernacular furniture would be impossible.

The overall improvement in material standards is apparent. Progress was far from even, and it would appear that advances in domestic furnishings were made most vigorously during the Elizabethan period and again in the early years of the eighteenth century. The former period is documented by inventories and is further illustrated by the comments of William Harrison on the changes which he had himself witnessed. Within the latter period 'the decade 1705–15 stands out as one in which most change took place' in both upper- and middle-class homes.[95] But change was neither uniform throughout the country, nor was it apparent at all social levels.

Certain categories of household goods, such as tables, chairs, forms, stools, beds and bedding, were now to be found everywhere and at all levels, but inventories do not, as a general rule, allow us to estimate their quality, except in so far as this is reflected in the valuations put upon them. Variation, both social and geographical, is most apparent in the occurrence of new and luxury goods. While tables, beds and cooking gear are almost universal, certain other goods, like books, clocks, pictures, looking-glasses and window curtains, have a pronounced local occurrence. The frequency with which essential and marginal items occurred has been analysed by Weatherill:

Table 5.1 *Percentage of inventories (1675–1725) containing:*

| | Essential goods | | |
	Tables	Cooking-pots	Pewter
London	92	81	92
Large towns	91	72	93
Other towns	92	70	94
Rural	88	69	93

| | Intermediate goods | |
	Table-linen	Earthenware
London	66	42
Large towns	55	45
Other towns	55	39
Rural	35	35

| | Luxury goods | | | | | |
	Books	Clocks	Pictures	Looking-glasses	Window curtains	China
London	31	29	41	77	43	13
Large towns	21	18	41	58	27	8
Other towns	23	20	23	50	15	7
Rural	17	17	5	21	6	1

Source: After L. Weatherill, p. 76

It is apparent that for all goods other than essentials the larger towns were the pioneers. Some non-essential goods had barely made their appearance in the countryside.

A closer examination of the geographical provenance of inventories shows that in certain parts of this country homes were on average better furnished than in others. London was consistently more adequately provided than the rest of the country, and, furthermore, showed a sharper increase in the volume of non-essential goods. Next came the south-east and, unexpectedly, the north-east. Much more backward were the Midlands, Cumbria, and, in all probability, the south-western peninsula, for which records were not examined.

Earlier in this book the correlation between the quality of housing and the extent of attached lands was discussed. The conclusion was that occasionally the correlation was high, but more often imperfect. A similar correlation can be made between social status and the furnishings of the home. Again, there is a contrast between those items, whatever their quality, in universal use, and those which have been termed 'luxury' or non-essential. In almost all respects the gentry and the better-off amongst merchants and traders possessed a greater range of the latter goods:

Table 5.2   *Percentage of inventories 1675–1725, containing:*

	Pewter dishes	Pewter plates	Books	Clocks
Gentry	53	41	39	51
Merchants	62	49	27	27
Craftsmen	55	30	17	17
Yeomen	41	20	18	19
Husbandmen	33	9	4	4

	Pictures	Looking-glasses	Table-linen	Window curtains
Gentry	33	62	60	26
Merchants	33	60	62	28
Craftsmen	15	36	49	13
Yeomen	4	20	35	5
Husbandmen	0	9	16	2

Source: After L. Weatherill, p. 184

It is evident from other sources that during the rest of the eighteenth century and during the nineteenth, for which there are no probate inventories, the volume of non-essential goods continued to increase, and at the same time to spread down the social scale to husbandmen and also to labourers, whose inventories are too few to have any statistical significance.

It is pertinent to ask, in the first place, why London and the larger provincial towns were so much better provided than small towns and rural communities, and, secondly, by what means the taste for such goods was diffused throughout the country. That London was becoming the centre of fashion and taste is in line with all that we know about the city at this time.[96] It was a port through which foreign goods, many of them of a luxury nature, entered the country and from which they were distributed. London was also where many others were manufactured. The city was spreading its commercial tentacles far into the provinces, and increasing numbers of people were travelling to London and becoming familiar with a more luxurious style of living than they could ever have known at home. Those who carried such goods back to their local regions became the subjects of envy or emulation amongst their neighbours. Such is the generally accepted model, but it must be remembered that all consumer goods have to be paid for, and that the cost of luxury goods was in most instances very high. A wider diffusion of such goods was dependent both on the cheapening of their manufacture and on an increase in purchasing power. What actually happened in these respects has been widely debated,[97] and space is inadequate here to review the arguments. It was not, however, a simple case of the convergence of costs of production and real incomes. There was, as always in such matters, an element of choice. Attitudes to consumer goods varied, not only through time but also from place to place. Fashions, like using the coffee-house as a social centre and taking tea in the afternoon, were adopted, each requiring a new material equipment for its satisfactory performance. Some succumbed to the new attraction; others did not, and in any one locality much depended on how the leaders of fashion acted and to what extent others imitated. With a limited disposable income, the individual had to decide how to use it.

Water-supply and sanitation

Progress in the provision of domestic comforts was not matched by the development of domestic conveniences. Both water-supply and sewage disposal remained primitive well into the nineteenth century, and those who gave so much thought and care to furniture design and wall decoration ignored almost completely those facilities which we now regard as essential for healthy living.

Water-supply was always haphazard, and varied from village to village, house to house. As a general rule, it was taken from a well, public or private, or dipped from the nearest river or stream. William Stukely described how the pump at his family seat at Holbech (Lincs.) was the only one in the parish, until he himself caused new wells to be dug locally.[98] The water-carrier long remained a humble but essential functionary in cities, and the water-bag was a not uncommon heraldic charge.[99] Pollution is not a problem peculiar to modern times. Few rivers and streams were as pure as they might have been, and contaminated water was not recognised as such until its taste made it undrinkable. In 1376 the inhabitants of the town of Penrith (Cumb.) complained that they had 'no water . . . save a little rivulet', in which the tanners were accustomed to soak their hides at all times of the year.[100] At Newcastle upon Tyne the river was so polluted in the late thirteenth century that all were obliged to rely on a single spring, which the king, doubtless in ignorance of the situation, had given to the Carmelite friary.[101] Nor were wells necessarily less polluted, since they sometimes lay close to cesspits and manure heaps whose effluent percolated into them. In 1555, a villager at Acomb (E. Riding, Yorks.) was officially warned not to allow the manure of his garden to corrupt the common well nearby.[102]

Andrew Boorde's advice was not to drink water at all; 'ale for an Englysshe man is a naturall drynke,' he wrote. Nevertheless, there were times when water had to be used. The best, he wrote, 'is rayne-water, so be it that it be clene and purely taken'.[103] But the collection of rain-water was not easy, and was possible only from large buildings with lead or slated roofs. It would have been impossible from the roofs of most cottages. Leaden water-butts, into which roof water could be directed by ducts or gutters, became common at great houses in the later seventeenth and eighteenth centuries, but little use could be made of rainwater in other contexts. Boorde judged 'ronnyng water' to be next in quality, but 'standing and well water should not be used'.[104] It was on well water that most people depended.

A piped water supply to towns was in many instances established during the Middle Ages, and certain religious orders, notably the friars, showed a conspicuous initiative in organising and constructing conduits. But the water was itself often taken from springs which were far from pure and was delivered through pipes that were often of wood, fouled with algae and accessible to insects and vermin. In rural districts water-supply was marginally safer, because there was less obligation to take it from sources close to cesspits and dungheaps. But, in total ignorance of the sources of infection, people would have been unlikely to have taken those precautions which would have been easy and effective. Not until late in the nineteenth century were significant improvements made in the domestic water-supply, and then only because the nature of infection and of its vectors had gradually become known.

Sanitary arrangements were throughout the pre-industrial period even more primitive and no less dangerous to health than water-supply. The introduction of chamber-pots and commodes was no doubt a great convenience, but it did nothing to alleviate the underlying problem. The best that the Middle Ages could manage was the monastic 'reredorter' – so called because it usually lay behind the dormitory. It consisted of a row of seats, built over a flowing stream, usually diverted from a river for this purpose. In castles, the euphemistically termed 'garderobe' was a small closet, often contrived in the thickness of a wall, with a vertical shute which merely discharged at the foot of the wall and was often impossible to clean out. There the accumulated excreta was, one hopes, periodically gathered up and disposed of (Fig. 5.6).

In the congested environment of towns the usual practice was to dig cesspits in the small gardens or even within the houses themselves. These were then covered with boards through which a small hole had been pierced. The case was brought before the London coroner of a man who fell through the boards, which had been

5.6 The clean-out opening at the base of the toilet chute at Old Soar Manor (Kent).

rotted by the damp, and was drowned in the contents below.[105] A similar anecdote appears in one of the stories of Boccaccio; it had evidently become part of the comic stock-in-trade. An ordinance of the city of London required that such pits be 'Sunk not less than $3\frac{1}{2}$ feet (1.07 m) from the boundary of the property, unless lined with masonry, which archaeology shows they very rarely were.[106] They were lined, if at all, with wickerwork (Fig. 5.7). Most latrines were private, and arrangements were presumably made to have them emptied at intervals, or, alternatively, to fill them in and dig fresh pits. In London there was a small number of public latrines, most of them discharging into the Thames, and there appear to have been similar crude and insanitary arrangements in others of the larger towns. The emptying of cesspits and the disposal of their contents was a disagreeable task, and in London, as in Paris and probably elsewhere, barges were used to carry it upriver where it could be used to fertilise vegetable gardens.[107]

In rural areas the problem was solved more easily. Trenches and pits were dug as far as possible from the house, and were filled in and replaced by others when necessary. They were frequently covered by a small hut, which could itself be shifted from one site to another. An earth closet such as this has continued in use in some areas into the present century. A Suffolk will of about 1463 referred to the 'newe prevy house ovir the synkke be [by] the dore in to the yeerd ward next the Facown [Falcon] wel'.[108] It was filled in, not, as might be supposed, on account of its proximity to the well, but because a parlour was to be built over it. At Salford (Lancs.), late in the next century, a man who 'hath erected a pryvie howse over his dytche lyinge within the close' of a neighbour, was ordered to remove it.[109] It is clear from court proceedings that shallow ditches, often cut along property lines to carry away storm-water, were also made to serve as totally inadequate sewers, and orders

162

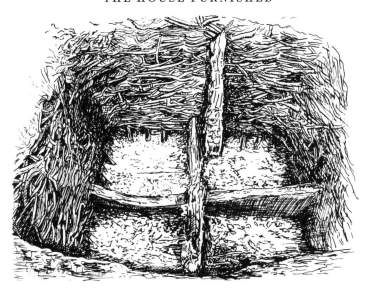

5.7 Domestic cesspit, lined with wickerwork, preserved in very damp soil.

to cleanse such ditches were recorded in court rolls with such frequency that one must wonder whether they were ever properly carried out.

Andrew Boorde's advice was to 'let the common howse of easement be ouer some water, or elles elongated [distanced] from the howse',[110] and this seems to have been the general practice, though, except on the most generous tenements, the distance could not have been very great. In his advice upon the planning of a great house, such as was being built in the middle and later years of the sixteenth century, he was more specific: 'let the pryue chambre be anaxed to the chambre of estate' – in other words, be within the solar block and close to the master bedroom. But he also contemplated a house of more than a single court, capable of accommodating a nobleman and a large retinue, with a commensurate provision of toilet facilities. 'If there be an utter courte made, make it quadryuyal, with howses of easementes' and, he added, a stable for 'horses of pleasure'. Care was to be taken that 'no fylth nor dong be within the courte', not, as might have been supposed, for reasons of hygiene or propriety, but 'so that all euyll and contagyous ayres may be expelled'. For the same reason he objected to snuffing candles. The fact is that people were becoming more sensitive to smells, and were less willing to tolerate the stench that must have prevailed in an earlier age in houses great and small. It may not be too much to suppose that people were beginning to associate disease with 'bad air' – *malaria* – and to assume that it could be identified by its unpleasant smell. This banishment of conveniences to a remote court reminds one of the sanitary arrangements in recent times in some of the colleges of our older universities. This increased provision of toilet facilities was, in turn, part of the general refinement of manners that took place during the age of the Renaissance.

The ultimate solution was the water-closet, and it is significant that the first essays

163

in this direction were made at this time. About 1580 Sir John Harington demonstrated a system by which excreta were flushed down a pipe and into a cesspit.[111] It was almost two centuries before the system was adopted, and then only in the houses of the rich. The reason lay not so much in the high cost of the system and the lack of craftsmen skilled enough to instal it, but in the inadequate water-supply. A patent for a water-closet, not unlike that constructed by Harington, was taken out in 1775, followed three years later by one for a valve to control the flow of water, and in 1782 by another for a water-trap to prevent smells from rising through the discharge pipe. The water-closet – the familiar WC – came into general use in the Victorian period only where a piped water-supply had been established and a system of sewers, constructed either of masonry or of glazed ceramic pipes, had been laid down.[112] These constraints gravely restricted its spread, and it did not reach all quarters of the larger towns until the end of the century or even the earlier years of the twentieth. Rural areas in the main continued to use earth closets and cesspits, though water-closets were not infrequently made to discharge into a cesspit which might serve a number of households (p. 367).

A topic almost entirely absent from wills and inventories is provision for personal cleanliness and hygiene. Soap appears on rare occasions in the stock of merchants and shopkeepers, but never in the inventories of cottagers.[113] Perhaps it was reckoned to be so small an item that it did not deserve a line in the list of household goods. There can be no doubt, however, that it was familiar to the well-to-do, even if they did not make excessive use of it. For laundry purposes lye was generally used. This was 'a concentrated alkaline solution made from the ashes of burnt wood'.[114] One occasionally finds a recipe for soap, tucked away in a manuscript commonplace book, alongside folk remedies and notes on preparing food. Soap was also manufactured in quantity from the Middle Ages onwards, generally by boiling together wood-ash, which provided the potassium, and animal fat. Such soap had an unpleasant smell, and this may have been a reason why so little use was made of it in personal ablutions.[115] The chief use for soap at this time was in finishing cloth. A better quality soap, in the manufacture of which olive-oil replaced tallow, was produced in southern Europe, and was imported in small quantities.

There was a perfunctory washing of hands at the dining-table in at least the better homes, and for this a ewer and basin were commonly provided and are listed in countless inventories. Thomas Coryat recommended the use of what we would call finger-bowls, and urged diners not to touch the dish, 'seeing that all men's fingers are not alike clean'.[116] But even this became less important, as, with the introduction of cutlery, especially of forks, fingers became less greasy.

Books of etiquette enjoined proper behaviour at the table, urging their readers to avoid spitting into the food, picking their teeth with their knives, and, when washing out their mouths at the table, ejecting the water back into the bowl from which others would drink.[117] The fact that this advice was thought necessary among the upper levels of society suggests that such rules were often ignored by the better-off and were unknown to the rest of society. There is no evidence that the peasantry washed regularly or that they ever did more than take a plunge in the river during hot weather. The coroners' rolls not infrequently tell of the death by drowning of men – usually young – who tried to refresh themselves in this way. Indeed, it is difficult for us, accustomed as we are to frequent washing and regular baths, to visualise the degree of discomfort that must have been experienced.

For the rich there were baths even as early as the twelfth century. They were, as numerous marginal and other drawings show, basically wooden barrels of the kind used for wine. A major problem in taking a bath was the organisation of a supply of hot water, and, when the bath had been taken, of disposing of it. It is not surprising that medieval drawings sometimes show two or three, irrespective of sex, in a single tub together. Such companionable bathing became popular in the later Middle Ages. Indeed 'stews', where tubs and hot water were available, became quite common, and it was even possible to enjoy a meal while squatting with one's friends in the warm water. Inevitably, stews encouraged promiscuity, and the name is today almost synonymous with brothel. For this reason the church frowned on their activities and public authorities suppressed them.[118] For some two hundred years public baths disappeared from the scene, and were revived only during the eighteenth century when it was supposed that certain hot springs possessed curative powers for an ill-assorted list of complaints. Such 'spas' attracted a wide range of people, not only hypochondriacs, but also those who preyed upon them. It has never been demonstrated that any of their ills were cured, or, indeed, that many of them had any really serious disorders to begin with. Nor can it be supposed that such baths made any significant contribution to the cleanliness of the nation. A Rowlandson drawing of the baths at Bath shows the bathers, up to their waists or even higher in the water, fully clothed and with their hats on.

The bath or tub continued to be used by the wealthier classes, who, despite reports to the contrary, never ceased to bathe, if only infrequently and irregularly. At the same time, a small basin, sometimes supported on a metal or wooden stand, became part of the furnishing of an elegant bedroom. When eighteenth-century cabinet-makers, like Chippendale and Hepplewhite, were called upon to design 'wash-stands' for the bedroom, and Wedgwood to make china basins for washing, personal ablutions had indeed become fashionable. But innovations of the later eighteenth century in the fields of both cleanliness and convenience were long restricted to the wealthy. They were expensive luxuries, the products of skilled craftsmanship. They were to be found only in the great houses of the countryside and in a few of the elegant town houses of the period. Their progression to the middle and lower classes was slow. Washing of hands and face under the pump, often in public, sufficed for most, and if the young wanted more, there was always the opportunity to take a dip in the polluted river. The reason was not altogether the high cost of bathroom and related fittings. The water-supply was totally inadequate until late in the nineteenth century to support the regular use of baths. At Bath, in the later eighteenth century, the public authority (p. 371) threatened to cut off the supply of water to a household which was thought to consume too much.[119] A piped water-supply was rare, even in towns, before the nineteenth century, and was unknown in many rural areas before the twentieth. The plumbing of waste-pipes and their connection with the sewer seems generally to have come later. A further problem was the heating of bath water. Medical writers advertised the merits of a cold bath, but in the British climate, this could be a painful experience. A bath called for a supply of hot water, which, before the introduction of the 'gas-geyser' in the last quarter of the nineteenth century, required an army of servants.

The diffusion of sanitary and washing arrangements spatially from London and the greater cities and socially from the wealthier classes, was, by and large, the achievement of the middle and later years of the nineteenth century. It resulted, as did most such advances, from innovations in a wide range of spheres, from the manufacture of glazed earthenware and iron casting to sheet metal-working, plumbing and basic chemistry. It is an instance, of the convergence of innovations to produce something new and useful. It typifies the way in which invention became exponential, with each invention interacting with others to generate further advances in widely differing fields.

Wealth and comfort

Wills and inventories are too diverse, too eccentric, too individual and too uncertain in their valuations to be used as measures of welfare and material progress.[120] They are, furthermore, documents that belong mainly to a social class, albeit a very broad class – those whose assets were worth more than £5. Wills clearly were not only made because they were required by both ecclesiastical and civil law. They were also a matter of convenience, a means of favouring one sibling over another, or of securing the future well-being of a widow or of a younger son. Wills were made not only to favour one person over another, but also to express disfavour for reasons that we may suspect, but cannot know with any degree of certainty. In some of the villages studied by Margaret Spufford, 'it was the poorer groups that produced most wills,' because greater care had to be exercised in apportioning their goods.[121]

Valuations given in inventories may approximate a fair market price locally, but they must always be suspect, and a fair market price in one part of the country could differ significantly from that in another. Furthermore, all valuations were subject to inflation in the sixteenth century and to fluctuations in the seventeenth and eighteenth.

Nevertheless, the reading of thousands of wills and the scrutiny of hundreds of inventories leads to the inescapable conclusion that there was material progress between the end of the Middle Ages and the later eighteenth century, but this progress was not experienced equally at all social levels or generally throughout the country. The rich, as judged by their chattels, do not appear to have been significantly better-off at its end than at its beginning, and one suspects that they invested a significant part of their increased income in buildings and land. Progress may also have been slight at the lower end of the social spectrum. There is not a

5.8 An 'ark', used for storing goods of lesser value.

shred of evidence in wills and inventories to show that the lot of the very poor had improved in any significant fashion during the period. Indeed, the administration of the poor law and settlement regulations suggests that in some quarters it may have become worse. Inventories, furthermore, are rarely explicit on the quality of furniture, making little distinction between the product of an experienced cabinet-maker and that turned out by the local carpenter or joiner, nor can one be sure that the appraiser was competent to distinguish between them. In short, one can count tables and chairs, beds and chamber-pots; one cannot measure their elegance or lack of it. In brief, one cannot measure the quality of life.

Only rarely does one come across inventories made at different times but relating to the same household, father and son, or grandfather and grandson inventories. Such inventories have, however, survived for the yeoman family of Beswick, living at Great Gristhorpe (N. Riding, Yorks.). They were drawn up respectively in 1612 and 1682.[122] A comparison between the two leaves the impression of a not inconsiderable material progress and of a rising standard of living. The number of chairs increased from two to fourteen; forms disappeared; settles came in; there were floor coverings and a clock at the latter date, whereas none had been mentioned before. Doubtless there were also small, unnoticed and probably immeasurable improvements in the fit of windows and doors, in wall-coverings, in the ease and convenience of stairways, and the equipment of kitchen, buttery and pantry, and in the number, arrangement and fittings of fireplaces. But all these would probably have escaped the far from discriminating eyes of the appraisers.

This revolution by small increments in comfort and personal possessions is of fundamental importance. Its effect was to convert the place where one slept and cooked into one in which one might live. The social consequences were far-reaching. During the Middle Ages, most people, except at the higher levels of society, passed much of their lives out-of-doors, rather than in their cottages. But

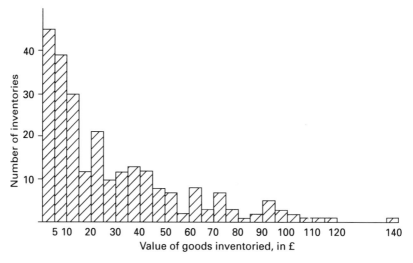

5.9 Appraised wealth, as recorded in Oxfordshire probate inventories, 1550–90. Based on M. A. Havinden, *Household and Farm Inventories*.

improvements in the structure and furnishings of houses and cottages encouraged people to spend more time in them, subject only to the long hours of work that were expected. The family grew more intimate; the alehouse and tavern became of less importance as a social centre, and drunkenness, a prevailing ill of traditional societies, was reduced. The attempts of the justices in the early seventeenth century to reduce the number of alehouses may have owed something to the growing puritanism of the period, but it also reflected a diminishing demand for their services. Domestic pleasures, including story-telling and group reading – the French *veillée* – increased. Natalie Zemon Davis has described the 'evening gatherings within the village community [in France] . . . especially during the winter months . . . Here tools were mended by candlelight, thread was spun, the unmarried flirted, people sang, and some man or woman told stories . . . Then, if one of the men were literate and owned books, he might read aloud.'[123] In Protestant Britain Bible-reading played a more prominent role than in much of continental Europe, but there was also room for chapbooks, small printed tracts which retold popular tales and folklore.[124] It is doubtful whether much of our own traditional lore would have survived without these evening sessions of reading and recitation in the cottages of the peasantry. But even this was dependent on some improved form of lighting, as well as on seats, cushions and other comforts, and such furnishings were not prominent in most cottages before the later seventeenth century.

How wealthy, one may ask, were those in traditional societies who have left wills? This question is difficult to answer, because wills in themselves tell us nothing about the value of what was bequeathed, and surviving inventories are much fewer than wills, and their valuations, as has been seen, are uncertain. Figure 5.9 is based on Oxfordshire probate inventories for the period 1550–90, short enough for the

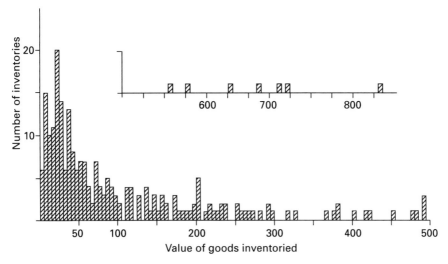

5.10 The appraised wealth of people in Mid-Essex, 1635–1749, on the basis of their probate inventories. No allowance is made for changes in the value of money during the period. After F. W. Steer, *Farm and Cottage Inventories of Mid-Essex*, Ess Rec Off Pubns, 8, 1950.

comparison of their values to have some validity.[125] It shows the estimated value of the chattels left by 258 testators. Of these 17.4 per cent were under no legal obligation to make a will nor for their executors to have their belongings valued, and 32.6 per cent had estates valued at less than £10. At the other extreme, less than 16 per cent left estates worth more than £50, but of these two had goods to the value respectively of £405 and £590. It was not by any means an egalitarian society, but if we exclude the half-dozen who left estates of over £100, the spread of wealth was not unduly great. The status of testators is not given in all instances, but is known or can be inferred in 220 cases made up of:[126]

		%
Gentry and clergy	6	2.7
Yeomen and husbandmen	145	65.3
Craftsmen and tradesmen	61	27.5
Labourers and domestics	10	4.5

Almost two-thirds were yeomen or husbandmen, but how many 'labourers and domestics', not to mention the poorest craftsmen, failed to make wills or to leave inventories we have no means of knowing. One thing is certain: surviving inventories do not represent a random sample of society.

Figure 5.10 represents the appraised value of the estates of 247 testators in Mid-Essex.[127] They range in date from 1635 to 1749, a period that was not characterised by any strongly marked inflationary trend, and are thus from 50 to 150 years later than those from Oxfordshire. The values recorded are very much higher than in the earlier record, a difference far greater than can be ascribed either to inflation or to the

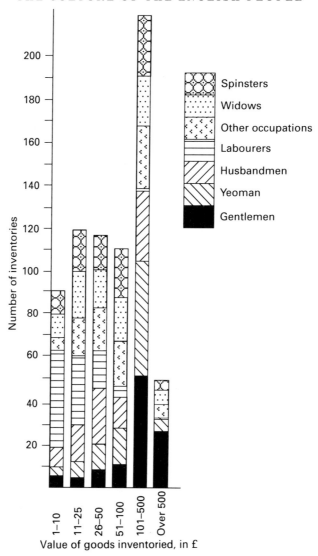

5.11 Graph showing the wealth and status of Worcestershire people for whom probate inventories are available, 1699–1716; after *Probate Inventories of Worcester Tradesmen 1545–1614*, ed. A. D. Dyer, *Worcs Hist Soc*, NS 5 (1967), 1–67.

aberrations of the appraisers. People just owned more goods. Houses were better furnished and more comfortable. About 44 per cent of the inventories were valued at less than £5, but 35 per cent at over £100, and the richest was worth £1873. The relatively poor were still the most numerous, but the mode had shifted from those with under £5 to those in the £20–£24 bracket.

The relationship of the size of the house and the quality of its furnishings to the status of its owner or occupier has been the subject of considerable debate (p. 99). The correlation of status with furnishings can only be very approximate. Figure 5.11

shows the social standing of those whose chattels were appraised in Worcestershire in the period 1699–1716.[128] There were 'gentlemen' with estates worth less than £10 and 'labourers' with over £100. Broadly speaking, however, gentlemen dominated the highest category; yeomen and husbandmen the intermediate range, and labourers the poorest. It is not difficult to visualise a decayed gentleman with an estate smaller than that of some labourers – a sort of 'barefoot' *szlachta*, but it is less easy to understand how a labourer, by definition landless, could be better off than many of the local gentry. Status was very important in traditional societies, and one must recognise that a husbandman or labourer who had made good, might still inherit the social standing of his ancestors, just as villein status lingered long after villeinage had effectively disappeared.

One must not read too much into these inventories. The law required that they be made by 'honest and skilful persons', but it is apparent that many appraisers were at best semi-literate, and that their knowledge of the value of goods was less than adequate.[129] But the most serious indictment of the use of inventories springs from the fact that the collections held in City and County Record Offices are not representative of the extremes of society. At the upper end of the social spectrum the rich were able to take their affairs out of the hands of the local archdeacon's court and to refer them to the Prerogative Courts of either Canterbury or York. At the opposite extreme was the far larger body which had no obligation and felt no need to make a will. Add to these the perhaps not inconsiderable number, even of the better-off, who died intestate, and the very large number of inventories that have not survived. Havinden's judgment is that in late sixteenth-century Oxfordshire from a quarter to a third of the population was too poor to make a will.[130] They constitute a submerged section of society. Their cottages, which are unlikely to have had more than two rooms, have mostly perished, and the only guide that we have to their contents is the very small number of wills and inventories which were drawn up, presumably for personal reasons, by the very poor.

Such an inventory was that of John Mason of Banbury, labourer, taken in 1574.[131] Apart from a heifer and four sheep, he left:

In the halle

A braspane, 3 kettlkes, one braspotte	5s.	0d.
6 peces of pewter	2	0
2 pales [posts] 2 loumes [tubs]		6
A table, one frame, a cheer with a cobard	1	8

In the chamber

2 bedstedes, 2 matterryssys, 2 cofares with a wyelle [spinning wheel]	10	0
6 pere of shetes	2	0
£1	1	2

One cannot judge the quality of these goods, but their valuations seem to be on the low side. This inventory points up what were clearly the priorities in traditional housekeeping at this time: bedding and cooking gear. Not until the latter part of the next century does one find any general evidence for a decent table and comfortable chairs in the humbler cottages.

Even at the higher social level of yeoman and gentleman inventories reveal a strange narrowness in the range of personal possessions. Beds and bedding again formed the most abundant and valuable group of possessions. The hall was often graced with a table and forms or benches, but the comforts of home tended more and more to be concentrated in the parlour. The hall had become either a place where one cooked over the central hearth or fireplace, or a sparsely furnished entrance room.

On the other hand, certain objects of a decorative or luxury nature became more common in the seventeenth century, and were as frequently found in the homes of the yeoman and husbandman as previously they had been in gentlemen's. Pewter – most often tankards for drinking – became more common; there was more brassware around the house; more china from which to drink the new-fangled tea;[132] candlesticks became more numerous, and there were silver spoons by the dozen. These, the only cutlery mentioned in early inventories, apart from kitchen knives, became so common that they must have been regarded as a sort of status symbol, the prized possession of the cottager, an heirloom to be passed on to a favoured son or daughter. Inventories are increasingly rare after the first quarter of the eighteenth century, and cannot be used to trace the social diffusion of china plates, as they replaced pewter, of upholstered furniture, curtained windows, wall-coverings and improved kitchen equipment. The volume of such goods, turned out by factories and foundries, increased as their retail price fell, bringing them within the reach of an ever-widening social spectrum. The consumer society had been born.

Conclusion

The period surveyed in this chapter, from the later Middle Ages to the eighteenth century, was characterised by an increasing specialisation in the use of internal space. The omnipurpose hall was abandoned. The parlour shed its earlier bedroom functions and became the principal room for socialising. At the same time, or somewhat later, a dining-room, largely reserved for eating, was separated off from the living space. Cooking was by slow stages banished to a kitchen, and, at least in the grander houses, the ancillary functions of brewing and making butter were allocated their own particular space. The insertion of an upper floor permitted the number of bedrooms to be increased, so that by the middle or later eighteenth century, a degree of privacy became possible for most members of a middle-class family. Indeed, even by the early eighteenth century 'sleep was considered to be a private activity, and adults were expected to sleep in their own beds'.[133] Evidence for the size of households and for the number of bedrooms and beds suggests that few, apart from married couples and small children, need have shared beds. Indeed, the feeling was gaining ground that it was slightly improper to do so.

Along with increasing specialisation in the use of rooms and the growing stock of furniture and furnishings came pride in their appearance. Amongst the upper classes there had always been some degree of emulation in the ways in which they presented themselves to the world. This desire to show off now became manifest amongst people of the middle and lower sort, and their homes became their show-cases. '... there was more to the inner lives of households than the satisfaction of physical needs. Moveable goods had expressive roles and could be used to draw lines in social relationships.' Certain parts of domestic space were used to present to the world a picture of their owner's view of himself. Display areas of the house came to be used for receiving visitors and for entertaining, a practice which became increasingly common during the eighteenth century, and, by the same token, certain types of activity were banished to the 'back' of the house. The home became, in its way, a piece of theatre, in which the public was invited to view the frontstage activities, while the necessary, but less elegant backstage activities were hidden from public view.

Architecture was made to contribute to the domestic drama, with its 'reception' rooms to the fore and kitchen, scullery and other offices to the rear (p. 108). Sleeping was a backstage activity, and, until bungalows became common in the twentieth century, was an activity only of the upstairs rooms. Old houses were adapted and new houses built in order to conform to the attitudes which were developing in the eighteenth century. By the mid-nineteenth century these concepts had been adopted in the terraced houses of the working class, with the 'front' room, reserved for visitors and family occasions, and their two or three small bedrooms upstairs.[134]

The furniture that was being made in the later eighteenth century and throughout the nineteenth century was designed for this social compartmentalisation. Dining-room chairs were made distinct from those for parlour or 'drawing'-room. The sideboard, from being a mere shelf, became a piece of furniture designed to take the accoutrements of elegant dining. Upholstered sofas and chairs made their appearance in those rooms in which people might be expected to sit for long periods, and light meals, like 'tea' and after-dinner coffee, which could be taken in such surroundings, were devised. Every such cultural development brought with it the material artefacts needed for its performance. From the mid-eighteenth century china teapots, cups and saucers began to be mass-produced in the English 'Potteries', and curtains and wallpaper, pictures and candelabra combined with comfortable seating to make the 'front' rooms places where one would take pleasure in sitting, conversing and receiving one's friends. We, or at least the middle classes, were entering the comfortable world of Jane Austen.

At the same time the darker world of Friedrich Engels and Charles Dickens, of Mayhew and Hollingsworth was emerging as industrial housing spread around the growing factories. Neither here nor in the cottage of the farm labourer were these developments in human comfort apparent. The house was still where one cooked, ate and slept. The worker had little leisure to do more, and furnishings were not such as to tempt him to spend longer indoors than he had to.

CHAPTER 6

FOOD, ITS PRODUCTION, PRESERVATION AND PREPARATION

Such a run of wet seasons as we have had the last ten or eleven years would have produced a famine a century or two ago. Gilbert White, *Natural History of Selborne*

In traditional Britain the choice of foodstuffs was severely limited. Most people ate only what their local area produced, and even then, they largely confined themselves to what it could produce most easily and abundantly. The volume of the crop was more important than its quality, for they lived for much of their lives on the edge of starvation. It was cereal crops which, under conditions prevailing in traditional societies, yielded most abundantly and most reliably, and it was on the breadgrains that most people depended for the greater part of their food supply.

The bread throughout the land [wrote William Harrison] is made of such grain as the soil yieldeth, the gentility commonly provide themselves sufficiently of wheat for their own tables, whilst their household and poor neighbors in some shires are enforced to content themselves with rye or barley; yea, and in time of dearth, many with bread made either of beans, peason, or oats, or all together and some acorns among ...[1]

The factors governing diet, that is the variety and the relative abundance of foodstuffs, were many. Among them the local soil and terrain were of foremost importance. Without anything beyond an empirical knowledge of agronomy and soil science, people had learned to adapt their cropping systems as far as was practicable to local conditions. Certain crops consistently grew better on a clay, a calcareous or a dry, sandy soil. Damp land was generally reserved for the cultivation of grass for fodder, and experience had shown that land at higher altitudes yielded only the poorest crops and was better left as rough grazing. In effect, people applied in the most rudimentary fashion the law of comparative advantage.

Climate and man

A second and scarcely less important parameter was climate and weather. Climate expresses the normal or expected atmospheric conditions, the warmth of summer, the cold of winter and the probability of frost or rain. Weather, by contrast, is made up of the day-to-day changes from sunshine to showers. Climate is broadly predictable, and on his expectations of it the farmer bases his annual routine. The weather, on the other hand, is unpredictable, except for the immediate future. Drought, severe frost, excessive rain, hail-storms and deep snow cannot be foreseen, except for a few hours ahead, and against them the peasant had no protection. Climate he could adjust to, but the vagaries of weather were beyond his knowledge and his understanding. It was weather, in the main, that caused an abundant crop one year and dearth another. There may have been – indeed there were – long-term variations in climate, and some have claimed for them a powerful influence on human destiny, but to the traditional peasant they were obscured by the fluctuations of weather. The day-to-day variations in weather were of an amplitude far greater than any slow, cyclic change in climate. The peasant was aware only of weather. What mattered to him was the extent to which the harvest in any one year departed from a vaguely sensed average. It was like the seven good years followed by the seven bad, except that there was no weatherman, in the shape of Joseph, to give him warning of what was to come.

Fluctuations in weather did not affect all crops equally. It might be autumn- or spring-sown crops that failed; excessive winter rain might be less disastrous on light soil than on heavy, and conversely the latter might crop better under conditions of drought. Only rarely was there a failure across the whole range of crops. As a general rule, what the peasant lost on his wheat he made up on his oats. Nature operates a kind of checks and balances. In bad years his food supply was reduced and its quality was poorer. He ate the horse's oats, and left his horse with the straw, but together, with difficulty and discomfort, they managed to get by.

Pre-industrial people were intensely interested in weather, as, indeed, they had to be.[2] It was, in any given place, the most important of the variables affecting their lives and livelihood. We no longer face dearth or famine as a result of a cool, wet summer, but we retain today a deep atavistic involvement with weather. Medieval chroniclers and early modern diarists and letter-writers referred so frequently to weather that it is possible to compile a broad-based record for its week-to-week, if not day-to-day fluctuations.[3] And even today it continues to make up a significant part of our conversation and our correspondence.

The effects of weather were thought to extend far beyond the scope of farming. A school of medical thought, associated especially with the name of the Dutch physician, Herman Boerhaave (1668–1738), attempted to relate all human ailments to the state of the weather, and his English pupil, John Huxham of Plymouth (p. 236), included a valuable weather record in the diary which he kept of his medical practice.[4] In France, the foundation of the first Office de Météorologie resulted from the epidemics of the 1770s.[5] Already some individuals had begun to keep quantitative records of temperature and rainfall, permitting a series to be projected back to the later years of the seventeenth century.[6]

If the mass of the population showed no interest in the historical record of weather, they nonetheless felt deeply the need for simple means of prognostication. Their observations of clouds, of the colour of the sky, of the behaviour of animals and birds, and of the order in which plants opened their leaves in spring became the basis on which they foretold the weather not only in the immediate future but for weeks ahead: 'When ye see a cloud rise out of the west, straightway ye say, there cometh a shower; and so it is. And when ye see the south wind blow, ye say, there will be heat and it cometh to pass.'[7] The Greeks personified the elements that made up the weather and turned them into gods who had to be placated. The Hebrews looked upon weather as the play of a benevolent deity: 'Hearken ye unto the noise of his voice ... He sendeth it forth under the whole heaven, and his lightning unto the ends of the earth.'[8] To the Anglo-Saxon peoples, living under a climate even less predictable than most, attempts to foretell or even to influence its changes assumed an even more important role. On the one hand, popular imagination devised a multitude of relationships between trivial natural happenings and changes in the weather:

> The hollow winds begin to blow,
> The clouds look black, the glass is low,
> The soot falls down, the spaniels sleep,
> And spiders from their cobwebs peep.
> Last night the sun went pale to bed,
> The moon in halos hid her head.
> The boding shepherd heaves a sigh,
> For, see! a rainbow spans the sky.
>
> .   .   .   .
>
> 'Twill surely rain – I see with sorrow.
> Our jaunt must be put off tomorrow.'[9]

On the other hand, they tried to influence the course of the weather with their charms and incantations, their bell-ringing and their masses. Witches and sorcerers attempted with their spells to bring about a storm or to avert it, and the church, inheriting their objectives if not also their techniques, tried to ward off bad weather when it threatened by their intercessions. In 1289 the Bishop of Chichester permitted every priest to offer prayers and institute processions whenever a storm threatened, without waiting for episcopal authorisation.[10] More recently, church bells were sometimes rung to avert thunder: '2d. paid the ringers when there was thunder',[11] and the Book of Common Prayer still contains prayers for a change in the weather. The Puritans sometimes claimed that prayers to the Almighty for rain or for its cessation were blasphemous, since they implied that God's original intentions were in some way improper.[12] Nevertheless, prayers to this end continue to be offered, and as late as 1976 some success was claimed by certain people, not excluding a cabinet minister, for their efforts in this direction.

Traditional societies were at the mercy of the weather to an extent that would be difficult to conceive today. Life was lived largely out of doors, and cottages gave but little protection from its severity. Neither rain nor snow brought any interruption to

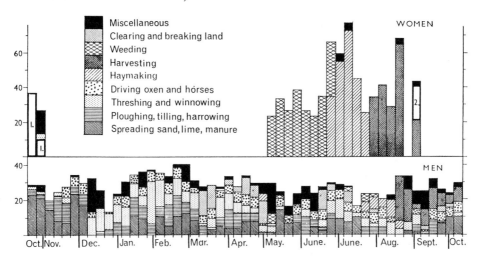

6.1 The weekly routine of a barton farm of the Buller family in Cornwall. Women's work on the land was significant only during harvest. Work was continuous except on Sundays and Christmas Day. Based on CRO, Buller Papers, Bu 21. From N. J. G. Pounds, 'Barton farming in eighteenth-century Cornwall', *Jl Roy Inst Cornw*, 7 (1873), 55–75.

their work on the land. 'I work hard,' said the ploughman in Aelfric's *Dialogue*, 'I go out at daybreak, drive the oxen to the field and yoke them to the plough. Never is winter so severe that I dare to remain at home; for I fear my master.'[13] The urban craftsman might rest on holy days and holidays, but those who worked on the land – and that was the vast majority – had an inexorable timetable, set by the course of nature. A daily record of each individual's activities on a group of very large Cornish barton farms in the mid-eighteenth century shows no interruption of their work except on Sundays (Fig. 6.1).[14] Work on the land went on from dawn to dusk every weekday of the year, and only on Christmas Day was there any reprieve. How the peasant must have hoped that threshing, a year-round activity normally carried on in the barn, would be kept for the worst days of winter! One can sense the hardships of the medieval peasant as in February he set out to prepare the fields for spring sowing or to cut wood for his fire, in the words of Piers Plowman:[15]

> And yet is wynter for hem worse,   for weet-shoed they gone
> Afurste and afyngered   and foule rebuked.

and in his despairing cry:

> Now Lorde sende hem somer   and some manere joye.[16]

For a society that lived always on the edge of subsistence even a small departure from the expected pattern of weather could spell disaster. There were many ways in which it could vary significantly from year to year. Autumns might be dry and favourable for ploughing, or so wet that the oxen sank to their bellies in the soil. In spring the fields might be frozen hard or so waterlogged that ploughing was impossible and autumn-sown grain rotted in the soil. Summers could be so wet and cool that the ears of grain might develop rust before they ripened, or so dry that the corn was parched before it had fully grown.

Departures from an arbitrarily conceived norm, in whatever direction, brought about a poorer crop. It is evident from a comparison of weather and harvest records that what the peasant feared most was a mild but very wet winter, continuing into a cool and rainy spring. This hindered both the germination of October-sown grain and the preparation of the fields for spring sowing in March. Only a degree less adverse was a cool, wet summer, today the despair of hoteliers on the British coast, which might hold back the ripening of crops until, in extreme cases, they were overtaken by the storms of autumn before they could be harvested. All these contingencies are abundantly documented, as are the sudden freaks of nature: the June frost, the violent hail-storm, the sudden deluge that submerged the meadows as hay was being gathered. These could, in some vague way, be understood, but the murrain that attacked the cattle or the fungoid or insect pest that ravaged a crop could not because its agency was unseen and unknown. It must, more obviously than other afflictions, be the work of some evil agent, to be averted only by a combination of prayers and sorcery, and traditional peoples were prepared to try both, often at the same time.

But how to measure the scarcities that resulted from these departures from the expected scheme of things? Until the government began in the nineteenth century to collect and publish statistics of agricultural production there was no means of estimating the yield of nature, except on a narrow and local scale. Estate records and tables of tithe payments are useful, but provide no continuous series. The price of grain can, however, be used as a surrogate, though no amount of manipulation can convert shillings per bushel into bushels per acre. Prices can be compared with the weather record, and, in general, the level of correlation is high. As Le Roy Ladurie wrote: 'waves of high and low price, of over production and deficit coincided almost exactly with the sequence of cold years about 1770 and of warm years around 1780.'[17] With bad weather and poor crops there usually went greater morbidity and a higher mortality.

The history of the western world has been punctuated by short periods of exceptional weather, when most crops failed. On rare occasions there might be two or even three such years in succession. At these times food shortages became extreme, and the price of breadgrains soared to heights beyond the reach of the mass of the population. None ate well or even adequately, and only those able to pay the inflated price of cereals could escape famine. Mortality was high, and even the birthrate fell, since conceptions were less common under conditions of near-starvation (p. 239). These were the *crises de subsistence* which occured at irregular intervals in all traditional societies. Such a crisis of extreme severity occurred over much of north-western Europe in 1315–17.[18] Others followed in the fifteenth and sixteenth centuries. The closing decades of the seventeenth century were a period of prolonged crisis. In the eighteenth century such crises became less frequent and less severe, and the last to affect Britain in any significant degree was that which followed the Napoleonic Wars and was due to the diminished insolation which followed the eruption of Mount Tomboro in the East Indies.[19] Famine crises were not, as a general rule, accompanied or followed by epidemic disease. Their high mortality was due to the exacerbation of those sicknesses which are common to all humanity. Intestinal and digestive disorders, in particular, were greatly increased as a result of eating tainted or indigestible foods.

The magic of growth

In addition to the physical constraints of soil and terrain, climate and weather, food production in traditional societies was also subject to the constraints of its social and economic milieu. It is a truism that the population was largely rural and on the whole self-sufficient. During the Middle Ages it is likely that some 80 per cent or more of the people lived in villages and hamlets and were employed on the land. But one cannot be precise; there was an agricultural element in every town, even the largest, and, in functional terms, towns graded imperceptibly into large villages, and large villages into small villages and hamlets. The size of the rural population, when the first census was taken in 1801, was proportionately a good deal smaller, but not before the census of 1851 can one be sure of the size of the agricultural population. In 1801 little more than 12 per cent of the population of England and Wales lived in towns of more than 10,000, and it is doubtful whether much over 20 per cent could be classed as urban.[20] A considerable part of the rural population, on the other hand, was no longer engaged primarily in agriculture, or, if they tilled the land at all, it was only small parcels on a part-time basis. They had become, in the terminology of the United States Census, 'rural non-farm', and were occupied mainly in domestic crafts or small factory industries.

The cohesiveness of rural society had long been disintegrating. The village or parish community had been held together, despite its frictions and jealousies, by a common need to protect itself not only against those who claimed some measure of control over it, but also against an unpredictable and untameable nature:

> Ar fewe yeres be fulfilled famyne shal aryse,
> Thorwe flodes and foule wederes frutes shullen faile,
> Pryde and pestilences shal much peeple fecche.[21]

William Langland's view would have been echoed by most members of any traditional society.

Society was profoundly unscientific in its view of nature. Of course, it had acquired a body of empirical knowledge. People knew what crops did best in a particular soil; it had learned to use marl and farmyard dung; it folded its sheep on the fallow, and took the first steps towards draining damp soils, irrigating the dry, and flooding water-meadows. But they could only use their environment as they perceived it. Yet their minds were not wholly without a sense of logic. Events did not just happen; they each had a cause. Misfortune had always to be ascribed to something, or, more likely, somebody, who was thus able to distort the proper course of nature. It was the duty of society to discover the cause and to root it out. The logic which could not find, or even conceive of, a natural cause was always looking for someone to blame.

The precautions which society took to protect itself against such ill-defined sources of misfortune were both general and particular. The former consisted of prayers and observances which aimed to obtain a good harvest and, in autumn, to ensure the return of spring after the hardships of winter. Their purpose was to ensure that nature would continue to pursue its accustomed course without interruption or deflection (p. 385). Then there were also the particular charms and spells. These might put a spell on a man's crops, make animals sterile or attract a bolt of lightning to his farm. The communal or general rituals are the more significant in the context of this chapter, though the one might merge into the other, and the 'cunning man' or white witch might well play a role in both.

Communal rituals were directed, by and large, towards ensuring the growth of crops and the continuing well-being of the community. They derived in many cases from pre-Christian times, and Christian invocations often sit uneasily on their pagan texts:

> Erce, Erce, Erce, mother of earth,
> may the omnipresent eternal Lord grant you
> fields growing and thriving,
> flourishing and beautiful,
> bright shafts of millet-crops,
> and of broad barley-crops
> and of white wheat-crops
> and of all the crops of the earth.
> May the eternal Lord grant him,
> and his saints who are in heaven,
> that his produce may be safe against every foe,
> and secure against every harm
> from witchcraft sown throughout the land.
> Now I pray the Sovereign who created this world
> that no woman may be so eloquent and no man so powerful
> that they can upset the words thus spoken.[22]

When the ploughman set out to cut the first furrow, he might recite:

> Hail to thee, earth, mother of men,
> may you be fruitful under God's protection,
> filled with food for the benefit of man.

This was, in effect, a pagan fertility hymn, addressed to the spirit of the earth – Erce or Erde, which has assumed superficial Christian overtones.[23] It is a spell, and, since one 'cunning man' might be able to remove the spell cast by another, the speaker appeals to a higher authority and this is where the Christian God came in – to prevent this from happening. Traditional societies practised countless fertility and harvest rituals, the latter conceived in part as thanksgiving for past mercies – the purpose of harvest festivals today – and in part as an appeal for continued good fortune in the future. Rituals varied greatly, and many of them were strictly local. The 'corn-dolly', a figure remotely human in shape, was plaited from straw at the end of the harvest and served as a fertility figure to ensure a harvest in the next year. Not unrelated was the Cornish custom of 'crying the neck' when the last sheaf had been tied.[24] Elsewhere, rituals surrounded the transport of the last load from the fields and the harvest supper which followed, that moment of relaxation that brought to an end the weeks of arduous toil by 'sunburned sicklemen of August weary', and initiated a short period of plenty before stocks began to diminish during the hardships of winter and the bitterness of spring. Such rituals disappeared in the nineteenth century, to be replaced, under the auspices of the church, by an altogether blander celebration, Harvest Festival.

Other rites were practised at the time when the crops were growing most vigorously. The Roman Robiglia was celebrated in spring for the express purpose of exorcising the spirit which brought 'rust' to the ears of wheat.[25] It was taken over by the church and became Rogation-tide, when the community processed through the growing crops to the accompaniment of appropriate litanies.[26] Another and quite different function was later appropriated to the Rogation festival (p. 385). Other rituals had as their purpose the proper ordering of the seasons. 'The flow of the seasons is not self-evident for the primitive mind, which considers it necessary to exert magical influence over the elements, the sun, the moon and the stars, to secure their proper movement.'[27] The celebration of the midwinter solstice shows how a ritual intended in the first instance to placate nature was taken over by Christianity as a religious festival and turned into a period of general rejoicing and merriment. Such a sequence of celebrations would probably not have been possible if it had not coincided with a time of the year when the land itself demanded little attention.[28] Christmas celebrations traditionally lasted until Twelfth Night – 6 January – when it is still the practice in many British households to take down the last of the Christmas decorations. Even this calendar custom was not wholly divorced from fertility rites, incorporating as it did the toasting of apple-trees – the 'wassail'.[29] The midwinter festival period was followed by 'Plough Monday', a celebration more overtly linked with fertility, when a plough, sometimes decked out with greenery, was paraded through the village or taken into the church for a ceremonial benediction.

Midsummer fires at the summer solstice complemented the midwinter festivals. That they consumed less time and were spread over only a very short period was due to the dictates of the farming calendar at this intense season of the year. The festival of the summer solstice was usurped by St John the Baptist, and its fires continued to burn in many places under the name of St John's Fires. It had not wholly disappeared earlier in the present century.[30]

It is impossible to convey the range and variety of seasonal customs whose purpose was in origin to ensure the smooth continuation of the round of nature. Some have been assimilated so completely to Christian practice and belief that it is almost impossible to detect in them any trace of their original fertility and agricultural associations. But in all one sees a primitive and socially necessary rite transformed first into a religious ceremony, and lastly into an occasion for feasting and jollification. They ceased in time to have any relevance to the procession of the seasons or to the pressing need to extract a livelihood from a harsh and unpredictable nature. The outward purpose of most calendar customs was to secure the continued growth and maturation of the crops, but they served also another and equally fundamental purpose. They brought – and held – the local community together. They overrode the jealousies and frictions of a small, inbred community, and were geared to one ultimate objective: its own security and survival. Society aimed to perpetuate itself, to continue to live as it supposed that it had always done. Its objective was stability, the continuing production of foodstuffs, sufficient in quantity and adequate in quality to allow it to subsist.

Fields and their cultivation

The medieval village community, like any comparable group of human beings, was shot through with jealousy and discord (p. 256), and was held together only by the powerful bonds of common agricultural practice, of common exposure to the hazards of nature, and of the common need to resist the claims and pretensions of their lords and masters. The cultivation of the soil and the rearing and protection of animals had to be a co-operative operation. A system had evolved – how it developed is beyond the scope of this book – of interlocking interests, of the common use of grazing, of the joint cultivation of the arable, with shared implements and draught animals, of common dependence on mill and woodland and warren.

This joint occupation by the village of its land and resources was governed by 'laws'. The peasant was restricted by sets of rules, those ordained by the church, those set by the manorial lord, and those deriving from a body of tradition and empirical judgments which the peasantry had itself put together over time and which it interpreted and applied with whatever modifications it deemed necessary. The conduct of the community – popular culture in action – is examined more fully in chapter 8. The immediate concern is with the constraints imposed by the community on the production, distribution and consumption of food.

The field-systems of traditional Britain had developed during the earlier Middle Ages, and, despite their appearance of ossification at an early date, they continued to be modified in detail until the great reordering of the land that took place in the eighteenth and nineteenth centuries. Much of Britain was open-field country (Fig. 6.2). The cropland of each community was divided into a small number of large open-fields, each made up of bundles or virgates of long, narrow strips (Fig. 6.3).

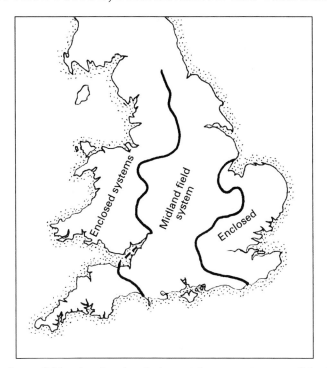

6.2 Areas of open-field and enclosed agriculture. After H. L. Gray, *English Field Systems*, Cambridge, Mass., 1915, folding map. The boundaries between the two systems were by no means as finite as shown here.

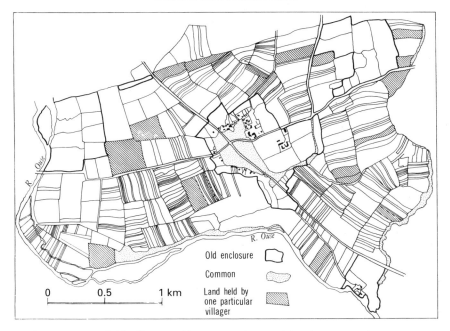

6.3 An open-field village, Goldington (Beds.), in the early nineteenth century.

This system reflected the early and piecemeal conquest and settlement of the land by small agricultural communities. It was a co-operative enterprise, with joint use of plough and oxen. The early conditions of land clearance were perpetuated in the intermixed strips of the villagers, and, one assumes, reflected a primitive sense of equality amongst the first cultivators. However suited such a field-system may have been to the social and physical constraints of the early Middle Ages, it was uneconomic and wasteful: 'economy', in Maitland's words, 'sacrificed on the altar of equality'. Peasants must have spent hours journeying with their plough and oxen from one strip to another, and consumed much of their energy in feuding with their neighbours about encroachments and rights of access. William Langland, in the *Vision of Piers the Plowman*, made Avarice claim:

> And yf ich ȝede to þe plou   ich pynchede on hus half acre
> Þat a fot londe oþer aforwe   fecchen ich wolde,
> Of my neyhȝeboris next   nymen of hus erthe.
> And yf y repe, ouere reche   oþer ȝaf hem red þat repen
> To sese to me with here sykel   þat ich sew neuere.[31]

That such offences were common is apparent from the records of manorial courts and even of Quarter Sessions. The court of the Rape of Hastings heard that one tenant had 'ploughed beyond his own land to [the complainant's] damage ... 13*s*.4*d*.',[32] or again, at Acomb (N. Yorks.) in 1622, another was indicted 'for plowing his strip of the headland in Follimell Field too wide'.[33] No less frequent were attempts to encroach on the highway. This was often a matter for the king's courts, to be determined by the Justices in Eyre or at Quarter Sessions. Occasionally a manorial court took cognisance; it was a matter of the status of the road in question. At Wakefield, R. L. 'incroached [*decurbat*] on the highway with a hedge and a ditch. The road is to be made up again ... fined 6*d*'.[34]

Rights of way across the open fields were a fertile source of dispute. At the manor court of Wakefield 'they say that Richard ... diverted a footpath leading towards the church from his own land on to the land of Adam. It is ordered that the footpath be put back into its proper place ... fine 2*s*.'[35]

Agricultural practice called for a common cropping system; ploughing and harrowing had to be accomplished at the same time in each great field, and when the crops were in, the gleaners, generally the most impoverished members of the community, moved across the fields, gathering such ears of corn as the harvesters had failed to bind and take away. The right to glean was a safeguard for the poor, and at the same time an obstacle to the reform of the cropping system. But even the right to glean did not belong to all. On a Wiltshire manor of the Bishop of Winchester a poor woman was fined for gleaning without her lord's consent.[36] The villagers' stock was turned loose upon the stubble of the 'lammas-lands' after harvest, to nibble such growth as remained and to contribute their modest offering of dung to the starved fields. No one might enclose such open land without the consent of all others who shared in its use. At Bedford in 1227 Reginald asserted before the

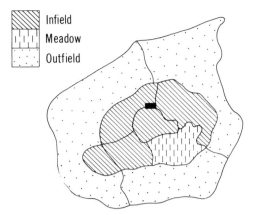

Infield
Meadow
Outfield

6.4 An isolated farmstead in Cornwall, practising an in- and outfield system. After the *Lanhydrock Atlas*, preserved at Lanhydrock House (Corn.).

Justices in Eyre that 'Thomas wold not be able to enclose that land because he himself was ever wont to have common there in every third year'.[37] It was a system of interlocking parts, and it stood or fell as a whole. That is why it took a higher authority – in the last resort, Parliament itself – to bring it to an end and to enclose the open-fields and common land.

But not all this country was occupied by open-field villages. In the south-east and the far west, for reasons partly social, partly environmental, the open-field system was adopted only fitfully, and was soon abandoned. It was suited to a large community, able from its own resources to furnish sufficient draught animals to pull the heavy plough. A thin and scattered population, such as was to be found in the hilly regions of the west and north, had neither the resources nor a large enough extent of cultivable land for open-field husbandry. The settlement pattern was more likely to be one of small hamlets and scattered farmsteads, and the economy to be based as much on animals and dairying as on ploughland and crops. The isolated farm or even the small hamlet was unlikely to have a heavy plough or a team sufficient to draw it. Instead it would have used a lighter plough, derived ultimately from the ard of the Celtic past, which needed only one or two draught animals, and could be turned within a small space. The field system which resulted consisted of small fields grouped around the farmstead, enclosed by a hedge or wall, and fertilised with whatever dung was produced nearby. It was often possible, with this assistance, to take a crop from the 'infield' almost every year, whereas more distant land, the 'outfield', could be cropped only intermittently (Fig. 6.4).

Such a system of cultivation seems to have prevailed in much of the hilly west and north of Britain, with only small islands of open-field cultivation. Here arable farming was intimately bound up with pastoral, for which the hilly terrain, poor soil and heavier rainfall made it more suitable. Pastoral farming is a very much less intensive mode of land-use than arable, and this alone would have made for more extensive but smaller human settlements.

But a pattern of small enclosed fields was also to be found in East Anglia and south-eastern England, where the climatic and topographical constraints met within the west and north were not present. The reasons must have been social and economic. If the open-field can be thought of as belonging to a certain phase in social development, when a maximum degree of co-operation was necessary to settle the land and to bring it under cultivation, then the south-east must have developed beyond this stage when the Anglo-Saxon peoples arrived and settled on land already cleared, and occupied fields already laid out in 'severalty'.

Those who lived in hamlets and scattered farmsteads had advantages denied to others who resided in clustered villages and cultivated their open-fields, subject always to the jurisdiction of the manor court and the constraints of its 'by-laws'. By contrast, they enjoyed a degree of freedom. The author of the French *Roman de Rou* captured the difference between them in the words:

> Li Paisan et li villain
> Cil des bocages et cil des plains,

thus contrasting the servitude of the villein with the freedom of the peasant. The peasant of the 'bocage' could, at least in theory, grow what he wished, unconstrained by the custom of a community. That they did not, in fact, experiment or innovate in their farming was because they shared the same concepts and prejudices as those who laboured in the open-fields. Wise counsels from the end of the Middle Ages urged the benefits of enclosing open-fields and converting them to small hedged fields and of replacing scattered strips with compact holdings. But it does not follow that those who cultivated 'in severalty' departed significantly from the crops and rotations in use elsewhere. Tusser, a strong advocate of enclosure, seems to have recommended it chiefly because it helped to reduce the internal frictions of the community:

> What footpathes are made, and how brode!
>   annoiance too much to be borne:
> With horse and with sattle what rode [road]
>   is made thorow e[ve]rie mans corne!
> Where champions [open-fields] ruleth the roste,
>   there dailie disorder is moste.
>
> .   .   .   .
>
> Again what a ioie is it knowne,
>   when men may be bold of their owne.[38]

But how many of those who cultivated a few enclosed fields were in any position to make 'bold of their owne'? Their degree of freedom led not to prosperity but to their extinction in the eighteenth and early nineteenth centuries.[39] In the context of this book, the long, slow decay of the open-fields must be related to the integrity of the village community. The open-field system had been the cement which held the community together. It consisted of a series of interlocking interests, change in any one of which would send shock waves through every other. Holding these disparate elements together called for strict discipline, which was exercised through the manor court at its regular meetings 'from three weeks to three weeks'. It oversaw the conveyance and inheritance of land; it ensured that every selion was ploughed and sown, that no household exceeded its 'stint' on the common or in the woodland and that every animal was put out on the fallow to the benefit of the soil. And it pronounced judgment in all cases of trespass and purpresture (encroachment), of rights of way and of neglect of the proprieties of village life. It provided the lubrication which eased the clumsy village mechanism and kept its disputes and animosities within bounds.[40] And when the manor court decayed and the open-fields ceased to exist, the village community slowly disintegrated and its popular culture, which had underpinned the whole system, withered.

A peasant society

The economy depicted in the preceding pages has often been described as 'peasant'. Peasant agriculture is generally assumed to be primitive, traditional and, by and large, self-sufficient. But the term also presupposes a certain type of relationship to the land. In a peasant society land is essentially familial; what matters is that it should be managed well and handed on undiminished to the next generation. It was not for the peasant to alienate his land or any part of it. He had a birthright in it, but what he did with it was a matter for the family to which he belonged.[41] He held his land in trust for posterity, and it was a solemn obligation on him to see to it that there would be both a posterity to succeed him and also a patrimony to support it. The medieval peasant envisaged, if he ever paused to think, a succession of peasants like himself stretching endlessly into the future, unchanged and unchanging except in so far as they were exposed to the accident of war and the buffetings of nature. This was the nature of peasant society. It was made up of social groups – village communities, perhaps – bounded and mutually antagonistic, segmented into 'units of high similarity and low mutual interaction'.[42] All such societies viewed neighbouring societies with suspicion, if not hostility, tempered only by the fact that their mutual contacts were few in number and limited in scope.

English individualism arose, Macfarlane has argued, when this nexus of the peasant and his land began to break down, when the peasant acquired a *personal*, as distinct from a familial right in land, and was able to sell it and to acquire other land in 'fee simple'; that is, to have as full and complete a right in the land as the law allowed. The slow breakdown of familial and communal authority over the peasant and his land was accompanied by the decay of the manor court and the abandonment of the open-field system. The court gradually lost elements of its jurisdiction to the Justices of the Peace, sitting at Quarter Sessions. The enclosure of the open-fields and common land put an end to the plethora of petty but nonetheless bitter disputes which had come before the manor court. Individual rights were asserted in the open-fields; common grazing was divided into private plots; rights in the meadow were appropriated to individuals. The causes and course of this breakdown of peasant society form too big a subject to be discussed here.[43] It is sufficient to say that the process began in the early Middle Ages and was not accomplished until the nineteenth century. When it was completed, the farming classes had been transformed into freeholders or leaseholders with a considerable measure of control over their own fortunes. As a living, functioning entity the manor had ceased to be. The village community remained, but only as a body of individuals, each intent on pursuing his own interests, on tilling his own half-acre in whatever way seemed best to him.

Yet Britain was not to become a land of small cultivators, of yeomen, each with a family-sized farm. The class of yeomen, conspicuous though it is in the records and in the popular imagination, is difficult to define. The term was an indication of status, and status was important in traditional societies. Legal documents were required to indicate the personal standing of everyone named in them. The yeoman was a free, land-holding man. He stood below the gentry, but a great gulf separated the poorest yeoman from those who bore the stigma of villeinage. His land may have derived from bundles of strips in the open-fields, concentrated and enclosed into a relatively compact unit; or it may have been part of the demesne farm, leased when its lord ceased to be resident; or it may have been put together piecemeal by inheritance, purchase and lease. The yeoman's holding may have been too small for subsistence, requiring to be supplemented by working on other people's land or by a domestic craft like knitting or weaving. It may, on the other hand, have been larger and more profitable than many a gentleman's estate. The term 'peasant' is applicable, if applicable at all, only to the lowest ranks of the yeomen.

The yeoman class was particularly vulnerable in the later sixteenth and the seventeenth centuries. 'Whereas in France and Germany,' wrote Habakkuk, 'the peasantry took over and absorbed the lord's demesne, in England the estate increased in size and absorbed the peasants' small holdings.'[44] The wealth which allowed the gentry and aristocracy to do this derived from many sources, but prominent among them were the profits of trade. For in England, in contrast with France and Germany, the upper classes entered freely and, on the whole, successfully into speculation and commerce. This coincided with the economic weakness of the humbler members of the landowning classes, many of whom were compelled to surrender their leases or sell their holdings. Estates thus came to replace smallholdings, and were divided and leased as large farms. The descendants of the yeomen and smallholders became, if they remained in agriculture at all, workers on the land of the gentry and large farmers. They were 'husbandmen'.

Crops and cropping systems

Social conditions underwent conspicuous changes between the later Middle Ages and the eighteenth century, but in the crops themselves and in the ways in which they were grown there was remarkably little difference. The same mix of cereals covered most of the arable land. The balance between them had shifted somewhat, but there was much peasant stubbornness in the face of new crops and improved methods. The enclosure of the open-fields was, as a general rule, imposed from above, but within the enclosed fields the same crops were grown as before and not infrequently the old rotations preserved.

Throughout medieval and early modern times, cereal crops were of two kinds, their difference determined by the length of their growing seasons. There were autumn-sown grains, mainly wheat and rye; and spring- or March-sown grains – the so-called 'three-month crops': barley and oats. The need to maintain the fertility of the soil dictated that these two groups should be grown in turn with fallow, and the traditional rotation was:

1 wheat or rye
2 barley or oats
3 fallow

The accepted view has been that over most of open-field England a three-course rotation prevailed. It has, furthermore, been assumed that this grew out of a two-course system, with alternating crop and fallow, which is assumed to have characterised Roman agriculture. It is difficult, even impossible, to discern evidence for such a conversion. Least of all can it be shown that a change from a two- to a three-course rotation was a response to rising population. The reality is more likely to have been that fluid agricultural conditions crystallised here into a two-course system; there into a three.[45] A further error that has frequently been made is to assume that any great field was sown in any one year with the same crop. This seems never to have been the case. Only the small bundles of strips – furlongs, as they were called – were cropped in the same way. This made for a far greater flexibility in rotation patterns than has generally been assumed.

This regime had been maintained on the open-fields because the cultivators could never agree on making any change. And on enclosed land the conservatism of the peasant ensured that change came very slowly. But change there was, in part enforced by the vagaries of nature, in part by the changing requirements of man. Crops sown in autumn might succumb to the winter's weather and have to be replaced in spring, or spring rains might so delay ploughing that some quick-growing catch-crop might have to be planted. Human preference, secondly, began in the later Middle Ages to bring about changes in the balance of crops, resulting over a long period of time in the reduction of the area under rye and an increase in that under wheat. In more recent time oats declined in importance, since their usual purpose was to feed the horses. Under 'normal' harvest conditions one might have expected an approximate equality between the volume of autumn-sown and spring-sown grains. This might result in an overproduction of certain cereals and an underproduction of others, since they were bound together in a system of joint production. From the sixteenth century a degree of flexibility was achieved by the occasional introduction of a 'catch-crop' on the fallow. This was commonly a fodder-crop, one of the 'artificial' grasses, or, at a somewhat later date, roots like turnips and swedes. On enclosed fields such variations in cropping were easier to achieve, and ultimately – by the eighteenth century – were widely adopted. In this way rotations came to be adopted with a four- or six-year or even longer cycle, in which the proportion of the wheat crop could be increased. But the breadgrains continued to dominate both the cropping systems and the diet. They were consumed not only in the form of baked bread, but also as a gruel, such as continues to be served today as porridge. True bread is made from flour and yeast, which forms small vesicles of gas and gives lightness to the bread. This is made possible by the presence of gluten, an albuminous substance in the grain which provides a kind of elastic 'skin' to enclose the gas emitted by the yeast. It is present in varying quantities in many cereals. It is most abundant in wheat but is absent from oats. There is gluten in rye, but very little in barley. Even in wheat, the amount varies from one subspecies to another, and is least in the so-called 'hard' wheats, from which pasta is made. The bread wheats (*Triticum vulgare, Tr. compactum*) are so called because their gluten is sufficient for the bread to 'rise' and become light and palatable.

The alternatives to bread in the strict sense were, first, 'flat' bread, made from barley, oats and sometimes rye, and secondly a kind of soup or gruel in which such cereals as were available were stewed along with vegetables and occasionally a piece of fat meat. The present-day descendants of these foods are respectively the oatcake and porridge. The kind of bread eaten in any particular place was determined by the nature of the cereals generally available. Ideally, bread was made from wheat; barley was used for malting and brewing, and oats were fed to the horses, but rarely did things work out quite like this. Much of the highly variable wheat production was eaten by the upper classes, and the mass of the population consumed a gruel or a hard and unpalatable loaf made from the coarser grains. The corrody, or allowance made to a pensioner of the Carmelite friary at King's Lynn in 1374, was made up of: '12 loaves of white bread and 2 of bran and 8 gallons of beer a week, [and] a quart of conventual pottage daily', as well as the use of a garden plot and 3000 'peats' yearly to heat his chamber.[46] This must be reckoned an above-average diet, with its combination of wheat bread with gruel and the added benefit of a garden in which the pensioner could grow vegetables and herbs. What is particularly noteworthy is the complete absence of meat and animal fats from the recorded diet.

Cropping systems and harvest conditions often made it necessary to substitute rye and barley and sometimes even peas, beans or bran for the breadgrains proper, using only a little wheat to give the bread some degree of lightness. The maltster was accustomed to using any variety of cereal, though he preferred barley. In hard times he might be ordered to use oats in order to free the barley for 'bread' making. The kind of bread eaten was a mark of status, the lord consumed wheaten bread, while his poor neighbours, in the words of William Harrison, were 'enforced to content themselves with rye or barley', or even worse.[47] At the Cologne abbey of St Pantaleon the oats from its estates were used to feed the horses of the lord abbot 'and any travellers who might arrive'.[48]

The balance of cereals in any one area was due in part to the weather during the growing season, but also to the soil and the prevailing climate (Fig. 6.5). Wheat grows best on a rich loam or clay, and barley, though less discriminating, prefers an

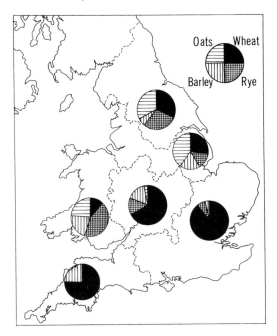

6.5 Regional distribution of the major breadgrains in the eighteenth century. A century earlier wheat would have been significantly less conspicuous, and rye much more so; based on Sir William Ashley, *Bread of our Forefathers*.

alkaline soil, but can tolerate low temperatures and a short growing season. Oats could be grown on indifferent soil and in poor climatic conditions, and rye would yield a crop even on the poorest of acid soils. These conditions influenced the regional distribution of both bread- and coarse-grains. We find everywhere that attempts were made to maximise the wheat crop, but the relative proportions of other cereals depended heavily on environmental conditions as well as on personal preferences.

The mix of cereal crops varied not only with soil and climate but also through time with improving agricultural technology and rising standards of living. The most conspicuous change was the increase in wheat consumption and the decline in rye.[49] Accounts for the Kettering manor of Peterborough Abbey for the year 1292 list the volume of field crops harvested on the demesne. More than half was of oats, much of which must have been fed to animals; rye was in second place:

Rye	54 quarters
Barley	25 "
Dredge (*dragium*)	15 "
Oats	$136\frac{1}{2}$ "

(Dredge was a mixed crop, possibly in this case, of barley and oats.)

191

In addition there was a small quantity of pease, beans and malt; there was no recorded wheat.[50] In the later Middle Ages and following centuries rotations began to be modified, reflecting in some degree the breakdown of the open-field system. A 'catch-crop' began to be taken on the fallow and departures from the traditional routine were made in order to obtain a greater volume of one crop and less of another.[51]

All evidence points to the fact that in earlier times rye had closely rivalled wheat amongst autumn-sown crops, but its cultivation declined rapidly during the seventeenth and eighteenth centuries. Ashley estimated[52] that about 1700 rye made up 40 per cent of breadgrains, but only about 5 per cent a century later. But there were strongly marked local variations. Harrison claimed that 'in champaign (i. e. open-field) country much rye and barley bread is eaten'. In Devon, on the other hand, rye was of negligible importance, and both here and in Cornwall bread was overwhelmingly of barley.[53] In much of northern England oats were important in the diet, and both here and elsewhere they were made into flat-cakes or gruel.[54] Piers Plowman lamented that he had only:

> two grene cheses,
> A fewee cruddes and creme and a cake of otes,
> And two loves of benes and bran ybake for my fauntes.
> ... I have no salt bacon
> Ne no cokeney [egg], by Crist, coloppes[55] to maken.[56]

But Andrew Boorde, writing in the 1540s, assumed that his readers, who would have been from the better-off and more literate classes, ate wheaten bread. He admitted, however, that 'Mastlyng breade is made, halfe of whete and halfe of Rye. And ... also ... halfe of rye and halfe of barley.'[57] By the late eighteenth century rye had largely been eliminated from the diet except in Wales, and oats remained significant only north of the Trent.

Bread made from wheat had to be baked in an oven, in which it could rise and assume the crusty exterior familiar to all who value 'real' bread today. The oven was masonry-built and usually dome-shaped (Fig. 6.6a). It was heated by burning wood *within* it. The ashes were then raked out and the unbaked loaves were put in by means of a long-handled 'paddle', an instrument which occasionally appears in household inventories. A bread-oven was a dangerous neighbour. One cannot know how many fires were kindled by the hot ashes raked from it, and for this reason it was scarcely ever found *in* cottages, and was far from common in the houses of the gentry. Most ovens were built free-standing and as far as practicable from other structures. Furthermore, in order to be economic an oven required to be used more regularly than a small household found necessary. The baker, who had an oven of his own, probably became the first retailer of ready-cooked food. Most communities had an oven which could be used by its members on payment of a small fee. Indeed, a manorial lord frequently claimed a monopoly of local baking for his oven, as he did

6.6 Primitive bread ovens: (a) as shown on a misericord, (b) as sketched by the author in Cyprus.

also of milling at the demesne mill. The Duchy of Lancaster held such a mill in its borough of Penrith (Cumb.). The Duchy accounts show small expenditures on its repair and a not inconsiderable income from its use by the burgesses.[58] Not until the eighteenth century, when ovens began to be built with a separate fire-chamber, can they be said to have become 'domesticated' enough to be constructed within the kitchen.[59]

Flatbread, made of oats, barley or rye, occasionally with an admixture of bran or beans, did not require an oven, a fact which recommended itself to the cottager. It was usual to brush away the ashes from part of the hearth and to place the 'cakes' on the hot stone. Sometimes an iron plate supported above the fire was used.

The alternative way of cooking and consuming coarse-grains was by stewing them in a pot, to which vegetables, seasoning and, when possible, animal fat had been added. The pot was either suspended over the hearth or set, sometimes on a 'trivet', amid the ashes. It is likely that such a gruel was permanently available, fresh water, corn, vegetables and other ingredients being added as need arose.

> Pease porridge hot, pease porridge cold,
> Pease porridge in the pot, nine days old.[60]

The food allowances, or corrodies, made to workers, dependants and pensioners were commonly expressed in 'loaves', suggesting that oven-baked bread was the commonest item of food. But such evidence is deceptive. Bread, most often of rye or of mixed grain, was indeed distributed on a large scale, but a careful examination of the records shows that it was more often than not provided by institutions, commonly monastic or manorial, which possessed an oven and baked bread on a large scale.

Manorial labourers, like the hired *famuli* and the boon-workers at harvest-time, to whom most of the records relate, would have taken their midday meal with them to the fields, and for this reason the cereals must have been cooked as bread or flatcakes. The peasant within his cottage was more likely to have had 'pease porridge' at every meal.

It is difficult to generalise regarding the consumption of breadgrains beyond saying that they made up by far the greater part of the diet of all except the richest segments of society. The mix of cereals consumed varied greatly, with wheat flour predominating among the better-off and oats among the poorest. In times of scarcity most social levels were obliged to stoop to the dietary standards of those below them, with the lowest turning to wild fruits and herbs which were not normally eaten. Except during years of scarcity, and these, it should be noted, occurred on average one year in five, the calorific intake of working people was adequate. But here again the evidence is slanted. It comes largely from estate records of allowances to farm servants. It does not relate to the cottager or smallholder, and it refers to working men, and not to their families and dependants. Hallam has calculated from a *compotus* roll of Peterborough Abbey, that in 1294 the abbey's servants on the manor of Kettering received daily:[61]

Table 6.1   *Food allocation, manor of Kettering*

	grammes
Bread	200.00
Oatmeal	3.35
Beans and peas	0.45–6.2
Cheese	3.2–3.6

Breadgrains thus made up from 95 to 98 per cent of the total calorie intake. This is broadly confirmed from other sources, though a small consumption of meat or of animal fat would have been usual. The protein level of the diet was adequate, but the absence of fruit, green vegetables, milk and eggs meant a serious lack of fats and of most vitamins. Vitamins A, C, D and K would have been largely missing and most people might have been expected to suffer severely from night-blindness, skin complaints, bleeding and rickets.

But the situation may not have been quite as bleak as this picture suggests. The cottager, almost by definition, possessed at least a toft, a small parcel of land, often only a fraction of an acre, on which he was free to grow whatever he liked, and what he chose appears, by and large, to have consisted of green vegetables, herbs and perhaps fruit. Piers Plowman claimed to have, in addition to coarse bread:

> ... percule [parsley] and porettes [leeks]   and manye plaunte coles [cabbages]
>
> .   .   .   .
>
> Al the povere peple   tho pescoddes fetten;
> Benes and baken apples   thei broghte in hir lappes,
> Chibolles [onions] and chervelles [chervil]   and ripe chiries [cherries] manye.[62]

In a normal year the weeks following harvest were a period of relative abundance. The harvesters themselves were usually well fed, and the harvest feast – to be distinguished from the ecclesiastical Harvest Thanksgiving – has continued to be celebrated into the present century. In the United States it has become institutionalised as Thanksgiving, and celebrated somewhat belatedly towards the end of November. The Christmas or midwinter feast took place while stores of food were still relatively abundant and following the autumn slaughter of surplus stock, but thereafter the store of food steadily diminished. The observance of Lent was, in secular terms, merely a recognition of shortage, and late spring, in so many respects a season of hope, joy and renewed growth, was paradoxically also one of scarcity and hardship. Piers Plowman wrote of his scanty store of food:

> By this liflode [food supply]   we mote lyve til
> Lammesse tyme.

But once the harvest was in:

> ... no beggere ete breed   that benes inne were,
> But of coket [quality bread] and clermatyn [white flour]   or
>   ellis of clene whete,
> Ne noon halfpeny ale   in none wise drynke,
> But of the beste and of the brunneste   that brewesteres selle.[63]

Such was the cycle by which people lived and ate, a short period of relative abundance followed by a long period when they saw their stocks dwindle and calculated anxiously the number of eating days to harvest. It is symptomatic that, though the winter solstice was celebrated with feasting, no trace of ritual eating accompanied the midsummer fires.

Superimposed on this expected annual cycle of abundance and scarcity was the unexpected and irregular occurrence of crop failure and famine. Though warfare could lead to the destruction of crops, and pre-emptive buying to scarcity and a sharp rise in prices, the chief reason for shortage was meteorological. In terms of weather, the margin between a good crop and total failure might be only a very narrow one. A late and unexpected frost, a single fierce storm of rain or hail, or conditions conducive to the spread of fungus or insect pests could each spell disaster for a particular crop. But complete failure usually arose from more spectacular and prolonged weather conditions than these. It is difficult to generalise because the course of weather (as distinct from climatic) history is not known in the detail that one might wish. But instances of really severe crop failure, such as those of the years 1315–17, appear to have resulted not from severe cold but from prolonged and heavy rainfall. Little was done – or could be done – before the nineteenth century to drain the fields by means of mole-ploughing or laying drainage tiles. Water which did not run off the surface or was not absorbed into the underlying rock was apt to lie in pools on the surface. Walter of Henley advised his readers to ridge up their selions so that the water might gather in the intervening hollows.[64] The problem was that the land could be neither ploughed nor sown under such conditions, and if the seed was already in the ground when the rains began, it was more likely to rot than to germinate. Although data are imperfect, it does appear that most of the great *crises de subsistence*, which have left so deep an impression on European history, were due essentially to prolonged rainfall in winter and spring.[65] Between 1224–5 and 1447–8 – a period of 224 years – no less that twenty-five harvests were outstandingly bad, some showing a deviation from the average of more than 40 per cent.[66] A truly disastrous harvest might thus be expected to occur in one year in ten, or perhaps a little more frequently.

Statistics derived by Titow from the Winchester rolls show that really good harvests outnumbered the bad, but that the bad deviated from the average very much more sharply than the good.[67] This conclusion is supported by Hoskins' study of the period 1480–1619, in which grain prices are taken as a measure of relative abundance or scarcity.[68] This means that for much of the time the peasant enjoyed a measure of abundance and security, but that these good years were punctuated at irregular intervals by years of extreme scarcity against which he had no means of protecting himself. It was these years of hardship that stayed in his memory and gave so powerful an edge to, for example, the allegory of *Piers Plowman*.[69]

Not by bread alone

The third ingredient of the popular diet, and the least susceptible of measurement, was made up of green vegetables, roots and fruit. These were, with the occasional exception of peas, grown mainly as garden crops, and rarely entered into any rotation before the eighteenth century. No regular record was ever kept either of their yields or of the labour expended upon them. They were, in theory at least, subject to tithe, but were rarely mentioned in the tithe records. Literary references to the cultivation and consumption of vegetables are more frequent. John Gardener, in the mid fifteenth century, showed:

> How he schall hys seedys sowe
> Of euery moneth he moste knowe
> Both of wortys [cabbages] and of leke
> Ownyns and of garleke,
> Percely, clarey [a salvia] and eke sage
> And all other herbage.[70]

Vegetables not only gave some body to a diet of weak gruel, but also contributed much of the necessary vitamins. Some herbs grew wild, and were gathered when in season. The old man's daughter in the 'Clerkes Tale',

> ... whan she hoomward cam she wolde bringe
> Wortes and other herbes tymes ofte,
> The whiche she shredde and seeth for hir livinge.[71]

And Piers, who could not rise to eggs and bacon, nevertheless had parsley, leeks and cabbages.[72]

Harrison, towards the end of the sixteenth century, noted that 'such herbes, fruits, & roots ... as grow yeerlie out of the ground, of seed, haue been verie plentifull in this land',[73] adding that in recent years they had become less popular. For the latter statement there is no corroborative evidence, and everything points to the increasing importance of vegetables in the sixteenth century. Indeed, Harrison himself commented on the liking of the upper classes for green vegetables. With the exception of legumes – beans and peas – vegetables were grown only on the small tofts attached to cottages or in the larger gardens met with close to great houses, castles and monasteries.

Vegetables were 'annuals'; their seed was collected each year and sown again for the next crop. They called for a well-manured soil, and were labour-intensive. The art of gardening was strongly developed, following the French example, during the later Middle Ages, and a number of treatises was written on the management of gardens. During the Renaissance, gardens, or at least those attached to great houses, became more formal and ornamental, and this may have been in Harrison's mind when he wrote that vegetables were becoming less important in his days.[74]

Some vegetables were of exceptional importance. No accounts of gardens fail to mention 'coleworts', 'wortes', or 'wurtys'. This was the general term for members of the *Brassica* genus, though the terms 'caboches' and 'cabogis' were in use before the end of the Middle Ages. They were then, as now, boiled, often with cereals and meat. Root-crops were also grown, and lists of vegetables often contained 'parsenepys', 'turnepez', 'carettes' and 'betes'.[75] They, like the brassicas, would have been added to the universal pottage. Their food value was low, but some were a good source of vitamins C and K. To the list of familiar garden vegetables the potato was somewhat reluctantly added in the seventeenth century (pp. 198, 218).

Andrew Boorde, who gave short shrift to garden vegetables, nevertheless thought highly of onions, garlic and leeks,[76] as also did Chaucer's Summoner:

> Wel loved he garlike, onions and lekes.[77]

They were mostly eaten as 'companage', a term used of everything that was taken to give flavour or interest to a meal consisting mainly of breadgrains. The onion appears to have been most used, until, under more prosperous conditions, it was displaced by cheese. Herbs, used in small quantities as flavouring rather than as food, were of particular importance, given the blandness of a farinaceous diet. In the course of the sixteenth century considerable advances were made in both the art of gardening and the range of crops grown. Harrison noted that the consumption of vegetables had increased amongst the upper classes, which had previously consumed an excessive amount of meat. They 'fed vpon [them] as deintie dishes at the tables of delicate merchants, gentlemen, and the nobilitie'. This newly acquired taste owed much to the Dutch, who came to Britain in considerable numbers towards the end of the sixteenth century, bringing with them their own more advanced ideas on the cultivation of gardens. It was possibly their novelty that appealed to the upper classes 'who make for their prouision yearelie for new feeds out of strange countries'. It has been claimed that the cabbage was introduced at this time, but *Brassica* is an extraordinarily varied genus and is subject to wide mutations. It is not impossible that a new species emerged at this time. In addition to the cabbage, the genus also included broccoli, brussels sprout, cauliflower, kale and kohlrabi, each of which developed many variants. But the most important, in the long run, of all newly adopted species was the potato. It is generally held that it was brought by the Spaniards from South America, and that it spread very slowly from the Mediterranean to northern Europe. The date of its adoption in Britain is uncertain, and its ascription to Sir Walter Ralegh has little to support it. There was, furthermore, some confusion at first between the potato and the sweet potato, which might well have been brought back from the North American colonies, but never took any firm hold in Britain.[78]

Animal products

Breadgrains made up the greater part of the diet of most of the population, but their inadequacy from the nutritional point of view was in some measure made good by a small consumption of meat and dairy produce. Records of medieval feasts show an inordinate consumption of meat, almost to the exclusion of other foodstuffs. But, except for the nobility, feasts were rare, and for most people there was no danger of consuming too much meat. This was due, in part, to the fact that animals, with the exception of the pig and, to a very limited extent, deer, were not bred for meat. Sheep were for wool, and cattle for draught purposes, and when their useful lives were over their carcases held little food value. Since both bulls and rams, castrated of course, could be made to serve the needs of agriculture, there was no inducement, as now, to kill off males soon after birth. There was a general revulsion against eating the flesh of the horse, the noblest of animals, whose chief task it was to carry its master to war. Only the pig was reared primarily for food, and this because it called for little by way of care and could be allowed to run wild in the woodlands, rooting for what food it could, and growing fat in autumn on acorns and beech-mast. One of the measures used in Domesday Book of the extent of woodland was the number of pigs that it could support.

Pigs bred frequently and prolifically, and the inability of the woods to support their numbers through the winter led to the autumn cull, when large numbers were

6.7 Most series of the Labours of the Months show the fattening and killing of pigs as an activity of November. Here men are seen feeding acorns to a herd of half-wild pigs.

killed and their carcases preserved by smoking or salting (Fig. 6.7). The opportunity to eat pork depended, by and large, on people's rights in the woodland, and these were often very restricted for most of the peasantry. We can probably assume that the gentry and the better-off amongst the peasantry ate pork or bacon on a more or less regular basis, while the poorer enjoyed at most a lump of bacon fat with which to enrich their pottage. Nevertheless, sides of bacon were not infrequently pictured hanging amid the rafters to 'cure'.

No doubt beef and mutton did occasionally enter into the diets of the humbler classes, but if other forms of meat were eaten they were more likely to have been rabbit and poultry. The rabbit had been introduced into Britain at the time of the Norman Conquest for the specific purpose of providing sport. The warrens, so jealously guarded by the gentry throughout medieval and early modern times, were inhabited mainly by the rabbit and hare. These provided food for the lord's table and were regularly poached by the lower classes.[79] Popular attitudes to poaching, engendered by shortages during the Middle Ages, have not changed significantly since that date. Poultry provided flesh as well as eggs, and both formed part of the obligations owed by many of the peasants to their lords as late as the eighteenth century.

Dairy produce played only a small part in diet before modern times. Animals were not bred to supply milk, and milk was available for only short periods after parturition. Milk, furthermore, had only a short life, and there was generally a popular antipathy towards drinking it. It can, however, be preserved in the form of butter and cheese, and it was probably as cheese that most was consumed. Butter was less important, perhaps because it was difficult to store and had a relatively short shelf-life. It was made at first in a churn of the vertical or 'plunger' type (Fig. 6.8), but this was gradually replaced in modern times by the rotating churn, in which

6.8 A plunger-type milk churn; after a wall-painting.

gravity was allowed to do much of the work of converting cream into butter. Cheese had the advantage over butter of being more easily transported and stored. In areas where animal husbandry was important, such as the grasslands of southern England and the moorlands of northern, there was a surplus of milk at certain seasons, especially in summer, though the quantities available were not large. The only practicable way of preserving it was to turn it into cheese. Cheese was made from the milk of cattle, sheep and, more rarely, goats. Considerable numbers of cheeses were made on the Bishop of Winchester's manors on the downland of Hampshire.[80] In the Yorkshire Dales rents due to Bolton Priory were sometimes paid in cheeses,[81] and the cheese-making tradition of Wensleydale is said to have derived from the land management of the Cistercian monks of Jervaulx.[82] It is evident, however, that the flocks were kept for wool production, and that cheese was only a by-product.[83]

Cheese and perhaps even butter were made at remote steadings in the Pennines, in the West Country, and in the Welsh hills. In many such areas the amimals were transhumant, spending the summer on the uplands and winter in the shelter of the valleys. The memory of these movements is sometimes preserved in place-names, especially in the hilly west. Havot in Wales and Laity (= milking-house) in Cornwall bear this connotation, and in England the place-name elements denoting 'milk', 'butter' and 'cheese' are not uncommon.[84] In continental Europe, especially

200

within the Alps, the seasonal movement of stock was accompanied by ceremonies in which the community bade farewell to its animals and migrant stockmen in spring and welcomed them back at the beginning of autumn. In Britain no such rituals appear to have developed, probably because the distances covered were short and contact could be maintained throughout the summer with the upland settlement. Nevertheless, transhumance played an important role in rural life, especially in the western and northern parts of this country. A doggerel poem of the seventeenth century, preserved in a commonplace book at Trebartha Hall in the Tamar valley, explains succinctly the role of upland pastures:

> But our best neighbour – and he's choice and good –
> Is the wild moor there's the best neighbourhood.
> It keeps vast herds of cattle, I profess,
> And flocks of sheep even almost numberless.
> Thus we our stock do summer on the Down,
> And keep our homer grass till winter come.[85]

It is evident that transhumance, apart from allowing use to be made of a marginal environment, served also to get the stock off the farmlands in summer so that a crop of hay might be taken for winter fodder.

Brewing, distillation and the drinks trade

The cereal harvest had to supply not only the breadgrains but also the basic requirement of the only popular drink of significance. Water was, of course, drunk, but much of the supply was contaminated,[86] and it was avoided by all who could afford to do so. The wealthier classes drank immense quantities of wine, imported from France or the Rhineland, but for the mass of the population the only alternative to polluted water was ale and later beer.

Brewing consists in the malting or germination of cereals, followed by their fermentation in water.[87] The process is relatively simple, and has been practised since very early times.[88] During the Middle Ages it was, in the main, a domestic pursuit, carried on by women who sold their brew to anyone who wanted it. Alewives and ale-houses were very numerous and the quality of their brew unquestionably bad. In 1267 the assize of ale was established, authorising the local court, whether manorial or burghal, to examine the quality of the ale offered for sale and to fix its price in the light of the current price of cereals. On those occasions when the quality of the ale was found wanting, the alewives brewing it were fined. This happened so regularly that the assize became in effect a tax on brewing.[89] At Colchester, for example, the number of alewives fined in 1356 for selling ale contrary to the assize was 115 in a town of no great size. The assize did not, of course, affect the private brewing of ale for domestic consumption, but this called for an apparatus of furnace and pans which ordinary households would have found it difficult both to acquire and to accommodate. Private brewing, to judge from inventories, was almost a monopoly of the great house.[90]

In the later sixteenth and early seventeenth centuries brewing passed increasingly from the alewife to the professional brewer, who sold his ale or beer to outlets such as inns, taverns and ale-houses.[91] All ale-houses were required by law to be licensed either by the justices or by a local authority. In fact, however, illicit ale-houses regularly traded, selling ale or beer obtained from brewers. There were, without doubt, far too many of them in most cities. John Ivie's 'Declaration' of 1661, written in justification of his actions while mayor of Salisbury, declared that his 'next careful chore was to suppress the alehouses which were above four score, licensed or not'.[92] Elsewhere in his tract he claimed that in the three city parishes there were 'above fifty inns' as well as over eighty ale-houses. The system of licensing ultimately reduced their number. In the West Riding of Yorkshire, it was claimed in 1638, there were about 2000 licensed ale-houses, as well as another 500 'that brew without license'. The writer added that the population was engaged chiefly in weaving and 'have their drink from the alehouse-keepers, and scarce one brews his own drink'.[93]

Brewing required not only water and a supply of malt, but also large vessels in which the wort was allowed to ferment. The latter are listed not infrequently in probate inventories of the seventeenth and later centuries, and were often kept in a separate room usually designated 'brewhouse'. A Lancashire inventory of 1583 listed, for example, 'the brewinge panne set now in the fornesse [furnace] in the brewinge housse'.[94] This came to be the common pattern in great houses, while those who lived in smaller houses turned increasingly to ale-house and tavern.

Barley was always the preferred cereal for malting, and, as the human diet came to consist more and more of wheat, this became the most important use for barley until, in very much more recent times, it began to be grown as an animal feed. But rye, oats and mixed grains were also used on occasion for malting. It was a matter of price and of the extent to which barley was absorbed into bread-making. Ale was fermented for only a short time, and its 'shelf-life' was brief. Its strength depended upon the ratio of malt to water used in the process. In general a quarter of malt yielded from 50 to 75 gallons of ale, but sometimes as much as 90 gallons of weak, or 'small' beer were obtained.[95] It was, in part, to guard against this kind of exploitation of the customer that the assize of ale had been instituted, though the fines imposed tended to become a general tax on alewives.

Brewing made heavy demands on a community's supply of breadgrains, especially as the consumption of ale was often heavy. Provision was often made in defining corrodies for up to 2 gallons a day. This may seem a more than generous allowance, even if we assume that most of it was 'small' beer with a low alcoholic content. This would have been the equivalent of about 10 quarters of grain a year. Statistics published by Dyer show that as much as 8 per cent of the total area under cereals might have been required to produce sufficient barley for malting purposes.[96] On the other hand, ale had a considerable food value, and this should be added to the calorie and protein intake of the peasant.

Ale was, by and large, a lower-class or peasant drink, the upper classes consuming mainly wine. Surviving accounts of gentle and aristocratic households nevertheless show how large were the quantities of ale and beer brewed and drunk. No doubt much of this went to servants and retainers, but in the later Middle Ages the quality of ale was improving, and there can be no doubt but that ale-drinking was far from unpopular amongst the upper classes. Improvements in the quality of the brew arose largely from an increasing use of barley malt and from the admixture of hops. Hops had long been known. They appear as *umblones* (Fr. *houblon*) as early as the ninth century on Carolingian manors in the north of France, where they may have been eaten as vegetables. They seem to have been introduced into Britain from the Low Countries, probably towards the end of the fourteenth century, and their use in brewing was recorded in Sussex about 1400.[97] Hops gave an added flavour to ale, which must without them have been a particularly bland and insipid drink. At the same time they gave the liquor, which we must now begin to call 'beer', a very much longer life. It is doubtful whether there could have been brewers selling wholesale to taverns and inns without the keeping qualities imparted by the use of hops. Beer ceased gradually to be brewed in small quantities for local and immediate consumption. From the sixteenth century its production passed to the brewers, who distributed it in casks, as they have since continued to do. This in turn led to the standarisation of the size of casks.[98]

The adoption of beer as a national drink did not go unopposed. There were those − as indeed there are today − who demanded traditional ale. For an Englishman, wrote Andrew Boorde, 'ale . . . is a naturall drynke . . . Barly malte maketh better ale than oten malte or any other corne doth.' Beer, he added, 'is made of malte, of hoppes, and water . . . And nowe of late dayes it is moche vsed in England', adding, however, that its use is dangerous.[99] In an imaginery debate between the English heralds and those of France, on the other hand, the former are made to say: 'we have good-ale, beer, metheghelen, sydre and pirry, beyng more holsome beverages for us then your wynes, which maketh people dronken, also prone and apte to all fylthy pleasures and lustes.'[100]

Whether serving ale or beer, the ale-house became 'the heart of the social world of pre-modern Europe'. Inns and taverns focused 'a galaxy of commercial, governmental and leisure activities', but these up-market establishments were greatly exceeded in number by the ale-houses. These were small, ill-kept and often rowdy. A survey conducted in 1577 found no less than 15,095 in England alone.[101] Before the Reformation 'church-ales' or 'scot-ales', organised for the purpose of making money for the church, had been occasions for heavy drinking and carousing. The Puritans set their faces against both drunkenness and the supposed misuse of the church. Gradually church-ales were abandoned, and the ale-house, 'one of the few quasi-public buildings in the community',[102] took over as the focus of social life. Where space permitted, old-style games and entertainments found refuge in the ale-house. The beer-drinking darts-player has a respectable ancestry.

The ale-house dispensed only ale and beer. Indeed, the only alternative drink

6.9 Early eighteenth-century bottles; after *The English Glass Bottle*, Truro, 1976.

before the introduction of the now familiar beverages, was wine. This was too expensive, too up-market for the ale-house and tavern, and is likely to have been available only in those inns which catered for the needs of the more well-to-do travellers. The homes of the gentry are likely to have contained a store of wine, but, until the bottle had entered into widespread use, wine was not of great importance outside the leading inns.

Although glass-blowing and bottle-making were known in the ancient world, and Roman bottles have been found in Britain, the art was subsequently lost, and was not reintroduced until the age of Elizabeth, and then by craftsmen from Venice. It was not until after 1660 that bottle-making was established on a significant scale. Early bottles were given a mark, denoting their ownership and the date of manufacture, by the addition of a small blob of glass which was then impressed with a metal stamp. Their shapes were individual, and were not standardised to the cylindrical form much before the later eighteenth century (Fig. 6.9). Some wine-bottles still retain the indented bottom which derived from the earliest methods of production. The bottle would have been of little value without a means of sealing it. This was achieved by the use from the eighteenth century of a cork made from the bark of the cork-oak (*Quercus suber*), and this, in turn, was dependent on trade with the Mediterranean.

The glass bottle effected a revolution in drinking habits. It not only allowed wine to be distributed more widely, socially and geographically; it also permitted provincial beers, whose merits often depended on local peculiarities of the water-supply, to reach the capital as well as other parts of the kingdom. Burton-on-Trent in the last analysis owed its importance to the introduction of a bottle made of tough, dark-coloured glass.[103]

When ale-houses and taverns began to diversify their offerings they turned to spirits. The distillation of alcoholic liquors was an outgrowth of medieval alchemy, and made use of the same apparatus of alembics and retorts. Wine was distilled in the later Middle Ages to produce 'burnt wine', *Branntwein* or brandy. Towards the end of the fifteenth century spirits began to be distilled, with the help of yeast, from beer.[104] The spirits thus obrained came to be flavoured with a variety of herbs and oils derived from flowers. Certain monasteries were particularly active in this field, and some have retained their reputation for liqueurs until this day. But it was gin, together with a crude *Branntwein*, which invaded the taverns and ale-houses of seventeenth-century England. 'Before brandy came over to England in such quantities as it doth now we drank good strong beer and all laborious people used to drink a pot of ale or a flagon of strong beer.'[105]

Gin was an invention of the Netherlands. Grain, imported from the Baltic, was used for the initial fermentation; the liquor was then distilled and flavoured with the juniper berry, in French *genièvre* and hence 'gin'.[106] In England the taste for gin was first acquired from drinking imported 'Hollands' gin. Then it began to be distilled here and was sold in quantities that were far too great for the health of the nation. Gin-drinking declined in the middle years of the eighteenth century almost as suddenly as it had developed. The unrestricted distillation and sale of gin were terminated by an Act of 1751. At the same time beer of a higher and more consistent quality began to be brewed by firms whose names remain familiar even today.[107] Porter was first produced at this time, and the names of Perkins, Whitbread and Worthington first appeared in taverns and on bottles.

In the later years of the seventeenth century both beer-drinking and the ale-house found another rival in the shape of the newly introduced beverages, coffee, tea and cocoa. The tea shrub originated in China, and tea — 'bohee' — was first brought to western Europe by the Dutch East Indiamen.[108] Coffee came in the first instance from the eastern Horn of Africa, but its cultivation spread to the Middle East, India and the East Indies. Both tea and coffee were expensive in England, and for that reason — such is the irrationality of human behaviour — became fashionable drinks. The coffee-house, of which there were said to have been some 2000 in London alone about 1700,[109] tended to replace the ale-house and tavern as a social centre, though catering in the main for a more affluent clientele. In the course of the eighteenth century the East India Company based in London acquired a virtual monopoly on the import of tea, which came very largely to replace coffee; coffee was, by and large, handled by the Dutch. The American colonists, thanks to the tea duty and 'Tea Party', changed from being tea to coffee-drinkers.

The preparation and preservation of food

Most foodstuffs become available only seasonally. The breadgrains have always been harvested in late summer; most fruits ripen at about the same time, and, though vegetables have a longer season, there was always a period when they were not available. Even the milk yield of farm animals fell away in winter, and meat was abundant only during late autumn, when the annual cull took place in advance of

6.10 The late medieval barn of Shaftesbury Abbey at Bradford-on-Avon (Wilts.). The space between the opposed 'transepts' was used for threshing, the doors being left open for the breeze to remove chaff and dust.

winter. If people were to survive, some means had to be found of holding surplus food from the times of relative abundance for consumption in periods of scarcity. This was a perennial problem, since many foods could not be stored for long.[110] The vast number of storage pits at Danebury demonstrate one way in which it was solved during the Iron Age. A few foodstuffs will keep naturally until the next harvest. Cereals, fortunately, have a relatively long life, and, if protected from damp and vermin, remain edible from one harvest until the next. This was an essential condition of settled agriculture. Much of the grain harvested in the damp British climate would nevertheless have deteriorated within a year without treatment. It was not uncommon to dry it in a kiln before storing it for the winter. Corn-drying kilns have been used since the Middle Ages or even earlier, and remained in use in Scotland and Ireland until recent times.[111] Corn intended for use as seed could not, however, have been treated in this way.

Cereals, whether or not they had been threshed, were customarily stored in barns, and the large medieval barns, generally though not always correctly called 'tithe' barns, that survive today were built to hold the manorial grain as long as might have been necessary (Fig. 6.10). The peasant enjoyed no such security, and was obliged to keep his small store within his cottage. Many of the cases of theft that came before the courts concerned grain stolen from peasant homes. It was the usual practice to thresh and grind the corn only as it was rquired. This meant that threshing was likely to continue intermittently throughout the winter and spring, and milling the threshed grain was almost a daily activity, since milled flour was difficult to store.

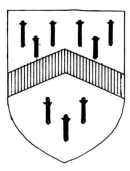

6.11 The shield of the Grocers' Company, showing a chevron between nine cloves.

Most foodstuffs were more perishable than cereals, and had a life which could be measured in days rather than weeks. There were, very broadly, two methods of preserving such foodstuffs: by dehydrating them and by bringing about a chemical change which would give them a longer life. Drying could assume many forms. It might be by simple exposure to the sun, a process which for climatic reasons could have had little value in Britain. Smoking was very much more important, and was particularly applicable to meat and fish. A significant part of the autumn cull was usually preserved in this way. Salting was a form of desiccation, and could be used for many foodstuffs. It called, however, for a supply of salt which was over much of Britain an imported and relatively expensive commodity.

Meat and fish cured in these ways could not be expected to last indefinitely, and the curing process itself was often less than perfect. Many must have been the occasions when people, both 'gentle' and peasant, were faced with tainted food. There was often no alternative but to eat it, its flavour disguised as far as possible with herbs and spices. Onions and garlic were much used, and those who could afford their higher cost would have made abundant use of spices. Foremost amongst the latter was pepper, followed by cloves, mace, cinnamon and ginger. Grocers were in origin dealers in pepper and other spices, and, in evidence of their business, the shield of the Grocers' Company bore a charge of nine cloves (Fig. 6.11). All spices in regular use had to be imported, and they constituted one of the principal cargoes carried by the Italian merchants from the Middle East. They were very expensive by the time they reached north-western Europe, and can only have been used in the kitchens of the rich.

The most important of the chemical methods of food preservation have always been fermentation and cheese-making. Fermentation consists in changing sugar into alcohol, and is sometimes used in preserving solid foods, as, for example, in making silage for animals and, in eastern Europe, in preparing *barszcz* from beet.[112] But the fermentation process is particularly suited to liquids. Malted grain is first 'killed' and is then fermented in water to which sugar or yeast have been added. Honey and many fruit juices can also be fermented in a similar way. The most important of the latter is the juice of the grape, though in Britain the apple and pear have been very important in some areas.

Cheese is the coagulated curd of the milk of the cow, sheep or goat. The process adopted in cheese-making varies in detail from one region to another, but consists essentially of the addition of either rennet or lactic acid to the milk. This process was discovered at an early date in human history, probably by a pastoral people who would have felt the need to preserve milk products from one season to the next. Within Britain the importance of cheese has varied greatly. In much of Lowland England animals were kept mainly for wool or for draught purposes, and their milk yield was of little consequence. In the Highland Zone, by contrast, animals were more important as a source of food, and, in order to make the greatest possible use of marginal land, they were often sent up into the hills in summer (pp. 200–1). Cheese became the only form in which their milk yield could be sent back to the lowland settlement.

With the breakdown of the open-field system of cultivation a more mixed pattern of farming began to develop. The growing of 'artificial' grasses and other fodder crops as 'catch-crops' on land that would previously have been left fallow encouraged animal-rearing. From the eighteenth century greater care was given to breeding, and stock began to be bred for specific qualities, of which milk yield was one. The result was not only an increase in the output of cheese but also greater refinement in its preparation. Cheese-making became an artform, reflected in the regional cheeses for which England, France and Italy are particularly noted. Before modern times cheese production had been on too small a scale, except in mountain areas, for it to have been of great dietary importance, despite its high food value. Its greater abundance in modern times permitted cheese to supplement and then to replace the onion, leek or garlic as 'companage', and the 'ploughman's lunch' became one of bread and cheese, as, in the popular view, it still remains.

Other substances are used today to prolong the life of foodstuffs, notably vinegar and sugar, neither of which was cheap or abundant in earlier times. Vinegar is made by allowing the alcohol within any fermented liquor to turn to acetic acid.[113] Any liquor can be used for this purpose, but traditionally vinegar has been obtained, as its name of *vin aigre* demonstrates, from wine. It has been used to preserve meat and fish as well as vegetables, a process generally known as 'pickling'. In Britain the use of vinegar has become important only in modern times, probably because the cost of the wine from which it was made had previously been too high.

Sugar can also be used to protect some foodstuffs, notably fruits, from putrefaction, as it continues to be today in the preparation of conserves. But before the nineteenth century, sugar, like vinegar, was too expensive to be used in this way in most households. Today physical methods – freezing, bottling, canning – hold the field, but they are the product of modern technology, and were not practicable before the latter half of the nineteenth century. Nevertheless, the bottling of fruit by a method close to that used today appeared in a manuscript recipe book of the early eighteenth century.[114]

Milling

Few items of human food, apart from ripe fruit, can be eaten and digested in their raw state. Most have to be ground, crushed or peeled before being cooked.[115] Of none was this more true than of the breadgrains. They could be softened by boiling, but it became apparent at an early date that it was desirable to remove the husk or pericarp.[116] This could be done by rubbing the grain between two stones, first the saddle quern,[117] and then the rotary quern.[118] The process lent itself to mechanisation, and most corn in Britain has, since the early Middle Ages, been ground in a mechanically operated mill with rotary querns. An advantage of the rotary quern was that it could be of almost any size, provided there was sufficient power to turn it. The stones of a mechanically powered mill could be 2 metres or more in diameter; those of a small hand-quern, only a fraction of a metre.[119] The quern, whether saddle or rotary, 'was an instrument of peasant culture ... of individual food production'.[120] It might be thought that it would have been part of the equipment of every household. The fact that it was not was due to the control over milling which manorial lords had been able to assert from the eleventh century onwards.[121] The mill powered by water or wind – the only agents available to turn it – represented a not inconsiderable capital investment. Only the lord was able to build one, and when he did so he reckoned to recoup his outlay by compelling his tenants to use it, in return, of course, for a fee.

Domesday Book lists no fewer than some 6000 mills, all of which were presumably powered by water.[122] There were on average twenty-two mills for each thousand of recorded population, more in the south and east, fewer in the hilly areas of the north and west, where greater reliance must have been placed on hand-querns.[123] The mills would have had their wheel set horizontally in the water, with a spindle to link it with the upper stone, or 'runner'. The lightly built millhouse was set above the stream which provided its power. It was vulnerable to every spate that occurred, and many were the mills that were swept away by floods. The vertically set wheel, which became general in the thirteenth and fourteenth centuries, marked a great advance (Fig. 6.12). It was more powerful and could accomplish more work, but, especially if it was an 'over-shot' wheel, required a mill leat, which drew water from a river, to service it. It represented a much larger investment than the small, horizontal wheel, and, in order to cover its cost, the lord became even more assertive of his rights over his dependants.

The windmill, at least in Britain, came very much later than the watermill, and was probably adopted at first only where there were no flowing streams.[124] The earliest windmill was the post-mill type, in which the house containing the millstones was mounted on a post about which it could be turned to allow the vanes to face into the wind (Fig. 6.13a). Its relative simplicity and ease of construction ensured that it remained in use until recent times. The tower-mill, built of timber or masonry, came later.[125] It was a more massive structure, in which the cap, which supported the spindle and vanes, was made to turn on rollers around the summit of

6.12 A late fourteenth-century overshot water-wheel. After the Luttrell Psalter, fo. 181.

(a)

(b)

6.13 Windmills: (a) a post-mill, as shown in the Luttrell Psalter, fo. 158; (b) tower-mill, from a
fifteenth-century window at Stoke-by-Clare (Suff.).

the tower. The post-mill was in use from the thirteenth century, but the tower-mill not for another century. The drawing (Fig. 6.13b) shows a tower-mill as depicted in a stained-glass window of the later fifteenth century in the parish church of Stoke-by-Clare (Suffolk).

Considerable care was given to the selection of the millstone. Its material had to be hard, with a naturally rough surface which would not wear smooth with use. It was essential, furthermore, that particles should not break off and become mixed with the flour. The best stones available in Britain were imported,[126] either burr-stone, an open-grained gritstone from the Paris Basin, or andesite, quarried in the Eifel, near Mayen, and shipped down the Rhine from Cologne – hence its common English name of 'Cullin' stone.[127] It was penetrated by a mass of tiny cavities, much like pumice-stone, so that, however much the stone was worn, its rough surface was retained. The most important native stone for the purpose was the Millstone Grit from the Upper Carboniferous series, though 'only a few restricted outcrops ... provide the necessary well-cemented, massive stone'.[128] The gritstone of the Derbyshire Pennines was much used, and millstones, cut on the moors, were transported over much of England.[129] Other types of stone were used, but were generally of inferior quality and were not carried far from the quarries which produced them. They include various grits as well as granite in the south-west. These were very much cheaper, but the expensive Cullin and burr were generally preferred.

The flour, as it fell from the rotating stone, contained the finely comminuted husk of the grain, or bran. To obtain the whitest flour this had to be removed by 'bolting' through a sieve with a very fine mesh. This was a laborious and far from satisfactory process, and most bread before the nineteenth century contained some bran.[130] Only in the nineteenth century, with the introduction of roller mills, was it possible to vary the extraction rate, and, when needed, to produce the whitest flour and the most appetising bread.

Food, élite and popular

'When grain was discovered,' wrote Linnaeus, 'the acorn became sour.'[131] Food is a necessity, but the variety of food eaten is a matter of convention. There have always been foods for the élite and foods for popular consumption, and the distinction between them has rarely borne any close relationship to their respective food values. It was to a large extent a matter of price. The rich could afford to buy expensive and exotic foods, and to eat them – and to be seen to eat them – became a kind of conspicuous consumption. Alexander Neckham advised his aristocratic readers to let the smells from their kitchens drift over the neighbourhood, so that all could be aware of how well they were faring.

Space has already been given to the location and design of kitchens and of other cooking facilities. Broadly speaking, the grand house came, quite early in the Middle Ages, to have a kitchen separate from the hall, together with its ancillary pantry,

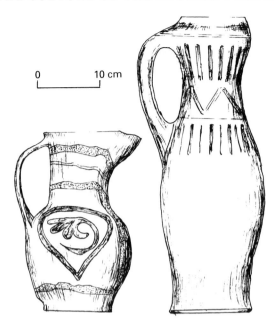

0   10 cm

6.14 Medieval jugs. These were made, used and broken in immense numbers. A thousand were ordered on one occasion by the king's butler at Westminster: L. F. Salzmann, *English Industries in the Middle Ages*, London, 1913, 117. They were used, among other things, for serving wine and ale.

buttery, brewery and dairy. In the cottage food continued to be prepared over the fire which burned in the hall, while in houses of intermediate standing, the preparation of food was moving from the hall to a kitchen located at its lower end. But wherever food was cooked the methods used were broadly similar. It was either boiled or roasted; only bread was baked. A series of four drawings in the Luttrell Psalter (Fig. 6.17a–d) shows the preparation and serving of a banquet, from the spit-roasting of meat and game and the boiling of a kind of pottage to serving the food at the lord's table. Liquid food was served in some form of mazer, while guests used their knives and fingers to slice off pieces of meat. Wooden trenchers served as plates, to be replaced in the later Middle Ages, at least in the homes of the rich, with silver and pewter. Today's breadboard is the lone survivor from medieval eating practices. Drink was served from jugs (Fig. 6.14) and drunk from goblets. In humbler households boiling became far more important than roasting, and countless illustrations show the pot, usually with handles for lifting and three legs to keep it steady on the hearth, seething amid the embers (Figs. 6.15 and 6.16).

There were for all classes of society times of feasting and times of relative austerity. The range between the good times and the bad was probably as great for the struggling masses as for the élite, though the best of popular diet may have been no better than the worst that the rich were called upon to eat. The populace had their good times after harvest and at Christmas, at weddings and, by that peculiar

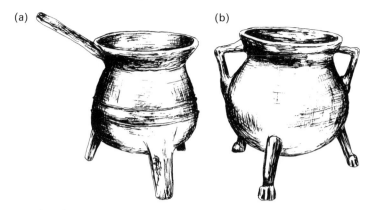

(a)　　　　　　　　　　　　　(b)

6.15 Late medieval cooking vessels; after examples in the London Museum. Both have tripod legs, but (b) also has loops for suspending it over the fire (see also Fig. 6.17).

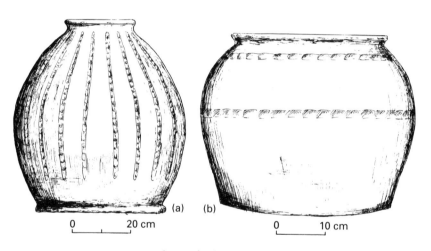

(a)　(b)

0   20 cm　　　　0   10 cm

6.16 Pots for (a) food storage, (b) cooking.

inversion of rituals, at funerals (Fig. 6.17). Their masters feasted at royal coronations, episcopal inductions and family celebrations. 'Food is the constant element in festival customs.'[132] It was food that made them memorable, and feasting became synonymous with festival. The record of these celebrations has contributed to the illusion that the Middle Ages were a time of 'coarse plenty'. For the poor and also for many of the not-so-poor celebrations were but interludes in a dull routine of unappetising and barely digestible food.

Some indication has already been given (p. 174) of the diet of the mass of the population, with the breadgrains in one form or another making up 80 or more per cent of their calorific intake. There were also roots and green vegetables, fruit in season, and very small quantities of meat and cheese. As one moves higher in the social scale, the food is the same, but the mix of its ingredients gradually changes.

213

6.17 The preparation, serving and consumption of food at a late medieval feast: after the Luttrell Psalter, fos. 206v, 207, 207v, 208; (a) boiling, (b) roasting, (c) serving (there was frequently a long journey from kitchen to hall), (d) the feast; note that the table consisted of boards laid across trestles.

214

Meat in its several forms – beef, mutton, pork, poultry, game – assumes a far greater role. The diary kept by Parson Woodford in the eighteenth century displays what amounts to an obsession with killing and eating animals. On one winter's day, he wrote, 'we had for Dinner Cod and Oyster Sauce, a fillet of Veal rosted, boiled Tongue, stewed Beef, Peas Soup and Mutton Stakes. 2nd Course, a rost Chicken, Cheesecakes, Jelly-Custards &.'[133] It would appear from this and other such diaries of the eighteenth century that this was the normal fare of the well-to-do gentry. At a higher social level the dishes would have been even more extravagant but broadly similar in their content. Similar also were the feasts prepared on great state and ecclesiastical occasions from at least the later Middle Ages onwards. Their exceptional nature can be judged from the care with which the menus have been preserved.[134]

This wide variety of dishes was certainly not served on a daily basis, but the diet of the well-off even in the Middle Ages, contained far too much meat, was lacking in green vegetables and milk products, and had little of the breadgrains. This type of diet, heavy on meat and animal fats, moved downwards socially from the upper to the middle classes, where we find it recorded in Woodford's diary, and ultimately to the lower classes as their Christmas feast or Sunday dinner.

Parson Woodford's dinner consisted of two courses, in both of which meat dishes played a predominant role. This was a perpetuation of a medieval tradition, according to which two courses were eaten, so much alike in most recorded menus that one wonders whether it was not one gigantic course punctuated by an interval during which dishes might be cleared and diners allowed to attend the calls of nature. Out of this ill-assorted mishmash a series of distinct courses gradually emerged. With the process of organising a meal went two others: the stabilising of the times for eating and the introduction into the diet of new foods and improved varieties of old and familiar dishes. It appears that at one time only two meals were taken during the day, the first at some time in the morning; the second early in the evening.[135] *The Babees Book* of about 1475 advised that 'ye shalle done [dine] at none',[136] and this appears to have been the general practice in the England of William Harrison. But already some had begun to take breakfast, usually a light meal of bread or pottage. The effect of this was to push the morning meal to a later hour, and in early modern times it appears to have been taken at around one o'clock or even later. William Vaughan's *Fifteen Directions to preserve Health* of about 1602 urged its readers to 'Eate three meales a day untill you come to the age of fourtie yeares ... betweene breakefast and dinner [let] there be the space of foure houres, and betweixt dinner and supper seauen houres.'[137]

Much, however, depended on status, occupation and other circumstances. The labourer almost certainly took a midday meal of bread and 'companage'. Only amongst a leisured and wealthy class was a dinner served of more than a single course of, at most, meat and garnishing. Alice de Bryene of Acton Hall, Suffolk, reckoned to sit down to the midday meal in the company of twenty to thirty.[138] The list of food consumed in the course of a single month in Dame Alice's household

(a)

(b)

6.18 The kitchen at the Cathedral Priory of Durham, showing (a) the vast fireplaces against the outer walls; (b) an exterior view, showing that the building was largely detached; (c) a plan; 'F' indicates fireplaces. From J. H. Parker, *Some Account of Domestic Architecture in England*.

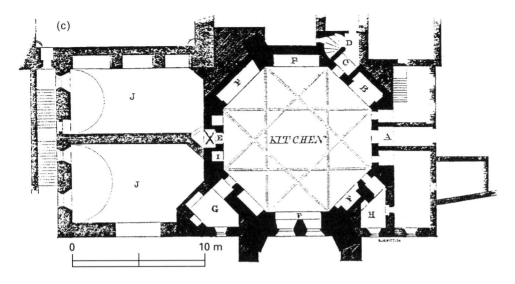

leaves no doubt that the meals consisted overwhelmingly of meat, poultry and game, and that a large part of the breadgrains consumed was in the form of ale.

The evening meal in households such as that of Alice de Bryene was similar to the midday meal, consisting mainly of meat, washed down with immense quantities of ale or wine. Amongst the labouring and yeoman classes supper was often more ambitious than the midday dinner, which had often been taken at the place of work. During the Middle Ages it often consisted mainly of gruel, thickened with cereals and flavoured with vegetables and meat or animal fat. The tendency during the sixteenth and seventeenth centuries was for the dietary standards of the gentry class to be adopted by lower social groups, with meat and poultry of increasing importance. Until the Reformation the fast days of the church seem regularly to have been observed. The household accounts of Elizabeth Berkeley, Countess of Warwick, for 1420–1 show that no meat was eaten in Lent; only bread, ale and fish.[139] The same record shows that the number of those taking breakfast was only about a quarter of those who sat down to dinner or supper, and one must presume that breakfast was a meal which one took if one really felt the need; it was not a social occasion.

By the mid-seventeenth century a system of meals and mealtimes had been evolved broadly similar to that of today, and with a comparable flexibility. The relatively long period between dinner and supper began in the late seventeenth century to be broken by a light meal which came to be known, from the beverage chiefly consumed at that time, as 'tea'. It is difficult to know whether it would have been institutionalised if there had not been a new-fangled drink in search of an appropriate occasion for its consumption. Certainly, in the United States, where tea ceased at an early date to be a popular drink, the tea-break has not become customary.

The gradual standardisation of mealtimes was accompanied by the division of meals into clearly differentiated 'courses'. This could take place only when the meal amongst the upper classes ceased to be overwhelmingly of meat, and after vegetables, fruit, pudding and cheese had begun to assume a more important role. This could not have been before the eighteenth century. The soup course, deriving from peasant diet, is one of the few instances of a food moving up-market. The 'sweet' or pudding course was made possible by the greater availability of sugar and the improved kitchens and ovens which made it possible to produce pastry, tarts and confections.

Cookery and recipe books had been known from the fifteenth century, many of them little more than household commonplace books, in which recipes were mixed up with health remedies and family details. Diana Astry's book was a collection of recipes which she had acquired from friends and acquaintances and had written out in a household book early in the eighteenth century for her own use.[140] In the course of the century such collections became more common, and showed an increasing use of vegetables, especially of newly introduced varieties like the cucumber, squash and pumpkin. They also suggest that a greater use was being made of sugar in cooking. The greater range of dishes that was required when a meal was divided into contrasting courses was the occasion for a spate of cookbooks – general, particular, specialised – which culminated in the countless editions of 'Mrs Beeton' in the nineteenth century, and has continued unabated until today.

A feature of the slow revolution in comestibles which took place in the seventeenth and eighteenth centuries was the introduction of new beverages and foodstuffs into this country. Most were expensive and were adopted first by the upper classes. Coffee, for example, 'after about two generations . . . passed from the highest classes to farmers, labourers and servants'.[141] In the early eighteenth century the 'cowcumber' and squash appeared as cultivated plants in the newly built conservatories and greenhouses of the gentry. The potato, on the other hand, entered the dietary spectrum at the lowest social level, and then only because famine conditions forced it on the attention of the poorer classes. From that humble level it has since worked itself up to the highest, though not without some assistance from plant-breeders in the course of the nineteenth century. Another item which entered into the diet of the poor in times of hardship but failed to become permanently established was buckwheat.[142] Wiegelmann has contrasted what he termed a *sinkendes Kulturgut* with an *aufsteigendes Kulturgut*, cultural traits which sank down through the social spectrum or rose from the bottom towards the top.[143] Social conventions are today shot through with such features, giving a pleasing variety and confusion to the alimentary aspects of popular culture.

The shortcomings of diet in pre-industrial Britain have already been discussed from the nutritional point of view (p. 194). It was inadequate in other respects. The methods of preserving food that have been outlined above were in many respects dangerous and standards of cleanliness in the preparation of food would be totally unacceptable today. It is impossible, amid the contorted language of clinical medicine before the later nineteenth century, to discern the symptoms of food poisoning, but they must have been present; descriptions of meals and of food preparation make that conclusion inescapable. The bacterial origin of most common complaints was not generally understood before the late nineteenth century. In earlier centuries unwashed hands and dirty vessels used in food preparation were wholly acceptable, because no one could see any harm in them. Much of the meat consumed must have been contaminated; fish sometimes took so long to travel from the coast that it must have been almost inedible, and if ergotism ceased to be general with the disappearance of rye from the diet, there were other fungoid infections of breadgrains. In times of scarcity the dangers were magnified. Harrison noted the dietary hardships to which the poor were put in times of scarcity (p. 174). It was not that the food which they ate was sometimes contaminated; it was just indigestible. Such items as the bark of trees and certain wild herbs were beyond the capacity of the stomach to deal with.

Added to bacterial contamination of food was its deliberate adulteration. Petty crime was extraordinarily crude and unsophisticated, because methods of detection were primitive. Adulteration of food was one of the commonest offences.[144] Nothing was easier or practised more frequently than adding water to beer. The assize of ale was an attempt to restrict the practice, and the frequency with which it was invoked served to show how common it was. Even bread was adulterated with lime and other substances, either inert or positively harmful. The greater availability of mineral salts in the eighteenth century led to their indiscriminate use. Copper salts were, for example, used to improve the colour of vegetables, especially when cooked.[145] Poisoning resulted from the use of copper pans in cooking foodstuffs containing an acid. Such abuses of the customer appear to have been most common in the cities, and travellers to London were often warned to beware of food sold by the costermongers who patrolled the streets. It was probably less easy to victimise people in the closed society of a village, where, in any case, the devious tricks perpetrated among the urban population would have been less familiar. Amongst the many hazards faced by traditional societies, food poisoning must be rated one of the more significant, even though its causes went unrecognised and the number of cases can never be known.

CHAPTER 7

IN SICKNESS AND IN DEATH

Times of great sickness and illnes, agues abounding more then in all my remembrance, last yeare and this also; feavers spotted rise in the contry; whether it arise from a distempered and infected aire I know not, but fruite rottes on ye trees as last yeare, though more, and many cattle die of ye murraine. Ralph Josselin's Diary, August 1647

People in pre-industrial Britain saw themselves as living always in 'the valley of the shadow of death'. Life was dominated by the prospect of death. Disease was rampant; malnutrition general, accidents frequent, and the expectation of life short.[1] Nowhere was this expressed more powerfully that in medieval iconography and illustration. And, since the only examples that most people were ever likely to see, at least before the later sixteenth century, were to be found in their local parish churches, it is to wall-paintings and stained glass that we must turn in the first instance. They all display a restricted number of motifs. Window-glass was made and the designs composed in urban workshops, but wall-paintings were spread over the rendered interior walls of churches by craftsmen who travelled from parish to parish with their limited repertoire of motifs which they repeated with little modification from one church to another.

Representations of mortality

These motifs were redolent of death. The wheel of fortune was a symbolic representation of the ages of human life, ending with death. Even more common was a depiction of the 'three living and the three dead', a morality which appears to derive from a French manuscript of the thirteenth century.[2] Three richly dressed persons meet three scantily clad skeletons (Fig. 7.1). The conversation between the two groups varied in different presentations, but consisted broadly of the three skeletons saying to the others: 'As you are we once were; as we are you will sometime be.' Related to this allegory was the 'dance of death', in reality a scene of skeletons dancing around human figures, well-dressed and prosperous, taunting them and demonstrating their ultimate fate. In the fifteenth century church art began

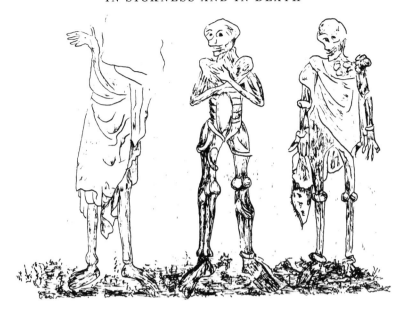

7.1 'The three living and the three dead' – a common late medieval morality. Here the three dead are seen as painted in the church of Tarrant Crawford (Dorset).

to reflect, with vivid realism, the physical aspects of death. Monumental brasses sometimes represented the deceased as a skeleton, clad only in a shroud (Fig. 7.2), and in monumental sculpture this motif was sometimes taken to horrifying extremes. The body might be seen lying on an altar tomb, armed or clad in liturgical vestments, while below might be the outstretched skeleton, maggots feeding on the remaining flesh.[3] The emblem of death, an old man with a scythe with which to cut down the living, made its appearance at this time.

The prevailing gloom was relieved by a coarse, rabelaisian humour and by the belief, even the conviction, that there would be a future life of peace, happiness and abundance if only atonement was made for the sins of this life. There was scarcely a will made in this country before the Reformation that did not lament human frailty and make provision for spiritual welfare after death. Petty sums were bequeathed for candles to be burned before the holy rood or on the altar of a particularly favoured saint. Gifts were made to those attending the obsequies of the deceased on condition that they prayed for his soul, and money was left for masses to be said on every conceivable occasion. Happiness in a future life was often purchased at a high monetary price. Money was allocated for masses by the trental – a daily mass for thirty days. A trental cost 10s. and a half trental 5s.[4] in the fifteenth century. In 1417 Richard Weyvyle of Sussex left the sum of £12 for 3000 masses 'to be celebrated for my soul in three days immediately after my death'.[5] The payment was well below the going rate, and the task of organising such a celestial bombardment might well have seemed superhuman. There were also instances of a thousand masses within ten

7.2 A shroud brass of 1499; from Aylsham parish church (Norf.).

days, and of another thousand 'within 3 or 4 days'. It is certain that towards the end of the Middle Ages a host of priests earned a precarious living by chanting masses for all who could afford the modest charge for their services. One only hopes that this effusive religiosity was judged in relation to the disposable wealth of the deceased.

Will and testament

Canon law required that every adult of sane mind should make a will.[6] Though modifications in the requirement were made by statute law, the will remained a religious instrument, and jurisdiction over it was held by the church courts. Wills were, as a general rule, made only when death seemed imminent. In will after will the testator declares himself or herself to be weak of body but still of sound mind and thus capable of apportioning the estate. The period that elapsed between the time when the will was drawn and its enrolment in the bishop's court was usually very short. In a collection of Essex wills of the fifteenth and sixteenth centuries the dates when they were both drawn and proved was in many instances given. The interval could be as little as 31 days, and the average was 53. Since the deceased was still alive at the former date, and probate was granted some days after death, the testator must have died soon after making the will.[7] The fact was that for most people any acute illness was likely to result in death, and was seen as a signal to make a will. People were not expected to recover, and if they did it was regarded as a miracle resulting from divine intervention.

222

A distinction was at first drawn between the *testament*, which devised the goods and chattels of the deceased, and the *will*, which related to real estate over which someone else — the lord of the manor or even the king — might have some jurisdiction and control.[8] Will and testament were not effectively merged until the sixteenth century, and a will devising land was not required to be in writing until the 1540s.[9] People remained free to make verbal dispositions of their chattels until 1837.[10] In a prevailingly pre-literate society the making of a will was a fearsome task, calling for the services of someone who could write from dictation. In towns there were professional scriveners, who could be summoned with their ink-bottles, pens and sheets of parchment. In rural areas there were often literate members of the community, capable of performing the task adequately, if not professionally. These would range from 'the lord or lessee of the manor, to the vicar, curate, church clerk or churchwarden, to the schoolmaster', or to anyone else who could claim some modest level of literacy.[11] If necessary, a notary was called in to inscribe a will which was later distinguishable by its superior calligraphy. Indeed, one can detect in collections of wills small groups, identifiable by their style of penmanship, as the work of individual but anonymous scribes. By the end of the seventeenth century the lawyers had, at least in the towns, 'effectively captured the business of making wills'.[12] thereafter 'the cold hand of the lawyer or notary' shows itself in their style and presentation, never to be relinquished until the present.

To what extent, it may be asked, did the will express the real motives and desires of the testator, or to what extent did it conform with current style? The opening religious invocation was, as a general rule, common form, but were the internal clauses influenced by the preconceived ideas, even by the greed, of the man who noted them down? That we shall never know, for it is certain that most of those who expressed their wishes to a scrivener were incapable of reading the final document and of judging whether it fully represented their desires.

Reservations which one might have regarding formal wills were all the more applicable to the oral or nuncupative will. It was spoken by the testator in the presence of witnesses who subsequently recollected and recorded what they thought they had heard. The nuncupative will was commonly expressed in the third person, and was authenticated by the signatures or marks of witnesses.[13] One must visualise a deathbed scene, with witnesses and potential beneficiaries urging the dying person to make this or that allocation of goods and perhaps reading what they wished into the incoherent speech of the dying. A nuncupative will of 1635 has at its end the words: 'The said testatrix suddenly failed of sence speech and life before shee coulde subscribe her hand hereunto.'[14] It is not surprising that a will had to be proved and its authenticity and reliability established before an ecclesiastical court.[15]

The normal procedure was for the executors named in the will to appear as soon as possible before the bishop's commissary or registrar, together with the will and an inventory of the deceased's chattels. If it was not disputed, and it rarely was, the will was then copied into a volume held at the registry. It is this copy that is most often used, the original will having been lost. But practice tended to vary between

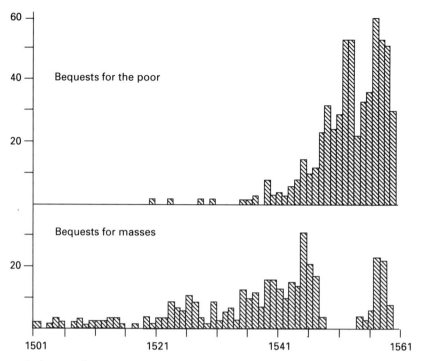

7.3 Graph showing the number and date of bequests for (a) the poor, and (b) masses. Based on *Transcripts of Sussex Wills*, vol. 1, Suss Rec Soc, 41, 1935.

dioceses. In some – Exeter for instance – the original will, together with the probate inventory, was held in the ecclesiastical court. The executors were then empowered, on payment of certain fees, to dispose of the estate of the deceased in accordance with the terms of the will (Fig. 7.3). There was still room for dispute, however, and cases arising from the interpretation of wills were heard in the same court, the consistory or archdeacon's, which also heard cases of bigamy, incest, paternity and all other breaches of the canon law.[16] For this reason the court earned the popular name of the 'bawdy court'.[17] The jurisdiction of the consistory extended, however, only to chattels, while matters related to land and feudal obligations were referred to the royal or honorial courts. In practice, however, with the decay of feudal modes of land tenure and the merging of 'will' and 'testament', cases involving land came increasingly to be handled by the ecclesiastical courts. In 1858 all probate jurisdiction was transferred by statute to the High Court of Justice.[18]

In chapter 5 considerable use was made of probate inventories, drawn up by two 'honest and skilfull persons' immediately after the death of the testator. The preparation of an inventory was not obligatory until after 1529, but was, nonetheless, sometimes made before that date.[19] Inventories were not enrolled in the bishop's register, and have, by and large, survived only when they were retained along with the original wills by the consistory court. On rare occasions the wills themselves were so detailed that they almost amounted to inventories. Usually, however, the testator, at least before the mid-sixteenth century, merely made provision for his or her spiritual welfare and left specific articles to named individuals. These were sometimes items of sentimental value – rings, silver spoons, the 'bed whereon I lie'. The residue was often to be sold and the money either given to the next of kin or allocated to specific purposes. Wills alone are an uncertain guide to the contents of a house or the possessions of its owner, but they offer deep insights into familial and social conditions and into the 'world-view' of the deceased. They demonstrate the feuds and antipathies within the family; feelings towards the church and community; care for dependants, and an intense desire that life should continue afterwards, unchanged or as little changed as possible.[20] A piece of furniture is to remain, unmoved, in perpetuity; a handmill is to 'be as an hayr lume [heirloom] perteynyng to the … mansion'.[21] One testator required that family portraits should *for ever* stand in the hall. The kindly regard for dependants was matched by the realisation that relatives do not always get along well with one another. The degrees of affection shown by parents to their children are shown in a will which left the household chattels to be 'devyded equally betwyxte my wyff and all my chylder, so that John my sonne have the worst part, and my wyff have the fether bed that we ii do ly in'.[22] All children evidently are equal, but some are less equal than others.

Early wills are dominated by an almost morbid fear of what will happen after death. Sums of money, sometimes very large in relation to the total estate, were left to buy wax for candles, to gild or decorate a pious statue, to make some repair to the parish church, or even to add a new porch or rebuild a tower, and, above all, to pay for masses for the soul of the departed. The cult of the mass was basically a late medieval development. The Fourth Lateran Council of 1215 affirmed the doctrine of transubstantiation, and later in the century the feast of Corpus Christi was initiated. The effect of these developments was to encourage the mass as the most powerful means of supplication and atonement. There was a change in Britain during the period of the Henrician Reformation. Provision for masses and candles gradually diminished, but care for the fabric of the church continued to be much in evidence. In general, however, acts of charity tended to replace the spiritual exercises of the pre-Reformation era. But there remained in many wills a backward glance towards the time when masses and good works held the key to the kingdom of heaven. The trend to Protestantism was interrupted under Mary (1552–8), and was then resumed at its peculiarly slow and deliberate pace under Elizabeth I.

Death and burial

The funeral came quickly after death. The corpse, wrapped in a shroud, was carried to the churchyard on a bier, such as many churches possessed for communal use (Fig. 7.4). The shroud might be of any fabric, until in 1666 Parliament ordained that it had to be of woollen cloth in order to support the domestic woollen industry.

7.4 A bier carried by apes: a satirical misericord.

Many a parish register is today accompanied by a book of certificates that the law had in this respect been complied with. This law was not repealed until 1814, but it was unpopular and seems to have been consistently flouted towards the end. Although there is sound archaeological evidence for the use of coffins throughout the Anglo-Saxon and medieval periods, they were only for the rich. Most people were buried in their shrouds. Coffins of lead or stone were used, but their cost was high, and their use limited. Wooden coffins came into use very much later. The funeral was, whenever possible, followed by some form of ritual eating, and some wills even made monetary provision for the distribution of food after interment. In this, as in many other respects, medieval Christian practice followed the example of pagan Rome. Even the rites to secure for the deceased 'comfort, refreshment and perennial renewal of life to their immortal spirits'[23] were comparable. Burial might be either within the church or in the churchyard. The former was in general only for the privileged, and usually called for a substantial fee to the church. It has been customary since prehistoric times to mark the places of burial of at least the more important members of society with a cairn, standing stone or other form of memorial. Romano-British memorials were in general less monumental but more informative, consisting often of a *stela* or inscribed and sculptured tablet. Some contained a statue of the deceased or even, in low relief, a domestic or business scene in which he had participated in life. In extreme cases a sarcophagus or a masonry-built monument might be erected, such as can be seen today in the tombs along the Appian Way to the south-east of Rome.

226

7.5 Churchyard cross, which served to sanctify the collective graves of those buried there. Only a fragment of the shaft survives. From Tong parish church (Shrops.).

Both Roman and Anglo-Saxon burials were mainly in cemeteries. Individual graves were generally unmarked, but the cemetery itself, at least after the coming of Christianity, might be dominated by a standing cross, many of which have survived. In the north and west of Britain they commonly assume the form of square arms within a circle, the whole supported by a shaft, often highly decorated with interlace, spirals and other motifs. Such cross designs, emasculated and executed in marble of uncertain origin, have during the last century again made their appearance in our cemeteries. In northern Britain crosses attained great size and artistic distinction; in the south-west they remained stunted and crude by comparison, perhaps because they were executed in the less tractable granite (Fig. 7.5).

Other forms of cemetery monument developed. During the eighteenth century the cemetery cross was replaced first by individual headboards and then by headstones. In some parts of Britain the 'house-tomb' or 'coped-stone' appeared in the eighteenth century, perhaps a symbolic representation of the new home of the deceased. Outdoor monuments were rare before the seventeenth century, but thereafter they became increasingly common. Elegant tombs and headstones of the eighteenth century survive in their tens of thousands, their decorative detail eroded by centuries of British weather and their inscriptions half obliterated (Fig. 7.6). From the eleventh century or even earlier the patrons and benefactors of churches began to be buried within their walls. Indeed, many of the great churches of the period were designed to be the repositories of the bones of their benefactors. Almost from the first the place of burial was marked by a stone let into the floor of the

7.6 The eighteenth-century grave-markers in the churchyard of Upwell (Norf.).

church, sometimes with an inscription recording the name of the deceased, sometimes with the outline of a human figure. In the twelfth century the figure began to be sculptured in a recumbent position. But inscribed slabs and outlines continued to be used, and in the monumental 'brass', with the figure engraved in a sheet of copper alloy known as 'latten', became a common type of monument from the late thirteenth century, socially somewhere between the sculptured effigy and the simple slab.[25]

The next step was to raise the figure above the floor level and place it on a so-called altar tomb.[26] The final stage was to enclose the tomb with a parclose screen, to raise a canopy above it, and to construct a private altar beside it at which masses could be said for the soul of the deceased. The building and endowment of such extravagant chantries ended with the Reformation, but the creation of family tombs, even grander and more flamboyant, continued through the seventeenth and eighteenth centuries. The earlier church monuments were placed as nearly as possible above the grave of the deceased. Post-Reformation memorials tended increasingly to be placed on the wall of the church rather than on the floors.[27] The reason is simple. The disappearance of the wall-paintings of the Middle Ages made room for them at the same time as the construction of wooden pews increasingly obstructed the floor space.

But indoor burials and monuments were for the élite whose ancestors were conceived as having built and endowed the churches. The lord of the manor, even if his family had alienated its rights of patronage, nevertheless retained certain

228

privileges which included that of burial within its walls. The ground beneath the floor of a church sometimes became as thickly populated as the cemetery around it. Burial within a church was, at the parochial level, controlled by a system of fees. The fee for breaking up the floor of the church and for burial beneath it was of the order of 10s. in the seventeenth century, while that for opening a grave in the churchyard was only about 1s.

Most people were buried in the cemetery, and an inscription on a tombstone at Kingsbridge (Devon) witnesses to the sense of deprivation and also of resignation which must have been felt by some of those who had been denied burial within the church:

> Here lie I by the chancel door,
> Here lie I because I'm poor.
> The further in, the more you'll pay,
> Here lie I, as warm as they.[28]

Wills not infrequently specified the desired place of burial, whether within or without the church. One asked to be buried near where 'I used to sit'. About 1530 Thomas Rawsby of Harnston (Lincs.) expressed in his will the desire 'to be buried in the "isle" [insula] of the parish church of Harnston, on the north side, if it can be done for 3s. 4d, otherwise in the churchyard'.[29] More than a century later Thomas Broke of Thorncombe (Som.) asked to be laid 'in the churchehey [-yard] of the parysch churche . . . as men goth over into ye churche at ye south syde ryghte as they mowe [may] stappe [step] on me and a flat playne stone save my name ygraved yarin that men mowe the rather have mynde on me and pray for me'.[30] John Portman of Taunton in 1521 requested burial 'nigh the pulpit', as if wanting to listen to sermons for all eternity.[31] Others called for burial close to the altar, as if that conferred some kind of grace on the deceased. Even for the great majority who were interred in the churchyard the place of burial still held some importance. The area north of the church tended to be avoided, perhaps because it lay in the shadow of the church and was associated with the dark, cold spirits that come from the north. But burial on the north side had its compensations. A tombstone at Epworth (Lincs.) records:

> . . . that I might longer undisturb'd abide,
> I choos'd to be laid on this northern side.[32]

The graveyard had only a restricted area, and had in many instances been in use from the twelfth century or even earlier, and could have seen the burial of thousands of corpses.[33] Graves were relatively shallow before modern times, and were usually unmarked except for the low mound of earth which resulted from the disturbance of the soil, and quickly subsided. The digging of one grave necessarily cut into previous burials, often revealing bones, though not everyone could identify a skeleton with the facility displayed by Hamlet. The diary of a Yorkshireman, one Arthur Jessup (1729–42) recorded that the churchyard of Kirkburton (W. Riding, Yorks.) 'is so full thronged with graves that the Sexton hath often publicly declared he scarcely knew where to put down his spade'.[34] At Lostwithiel (Corn.) a rough plan of the churchyard was made in the late eighteenth century with the positions marked on it of those burials that could be remembered. Successive burials raised the level of the soil, so that a cemetery may today stand a foot or two above what may be termed the natural ground level.

Churchyard graves were, as a general rule, unmarked before the eighteenth century, though a few headstones survive from the medieval period. A Lincolnshire will of 1532–4 records the desire for a stone memorial, though in this instance there appears to have been an element of local rivalry. Thomas Peper of Spilsby asked 'to be buried in the church yerd ... I wyll have a free stone to lay upon me whan I am buryed, lyk Robert Godrykes.'[35] The use of headstones began to spread late in the seventeenth century, and became general in the eighteenth amongst all families that could afford their not inconsiderable cost. Amongst the earliest were headboards, recording the name of the deceased. Most of these have now rotted and disappeared, and have been superseded by headstones and stone slabs.[36] During the eighteenth century headstones achieved a high degree of artistic refinement. In some churchyards, notably Painswick (Glos.) and Upwell (Norf.) large assemblages of such monuments have survived, though everywhere time has dealt harshly with their sculptured detail. In some cemeteries headstones of this period often show a degree of similarity in style that suggests that there was a local craftsman who was expert in producing them. In the nineteenth century the vogue for churchyard monuments intensified as the level of taste displayed in them deteriorated. The ugly sculpture, crude lettering and banal sentimentality expressed show how quality was sacrificed in order to satisfy an expanding mass market.[37]

All outdoor monuments and not a few within the shelter of churches are subject to continuous weathering and erosion. They are not only part of this country's heritage, but also a not unimportant source for local and family history. It is clearly impractical to give to them the care and attention that they deserve, but they should at the very least be photographed and recorded. The current practice of rearranging them around the boundary fence of the churchyard is to be deplored.

There was, as countless wills demonstrate, a powerful demand for a 'good funeral'. The number of men handling the bier and of mourners following it became a kind of posthumous status symbol, immune to all theological objection. In the eighteenth century the emphasis tended to pass from the ceremony itself to the church or churchyard momument, which became increasingly elaborate. Burial was not a sacrament of the church; sacraments were administered only to the living, and in the medieval church the last to be received was extreme unction. The body was borne to the church on the shoulders of the mourners, but sometimes on a wheeled bier, with a pause at the 'lyche' gate where it was met by the priest.[38] The committal was preceded by the *dirige Domine Deus meus*, commonly known as the 'dirge', and was accompanied by prayers,[39] and was usually followed immediately by a requiem mass celebrated within the church, and, of course, by whatever sequence of trentals and obits the deceased might have provided for.

7.7 Phlebotomy, or blood-letting, as illustrated in the Luttrell Psalter, fo. 61.

The practice of medicine

Most people died following a fairly short illness. Any sickness was likely to be fatal and to prompt the hurried dictation of a will. Traditional societies lacked a knowledge both of the physiological basis of life and also of the pathogenic origin of disease. Sickness was something that happened. Of course, it had a cause, but this they sought in the malevolence of spirits, in the wrath of God or in the balance of humours within the human body.[40] To the mass of the people magic provided the principal means of averting or of curing illnesses. To the more sophisticated, who could comprehend the elaborate medical system which derived from Galen, the remedy lay in devices like bleeding and vomits, which were held to adjust the balance of the humours (Fig. 7.7). For most people magic was both more accessible and very much cheaper.

Not until late in the eighteenth century was it generally thought that environmental conditions could have any influence on the incidence of disease.[41] In the 1830s the views of Edwin Chadwick (p. 371), that disease was in some way linked with filth and squalor, began to be accepted. But, even so, it was supposed that it was spread by exhalations or miasma arising from the earth, in short 'malaria'. It was not until the last quarter of the nineteenth century, the age of Pasteur and Lister, and beyond the time-scale of this book, that the microbial origin of disease began to be entertained by the more advanced thinkers. Amongst the masses belief in miasma and magic continued even longer.

It is a commonplace of social history that in traditional societies the death-rate was high and expectation of life short. A quarter of those born may have died within a year, and little more than half would have reached sexual maturity and contributed to the next generation. The 'net reproduction rate' hovered around unity. People did not need the biblical injunction to 'be fruitful and multiply'. It was apparent to all that it took many births to ensure that parents had heirs to inherit their land and to care for them in their old age. Data on birth-rates, mortality and longevity have in recent years been gaining in volume and precision. They are derived, by and large, from an analysis of the registers of baptisms and burials that were in 1538 ordered to be kept in every parish of the land.[42] Records had occasionally been kept before this date, but this was the first occasion when this became a general requirement. There was a degree of resistance and the instruction had to be repeated before the end of the century. Early recording was unsystematic; documents have been lost, and in some parishes registration was not even begun for many years after Thomas Cromwell's original ordinance. Near the end of her reign Elizabeth ordered the record to be kept in a parchment book, and this is why we find in many parishes that registers from previous decades have been transcribed by a professional scrivener in a clear and legible hand. In the Commonwealth period registration was spasmodic and was in some parishes interrupted, and even later insufficient care was sometimes taken to ensure that the registers were a full and accurate record of baptisms, marriages and burials in each parish.[43] Nevertheless, there are no other records as full and as comprehensive as the parish registers from which to compile a history of the population of this country.

A simple 'aggregate analysis' can be made to yield a comprehensive picture of changes in natality and mortality (Fig. 7.8). Since these are, along with migration, the only parameters of population change, the aggregate population of this country can be projected back to the time when registers were first kept.[44] But the registers can be made to yield more than aggregate statistics. In a society which was less mobile than that of today the registers allow us to establish the size of a family that resulted from a marriage, to find out how many children survived to adulthood, and the time that elapsed between successive births. We can determine the average age at death and the frequency with which widows and widowers remarried. The family can, in fact, be reconstituted, and the structure of society analysed. The statistical framework derived from registers can be filled out by using wills, diaries, conveyances and letters, as well as from public documents such as records of hearth, poll and other taxes. Taken together, these sources provide a window into the social life and popular culture of the people of Britain from the later years of the sixteenth century onwards.[45]

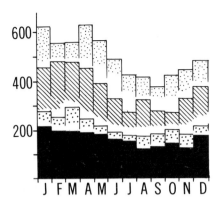

7.8 Histogram showing seasonal variations in morality in four Cornish parishes. Aggregate figures for each month were used for the period 1600 to 1800. The record shows a consistently high mortality in winter and early spring, and a low morality in late summer. Based on the parish registers of the parishes.

The primary concern of this chapter is with mortality, morbidity and popular attitudes to death and illness. The premonition of death was usually strong, and wills were most often made on the deathbed, as is demonstrated by a comparison of their dates and those when they were presented to the bishop's commissary for registration (pp. 222–4). The nature of disease was unknown before the later years of the nineteenth century. Such medical knowledge as there was derived from the writings of Galen and Hippocrates. Health was thought to depend on the balance of the humours, and it was the function of the medical practitioner to ascertain in what ways this balance had been disturbed and so to correct it. A medical terminology grew up which bore no relationship to the modern anatomical and etiological concept of disease. It was devleoped to define the symptoms, and cannot be translated into the clinical language of today. It is, indeed, almost impossible to translate into current medical terminology the terms used before the nineteenth century. A complaint diagnosed as 'malignant bilious petechial putrid fever' has no meaning in current medical terminology. It belongs to an entirely different system of thought.[46]

A few diseases, however, were instantly recognisable, and were given names which have since remained in popular use: plague, smallpox, together with the 'greater' pox, and perhaps pleurisy, mumps, measles and 'scarlatina' or scarlet fever. It is very doubtful whether doctors ever achieved anything beneficial by their blood-letting, purgatives, vomits and clysters, and in many instances they must have made the patient worse. It is perhaps fortunate that their fees were high and that few could afford their services:

> For gold in phisik is a cordial,
> Therefore he lovede gold in special.[47]

Medicine was practised in pre-scientific times by a hierarchy of practitioners, from among whom the professions of physician, surgeon and apothecary eventually crystallised. The nature of Anglo-Saxon medicine is revealed in surviving leechbooks and charms.[48] They derived from many sources. Some came straight from Galen's writings on anatomy and physiology and from the herbals (*Materia Medica*) of Dioscorides (first century AD). Others owed their origin to Germanic folklore, now best preserved in the Icelandic Sagas and Eddas, and to a surviving substratum of Celtic lore. The contribution of Christianity was slight: the substitution of saints' names for those of pagan gods and spirits, and occasionally the addition of a doxology at the end of a charm.[49] It is not clear who practised this particular form of magic, but whoever it was he was presumably literate, and perhaps also literate in Latin, and this suggests someone of the priestly class. It was certainly within the church that the leechbooks, or lists of prescriptions and charms, were written down. In the contemporary view, medicine, like religion, was a form of magic, and no attempt was made in logic to distinguish between them. Belief in spirits was universal. Sickness was due to an evil spirit, which had to be exorcised. The process of curing consisted in the first place in the use of certain substances: herbs, wine, salves, which may in some instances have had a medicinal value, and secondly in the appropriate rituals, which had none. Herbs had to be gathered during specific phases of the moon; they had to be taken from particular places, and prepared in prescribed ways. There were magic numbers and certain words had particular significance. Some had the ingenuity of a modern acrostic. The word *sator*, meaning 'father' or 'creator'[50] was thought to be particularly efficacious in childbirth if used as a charm:

```
S  A  T  O  R
A  R  E  P  O
T  E  N  E  T
O  P  E  R  A
R  O  T  A  S
```

Its miraculous power was held to lie not only in the fact that the words could be read in every direction, but that the letters themselves made up:

in which the A and O (alpha and omega) represented God.[51] A cure as sophisticated as this could have been manipulated only by a person of some education, and it disappeared from the popular practice of medicine.[52] On the other hand, the latter retained words and phrases that had become totally meaningless, such as those used by the quack and the conjurer today.

After the Anglo-Saxon period popular medicine diverged from the academic pursuit as taught and practised in the universities and larger monasteries.[53] The medieval physician in the latter sense based his practice on the writings of Galen, who maintained that health was dependent on a correct balance between the 'humours', which, if disturbed, could be restored only by bloodletting or venesection. This was part of a complicated system which took account not only of the seasons of the year but also of the veins appropriate to each complaint. Such cures were supplemented with herbal remedies, which may in themselves have done little harm, and also, from the time of Paracelsus (c.1490–1541), with mineral substances, some of which were a great deal more dangerous. Physicians also made use of 'cures' which must be classed as magical, though they would have recognised no logical difference between magical, herbal and narrowly medical remedies.

This type of medicine continued with little change except of emphasis into the eighteenth and even the nineteenth century. The simple, if erroneous, assumptions of Galen became enveloped in a verbal fog which may have served to disguise the ignorance of doctors but must certainly have left their patients utterly bewildered. Doctors rarely made house-calls, and were visited by their patients only infrequently. Instead they diagnosed and prescribed by letter, and some of their surviving correspondence gives an insight into their interpretation of the body's humours:

The crick of your neck, the pain of your toe, the swelling of your knees and the trembling of your joints which you call the palsy are all from one and the same cause. The hotter temperature of your liver is not only the fountain of the hot and sharp humour of choler surcharging the mass of blood from whence comes that preternatural heat which you feel, but also the serious watery humour (which dilutes the mass of the blood and by his tenuity makes it apt to be carried from place to place) is unnaturally salt and sharp which, being an excrementitial part of the mass, is from the same separated and voided by urine, by sweat, or insensible transpiration.[54]

So careful a diagnosis no doubt deserved a large fee, even though it was delivered by letter. The mass of the population could no more afford the fee than understand the mumbo-jumbo which earned it. Popular medicine was simpler, cheaper and no less ineffective than that dispensed by the physician to his well-to-do clientele. It derived from the charms and cures of the leechdoms, supplemented and distorted by folk remedies of every kind.

Many of these cures were based upon a degree of empirical knowledge and may not have been wholly useless. The author once discussed folk medicine with a very elderly American, who claimed that his father, a farmer in southern Indiana, always kept in the barn a pan of jelly on which a mould had been allowed to grow. This was always applied to any wound sustained by a farm animal, with, it was claimed, complete success. This must have been at least half a century before penicillin is generally held to have been discovered. Many a commonplace book of the seventeenth or eighteenth century contains folk remedies for various disorders. As a general rule they involved the use of herbs and mineral substances. The former may occasionally have been efficacious but were generally neutral, but the use of minerals could be very dangerous indeed. William Carnsew, a late sixteenth-century Cornish squire, was deeply interested in medicine, as were many of his contemporaries. His diary shows him reading widely in the medical literature, all of it in the Hippocratic tradition.[56] But he was willing to blend 'scientific' with folk medicines. He would prepare a potion for his friends whenever they seemed to be unwell, and even mixed a concoction to cure his son's toothache. But his favourite cure was a mineral substance which he called 'styby'. It was almost certainly stibnite (antimony trisulphide).[57] On one occasion he gave the substance to a neighbour, noting in his diary that 'she was nott myche molestyd but [it] wroughte soo as she hadd 3 vomyttis, on[e] stoole and Ame[n]dyd'. He was fortunate on this occasion. At a different time he clearly overreached himself. He gave a similar potion to the vicar. Three days later the vicar was 'extremly sycke', and five days later he was dead. But Carnsew would never have admitted that his own concoctions had contributed in any way to his death. Medical interests were uppermost in his mind. He watched 'hym openyd' and diagnosed his sickness as 'a putrefaction of hys Longis'.

How many people suffered thus from the well-meaning but completely uninformed manipulation of herbs and minerals no one will ever know. In many instances they must have hastened a death that was inevitable; in others they doubtless killed those who were scarcely ill at all. The volume of quack medicines consumed must have been immense. Almost everyone was sick for much of the time. The diary kept by Ralph Josselin, vicar of Earl's Colne (Essex) between 1616 and 1683 is a dreary catalogue of the illnesses of himself and his family.[58] His daughter contracted an indeterminate ailment: 'wee apprehend it was the spleene, wee applied an oyntment to it, a plaister of halfe an ounce of oyntment of melilot [a variety of clover] for the spleene, and also 3 spoonefuls of juyce of red fennell clarified with 6 spoonfulls of beare and swetned.' The medication in this instance was probably entirely neutral. Josselin was himself sick for much of the time with 'rheums', stomach disorders and what appears to have been an ulcerated navel.[59]

Another diary, this time specifically medical, was kept by John Huxham, a Plymouth doctor, during the first half of the eighteenth century.[60] He had clear views on the etiology of disease, but little knowledge of how to cure it. They all derived from the weather, he supposed, and his diary is compounded of those two essentially British topics of conversation, one's health and the weather. His medical terminology cannot easily be rendered into English, though on other evidence one might guess that 'peripneumonies' was bronchitis and the 'ulcerous sore throat' diphtheria. But even he could at times find no name for a complaint, diagnosing it merely as 'great lowness of spirit'.[61]

Four hundred years earlier the situation was little different; why, indeed, should one expect it to be, when medical knowledge derived from the same body of ancient lore? There was a rich variety of medical terms, none of them having any precise or clinical meaning. *The Vision of Piers Plowman* visualised a stream of complaints that 'cam out of the planetes':

feveres and fluxes,

Coughes and cardiacles;   cramps and toothaches

Rewmes and radegundes   and roynouse scalles,

Biles and bocches   and brennynge agues,

Frenesies and foule yveles   forages of Kynde

Hadde ypriked and prayed   polles of peple

Largeliche a legion   less hir lif soone.[62]

Beside the élite or official medicine of the doctors, trained and authorised to prescribe and administer cures, and the grey area of the folk medicine of herbals and minerals, there was a third medicine. It was a popular medicine to which even the élite sometimes resorted when their own cures proved ineffective.[63] It was the medicine of magic; its practitioners were witches and 'cunning men', and its instruments were charms and spells. It probably held a wider appeal than either of the other forms of medical practice.[64] Its lack of any logical or scientific foundation was its recommendation, for opinions arrived at illogically cannot be refuted by logic. Yet magic is difficult to define. 'When Sir Christopher Hatton sent Queen Elizabeth a ring to protect her against the plague or when Elias Ashmole wore three spiders to counteract the ague, they were not resorting, strictly speaking, to magic, but employing a purely physical form of treatment.' It derived, as Keith Thomas has emphasised, from a Neoplatonist view of 'correspondences and analogies' between different parts of creation.[65]

Superficially regarded, such precautions may have differed little from the belief held by some today that the wearing of copper has some protective power. Robert Burton, the anatomist, admitted that 'the toothache, gout, falling sicknesses, biting of a mad dog and many such maladies [were] cured by spells, words, characters and charms'.[66] Such medicine had much to recommend it to simple people. They could see no rationale in the adversities which overwhelmed them. The causes of illnesses were hidden. Sickness was a 'happening', without visible cause or apparent reason. It might therefore be terminated by spell, incantation or ritual superficially quite unrelated to it. At this time the intellectual gulf between the narrow élite, which distrusted charms and incantations and wrestled with the medical system bequeathed by Galen, and the masses who accepted the validity of magic was widening. Thomas Hobbes (1588–1679) wrote a generation later than Burton and showed himself a true sceptic: 'As for witches, I think not that their witchcraft is any real power,' adding that they were, nevertheless, justly punished, not for the harm they did, but for their 'false belief they have that they can do such mischief'.[67]

The services of the witch or 'cunning man' were, unlike those of the doctor, relatively cheap. Occasionally they were performed as a 'service' or at most for a little food. Witches and wizards were local people, as the doctor, all too frequently, was not. And the use of spells and incantations, furthermore, was a welcome alternative both to painful surgery and to the purges and phlebotomy which were then only a degree less unpleasant.

Morbidity and mortality

What, then, were the causes, in so far as we can reconstruct them, of illness and death, and what were the changes in the parameters that led to the 'vital revolution' and the sharp increase in population that took place in the late eighteenth and the nineteenth centuries? One may look for two sets of factors, the one environmental, the other epidemiological. The two, of course, were never wholly distinct, and there can be no question but that improvements in physical conditions of life were attended by a decline in epidemic disease and an increase in longevity.

Underlying all patterns of death were those perennial causes: cancer, heart disease, pulmonary infection, and senility in all its forms. The fact that they have become statistically more important in modern times serves only to emphasise the fact that other causes of death have become less so. The high mortality that occurred during every outbreak of, for example, plague cannot be wholly attributed to the epidemic itself. A fraction of the deaths would have occurred in any event from unrelated causes. Nevertheless, epidemic disease was a frequent but irregular occurrence, and was the chief cause of the extraordinary peaks – crises de mortalité – which occur in burial records. There were in addition those complaints which tended to occur seasonally, but cannot be termed epidemic. Bronchitis and other pulmonary complaints were always most serious in winter and early spring, as, indeed, they remain today. During the heat of summer, when sanitary conditions were often at their worst, bacteria multiplied more rapidly and the risk of infection was greater, especially amongst the young. In winter, crowded domestic conditions favoured the spread of typhus. In none of these instances, however, is it possible to envisage an epidemic sweeping across the country, if only because the source was local and people did not, in general, carry the infection with them as they travelled.

The spread of disease is dependent on vectors or agents, most often insect- or water-borne, which carry and spread the pathogen. The bubonic plague was disseminated by the black rat (Rattus rattus) and the flea (Xenopsylla cheopis) which carried the infection from the rat, the essential vector, to the human host and from one infected human being to another and also back again to the black rat, in whose bloodstream it incubated.[68] The cholera pathogen multiplies in the human body and is excreted with the faeces. It can be passed from one human being to another only by drinking water or consuming food that has become contaminated by it.[69] Typhus is carried by the bodylouse, but smallpox has only a human vector, and is passed on the breath from one person to another. It can thus be isolated by strict quarantine, and has, in fact, been eliminated during the later years of the present century.[70]

In all complaints, with the possible exception of those directly related to ageing, environmental factors must have played a significant if not dominant role. These can

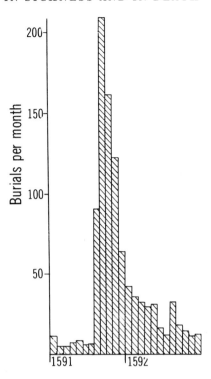

7.9 Histogram showing plague mortality in Exeter, 1591–2. Based on Ransom Pickard, *The Population and Epidemics of Exeter*, Exeter, 1947.

be summarised as (1) climate and deviations from the climatic norm, (2) diet and nutrition, (3) the quality of housing, together with the adequacy of clothing and heating, and (4) hygiene and sanitation. Climate and the vagaries of the weather clearly had a direct influence on physical welfare, as is demonstrated by the increased morbidity and mortality in late winter and early spring. 'Cold weather', wrote Wrigley and Schofield, 'may be killing the older population through pneumonia, bronchitis, influenza and other respiratory tract diseases, which are rapidly lethal. In summer hot weather may be killing infants and young children through digestive tract diseases, which are debilitating, but take longer to kill.'[71] In London adult mortality was greatest in winter, while that of children showed a less pronounced peak in late summer. Late summer was also the season when bubonic plague was most likely to occur, since it was then that its vectors were most active (Fig. 7.9). But the effects of climate are, in the main, mediated through agriculture and crop returns. Harvest fluctuations are attributable *mainly* to climatic irregularities.[72] Only a small fluctuation made the difference between dearth and abundance. There was little food in hand to cushion the effect of a bad harvest, and by the following spring its effects were being shown in varying levels of undernourishment or starvation. There is no general measure of the productivity of crops before the late nineteenth century, and one is obliged to use the price of grain as a surrogate.[73] A high price meant scarcity, and the higher the price rose, the more the breadgrains passed beyond the reach of the poorer members of society. In extreme cases, this could lead to a *crise de subsistence* and this in turn to a *crise de mortalité*.

An adequate human diet must contain a certain level of calories and protein, as well as particular vitamins and trace elements. The calorific content of traditional diets was always high, and under conditions of dearth it was the level of protein consumption that was the first to fall below an acceptable level. Starvation takes many forms. Protein deficiency gives rise to diseases such as kwashiorkor, pellagra and beriberi, which have not normally occurred on any significant scale in Britain. Lack of certain vitamins may affect vision, the production of blood and the formation of the bony structure of the body (rickets). Outward symptoms of acute starvation include loss of weight and of hair and teeth, the absorption of muscle, a bloated stomach (oedema), a general sense of weakness and, in its terminal phases, the 'bloody flux' or bleeding diarrhoea.[74] It has also been found that there is a well-marked inverse correlation between the price of grain and the number of conceptions.[75] There is little doubt but that famine conditions inhibit ovulation,[76] and that the birth-rate can be expected to drop after any subsistence crisis.

The increase in population that began in the middle years of the eighteenth century – the 'vital revolution' as it has been called – has been ascribed to a number of radically different factors.[77] It has been attributed to an improvement in diet, to better hygiene and public health, to the elimination of diseases like the plague and to the containment of others like smallpox. All these factors played their part, and no convincing case has yet been made out for the overwhelming importance of any one of them. Nevertheless, the significance of malnutrition in limiting population growth has had powerful advocates.[78] Famine-induced amenorrhoea was without question a harsh reality, but the question of whether prolonged malnutrition, as distinct from short-lived famine, was a major factor in the death-rate must remain not proven. That it contributed to morbidity, loss of energy and of resistance to disease can hardly be doubted, but it has been shown for London that there is no significant correlation between bread prices, a surrogate for lack of food, and outbreaks of the major identifiable diseases.[79] Typhus, in particular, has been associated with famine, but it was in fact a disease of squalid and crowded conditions, in which its vector, the body louse, could thrive and multiply.[80] It seems that only in extreme conditions of malnutrition, amounting to famine, was the capacity of a population to reproduce itself significantly curtailed.[81]

To what extend, then, was the population growth of modern times induced by the elimination or significant reduction of certain epidemic diseases? A case has been made for the conquest of the bubonic plague. It had been endemic in these islands from 1349 to the later years of the seventeenth century, erupting at intervals into fierce and devastating outbreaks. Mortality from the plague had been very severe, but the last major outbreak in this country was in 1665, and the last in western Europe in Provence in 1720. It remained endemic in the Balkans into the nineteenth century,[82] and is still present in parts of the Far East. The elimination of the plague had removed a major constraint on population growth, but it was not until long after the last victim had died in Britain that the population began to increase significantly. A stronger case has been made for smallpox as a major constraint on growth.[83] This disease became common in the seventeenth and eighteenth centuries, and accounted for a significant proportion of deaths. Furthermore, it severely disfigured those who had contracted it and survived. Lady Mary Wortley Montague, in a famous letter from Turkey in 1717, advocated *inoculation*, as practised in the Ottoman Empire, as a means of acquiring immunity.[84] This method of protection became very popular. It was cheap and easy, and the overseers of the poor sometimes paid a doctor to inoculate all who lived in the local poorhouse. But it was an uncertain remedy, and the consequence was not always a mild and innocuous form of the disease. An entry in the parish register of Wendron (Corn.) records that the deceased had died of smallpox 'in the natural way' and not as a result of inoculation.[85]

Things changed after Edward Jenner had in 1796 made public the results of his experiments with pus derived from a cow infected with cowpox. A successful *vaccination* gave immunity for a long period, and immunisation by this method became a statutory requirement in Britain and in a number of other west European countries. In the nineteenth century vaccination must have contributed significantly to a lowering of the death-rate. 'The mortality in London from smallpox in the last thirty years of the eighteenth century had ranged between 17 and 20,000 per decade.'[86] It fell abruptly during the next century, by which time the population was expanding at an increasingly rapid rate.

The view that population increase during the eighteenth and early nineteenth centuries was due in significant measure to medical advances has been dismissed (p. 248). 'Except in the case of vaccination against smallpox (which was associated with 1.6 per cent of the decline of the death-rate from 1848–54 to 1971) it is unlikely that immunization or therapy had a significant effect on mortality from infectious diseases before the twentieth century.'[87]

If medical reasons can, by and large, be excluded, the diminishing death-rate and the growth in population from the middle years of the eighteenth century must be ascribed to environmental and social factors.[88] The productivity of agriculture increased more than was necessary to support a growing population. The quality of the diet was, on average, improved, and one must assume that there was less sickness. Unfortunately, morbidity, unlike mortality, is not susceptible of precise measurement. *Crises de subsistence*, which had been a recurring feature of western society since the earlier Middle Ages, became less frequent and less severe after about 1740. Harvests continued to fluctuate, as, indeed they still do, but generally within acceptable limits. Shortfalls in the eighteenth century were sometimes large enough to cause considerable discontent, though food riots were, as a general rule, due more to a breakdown in the mechanism of distribution than to any absolute shortage.[89] Famine mortality declined, but one must remember that for everyone who died of malnutrition there were many who were sick for long periods and some who suffered some permanent disability such as rickets, as a result of it. The irregularity

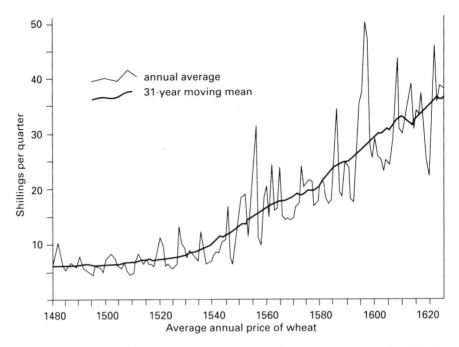

7.10 Graph showing the fluctuations in the price of wheat, 1485–1625; based on W. G. Hoskins, 'Harvest fluctuations'. Price is used here as a surrogate for abundance or scarcity.

and uncertainty of the harvest was a fact of life, and, until this unevenness in the supply of breadgrains could be evened out by supplies from other countries, there was periodic hardship. The margin of subsistence was too narrow for a stock to have been accumulated, even if methods of food preservation had made this possible. Figure 7.10 shows the fluctuations in the price of grain during the century and a half from 1485 to 1625.[90] A statistical examination of the figures shows that, although harvests were more often above average than below, the negative departures from the mean were far more extreme than were the positive. Seven of the years represented here were characterised by 'dearth', when the deviation was more than 50 per cent. In the absence of accumulated stocks, famine and increased mortality were the inevitable consequences.

Evidence for food supply is derived largely from the volume of breadgrains supposed to have been available. But there were other items in the diet, no less important than cereals, though less susceptible of measurement. The intake of protein was small for the mass of the population, and was often below the level which would today be considered necessary. Cheese was eaten, but there seems to have been a widespread antipathy to milk, which was 'full of vapours and led to wind, colick and palsies'.[92] Fruit and vegetables were eaten only when they were in season, mainly from early summer until early autumn. For the rest of the year the intake of vitamin C was probably minimal, and much of the population must have been 'in a pre-scorbutic state by the end of winter'.[92] The shortage of animal

242

products in the diet contributed to the lack of vitamins of the B group, and thus to anaemia and the 'lowness of spirit' mentioned by John Huxham. Lack of vitamin A, present in liver oils, both animal and marine, and also in vegetables like carrots, spinach, kale and turnip greens, contributed to xerophthalmia, or night blindness, and to other disorders of the eye.

Vitamin deficiencies cannot be said to contribute to epidemic disease or even, with the exception of that of vitamin C, which prevents scurvy, to lead to death. Yet their presence is essential for a normal healthy life.[93] Their absence from traditional diets can be readily demonstrated. In some instances the foods which contained them were not available; in others there was a deep-seated but quite irrational prejudice against them. Nor was vitamin deficiency limited to the poorer classes The latter could not afford the citrus fruits, chief source of vitamin C, but, on the other hand, the low extraction rate of their milling practices ensured that they consumed much of the bran and with it sufficient thiamine or vitamin B. The wealthy classes of their own volition consumed a diet which was made up largely of meat, poultry and game, and was grossly deficient in vegetables, milk products and coarse fibres.

Constraints of the environment

In addition to diet and food supply, the environmental constraints on human well-being included the physical conditions of living: housing, clothing, heating, sanitation. All these factors influenced health both directly and through the pathogens and their vectors which they encouraged. Cottages, timber-framed and panelled with wattle and daub, provided shelter for insects and vermin; floors of beaten earth were damp and cold for much of the year, and shuttered windows and ill-fitting doors allowed the cold blast of winter to blow through them. This may have helped to dissipate the smoke and the smells, but it also contributed to 'colds' and encouraged people to huddle together for warmth, thus allowing parasites like the flea and the body louse to move freely between them and infect the whole household. Personal habits did nothing to improve matters. People spat and defecated wherever they chose; Andrew Boorde's warning in this respect has already been quoted (p. 148).

The dangers inherent in the uncertain supply of water have already been mentioned. Boorde claimed that only fresh rainwater was wholly reliable, but this was always difficult to collect and to store. Not until the eighteenth century do leaden downpipes from roofs and leaden water-butts make their appearance on any considerable scale. In their total ignorance of the nature of infection, people saw no reason for going to the trouble of keeping their water-supply separate and distinct from their sewage-disposal systems, and it was not until the later nineteenth century that public opinion became any more enlightened in this respect. It is surprising that a people, habituated to think that infection was in some way attributable to miasma or 'bad air', took so little notice of the foul smells amid which they spent much of their lives. Apart from the rare complaints of lavatorial smells, chiefly in the

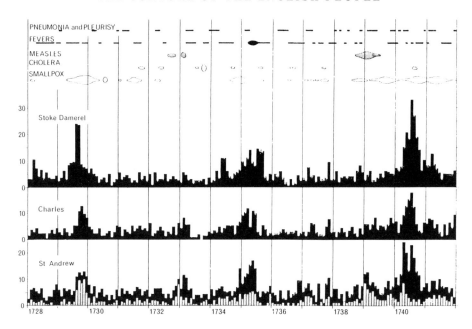

7.11 Mortality in the three parishes of Plymouth, compared with the evidence for identifiable diseases, as described in the diary of John Huxham. The vertical axis shows monthly mortality.

uppermost levels of society, there was little contemporary note of this particular form of nuisance. People had become accustomed to the smell of unwashed bodies and the stench of cesspits around their homes: it was part of life.[94]

All the evidence, both literary and archival, points to a high mortality and a short expectation of life. The major epidemics which contributed so importantly to this situation are well documented; their clinical detail was well known, and they can today be identified with some degree of certainty (Fig. 7.11). Until late in the seventeenth century, the most awesome was without question the bubonic plague. Its symptoms were obvious, its incubation period short and its progress across the country, like an advancing wall of death, could be anticipated.[95] Quarantine, as was discovered at an early date, gave some protection, but against the sickness itself no potion or charm was effective. The plague entered deep into people's imaginations. There can be little doubt but that the symbolism of death, which became so prominent in the later Middle Ages, owed much to the imminence of the plague, as also did the conspicuous hedonism on the one hand and the masochism of the Flagellants and similar groups on the other.[96] Fear of death prompted what Ziegler has called 'the frenzied charity' by which the rich strove to ward off the fate which they foresaw, by the endowment of chantries and charities. The times were out of joint, and the shock of the plague's inexorable progress led many to question established values and institutions. Both the revolts of the peasants and the rise of the Lollards owed much to its depredations. 'Wyclif was a child of the Great Plague in

244

that his generation had suffered and learned through its sufferings to doubt the premises on which its society was based.'

The plague was endemic in these islands from 1348/9 to 1665 or shortly afterwards, when its disappearance was almost as sudden as its arrival had been. The etiology of plague has become familiar only in recent years. Its pathogen bred in the bloodstream of the black rat and was carried to its human victim by the flea (p. 238) It is easy to assume that its depredations were encouraged by the physical conditions, conducive to both rat and flea, amid which most people lived. But the disappearance of plague did not follow any significant improvement in the physical conditions of life. There is at least the possibility that the black rat became extinct in Britain, and was replaced by the brown or grey rat (*Rattus norvegicus*), which appears to have had a degree of immunity to the plague bacterium. The symbiotic chain of rat, flea and human being may thus have been broken without either medical or environmental intervention.[97]

No other epidemic disease aroused such fear or occasioned a comparable mortality before the cholera epidemic of the early and middle years of the nineteenth century, but smallpox, typhus, syphilis, the 'English sweat' and tuberculosis were each responsible for great suffering and considerable mortality. Smallpox may have been present during the Middle Ages, but does not appear to have become epidemic before the later sixteenth century.[98] It was transmitted on the breath, and could spread very rapidly because there was no independent vector. Greater human mobility and more frequent personal contacts served only to increase its virulence. One isolated community might be completely free of it, while another, through a chance intruder, might be completely devastated. In this respect it closely resembled the plague. On the other hand, an attack however slight, could give immunity to those who survived it, and this fact became the basis first of inoculation and then of vaccination (p. 241). It was, after the plague, the most widespread, most visible and most feared of all diseases that afflicted traditional societies.

Typhus and tuberculosis were part of that spectrum of diseases which were always present yet rarely grew to epidemic proportions. Both were diseases of cramped, crowded and insanitary conditions. The former was spread by the body louse (p. 238), and the latter by the sputum of an infected person. Typhus could ravage a prison population or soldiers living in the foul conditions of warfare – hence its common pseudonyms, gaol- and trench-fever. Tuberculosis was also a product of squalid, crowded and insanitary conditions. Its pathogen could not survive in bright sunlight, so that the disease spread most rapidly in the dark, dank basements of early nineteenth-century industrial housing. Environmental change, not without the assistance of modern drugs, has, at least in Britain, put an end to both. Better personal hygiene, clothing that can be laundered frequently, and cheaper and more abundant soap have been preconditions of their disappearance.

Other diseases which formed that background of morbidity during medieval and early modern times were leprosy, syphilis, measles and a host of fevers and infections of the pulmonary and digestive tracts. They are difficult to recognise in records that lack all clinical precision, and their names can at best designate one of a host of unrelated diseases. Leprosy is a case in point. It appeared as a significant disease in the Anglo-Saxon period, but seems to have died out by 1400 or soon afterwards, when leper-houses were converted to other uses. Despite common opinion, it was not readily contagious, and there can be little doubt that the primitive quarantine insisted upon during the Middle Ages sufficed for its elimination. It was rarely fatal, but was disfiguring and could lead to the loss of fingers and toes. It was probably the ugliness of the leper that instilled so great a dread into the medieval mind. Unfortunately, there was a tendency to regard any serious skin complaint, including acne, skin cancer and even scabies, as leprosy, and many must have been incarcerated in leper hospitals without any clinical justification.

Syphilis, *morbus gallicus* or the 'great' pox erupted with great suddenness at the end of the fifteenth century to join gonorrhoea and other sexually transmitted diseases.[99] It remained serious despite the fact that its etiology had become known empirically soon after the disease first appeared in the army of the French King Charles VIII, who was campaigning at the time in Italy. Measles appears also to have been a common and generally recognisable complaint. Huxham identified two minor epidemics of measles in Plymouth, and both coincided with a high child and infant mortality, as recorded in the parish registers of the town.[100] It is difficult, if not impossible, to identify the various febrile complaints of which 'fever' was the most general symptom and also the most common name. Many, like influenza, were not particularly serious, but some could erupt into major epidemics with heavy mortality. The 'English sweat', which first appeared about 1485 and disappeared in the middle years of the next century, may have been a form of influenza, which, as is well known, is capable of sudden mutations. In addition, complaints of the digestive tract were, if one may judge from allusions in diaries and letters, extremely common and at times very severe. They can probably be classed as diarrhoea and gastroenteritis, and would most often have been picked up from infected water and food (p. 370). More serious complaints, like dysentery, typhoid, and, after about 1832, the most dangerous of them all, cholera, could also have derived from infected food and drink.

Cholera had long been endemic in Asia, but, owing to the slowness of transport, its bacterium had not been able to reach Britain in an active condition before about 1832.[101] It was spread when the faeces of an infected person entered the water-supply, and this was most likely to occur in the greater cities. Its etiology was explained by John Snow, a London physician, who demonstrated that the Soho outbreak of 1854 had its origin in the infected water taken from the Broad Street pump (Fig. 7.12). Yet it was a remarkably long time before his findings became known and were acted upon by public authorities. Vulnerability to any of these complaints may have been increased by undernourishment, but it is apparent that a major reason for their virulence was environmental. Their reduction, if not complete elimination, has been effected by removing the physical conditions – filth, squalor, overcrowding – which favoured the spread of their pathogens. Above all, a

7.12 John Snow's map of 1854, showing the location of cases of cholera in Soho, London, in relation to the Broad Street pump.

supply of water, free from contamination by sewage, has been a prerequisite for any improvement, and this was not achieved in much of Britain before the middle years of the nineteenth century and, in some areas, the early years of the twentieth. The increase in the practice of taking baths must have done something to reduce the risk of infection through parasites. It must, however, be added that no commensurate progress was made in the laundering of clothes. In any discussion of morbidity a distinction must be drawn between rural and urban living. There are two aspects to the question. In the first place a rural population is more widely scattered than an urban. Human contacts are necessarily less frequent, and, since most diseases are spread from person to person either by direct contact or by means of a vector, their spread is necessarily slower than in a more congested urban society. It can thus be assumed that both morbidity and mortality are lower in a rural environment that in an urban. In the second place, urban population can be assumed at some stage to have derived from the countryside. Urban growth has been fuelled by the immigration of country people. Habits of sanitation and hygiene which might have been tolerable, if not wholly desirable, in a rural setting could become positively dangerous in a town. Cholera, for example, was by and large an urban disease, because the wells which were a major source of water could not avoid being sunk close to cesspits which received domestic sewage. A rural community, especially if it maintained few contacts with the outer world, might remain free of infection even during a period of epidemic disease. Conversely, as the case of Eyam (Derby.) in 1665 demonstrated, a remote community that did become infected might be isolated and its inhabitants largely wiped out.[103] The diffusion of disease is intimately linked with human mobility and the frequency with which people meet or are in contact with one another.[104] Urban rates of mortality and presumably of morbidity have been consistently higher than rural throughout the period for which evidence is available. It is doubtful whether, in the pre-industrial age, any urban population could have sustained itself without an inflow from rural areas.

Demographic history

It is not the purpose of this chapter to trace the changes in gross population of this country. That has been done with great thoroughness and expertise by a number of scholars.[105] It is sufficient here to present a simple graph of aggregate population in England and Wales and to comment briefly on it. The total population of any discrete area at any time must be made up of total births minus total deaths that have occurred within it, corrected for in- and out-migration. Fluctuations in the total must be due to variations in these parameters. Figure 7.13, taken from the work of E. A. Wrigley,[106] shows aggregate births[107] and deaths in the parish of Colyton (Devon.) from 1550 to 1830, and demonstrates the extreme variability of these parameters of population. It shows an initial period of over eighty years when births consistently outnumbered deaths and the population must be assumed to have increased steadily. This was followed, about 1640, by a period of similar duration when deaths usually exceeded births. A period of half a century followed when births and deaths were more or less in harmony. A fourth period, beginning about 1785, was characterised by birth-rates consistently higher than death-rates. The pre-industrial period must have ended with a steeply rising population. These data apply, of course, to a single rural parish, but there is, in Wrigley's words, 'reason to expect that the Colyton mortality [and natality?] may prove to be repeated in many parishes' – perhaps in most.[108] It is not easy to explain fluctuations in natality and mortality as extreme as these shown in Figure 7.9 in terms of either epidemic disease or environmental change, though improved sanitation and hygiene must have played a role in the increase after the 1780s. Harvest fluctuations, and hence the supply and price of foodstuffs, remained important, but were damped down after the 1740s. There were henceforward no *crises de subsistence*, and apart from a period of scarcity in 1816–17, due to abnormal weather conditions which are now well understood,[109] there were no years of general scarcity. One must look for other factors. Amongst these were the reduced marriage and birth-rates during much of the seventeenth century. There is reason to suppose that average age at marriage was

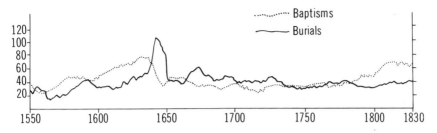

7.13 Graph showing aggregate annual baptisms and burials in the parish of Colyton (Devon); after A. E. Wrigley.

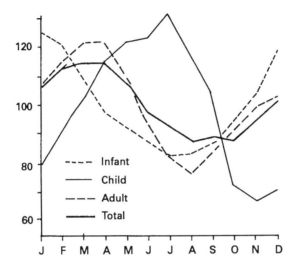

7.14 The seasonal pattern of mortality in Ludlow (Shrops.), 1577–1619, showing the distinctive pattern of mortality amongst children; after R. Schofield and E. A. Wrigley, 'Infant and child mortality in England in the late Tudor and early Stuart period', *Health, Medicine and Mortality in the Sixteenth Century*, ed. C. Webster, Cambridge, 1979, 61–95.

higher during the period of reduced natality, and that the size of completed families was in consequence smaller. There is also reason to suppose that there was a voluntary restriction on births during this period.[110] though this is extraordinarily difficult to evaluate.

Aggregate mortality figures tell us a great deal about the movement of total population, but it is no less useful to examine age-specific mortality. The high child mortality in Plymouth during the first half of the eighteenth century, arising largely from epidemic measles, has already been mentioned (p. 244). The question of infant and child[111] mortality is of great importance because it affects the size of the next generation of parents (Fig. 7.14). It can be determined only by the laborious method of family reconstitution on the basis of parish registers, and is even then susceptible of a margin of error through migration and the inadequate registration of births.

7.15 The search for head-lice, as shown in a carved misericord. The louse was the chief vector of typhus.

Still-births were not registered and the burial of infants who died before baptism frequently went unrecorded. Infant and child mortality, as reconstructed from the registers, was high in the pre-industrial era. It was highest in the later years of the seventeenth century, but although it tended to fall in the course of the eighteenth,[112] did not diminish significantly until well into the nineteenth. The proportion of live births that died during infancy in one parish in the city of York in the later sixteenth century amounted almost to a quarter.[113] In a group of Worcestershire parishes comparison of baptismal with burial records showed that a tenth of all baptised children died during infancy and a further quarter to a third during childhood.[114] It is apparent that without this infant and child mortality the adult population *could* have been increased a decade or two later by nearly 50 per cent. The effect that this would have had on the size of future generations needs no emphasis. It is important, therefore, to look more closely at the question of infant and child mortality in traditional societies.

Children suffered no less than adults from epidemic disease and there is some evidence that plague mortality 'was less serious amongst young adults than amongst children, and that children suffered very much more than other age-groups'.[115] It is well known that children are in addition at greater risk from dysentery and other diseases of the digestive tract. It has already been pointed out that mortality from these causes amongst infants and children is particularly high in summer and early autumn.[116]

Statistics of still-births and of infant deaths before baptism are quite unsatisfactory. On the other hand, if a newly born infant seemed unlikely to survive, it was usual to send for the priest and have it baptised privately. Alice Thornton's autobiography describes how her fifth child, born in December 1657, died 'before we could get a minister to baptize him, although he was sent for'.[117] The number of such instances is likely to have been high, and may help to account for the relatively long intervals that sometimes occurred between successive births. Mrs Thornton also recorded that as her sister, Lady Danby, 'drew neare her time for delivery of her sixteenth child ... ten whereof had bin baptized, the other six were stillborn when she was above halfe gon with them, she haveing miscarried of them all uppon frights by fire in her chamber, falls, and such like accidents happening.'[118]

Baptismal registers often record the 'private' baptism of a child within hours of its birth, and John Mirc's manual for parish priests, written about 1450, recommended the baptism of the child, if the birth was very difficult, as soon as its head appeared in the birth canal:

> And thaghe the chylde bote half be bore,
> Hed and necke and no more,
> Bydde her spare neuer the later
> To crystene hyt and cast on water.[119]

Canon law recognised baptism by a layman or even by the midwife as valid in such an emergency. A reason for the tight control which bishops exercised over midwives was that they might be called upon on such occasions to perform the rite.[120] Death of both mother and child in childbirth stood at a level that would be intolerable today. Nicholas Assheton of Downham (Lancs.) wrote in 1618: 'My wife in labour of childbirth. Her delivery was with such violence, as the child dyed wthin half an hour, and, but for God's wonderful mercie, more than human reason could expect, shee had dyed; but hee spared her a while longer to mee.'[121] In 1687 Elizabeth Cellier, a practising midwife of uncommon education and skill, who had attempted to secure the better training of members of her profession, wrote at length on their inadequacy. Within the past twenty years in London 'above 6000 women have died in childbed, more than 13,000 children have been abortive and about 5000 chrysome [less than one month old] infants have been buried ... above two-thirds of which, amounting to 16,000 souls, have in all probability perished, for want of due skill and care, in those women who practice the art of midwifery'.[122] Alice Thornton, who gave birth to nine children, poignantly expressed the woman's viewpoint: 'about a fortnight before my delivery, when my travell began upon me, and then the panges of childe-beareing, often remembring [reminding] me of that sad estate I was to passe, and dangerous pirills my soule was to find, even by the gates of death. Soe that I being terrified with my last extremity, could have little hopes to be preserved in this ... if my strength were not in the Almighty.'[123] The fact is that most pregnant women firmly believed that their chances of surviving childbirth were always uncertain.

In ordinary families the intervals between successive births were often from two to three years, probably because mothers were breast-feeding their infants, rather than through any deliberate family limitation. Among the upper classes, where the use of wet-nurses was common, births were more frequent. Sir John Bramston, who was married in 1635, wrote of his wife that 'she was a very obseruant wife ... She was mother of tenn children in the twelve yeares she was a wife.' She died young, leaving only two of her six sons. Alice Thornton, explicit as ever on family matters, wrote: 'it was the pleasure of God to give mee a weake and sickely time in breeding, from the February till the 10th of May following, I not having fully recruted by last September weakenesse ... The birth of my ninth childe was very perillous to me, and I hardly escaped with my life.'[124] Less frequent childbearing might have been far better for the health not only of the mother but also of the children themselves.

The reasons for these traumatic experiences lay in part in the abysmal lack of medical knowledge; in part in the complete failure to recognise the importance of hygiene and of conditions as nearly aseptic as possible. Midwives, who alone attended births, were quite incompetent to handle many of the problems that arose, even in normal childbirth. Alice Thornton described the breech birth of one of her children: 'the childe comeing into the world with his feete first, caused the childe to be allmost strangled in the birth, only liveing about halfe an houer'.[125] Midwifery was, throughout the Middle Ages and early modern times, the most neglected aspect of medical practice. Indeed, it was regarded as a manual craft, not as a branch of medicine. An engraving of about 1580 shows a woman, fully clothed, giving birth, attended by three other women, while the doctor could find nothing better to do than to sit at the window, observe the stars and cast the child's horoscope (Fig. 7.16). The midwife, or *sage femme*, had been trained, if at all, only by other women who had been similarly employed. They had been licensed by their diocesan bishop, but a bishop's licence was no alternative to medical training, and appears to have been instituted primarily for the purpose of controlling infanticide and ensuring that the child was baptised. Episcopal licences examined by Forbes contain evidence for the midwife's good character; never for their technical competence. The safety of the child's soul was of far greater consequence that the physical life of the mother or even of the child itself, and so it remained, at least in the eyes of the church, until far into the nineteenth century.

Obstetrics was, according to Garrison,[126] the worst aspect of medical practice. The primitive superstition lingered that giving birth was an 'unclean' act, and could be relegated to any odd corner of the house, and any old and soiled bedding could be used on the assumption that it would be made worse in the process. Cleanliness was never considered necessary, though empirical evidence might have taught people that it mattered very much. To most people incantations and spells were far more significant. The church required the mother to be 'cleansed' or 'churched' after delivery both to give thanks and to be 'purified'.

In the course of the eighteenth century certain changes were made. Forceps began to be used in delivery, but the slight evidence that is available suggests that they did nothing to reduce mortality because no care was taken to ensure that the instruments themselves were clean.[127] In the mid-eighteenth century lying-in hospitals began to be established, first in London and then in towns throughout the provinces. Their effect was to increase the mortality rate.[128] One case of puerperal fever in such a hospital usually meant that infection remained in the building, its beds and bedding.

7.16 Engraving of about 1554, showing a woman giving birth, attended only by midwives, while the doctor observes the stars for portents. From Jacob Rueff, *De conceptu et generationis*, 1554.

Maternity hospitals, in fact, earned the name of 'gateways to death', and cases are known of pregnant women pleading to be allowed to have their children at home. A significant improvement could only come from greater attention to hygiene. A practising doctor in the 1770s claimed that he had not lost a patient through puerperal fever because he had insisted upon scrupulous cleanliness and good ventilation.[129] But it was to be a long time before such attitudes reached the backwoods doctors and midwives of rural England, and even longer before they could conceive of pathogenic infection and aseptic conditions. In the meantime, infants continued to die and women to suffer until far into the nineteenth century through the backwardness of gynaecological and obstetric practice and the unwillingness of doctors to interfere with the midwives' ill-managed monopoly.

CHAPTER 8

THE COMMUNITY OF PARISH AND VILLAGE

> To exist, one had to belong to an association: a household, a manor, a monastery, a guild; there was no security except in association, and no freedom that did not recognise the obligations of a corporate life. One lived and one died in the style of one's class and corporation.
> Lewis Mumford, *The Culture of Cities*

Few people lived alone, or, indeed, had any desire to do so. Everyone looked to membership of a group for mutual help in bad times and support in old age. Even the state in medieval England required people to be linked in small groups or tithings, so that each could vouch for the others' good behaviour. It is not that man is a particularly sociable animal: association has been forced upon him by the physical conditions in which he lived. Almost everyone is, by the accident of birth, a member of a family, of a more extended kinship group and also of a local or village community. One might leave the latter, and, perhaps with difficulty, gain acceptance in another, but family and kinship could not be replaced. Members of a family and families within a community were bound together by ties of mutual dependence. Although no family or community was ever without its internal frictions and disputes – the records are full of them – as a general rule they were never pursued to the point at which they interfered with the operation of community institutions and the performance of the agricultural routine. Society had its inbuilt mechanisms for reducing the frictions and feuds that were inevitable between families and kinships. Both family and community were governed by a body of customs, practices and observances. Sometimes these were written down as village 'by-laws',[1] but more often they were held in the collective memory of the community. These communal codes of behaviour originated so far back that, in the formula of later documents, 'the memory of man was not to the contrary'. Their original purpose may have been to ward off danger or to secure the proper cultivation of the fields; their effect was to bring the community together in ritual acting and feasting and in the common interpretation of their own village codes and their practice of a common agriculture. It is part of our accepted wisdom that the village community in traditional societies consisted of a 'group of people striving for common objectives', and, like much

255

8.1 Village gossips, from a wall-painting in Peakirk parish church (Northants). The devil hovers above their heads, while they themselves grow horns.

accepted wisdom, it is totally wrong. Belief in such communities, wrote Macfarlane, 'is one of the most powerful myths in industrial society'.[2] It is as if members of modern fragmented and divided society looked back nostalgically to an age when feuds and social divisions did not exist. The romantic concept of a peasant society, living in harmony with itself, was expressed by the nineteenth-century German historian and folklorist, Tonnies, and was disseminated by those who, mainly for social reasons, found it acceptable. Belief in 'community' has in recent years come under vigorous attack from many quarters.[3] Lawrence Stone has characterised life in the Elizabethan village in the bitterest terms: 'filled with malice and hatred, its only unifying bond being the occasional episode of mass hysteria, which temporarily bound together a majority in order to harry and persecute the local witch'. He wrote of the overwhelming evidence for 'the lack of warmth and tolerance in interpersonal relations ... the extraordinary amount of back-biting, malicious slander, marital discord and unfaithfulness, and petty spying and delation which characterized village life' (Fig. 8.1).[4] The very closeness of this 'tightly knit, intolerant world', forced upon it by the need to till the fields, resist the pretensions and claims of its lords and masters, and confront the harsh realities of nature, intensified its internal discords.[5] Violence was far from absent, but strife showed itself most often in defamation and slander. The many cases that came before the courts show a range of obscenities and vituperation that would do justice to the proverbial trooper. People affected to be very sensitive to such insults, and the 'contemporary Englishman was unusually willing to protect his reputation by waging law'.[6] 'Resort to the law ... was commonly the pursuit of private warfare by other means.'[7] Yet relatively few such cases came to judgment, and when they did the plaintiff commonly demanded nothing more than recantation and apology. It was enough to humiliate one's enemy. John Bossy has shown how the frequency and destructiveness of disputes itself brought about a mechanism for arbitration and reconciliation. Contemporaries 'were anxious to maintain some sort of harmony in their communities, and saw a bitterly contested lawsuit as a threat to that harmony'.[8] At the same time, it became the objective of families and individuals to extend the circle of those who were bound to them by ties of kinship and friendship – *consanguinei et amici* – and thus to reduce the possibility of feud.

One should not therefore see the structures of village or communal life as woven of friendship and co-operation and watched over by a benevolent church. One finds, rather, devices to minimise hostilities and reduce feuds, thus allowing the community to lurch from one social crisis to another, always on the brink of disintegration, but always saved by short-lived reconciliation and compromise. The church, whether the Catholic church or the fragmented churches of post-Reformation Britain, had their ways of minimising strife.[9] Moral suasion played a role, but was supplemented by social institutions which matured in this divided society. Foremost amongst them was marriage itself. A marriage customarily brought together members of two kinships, which might or might not have been on terms of mutual hostility. The kiss of peace, now an optional element in the marriage service, was in origin the symbolic bringing together of two such groups. Shakespeare, so much closer to this *mentalité* than we can ever be, demonstrated in highly dramatic fashion the reconciliation of the feuding kinships of Montagu and Capulet.

The rite of baptism served much the same purpose. Over and above its theological importance, it was a means of extending the kinship group and thus of reducing the scope for feud. It not only strengthened the bonds between existing parental groups, but introduced new relationships in the shape of the 'godsib', or godparents, for the number of godparents was not formerly limited, as it is today, to three; nor were godparents necessarily chosen from within the kinship. Their selection was a means of 'making firm connections between the kin whose relationship might otherwise have been too distant to be effective, or of establishing them where they had not existed hitherto'.[10] Godparents from without the kin thus became, as it were, 'honorary kinsmen'. One does not attack or feud with one's kinsmen, and to widen the kinship in this way was tantamount to reducing the opportunity for feud. Piers Plowman refers to:

alle that beth myne hole bretheren   in blood and in baptisme.[11]

In other words, his brethren included both his natural and his spiritual kin.

Not infrequently children were chosen as godparents, despite their manifest inability to discharge the obligations which the church today lays upon them. The purpose is clear: 'to lay the foundations of a new group which would sustain the child in his or her adult life and perhaps make up for the ravages of death among brothers and sisters' and, it must be added, parents: '... a formal system of friendship', wrote Bossy, 'implied a formal system of enmity.'[12] It was the role of extended kinship groups and fraternities to give a sense of security and material support to its members, and, in doing so, to reduce the scope for hostility by reducing the number of groups which might come into conflict. Fraternities and kinships were like oases of relative peace amid the troubled scene of the local community. Ideally they should have been numerous and complex enough to have induced a sense of tranquillity and brotherly love throughout. In fact, they were not. Nor did calendar customs, Rogation Day rituals and church-ales always induce that sense of community that some have postulated, though the unrestricted consumption of alcohol on these occasions may have induced, as it has continued to do, a bibulous cordiality and a feeling of well-being.

Village, parish and church

Since the earlier Middle Ages most of this country has been divided into parishes, units of ecclesiastical administration and pastoral care. It was long before their boundaries were firmly and incontrovertibly established, but everyone claimed to belong to or was claimed by a parish. It would be an exaggeration to say that the parish was the ecclesiastical expression of the village, but there was a high level of conformity between the community of the parish and that of the village.

The village, as it evolved during the Middle Ages, was a group of cottages and farmsteads, with, somewhere in its midst, a church and probably also a manor-house, seat of the local lord and centre of his estate management. It might be clustered round a 'green' or strung out along a road. It might be ringed with satellite cottages and hamlets, or it might consist of nothing more than a scatter of farmsteads. These variant forms (Fig. 8.2) are each characteristic of some part of this country. They are differing responses, on the one hand, to contrast in the environment: soil and vegetation, climate and relief, and, on the other, to the social structure and the economic organisation of those who created them and shaped their growth. Each has resulted from the way in which a particular group of people – clan, kinship, family – perceived the land and used its resources, and from the ways in which succeeding generations have continuosuly shaped and moulded it (Fig. 8.3).

Over most of England and Wales the parochial structure was superimposed upon a pattern of human settlement. But, once established, it displayed a remarkable durability. Minor changes in the parochial map were made in the later Middle Ages, reflecting, in general, local changes in population and prosperity. A few large parishes were divided, and sometimes a couple of small and impoverished parishes

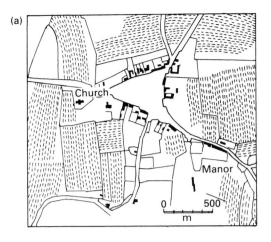

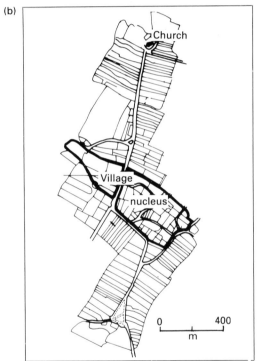

8.2 The predominant types of village settlement: (a) a 'green' village, Eltisley (Cambs.); (b) a 'street' village (Cottenham, Cambs.), which grew as a ribbon development along roads leading from the original settlement. Based on J. R. Ravensdale, *Liable to Floods*, Cambridge, 1974.

might be merged, as happened to the two Norfolk parishes of Framington Pigot and Framington Earl. In 1505 Framington Pigot was declared to be 'unequal to the support of a rector, owing to a pestilence, sterility of the land, ruin of buildings, and the fewness and poverty of the parishioners'. At the same time Framington Earl was

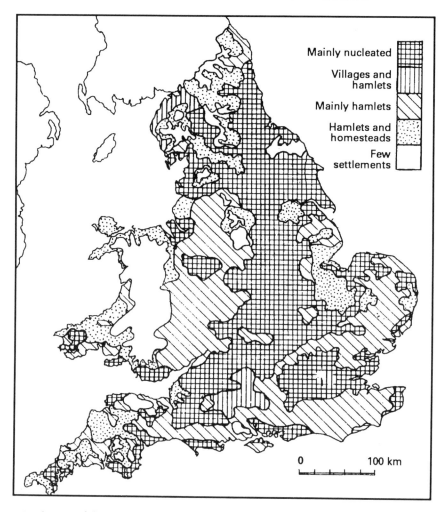

8.3 Distribution of the main types of rural settlement; based on H. Thorpe, 'Rural settlement', *The British Isles: A Systematic Geography*, ed. J. Wreford Watson and J. B. Sissons, London, 1964, 358–79.

declared to be 'unequal to the support of a rector'. Furthermore, the titheable lands of the two parishes were so intermixed that 'every autumn disputes were caused'. The bishop's court found accordingly that one chaplain would suffice for the two, but, despite their poverty, both churches remained in being, as they continue to do today.[13] By and large, however, the patterns of civil parishes recorded on the later editions of the now defunct 1-inch Ordnance Survey maps reflect fairly accurately the late medieval parochial pattern (Figs. 8.4 and 8.5).

Until modern times all who lived within its bounds would have acknowledged the parish as the primary unit of human organisation after the nuclear family. Until the Reformation it represented the jurisdiction of the universal church, and for a

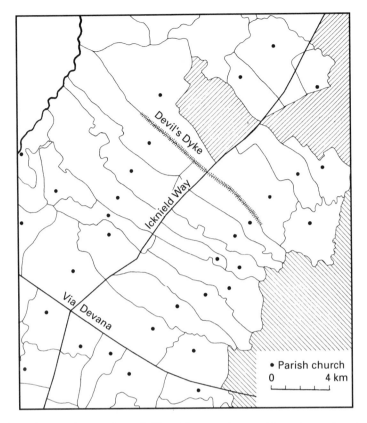

8.4 Map of parishes north-east of Cambridge. Most are elongated in order to share in the varied resources of the area. Note that the Roman road (Via Devana) and the Anglo-Saxon Devil's Dyke both serve as parish boundaries.

generation or two afterwards most would have recognised the authority of its successor, the Church of England.[14] So definite and so durable had the parish become as the primary subdivision of the country that it attracted to itself countless civil functions. Indeed, Christopher Hill has written of the 'secularization of the parish'.[15] It became responsible for the maintenance of roads and bridges within its limits and for the support of its own poor; for the levying of taxes and the conduct of the early census. Yet, through it all, the parish remained fundamentally a unit of ecclesiastical administration and pastoral care.

The break with Rome brought about certain outward changes in ritual and observance, but change came slowly in the popular aspects of religion. Deep down, the Reformation had little immediate effect. The popular world was not greatly concerned with the niceties of doctrine; more with magic and the seasons and the welfare of the crops. This is not to say that there was not a minority, mainly middle-class and literate, which argued deeply about grace and predestination. The Puritans might denounce what they terms the 'idolatry' and superstition of the old religion,

261

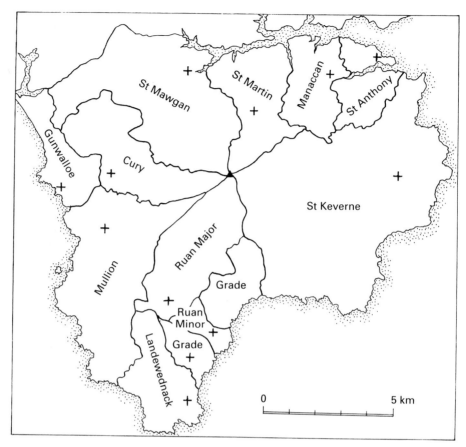

8.5 Map of parishes in the Lizard Peninsula (Corn.). Six out of the twelve extend to Dry Tree, in the middle of Goonhilly Downs. All except two incorporate a section of the coast. Dry Tree must have been a medieval landmark; it appeared as *arbor sicca* in medieval charters.

but their own belief in magic, sorcery and witchcraft was undiminished and, indeed, inspired one of the most ferocious of all pogroms against witches. But this was as much a reflection of social stresses within the community as of any deep belief in the powers of darkness and magic.

At the focal point of each parish lay its church. The church might be surrounded by a village lying wholly within its parish, or a village might be shared by two parishes with their respective churches, or the church might stand in splendid isolation in a landscape of hamlets and scattered farms (Fig. 8.6). The physical relationship of the pattern of human settlement to church and parish was of little fundamental importance. The parish church attracted the tithes and oblations, the loyalty and, in a vague way, the worship of its parishioners. It was their church, the only enduring monument to their own past to be found in their midst. They met, stood, or knelt in the nave, which they and their forebears had built. Here they met to discuss business

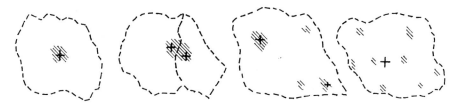

8.6 Schematic diagram showing the possible relationships between parish and village. Villages are indicated by cross-hatching, churches by crosses.

matters and here, in the great chest with its multiple locks, they might keep such valuables as they possessed, like the copy of the court roll that constituted their title to the land they cultivated, or an heirloom of silver or a few gold coins.

At the beginning of their lives they had all been brought to the church to be baptised at the font which stood just within the main entrance. This was something more than a rite of passage marking their admission to the Christian community; it was a link with the past, for previous generations had all been dipped in the consecrated water of that font, and in the future their own children would submit, no less noisily than they had done, to the same ritual. It stood as a symbol of the continuity of life. They would never willingly let it be destroyed, and if it had to be replaced, it would most likely be buried in consecrated ground.[16] Amongst the symbols with which it might be decorated were the tree of life, seen in the vision of St John, and the serpent which had been defeated by the sacrament that had been performed there. At its corners there might be face-masks, which must derive from the pre-Christian cult of the head (p. 395), but which were no doubt seen as witnesses to the rite of baptism and as protectors of the new initiate. At the font they had been given a name, and had become persons with an identity which would remain for ever their own. At the church porch they would be married, and after death they expected to be buried, not within the shadow of the church, for that would be on the north side, from which evil influences were believed to come, but somewhere within the hallowed ground illuminated by the sun.

The community of the parish had built the church, not, as a general rule, with their own hands, though there were occasions when this did happen, but with their donations and bequests.[17] The tithe — one-tenth of nature's bounty, which they were under an obligation to give to the church — went to the rector, who was supposed to use it for his own support, for charitable purposes, and for building and maintaining the chancel, which was always seen as the peculiar sphere of the priest within the whole fabric of the church. The parishioners themselves looked after the nave: this was their own exclusive domain. They raised money for it by church-ales and church-rates; they gave during their lives and bequeathed money after their deaths, and more often than not they made the nave a larger, grander and more elaborate structure than the rector could ever aspire to in his chancel.[18] The church-rate, which had been levied occasionally before the Reformation, became general thereafter, and was a variable assessment on the parishioners for the purpose of maintaining their own part of the church. What ill will there was between the two partners, spiritual and secular, who shared both the church and the obligation to look after it, one can only sense from the records, and it was not inconsiderable. The diocesan bishop had, in most instances, jurisdiction in these matters, and exercised it through periodic visitations by himself or his archdeacon. The bishops' records often distinguished between nave and chancel in reporting on the condition of churches. Complaints were most frequently of the condition of the chancel: 'at Wistow the chancel was exposed to rain . . . at Market Harborough the walls of the chancel showed decay.'[19] Visitations conducted after the Reformation showed no conspicuous improvement, and everything points to the continued neglect of the chancel by the rector. Evidently the patience of the parishioners was at times sorely tried, and at Hesket (Cumb.) the chancel was reported to have been 'repair'd at the publick Charge of the Parish'.[20]

Nearly half the rectories in this country were in lay hands after the Reformation. During the Middle Ages, they had been appropriated to religious foundations, most often monastic, and at the Dissolution had passed, along with other assets of the dissolved houses, into the possession of laymen, 'lay rectors' as they were termed. The latter continued to receive the tithes and certain other dues, but, like their monastic predecessors, were obliged to provide a vicar who would discharge the rectorial obligations vicariously. Before the Reformation it was the monasteries that neglected their charges: 'what care they if it rain on their altars,' wrote William Langland. After the Dissolution, it was the 'lay' rectors who in many instances, but, it must be emphasised, far from all, misappropriated the income which they had received as tithe. Tithe payments were in 1836 commuted for a fixed monetary payment, which, with inflation, has since diminished almost to a vanishing point.

One must beware of thinking of parishioners as motivated only by piety or the need they felt to atone for their sins on earth. Such thoughts may have been present in varying degrees, especially towards the end of the Middle Ages, when the imminence of plague induced a sense of impending doom, but their motives went much further than this. 'The parish church was [the] heart of the late medieval village. It was even then a legacy of the past, the repository of communal memory.'[21] And the communal memory reached far back to a pre-Christian past and to a time when the prevailing culture can very loosely be called 'Celtic'. Celtic peoples at one time inhabited much of Europe, and a Celtic substratum is to be found in folklore and folk art over much of the continent. One can, furthermore, detect in the iconography of the Middle Ages a gradual waning of pre-Christian concepts and motifs as they became overlaid or transformed by the doctrines of the church: 'the villagers' religious life was dominated less by new innovations in penance, preaching or the mass, than by folklore and traditional values handed on more-or-less intact for centuries'.[22] Pagan or pre-Christian aspects of culture have survived until the present in slow process of transformation, attenuation or bowdlerisation. 'In its totality the pagan universe was a large, loose, pluralistic affair, without any clear unifying principle. It encompassed superhuman beings and forces, witches and wise men, and a mass of low-grade magic and superstition.'[23] The church tolerated this world-view. Its magic was 'an inferior form of religion' and is creatures were humanised as saints and martyrs. It mattered little that there never was a St Michael, a St Christopher or a St George. These were personifications of forces that were common to both pre-Christian and Christian cultures; they appealed equally to the subconscious in both.[24]

The medieval decline of the folkloric element in religion culminated in the Reformation and Counter-Reformation. Both attacked 'the popular folklorized Christianity inherited from the Middle Ages', and at the same time 'they shifted the accent from religion as an attitude – as "faith" or "piety" or "religiousness" – to religion as belief. Christianity in their hands hardened and materialised into articles of belief, its defining act becoming intellectual assent to a creed.'[25] The change was typified on the interior walls of parish churches by the replacement of paintings of saints, the gospel story and the moralities by the tedious narration of the Apostles' Creed and the Ten Commandments. Fantasy, allegory and symbolism gave way to fierce dogma; henceforward justification was to be by faith alone. At the same time, in continental Europe, the Counter-Reformation instituted 'a system of parochial conformity similar in character . . . though more comprehensive in its detail'.[26] In its efforts to break down 'the internal articulations of . . . society, the church set itself to destroy the kinship and to control the family' – a movement to which we shall return in the next chapter.

But the 'collective unconscious' – to use the expressive phrase of Carl Jung[27] – lingered on, however overlaid it may have become. It is with us still, depersonalised and expressed in popular and often meaningless prohibitions and injunctions. No longer, as a general rule, does a church which has lost all pretension to universality presume to dictate or to prohibit the observance of customs which time has hallowed and society has deprived of their true meaning.

The rituals of everyday life

One must distinguish, in theory at least, between popular culture in the strict sense and the culture of the élite, between, in Redfield's words, the 'little tradition' and the 'great'.[28] The distinction between them was always blurred, the one borrowing extensively from the other. The élite participated in popular tradition, taking over popular art, song and certain other aspects of culture, often sanitising and bowdlerising them in the process. Popular culture borrowed no less extensively but probably more consciously from the élite. Both cultures were expressed in the conventions of daily life, in art and iconography, and in games and play in its widest sense. If this distinction between élite and popular culture was not apparent in literature before modern times, this can only have been because literature *stricto sensu* was almost unknown in the latter.

Popular culture was expressed in three ways: in rituals and custom, in visual representation, and in the *mentalité* or world-view of the people. All were reflected in

8.7 A bench-end showing a fox, garbed as a priest, preaching from a pulpit; Thornham Parva (Suff.).

the customs and practices of ordinary people and demonstrated their simple, psychological imperative for recreation, amusement, company, the need to find some form of escape from the oppressive hardships of everyday life. For most people before the social revolution of the eighteenth and nineteenth centuries life was 'nasty, mean, brutish and short'.[29] The mind could not tolerate its endless drudgery and uncertainty without the expectation of periodically escaping from its rigours. Festivals and, above all, 'carnival' provided that escape (p. 389). Authority in the shape of the church, the manorial lord, even the organs of the state, was overpowering and oppressive. It could be supported only by satirising and ridiculing it, by representing the preacher as a fox (Fig. 8.7), the physician as an ape (Fig. 8.8) and by other forms of role-reversal and make-believe.

The forms assumed by popular culture were capable of endless variation, for in detail it was local or at most regional. Its universal aspects were modified, undergoing 'a process of unification within [their] own area through the mutual control and reciprocal influence of its bearers', creating in von Sydow's

8.8 A bench-end showing a physician, represented as an ape, examining a urinal bottle, a common method of diagnosis; from a bench-end in Suffield parish church (Norf.). The ape is shown wearing academic dress.

terminology, an 'ecotype'.[30] This is seen most clearly in the folk art with which people decorated their churches and their homes. Individual motifs might be characteristic of houses within a particular village or of a group of neighbouring churches. Language, too, was local in its vocabulary, syntax and inflection, changing, however slightly, from one region to the next. Imitation and mutual borrowing explain the homogeneity within a small area in one respect or another. Minute differences in culture between areas as small even as a parish could be readily translated into distrust and hostility. Local rivalries rarely have any basis beyond petty and superficial differences. The reason given by the French villagers of Minot (Côte d'Or) for their dislike of their neighbours of Moitron, only 4.5 km away was that from that direction 'came neither good winds [the cold north-easters of winter] nor good people',[31] an instance of the transfer of characteristics typical of popular culture. Local hostilities rarely had a rationale more logical than this.

Popular culture is repetitive; its rituals come at regular intervals of time. Folk-memory retains a picture of how they should be performed, but the fact that it is dependent only on memory means that it can embody slight but cumulative changes from year to year. The calendar customs of the nineteenth century bear only the slightest resemblance to those of two or three centuries earlier. Modification and change were, by and large, unconscious; the participants would be likely to regard any deliberate change as a break with tradition, negating the purpose for which the ritual was instituted in the first place. Popular culture was acted out in a form of play, though earlier peoples never drew any clear distinction between work and leisure.[32] Leisure activities had for them a social content; their ultimate – though forgotten – purpose was the welfare of the crops or the preservation of the community from the evils that threatened it. Man played the order of nature as it was imprinted on his consciousness,[33] but play it he did, and he derived both pleasure and satisfaction from the rituals which he performed. Taken together, these pageants and rituals constituted 'a second world and a second life outside officialdom, a world in which all medieval people participated more or less, in which they lived during a given time of the year ... To ignore or to underestimate the laughing people of the middle ages also distorts the picture of European culture's historical development.'[34]

There is a tendency, wrote Homans, for 'any group of men ... to complicate the conditions of life and to make them more interesting ... to build up their social life over and above that required by the original purpose ... providing an outlet or vehicle, sanctioned by tradition, for this elaboration upon the activities of daily life'.[35] This he termed 'superfluous behaviour'. Much of the play-acting in popular rituals was superfluous behaviour; it went far beyond the limits set by the original religious motives for the ceremony. And in no way were the bounds of normal behaviour so far exceeded as in 'carnival', the festivity which preceded the Lenten fast. Indeed the very name, probably deriving from *carnem levare*, the putting aside of flesh, betokens an orgy before a period of abstinence. Such rituals can be documented from as early as the twelfth century, and are met with still in the more structured ceremonies performed at Nice and New Orleans. In the village community they also became a rite of passage (p. 404), in which the youth gave free rein to their sexual instincts and their urge to displace their elders. The play element asserted itself 'over an original and sometimes conjectural, religious purpose'. This has been the inevitable course of 'carnival' and similar celebrations. 'Peasant tradition ... was remoulded in conformance with current notions about civilization, and what had originally been sacred became a mere diversion emptied of its religious content but perpetuated as a survival by the momentum of highly integrated peasant life.'[36]

The dance was an essential part of primitive and traditional rituals. The rhythmic movement of a group of people, all acting in unison, was a mode of afffirming 'social unity and occurs on all occasions which are socially important'.[37] It has strongly religious overtones; the Jews 'danced before the Lord', as, indeed, they continue to do. Dancing has come to have sexual overtones, but traditional dances were often performed by men or women separately. The dance that developed in the nineteenth century had precise gyrations and carefully co-ordinated footwork; the traditional dance had none of these features. No one who has watched a *kola* being danced through the streets of a Balkan village can have any doubt of its spontaneity or of its lack of precise forms. It was not a learned activity; any movements would do. It was a spontaneous expression of joy, or relief from tension, of celebration, even of religious ecstasy. At the same time it could be an enjoyable experience, and for this reason it has continued to excite the human mind long after it had ceased to give unity to the community or to do reverence to the community's gods.

Some time in the late fifteenth or the sixteenth century the dance, as it were, came in from the cold. It ceased to be a monopoly of the masses, to be indulged in on occasions which were basically religious. It became an entertainment for the royal court in France and was quickly imitated in England. The names of the dances – *branle* or *brawle*, *allemande* or *corrente*, *Ländler* or *Waltz* – all betray their peasant origin. The dance was an element of popular culture that moved socially upwards, losing its coarser elements in the process. It is this refined dance which ultimately spread back downwards as a sanitised social activity.[38]

Ritual feasts and celebrations had an intensely local character because, although the cycle of nature might be universal, the spirits that had to be placated and the saints to be honoured dwelt locally. Their dedications served not only to individualise the churches and their parishes but also to identify them indissolubly with a particular saint. Neighbouring Italian parishes, both dedicated to the Virgin Mary, disputed with one another which Virgin Mary was the more powerful, which held the stonger magic. Both were the spirits of their respective places, and, since not even spirits could be in two places at the same time, they could not therefore be one and the same.

The parochial saint had his or her name-day, when masses were said and rituals performed in the saint's name. These became calendar customs unique to a particular parish, and, because they formed part of the individuality of the parish, they lingered on, stripped of their religious content, into the present age. There were other calendar customs, briefly catalogued and discussed in chapter 10, all having the double function, the ritual placation of the spirits that drove the seasons and the practical object of achieving unity within the community.

The visual evidence

It is not easy to recapture the play-acting and the festivities which formed so important a part of popular culture in any particular community. Unless they were described or recorded at the time, they have vanished. The feeble customs of today are either the gentrified versions of what once happened or they are unauthentic revivals. The visual aspects of popular culture, where they have survived, are more authentic and probably bring us as close as we are likely to get to the mental processes of people who lived half a millennium or more ago. Even so, they are often ambivalent, and some seems to defy rational explanation or interpretation. Many such representations could once have been seen in the churches, more especially the parish churches, which served the needs of ordinary people and expressed their modes of thought. But even the visual image has suffered. Much, especially that which had an overtly religious connotation, was destroyed during and following the Reformation. Wall-paintings, for example, disappeared under coats of white-lime. Churchwardens' accounts record the expenditure for this purpose: 'for x Lode of lyme for white weashinge for the hole churche';[39] 'for wasshinge out the images for iii days and a halfe';[40] 'pweyntyng of the chyrche'.[41] In some cases the 'images' have been retrieved from beneath their layers of white-lime to reveal not only a primitive representation of the main elements of the biblical story but also moral admonitions and echoes of a much older and more primitive past. It is remarkable that the removal of these forms of decoration aroused so little opposition within the community. It is possible that it all happened so gradually that resistance could not easily be organised. It is unlikely that the parishioners had come to regard them as irrelevant when, as churchwardens' accounts demonstrate, they had paid for them to be repainted only a decade or two before.

A second wave of destruction followed, mainly in the seventeenth century, and was aimed not so much against the evidences of the Catholic faith, which had in the main already been obliterated, but at everything in the church that was secular or sexual. Popular culture was coarse in the extreme, and the Puritans took exception to all that seemed to profane their house of worship.[42] Images and pictures which had no acceptable theological content, were mercilessly destroyed, just as the colourful churchales,[43] carnivals and charivaris disappeared from the streets.

> Thou hast conquered, O pale Galilean
> And the earth has grown grey from thy breath.[44]

It is doubtful whether this orgy of destruction was wholly the work of reformers and fanatics. A wave of destruction for the sheer joy of it appears to have accompanied most religious disturbances, as if the sanctions which serve to bind society together had on these occasions been loosened. There have always been vandals who derived some perverted pleasure from knocking the heads off statues and throwing stones through windows. They are with us still, and they also are part of popular culture.

The motifs which delighted the eye of the medieval peasant will be discussed later (p. 390). Their number and variety are immense, but their meaning is never simple. They overlap; they bear changing and conflicting interpretations. Some represent a coarse, erotic humour; others hark back to the Celtic symbolism of the head or to woodland figures; yet others are grotesques of almost frightening proportions. Some linked up with the dramatic performances presented at popular festivals, so that the pageant of popular art formed a continuous whole, from which the peasant derived instruction or consolation or just simple, earthy amusement. The glazed windows, the wall-paintings and the sculptured bosses and capitals constituted the only 'book' available to the peasant, certainly the only one he could 'read'. One must visualise the priest guiding his flock from mural to window to sculpture, commenting on the biblical narrative which they portrayed or the moral lapses which they pointed up. This is implicit in the sermons that have survived from the later Middle Ages,[45] as well as in manuals written for the guidance of parish priests.

The medieval church had inherited a rich body of imagery and symbolism. Some of it derived from the classical culture of Rome; more was inherited from Celtic culture which had at one time pervaded much of Europe, and superimposed on these cultural strands were elements of Germanic popular culture imported by Angles, Saxons, Jutes, Danes and Norsemen. All were merged to form an ambivalent body of folklore, more an attitude than a perceived body of belief, and, for that reason, less easy to expunge from the minds of the people.

The erotic was always prominent in folk art. Sculpture, in particular, could be sexually explicit, and much of this survived the Reformation because it appeared to have little or no religious connotation. Erotic sculpture has survived in Britain perhaps because later generations failed to recognise it for what it was. It is probably no exaggeration to say that at one time scarcely a church was without its erotic figures, generally carved in stone in capital or corbel, or in wood in misericord or bench-end.[46] They are today less common in Britain than in France or Spain, but among them is that explicit depiction of the human genitalia, sometimes male but most often female, known by the corrupt Irish name of *sheela-na-gig*. Occasionally, as at Whittlesford (Cambs.), both male and female forms occur in the same composition. The seventeenth century was intolerant of such folk art, and a quantity of it, impossible to estimate, was destroyed.

The eighteenth century was more tolerant. Popular art was seen as barbaric rather than sacrilegious or obscene. Grotesque heads were replaced with smooth-faced children. Nevertheless, a degree of eroticism did, in fact, survive into the nineteenth century, when it was submerged beneath Victorian prudery and artistic humbug. But, by and large, it was élite art which spread into churches as well as homes after the seventeenth century. It was broadly classical in its inspiration, and reflected the wealth and the local power of the squirearchy who had acquired the patronage of churches and parishes. In some degree the parish church severed its links with local culture. It became gentrified, and one cannot fail to see in this at least one reason for the failure of the established church to satisfy the spiritual needs of more than a part of the population, and for the growth of nonconformity.

Victorian antiquaries tended to explain these carvings as 'fertility figures', as if the end justified the indelicacy. No one can doubt that many such carvings, like ancient Isis or Ishtar, served this purpose, but these were never as aggressively erotic as the *sheela-na-gig*. To Margaret Murray the *sheela* seemed divine, or at least to have had divine attributes, as 'shown by the fact that the figures are almost always found on Christian churches'.[47] In fact, there is nowhere else where they could have survived, and in church sculpture they are invariably found among grotesques which have no obvious fertility significance. The often-cited *sheela* at Kilpeck (Hereford.) is carved in one of the corbels which run round almost the whole church, just below the eaves

(Fig. 11.3).[48] The other corbels mostly show only grotesque heads. It is probable that this *sheela* came to be used as a fertility symbol, but it is highly unlikely that it was conceived as such in the first place. It challenges comparison with the graffiti found today on the backs of toilet doors, and no one dare say that these serve that purpose. They are pornography, from which some derive a prurient pleasure. The same is probably true of the erotica of the Middle Ages.

A world-view

The attitudes and perceptions of traditional people underwent no significant change before the scientific revolution, which cannot be said to have begun before the late seventeenth century. Even then the popular view of the world began to give way to a more sophisticated outlook only amongst the educated minority. The impact of science on popular culture did not become apparent for at least another century. Popular culture had been a product of the interaction of Christianity with pre-Christian cultures – a case of 'internal acculturation'. From this double process there arose the two cultures, popular and élite. 'The culture common to all people in a pre-class society becomes the culture of the "common people" in a class society, counterposed to the "official" clerical culture; it becomes a persecuted culture driven back to the periphery of spiritual life.'[49] The 'golden age' of medieval Christianity, wrote Delumeau,[50] 'is a legend. The religion of the mass of the people in the west has been confused with the religion of a clerical élite.' Their respective world-views may in some respects have overlapped, but they were fundamentally different. Gurevich may perhaps have underrated the degree to which popular culture infiltrated that of the élite. Elite culture was, in fact, only popular culture that had been filtered, cleaned of its original coarseness, and reinterpreted in the light of newer and more sophisticated thought processes. It continued to absorb elements of popular culture, passing them through its screening process, emasculating them and separating them from their original folk contexts.

The creation of an élite culture was, by and large, the achievement of the church. As the Middle Ages wore on the church became increasingly intolerant not only of heresy, which itself often had a populist element, but also of localisms in practice and belief. the penitentials of the later Middle Ages, analysed by Gurevich, show the church in competition and conflict with popular and local magic.[51] The church 'collided with an alien universe determined by powers which had no relationship to the Christian god or, perhaps, to any god at all. They were primordial and primary ... powers which united man and nature in a complex intercourse and continuous change.'[52] Goering speaks of the attempt 'to break down the long *de facto* traditions of local loyalties and customs, and to ensure that the local priest would see himself as an integrated part of a larger Church'. This process began in the twelfth or thirteenth century, and aimed to make the parish priest 'the bishop's true and full vicar in the parish ... a key figure in bringing outside culture and discipline into the local parish'.[53] But not until the Counter-Reformation of the later sixteenth century did the church achieve any conspicuous success, and by this time Britain no longer formed part of Catholic Europe.[54]

The Reformation in Britain was accompanied not only by a change in doctrine but also by a shift in social emphasis. The church at the parochial level became secularised. This was an unintended but inevitable consequence of the course of the Reformation in Britain. Almost half the parochial rectories passed, with the Dissolution of the monasteries and the secularisation of their assets, into the hands of the laity, most of them members of the gentry.[55] The social origins of pre-Reformation parish priests had, as a general rule, been humble, and their educational attainments modest. There was almost certainly an improvement in their intellectual quality towards the end of the Middle Ages, but they remained attached more to the lower than to the higher end of the social spectrum. The Reformation brought about no immediate change, but in the course of time the aristocracy and the gentry gained some degree of control over the church at the parochial level, just as they had long done at the higher levels of ecclesiastical administration. In short, they became the patrons of livings and 'presented' their incumbents (p. 264). When, as was often the case, the patronage rested with the local squire, secular control of the church was almost as complete as it had been before the reforms of the late eleventh century. The patronage of parish churches by members of the gentry meant not only that they appropriated the tithe income of their parishes, but that they usually presented men like themselves, even members of their own family, to the churches which they controlled. The church at the parochial level became gentrified.

The reformers are seen generally as rebelling against the centralising, fundamentalist tendencies within the church. This they certainly did, but only on narrow theological grounds. They were no less authoritarian and fundamentalist in their own way, no more tolerant of local idiosyncrasy in practice and belief. (p. 413). Protestantism in both its Calvinist and Lutheran forms, like post-Tridentine Catholicism, strove to suppress or to eradicate the popular culture of the later Middle Ages, and in large measure they both succeeded.

What, then, were the characteristic features of the popular world-view? In the first place, it was a narrow and restricted view. Mobility in the pre-industrial period has no doubt been underestimated, but the proportion of the rural population that made journeys further afield than their neighbouring parishes or the nearest market-town was relatively small. From the Renaissance onwards more people travelled farther and more often, but it was most often the gentry which became aware of distant places and culture. The mass of the population, at least before the radical social changes of the eighteenth and later centuries, saw little of the world beyond their own physical horizons.

Their world was made up of three zones, best conceived as concentric.[56] The first comprised their own community, whose members would have been familiar to them and with whom they were linked by ties of mutual dependence (p. 267). Surrounding this intimate zone was a 'foreign' but at the same time familiar zone, distrusted, but nevertheless drawn into their own circle of endogamous relations.

This second zone might extend the distance of two or three parishes. Beyond was truly foreign country, with which our community preferred to have no contact and of which it claimed to have little knowledge. Relations with the intermediate or second zone might extend to mutual help in emergency, but were more often agonistic and based on rivalry or hostility. The communal boundary was a zone of friction, because it marked the division of resources. It was likely to have been initially an area of woodland, moorland or rough grazing, within which property rights were undeveloped or ill-defined. Definition first became necessary when a tithe of the animals which grazed there or of the timber cut in the woods was demanded by the parish rector on one side or the other. Most often, since this was, in the immediate context, an ecclesiastical dispute, the diocesan bishop adjudicated and delimited a communal or parish boundary. Its demarcation by means of trees, cairns, standing-stones, roads or streams, came later, together with the practice of 'beating'[57] the bounds to impress on all and sundry the limits of their own territory, the boundary between the familiar and the foreign.

Local courts and local law

The local community was in many respects self-governing. It never enjoyed complete control over its own affairs, but, through the manor court and the periodic meetings of the parishioners – the later parish council – it could influence those decisions which it did not itself make. The lord of the manor was often an absentee and rarely attended the meetings of his own court. His local representative, his steward of *senescallus*, presided. He was a local man, and, though paid to represent the interests of his master, he was not unaware of the rights and interests of his neighbours, whom, at a purely personal level, he could not afford to alienate. Indeed, the courts were governed by custom – manorial custom – which supplemented and filled out the law of the land, and those who knew and understood local custom most fully were the villagers themselves. They knew who had rights in meadow, common and woodland, where local property lines ran, and whose turn it was to perform the duties of rounding up stray animals and serving as local constable. They 'presented' offenders at the manor court, which met 'from three weeks to three weeks' or less frequently. They heard the cases, in which they were as much witnesses as judge, and reached their verdicts, leaving the stewards to execute them. Cases were often contentious, but only rarely did they escalate into disputes between the villagers and their lord. It was the villagers themselves who were most often the interpreters of their own 'laws'. These were 'the custom of the folk . . . the possession of the people, preserved in the memory of men who for the most part neither wrote nor read'.[58] They were, in the memorable words of Helen Cam, their own 'law-finders and law-makers'. In 1329 the villagers of Darnhall (Ches.) protested that it was not lawful for their lord, the Abbot of the monastery of Vale Royal in Cheshire 'to punish them for any offence except by the assessment [judgment] of their neighbours'.[59] Theirs was a rough justice, but it was very far from being an arbitrary one.

On most manors there was in fact more than one court, or perhaps the same court was held under two or more titles, and exercised more than one group of not very clearly differentiated functions.[60] The hallmote, also known as the court leet or *curia legalis*, was the lord's court, and, as its name implies, customarily met in the hall of the manor-house. The lord's tenants, both free and unfree, were obliged to attend, and were fined if they absented themselves without good reason. Proceedings always began with 'essoins' or excuses for those who were not present. It dealt with petty cases of trespass, damage, nuisance and the like. The penalties which it could assess were generally light, consisting of little more than a fine. The court also recorded the transfer of land – at least of unfree and copyhold land – from father to son and from one tenant to another. In addition to the manor court *sensu stricto* was the View of Frankpledge.[61] This was, in theory, a sheriff's court, but it had in very many instances passed into the control of the manorial lord. At the heart of the View was the tithing, a group notionally of ten or a dozen men, usually heads of households, who stood surety for one another and 'presented' one another's peccadilloes to the court. It was a means of policing the community, the tithing serving as a presenting jury. It had its origins in Anglo-Saxon England, and continued to operate until, at the end of the Middle Ages, it was effectively superseded by the Justices of the Peace.

Both kinds of court were a source of profit to those who possessed the right to hold them. 'Profits of court' were a regularly recurring entry in the ministers' accounts for the manors in their charge. It was thus to the lord's advantage for his steward to secure convictions, but custom dictated that judgment lay with the assessors who made up the court. There may have been miscarriages of justice, but rarely could it have been said that a man was not convicted by the judgment of his peers. A record was kept of the proceedings of the court, and these survive in the large numbers of court rolls, varying greatly in fullness and clarity. There were few who were competent to keep such a record, and the obligation seems to have fallen most often on the parish priest, who was likely to have been the only literate member of the community. The priest in *Piers Plowman* is made to say:[62]

> Ich haue be prest and person   passyng therty wintere
> ut can ich nother solfye ne synge   ne a seyntes lyf rede
> Ach ich can fynde in a felde   and in a forlong an hare,
> And holden a knyȝtes court   and a-counte with the reyue
> Ach ich nought constrye   ne clergialliche reden

The care with which some court rolls were kept, however, suggests a somewhat higher level of literacy than was assumed in the poem.

The manorial court tended to lapse with the decay of the manorial system in the later Middle Ages and sixteenth century, and many of its functions were taken over, under the aegis of the state, by the council and officers of the parish. Nevertheless, there were manors in which the courts continued to be held and to do business through the seventeenth and into the eighteenth century.[63] Where this happened,

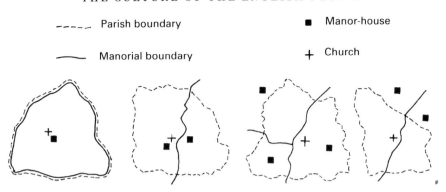

8.9 Schematic diagram showing the possible relationships between parish and manor.

however, the court is usually found to have taken some of the functions generally performed elsewhere by the parish council.

Most people, at least in rural areas, fell under some kind of manorial control, and were also, at least until the system collapsed, members of a tithing. At the same time everyone belonged to a parish. The parochial system was complete by the thirteenth century, and the whole country was divided into parochial units, each conceived as adequate to support both a church and a priest to serve in it. Parish boundaries had become established and were to remain fixed until at least the recent past. The fixity of parochial structure contrasted with the fluctuating fortunes of the manor, likely at any time to be fragmented or to acquire additional land, to be divided between heirs or to be merged with another. From late in the thirteenth century the central government began to use the parish, instead of the manor (which had been used in Domesday Book), as the chief local unit for public administration: for collecting taxes, maintaining roads and bridges and, from late in the sixteenth century, for looking after the poor. It was the parish, therefore, which became 'the institutional focus of such peasant business as transcended or violated manorial interests and the parish church was the meeting place'.[64]

There had at one time been a kind of conformity, if only approximate, between manor and parish, but as the manor became more fluid, the parish, on the other hand, adopted the rigid pattern which it has retained. A parish might come to encapsulate more than one manor, or a manor might extend beyond the parochial limits and incorporate parts of neighbouring parishes. There have been endless variations on the theme of permanent parish and fragmenting manor (Fig. 8.9). And yet the rigidity and permanence of the parish must not be exaggerated. Small parishes might merge and large be divided; the examples of the Framinghams has already been cited (p. 258). On the other hand, the population might grow in numbers and wealth, and secondary foci might be created in addition to the primary village; these might, in their turn, claim the right to have a church with its sacraments for themselves. Such a claim never went unopposed. To carve a second parish out of the territory of the first would be to deny the latter part of the tithe, fees and oblations which it had been

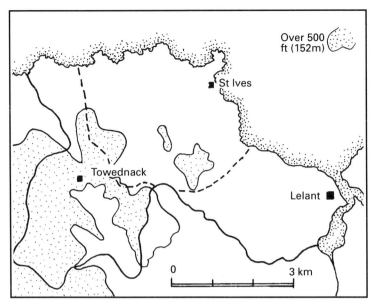

8.10 The large medieval parish of St Uny Lelant (Corn.). St Ives and Towednack were chapels-of-ease.

accustomed to receive. The inhabitants of the would-be parish might appeal to the bishop with horrendous stories of how their distance from their parish church was imperilling their souls. Those of the 'chapelries' of Towednack and St Ives, within the large parish of St Uny Lelant (Corn.) complained 'that they lived, for the most part, four, three or (at least) two miles from the Mother Church ... the roads being mountainous and rocky, and liable in winter to sudden inundations, so that they could not safely attend Divine Service or send their children to be baptized, their wives to be purified, or their dead to be buried; the children often went unbaptized, and the sick were deprived of the last sacraments' (Fig. 8.10). They added, furthermore, that they had already built two chapels at their own expense, had enclosed cemeteries and could well afford the cost of a priest.[65] In this instance the vicar of Lelant resisted the claims of his parishioners. The case went to Rome, where Popes Alexander V and John XXIII (a schismatic pope) pronounced in favour of the people, and the Bishop of Exeter authorised the celebration of the holy office in the two chapels.[66] Those who know the terrain in which this drama was set will not only sympathise with the parishioners – for Cornish miles are long and hard – but will recognise that the sacramental issue was not the only one. The relative isolation of the communities from one another gave each an individuality that resulted in distrust if not hostility towards the rest.

No bishop could ever have regarded appeals like this as more than pieces of transparent special pleading. Yet many, in fact, yielded. The second church was, as a general rule, allowed to have all the sacraments with the exception of baptism and burial, the distinguishing marks of parochial status. The new church was generally expected to manage on the donations of its handful of faithful, who were expected to maintain the whole of its fabric. In the chapelries of the parish of Bakewell (Derby.) 'the parishioners are to keep both nave and chancel, and to provide both chalice and missal'.[67] On rare occasions a division of the parochial tithe was agreed upon, and such compromises were recorded in detail in the bishops' registers. But the status of the second church was, as a general rule, rarely more than that of a 'chapel-of-ease', with nothing more than the hope that some day it might graduate to the status of parish church. All too often the chapel struggled, with insufficient income, for survival, rather like impoverished churches, deserted by their congregations, at the present time.

The parish and its church aroused an intense loyalty in most parishioners, though this began to fade in the later seventeenth century. Its boundaries constituted, for the medieval parishioners, a kind of mental horizon, beyond which all was *forinsecus* – 'foreign'. People from beyond these unseen limits were rarely made welcome; they were not taken to the hearts of the community and allowed to share in such privileges and endowments as it might possess. The stranger was not placed in a tithing, like other folk, and might even be required to have a surety, a 'mainpernor', who could vouch for his or her good intentions and ensure that he, in a widely used phrase, *decetero, bene et fideliter se habebit dum fuerit residens in ville* ('conduct himself decently, well and faithfully while resident in the town').[68] Raftis is, however, at pains to show that there was, in spite of this, a not inconsiderable movement from manor to manor, and that in the course of time migrants did become accepted, though the process was slower and less certain than that of acquiring a new nationality today.

Every parish had its organs of self-government, though these might differ greatly from one to another. The parishioners formed a kind of government separate from and not infrequently at odds with that of the manorial officers and court, even though the same people were likely at some time to serve in both. The parish chose a constable, an overseer of the poor and one of more churchwardens,[69] even before these offices were regularised at the end of the sixteenth century. They tended to be filled from the small number of better-off members of the community, a sort of oligarchy of prosperous farmers and craftsmen.

Relatively few records of parish administration have survived, and, in all probability, few were ever kept. Foremost amongst such records, however, were the parochial registers of baptisms, marriages and burials, made obligatory in 1538 and kept with some regularity from later in the century, and the accounts kept on behalf of the parish by the churchwardens.[70] Incumbents who performed the ceremonies were responsible for the former, though the register appears more often than not to have been kept by a lay person who received a small fee for his pains. The elected churchwardens kept the parochial accounts in their own far from orderly fashion. The office of churchwarden first appeared in the later Middle Ages, and was a response to the obligations placed on the community to maintain those parts of the church which were not the specific responsibility of the rector.[71] The earliest surviving accounts date from the early fifteenth century.[72] A canon of 1571 prescribed that there should be two wardens, one nominated by the rector or vicar, the other elected by the parishioners.[73] Their duties were, first and foremost, to look after the fabric of the church and to collect money for this purpose. But, according to local circumstances, their duties usually extended far beyond this. They organised church-ales and other means of raising money; they levied and collected the local 'rates'; they administered the parish stock (p. 285); they provided for the poor and indigent, and, on occasion, turned their attention to roads and bridges within their bailiwicks. The churchwarden had become 'the local odd-jobman for administrative purposes'.[74] Some of these multifarious duties had been inherited from the manor court as it passed into desuetude; others were to be streamlined and reorganised by Elizabethan legislation. All were to remain the obligations of the ecclesiastical parish into the nineteenth century.[75] The records which the churchwardens kept were sometimes little more than jumbled lists of petty receipts and expenses.[76] The most orderly of them, on the other hand, were the carefully written and audited accounts which were submitted annually to the parish council. Almost always, however, they were incomplete, since certain categories of parochial income that had been wholly allocated to specific purposes were often omitted from the accounts.[77]

A divided society

Parochial records reveal a society torn by jealousies and discords and divided by class. The apparent unanimity of parish decisions gives an entirely false picture of democracy in action. The community was riddled with factions. There were families which gave, as the reason for not attending church, the fact that their rivals would be present. There was, indeed, much to quarrel about: the sale and inheritance of land, broken engagements and marriage settlements, and the support of illegitimate children. Add to these the strictly agricultural sources of dispute: encroachment on a neighbour's land; overgrazing of the common; illicit gleaning; and defaulting on communal obligations to fence the churchyard or to perform customary tasks like cutting and spreading rushes on the church floor. Then there were disputes which arose both from the boisterous behaviour of the young, who threw stones through windows and upset the decorum of their elders, and from the overindulgence of the old. Things have not greatly changed, though in a wealthier and more mobile society such causes of dispute may today seem trivial.

In no aspect of communal life was division more apparent than in the provision of seating within the parish church. It was the practice in the earlier Middle Ages for the congregation to stand or kneel during service, and many were the complaints of the filth and unevenness of the floor. The less robust 'went to the wall',[78] where there was commonly a stone bench, a sort of raised plinth intended to serve as a seat (Fig. 8.11). Rushes were commonly strewn on the floor, and when for some reason this practice lapsed, the parishioners of Capgrave (W. Riding, Yorks.) complained that

8.11 Stone seat at the base of a pillar in Hythe (Kent) parish church, used by those unable to stand during the long services.

there was 'scarce anything [on which to kneel] except the bare ground itself'.[79] The earliest seats were for the use of the priests and acolytes, but in the later thirteenth century wooden seats began to be provided for the laity. At once there were disputes about their use. 'Alas,' wrote Bishop Quivil of Exeter in 1287, 'we have heard that, on account of seats in churches, the parishioners are often vexed, two or more persons claiming one seat.'[80] He ordered that only 'noble persons and patrons' might claim any proprietory right in a seat. But disputes of this kind continued and became more violent as more and more churches set up benches within their naves. At Wakes Colne (Essex) it was reported in 1594 that 'there is great disorder in the placing of the parishioners in their pews, the rich with the poor and not according to their calling [status]'.[81] At the Archdeacon's Court of the Diocese of Oxford, in 1584, one respondent stated that as she was taking

her seate at the beginning of evening prayer the sayed Barbara iostled further into the seate and wolde not lett her come into her own place there, wherpon this resapondent sayed unto her, yf yowe will not lett me come unto mye owne seate I will sitt upon yor lappe ... and therevpon grewe ffurther woordes of inconvenience betweene theime, as whore and basterd & suche lyke ...[82]

Such 'broyles about seates' occupy a conspicuous part in the presentments before every consistory court, because seating in the church was the most conspicuous, indeed the only way by which status could be incontrovertibly demonstrated in the small, closed rural community. In many instances the pew became attached not to the family which customarily used it but, like labour obligations in the Middle Ages, to the land itself. This inevitably raised problems, as, for example, when one of presumed lower status took over a farm from one of higher. In the end, it was status that determined one's proximity to the altar and pulpit, as it did one's place of burial within the church or churchyard. The churchwardens generally had the ordering of seats, a thankless task which led to much rancour within the community. At St Ebbs, Oxford, in 1663, Francis Taylor, a cobbler, and John Mares, an ale-bearer, 'did remove themselves . . . out of the seate used by them . . . into a higher seate there not soe fitt for them as theire said former seate because that in the showe of the world they nowe sitt above their betters'.[83] The assessment for church-rate was generally said to have been based on the extent of land held. At Lambeth (Surrey), however, the church-rate itself 'was based on the position of the pews occupied by the parishioners',[84] which probably amounted to much the same thing.

The more privileged within the parish were accustomed in the seventeenth and eighteenth centuries to construct large box-pews for themselves, their families and their dependants, but among the humbler members of the community the men were generally seated apart from the women, the men to the south and the women to the north of the central aisle. This is why we occasionally find in a churchwarden's account that a husband has paid for a seat for his wife without any mention of his own.[85] There is even a case of one aspiring member of parochial society cutting away part of the baptismal font in order to obtain sufficient space to construct his pew.[86] It was usual for at least the better-off to pay for their seats, and pew rentals constituted a not inconsiderable source of parochial income. In 1454–5, 6d. a seat was the flat rate at St Ewen's, Bristol. At Ashburton (Devon.) a half-century later the price of a pew varied from 4d. to 8d. a year according, one presumes, to its nearness to the altar. In some churches – Ludlow parish church was one[87] – parishioners were accustomed to purchase what can only be called a kind of leasehold on their pews, and when a member of the gentry built a large box-pew for himself and his family he commonly purchased the necessary floor space.

Such was the importance of a claim to a particular seat within a church that it became a common practice in the eighteenth century for the churchwardens to prepare a seating plan, as if attendance at church was a kind of dinner party. Such a plan was drawn up for Clayworth (Notts.) in the late seventeenth century.[88] A comparable plan, with occupants' names written against their seats, survives for the borough and parish of Lostwithiel (Corn.) and is shown in Figure 8.12,[89] and the seating in the church of Myddle (Shrops.) was made the basis of a unique study of the social structure and internal frictions of the parish about 1700.[90]

During the Middle Ages the obligation to attend church was taken for granted. When there was absenteeism it was for personal reasons; questions of theology and doctrine rarely entered into it. The Protestant Reformation of the sixteenth century intensified differences and, indeed, created a veritable schism in some communities. But popular attitudes had not changed. Unanimity was essential if the new magic, like the old, was to work, and, since opposition was both more visible and more voluble, steps that would have been unthinkable in the Middle Ages were taken to

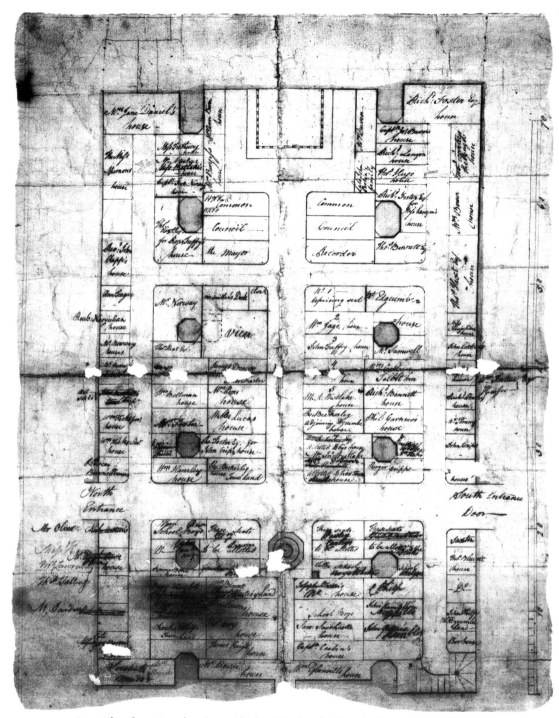

8.12 Church seating plan, Lostwithiel parish church (Corn.). Cornw Rec Off P128/6/2.
Courtesy Cornwall County and Diocesan Record Office.

root it out. In particular, the state intervened to compel church attendance and at least an outward compliance with the law.

The accession of Elizabeth was followed immediately by an Act of Uniformity, which restored the Second Prayer Book of Edward VI as the sole liturgy and imposed penalties, more or less severe, on those who promoted the authority of any foreign potentate or prelate, and this, of course, could only mean the Pope. Some thirteen years later further legislation was enacted against the practice of the Roman Catholic faith, and 'recusancy, or deliberate abstention from the Anglican service, made its appearance'[91] as a regular feature in English life. The Catholic powers at this time constituted a grave threat to the security of this country, giving further point to the demand for religious conformity.

But late in Elizabeth's reign, and during those of her successors, James I and Charles I, the political decline of the Catholic countries removed the threat if not also the fear of recusancy. At the same time the religious structure of the country began to be threatened from the opposite direction, by groups which can collectively be known as Puritans. The main instrument of Catholicism had been the priesthood and the sacraments; that of the Puritans was preaching. The sermon had also assumed much greater importance within the Anglican church during the previous century, as is demonstrated not only by the volumes of sermons that were printed but also by the money spent on building and improving pulpits.[92] The government's efforts to control these activities and to restrict unauthorised preaching met with little success. Henceforward any community was likely to be torn in both directions, by the recusants with their secretive practices and refusal to attend the Anglican church, and by the far more public preaching and proselytising of the Puritans.

The dialectic of the first sixty years of the seventeenth century was followed by the reassertion, soon after the Restoration in 1660, of the supremacy of the Anglican church. 'Conventicles', or nonconformist meeting-places, were banned, and public office was restricted to those who adhered to the established church. The law seems never to have been strictly enforced, though non-attendance at church and refusal to have a child baptised figured very prominently in the presentments made by the churchwardens on the occasion of the archdeacon's periodic visitations. The penalty was at most penance, and even this proved difficult to enforce. Public opinion in time became more tolerant, and the disabilities of nonconformists, both Protestant and Catholic, were gradually removed during the nineteenth century, and were totally abolished before its end.[93] It was during the seventeenth century that bishops and others attempted to enumerate those who in one way or another dissented from the established church. The Compton Census of 1676, named after the Bishop of London, who collated the returns, was the most extensive and, despite many estimates that cannot be wholly trusted, the most reliable.[94] But many bishops called for the numbers of communicants, recusants and dissenters in the articles which preceded their visitations. The arrival of a Dutch Calvinist on the English throne in 1688 and of a German Lutheran in 1714 made the earlier legislation somewhat inappropriate. It was not repealed, however, but, in typically English fashion, was in most respects ignored.

Nevertheless, many communities were irreparably divided. To the old divisions amongst the peasantry, based on land and wealth, were added those deriving from religious affiliation. The Puritan sects ripened into denominational groups, and from late in the seventeenth century began to build meeting-houses and to attract certain segments of the local community, most often those who were in one way or another aggrieved with the establishment. But the interplay of self-interest and religious conviction, of animosity and group solidarity, assumed so many forms that it is impossible to generalise. There can be little question, however, but that the social element in nonconformity was as big as the theological.

The duties of the churchwardens included the management of parochial assets and the maintenance of the fabric of the church, or at least of those parts for which the rector was not legally responsible. By canon law the chancel was built and repaired from the rectorial tithe. The parishioners were alone accountable for the nave in which they sat, and for the tower and porch. But the churchyard was part of the incumbent's freehold, and he received the fees payable for interments. Before the reorganisation of church finances in modern times, the rector was sometimes able to evade his responsibilities for chancel and churchyard.[95] The complaint of the people of Huddersfield, that 'ther Chauncell is in decaie and almost downe and ... many tymes it hath bene presented but no reformation had',[96] is repeated over and over again in every consistory court record. A visitation of churches in the diocese of Carlisle, early in the eighteenth century, revealed an appalling state of affairs, due both to the small income of the incumbents and to the poverty of the region. Of Holme (Cumb.) it was reported that 'the Inside of the Church was full of Water the Rain falling in plentifully everywhere', and, in a vain attempt to stem the decay, the parishioners 'took the Lead from the South Isle ... to cover that on the North'.[97] On the other hand, parishioners often took a great pride in their church, and gave or bequeathed, in the aggregate, large sums for its maintenance. The evidence of wills alone shows that £2287 (about £800,000 in present-day terms) was bequeathed for the building of Lavenham (Suffolk) church between 1485 and 1540.[98] This writer has, however, yet to find any unambiguous evidence for parishioners voluntarily giving money to restore the rector's part of the church. Donations and legacies for the maintenance of the church tailed off after the Reformation, but any shortfall in this respect was probably made good by the income from church-rates and the rental of pews. The church-rate was disliked by all and strenuously resisted by some, the reason generally given being hostility to the established church. Delinquents were liable to be called before the bishop's court, which alone had jurisdiction but possessed little power to enforce its judgments. At a Yorkshire parish William Kirkebiue 'denyes to pay his cesmente to the reparacion of the church',[99] and there was little that the church authorities could do about it. There were many like him, and the fabric of parish churches decayed sadly during the eighteenth century. Such failures to support the focal institution of the parish can only have added to the rancour which was rife amongst parishioners. Breaches of church discipline were required to be reported by the churchwardens to the bishop's consistory to be judged by his officials. Some of the petty offences that were thus 'presented' may seem to us more risible than serious, as they may well have done to many of the parishioners. There can be little question but that the enforcement of the church's code of conduct contributed significantly to the divisions within a parish, and the incumbent's frequent and personal attacks on 'dissenters' can only have increased the inevitable ill-feeling.

Parochial charities and church stock

In most parishes there was a parish stock, a varied assemblage of land, animals, chattels and money which had over the years been bequeathed to the parish. Wills often record such small endowments. Management of the stock was usually left to the churchwardens, occasionally to a self-perpetuating group of trustees. Such records as they have left were commonly incorporated into the churchwardens' accounts, but occasionally one finds an independent accounting. At St Mabyn (Corn.) its administration was recorded in a small notebook.[100] Loans were made to parishioners in need, but only, it would appear, if there was some prospect that they would be returned. Objects were lent on paymnt of a small sum as rent. At the Bedfordshire village of Clifton 'the cherche cowe ys lett after thys maner'. There followed the rules by which the services of the cow might be had; usually it would appear from another source, for the provision of milk for a widow or a poor family.[101] The stock might also include items of a more general use to the community, such as water-buckets and iron rakes for tackling a cottage fire. At Morebath (Som.) the wardens submitted a regular account for 'the Store of Sent Sonday',[102] and in a visitation of Carlisle diocese it was noted at Ravenstonedale that 'they have a good poor-Stock, well preserv'd and employ'd',[103] and, it would appear from the fragmentary accounts that survive, this was generally the case. The bier, used for transporting corpses to the cemetery and the cloth to cover them, were usually reckoned to be part of the parish stock. The parish stock was indissolubly linked with parish gilds, which in many instances served as its guardians. At Morebath, for example, a number of sheep were in 1522 given respectively to the 'Store of Sent Jorge', the 'Store of Sent Antoni' and the 'Store of our Laydy'.[104] Parish gilds were primarily social and religious. They provided for masses for deceased members and burned an inordinate number of candles for their souls, but they also gave more material help to their widows. They participated actively in church-ales and less publicly in dinners and festivities which were peculiar to themselves. Some gilds acquired considerable wealth, which enabled them to add chantry chapels to their parish churches, and to make provision for a priest, and even, especially in urban gilds, to erect a substantial 'gild'-hall. A survey of gilds was conducted in 1389, and the returns made to the royal Chancery show a total of over 500. There were many more which made no return or whose returns have been lost.[105] Their functions have today in some degree been taken over by the state, but their role is also in part filled by such organisations as Rotary, Kiwanis and similar societies.

A community might have two or more gilds, with different dedications, each representing a particular group of craftsmen. At the village of Croscombe (Som.) there were no less than six such gilds, two of them, the Webbers (weavers) and the Tuckers (fullers), clearly identified with individual crafts; the others were the 'Young Men', the 'Maidens', the 'Archers' and the 'Hogglers'.[106] There is even a brief mention of the gild of 'their wives'. Parish gilds were no doubt fluctuating bodies. Some were ephemeral and most ceased to exist at the Reformation since their activities had been closely associated with chantries which had been dissolved.[107] The account books of the Gilds of St George and of St Mary in the parish church of St Peter, Nottingham, for the period 1459 to 1545–6[108] show how broad was the spectrum of activities in which they engaged. They possessed a not inconsiderable amount of silver and pewter, and continued to purchase silver for the manufacture of plate. They earned a small income by lending table vessels, and even received 16d. 'for hire of pewter vessels for use in the house [presumably Nottingham Castle] of the lord King'. One gild made payments for glazing the windows of the hall 'in which the feast of the brothers and sisters was held',[109] evidence that some gilds were not exclusively male. At the same time the two gilds combined to build a new aisle for their parish church.[110]

The charitable activities of the churchwardens were not limited to the management of the parish stock and the occasional supervision of a parish gild. Even before the Elizabethan Poor Law of 1598 they had some responsibility for the indigent and destitute of their community.[111] They made occasional gifts and loans, sometimes from parochial income, sometimes from parish stock. After 1598 the system was regularised, and a parish rate was instituted and administered by the local poor law officers. These commonly belonged to the same village élite from whom the churchwardens and constables were drawn, and most of the leading personages would have taken their turn in filling all these offices. The parish was responsible for its own poor, but always took very great care not to be burdened with paupers for whom it had no legal responsibility. This was the primary reason for the close examination of the parentage of any illegitimate child born within its limits. No intruder who was likely ever to become chargeable to the local rate was tolerated, and he or she could after 1598 be legally moved on until the potential pauper reached his or her original place of residence.

Parochial charity was not always so restricted. Occasionally gifts were made by the wardens to individuals from outside the parish, but always, so it would seem, because they had suffered a calamity for which they were in no sense responsible. At Shillington (Beds.) six pence were 'given to a poore woman that had great losses by fyar'.[112] From the later sixteenth century it became a common practice to take collections for groups elsewhere who had suffered some grave misfortune. This would be read in church and contributions solicited. In 1596 the parish of

South Newington (Oxon.) raised the princely sum of six pence 'to a brief for burning of certain houses'.[113] In the seventeenth century the practice became more widespread. It is well documented for Clayworth (Notts.).[114] In 1676 the rector recorded that 'I read a letter of Request for a fire at Scrooby & there was collected there upon 7s. 10d.' Thereafter briefs became more frequent and the generosity of parishioners less conspicuous. Within the next twenty-five years 71 briefs were received, no less than 54 of them to assist people whose homes had been burned. One was for sufferers from an earthquake, and one for the rebuilding of the church of West Halton (Linc.) which had fallen down. In general, such appeals were likely to raise from 2s. to 5s. A feature of the response to these briefs was not so much the compassion displayed as the widening of the mental horizon of the parishioners. There was a slowly emerging awareness that people a hundred miles and more away, who would have been alien to their society only a few generations earlier, needed their help, and, if they themselves had been in a similar situation, would have responded to their own appeal. These briefs marked a stage in the breakdown of the sense of isolation of the rural community. The practice of taking collections for specific and often non-religious purposes cannot be said to have wholly disappeared from formal church observations even today, though good causes are now more likely to be within the Third World than nearer home.

The church itself had at one time been the scene of charitable and recreational activities. But before the end of the Middle Ages property began to be acquired and used for these purposes. Most often it had been bequeathed to the community and amounted to nothing more than a simple cottage. All too often the community could not afford to keep it in order, and occasionally even its ownership was disputed in the courts. At Cheddington (Bucks.) a house which had been given to the parish had 'fallen into delapidation, and the parishioners did not dare repair itt, because a certain William Couclyff claimed it'.[115] The 'chyrche hows' came to be used for village entertainment, especially after these activities had been driven from the church. The church house at Boxford (Suffolk) even contained an oven for communal use.[116] At South Newington (Oxon.) the community actually built its own church house,[117] and this seems to have been increasingly the practice as the church ceased to be used for secular purposes. In the course of the nineteenth century a church or village hall became a common, almost an invariable, feature, replacing the church as the social centre of the community.

Fun and games

The medieval community had derived much of its sense of unity from common participation in carnival and other regularly recurring festivities (p. 389). Most of these practices declined after the Reformation. The reasons were many. Some had taken place on Sundays, the only day of the week, apart from certain saints' days, when most people were free to participate in them, and such abuses of the sabbath were now strenuously discouraged (Fig. 8.13). At Lawton (E. Riding, Yorks.)

8.13 Wall-painting in Breage parish church (Corn.), showing a suffering Christ surrounded by the tools of the trades. This represents his grief that people used these tools on Sundays. Amongst them is a playing-card.

'there was a Maypole sett uppe upon Lawton Grene upon a Sabbothe or holly daye, where a pyper and dyvers youthe were playinge and dauncinge.'[118] The consistory court to which this was reported was, not unexpectedly, severe on such a profanation of the sabbath. In their presentment of abuses the churchwardens frequently had occasion to note that games were played in the churchyard – an easy matter when there were no tombstones to stand in the way – and that balls were even hurled through the windows of the church. At Goring (Oxon.) 'some of the towne did use to boole in the procession waye', that is, the footpath leading to the church door.[119] It was also reported that in a Yorkshire parish five or six persons 'Plaid at bowles on Whitsonday in the churche yarde', and were severely reprimanded.[120] In the later seventeenth century people were presented before the Bishop of Durham's court for 'playing football, nine-holes [and] driving sheep' on the sabbath.[121] The frequency of such presentations is testimony to the boisterousness of youth, which authority from that day to this has utterly failed to repress.

Many such holiday activities had religious overtones. The ritual enactment of dramas and dances – now gentrified as morris-dances – was an integral part. The churchwardens of Ashburton (Devon.) paid 'for painting the players' clothes and making the tunics ... for chekery [chequered cloth] for making the said players' tunics ... And for making players' staves and for crestes on their heads at the feast of Corpus Christi'.[122] At Northill (Beds.) 3 shillings were given to the 'morysse dauncers towerd ther shoues [shoes]',[123] and again 'for 7 payre of dansynge showes 5s. 10d.'[124] Such play-acting tended everywhere to disappear in the late sixteenth and early seventeenth centuries because their convivial and social aspects could not readily be separated from the religious.[125] But they did not vanish completely. The Lord of Misrule may never again have reigned as he had once done, but his presence was clearly condoned by some churchwardens who failed in their duty to report him to the archdeacon. At Wooton (Oxon.) they were themselves 'presented' 'for not presentinge of evell rule done in the churche by the Lord and Ladie on Midsomer day. The [churchwardens in reply] state that theare was noe lord or ladie this year ... but on Midsomer day last at evening prayer the youth were sumwhat meerie together in crowning of lordes.'[126]

The most persistent of such occasions for jollification were church-ales. Much as the Puritans frowned upon them, they were nevertheless obliged to tolerate them for the economic benefits which they gave. They were like whist-drives and jumble-sales today, means of raising money for parochial and church purposes. At Boxford (Suff.) they were said to have been by far the largest source of parochial income,[127] and nowhere was it possible to ignore the income which they generated. The ale was generally brewed by parish officers, sometimes from malt received as a levy on parishioners, and was sold to all who participated,[128] and any malt that remained after the festivities was also sold for the benefit of the church.[129] Vast quantities of ale, as well as of more solid food, were consumed on these occasions, and considerable sums of money were raised.

At Northill (Beds.) the expenditure on a church-ale in 1561 was carefully itemised in the churchwardens' accounts:[130]

for spysse and frutte for bakemeats	3s. 2d.
for hoppes to brewe the bere withall	1s. 8d.
for layed out for weate	7s. 4d.
for layed out for the 2 dormes [probably dormant tables] and the menstrell	11s. 0d.
for the makeng of the moryscotts	2s. 4d.
for the morysse dauncers towerd ther shoues	3s. 0d.
Item gevyne to the bruers of the bere	4s. 0d.
	29s. 6d.

The record does not state what the income was from these festivities. At Marston (Oxon.) in 1547 26s. was earned 'at theire Witsondays ale',[131] but the sums raised were usually a great deal less than this: at South Littleton (Worcs.) in 1554, only 2s. 3d.[132]

A parish was usually proud of its church-ale and happy with the profit that it brought. Indeed, there were occasions when one parish, in an unaccustomed excess

8.14 A game of shuttlecock, from a misericord.

of goodwill, invited representatives of neighbouring parishes to attend, but, since the purpose was to raise money, required them to buy their own drinks.[133]

The more extensive use of the church-rate and the imposition of pew rentals in the course of time removed the monetary incentive for this particular form of celebration.[134] Archbishop Stratford had in 1342 authorised the levy of a rate on property for the purpose of maintaining the fabric of at least the parishioners' part of their church. But payment could not be enforced except by the ineffective church courts, and attempts to give it legal validity were repeatedly resisted by Parliament. Indeed, 'the first statutory recognition of [its] existence was in the act for [its] abolition'.[135]

A more charitable view of church-ales was expressed by Peter Mews:[136]

> The churches much owe, as we all do knowe,
>   For when they be drooping and ready to fail
> By a Whitsun or Church-Ale up again they shall go,
>   And owe their reparing to a pot of good ale.

But this was in 1671, when the restoration of Charles II had brought with it a more rational attitude to the pleasures of village life. By this time, also, churchwardens had begun to tap other – and theologically less compromising – sources of income like church-rates and pew rents.[137] The latter have continued in some churches into the present century, but the church-rate was made illegal early in the nineteenth century.[138]

8.15 A ball-game from a late medieval misericord.

The playing of games, most of them ball-games, was universal in pre-industrial communities. We must visualise them as ill-organised displays of physical activity, even of bravura, which readily degenerated into rowdyism and could on occasion cause considerable damage. They were probably not strongly competitive, and consisted mainly in kicking or throwing a ball about. There was little by way of rules, and the games served primarily as an outlet for youthful high spirits. Nor was there usually any element of team spirit. A London coroner's roll recorded[139] that two men, who had been drinking, agreed to wrestle. One then desisted, saying that his clothes were torn. The other handed him a vest, whereupon 'they wrestled with all their strength and gripped each other in such a way that [one's] right leg was broken',[140] and he died.

Many games, however, consisted merely in kicking or throwing a ball, and it was from these totally unstructured activities that most nineteenth-century games emerged. Occasionally such contests were staged with the young men of a neighbouring parish. Such was the 'hurling' contest between the men of St Columb Major (Corn.) and those of the surrounding parishes, which continued to be held into the present century. Such games sometimes assumed the proportions of a pitched battle, which reflected and exaggerated the depth of feeling between neighbouring parishes.

It became the practice in East Anglia, and possibly also elsewhere, to set aside a tract of land for games and probably also the performance of plays and other rituals. The memory of its purpose has survived in many villages in the eastern counties as a field-name: 'camping' ground or close. The word 'camp' was cognate with the Germanic *kampfen*, meaning to fight, and is indicative of the kinds of contest that took place there. In Yorkshire the comparable term 'garry', from the French *guerrier*, was used.[141] In almost every case the 'camping ground' was close to, even contiguous with, the churchyard, suggesting that the game ritual was linked in some way with the religious. Games were played on the occasion of certain church festivals, Shrove Tuesday, for example. It is likely, furthermore, that they had been played either within the churchyard itself or across open fields to the grave damage of the crops, and that this may have led to the attempt, long before the end of the Middle Ages, to restrict the damage they were likely to cause to a small field.

The games played in the churchyard and the street were only part of a broad spectrum to play which ranged from staged religious drama to boisterous and inebriated dancing, such as that shown in some of Brueghel's paintings. The social importance of play cannot be exaggerated. Life in traditional societies 'was brimful of play; the jouous and unbuttoned play of the people, full of pagan elements that had lost their sacred significance and been transformed into jesting and buffoonery'.[142] It served many functions, none of which would have been clearly perceived by its participants.

Play, in the first place, has 'the power to create a coherent sense of experience which [was] radically different from that of everyday life. It can oppose a new and temporary order to the conventional routine; it is able to dissolve normal restraints, sanction what would on other occasions be impermissible, and sometimes allow for fantasies which seem but madness, to be actually realized.'[143] It was part of the routine of role reversal which characterised all societies. It represented an escape into 'a distinctive world of culture and consciousness', a relief from the dull, exhausting and oppressive routine of work.

Games, secondly, were rooted in the agonistic basis of cultural life, the spirit of competition between individuals, between the societies which they comprised, and between humankind and a savage and unpredictable nature.[144] Man acted out the order of nature, fought with it, and, in play at least, conquered it. In this must surely lie the roots of such 'sports' as bear-baiting, badger-baiting and fox-hunting.

Associated with such agonistic activities there seems always to have been an urge to destroy. This may at one time have represented the elimination of opposition, the destruction of the property of an 'enemy', or the killing of a quarry. It could also embody an element of bravado, of showmanship, of conspicuous consumption, whose purpose was solely to demonstrate the 'nobility' of the person whose possessions were thus wasted. The potlach of the Nootka Sound Indians of British Columbia[145] may be an extreme example, but less extravagant instances were not uncommon in all traditional societies, not excluding our own.

Games, thirdly, gave coherence to the groups which played them, not only to the participants but also to those who supported them, encouraged them and entered vicariously into the sport. One cannot be sure that the concepts of 'team' and 'supporters' had emerged much before the early nineteenth century: probably not. But after they had appeared there can be no question of their importance in lending a kind of unity and purpose to a society. It could be argued that, in a traditional society, the bonds which held it together were sufficiently strong not to need the further impetus provided by 'conflict' with other communities. This, however, is not the case with post-traditional societies. These societies lacked cohesion and needed such institutions as sporting clubs with which to identify, in order to give

8.16 A stick-and-ball game, ancestor to the modern hockey, in the great east window, Gloucester Cathedral.

them meaning and purpose and a sense of unity, and this remains today their principal justification.

The practice of games, lastly, derives from remote antiquity, when they served neither as a social bond nor as an expression of *joie de vivre*. They had a ritual significance, but the ritual of games has always called for both space and leisure. Games were played in the streets, on the 'greens', which provided the only open spaces within village settlements, and most often within the unobstructed space of churchyards. The many presentments for playing games in the churchyard always seem to have related to Sundays. It is impossible to tell whether, in the minds of contemporaries, the offence was the desecration of the churchyard or of the sabbath.

This raises the question of how much leisure people might have had for outdoor games. The working day was long, and there was never any question of regular time off until late in the nineteenth century. The only times when most people were able to enjoy any leisure during the daytime were on Sundays and certain church festivals. If games within the churchyard had been tolerated during the week, it is likely that only the very young would have been able to participate. There was, in the course of the week, no slot into which organised play could be inserted, and team games for the mass of the population had to wait until Parliament had instituted a half-day's holiday on Saturdays. Society in this country has had to pay dearly for the puritanical objection to any supposed misuse of the sabbath.

What, then, were the games which engaged the attention of people, both old and young? One must distinguish between what, for lack of a better term, may be called 'field' sports, and those which engaged individuals rather than groups, and could be played indoors. The latter included a variety of board and card-games as well as games of chance. This distinction had clearly been made long before Christian times. The Irish epic, *Tain Ba Cualnge*, described how the chieftain watched the young men playing ball-games (Fig. 8.16), while their less agile elders played board-games

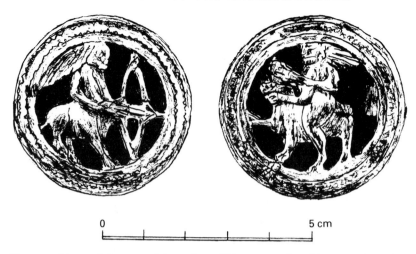

0   5 cm

8.17 Pieces used in a *tabula* game of the early twelfth century, found in excavating Gloucester Castle.

such as *brandub* and *fidchell*.[146] In the course of excavations on the site of Gloucester Castle the board and pieces for the game of *tabula* were found (Fig. 8.17). A rectangular board was covered with small bone panels. The 'pieces' were round counters, also of bone, all different and carved with human and animal figures, not unlike those met with in architectural bosses and capitals.[147] The game in question was probably an early form of backgammon. Such a game is shown in progress in the Luttrell Psalter of the early fourteenth century.[148] Games of chance were important, as is shown by dice recovered from Celtic sites. In a case before an Essex consistory court the defendant 'admits playing ball, but denies dice during sevice',[149] as if gambling were more heinous than a boisterous ball-game (Fig. 8.18). Such games were played one-on-one. They could be used to fill short periods of leisure and called for little by way of equipment. Card-games appeared at an early date, and appealed to the gambling instinct present in most people. A minatory wall-painting of a suffering Christ, surrounded by artificers' tools, contains, in one instance, a playing-card as a warning to those who would profane the sabbath by either work or play.[150]

The *Tain* describes how a boy set out to join the court of a chief:

The boy . . . took his playthings. He took his hurly stick . . . and his silver ball; he took his little javelin for casting and his toy spear with its end sharpened by fire; and he began to shorten the journey by playing with them. He would strike his ball with the stick, and drive it a long way from him. Then, with a second stroke he would throw his stick so that he might drive it a distance no less than the first.[151] He would throw his javelin and would cast his spear, and would make a playful rush after them. Then he would catch his hurly stick and his ball and his javelin; and before the end of his spear had reached the ground he would catch its tip aloft in the air.[152]

A pottery mould, found in the English Midlands, shows a human figure in the act of

(a)

(b)

8.18 A board-game, from the Luttrell Psalter, fo. 76; it looks like the game called 'nine men's morris'; see J. T. Micklethwaite, 'On the indoor games of school boys in the Middle Ages', *Arch Jl*, 49 (1892), 319–28; (b) two gamblers playing a dice-game appear to be quarrelling; from a misericord in St George's Chapel, Windsor Castle.

striking a ball with a curved stick,[153] and a similar figure is represented at a very much later date in the great east window of Gloucester Cathedral (Fig. 8.16). The action of the small boy in hitting his ball along the road with a curved stick could be interpreted as the earliest form of golf or even of hockey. Indeed, the ball-and-stick

8.19 Rubbing of a graffito showing a hobby-horse, in Wallington parish church (Herts.).

game, along with football, must have been the most popular of field-games. A decree of Edwad III of 1363 roundly condemned *ludos inhonestos et minus utiles*, including amongst them *canibuca* or *cambuca*, a stick-and-ball game, and required that people should practise archery instead.[154] The reason given was not that they led to an abuse of the sabbath, but that they interfered with the practice of archery. This, on account of its military significance, seems never to have been discouraged, even on Sundays.

Toys differ from games in that they generally lacked the element of competition and struggle present in the latter. Yet the distinction is an arbitrary one. A ball can serve in a competitive game, and, tossed about by the boy in the *Tain*, it becomes a toy. Toys derive in the main from adult activities of everyday life rather than from past rituals, and are discussed later (Fig. 8.19). Hunting has always been practised by traditional societies. At first, its purpose was that of providing food, the human animal preying on game animals, as the latter in many instances did upon smaller creatures. Even in classical times, however, hunting as a means of livelihood began to yield to hunting as a pleasurable pursuit. Hunting the deer or the boar remained the preserve of the élite; humbler members of society trapped or snared birds and the less obtrusive animals like the rabbit and the hare. This is not the place to examine the legislation which sought to restrict the pleasures and profits of the chase to the upper classes who alone possessed rights over the land. It is enough to say that the upper classes hunted, while the lower poached. Many were driven to poaching, despite the harsh penalties imposed, by economic necessity. Poaching was, in the popular view, the least dishonourable of all felonies.

Beside the hunt for a restricted number of animals which were held to have a food value, there was a determined effort to exterminate those which were deemed by an ignorant populace to be vermin. Foxes were likely to kill poultry, but no such charge could be levelled against the hedgehog and the badger. The hunting of these and of other small animals became in many rural areas a pursuit of boys, who received a reward from the parish officers for each dead animal they brought in.

The hunting of certain animals, generally with dogs, was upgraded during the later Middle Ages and early modern times to a ritual in which few could afford to take part. Except in the marginal case of deer-hunting, the excuse that the hunter was engaged in providing food for the table had no basis. Hunting became a game in which the hunter pitted himself against the wild creatures which were forced involuntarily to take part in the unequal contest. Only recently has the huntsman compounded his offence with the egregious claim that he is thereby contributing to the good of the environment by helping to maintain the balance of nature which he had been the first to disturb.

Vast areas of medieval England were set aside for hunting by the king and his nobles. This does not, however, mean that these lands were withdrawn from ordinary settlement and cultivation but, only that they were subject to 'forest law' and that game within them was reserved for exclusive pursuit by the monarch and those whom he had designated. In the course of the later Middle Ages this status was gradually lifted from most of them, though the term 'forest' still attaches to large areas, including parts of Salisbury Plain, which had never been forested in any strict sense of that term. Not unrelated to hunting was the baiting of live animals, generally with dogs bred for the purpose. This was always a lower-class 'sport'. Though now illegal, it continues to be practised secretly by a certain subculture. Animals, notably bears, were used in the medieval 'carnival', but there is little evidence that in doing so they were deliberately misused. The baiting of animals, on the other hand, seems to have developed in modern times as a vicarious form of hunting for those unable to indulge in the real thing. But bloodsports of all kinds had a following in early modern times which spanned all classes. The early eighteenth-century diary of the Lancashire squire Thomas Blundell shows him addicted to them. No evening's entertainment was complete without baiting or cockfighting, and, as a special amusement for Shrove Tuesdays, he always put on 'throwing at the cock', and in this he was far from alone. The Revd Henry Newcome, a Puritan divine who denounced maypoles and church-ales, could nevertheless send his children to take part in 'ye shooting of ye cocke' and prayed 'yt God would preserve ym' from harm in the heartless crowd which participated.[155] Baiting seems, furthermore, to have become as much an urban as a rural 'sport' because it requires relatively little space. All such activities tended to become vehicles for gambling. Hunting was least suited for betting, but animal fights were well adapted, and it is probably true that many were organised primarily for this purpose.

Games belong to all societies and to all ages. The *Tain* distinguished between those of youth and the more sedentary pursuits of the older generation (p. 293). The more active and violent games were for the young, board- and gambling games for the older age groups. Play was an essential element in the development of children, and children's games arose, in large measure, from the unconscious imitation of their elders. Rituals enacted at religious festivals were imitated, and it is likely that skipping-games and the hobby-horse originated in this way. Hunting was reflected in games involving searching and chasing. 'Modern games often contain fossilized relics of ancient belief.'[156] Adults, often unconsciously, passed on their own pursuits in modified form to the young. The cult of the miniature is a case in point. 'The ambiguity of the doll and the replica continued during the Middle Ages ... This taste for representing in miniature the people and things of daily life, nowadays confined to little children [is it?], resulted in an art and an industry designed as much to satisfy adults as to amuse children.' The history of the doll (p. 318) is a case in point. Children's games appear, in general, to be imitative, the aping of rituals and other activities of their elders. They were often perpetuated long after the latter had abandoned them. The only distinction lies in the fact that adult games are more overtly competitive.

The extent to which children participated, if only as spectators, in adult entertainment is far from clear. It would appear that, in general, they did, as, indeed, they do today, but there were occasions when they clearly were excluded. A churchwarden's account for the parish of South Newington (Oxon.) records that in 1649 only two from each family might attend the parochial festivities, because, in the past, 'the intrusion of so many children' had occasioned 'much disorder'.[157]

Children's games and children's toys have continued little altered from the Middle Ages to the nineteenth century. Their range has broadened, and the adjuncts of play have increased immeasurably. The chief development in adult play has been an intensification of the competitive aspect, the organisation of team games, and, as a corollory, the formulation of rules. Rules first appeared in the more élite pastimes. Hunting came to have its rituals and its seasons, while football remained little more than a local brawl.

Last to be regulated were the mass-participation sports. Football and hurling, for example, had long been played, but only according to local custom. They were condemned by both church and state, by the former because they were played on the sabbath, and by the latter because they interfered with archery practice.[158] By the seventeenth century the latter excuse ceased to have much relevance, and it was to oppose the sabbatarians that James I issued his ordinance on sports in 1618, later reinforced by the Laudian injunctions of Charles I.[159] In it the king pointed out that if 'his subjects were debarred from lawful recreations upon Sundays after evening prayers ended, and upon Holy-days . . . the meaner sort who labour hard all the week [would] have no recreation at all to refresh their spirits'. He ordered that 'no lawful recreation shall be barred to our good people' after Sunday service, and that those who wished to indulge in 'dancing, archery, leaping, vaulting . . . [and] May-games, Whitsunales and Morris-dances' should not be prevented by 'Puritans and precise people'. Unfortunately, the Puritans prevailed, and village games and sports were prohibited on Sundays. Although the law was later relaxed, the pattern had been broken, and an unofficial prohibition of Sunday sport prevailed throughout the Victorian period. It was only when teams from different places began to compete – and this was, by and large, not before the nineteenth century – that some consistency in their practice became necessary. Rugby football emerged, so it is commonly supposed, when a schoolboy carried the ball on the playing-fields of Rugby School instead of kicking it, as was customary. But there can be no question that in the rough village games the ball had been both carried and kicked long before this. It was, however, another half-century before its code of rules was drawn up. Cricket had acquired a degree of respectability more than a century earlier. It grew from a stick-and-ball game, such as was played by the young in every community in the country. It was taken up by the gentry in south-eastern England, who developed it early in the eighteenth century into an elegant and time-consuming sport. It was the long period of time required for the completion of a game that restricted it to the leisured classes. This began to change only in the latter half of the nineteenth century when the working classes were first able to give a half-day, other than Sunday, to a competitive game.

It was at this time that football played according to the Football Association code began to emerge from the hurly-burly of the village ball-game. The reason again lay in the increase in leisure that arose as Parliament reduced the length of the working day, and legislated for a shorter work period on Saturdays. The formation of the Football Association in 1863 and of the Football League twenty-five years later effectively confirmed 'football' as both a spectator and a participatory sport.

Fishing has in modern times become one of the most popular of participatory sports. That it has always been important is evident from the role of fish in the human diet. A distinction must, however, be made between fishing as a subsistence activity and fishing as an enjoyable pursuit for a fine summer's day. This is difficult, because fishing for pleasure usually yields a small quantity of food. It may, however, be assumed that the operation of fish stews on an early manor or at a monastic site was exclusively to provide food. But there is good evidence that, even in the Middle Ages, men did go out with rod and line for the pleasure of sitting on a cold, damp river bank, waiting for a bite.

Clocks and bells

Traditional societies had but an imperfect concept of time (p. 407), and not until the sixteenth century did a precise means of measuring time become available to most rural communities. Mechanical clocks had long been known, but they were uncertain in their operation and very expensive, and were to be found only in the richer monastic foundations. In the course of the sixteenth century, a simple clock, operated generally by weights and a pendulum escapement, became available. It was beyond the means of peasant or yeoman households, but well within the reach of a prosperous community. Churchwardens' accounts report in increasing detail the cost of purchasing a clock and of keeping it in working order. Early clocks had no dial; their purpose was to sound the hours and thus to give an aural warning to parishioners of the passage of time. The earliest clocks were to be heard, not seen. At Walsall, for example, there was a 'lytull watche',[160] which was an alarum attached to the clock's mechanism.

The earliest reference to a clock installed in a parish church, found by this writer, was at Croscombe (Som.) in 1483–4: 'payd to Bronch for kepyng of the cloke 4s.'[161] One may be sure, however, that there were clocks long before this date in parishes less remote and more prosperous than Croscombe. The cost of 'kepyng of the cloke' was high. In parish after parish we find that someone was being paid a not inconsiderable sum to tend it.[162] At Ashburton (Devon.) the duty devolved upon one Richard Sexton, who doubled as grave-digger, at 10s. a year.[163] Sums of half a mark to a mark for repairs were not uncommon. At Boxford (Suff.) 11s. 7d. was 'payd to the clokemaker for mending of the Cloke and For hys mett [meat]'.[164] The appointment of the local blacksmith to look after the village clock may help to explain why its performance was so irregular.

Closely connected with the parish clock were the church bells. These, like the clock, became an object of local pride as well as of utility. Church towers were built to contain them, and their maintenance – the provision of new wheels, clappers and bell-frames – constituted a drain on the parochial purse only a degree less heavy than that of the clock itself. Furthermore, bells had at intervals to be recast, an expensive process for which a mould was sometimes made even in the very floor of the church.[165]

Bells served many purposes. They were used to summon parishioners to mass and, after the Reformation, to morning and evening prayer, an important consideration when most households had no clock. At Eardisland (Hereford.) in 1397 two women servants of the vicar both rang the bells and helped him in the celebration of mass, which was declared to be 'contrary to proper church behaviour . . . a scandal . . . and a dark suspicion that [they] cohabited with the vicar'.[166] A bell was tolled at funerals, but only on payment, at least in the sixteenth and seventeenth centuries, of the not inconsiderable sum of 12d.[167] Bells were rung on the occasion of national celebrations, as, indeed, they still are. They served to articulate the passage of time, until the regular chiming of clocks within the home took their place, and they were used to give out a warning when danger was perceived to threaten the security of the community. They were even rung to avert the threat of a thunderstorm, but in this they had ceased to be used to convey a message and instead assumed the magical role of influencing the weather.

CHAPTER 9

THE FAMILY

The family is the first refuge of the individual when the state fails him.

Georges Duby

The family was an open-ended, low-keyed, unemotional, authoritarian institution which served certain essential political, economic, sexual, procreative, and nurturant purposes.

Lawrence Stone

In 1676 the Reverend William Sampson was inducted into the living of Clayworth in Nottinghamshire. From the first he kept a diary in which he recorded significant events within his parish.[1] Very wisely, he began by compiling a list of his parishioners. He counted 401 heads, and noted that there were 'no popish recusants ... nor are there (thanks to God) any other dissenters'. Twelve years later he compiled a second list, this time with greater care and 'according to ye Order of Houses & Families, down ye North side of ye town, & up ye South-Side, and lastly those of Wyeston', a hamlet nearby.[2] In his second census he was at pains to give the occupations and interrelationships of those who made up the 91 households within the parish. The result is a complex pattern of familial structures. Of the 91 households the great majority were nuclear, each consisting of parents and children with at most a servant living in. Thirteen were headed by a widow or widower with children. There were only four single-person households, three of them widows, one with a servant living in.[3]

There was little evidence in Clayworth that the extended family included grandchildren and other relatives, but in no less than 26 there were servants, some of whom must have been farm labourers. Two households, headed respectively by a 'housewright' and a 'blacksmith', each contained a journeyman, and in four there was a resident apprentice. But as for extended families, one can point to only four instances, and these were small, containing at most grandchildren and a sister and her children. On the other hand, the nuclear families show a perhaps unexpected complexity. No less than 26 contained one parent, usually the man, who had been married before, and in four cases both parents:

Men previously married once	19
,, twice	0
,, three times	3
,, four times	3
,, five times	1

In several of these cases children of the previous marriages were cohabiting with those of the present marriage. Overall, 26 men had been married previously, but only three women.[4] By contrast, the census listed 17 widows but only three widowers. One might deduce from this that the ravages of childbearing cut severely into the total of women in the middle years of life, but that those who had outlived this phase might anticipate a long and healthy old age. This interpretation is in line with what we know of the family in traditional society.

It would be unwise to generalise from Clayworth. Both local custom and family structure could vary greatly, not only among regions but also between parishes within a few miles of one another.[5] The evolution of the family and of familial structures, like most other human institutions, shows a progression from the complex towards the simple. There was over time a general simplification, in the course of which many of the original features were relegated to the status of archaisms or survived only in remote and culturally deprived areas. In marriage and inheritance, in attitudes to bastards and paupers, in the treatment of aged parents and younger children, there was an infinite range in the shades of practice and opinion. There was, for example, no sharp boundary separating partible from impartible inheritance. Practice varied with social class, and it is difficult to resist the conclusion that over much of the country the practice was, in Margaret Spufford's phrase, one of 'semi-partible inheritance'. The patchwork quilt of popular custom was not characterised by sharp divisions between contrasting colours, but by gradations from one shade of practice to another. In this chapter it will be possible to paint only with the broadest brush strokes the chief lineaments of familial culture in pre-industrial societies.

A peasantry?

'... the basis of the rural economy throughout the whole middle ages [and, it might be added, much of modern times] was the holding of the peasant family.'[6] Its surplus production supported 'the whole social and political superstructure of nobles, clergy, towns and state'.[7] It is with the peasant family that we are primarily concerned in this chapter. The accepted model is that of families bound to the soil – *adscripti glebae* – unable to leave it because their labour and dues, by virtue of which they held their land, were necessary to support their lords at the level to which the latter had become accustomed. Such a view is, of course, too simplistic; there were 'degrees of unfreedom', which varied both spatially and through time. Freemen – *liberi homines* – were to be found working on the land in all parts of the country, but were especially numerous in East Anglia and Lincolnshire, where they can be seen as heirs of the Danish settlers. By contrast, serfs, the *servi* or slaves of Domesday Book, were relatively numerous in the west. One can discover much about earlier settlement and the ethnic composition of the population from its status.[8] Many factors impinged on the status and well-being of the villager, some of them generated within his own society; others originated outside and were totally beyond his control. Amongst the latter were the vagaries of the weather and their unpredictable impact on food supply; the spread of epidemic disease and warfare. Amongst indigenous factors were the size of the family, the modes of inheriting peasant holdings and of supporting dependent members of the family. Some of these factors have already been discussed (pp. 327–34). All changed through time and varied over space, and it is against their interaction that we must see the changes in the status and the material welfare of the peasant.

The peasantry made up a large part of rural society at some stage in the development of all western societies, and is still of immense importance throughout the Third World. But how to define a peasant? The peasant was not merely a smallholder, cultivating his land primarily for the subsistence of himself and his family. It is generally assumed that his attachment to the soil – *his* soil – went deeper than this.[9] This attitude to the land derived from times long before the forms of feudal land tenure had been developed. The early Irish Laws represent a social structure which must once have been widespread. Together with the Welsh Laws, they offer a picture of kindred groups, each with its prescribed territory within which it settled, grew crops, grazed its stock and cut its timber.[10] The community's land belonged to the whole community; every member had a claim to support from it, 'from generation to generation'.[11] Membership of the kindred was defined by descent from a common ancestor a number of generations back. Hence the interest in genealogy manifested by early societies. The man who cultivated a tract of the community's land was in the position not of owner but of steward, and the good steward was at pains to care for his land, never to impoverish or alienate it, and always to pass it on undiminished to the next generation. The peasant *mentalité* conceived of a fusion, if that were possible, between the cultivator and his land, the two inseparable, each inconceivable without the other.[12]

Each member of a kindred had 'a birthright in the land, but a single individual had little or no right to claim a specific share as "his" or "hers" and to do what he or she willed with it'. Least of all could the peasant sell his land or alienate it in any way. He was expected to marry and to have children, but only so that the kindred might be perpetuated in the lands of its ancestors. Cicely Howell claims that this attitude towards the land 'was strong in England in 1700'.[13] It can certainly be recognised in rural attitudes to common grazing and woodland and to its wild life, which was seen as primarily for country-folk to poach. But this view began to yield at some time during the Middle Ages to the view that 'an individual has rights to property as against other individuals', and this change, Macfarlane argues, lies at the root of individualism today.

The reasons for the change were many and complex. First and foremost must be the feudal view of the land as held by one person or another in return for service. It is not relevant to discuss the extent to which feudalism in Britain antedated the Norman Conquest. That event put the king firmly in control of the land, which he proceeded to allocate in discrete units to his followers. The latter in turn endowed their dependants, until, at the lowest level of the feudal hierarchy, the local lord was owed the services of those who occupied and cultivated the land which had been placed under *his* control. The land was tilled for *his* benefit; its cultivators were in varying degrees *his* men, and if they enjoyed a kind of security of tenure and expected to pass on their strips and rights to their heirs, this was only by custom, not by law. What happened in England in the eleventh and twelfth centuries may have been not unlike the way in which western conquerors and settlers occupied communal and tribal land in North America or Africa, in utter ignorance of the way in which the people, and not their leaders, had customary ownership of it. Custom in Britain derived from primitive landholding, from Celtic law. Feudal control had been imposed only in recent years, and law and custom continued to coexist. Bracton recognised the importance of custom,[14] and there seems to have been a general realisation that it would be unwise to do any great violence to it. Manorial and village 'laws' or customary practices were often recorded, dealing in large measure with the use of common land and other such shared 'rights' of the community. Nevertheless, there was conflict between custom and law, and from the conflict there emerged, dialectically, the practice of individual ownership of land, with the right to divise it by will and even to sell it in the market. Despite the unfree status of the villein and the lord's control of the soil, a market in peasant land had developed by the mid-thirteenth century, together with a wide range in types of tenure.[15] Nevertheless, Razi has demonstrated that on the monastic manors of Halesowen transfers of land before 1349 were mainly within the kinship. After the Black Death, with its heavy mortality and the greater mobility which followed, land transfers were more frequently made to immigrants and others who were very distantly related, if related at all.[16] The Great Plague was here an important factor in breaking down the kinship. Much depended, as Dyer has emphasised, on the availability of land and on its physical condition. A tenement might be let to an outsider because there were no relatives waiting to take it on.

If the dominant criterion of a peasantry is the familial ownership of land which cannot be alienated from the kinship group, then England had ceased to be a peasant country at an early date. The kindred had been obliterated by feudalism, and from them both had emerged English individualism. This seems to be the dialectic of Macfarlane's argument, and his conclusions would appear to invalidate the comparisons that are frequently drawn between the English rural classes and the peasantry of continental Europe. On the other hand, the earlier modes of tenure continued to be practised in Wales, perhaps until the end of the Middle Ages. The Welsh Laws make it clear that the 'owner' of a piece of land 'could not defeat his descendants' right to succeed'. By the later Middle Ages his property would very likely have consisted of a piece of 'appropriated' land which was under some form of cultivation, and an undivided share of the common land. Rights in land were periodically revised and new allocations made, as necessitated by fluctuations in population and family size.

Kinship and the nuclear family

The role of the kinship, as distinct from the conjugal family, in the social history of this country has given rise to a debate which still continues. The kinship, simply defined, was the body of people, both blood relatives and affines (i.e. linked by marriage), who stood outside the nuclear or conjugal family. Marriage had the effect of linking together two kinships. How far the kinship was seen to extend, or how many generations back one should go in tracing its ramifications were questions which have never received any clear answer. At a more practical level, the kinship was a group within which one did not marry, and no one who has read the Table of Kinship and Affinity printed in the Book of Common Prayer or exhibited in churches can doubt that it encompassed a very wide circle whose remoter fringes might well have been unknown to any one individual. The church, which had jurisdiction over matrimonial matters, tended generally to take a liberal view; otherwise there could have been no legitimate marriage within many small communities.

As an institution the kinship is of great antiquity. It was at the height of its importance when the organs of the state were weakest. It flourished on the Scottish Borders, where 'surnames' fought and avenged one another under conditions which approached anarchy. By the thirteenth century it had disappeared from most of England, but, with its related institution, the blood-feud, was still active in Wales in the later Middle Ages.[17] In the Middle Ages, the Welsh were preoccupied with their lineages, with the bloodline which linked them with their kin. Every man could expect the support of his kin in his disputes, and conditions changed only when, in the more settled conditions of modern times, the courts assumed the role of terminating disputes and punishing crime.

In England these changes occurred at a much earlier date than in the Celtic west. The private settlement of disputes and the exaction of *wergild* or blood money did not outlive the Norman Conquest. The kinship ceased to be of judicial importance, but did the kin remain important in everyday social relations? The medieval rural community was close-knit and mutually dependent, but was it the kin or 'cousinhood', those linked by blood or marriage, through which this relationship was maintained, or did one just turn to neighbours in case of need? Did relatives, however distant their relationship, help support one another in times of difficulty and stand surety and make loans in adversity? An analysis of interpersonal relationships in a Suffolk parish shows that they did, but only to a very limited degree, and that such relationships within the kin were significant only amongst the middle ranks of the peasantry.[18] The Anglo-Saxon kinship had been important, not so much in settling disputes as in providing support for those who had become involved in them. In a sense this role was assumed by the medieval system of frankpledge. All able-bodied men were expected to belong to a group, or 'tithing', who watched over each other's activities. There is no evidence whatsoever that a tithing was ever drawn from a particular kinship, and one must conclude that, with the abandonment of the blood-feud and *wergild*, the kinship had lost its primary *raison d'être*.

On the other hand, Miranda Chaytor has claimed that in County Durham, specifically within the community of Ryton, elements of the kinship relationship lingered on until the sixteenth and even the seventeenth century.[19] There was, she wrote, 'a flow of loans, goodwill and obligations' between the households in a loosely conceived kinship. This has, however, been criticised by Wrightson. He claims that the supposed kinship system was in fact a series of *ad hoc* arrangements and that in reality the nuclear family was always the dominant social institution.[20]

The decay of the kinship must be related both to the high level of mobility which developed, especially in the later Middle Ages, and, above all, to the organs of state which made such an institution unnecessary. Ralph Josselin, parson of Earl's Colne (Essex), who kept a detailed and intimate diary during most of his life,[21] showed little 'interest in lineage and [a] very restricted recognition of kin'. This is in line with the evidence collected by Wrightson for the nearby parish of Terling.[22] Mobility had destroyed any extended kinships there may have been. One's close associations were with members of one's nuclear family or with near neighbours. Neighbourliness had, by and large, replaced dependence on kin. How many people today still retain second, third or fourth cousins amongst their close associates or depend on the distant relatives of their 'in-laws'? From the sixteenth century, or even earlier, the nuclear family of parents and children has been the dominant social institution in this country,[23] as, indeed, it has continued to be into the present century.[24]

At Clayworth some 75 per cent of households could have been termed nuclear, and of those which were in any sense 'extended' we find only the addition of a close relative, an apprentice or a journeyman. The extended family, as exemplified, for example, in the *Zadruga* of the southern Slavs, has never, at least in historical times, been a feature of this country.[25] In a primitive society custom dictated that the land should never leave the possession of the kindred. After death it was obvious who should inherit. A will was not necessary, and any will which conflicted with custom would very likely have been ignored. In a feudal and post-feudal society the situation was far less clear. The head of the household was no longer obliged to provide for all its junior members after his death. He was free to divide up the bundle of rights and properties which he held as he saw fit, and how he chose to do so is the stuff of which wills were made.

But first, the structure of the nuclear family. This is very difficult to penetrate before the mid-sixteenth century owing to the lack of any consistent body of data. Thereafter it is facilitated by parochial registers of baptisms, marriages and burials;

by wills, and by such accidental survivals as the Clayworth census, and, of course, by personal records like diaries and letters. From these can be constructed a picture of the family, ranging from age at marriage to the size of the completed family, retirement and death. For the Middle Ages one knows in some detail the fortunes of noble families, but only because their lives were a matter of public record.[26] But the reconstitution of peasant families is difficult, and is dependent on the survival of a good run of manorial court rolls and other manorial documents. In 1538 Thomas Cromwell issued an ordinance requiring all parish priests to keep a record of baptisms, marriages and burials.[27] In few parishes was this injunction adequately observed from the beginning. Further orders towards the end of the century brought about some improvement, but in most parishes there are significant gaps during the Interregnum and also at other times owing to the laxity of incumbents and local officials. Nevertheless, these registers are being used with considerable success in the reconstitution of families. The accumulated data show how people behaved, their age at marriage, the number and spacing of their children, how many of the latter died before adulthood, and their expectation of life.[28] This chapter has drawn heavily on evidence derived from the analysis of parish registers, in which the author has participated to only a small degree.

Betrothal and marriage

Marriage was a social necessity. The evidence shows that only the young and the very old had no living spouse, and that the death of one partner was quickly followed by marriage to another. Those eligible to marry who, for one reason or another, chose to live alone, were always suspect. Witches were always solitary. Only within the family could one achieve some degree of support and security. It is commonly said, in part, it would seem, on the uncertain evidence of Shakespeare, that age at marriage was very low, and that many, especially women, were first married in their teens. Nothing could be further from the truth. By the simple process of comparing the date of marriage with that of the baptism of the two partners, provided that it can be obtained from the registers, age at marriage can be established.[29] Furthermore, when a marriage was by licence issued by the diocesan bishop, the age of both partners had to be specified. Laslett has shown that the average age of women marrying for the first time was 24 and that of men 31 in early modern times. There are, of course, well-documented cases of childhood marriages, chiefly amongst the upper classes, but the age of puberty was not lower and may have been higher than today, and such marriages could not have been consummated for a considerable period. In some instances the marriage had been annulled before this could have happened.

Marriage was generally thought of as for life. This was not altogether because it was the teaching of the church, but because society could not readily accommodate and provide for divorced persons. Annulment was the usual way out of a difficult situation – the assertion that there had never been a marriage in the eyes of the

9.1 Married bliss; after the Luttrell Psalter, fo. 60.

church. But this called for persuasion in the right quarters and the expenditure of not a little money. It was not a course of action available to the mass of the population.[30] Apart from annulment, there was only one way of terminating a marriage: the separation of the parties with the formal consent of a church court. In such cases, the remarriage of either partner was forbidden. There were, of course, illicit ways of effectively terminating a marriage. One partner or the other might abscond, and if he or she got far enough away, rumour of a previous marriage might never catch up with them.

Partners in a marriage were expected to live together. Failure to do so was deemed to be a matter for the church courts, which could impose penance and require them to cohabit. There are numerous instances in the proceedings of the archdeacons' courts of couples who had been presented for failing to do so. Underlying all such judgments was the fear that one or other would procreate illegitimate children who would be likely to become a charge on the parish. In one instance a court was persuaded that failure to cohabit was due to the fact that the man was employed outside the community and was able to return home only infrequently.[31] No doubt most marriages in traditional societies arose from the mutual attraction of the two people, but there have always been 'arranged' marriages in which family fortune has played a more important role than mutual affection; even when there was deep love between the partners, a broker, a kind of benevolent Ketzel, was necessary to sort out matters of dowry and inheritance.[32] Piers Plowman describes how matters were handled:

> The wif was maad the w[y]e   for to helpe werche,
> And thus was wedlok ywroght   with a mene persone [intermediary]
> First by the fadres will   and the frendes conseille,
> And sithenes by assent of hemself,   as thei two myghte acorde;
> And thus was wedlok ywroghte ...[33]

It was important that the marriage should not only be desired by the partners to it, but also be acceptable to the kindred — by 'frendes conseille'.

Marriage was, as a general rule, preceded by betrothal, and it was in the latter that the 'mene persone' was most active. Betrothal was a far firmer contract than engagement today. It was 'not a mere promise of marriage . . . but part of the actual marriage, and in practice the vital part ... the effect of betrothal was that neither party could remarry while the other was alive'.[34] The betrothed did not usually cohabit, but intercourse frequently followed, if, indeed, it had not already taken place. The church disapproved, but was in general powerless to act, and society at large usually condoned. Nevertheless, at West Wittering (Sussex) the church court in 1621 imposed a sentence of penance for 'incontinency before marriage except that it be held a lawful yssue which is borne in [within] the nynthe moneth [month]'.[35] English law, however, seems never to have recognised that a subsequent marriage conferred a retrospective legitimacy on children actually born before the marriage of their parents. But at the popular level pre-nuptial intercourse was taken for granted. Less than 5 per cent of those who produced a child within nine months of marriage actually appeared before a church court on such a charge, simply because the churchwardens did not want to know. The evidence of parish registers suggests that a third of all brides were pregnant at the time of their marriage.[36] Whatever the church said, society as a whole seems not to have disapproved. After all, no man wanted to marry a wife who was incapable of bearing children, and society acquiesced in a 'trial run' before marriage.

The practice of 'bundling' is often cited in this regard. It consisted in young people of different sex sleeping in the same bed, but prevented by clothing or even a wooden barrier from close physical contact. It was once common in Wales and also in New England and the Appalachian region in the United States. It has commonly been explained in terms of lack of space, and hence of beds in the traditional cottage. Kinsey[37] regarded it as a way in which society tolerated or even encouraged premarital intercourse as a means of testing the woman's capacity to conceive.

There were, however, two matters on which society felt a great deal more strongly: incest and bastardy. Incest was in origin an offence only in canon law, which derived many of its prohibitions from Jewish law. The Pentateuch had prohibited marriage within certain degrees, which were extended by a council of the early church to include almost every definable degree of consanguinity and affinity. Affinity was even taken to include 'spiritual affinity', such as that between godparents and godchildren. This probably derived its rationale from the fact that godparents were assimilated to the kinship, and marriage was expected to be outside the kin (p. 306). Although the extremities of canon law were in the course of time moderated, the church courts continued to cast their nets very widely. Within a small rural community the degree of consanguinity was inevitably high, and it was for this reason, one must assume, that early societies encouraged marriage outside their own limits. Nevertheless, canon law remained rigid. It inspired the Table of Kinship and Affinity which appears in the Book of Common Prayer of the Anglican church and was until comparatively recently exhibited in every parish church in the land as a warning to those who would violate it. So complex were the prohibited degrees that there must have been many who failed to comprehend their ramifications. At Rougham (Suff.) about 1290 Richard son of Thomas committed incest with a blood relative, and, when taxed with the offence, brought to court six witnesses who all testified that 'he was not aware of the relationship'.[38] The court accepted their statements, but the marriage was nevertheless annulled.

Cases of incest are relatively rare in consistory court proceedings, probably because people were aware of the closer degrees of affinity and no one cared about the more distant. At Wadsworth (W. Riding, Yorks.) a man was in 1743 indicted for marrying his aunt,[39] but one must assume that most people were able to evade 'the feeble coercion of the spiritual courts'. Incest did not become an offence in secular law until 1908, and then only within strictly limited degrees. According to Emmison, people had by the sixteenth century ceased to view incest with the horror that had previously been displayed,[40] and only during the period of Puritan domination was the law tightened and rigorously enforced. It seems unlikely that fear of incest owed anything to its genetic consequence, though a certain empirical knowledge of the consequences of marriage between close blood relatives may have been acquired. The acceptance of the modern law on incest probably owes more to the development of biological science than to the Pentateuch.

Bastardy concerned people much more deeply, because, unlike incest, it touched their pockets. Illegitimate children often had fathers who were either unknown or could not be found. Their support, unless their mothers had some means, which was highly unusual, devolved upon the parish, and, after the enactment of the Elizabethan Poor Law, was paid for out of the poor rate. There can have been few parishes in the seventeenth and eighteenth centuries in which there were not a few persistent offenders who became a charge on the local rates as they brought into the world a series of bastards of somewhat doubtful paternity. In making entries in their registers incumbents, or their parish clerks, were required to indicate the parentage of the child who had been baptised. The usual formula was: 'Mary, the daughter of William and Alice B...' The baptism of an illegitimate child was likely to have been recorded as: 'John, illegitimate [or bastard] son of Joanne'. This writer has sometimes found the name of a particular unmarried mother occurring in the register with a monotonous regularity – 'repeaters', Laslett called them. In one instance the parson, doubtless with one eye on the level of the rates, exploded on to the register: 'This is the fourth bastard this woman has born.'

It might seem easy to count the number of illegitimate children born within a particular parish. But there are problems. The statistics are of baptisms, not of births, and it is not impossible that a marginally higher proportion of illegitimate infants would die at or soon after birth than of legitimate, who might be expected to receive better attention during parturition. A further problem is the number of prenuptial pregnancies (p. 313); some 30 per cent of brides were pregnant over the three centuries from about 1550.[41] What the records cannot tell us is how many of these conceptions occurred after betrothal. The ambiguity of the distinction between betrothal and marriage ensured that the church courts never viewed prenuptial pregnancy too seriously, while public opinion openly condoned it. The child did not come into the world fatherless, and the question of its support from the public purse did not arise. In addition to the pregnancies that occurred after betrothal but before marriage, there must have been a number – how many we have no means of knowing – of what may be termed 'shotgun marriages'. It must always be recognised that in the small, open society of the traditional parish or village there were few secrets. At Ross-on-Wye in 1397 a list of men was compiled, together with the names of the women with whom they had committed fornication.[42] If a girl became pregnant, her neighbours would have had a shrewd idea of who was responsible. The mere fact that a bastard was likely to become a financial liability on them all ensured that the man would be under very great pressure to marry her. Morality has always had a sharp economic edge.

There thus remained a hard core of cases in which eventual marriage did not give a retrospective respectability to incontinence. In some instances the man absconded; in others the woman was known to be promiscuous. At Graffham (Sussex) the churchwardens presented to the Archdeacon's Court Joane H. as 'an incontinent person, a gadder up and downe, a common carrytale, a maker of lyes, one that hath contracted herself to 2 or 3 knaves and is marryed to none'.[43] It is noteworthy that in this case the accusation came from one of the parishioners. One can imagine his red-faced indignation as his moral sense was offended and his pocket touched.

A final question relates to the popular concept of marriage. The 'arranged' marriage was never an accepted practice in Britain, nor was it countenanced by the common law. But much was at stake in a marriage, over and above the happiness of the couple at its centre: 'marriage initiated a cycle in which *people* and *property* [my italics] moved from one household to another ... a flow of loans, goodwill and obligations between households'.[44] To this extent the goodwill of both families was highly desirable, if not positively necessary. A marriage had the power to resolve the differences between feuding kinships, a fact which lent itself to very effective dramatic representation. It was in the inter-family negotiations regarding property settlement that the 'mene persone' and 'frendes conseille' were most needed.

The role of the church in marriage was a relatively late development; it had previously been a matter for secular negotiation between the partners and their families. Indeed, the Catholic church was always ambivalent towards marriage, recognising its necessity, but always claiming that virginity conferred a nobler status. There was no general agreement that the act of matrimony was a sacrament and that it conferred grace, before the time of Thomas Aquinas, and it remained the only sacrament of the church, barring only baptism in exceptional circumstances, performed by lay persons, the priest being present only as a witness.[45] For this reason it was in the Middle Ages performed in the porch of the church. Chaucer's Wife of Bath had acquired her numerous husbands in succession 'at chirche-dore'.[46] The rite was later moved into the church, where it was customarily followed by a mass. The Anglican church, in the Book of Common Prayer, showed itself reluctant to regard marriage as a sacrament. The Puritans considered it a matter to be negotiated and settled between the parties themselves and their families, and during the Interregnum Parliament disallowed religious marriages. There remained after the Restoration of 1660 an undercurrent of opposition to the ecclesiastical control of marriage, and clandestine marriages remained relatively common and generally legal. It has been estimated that such irregular unions 'may have accounted for at least a fifth and perhaps as much as a third of all unions in the first half of the eighteenth century'.[47] English civil law accepted the validity of such marriages, except during the period from 1753 to 1823. Hardwicke's Marriage Act of 1753 called for parental consent for the marriage of anyone under the age of 21, and prescribed that the ceremony should take place only in a proper church and after the calling of banns on three successive Sundays. The validity of civil marriage was reasserted in the Marriage Act of 1836, and twenty years later the feeble and ineffective jurisdiction of the church courts in matrimonial matters was finally terminated.

Public opinion in these matters was, generally speaking, more liberal than either church or state. It condoned civil marriage long before it was recognised by authority, and even closed its eyes or asked few questions regarding cohabitation. A Welsh parish register of 1686 recorded:

Edward Parry who liveth still with his concubine unmarried.[48]

One suspects that this was condoned by the neighbours, and that if the couple had moved to another parish the fact might not even have become known. It is impossible to obtain any statistical evidence in such matters. In addition to those couples who chose to live together without the blessing of the church, there were others who cohabited while married to other partners. As Laslett has commented, 'consensual unions between partners indissolubly married to other peresons may well have been fairly common. This was, after all, the only choice open to spouses whose marriages broke down and who were unwilling to live for ever alone.'[49]

Continually we find that public opinion within the community was more tolerant and more charitable than officialdom in either church or state.

Until 1837 a marriage could in England and Wales (the law was different in Scotland) be contracted only in a church of the Anglican communion, though exceptions were made in favour of Quakers and other sects. There were those whose religious convictions prevented them from accepting this practice. Cohabitation may have followed a mutual agreement which would today be acceptable in law, but in the eyes of the church the marriage was not legal and the children who sprang from it were deemed illegitimate. It is possible that many who before that date would merely have cohabited would thereafter have accepted a civil marriage. It is not without significance that the latter was most common in the peripheral areas of the south-west, Wales and north, not notable for their loyalty to priest and established church.

With these reservations, one may, following Laslett, claim that in traditional societies from 2 to 5 per cent of all births were illegitimate.[50] But illegitimacy moved in cycles. From less than 2 per cent about 1550, the proportion rose to more than 3 about 1600, and then dropped to its lowest level – about 1 per cent – during the Commonwealth, before rising to its maximum of over 5 about 1800. It is difficult to resist the assumption that the relative laxity in morals of the Elizabethan period and again in the eighteenth century was reflected in a greater degree of promiscuity and hence a higher proportion of illegitimate births. On the other hand, it is possible that social pressures during the Commonwealth led to a greater number of forced marriages, so that premarital conceptions would appear as legitimate births. It is unlikely that human nature could have changed over three centuries as much as the bastardy statistics suggest. Indeed, the sheer difficulty of obtaining a divorce or even the annulment of a marriage would suggest that extramarital liaisons would have been fairly common. The slender evidence suggests that this was indeed so, but unless they resulted in a birth recorded as illegitimate, there could be little evidence. There were very few men, or women for that matter, who had the inclination, or even the ability, to commit their sexual life to paper with the candour of a Samuel Pepys. That there were prostitutes in towns, if not also in the countryside, for those who needed their services is obvious. There were even pimps who prospered by them in the later Middle Ages. In 1497 a certain P. M. appeared before a church court, accused of being 'a common procurer [who] has especially arranged lewdness between J. G., an Easterling[51] and various suspect women'.[52]

There was a full realisation of the dangers of venereal disease – *morbus Gallicus* – which had been spread from Italy at the end of the fifteenth century. It fell to the church courts to eradicate it, as if it were vulnerable to excommunication and penance. At Banbury in 1616 a man was 'burned with a whore but by whom wee know not'.[53] If they had discovered her the courts would have been powerless to take any significant action. Shakespeare repeatedly makes play with the word 'burned' in contexts that his listeners would have readily understood. There can be no doubt that syphilis was widespread, and that its etiology was familiar. It aroused a general fear, but, like AIDS today, led to only a marginal decline in promiscuity.

Childbirth and childhood

In the medieval church marriage was prohibited by canon law during Advent and the Christmas festivities; from the beginning of Lent to the octave of Easter, and again from Rogationtide to Trinity Sunday. Marriages could thus not be allowed to conflict with the three great festivals of the church. Not surprisingly late spring and early summer became and have remained the favoured times for weddings, despite the fact that there are no longer any effective constraints. The Book of Common Prayer declared the primary purpose of marriage to have been the avoidance of fornication and the procreation of children, though it added the mutual help and support that the married couple could give to one another.[54] This would have been the opinion of most traditional societies. In register after register we find that the first child of a marriage was baptised within a year. Indeed, on the assumption that baptism followed within a week or so of birth, a high proportion of all conceptions must have taken place between April and July.

Childbirth took place almost always at home, attended, if helped at all, only by the local *sage femme*. It was surrounded by mysticism and squalor (p. 252) and the outcome was all too frequently the death of both mother and infant. The foundation in the course of the eighteenth century of lying-in hospitals was thought to be a means of reducing this mortality. That, however, seems not to have been their effect, at least in the absence of aseptic and hygienic conditions.

Childbirth was necessarily private, but under no circumstances must it be secret. Society, always fearful of having an unwanted mouth to support, suspected that secret births were also illegitimate. The midwife, on being licensed by the bishop (p. 251), was enjoined

not [to] deliver any privately or clandestinely to conceal the birth of the child. If you help to deliver any whom you suspect to be unmaryed you shall acquaint the Ecclesiasticall Court ... therewith and before you yield your assistance or helpe you shall perswade and by all lawful means labour with them to declare who is the father of the said child.[55]

It is doubtful whether, under such circumstances, many women would have refused to tell what they knew.

The child who had survived the trials of birth faced other dangers only a degree less severe during the first years of life. In addition to the risk of childhood diseases, there were the physical dangers present in small cluttered homes, in which elementary safety precautions were often ignored. Add to these the fact that most small children would not have had cradles, but would have shared their mothers' narrow beds.[56] Overlaying was a persistent risk, but how to distinguish between the accidental suffocation of a child and its deliberate destruction? Such cases lay in that grey area between manslaughter and murder. The woman was usually indicted for the latter, and was saved by the impossibility of proving intent. My student, David Clark, who made a study of the cases of overlaying that came before the Essex Quarter Sessions in the seventeenth century, claims that the verdict was usually one of accidental death.[57] The woman was often saved by the testimony of neighbours that she was of good repute and that the child, without ever having been subjected to any kind of medical examination, 'died of sickness'. In one case it was alleged that the parents rolled upon and suffocated the infant while having intercourse. It must, however, be remembered that attitudes to children and to child deaths were casual, not to say callous. A high child mortality was expected. Parents rarely showed any profound affection, and one more dead child was not a matter of great moment to either parents or community.[58]

Baptism followed closely on birth. The older view that the ceremony should be performed only at Easter disappeared early from the Catholic church along with the adult baptism of converts.[59] The acute danger that a child might survive only for a few days or even hours made early baptism essential. Hence the authorisation for midwives to baptise a child who seemed unlikely to survive. The church required that the infant should not wait 'longer than the first or second Sunday after birth', and baptismal registers show how often a priest was called to a cottage to baptise an infant thought to be in imminent danger of death. Society felt strongly on this matter, and numerous presentments by churchwardens are recorded either of late baptism or of a complete failure to have an infant baptised.[60] As a general rule the infant seems to have been baptised with what might seem unseemly haste. An Act of 1653 required that the date of both birth and baptism be recorded. This law was inadequately observed and soon came to be ignored, but in some areas sufficient evidence was accumulated to show how rapid was the procession to the font. In three Gloucester parishes, a quarter of all baptisms took place within two days of birth, and half were within seven days. Only 10 per cent of infants had not been baptised within three weeks of birth. In the York parishes for which data are available the median time lapse was six days, and in London, seven.[61]

There are many popular misunderstandings regarding the fertility of women in traditional societies. They did not, except in very unusual cases, bear a child every year, nor did their completed families run to a dozen or more children. Prolonged breast-feeding was normal, except among the upper classes, who employed wet-nurses, and this had the effect of reducing the likelihood of conception. The intergenesic period — the length of time elapsing between successive births — was rarely less than two years, and an average would appear to be close to thirty months. Furthermore, this period tended to become longer with the woman's increasing age. Nor was the completed family as large as is commonly supposed. There is abundant evidence, from the mid-sixteenth century onwards, not only that the nuclear family was normal, but that there were at any one time on average rarely more than three children. This, however, is not a measure of the size of the completed family; it represents a cross-section through society, with some families completed and others yet to be begun. Some children would certainly die before reaching adulthood, and the oldest might already have left home when the youngest was born. Occasionally a very large household resulted from the marriage of persons who had both been married previously and had had families by their previous spouses. The Clayworth census gives instances of this.

Another illusion is that the poorer and labouring classes produced bigger families than others and certainly larger than they could afford to support. Literary allusions are legion, but literature is all too often liable to mistake what may be conspicuous and unusual for the normal. On the basis of family reconstitution for one hundred parishes Laslett has calculated the mean size of the groups of children in the completed families of:[62]

Gentlemen	2.94
Clergy	3.53
Yeomen	2.76
Husbandmen	3.10
Trades- and craftsmen	2.90
Labourers	2.70
Paupers	2.34
Others	2.31

Labourers and paupers come almost at the bottom of the table. Most prolific were the clergy, so that Trollope's characterisation of the Reverend Mr Quiverful was not wide of the mark.

Childhood was the most dangerous period in the life of everyone. On the basis of a family reconstitution for the parish of Colyton (Devon.) Wrigley has estimated that infant[63] mortality rates ranged from 120 to 140 for each thousand live births in the sixteenth century, and that this changed little before the mid-nineteenth century.[64] Furthermore, between 50 and 60 per cent of these deaths occurred within the first month of life. Thereafter the death rate declined, and once a child had reached the age of 6 or 7 it could reasonably expect to live into middle life, if not old age.

The sources tell us little about childhood as such. Only when children met with accidents or aroused the anger of their elders by their rumbustious play do we find a small window into their world. That they had toys and played with them on the floor of the hall and not infrequently fell on to the hearth or overturned a seething pot set amid the ashes is apparent from the coroners' rolls. That they had some ill-organised ball-games which they played in the churchyards (Fig. 8.15) can be demonstrated from the proceedings of the ecclesiastical courts. But of their relations with their parents and kin we know remarkably little except for the upper classes, whose lives had become a matter of public or private record. We know that the children of the aristocracy and perhaps also of the gentry were fed for a very long time by a wet-nurse, and that the poorer classes were not. We know also that until the eighteenth century parents showed little affection for their children, who were

9.2 A man takes liberties and has a plate thrown at him. After a misericord in Hereford Cathedral.

left, by and large, to fend for themselves, and if one of them died of illness or as a result of an accident little grief was shown; one child more or less made little difference, and a high mortality amongst children was to be expected. The affective family did not appear before the eighteenth century, and then only among the wealthier classes which had the time and money to spend on their children.

At a humbler level we can only guess that the toys with which they played were crude imitations of the objects and artefacts used by adults. Graffiti suggest that a child might exercise his mind by playing with his hobby-horse (Fig 8.19), and doubtless there were many other improvised playthings. Today the child is amused and instructed by countless models of objects of the adult world, of which mechanical toys, dolls and diminutive household furnishings are amongst the most widespread and important. But models – dolls in particular – had an ambiguity which they have long since lost. They represented in miniature 'the people and things of daily life ... [they] resulted in an art and industry designed as much to satisfy adults as to amuse children'.[65] From the sixteenth to the early nineteenth century the doll was 'used by the well-dressed woman as a fashion model', and only when she had finished with it was it handed down to junior members of the family. 'Childhood was becoming the repository of customs abandoned by the adults.'[66] It is doubtful whether toys designed specifically for children were to be found much before the later years of the eighteenth century, and then only in the homes of the upper classes.

Children were from a very early age treated as young adults. They were dressed like their elders, and they played as nearly as possible with the tools of adulthood; from an early age they learned to gamble and play at dice. There was little schooling for the majority of the young. In most towns there was a grammar school, founded in the sixteenth or seventeenth century and dedicated to instruction in the classical languages, and in many villages a schoolmaster of doubtful learning and competence instructed children placed in his charge at a small weekly fee. In this way many acquired a very rudimentary reading skill and a modest acquaintance with arithmetic. Most, on the other hand, were exposed from an early age to the harsh realities of life. There was no need for sexual education. Most were well aware of sex long before puberty allowed them to practise it. The doctor employed by the French king, Henri IV, for his son, the future Louis XIII, left a journal [67] in which he described how the prince was introduced to sex while still an infant.[68] There is nothing quite as revealing in England, but in the small, congested cottage there was no possibility of sexual privacy. All children must have witnessed it, and not infrequently found themselves in the same bed with their parents who were practising it. Lack of space meant that children of both sexes often shared the same bed, under conditions which made intimacy and incest almost inevitable. This was, of course, one of the reasons why many children were sent away from home as soon as they had reached puberty. Change came for the upper classes in the sixteenth and seventeenth centuries with the building of larger houses with rooms arranged on a corridor principle (p. 108), but lower in the social scale there was little improvement before the late eighteenth or early nineteenth century.

Puberty and marriage

In Britain the coming of puberty was not marked by any particular ritual.[69] Baptism may once have served this purpose, but this rite was pushed back to childhood at a very early date. Perhaps the sacrament of confirmation, once it had been separated from baptism, came as near as possible to a puberty rite.[70] Children's advance to young adulthood was marked, rather, by longer and harder work. Some, even in rural areas, were apprenticed to local or even distant craftsmen at a very tender age, 10 or even less, and in most instances lived in the homes of their masters. The Bristol apprentice books[71] show that children from quite distant villages were sent to urban craftsmen to learn a trade. It is not difficult to imagine how these youngsters felt, alone in a distant city, with no relative or kin at hand and prevented by distance from returning home at any time during the year. Children whose fathers were yeomen, smallholders or husbandmen worked on the land, and doubtless looked forward to the time when they would marry and farm the same acres. A few absconded. Cities from the early Middle Ages had constituted an open gulf into whose anonymity the refugee from the countryside could fade, unnoticed and forgotten. Some, for whom a smallholding of a yardland or less could not provide a living, became the servants of the better-off, with little prospect of ever rising above this status. A feature of most surveys of household size is the larger number of servants, both male and female. Amongst the upper levels of society it had long been the practice for young men to serve in the households of other members of the nobility and gentry. There they were expected to learn the etiquette which surrounded the greater families of the land. Handbooks were written for their guidance, outlining in precise detail how they should conduct themselves at table or in the presence of their superiors.[72] After the sixteenth century such young gentlemen turned increasingly to the church, the law and commerce. At a humbler level many of those who could not be profitably employed at home became servants. There was no pretence that they were learning anything, even though the Poor Law papers repeatedly stated that young people were being apprenticed to 'housekeeping'. Most became domestic drudges. One is constantly surprised at the number of households that could afford to keep at least one servant, demonstrating that servants consituted an abundant and therefore cheap commodity throughout early modern times. In the hundred communities which provided the basis for Laslett's research, nearly 30 per cent of all households had one or more servants.[73] In the parish of Clayworth (p. 302) there were 35 male servants and 24 female, together 14.7 per cent of the population of the community. Twelve years later the totals were respectively 29 and 32, together making up nearly 15 per cent.[74] One is tempted to suppose that male servants worked on the land, or at least out of doors. This may not always have been the case, and literature, especially fiction, of the pre-industrial period is filled with the doings of devious characters employed as valets, porters and domestic servants.

In English society the young man expected to leave his family or his employer's home when he married and set up home on his own account. For this reason, if he were provident, he needed some secure means of livelihood, a craft or an assurance that he would shortly take over his father's holding. But this may not always have been possible. Accordingly, 'in pre-industrial England marriage came relatively late'.[75] In general, men married at between 25 and 30.[76] There were, however, notable fluctuations, depending chiefly on their ability to establish an independent household. Age at marriage seems to have increased during the eighteenth century, perhaps in response to a bigger population and a more vigorous competition for a livelihood.[77]

As a general rule women married younger than men, commonly by two or three years.[78] This was important for the size of their completed families, since they lived a longer part of their fertile period within marriage. It also, together with the fact that women's expectation of life, at least after their childbearing period is over, is greater than that of men, accounts for the relatively high proportion of women amongst the aged.

The age at which menarche occurred was probably later than it became in the twentieth or even the nineteenth century.[79] Earlier sexual maturity came probably with improved diet and physical conditions. In any event, a considerable time elapsed between sexual maturity and marriage for both women and men.[80] Laslett has commented on the problem facing any paterfamilias with a daughter of marriageable age. Literary evidence, for what it is worth, suggests that 'illicit love' was considerable, but, on Laslett's showing, the illegitimacy rate, though variable, tended to be low.[81]

The question of birth control, both within and outside marriage, is as difficult as it is important. It was never condoned by the church, whether Catholic or Protestant, but church authorities were unable to determine when it had taken place and, in the complete absence of evidence, were powerless to punish it. According to Keith Thomas charms to prevent conception were comparatively rare,[82] though late in the seventeenth century astrological 'sigils' or talismans for this purpose were being sold to servant girls – always a vulnerable class – at 4s. a time.[83] Potions were used both to prevent conceptions and to promote abortions, with what degree of success one cannot judge. The evidence for the practice of birth control is entirely circumstantial and statistical. It lies in the departure of the pattern of births within marriage from that which might be expected under conditions of unrestricted fertility. Wrigley has demonstrated from his family reconstitution for the parish of Colyton (Devon.) that married couples wanted children, but not too many.[84] The spacing of births in the early years of marriage can in general be termed normal, but thereafter the intergenesic periods become longer, and the last birth was commonly well before the presumed onset of menopause.[85]

Birth was enveloped in a cloud of folklore and magic, which had, of course, no influence on the course of events, except in so far as prophecy can under some circumstances become self-fulfilling. There was magic to bring about abortion and to achieve a healthy birth; to promote conception and to prevent it. No doubt such services were requested of the witch or 'cunning man' by those directly involved. But it was also assumed that such results could also be brought about by a third party for reasons of spite. As late as 1680 a certain Ann was found guilty by a church court in Scotland 'of using charmes and superstitious ceremonies ... to the end that she might render the said Alexander impotent to his own wife'.[86]

Adulthood

The estate of marriage was normal, and if it was postponed this was usually for economic reasons. It is noteworthy that on the death of a spouse, the surviving partner usually remarried within a very short period of time. This may perhaps have been to secure the welfare of any children there may have been by the first marriage, but it was above all because it was difficult, even impossible, to live alone. The man worked in the fields or at his craft for very long hours; he had to have someone to prepare his meals and look after his house. Women, on the other hand, had few opportunities for employment other than that offered by domestic work, and in this older women are likely to have been crowded out by the young. The impression that one gains from parish registers is that remarriage was more common in traditional societies than it is today.

The expectation of life was, by current standards, low, but it varied both spatially and through time. In pre-industrial England it was about forty years at birth. Analyses of traditional communities show not only a very high proportion of children – 45 per cent or more, but a low average age for the population as a whole, generally 25 or 26.[87] As a result, a high proportion of children, especially the younger members of a family, would have lost one or both parents before they had reached adulthood and were able to fend for themselves. Illegitimate children form a special case, because they had from birth effectively only one parent. They appear, however, to have been relatively few just because 'bastards died so quickly'.[88] They were unwanted by society and were probably the most deprived of all its members. But orphans – those who had lost one or both parents before the age at which they would have left home – were far more numerous. Indeed, their numbers posed an acute problem for traditional societies. At Clayworth they made up almost a third of all children in both 1676 and 1688:

Table 9.1   *The number of orphans*

	1676	1688
Total children	154	162
Orphans, one parent	50	56
Proportion of orphans	32%	32%

A series of local analyses made of communities in the period 1599 to 1811 shows a range of from 7 per cent orphans to 36, with an average of about 20. We should not be wide of the mark if we said that in traditional societies at least one child in five was orphaned.

It is difficult to discover how orphans and bastards fared in a traditional society. At Clayworth in 1688 well over a half were living with a step-parent, sometimes together with siblings of a later marriage. It would be surprising if, in one way or another, consciously or otherwise, they were not discriminated against. The great popular appeal of the Cinderella story is testimony to this kind of domestic situation. On the other hand, there is evidence in wills that children in general and orphaned children in particular were sometimes provided for.

Old age in traditional societies

Men who worked long hours in field or workshop and women who had borne half a dozen children in primitive physical and medical conditions and had seen half of them die in infancy, were apt to grow old early. At 50 or 60 they were aged and many were unable to work and had become an encumbrance on society, which had few institutional means to provide for their welfare. The problem was eased, of course, by the fact that the geriatric classes formed a very much smaller group than they do today. It is impossible to say with any precision what proportion of men lived long after their physical powers had deteriorated to the point at which they were no longer able to do any serious work. It might, before the Industrial Revolution, have been no more than a quarter or a third. The position of women was somewhat different. In the sense that a housewife's work is never done, they had no opportunity to retire, and most continued to run a household, however inadequately, until overtaken by death. Given the fact that the expectation of life for women was up to two years longer than for men, it is not surprising that the number of widows greatly exceeded that of widowers. At Clayworth in 1676 there were 24 widows but only 7 widowers. The number of lonely old women, subsisting at or below what may have passed as the contemporary poverty line, must have been very considerable. How, then, did traditional societies provide for their aged and ageing?

Most marriages in the traditional society of medieval and early modern Britain were both stable and fertile. They lasted in general some twenty years, and a few could endure for thirty-five years or more before one of the partners died.[89] The probability was that they would have grown children capable, though not always willing, to give them help and accommodation. The number of elderly and aged[90] without living kin must always have been small. The obligation to support these few fell upon the community, which discharged it with varying degrees of charity and concern. Parish gilds commonly assumed some responsibility for their aged members and also for their widows.[91] Churchwardens' accounts sometimes record small payments for their welfare. Most gilds disappeared at the Reformation, and their task was then assumed by private charity. Late medieval wills showed overall an immense investment in the future life in the shape of obits, trentals and candles. This ceased in the mid-sixteenth century, and private charity tended thenceforward to be directed towards provision for the bereaved and the poor (Fig. 7.3). The great majority of Britain's endowed almshouses were established during this and the next century. This was an 'age of secularism', when the 'central preoccupation [of charitable donors] had become not the state of faith, but the plight of the poor'.[92] The emphasis in such bequests was usually on the sick and the aged or else on schools and education. A further feature of such endowments was the favoured position which they gave to women. Some almshouses were exclusively for women, and in mixed houses women were sometimes given a more ample provision than men. At Chenies (Bucks.) Anne, Countess of Warwick, in 1603 endowed a 'hospital' for four men and six women. One is tempted to suppose that the donor had some realisation of the sex ratio amongst the aged.

Such charity was discriminating in so far as it was exercised within a very narrow area, usually the village or parish in which the donor lived or had a special interest. Since such endowments were made only by the aristocracy and occasionally by the gentry and the better-off members of the merchant and yeoman class, the poor benefited proportionately more in the wealthier parts of the country, where, it could be argued, they needed it least. But such provision for old age – by the parish and endowed almshouses – was a means of last resort. The general assumption was that children would support their aged parents, and this assumption was written into the

Elizabethan Poor Law. Other relatives – brothers, sisters, cousins and those even further removed – had no statuary obligation. So much for the role of kin and the extended family: they had disappeared from the English social structure.

Parish surveys and registers may give some idea of the numbers of the elderly requiring support, but only wills can show how in fact they were helped, and even here the evidence is only partial. We have, broadly speaking, two possible scenarios:

(1) Both spouses alive, but the man aged and unable to work and his wife perhaps bedridden and unable to attend to domestic duties.

(2) One spouse surviving, perhaps able to tend to his or her own needs, but often needing support.

In the case of the former, information is difficult to come by since, as neither has died, there are no wills to throw light on the domestic situation. Information has to be sought in the agreements reached between parents and children. As a general rule, the father gave up, wholly or in part, the management of his tenement or his craft, while retaining his house or at least a room or two within it. Sometimes the prospective heir was required to make some contribution to his parents' support.

On the other hand, wills throw a great deal of light on the situation in which the husband died, leaving the widow to inherit part of his possessions. The reverse is less clearly demonstrated, in part because women tended to outlive their husbands, in part because the family's possessions were vested in the husband, who alone made a will. What happened in the poorest households is unclear, because they generally had few possessions and had no testamentary obligations. It is from this class that the inmates of hospitals and almshouses appear mainly to have been drawn. The division of an estate between a widow and her children was always a difficult and sometimes a contentious matter. A feature of Elizabethan wills, wrote Emmison, was 'the kindly care shown by many a dying man for his wife'.[93] Continuing provision for accommodation and support was often difficult from the income from a small tenement, and the testator had to be very firm in defining his wife's rights.

Richard Hamond of Waddington (Lincs.), who appears to have had no male heir, willed 'that my wyffe have a bedroome in my house duryng her lyff yff so be that she and my sayd cosyn John can agre togeder',[94] and again, Thomas Smyth's widow of Deeping St James (Lincs.) was to continue to live in the family home 'so [on condition] that John my sonne be not put from [the] house that I dwell in, but that hys dwellyng may be in it with my wyff so long as they can agree'.[95] This question of the widow's ability to get along with the new occupant of the family home must have been deeply worrying to a dying man. What was to happen if the relationship broke down we are not told. One assumes that in most instances the heir had no alternative but to acquiesce with whatever grace he could manage in the widow's continued use of some part of the property.

This was institutionalised in the practice known as 'freebench', which became 'a remarkably powerful tradition in English life'.[96] The custom varied in detail but, broadly speaking, the widow was entitled to a fraction – commonly a third or a half – of her late husband's estate during the rest of her life. There are many instances of able-bodied widows continuing to farm their moiety of the holding, especially if they still had younger children to support. But it seems, on the evidence of wills and court rolls, that men used 'their wills to encourage their widows and sons to share control of undivided farms'.[97]

At Great Parndon (Essex) a yeoman left his tenement to his son, but his widow was to have accommodation with 'free egress and regress to the fire in the hall to dress her meat and into the kitchen to brew her drink, bake her bread and wash'.[98] Evidently many a widow was able-bodied and fully competent to manage her affairs. At Sibsey (Lincs.) the widow was required 'to kepe the forsayd house in good and sufficient reperell [repair]'.[99] Or the widow might have 'my house in Newton (Lincs.) duryng her lyff, and aftyr her decease to remayn to William my sonne and to heyres of his body'.[100] The last clause, which looks suspiciously like an entail, had no binding effect in law. Sometimes the provision for a widow could be very precise: 'I will that she shall have the great new chamber and the two little chambers towards the great gate several [separately] for her life',[101] or 'my wife to have her dwelling in ... the two chambers with the soller [solar] in the north end of the hall'.[102] Provision might even be made for the widow's animals, presumably a milch cow: 'my wife to have room to tie up two beasts and place to bake in the oven without disturbance'.[103]

Sometimes additional building was necessary before appropriate accommodation could be made available: 'I will that my executor shall set up [raise by an extra storey] the roof of my kitchen with such goods and timber as is mine, and then my wife to thatch and daub it at her own costs',[104] or, again, Robert Farrant of Hadstock (Essex) 'shall have the chamber at the gate and my son shall build a chimney [i.e. fireplace] in the same for her'.[105] On the other hand, we have the widow who, until his death, must have been looked after by her husband: 'the resydue ... to Agnes my wyff ... I mak my sone, John Wryght, over sear with my brother Robert in federance [support] off my wyff because she is agyd and may not labor, and he to have for hys pane and labor xs.'[106] Such simple and pathetic requests were common in wills before the Industrial Revolution; they go far to refute the view of traditional society as heartless and cruel to those no longer able to fend for themselves. Careful provision also appears in some wills for a surviving parent. William Eyre of Saleby (Lincs.) left instructions that 'my mother shall have her lyffyng with my wyff as long as her lyff shall contynew, so she beyng contente therwyth, yff not then she to have money and stuffin penyworthys to the valuewe of xls. and one cowe, wich she will choys, to fynde [support] her with'.[107] At Cossington (Som.) a son and heir was required to provide 'food and clothing' for the testator's sister.[108]

The will was in origin an expression of desire, and related to real estate over which the testator had no control. The testament, on the other hand, related only to chattels and was legally binding. After 1536 the two were effectively merged, and the testator was enabled to divise his property as well as his belongings. It must, however, be remembered that his right in land might be for only a term of years or for specified 'lives'. Wills, in so far as they relate to chattels, display an infinite variety. In their phraseology one can detect the petty jealousies and suspicions which arise in most families. One sees the special favour with which a particular son or daughter was viewed in the disposition of some treasured article of household goods. One learns which neighbours had been kindly disposed by the bequest, for example, of a watch or 'my little clock', and we detect also that streak of vanity which is present in all of us. Many wills called for the burial of the deceased in the most conspicuous part of the church or churchyard: 'afore the myddist of the altur there whereas the prest shall alwais [at] the tyme of consecracion stand even over and upon my harte';[109] or before the image of St Erasmus, bishop and martyr, in the church of St John, Glastonbury (Som.),[101] or close to the porch by which people entered and left the church. Thomas Broke thus asked to be buried 'in the churchehey [yard] ... of Thornecombe (Som.) as men goth over into ye churche at ye south syde ryghte as they mowe [may] stappe on me and a flat playne stone [with] my name ygraved yarin that men mowe the rather have mynde on me and pray for me'.[111] How much they loved to have their names, or at least the crests and marks by which they were known, displayed in public view! In the frieze which runs around the nave of Long Melford (Suff.) church are recorded in flushwork the names of those by whose generosity this great building was erected. In 1441 William Wenard of Exeter left 8s.4d. to each parish church in Devon and Cornwall 'on condition that my name be written on a certain glass window or in a certain public place of each church so that it can be seen by all men, as well friends as enemies, that when they see my name publicly written they perchance by induced more quickly to pray for my soul'.[112]

Most set great store by a good funeral, with pomp and a vast gathering of mourners. Before the Reformation it was not uncommon for those who could afford the extravagance to prescribe and pay for the dress of those who carried the corpse; the number of tapers that accompanied it, and, of course, of the masses that were to be said by the trental[113] and the hundred. Richard Groos of Wells (Som.) left '1d. or one loaf of the same price [to] every poor person ... [even] boys coming on the day of my burial',[114] and John Brygon of Exeter required that 'on the day of my burial all the poor shall have victuals sufficient for their dinner, and that each ... on leaving shall have ... $\frac{1}{2}d$.'[115]

On the other hand there were instances where such immoderate expenditure was firmly prohibited. Richard Clarke of Lincoln, described as a gentleman, would have no bell-ringing,[116] andSir Henry Lucas of London firmly declared: 'I do not wish for either candles or tolling of bells.'[117] John Stourton of Preston Plucknet (Som.) 'firmly prohibit[ed] that any great cost be incurred on the day of my burial, no further cost on the day of my anniversary, except such as must of necessity be borne, but that what is usually spent in these uses should be distributed among the poor'.[118] Taste and preference were as varied as they are today, and then, as now, there was a tendency for those whose estates could most easily have borne the cost of an extravagant funeral to be content with the plain and simple.

Running through the thousands of wills which I have read is one constant theme: the presumed immutability of family and society. No concept of growth, development or change is ever expressed. An endowment might require that tapers be burned on the occasion of the testator's obit *for ever*; furnishings might be made part of a house, inseparable from it *for all time*. 'I leave all the old family pictures which are or were in the great parlour at Spurstow [Ches.], and mine and my late dear husband's picture to be kept and remain in the great parlour ... *from generation to generation*' (my italics).[119] Thomas Vincent of Great Tey (Essex) left to his son 'all my tools ... my timber wrought and unwrought, with all my hewing block, planks, shelves, trestles and other engines. I will that he shall work the said timber in the shop where I work, so that he may maintain a fire in the house with the chips and other things arising thereof'.[120] Well might he have asked with A. E. Housman:

> Is my team ploughing,
> That I was used to drive
> And hear the harness jingle
> When I was man alive?

and heard with quiet satisfaction the poet's reply:

> Ay, the horses trample,
> The harness jingles now;
> No change though you lie under
> The land you used to plough.

The immutability of the world they had known seems to have been a vicarious kind of immortality, for these people could not really understand any other.

Tenure and inheritance

The peasant, we are told, conceives of immortality as the inseparable bond between his ancestors, himself and his descendants, on the one hand, and the land which they in turn held, tilled and loved. Their most earnest endeavour was always to keep the land – their land – within the family, to treasure and protect it and to pass it on, undiminished and unencumbered, from one generation to the next. The peasant had no concept of a private or personal interest in it which could be alienated or sold. The land which he tilled was held in trust for future generations. 'It was only with the greatest difficulty', wrote Macfarlane, 'that the idea that property could be divided between all the heirs was introduced.'[121] It may be that a fully communal system never existed in England,[122] but the stage at which a holding was divided between heirs – partible inheritance – is well documented. But, however widely it may at one time have been practised, its sphere was progressively narrowed, and in modern times it remained significant only in East Anglia and the south-east.

A peasant society is characterised not only by the identification of the family with the land which it cultivated but also by its high degree of self-sufficiency. It was not primarily a money economy, and few goods either left or came on to the peasant holding. English society, however, ceased relatively early to consist of self-governing units. Money in very small denominations – the *sceatta* – passed among the Anglo-Saxon cultivators, and at an early date the English became 'an open, mobile, market-oriented and highly centralized nation'.[123] Any chance that England might have become a peasant country disappeared when a 'natural economy' melted away under the influence of market forces.

The Domesday Survey (1085–6) recorded a population that was overwhelmingly rural and agricultural, and of the rural population the great majority was in varying degrees unfree. They were bound to the soil. But this attachment to the soil was different from that which characterised a free peasant. Except in the case of the class of freemen or *liberi homines*, and sokemen, the land was not theirs. They held it of their lords, and in return for its use they contributed their labour and services on their lords' demesne. If the peasant had acquired any degree of security it was only because his services were necessary to his lord. And so a holding was allowed to pass from father to son, because this seemed to be the simplest and least troublesome way of securing its continued cultivation and a future supply of labour. Convenience ripens within a generation or two into custom, and in a traditional society custom has almost the force of law. In theory most men held their land at the will of their lord, but in practice the security of the peasant was such that he could buy, sell and exchange his 'rights' in small parcels of land. A large collection of charters recording land sales in the twelfth century shows 'an active market in peasant property'.[124] Evidence from the Huntingdonshire village of King's Ripton also demonstrates an active land market in the late thirteenth and the fourteenth centuries. Parcels of land alienated were generally very small. Though free tenants were active in the land market, we also find unfree tenants exchanging land and devising it by will. This evidence contradicts 'the impression that familial plots ... were somehow static or permanent appendages of a single household'.[125] Such changes in landholding were made necessary by alterations in family size and structure. They do not necessarily denote a system of partible inheritance, but they emphasise the fluid nature of the holding and the readiness with which its extent or even its precise location could be changed. There is nothing in this that suggests that undying bond between the peasant and his land that, we are told, existed among, for example, the French peasantry.[126]

Evidence for this local land market is to be found in the court rolls, which recorded the business conducted in the manorial court. One gets the impression that all that the lord (or his steward) wanted was to be informed of what was happening. Indeed, the records of the court came to be themselves evidence of a right to hold land. For this the peasant was given a copy of the relevant part of the roll as proof of his title, and his tenure came to be called 'copyhold'. As a general rule, villein tenures, which made up some 55 per cent of unfree holdings at the time of Domesday, developed into copyholds. But there were varieties of copyhold, depending upon the conditions set by the court.[127] The tenant might have security for life or even for a number of 'lives'; it might be for a term of years, and if it was renewed this might be only on payment of a 'fine' of extortionate amount.[128]

On the other hand, legislation was coming to the rescue of at least some of the copyholders or customary tenants. The king's courts from the mid-fifteenth century began to give protection to a copyholder threatened with expulsion by his lord.[129] 'The copyholder', in Raftis' words, 'shaded toward freehold.'[130] But the apparent security of the copyholder in the end proved illusory. How often do we find that legal status has been undermined by social and economic circumstance. In England, over the next two centuries, copyholders disappeared and with them what passed in England as a peasantry.

The disappearance of the peasantry has been the subject of prolonged debate. England has, in this respect, been contrasted with France and with much of western Europe, where a true peasantry has remained significant until recent times. The enclosure movements, which brought the system of open-fields and of common land to an end, has been blamed, but in fact the peasantry was almost extinct when the great wave of enclosures took place in the eighteenth and early nineteenth centuries. The reason lies rather in the continued survival of the manorial demesne, the home-farm of later times. The lord may no longer have wanted to cultivate it himself, and it generally proved profitable to lease it to a 'farmer', and to live in a great house, rural or urban or both, on the rents it provided. And if the demesne could be made to yield so well, there was surely advantage in extending it and incorporating the lands of copyhold tenants as and when it proved practicable to do so.[131]

There were many ways, extra-legal if not positively illegal, of forcing a copyholder to surrender the piece of paper which was the title to his land. Less favourable conditions might be imposed; rights of common on the waste and in the woodland – a necessary supplement to his holding – could be restricted, or he could be driven from the land by a combination of menaces and bribes.[132] Copyhold lands, consolidated into manageable units, could then be leased at a fixed rent for a term of years. Rents could be raised in line with inflation whenever the lease came up for renewal, and there was no longer any appeal to the manor court or obligation to conform with local custom.

Social changes in the sixteenth and seventeenth centuries intensified the process. Money made in commerce or at the law was often invested in land, and it may not have been difficult to persuade a struggling copyholder to sell out to a man from the city. Then, too, people of humbler status than the merchant and the lawyer were found laying acre to acre in the hope that before they died they might have a respectable farm and be entitled to call themselves 'gentlemen'. Ralph Josselin, who for much of the seventeenth century held the living of Earl's Colne (Essex), was able out of a relatively small income to acquire a substantial holding which he bequeathed to his heirs.[133]

The copyholder who had inherited nothing more than a medieval yardland, faced grave problems in the inflationary times of the sixteenth and seventeenth centuries. It was a period of slowly rising population, so that each generation had to provide for a larger generation to follow. Fathers – by no means all, of course – had younger sons to provide for and daughters to endow with a marriage portion. They might shave off a small part of their tenement to endow a younger son, and there was all too often a widow for whom to make provision.

Margaret Spufford has analysed the inheritance customs in three contrasted parishes in Cambridgeshire, one of them on the chalk, a second on the clay, and the third on the edge of the Fen. In all three areas fathers struggled 'to provide for all their sons ... Even where primogeniture was the rule as much as possible seems to have been done for other children.' This process hastened the 'breakdown of the larger peasant holdings [and] tenants with traditional farms were squeezed out in the late sixteenth and seventeenth centuries, whilst the number of cottagers increased rapidly'.[134] Middling-sized holdings very nearly vanished, their land passing into the possession of the gentry, traditional or self-made, who thus laid tenement to tenement in order to build up an estate.

Despite the fact that the practice of primogeniture prevailed over most of England, attempts were commonly made to separate off a parcel of land to support a younger son. The division between the principles of primogeniture and of partible inheritance was very unclear. Primogeniture appealed to the landlords because it enabled them to keep a tighter control over their lands, and to the lawyers who liked its precision. But in the popular mind there lingered still some vague idea of the kinship, that broader group which had somehow to be accommodated within the family's traditional holding. This was more easily done in some parishes than in others. In Chippenham (Cambs.), a traditional open-field community spread across the chalk of eastern Cambridgeshire, there was little scope for the creation of more smallholdings by the division of the larger. An irreducible minimum had been reached, beyond which younger sons could expect only to become landless cottagers or to migrate. At Willingham, however, the arable lands along the Fenland edge were supplemented by resources in fish, wildfowl and summer grazing to be had out over the Fen.[135] These allowed a family to subsist on a very much smaller tract of farmland. The division of holdings could thus be carried very much further, because each parcel could be supplemented by rights in the still unreclaimed Fenland. Willingham became – or remained – more nearly a peasant community than either Chippenham or the intermediate parish of Orwell.

Thus the copyholder, descendant of the medieval villein, passed from the scene, and his descendants were to be found in the urban proletariat of the nineteenth century; in the landless farm labourer and estate employee, and in the émigré to new lands beyond the seas. His tenement, enclosed and cultivated in ways more advanced than he could ever have conceived, now formed part of the estate of a gentleman who perhaps sat in Parliament and invested in overseas trade.

There had always been on the fringes of rural society a class of cottagers who held no land of any significance and claimed, usually with the little legal warrant, rights of common for their few miserable animals. They made no will because they had little to leave, and we lack the insights that wills can give into their way of life. They were, as a general rule, dependent on casual employment on the land, and, when this failed, they turned to the parish for relief. Some of them were the last of the copyholders, squeezed from their holdings or obliged to sell their titles. Others derived from a landless class of less than villein status. A few had, no doubt, through a combination of misfortune and mismanagement, slipped down the social scale from the status of yeoman or even gentry. It was a fluid society in which as many were downwardly as upwardly mobile. If the copyholder found it difficult or even impossible to hold out against the pressures – economic and social – to which he was exposed, it is difficult to visualise the abject poverty of those at the bottom of rural society.[136] It is tempting to suppose that it was from these classes that industrial workers were drawn. The developing factories of the eighteenth century were indeed the 'promised land' on the far horizon. But it is likely that many lacked the knowledge to migrate to them and the resilience to adapt to new surroundings and a radically different kind of work from that to which they had long been accustomed.

As a result of these changes in the structure of rural society copyhold land became leasehold. Share-cropping, so common in western Europe under the name of *métayage*, was very rare in Britain. Far more common, and, in fact, general in the West Country, was leasehold for a term of two or three lives. The tenant took the land at an agreed rent, which was often very low, on payment of an 'entry fine', which was variable and generally high. The land was his for the duration of the lives of, generally, three named persons.[137] Most often the tenant designated himself and his expected heir. Sometimes he added his wife or a complete outsider who appeared to be both young and healthy. The changing value of the tenancy was reflected in the variable fine rather than in the rent, which was fixed and tended in real terms to decline. Even so, the practice varied from one manor to another. The Warden of New College, Oxford, in the course of his perambulation of the Wiltshire estates of his college, found at Stert that 'the custome . . . are three lives and a widowes estate', while at Colerne 'two lives only are granted in this Mannour'.[138]

Leasehold for lives probably began as an attempt to ensure the well-being of the tenant, his wife and his son and heir. It did not permit the inheritance to be divided, and the son would often be left with the problem of devising some way of looking after *his* heir. The most common solution was to pay a fine to the lord in return for permission to add another 'life' to the lease.

There were yet other forms of tenure. The church had held land in frankalmoin, subject only to the obligation of offering prayers for the soul of a former benefactor. Such tenures, by and large, disappeared at the Reformation. Tenure by sergeanty, the obligation to perform some trifling service, usually for the king should he ever pass by, also became defunct in the sixteenth century. Tenure by knight service, the duty of providing one or more armed knights to fight for the king for, as a general rule, a period of forty days in each year, should he ever demand it, had long been obsolete when it too was terminated by law in 1660.[139] All these forms of tenure were transformed into estates in fee simple, the fullest and most complete form of land ownership known to English law. The holder of land in fee simple was free to sell it or to devise it by will to whomsoever he wished. He was free to divide it between heirs or to entail it so that it descended intact from generation to generation.

The tendency was thus for the complex forms of land tenure of the Middle Ages to be simplified and, in effect, reduced to two, fee simple or free socage, as it was sometimes called, and leasehold. Leasehold, whether for lives or for a term of years, was usually held of someone who in turn held the land in fee simple. In the last resort land bore only those obligations placed on it by the state: the duty of paying the land tax, tithe and whatever local assessments there may have been.

The law says little about who may inherit a family's holding or indeed the chattels of the deceased. It is all a matter of custom. 'The inheritance system of any society ... is the way by which property is transmitted between the living and the dead and especially between generations.' How it was transmitted, whether intact or divided between kindred and affines, whether confined to males or extended to females, whether agnatic or uterine, was 'related, in complex, subtle and sometimes contradictory ways to the social and cultural patterns, to institutions and *mentalité*, to the formal and informal structures of the people'.[140]

The generally accepted model is that in origin land and even the stock and farm gear belonged to the community, and that the family had nothing more than a life interest in it. There could be no will, because its temporary occupant had no discretionary power to devise it. Only when private rights in land began to be established could the question of inheritance arise, and even then it was custom rather than the will of the peasant which determined where the land and chattels should go. The written will, definitive evidence of the intentions of the deceased, had furthermore to await the growth of literacy, and the oldest surviving English wills are not earlier than the later Middle Ages, though there remains a handful of Anglo-Saxon documents of this kind.

Private rights in chattels were established before those in land. The will *sensu stricto* related only to land and was an expression of a desire that it should pass to a designated heir. It was for a court, usually the manor court, to make the final decision. The testament, on the other hand, related to chattels, over which the testator had come to have complete power of disposal. In reality, private rights in land had been intensifying despite legal theory, and by the sixteenth century, when the will was merged with the testament, the testator had a theoretic freedom to choose an heir and to divide his inheritance as he wished. It is commonly said that England, along with much of north-western Europe, was an area where primogeniture prevailed, that the eldest surviving son succeeded to whatever land there may have been, and that younger sons and daughters had no rights of inheritance. By contrast, in parts of France and Germany the practice of partible inheritance was generally observed. The land, and by implication what went with it, was divided, though not necessarily equally, between heirs. Reality was less clear-cut. It was no doubt more convenient for a lord if his dependent tenements were passed intact from father to son. It made for easier and more profitable management. But usage, deriving from earlier practices within the kinship, always looked in a more kindly fashion on daughters and younger sons. Law, as interpreted in the courts, was in consequence always tempered by custom, which had a greater regard for individuals.

In practice the totality of an estate began to be divided as soon as a daughter was married. By tradition she brought to her marriage her *maritagium* or marriage portion. This might be in land, chattels or money, or in any combination of the three. This remained in theory the property of the wife, though it was likely to be managed by the husband or absorbed into his estate. In theory, too, it reverted to her family should the marriage break up, and, if her husband died before her, it was intended to give her some support in her widowhood. Less formally, a father might endow his children before his death, laying out money for their apprenticeship or to furnish them with a small parcel of land. He might decide to withdraw gradually from the cultivation of his lands or the practice of his craft, leaving his heir to inherit by slow stages, while he continued to live in the family house or in some part of it. Unless such intra-family arrangements were confirmed by the manor court or by a legally binding document – and this seems to have been unusual – we can have no knowledge of them. Nor do we know of the frictions that must have arisen as the son diverged from his father's customary practices or when younger children found themselves cut off with the proverbial penny.

When the father came to make his will he had complete freedom to devise his estate as he wished, subject only to the requirement that his wife, if she should survive him, should have her 'freebench' or 'widow's estate'. There was no legal obligation to leave land and goods to children, and it was in the father's power to disinherit a son if he wished to express his displeasure. Nevertheless, a system approximating that of primogeniture became general in England, but this was more a matter of custom and convenience than of law. An agricultural holding might have become so small that further division was impracticable, but the minimum economic size of a holding was a matter of local circumstance. There were conditions under which a less than minimal holding could provide a livelihood if it was supplemented in some way, as the tenements in Willingham (p. 330).

The simplest and most common adjunct to a very small holding was the practice of a domestic craft. Joan Thirsk has demonstrated how cloth-working might be made to yield a supplementary income, and allow a family to subsist on a great deal less than the traditional unit of land.[141] The practice of partible inheritance thus remained important in East Anglia, where weaving and other aspects of cloth-working gave additional employment. But, generally speaking, the practice of partible inheritance prevailed only in areas where land remained relatively abundant and common land extensive. This was notably the case in the hilly regions of Britain, where hill-grazing supplemented the arable bottomlands. In forested regions, notably Rochingham Forest and the Weald of Kent, partible inheritance was also practised, since a diminutive farm could be supplemented by extensive common and woodland grazing. Fenland could also be used to supplement the more formal cultivation of the land, as in the case of Willingham. A similar social development took place in the Fenland of southern Lincolnshire.[142] But 'partible inheritance could survive . . . only so long as commons and waste were large and provided a reserve of land on which succeeding generations could draw for their living'.[143] A point was eventually reached at which a holding could be no further reduced, and at this point the practice had to be modified or abandoned.

There seems to have been a close connection between the practice of partible inheritance and population growth. The view that, since all sons would be provided for, the parents were thereby encouraged to have more children is far too simplistic. It implies, furthermore, an attitude to family planning that probably did not exist. The effect of tenurial conditions was far more subtle. The prospect of an inheritance encouraged younger sons to remain at home, but there was the prospect that they might marry and set up home at an earlier age than they might otherwise have done if some supplementary income was available. Age at marriage was always one of the most significant parameters in population growth. Sons who left the family and migrated to a perhaps distant town would enter the lower ranks of the labour force. Marriage might be difficult until they had established themselves, and this could have been delayed until middle life. An abundance of land, together with the practice of partible inheritance, could thus readily account for early marriage and a sharp rise in population.

Primogeniture is often represented as the opposite of partible inheritance, as if inheritance was necessarily by the one system or the other. In fact, they are only the extremes of a very broad spectrum. Whatever lawyers and manor courts felt about it, a man's primary concern, at least in England, came to be the welfare of his family. 'Even where primogeniture was the rule, as much as possible seems to have been done for the other children,'[144] and, even if the holding had already reached an irreducible minimum, he might still burden it with financial lien in order to set up a younger son in business or a craft. 'It is difficult', wrote Margaret Spufford of the sixteenth and seventeenth centuries, 'to conceive how a labourer's cottage could bear such an annual burden on top of the rent when the wages of agricultural labourers were steadily losing purchasing power.'[145] Even Bracton, a lawyer who favoured the custom of primogeniture, was obliged to admit that it meant only that the eldest son had the first choice among the parcels of land to be allocated.[146] Homans stated categorically that 'unigeniture[147] was the product of estate management'.[148]

It may have been usual to favour the oldest son over his brothers, but the custom, known as Borough English, of allowing the youngest to inherit the major part of an inheritance, was well established in some localities.[149] It was the practice in certain forested areas such as Northamptonshire and the Forest of Dean. It was recorded in the parish customs of Dedham (Essex),[150] and probably represented a form of partible inheritance, in so far as the older sons had already been provided for and had left the family home, thus leaving the youngest to inherit what remained.

The nuclear family

The role of the family has been a sadly neglected aspect of history. Since there could be no human history without the family, its importance has perhaps been taken for granted, and was, until comparatively recent times, almost wholly ignored by historians. Yet the family has been a very variable institution. One can, up to a point, measure its size, the age at marriage of the parents, and the spacing of children. It is less easy to gauge the cohesiveness of the family group – the nuclear family; its relations with relatives and affines; and it is almost impossible to estimate the degree of affection which its members bore to one another. Was marriage, for example, an institution of convenience, or was it held together by bonds of genuine affection? To what extent was it disturbed by external liaisons, and were children wanted or were they the price that had to be paid for intimate relationships? Answers are never easy or simple and they depend, furthermore, on the period and the region in question.

Although the myth of the extended or 'stem' family has now been banished from the serious study of household and family in this country, the concept of the kinship group nevertheless survives. Its presence is implicit in the Table of Kinship and Affinity which was once exhibited in every church of the Anglican communion. The kin was the group within which one did not marry. The perception of kinship varied with circumstances. According to Arensberg's study of society in County Clare (Irish Republic) in the 1930s, third cousins were felt to be 'very far out'.[151] Marriage at this distance was in theory prohibited, but was, in fact, permitted by the church whenever proper cause could be shown. And a proper cause might be that everyone in the community was related within this degree of affinity with everyone else. There was, Arensberg noted, no feeling of horror at such a marriage, though it might have been a matter of amused comment. This was the attitude in the south-west of Ireland earlier in the present century. It might be assumed that it prevailed generally in traditional society at an earlier date.

However great was the importance of the kin in earlier societies, the tendency was for it to decline before that of the nuclear family. The extended family, which bore a certain resemblance to the kinship, was never significant in Britain, and the only rival to the family as the focus of an individual's attachment was the community, and this tended, like the kinship, to be of diminishing importance.

There seems to have been, especially in France, 'a series of contractions and expansions in family size and solidarity'.[152] A small nuclear family reflected the degree of security afforded by public authorities, whether the state itself or feudal lordship. By contrast, a state of war or of insecurity was reflected in a more extended family, with relatives and affines living alongside the conjugal group.[153] In south-eastern Europe, where the extended family was exemplified as nowhere else in the western world, the home itself was often protected, giving rise to the *kula* or tower-house. It would be interesting to know to what extent the development of pele-houses and bastles in northern England was accompanied by the emergence of a more extended family structure.

That children were wanted, rather than being the accidental product of marriage, is demonstrated from the records. Fertility figures were common, especially in churches, though not as common as is often supposed. The first child was often born within nine months of marriage and usually within a year (p. 310). The spacing of the next two or three is generally consistent with breast-feeding and unrestricted intercourse. Thereafter the intergenesic periods usually lengthened. Many demographers interpret this as evidence of birth control, probably by the method known as *coitus interruptus*. Society expected a woman to have children, though it did little to relieve the anguish or reduce the dangers of childbirth (p. 252). Various charms and prayers were used to reduce both, as well as to bring about conception in women who had been infertile. Some 'cunning' persons even claimed to be able to induce a pregnancy without *coitus*.[154] There were, on the other hand, cases of women driven to the limits of sanity by their inability to conceive. In Oxfordshire a man and his wife were presented by neighbours before the Consistory Court for having a cradle beside their bed 'as if a child was in it'.[155]

This desire for a family contrasts with the lack of care taken of children. Birth was traumatic for both child and mother, but the dangers that faced the child during the first few years of life were far greater. Accidents were frequent and often fatal. The mother's carelessness may have been to blame, but it was very rare for her to be indicted for infanticide. Indeed, the courts treated the deaths of children very lightly, and the death of a bastard, even when murder was suspected, aroused little consternation. It is difficult to demonstrate the extent to which infanticide was practised, because drowning or overlaying could so easily have been the result of accidents. Newly born children counted for little, and a high infant mortality rate was a fact of life. Abortion was tolerated and called for little censure, because of the uncertainty of the stage at which life began and the certainty that an unbaptised child in any case had no soul.[156]

This almost casual attitude towards children extended also to youth. There was little attempt to provide a child with activities suited to its age, and none to educate him or her in any literary fashion. This totally inadequate apprenticeship for life ended in the early teens. Boys were considered mature at 14, and girls were able to marry at 12.[157] In aristocratic circles boys might be sent off on crusade, and girls be precipitated into a nunnery if no suitable marriage could be found for them. But the history of the peasant family was in many ways different from that of the well-to-do. Children of the former did not set off to fight the Turk, and very early marriage was out of the question. But adulthood came early nonetheless, and children graduated almost directly from infant pursuits to those of grown-ups. Child labour was not a creation of the Industrial Revolution; it had always been practised. Aristocratic children were sent at the age of 6 or 7 to serve in other noble households. Apprenticeship began as early as 10, and small children were employed on the land in any capacity that did not call for great strength or manual dexterity. In one eighteenth-century farm account 'scaring bards' at a penny a day was common occupation for children not sufficiently developed to do more.[158]

Change came during the period of the Renaissance, and it is then that the 'centuries of childhood' may be said to have begun. Italian art, as Ariès has emphasised,[159] began to represent children as children, and not as small, gnome-like grown-ups. It is possible that representations of the Virgin and Child brought home to people that a child was a child and not an underdeveloped adult. At the same time the child progressed to centre stage. Family groups were painted, and in monumental sculpture it became customary in the later sixteenth century to show the whole family on funeral monuments erected to the parents. The schooling of children begn to be taken more seriously. Schools were founded in the small towns of England and Wales; the rich engaged tutors for their sons if not also for their daughters, and books especially written for children came off the presses in increasing numbers. Toys were designed that were more than miniature replicas of adult weapons and tools. The jigsaw puzzle was invented in 1762 and children's dice and board-games began to appear soon afterwards.[160] The family portrait became common in the richer homes in the seventeenth century, and in the eighteenth children began to occupy a canvas in their own right and not merely as adjuncts to a conjugal pair. At the same time schools became more numerous, and the schoolmaster, however unlettered and unskilled, was to be found in many villages.[161] These new attitudes to childhood and children were at first restricted to the wealthy and leisured class. Only they could afford not to set their children to work at an early age. Yet this new attitude was not accompanied by any development in domesticity. Parents did not, as a general rule, set aside a period each day to be with their children and to talk with them. It seems, rather, that the aristocratic mother put her children out to a wet-nurse and in fact saw very little of them. If in the eighteenth century they no longer went off to serve in other noble households, they were sent to boarding-schools, to live in harsh conditions and under a strict discipline, and to sleep in dormitories in the company of boys of their own age.

Society's attitude to children are well illustrated by the toys they were given (p. 318) and the clothes they were made to wear. Not until the seventeenth century was there any significant difference, other than size, between the clothes worn by children and those of their parents. In the course of the eighteenth the differences became more conspicuous, but not until the nineteenth did children's styles, radically different from those of adults, at last make their appearance.

It is possible to measure the cohesiveness of the family in the past only by the open expressions of its members. Wills give some idea of the regard with which men (who made most of the wills) regarded their wives. The fact that married couples stayed together until death parted them has little relevance. Divorce was impossible and legal separation difficult. Even living apart from one's married partner was treated as an offence by the church courts, and married women were almost unemployable, except on the land and in factories, which, from the early days of the Industrial Revolution, made heavy use of female labour. Social pressures to maintain the conjugal home were great, even though internal rancour and disputes may have made this difficult. Stories, both literary and legal, of the shrewish wife were sometimes so gross that the marriage relationship must have been very difficult to maintain. But popular opinion in favour of marital stability was able to express itself in ways that would not be tolerated today. Blundell of Corby (Lancs.) noted in his diary in 1722 that 'there was a Riding for Ann Norris who had beaton her Husband, they called here in their Round. Henry Swift was their Rider.'[162] Readers of Thomas Hardy will be familiar with the 'skimmington ride' as a means of ridiculing marital infidelity or breaches of domestic harmony.[163] On the other hand, expressions both of conjugal affection and of regard for children are common in letters and diaries. Sir John Bramston (1611–99) wrote of his wife that 'she was a very observant wife. I scarce ever went on a journey but she wept … She was mother of tenn children in the twelve yeares she was a wife, fower daughterss and six sonnes, tho' when she died she left only two sonns [and] two daughters.'[164] The concern shown by some husbands when their wives were in labour also shows how close their relationship could be (p. 251).

There is abundant evidence, however, that the family was seen primarily as a mechanism for procreation and the supply of domestic labour. At the higher social levels marriages were commonly arranged for family or political reasons. No doubt real affection could develop in time, but external liaisons by both partners were in part the consequence of the lack of conjugal affection and in the eighteenth century aroused little comment. At lower social levels marriage was more likely to arise from the mutual attraction of its partners simply because there was less likelihood of there being family lands to protect or extend or political alliances to secure. Nevertheless, the cohesiveness of a marriage varied not only from one social class to another but from one generation to the next.

What Stone calls the 'companionate marriage', in which the partners displayed true affection and mutual support, was comparatively late in appearing. It was a luxury which society could not afford until modern times. It was preceded during the later Middle Ages and early modern times in both upper- and lower-class households by the open family, in which there was no privacy and little cohesiveness or affection. Each family was watched by every other in the community, and the nuclear family was half-submerged in kinship.

In a traditional society everyone belonged to three overlapping groups, the family, the kinship and the community. 'So long as the social life of the village community flourished,' wrote Joan Thirsk, following the arguments of the French sociologists, 'it swamped and stifled the life of the family and inhibited the growth of family solidarity.'[165] But much depended on the economic standing of the family and its physical relations with the rest of the community. In a predominantly pastoral society, with a scattered settlement pattern, a degree of isolation and thus of cohesiveness was forced upon the family. In a nucleated settlement close association between familial groups was easier and co-operation between them essential for the running of village affairs. Mandrou has argued[166] that in winter families were obliged to share one another's homes in order to keep warm. It was in such evening gatherings that local popular culture was perpetuated: '… an evening gathering within the village community [where] tools were mended by candlelight, thread was spun, the unmarried flirted, people sang, and some man or woman told stories ... Then, if one of the men were literate and owned books, he might read aloud.' It is impossible not to see in the strengthening of familial bonds an important reason for the decline of the sense of community and thus of the legacy of popular culture of which it was the bearer.

This assertion of the conjugal family as the primary unit of human organisation and control during and after the Reformation may have been coincidental. The effect, however, was to reinforce its importance. 'For Puritans the lowest unit in the hierarchy of discipline was not the parish but the household ... The Reformation, by reducing the authority of the priest in society, simultaneously elevated the authority of lay heads of households.'[167] Puritan writers, especially during the first half of the seventeenth century, repeatedly emphasised the importance of the family and, in particular, of its male head, who was encouraged to conduct family prayers and to adopt an arbitrary and dictatorial attitude to wife and children. Paterfamilias became parish priest writ large. The whole theological structure of Puritanism was patriarchal.

Medieval practice had allowed women a far greater degree of freedom than is commonly supposed. This is demonstrated in landholding and inheritance practices, in family life and before the law. The effect of the Protestant Reformation and, in particular, of the development of Calvinist theology, was to reverse this. At its root lay the doctrines of predestination and of original sin. The child had been conceived in sin, and its evil nature could be combated only by the most vigorous of repressive measures. Since sin had come into the world through the actions of Eve in tempting Adam, women were henceforward to be placed under the domination of men. With the ending of the Catholic priesthood, the father and head of the household became the chief intermediary between his family and God. Ideas of male dominance were in time stripped of their theological underpinning but nevertheless survived into the nineteenth century, when legislation was introduced to reinforce the effects of customary practice. Only now is society emancipating itself all too slowly from the legacy of Puritanism.

At the same time, the doctrine of original sin, which had been held throughout the Middle Ages in a relatively innocuous and tolerant form, received a sharper edge. Mankind was born in sin, inheriting, as it were, the original sin of Adam. Even infants, 'though they have not yet brought forth the fruits of their iniquity ... have its seed; nay, their whole nature is a sort of seed of sin, therefore it cannot but be hateful to God'.[168] Children were therefore repressed, their natural instincts inhibited and their intellectual growth stunted. Of course, not all either subscribed to or practised the kind of familial control implicit in the assumptions of Calvin and his followers. In attitudes to children, as in the treatment of women, the *a priori* assumptions of Protestant theologians came in time to be moderated or abandoned, but their legacy in the sadistic treatment of the young survived into the present century.

339

In the last resort, the reasons for the intensification of family life and the development of the 'affective' household must be sought in material conditions, in the increasing conveniences and comforts of domestic life, which brought people together in their own living rooms (p. 173). Social attitudes cannot be divorced from domestic furnishings and architecture.

CHAPTER 10

THE CULTURE OF CITIES

Funny you can be so lonely with all these folks around.   Kurt Weill, *Street Scene*

When I come out of the country hither to the City methinks I come into another world,
even out of darkness into light.   Sermon at St Paul's, 1571

The popular culture of cities and towns is, by its nature, a derived culture. Towns
were a relatively late development; they could arise only when agriculture had been
sufficiently developed to yield a surplus for their support, and the ratio of urban to
rural population in traditional societies has always been low. Towns derived not
only their basic food supply from the countryside, but also their population. Urban
death-rates were generally higher, and birth-rates lower than in the countryside, and
the net reproduction rate was for much of the time less than unity. There thus had to
be a migration from the country to the town, and the vast number of locative
personal names, indicating a village or place of origin, gives some idea of the
distances covered by the migrants.

Many towns had no precisely known point of origin. They had grown in response
to human needs, and in some form or other seemed to have existed from time
immemorial. Some had been established by the Romans, had decayed and had been
abandoned, leaving only an infrastructure of roads and the rumour that there had
once been a city. Gradually, during the post-Roman period, most such sites were
reoccupied, but when and by whom we generally have no means of knowing. They
once again became towns, often with a monastic foundation to hasten their growth.[1]
During the Anglo-Saxon period, gatherings of merchants, who needed protection
against the raids of the Danes, gave rise to another group of settlements, some of
which grew in time to the size and status of towns. Almost all the towns surveyed in
Domesday Book belonged to one or other of these two categories, and are often
called 'organic' towns from their lack of any clear-cut foundation.

A third kind of towns was created by territorial lords in the later Middle Ages
because they saw potential profit in them. They let it be known that here was not
only economic opportunity but also a burgage plot to be had at a modest rent,
together with freedom from servile obligations. These were 'planted' towns. Their

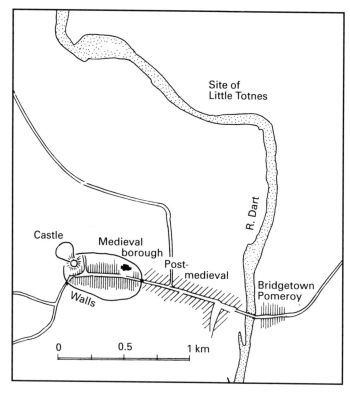

10.1 The borough of Totnes and its satellites, neither of which became functioning boroughs.

privileges were guaranteed by charter, and, in many instances, their street plans were laid out and plots marked off in advance of settlement.[2] By contrast, the 'organic' town had grown slowly as economic opportunity offered. It had no founding charter; its rights were prescriptive, and had to be confirmed retrospectively, usually by the grant of a royal charter. London, Bristol, York and Norwich belong to this category; Ludlow, Totnes, Richmond and Bury St. Edmunds to that of 'planted' towns.

The expectations of many a lord must have been raised by the prospect of having a town and of profiting from its rents, fines and tolls. But their hopes were all too often dashed. There was a limit to the number of potential burgesses and the volume of urban services that society either needed or could support. Many an incipient town proved to be stillborn. The town of Totnes (Devon.) grew up below the castle of Judhael of Totnes, and its main street sloped down the hill to the river Dart, where seagoing vessels could tie up (Fig. 10.1). Its apparent success became a model for others. A neighbouring lord, de Pomeroy, was tempted to found a town on his own land across the river from Totnes, and yet a third settlement was established a mile or two up the river. Alas, there was business enough for Totnes, but Bridgetown Pomeroy never grew to be more than a cluster of cottages and the third never made it that far.[3] Devon is strewn with such false hopes, such *villes manquées*. According to Hoskins there were once no less than seventy places in the county with the title and aspirations of a borough.[4] Of these only twenty were still boroughs for taxation purposes in the Middle Ages, and several of these were sinking even then to the status of villages.[5]

This raises the question: what consituted a borough or town? Strictly speaking, a borough was a place which had been incorporated by charter, granted most often by the king, exempting it from the manorial regime which prevailed throughout rural England, and giving it limited rights of self-government. The charter conferred the right to hold a weekly market and usually an annual fair. It also allowed the townspeople to have their own court to settle disputes and to punish petty misdemeanours. But permission to have these rights by no means assured the ability to enjoy them, and a large number of legal boroughs throughout the country proved to be unable to sustain the privileges they had gained.

In an entirely different sense, a town or borough was a settlement whose dominant functions were non-agricultural. It contained merchants and craftsmen, and it provided services. But not even the most prosperous town in traditional societies was ever divorced completely from the land. Its citizens often owned and not infrequently cultivated the surrounding fields (Fig. 10.2). They milled grain and tanned hides from nearby farms. Farm produce was sold in their markets, and their more prosperous citizens invested in rural land and enjoyed the rents which accrued. But to be a functional or economic borough, a significant part of the population had to be engaged in craft industries or employed in trade. It had to have a 'basic' occupation other than agriculture.[6] Another segment of its population would have been engaged in what would today be termed tertiary or 'service' industries. Their business lay in transporting merchandise, in providing accommodation for travellers, in offering legal and administrative services. From this commercial élite were usually chosen the borough's functionaries – mayor, aldermen and the wardens of gilds – who served in a part-time and honorary capacity. And in all except the smallest towns there was usually a spiritual establishment of monks, canons or friars, not to mention a host of poorly paid priests who sang masses and celebrated obits for a petty reward. It is not easy to estimate the size of this ecclesiastical population, although, of course, one can enumerate the parish priests, formally entrusted with the cure of souls and one can estimate the approximate numbers in the religious orders.

A further complication, and a peculiarly English one, was the parliamentary borough, which was called upon at intervals to send two representatives to Parliament whenever the king summoned it to meet at Westminster or elsewhere. The distinction was an arbitrary one. The crown sent writs to individual towns. The basis of their selection, never logical in the first instance, became increasingly erratic. Although most important towns of medieval England were called upon with some regularity, there were many smaller ones whose representation was spasmodic and, since the borough bore the expenses of its members, reluctant. There were some

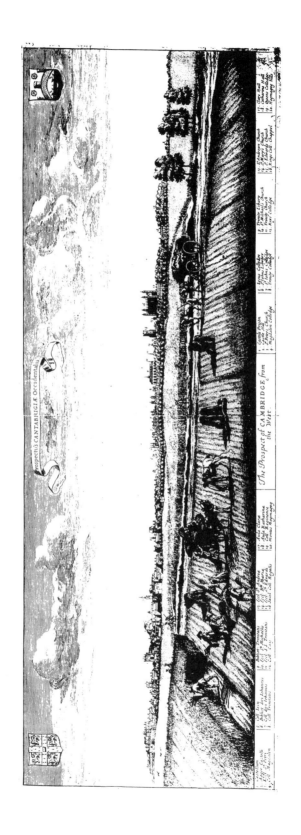

10.2 Cambridge fields: the open-fields of the town reached close to the built-up area. Evidence can be seen in the foreground of open-field strips, or selions. From David Loggan, *Cantabrigia Illustrata*, 1690.

parliamentary boroughs which withered until only a few cottages remained. Such 'rotten boroughs' were mostly disenfranchised in the Great Reform Bill of 1832. The status of the parliamentary borough was an accident of history, and has no relevance to the substance of this chapter.

An urban population

Our concern here is with the economic or functional borough, since only that stood in contrast with rural settlements, and only in the functional borough can a distinctively urban culture be said to have prevailed. One can, though only in the broadest outline, trace the growth of urban population from the time of Domesday Book until the beginning of the nineteenth century, when the decennial censuses began to provide reliable data. Even so, Domesday references to towns are frequently ambiguous, and their total population uncertain. Darby found evidence for a total of 112 boroughs, including London and Winchester, for which the surveys are no longer extant.[7] But it is difficult to translate the *burgenses, mansurae, hagae* and other such terms, which must each have denoted some form of household or tenement, into firm totals of the number of burgesses. On the evidence of Darby's urban statistics I would put the total urban population at not less than 100,000.[8] On the assumption that the total population of England was of the order of 1,350,000, urban population cannot have greatly exceeded 7.5 per cent. There are no comparable estimates of urban size before the Poll Tax of 1377. The latter purported to enumerate all adults, but omitted priests and members of the religious orders, as well as those too poor to pay. While it is possible to make a correction for the young and for the church, it is difficult to say how many were classed as 'poor'. It might, however, be suggested that urban population amounted *in toto* to 300,000 to 350,000 or about 14 per cent of a greatly increased total.

During the next two centuries urban population fluctuated under the influence, on the one hand, of epidemic disease which must at some time or other have ravaged most towns, and, on the other, of changes in the basic economy of the country. Some towns decayed with the decline of craft industries, notably weaving, which had been their mainstay. Others, and notably the port towns, grew with the expansion of trade.[10] Although there is no general source of urban statistics, there survive for many towns lists of burgesses and freemen, of tax-payers and burgage-holders. Taken together, these suggest that there was a slow growth in urban population in the sixteenth and seventeenth centuries, and a much sharper expansion in London, but the first census of 1801 suggests that its total could have been little more than a fifth.[11]

Urban population increased very much faster than the population as a whole, and this could only have been achieved by a large-scale immigration. At any one time a high proportion of the inhabitants of any major city was made up of immigrants. They had mostly been born in the countryside, and had moved to the 'promised land' of the city. There are no quantitative data for the composition of urban population before the census of 1841, when the enumerators were required to note the occupation and the county of birth of each person counted. Ten years later, the question was more specific; it called for the actual parish or place of birth. Urban growth was rapid at this time, and one would expect an even higher proportion of a towns population to have been born elsewhere.

An examination of the enumerator's books of the small Cornish borough of Lostwithiel for the year 1851 shows that, of heads of households, only 29.5 per cent of the men and 21.5 per cent of the women had actually been born within the borough. The rest had migrated from other parts of the county or from beyond the Tamar. Some had come from as far afield as Kent and Northumberland.[12] The proportion of immigrants in the population would have been much lower in the seventeenth and eighteenth centuries, when urban growth was slower.

Immigrants to a town brought with them a *mentalité* different from that of long-time urban-dwellers. It was not merely that the infrastructure of the village – its water supply, sanitation and food supply – was different from that of the town and in general allowed for a greater latitude of conduct. It was rather a difference in outlook. The countryman was accustomed to the security conferred not only by family and kinship but by the rural community at large. This support was suddenly snatched away from the immigrant, since it was generally individuals from the younger age-groups in the greatest need of support, who made the transition from country to town. Many were country boys apprenticed to urban craftsmen, with little if any opportunity to return home to visit parents and relatives.[13] Most significant, perhaps, was the number of young women who migrated to towns to seek work as servants. Some returned to their villages to marry, but many must have been absorbed into an urban 'subculture'.

The immigrants found themselves alone in a culture superficially similar to, yet strangely different from, that to which they had been accustomed. They must have felt isolated and alone amid the urban crowd, and many a young person must, as in the apocryphal story of Dick Whittington, have felt that bare subsistence in the home village was preferable to the loneliness and unknown dangers of life in the city. In the words of Louis Wirth, 'urban life consists in the presence of close physical proximity coupled with vast social distances' between people.[14] The culture of cities is made up, in part, of attitudes and artefacts inherited from the countryside, superimposed on which are the institutions and relationships created in order to fill this social void in people's lives. We must conceive a footloose people who, for whatever reason, had left the relative security of their homes and villages for the lottery of the town, and had, in varying ways, created new institutions and relationships for their own protection and well-being.

Domesday evidence shows that a few towns were already large, by medieval standards, with 3000 or more inhabitants before 1100, and before the end of the Middle Ages there could have been a dozen with over 5000. Nevertheless, most towns remained small, with little more than one or two thousand inhabitants even as late as the eighteenth century. Such towns had retained many of the features of the village. They were inward-looking, for very few ever achieved any national or even regional significance. Theirs was a 'face-to-face' society.[15] The citizens knew one another, and any newcomer would quickly be recognised as such and made unwelcome. The immigrant could not fade unnoticed into the anonymity of the crowd. Many of the planted towns were little more than villages writ large, and some never achieved the size even of a large village.

It is with the larger 'organic' town that this chapter is mainly concerned, because only there does one meet with social problems and solutions that were specifically urban. The structures and institutions of the village provided in some ways the models for the town, but they had to be modified, skewed as it were, to fit the new environment. In this sense the culture of towns was a bastard culture. It was less conservative than that of the village, more ready to accept technical and cultural innovation than the countryside. It was more exposed to external influences than the village, just because it received immigrants, dealt with foreign traders and carried on business with other towns. Cities were the principal agents of change in western society.[16]

Urban culture in traditional society is examined here under three heads. First are the institutions which were fashioned to satisfy the psychological needs and social and economic requirements of its citizens and to carry on the business of governing the town. The second is the *mentalité*, the outlook or world-view of the townsman, and the ways in which it differed from that of the country-dweller. Lastly, there are the structures and arrangements which were created to serve the physical needs of the citizens: housing, the supply of food, water, sanitation, fire-protection and security.

Social structures

The traditional town was full of small corporations, each providing in some small way companionship and security for its members. The town was itself governed by a body made up usually of an oligarchy of citizens of 'the better sort'. Subject in varying degrees to this patrician class were the town and parish gilds, in most of which the city fathers played some role as members or leaders. Then there were the lesser associations which managed individual charities, chantries and almshouses. In all small towns and, indeed, in most large ones, a group of rich and powerful citizens spread their tentacles widely. They dominated town government, and usually had a controlling voice in the management of most other associations. They could exclude newcomers from gild membership, from the freedom of the town, and from the benefits of local charities, and, until the municipal reforms of the first half of the nineteenth century, they could perpetuate themselves and their class in positions of power and authority.

Almost all such associations had some form of religious basis, and many had, as their stated purpose, the maintenance of a light before a shrine, the singing of masses, or the performance of a religious play. The role of women in gilds is less

347

clear. Most gilds appear to have been male-dominated, but in none does there appear to have been any deliberate policy of excluding women from its privileges. There were, however, some craft gilds, smithing, for example, to which few women would have wanted to belong, but in some of the more socially oriented gilds women appear to have played a not inconspicuous role.

Church and parish

The parish and the community of its parishioners was one of the foremost of such social structures. The parish church, together with the religious and social obligations which focused upon it, had been a unifying force within the rural community. Together they gave a degree of security to the individual, and it became one of the first tasks of newcomers to the town to replicate, in this very different environment, institutions analogous to those which they had left behind in the countryside. The creation of a 'neighbourhood' church not only served the spiritual needs of those who lived nearby but also brought them together socially, creating a 'little community' amid the faceless mass of urban-dwellers. This is as true of the urban church of the Middle Ages as of nonconformist chapels in the growing towns of the nineteenth century. One must never underestimate the spiritual needs even of the humblest members of urban society, but spirituality has rarely been dissociated from sociability. Those who prayed together usually did business and played games together.

The Church of the Holy Sepulchre in Cambridge may serve as an example. Between 1114 and 1130 a group of citizens – we even know the names of three of them – obtained from the Abbot of Ramsey a parcel of land on which to build a church.[17] They built handsomely. News of the Crusade and of the capture of Jerusalem had reached them, and they erected a round church on the supposed model of the Holy Sepulchre and with the same dedication. Despite misguided restoration in the nineteenth century, it survives substantially as Anger the Bearded and his friends had left it in the early twelfth century.[18]

We know of this minor incident only because of an almost casual entry in a monastic cartulary. What we cannot know is how many such churches were built by simple people who felt an overwhelming urge to act together. One can be fairly sure that many of the numerous churches of, for example, later medieval Winchester or Norwich had arisen in this way. Nor can we tell how many, far less pretentious than the church of St Sepulchre in Cambridge, were built and were then lost because their founders, or their descendants, lacked the money to maintain them or the social need to keep them.[19] In all our older cities there are 'lost' churches, whose short-lived purpose it was to provide a bond between the disparate elements which went to make up the population of early towns.

The fundamental problem of urban churches was that they were urban; that they lay in built-up areas and were surrounded not by cultivated fields but by houses, streets and markets. The basic support of the rural church was the predial tithe, and

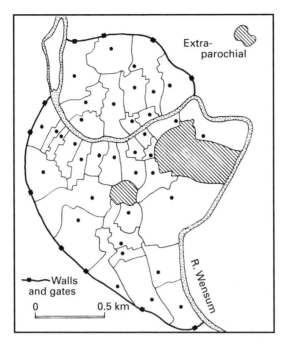

10.3 Map of urban churches and parishes in Norwich in the later Middle Ages, based on 'Leet jurisdiction in the City of Norwich', Seld Soc, 5, 1895, and N. P. Tanner, *The Church in Late Medieval Norwich 1370–1532*, Toronto, 1984.

one-tenth of everything that grew or lived within the parish could amount to a very considerable sum in monetary terms. It must be admitted that some part of the tithe that was collected was often diverted to other ends, but those who received it generally recognised, however grudgingly, their obligations to the parish and its church. Many – perhaps most – churches in the larger towns received no predial tithe, because their narrowly circumscribed parishes yielded no agricultural produce (Fig. 10.3). Canon law required the payment of personal tithes by those who cultivated no land and received no increase of nature. But in an age when most people were, in contemporary terms, self-employed, it was very difficult to assess the value of their employment and even more so to collect one-tenth of it. In fact, personal tithes seem rarely to have been paid, and the urban parish church was fortunate if it could make some kind of levy on its parishioners in lieu of payment.

In consequence the urban church was heavily dependent on the piety and the generosity of individuals, and a neighbourhood church in a poor quarter of town had very few to whom it could turn for support. Many must have succumbed, and even more remained impoverished and architecturally undistinguished. Episcopal visitations not infrequently mention the poverty of urban parishes, the poor condition of their churches, and the small income of their incumbents. These circumstances help to explain the immense range to be found in the structural quality of urban churches. The older towns of England were, with very few exceptions, 'overchurched'. Many of the churches can have had only a very small following; they were gild, chantry or private chapels. Most important were the parish churches, which, in a city like Norwich, could have numbered as many as 50 in the later Middle Ages;[20] London had about 130 parish churches,[21] Winchester about 60,[22] and York 37.[23] But amongst them one, or at most two or three, stood out by reason of their size and splendour. They often lay close to the most important market and near the homes of the more affluent members of the urban society. They were the churches which the latter frequented and upon which they lavished their wealth in a kind of competitive piety. They gave during their lives, and in their wills not infrequently bequeathed the money to rebuild or extend the fabrics, and after death they were buried within the walls. They were not modest donors, and rarely was their generosity allowed to go without public record. One cannot look at the great churches of Bristol or Fairford or Lavenham without asking who paid for this display, and the answer is often self-evident in the glass of the windows, the statuary or the monuments. Even in the smallest towns the single church was often embellished in similar fashion at the expense of one or other of the local families: Chipping Camden (Glos.) by the Grevilles; Lavenham (Suffolk) by the de Veres and Sprynges, and Long Melford by a galaxy of clothiers whose names, set in flushwork, continue to decorate the parapet of the church.

We must assume that many, perhaps most, urban churches began as neighbourhood chapels, created and maintained by those who used them. They were a spontaneous growth, and their function was as much social as it was religious. The neighbourhood community was drawn together in the creation of a church, as the rural had been by the common experience of tilling its fields and doing suit at its manorial court. The urban church reflected the 'identifiable style of one's class', and churches, as a group, became as hierarchically structured as the urban society which created them.

Gilds and friendly societies

Gilds and friendly societies each served a narrower group than the parish. If the parish corresponded with the village, the gild was more like a kindred group, an association of people with something more in common than mere propinquity. Such associations were known in Anglo-Saxon times, and there was a *cnihtengild* (knights' gild) in tenth-century London.[24] After the Norman Conquest gilds proliferated. First to appear in many towns was the Gild Merchant, an amorphous group of those who, in contradistinction to agriculturists, pursued the essentially urban occupations of buying and selling.[25] The gild had a monopoly of business within the town. An Oxford charter expressly stated that 'none who is not of the gild shall do any business in the city or suburbs'.[26] Its purpose, like that of many others, was to preserve the exclusivity of the established urban craftsmen and tradesmen.[27] One must not think of the Gild Merchant as separate from the city government. Towns were too small to have separate and conflicting authorities. They were made up, broadly speaking, of the same people, now meeting for one purpose, now for another. Some important towns, amongst them London and Norwich, seem never to have had a Gild Merchant.[28] Instead the regulation of crafts and trade must have remained with the administrative council and its courts until such time as it was devolved upon the individual craft gilds. Better known because later in date and more fully documented were the craft gilds, each of which embraced all who followed a particular craft or, perhaps, group of related crafts. Their declared purpose was the maintenance of standards of workmanship and the proper training of those who were to enter the brotherhood of craftsmen. In reality, craft gilds showed themselves to be producer- rather than consumer-oriented.[29] Their monopolistic role gave them a position of power which was not infrequently abused. It cannot be denied that they sometimes acted in restraint of trade and at best represented only a narrow sectional interest. In fact, the exclusivity of gilds declined in the seventeenth and eighteenth centuries, and the Municipal Corporations Act of 1835 made all such restrictions and prohibitions illegal.

The economic functions of gilds were underlined and strengthened by their convivial, charitable and religious activities. Religious obligations were always present, even in the most mundane of gilds: the maintenance of lights in a chapel, the celebration of the obits of deceased members, participation in religious plays and processions. Some ostensibly religious gilds hid a form of craft organisation behind their dedications and religious observances. No clear line can be drawn between the religious, the charitable and the economic functions of gilds. They shared in varying degrees in all these aspects.

Only in a few of the larger towns were most crafts represented by their own gilds. London was the extreme case in Britain. In 1422 the Brewers' Gild compiled a list of crafts – no less than 111, in addition to their own.[30] In 1518, 47 companies participated in the city watch.[31] These numbers were greatly exceeded in Paris, which was, in any case, a very much larger city.[32] Many crafts were absent from the smaller towns or were practised by so few that they could not possibly have constituted a separate gild. Gilds established under such circumstances were of the nature of umbrella organisations, each representing a group of related crafts, such as the smiths, metal-workers and clothworkers. There are trades unions today with such broad, undifferentiated coverage.

The majority of medieval gilds, however, had no specific craft basis. They may have served as a forum for the discussion of business matters, but their overt purposes were religious and charitable. They were associations of like-minded people. In most instances their purpose was narrow and local. There were gilds for organising processions, for presenting religious plays, for revering a particular saint or for educating the young; 'all objects of common interest for which nowadays special societies and associations provide . . . caused all who were interested in them, to unite themselves to religious gilds.'[33]

Gilds were by their nature exclusive, and as they elaborated their rituals and broadened their social activities, so they became more and more restricted to the better-off members of society who alone could afford the banquets and the robes that were worn on these occasions. If many of the parish churches did little to draw the lower classes into their corporate life, the gilds did nothing. At the Reformation all gilds whose purpose was primarily religious were dissolved, and the spiritual exercises of others were truncated.[34] From the sixteenth century, when the government began to assume greater responsibilities in the management of the economy, the regulatory functions of the craft gilds diminished in importance, and in the course of time gilds either disappeared or declined to the status of élitist dining societies.

Most churches and gilds thus came gradually to be restricted in membership as they tended increasingly to cater for the needs of the urban establishment. The problem was to create comparable forms of association amongst the unattached and floating population which was being continually fed into the towns from the countryside. In the modern period such associations have proliferated, helped by the slowly increasing literacy of the urban proletariat. Every minor shade of opinion, every gradation of economic interest came to be reflected in the formation of associations, some officially countenanced, a few eminently respectable, others in some measure heterodox if not actually illegal, and many of them short-lived. In the growing industrial cities from the middle of the eighteenth century, a wave of chapel-building, comparable with that which took place in the early medieval town, spread through the working-class districts. Chapels provided companionship and consolation to the uprooted masses, while friendly societies, often with romantic and backward-looking names, like Foresters, Oddfellows and Buffaloes, revived some of the charitable functions of the defunct system of gilds. At the same time, co-operative societies, which claim to derive from the Rochdale (Lancs.) Pioneers of 1844, helped the masses by retailing their basic necessities as cheaply as was practicable.

Gilds and parochial institutions constituted 'little communities' within the broad mass of the urban population. The larger the town, the more important it became for people to have some *point d'appui*, some focus; to belong to some face-to-face group, within which they were known to one another, could rely on mutual help in adversity, and, within limits, could trust one another.[35] de Tocqueville characterised the village as 'the only association . . . so perfectly natural that wherever a number of men [and women] are collected it seems to constitute itself'.[36] Parish and gild in their own inadequate ways had served the same purpose in towns: they were 'urban villages'. The essential difference between them and the society of the real village was their relative exclusiveness. Within the town there were always people who had been left out. The structure of urban society itself generated an 'underclass', which could on occasion, depending on the local social and economic situation, become large and dangerous.[37] That of the village did so to only a very limited degree.

The urban mentalité

No clear divide separated the traditional town from the village. There was a gradation in size from the one to the other, and even in function the distinction was anything but clear-cut. 'The urban community', in the words of Clark and Slack, 'was permeated by the countryside: gardens and orchards, oast-houses, pigs and poultry flourished within the limits of the largest towns, while the countryside crept to the back-door of houses on the High Street of the smaller centre.'[38] The town was enclosed within its fields; its citizens grazed their animals on its common land and ploughed their strips, and craftsmen deserted their workshops to toil in the fields at harvest-time. It would have been difficult to 'abstract any element and label it distinctively urban',[39] Was, then, the *mentalité* of the urban-dweller any different from that of the countryman?

If we except the smaller towns, whose generally face-to-face character was not dissimilar to the intimacy of the village, there was, indeed, a contrast between the extremes of village and town. Within the latter there was a kind of anonymity, the loneliness of the crowd. The mutuality of the village may not have disappeared completely, but it was greatly diminished. One might starve to death, unnoticed by one's neighbours in a large town. There might be shortages in a village, but it was a condition in which all in some degree shared. This was due, in part, to the fact that the countryman was in large measure self-sufficient; he grew much of what he ate; he was far less dependent than the town-dweller on a money economy. If crops failed, all in a village tightened their belts. In a town the rich continued to buy food at inflated prices; the indigent and the deprived ceased to be able to buy at all.[40] Well might the townsman gaze

> fondly country-wards ...
> Loathing the town, sick for my village home,
> Which never cried, 'Come, buy my charcoal,
> My vinegar, my oil, my anything',
> But freely gave us all.[41]

The words are Aristophanes', but they reflect what must often have been a feeling of regret at having left the countryside. At the same time, in the village, the town must sometimes have seemed the 'promised land'[42] to the impoverished husbandman or landless younger son. Attitudes were ambivalent. Only the rich could enjoy the benefits of both town and country, as when the well-to-do invested their profits in rural land, and hoped that their descendants might one day achieve the status of country gentry.

The conservatism of the countryman has no doubt been much exaggerated. His unwillingness to make changes sprang in part from the interlocking social and economic structures within which he lived. But change was, by contrast, built into the urban environment. Urban society, or at least its upper and middle ranks, was

353

entrepreneurial. Fortunes were gained not by following a routine, year in year out, like that of the peasant. The townspeople throve on change; they took risks, and, when fortune favoured them, they made large profits. They acquired property, which they leased; they engrossed, forestalled and regrated, and committed every sin in the book, which they hoped to expiate by their provision for masses and their bequests to the church. The wheel of fortune was a favourite medieval allegory, but it was one which was applicable more to the urban- than the country-dweller.

The Reformation brought changes to the town, but attitudes to risk-taking and change were not amongst them. Instead, it was that readiness to accept change which contributed to the more ready adoption of the reformed faith in the towns than in the countryside. When the preacher, in the quotation at the head of this chapter, moved from the darkness of rural areas to the light of the town, it was a spiritual light which beckoned him, a more general acceptance of the articles of the new faith. The 'dark corners of the land', where the old religion lingered on, were in the countryside, not in the towns.

An urban population was more rigidly structured by class than that of the countryside. A social class, in Sjoberg's words, 'is a large body of persons who occupy a position in a social hierarchy by reason of their manifesting similarly valued objective criteria . . . kinship, affiliation, power and authority, achievements, possessions and moral and personal attitudes'.[43] There was mobility between classes in an urban society, but the system was perpetuated by the fact that people were continually being fed into it at the bottom, where they replaced those who had succeeded in climbing above the lowest rungs.

Although the population of every town constituted a spectrum from the rich and powerful to the poorest, this range can for convenience be divided into (1) the élite or patrician class; (2) the urban middle class of craftsmen, petty traders, journeymen and others in established if not lucrative positions, and (3) the submerged class, which Sjoberg, not altogether correctly, terms the 'outcast' class.[44]

The presence of an urban élite is apparent in most towns from a relatively early date, though it is not always easy to distinguish it from the urban middle class. We are not concerned here with its origins, rather with its social role within the town. It was always numerically small, often no more than 5 to 10 per cent of the urban population. It is commonly assumed that its wealth derived from trade, but it is becoming clear that it never wholly relinquished its grip on the countryside, and, in the later Middle Ages and early modern times it tended to invest its profits in rural land. Its members often married into rural land-owning classes, and many prosperous patrician families disappeared from the urban scene after a generation or two, absorbed, or perhaps reabsorbed into the rural gentry. The illustrious urban families commonly had only a short career within the towns. The records show them prosperous and dominant for two or three generations. Then they disappear, if they had been successful, into the ranks of the gentry and aristocracy, or, if less so, back into the near anonymity of the urban middle class.

Within towns this élite, ephemeral and changing though it was, constituted the chief employer of labour; it controlled at least the more important of the gilds: those engaged in the more upmarket crafts and long-distance trade, and it often acquired a large part of urban housing. In the small borough of Lostwithiel (Corn.) 6.5 per cent of the burgesses had in 1332 gained possession of no less than 35 per cent of the 391 burgage plots, and one of them, Thomas Queynte by name, held 18, while Serlo Queynte, undoubtedly a relative, held 11.[45] Some 8 per cent of the borough would thus seem to have been in the possession of one family. It is symptomatic of the changing fortunes of urban families that, within half a century, the name of Queynte had disappeared from the records of the town.

Most towns came to be administered and their gilds regulated by a mayor or portreeve and common council, often, but by no means always, made up of 24 members. At Lincoln a majority of this body consisted of 'substantial citizens, owning property or belonging to families known to hold property'.[46] Although lists of councillors are not infrequently met with, it is not always possible to determine the social and economic status of those named. Occasionally, especially in the smaller towns, the lists must often have included the names of men of modest wealth and standing.

There was no equality even amongst the freemen of a borough. In the larger towns certain gilds or 'mysteries' carried a disproportionate weight in the town's governance, and nowhere did this become more conspicuous than in London. In general those mysteries which were engaged in import and resale, such as the mercers, grocers, vintners and fishmongers, together with a few crafts which were by their nature restricted to the better-off, like goldsmiths and drapers, acquired very considerable political power within the city. They came to constitute the group of 'greater mysteries', from whose members the aldermen of the city were chosen and the lord mayor elected.[47]

The more numerous 'lesser mysteries' tended to form groups, each made up of crafts linked together by the materials they used or the markets they served. The clothworking crafts – weavers, dyers, fullers, shearmen – were dominated by the greater mystery of the drapers, and the glovers, pursers, pouchmakers and other workers in leather by the cordwainers. In all such groups of related crafts one gild, usually one of the greater mysteries, tended to assume a position of pre-eminence, its members often serving as middlemen for the goods produced by others. In this way they acquired wealth and power within the city, and used it to further their own economic interests.[48]

Gilds, whether in London or the provinces, were governed by their masters, the body of independent traders and craftsmen. To become a master it was necessary to serve an apprenticeship, most often for a period of seven years, at the end of which the man was admitted to the gild and usually also to the freedom of the town. But the 'master' was often served also by a journeyman and servants. These had in many instances never been apprenticed and had no prospect of ever becoming masters. They might be new arrivals from the countryside or men whose parents had been unable to afford the sometimes large premium for their apprenticeship. They formed a body of wage-labourers, hovering dangerously on the margin of the urban 'underclass'. Nor did the apprentice always have a secure future. There were masters who failed to register their apprentices or to present them for the freedom of the town on the completion of their time. These young men might also merge, along with day-labourers, into the body of underprivileged and exploited who formed the third category of the urban population.

Every town had its underclass. In small towns it might be no more than a handful of unfortunates, over whom the overseers of the poor kept a watchful eye, giving them whatever support seemed to be absolutely necessary, but striving to prevent them from becoming too great a burden on the town's rates. In large towns it was an amorphous group which lived precariously on a blend of charity and casual employment. Servants, street-cleaners, dung-carriers were drawn from this class. The younger amongst them might hope for an apprenticeship at some unrewarding trade, if town officials could be induced to put up the premium required. There is evidence from Coventry of such pauper children being apprenticed as chimney-sweeps,[49] a craft which they would be obliged to abandon as soon as they grew too big to climb through twisting domestic chimneys. They were merely cheap – and temporary – labour for the master-sweep, who nevertheless demanded his premium for setting them about their dirty and dangerous task.

The very poor were often disease-ridden. They aged quickly, and in their latter days could hope only to be taken in by a local poor-house. It is difficult to form any estimate of their numbers. In the eighteenth century, some 10 per cent of the population of the Breton town of Vannes was classed as *mendiants* or *indigents*.[50] It is unlikely that the proportion could have been significantly less in the larger towns of pre-industrial England. The conditions in which this lowest class lived further deteriorated with industrial development in the later eighteenth century and the growth of industrial towns in the nineteenth. The able-bodied of both sexes were absorbed into factories and mines, where their conditions of work were described in minute and harrowing detail by social writers and Parliamentary Commissioners. The lot of those incapacitated or too old to work – of whom there were relatively few – was even worse; they became the forgotten people of industrialising Britain.[51]

The physical scene

It is not easy to estimate the size of towns before the first census in 1801 gave some precision to the data. The uncertainty of Domesday statistics has already been mentioned. The Poll Tax of 1377 offers less room for error, but thereafter, for more than 400 years, there are no sets of data which allow a comparative study to be made.[52] Instead, we find individual estimates, some based on tax or rent-rolls; others, like those submitted in answer to enquiries initiated by the bishops, little more than guesses. One can only say that in the later fourteenth century most towns of regional importance had from 2000 to 5000 inhabitants; that a few, like Bristol, Coventry, Norwich and York, had up to 9000,[53] but that London towered above them all with some 35,000.[54] The primacy of London was accentuated during the following centuries. The population of England approximately doubled between 1500 and 1700; that of London increased fourfold, and the city cast its web of influence ever more widely over much of England.[55] The more important provincial towns also grew faster than the population as a whole, and by 1700 most ranged from 6000 to 10,000.[56] This selective growth was accentuated during the eighteenth century, and when, in 1801, the first official census enumerated the urban population, there were 47 towns of more than 10,000, 12 of them with over 30,000, and five in excess of 50,000.[57] Growth had been very much less marked in Wales, where only Swansea had reached 10,000 by 1801.

The size of a town is in some degree a measure of the social problems which it faced. As towns lost their sense of intimacy, so they became ever-growing hives in which the individual was lost. They became at best assemblages of 'quarters': élite, commercial, working-class, and most citizens would have identified with only a narrow area or a small section of the population. Their social focus became the chapel or the tavern.

Physically, the town has always consisted of streets, lined with buildings, private and public, administrative and industrial. Their pattern has assumed many forms, and the layout of each is unique. Nevertheless, certain regularities are apparent. A minority of British towns – and a large majority of those in continental Europe – were enclosed from a relatively early date by a wall, which gave them some protection and served to contain their spread. Walls survived long after their period of usefulness had ended. It is difficult to say how protective they may have been; there were virtually no urban sieges in Britain. An inquisition of 1283–4 sought to determine whether the town walls of Scarborough might be used as a quarry. A jury of local men declared that without them they would be exposed to pillage by the king's enemies, namely the Scots.[58] The walls seem never to have been called upon to perform this service either here or in most other walled towns of England, and their retention seems rather to have been for reasons of pride rather than protection.

Walls, with restricted openings through them, hindered the circulation of people and goods. Those who were free to decide where they would live commonly chose a site within the walls, and suburban areas were commonly characterised by poorer homes and inhabited by the least affluent. On the other hand, the congestion which characterised the walled area drove some tradesmen to seek the greater space and lower land values to be found without. There are even instances of markets being shifted from the barely accessible town centres to places outside the gates.[59]

Most organic towns were walled, their defensive line deriving in many instances from the fortifications of the later Roman Empire. Even those which had no walls, like Cambridge and Ipswich, nevertheless enclosed themselves with a ditch and bank. The last English town to erect walls was probably Coventry, where the walls were built in the fourteenth century. But the 'planted' towns were different. Relatively few, except in Wales, were ever walled. Many consisted of little more than one long street, which widened at some point into a market-place. They were open-

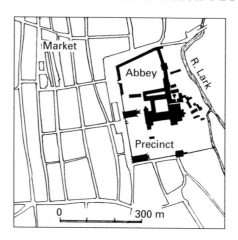

10.4 Plan of Bury St Edmunds, a 'planted' town with a rectilinear street plan.

ended. They could expand in one direction or the other, though always the most prestigious dwellings were grouped close to the market-place and the church, and the poor lived mostly at the extremities of the 'High' Street. In such towns burgage plots were laid out with their narrow frontage on 'Main' Street, reaching back sometimes 100 metres or more to a lane aptly called 'Back Street'. Sometimes houses, usually of a meaner sort with very little land attached to them, might in the course of time be built along the back streets. Alleys might be opened, often known by some such local name as 'wynd' or 'ope', linking them with the main street.

In older and generally larger towns this process of division of plots and infilling of the spaces behind the houses on main streets went even further, with the creation of 'courts', until it posed a grave threat to health and even to life. This process was not restricted to the older towns, hemmed in by their walls. Many of the industrial towns, which had been little more than villages in the seventeenth century, grew rapidly and developed a level of congestion even greater than that to be met with in the older ones. The basic reason was the need to live close to the factories which were the chief source of employment. But the principal reason for the conditions which appalled Engels in the mid-nineteenth century was, on the one hand, the developers who found profit in crowding as many shacks as possible on to every scrap of land, and, on the other, the poverty of those who could afford nothing better.

One thinks of the limits of a street or of the boundary lines of properties as fixed and immutable, preserved for all time on maps and plans. In traditional societies they were not. It was not only in the fields that a man might usurp an inch or two of his neighbour's strip. Encroachments — 'purprestures' they were called — were much more common in towns. The growing congestion sometimes made it impossible to add a chimney-stack or dig a cesspit or discharge rainwater from one's property without encroaching on the land of another. Disputes were bitter, and the cases that came before the courts were only those that could not be settled in any other way.

358

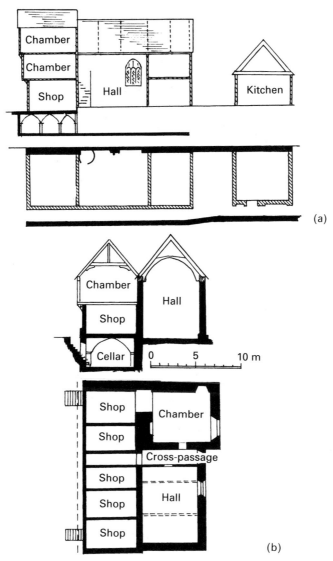

10.5 Town-house plans: (a) High Street, Exeter, (b) Tackley's Inn, High Street, Oxford.

But the easiest and most common kind of purpresture was at the expense of the street. It could take many forms. The simplest and the least easy to control was the 'jettied' upper floor of a house which was made to project over the road. This became a normal practice, and little was done to restrict it. In London a horseman was killed by striking his head against the jetty of an upper floor. More subtle was the process of gradually incorporating into the house part of the area thus overhung by the jetty.[61] Many town houses had cellars, used by merchants and craftsmen for storage. It was dangerous but convenient to construct two or three steps leading down to the cellar entrance in the road itself (Fig. 10.5). These constituted unprotected pits into

359

which the pedestrian might fall. The London Assize of Nuisance contains many complaints of the practice.[62] Not unrelated to simple encroachment on the street was the practice of depositing in the middle of the road such household or business waste that could not be disposed of in any other way. There were times when the accumulated waste obstructed the road, and always it attracted vermin and the pigs which, as late as the eighteenth century, were allowed to scavenge through the streets.

In one way and another, by new construction, by the encroachment of old, and by the failure of weak civil authority to enforce its own regulations, the shape of the traditional town was slowly changed. Streets narrowed until, in more recent times, drastic steps have had to be taken to widen and straighten them.

Life and limb

Coroners' rolls provide deeper insights into urban living than almost any other category of document. From late in the twelfth century it became the duty of the coroner to hold an 'inquest' into the cause of every death that was not clearly from natural causes.[63] As his title indicates, he kept the pleas of the crown, and his task was to see to it that the king received all that was in law due to him in consequence of the death. This consisted of the possessions of a felon, and, if the death was judged to have been accidental, the instrument, or *deodand*, which had been its immediate cause (p. 135). In consequence, coroners' records noted in some detail the circumstances in which a death had occurred. The coroner had always more business in towns than in the countryside, because causes of death were so many, so varied and their occurrence so frequent.

Accident in the home or workshop was no less common than in the street. Children and even adults fell into dyers' vats and brewers' cauldrons in their scores. Building workers slipped from scaffolding and pedestrians fell into basement stairways. Flimsily constructed buildings collapsed, and, in houses which were in the main timber-framed, there was the constant danger of fire. Rivers – and most towns in Britain lay on a river – claimed countless victims: they fell from bridges or were drowned while bathing, or were precipitated into the river by the collapse of toilet seats which had been constructed to project over the water.

Urban housing

The earliest town houses differed little, if at all, from those to be found in the countryside. They were small, timber-framed and thatched. Change came slowly, and it was not until after the Norman Conquest that, with increasing wealth, houses became larger and more complex in their design and construction. The urban scene in general placed constraints on building that were unknown in the countryside. In the first place, urban space was limited and tended to become valuable. Any 'developer' was obliged to make the most of it by adopting what would today be called a high housing density. This was especially the case in the older towns of pre-Conquest origin. In the 'new' towns space was as a rule more abundant, and the burgage plot was large enough for house construction. But in the more successful of them, plots were divided and subdivided until they too displayed a degree of congestion comparable with that to be found in the older towns.[64] At Hull (E. Riding, Yorks.), for example, within a few years of the town's foundation by Edward I, the records no longer spoke of 'plots'; they had become 'tenements'. There was no more any question of one house to the plot: 'a number of apparently single properties were in fact parcelled out among subtenants who were each developing their own share ... This ratio [4 to 1] of tenants to fee farm property [i.e. burgage plots] is supported by the Poll Tax ... of 1377 which [implies] that each property in the 1347 rental must have housed ... 2–6 households.'[65] A not dissimilar division of the original plots took place in King's Lynn, where, it has been calculated, the average frontage width had been halved by the late thirteenth century. There is evidence also that the elongated plots were split across the middle, giving rise to small plots lying behind the street and reached from a back street.[66] There is evidence no less for the concentration of part-tenements in the hands of individuals who, so it would appear, were attempting for whatever purpose to establish a block of land under their own control (p. 355).

Closely related to urban congestion were the danger of fire and the problem of disposing of sewage. The former was reduced in some towns by building regulations, but the latter was not realistically faced in most before the nineteenth century. The well-known housing ordinance of London of 1189 has already been cited (p. 132). This was the first, and probably one of the more successful attempts to require the use of non-inflammable materials in urban building construction. That other consequence of urban congestion, the difficulty of constructing sanitary facilities and of disposing of excreta, will be mentioned later (p. 366). These two themes form a thread running through urban history from its earliest times until the later years of the nineteenth century.

The second major constraint on building lay in the purposes to which these buildings were to be put. Unlike the rural cottage, many – perhaps most – urban houses served other uses than simple residence. They were used commercially and industrially. Most craftsmen in medieval and early modern times worked at home. There were a few crafts, prominent amongst them tanning, brick-making and milling, which by their nature required a separate and specialised location. The London records show that not only were forges sometimes set up in the public thoroughfare,[67] but that a forge was even built within a tenement. The noise of sledge-hammers shook the walls of neighbours' houses as well as keeping them awake at night, while 'the stench and smoke from the sea-coal used in the forge penetrates their hall and chambers'.[68] Few industrial uses of domestic accommodation were as extreme as this, but many properties were used for weaving, dyeing and baking, while every small tradesman lived 'over the shop'.

One cannot know with certainty exactly where domestic crafts were actually carried on within the house. The armourer, whose activities proved such a nuisance to his neighbours, had built his forge in the court behind his house, and it would seem that the backyard was the most frequent locale for the baker's oven, the dyer's vat and the brewer's 'lead'. But many crafts were carried on within the house, notably spinning, weaving and shoemaking. The house had in both plan and elevation to be adapted to these activities.

Town houses were in plan very broadly of two types, depending on whether their long axes were parallel or at right angles to the street. The smallest two-celled cottage might have been built on a standard plot parallel to the street. But if a house of central-hall plan, with projecting wings, was desired, then the plot had to be a great deal wider than was usually the case. Such houses were indeed built, and many have survived from the later Middle Ages and the sixteenth century in towns that have not suffered from drastic rebuilding. They were, as a general rule, the homes of the wealthier urban 'dynasties', and are especially noticeable in the smaller towns of East Anglia, where they are – generally correctly – associated with the entrepreneurs of the clothing industry.

More often, however, especially if the house was to be of more than minimal size, it had to be set at right angles to the street and allowed to extend back into the court behind. A narrow passage, sometimes arched over, might be left in order to gain access to the rear of the building. Usually houses were made to butt against one another, each presenting its gable end to the street.[69] In these circumstances the fire hazard was at its greatest, and in London at least, some pains were taken to ensure that the party walls were of masonry construction. Such a house, illuminated only from the front and back, would have been very dark, further limiting its use for craft purposes. Sometimes a single wing, occupying only part of the width of the plot, was made to project backwards, and in this case it was possible to have windows along its side (Fig. 10.5a). How to contain the essential features of a medieval house, together with shop and workshop where necessary, on a small site, must have exercised the minds of medieval and early modern builders. The examples which survive may not in all respects have been typical; they were in all probability the grander houses and had been more stoutly built than others.

Many medieval houses had been built above cellars or undercrofts. These were often sunk as much as 2 metres below the road surface and were generally built in stone. Many such cellars have survived, while the buildings raised above them, usually timber-framed, have disappeared. So numerous are the remains of such cellars that one is tempted to regard them as typical of the medieval town house, which, in fact, they were not. As a general rule they were entered by steps directly from the street (p. 359), and were effectively without illumination. The purpose of cellars is not always clear. They were too dark to have served any industrial purpose, and were probably used for storage.[70] The smoke of the forge already mentioned, so it was alleged before the London Court of Nuisance, spoiled the wine and ale in neighbouring cellars.[71] But, as Quiney has pointed out, if all cellars were used for storing wine casks, Londoners must have been 'unbelievably bibulous'. Access to cellars was in many instances too difficult for woolsacks and other bulky goods to have been stored there.

Above the basement level the house was often of an L-plan, with a narrow wing reaching back on one side of the plot. This allowed for illumination, and also left a small court free of obstruction. Some of the houses surviving on the old quay at Ipswich have this plan. As a general rule the hall stood end-on to the street, and its illumination was from this direction. Behind it lay the kitchen and domestic offices, and above, on a jettied first floor, the chambers. But this plan, which can be regarded as the first derivative of the simple solar–hall–kitchen plan of the rural dwelling, underwent many adaptations to adjust it to the site and to the functions which it was to serve.

The first modification was to make the ground-floor room against the street into a shop. The medieval shop often served also as a workshop, artefacts being fabricated under the eyes of the client. Shops were often very small, commonly no more than 3 m by 2 m.[72] Against the street was a window, closed by a shutter which could be folded down to make a display area. Alternatively, a wooden stall might have been built against the shop front, encroaching on and narrowing yet more the already narrow street. The placement of the shop left no room for a hall, except the dark area behind it or on the floor above. The latter appears to have been a common solution, and a second floor might provide space for chambers. In late medieval times this would have been the house of a man of substance.[73] Heating such a house and cooking for its inhabitants was both difficult and dangerous, and in many instances more or less detached kitchens seem to have been erected behind.

This was the typical town house of any well-to-do citizen. It was to be found along the main streets around the market-place. Such houses stood cheek by jowl, each individual in its decoration and in the facade or gable-end which it presented to the street, but all conforming broadly to a plan which reconciled domesticity with trade. As more space came to be required, the house might be extended back into the yard behind, or – probably a more expensive course – an extra floor might be added, jettying yet further over the street and casting longer shadows over the shops below. The jetty gave a small additional space to the room which it supported, but the chief reason for its employment was more likely to have been the pride and self-assurance of the man who had it built.[74] Immense care was lavished on the facades of such houses as they rose, floor above jettied floor, to a decorated gable with fretted bargeboards. In many such merchants' houses the upper floors seem to have been used for storage. In the many-storied houses of Amsterdam a crane or hoist was made to project from the gable, and window openings below were enlarged to allow large pieces of merchandise to be hauled in. Such a device does not appear to have been common in England, though there is evidence for it in Lavenham (Suff.), where upper floors may have been used for the storage of wool.

But not all urban houses conformed to this generalised pattern. There were humbler houses, more rural than urban in appearance, flimsily built and insubstantial: 'one-roomed huts . . . of cob or elementary timber framing, with thatched roofs'.[75] The town's élite crowded towards the centre so that such primitive housing was generally to be found on the periphery or in suburbs beyond the walls. Such houses have, without exception, disappeared, though their successors in the late eighteenth and early nineteenth centuries show how small and primitive such housing could be.

At the opposite extreme were the few grand houses. In some cases these were the town houses of rural gentry or even aristocracy. In London they were often courtyard houses, able to accommodate a large body of retainers. They had been built by nobles, bishops and the abbots of more important monasteries. They were usually intended only for temporary inhabitation when their owners were attending Parliament or the royal court, or carrying on their incessant litigation before the king's justices. But such grand houses were rare in provincial towns before the eighteenth century. Instead there were those of prosperous merchants and local gentry. More often than not they lay parallel to the street rather than at right angles, and of necessity occupied a plot much wider than most. It seems that two contiguous plots were sometimes acquired for their construction. They were generally of central hall plan, with solar and kitchen blocks. They were commonly set back from the street, with a small enclosed court in front and a garden behind. Both the Bridewell and the Strangers' Hall in Norwich were of this plan.

Building materials and construction

Until comparatively recent times urban houses were constructed mainly of wood, with wattle and plaster filling the interstices of the framing. In the earliest of which there is archaeological record, the posts were set directly in the soil.[76] Sill plates, resting directly on the ground, were then used. But the rapid deterioration of wood in direct contact with the soil led to the adoption of plinths of stone or, at a later date, of brick. Some of the building contracts printed by Salzman[77] required that the structure be raised on stone foundations, and we may assume that by the end of the Middle Ages all new construction of the better sort had masonry footings. The house was usually framed in oak, strengthened with braces. Many late medieval contracts specified the scantling of the timber to be used, and some of these were generous in the extreme. This must not be taken as an indication that good constructional timber was abundant. It was not, and when the dimensions of timber were prescribed it was probably to prevent the carpenter from getting away with less substantial materials.

The urban builder had always to balance the relative cheapness of timber construction against the fire hazard which it posed. The equation varied from one part of the country to another. Greater use was made of stone in the Cotswolds and in other parts of the 'Stone Belt' than elsewhere. Today timber-framing is almost completely absent from the urban landscape, but appearances can be deceptive. Even at Burford (Oxon.), close to some of the most highly esteemed limestone quarries in this country, much of the local building was still at the end of the Middle Ages in timber, and 'even when stone began to be more freely used, it was not as a rule employed above the ground floor ... the upper parts of the house being still of timber with wattle and daub filling'.[78] Today the houses along Burford's main street are faced with ashlar of a high quality, but anyone who ventures through the passages and alleys which separate them finds evidence for timber-framing. Within the whole of the excavated area of Winchester Biddle found evidence for only three stone-built houses.[79]

If stone was little used in domestic building, even in towns within the 'stone belt', one might expect it to have been totally absent elsewhere. In fact, there was a sparing use of stone in many towns in the later Middle Ages and early modern times. The reason probably lies in the fact that oak of a quality suitable for good framing had become scarce around the more populous centres such as Norwich, Stamford and King's Lynn. Good stone was imported whenever possible by river and coastal craft from, in particular, the 'Stone Belt' (Fig. 3.28). Most of it was used in the building of churches and public buildings, but it is evident that it was also used in the ground floors of the better houses as well as in their basements. Some use was also made of less desirable materials such as flint, clunch, carstone and septaria in East Anglia, of Kentish 'rag' in the south-east, of Lias in the West Country, of Millstone Grit in the northern counties, and of hard and intractable Palaeozoic rocks in Wales and the south-west. In London, where most of the building before the Great Fire had been of timber over a masonry cellar or stone footing, there were other uses for stone. A judgment of 1558 required that a watercourse, constructed across a yard in the city of London be of 'lead or hard stone of Kent'.[80]

Thatch of straw or reed was the commonest of traditional roofing materials, despite the fire danger which it posed. From the later years of the twelfth century Londoners were encouraged to roof their houses with some non-inflammable material. A variety of materials thus came gradually into use. First were the 'slates' made from fissile limestone and sandstone. The best were quarried in the Cotswolds, near Stonesfield (Oxon.), and 80 miles (130 km) to the north-east, at Collyweston (Northants).[81] The Pennant sandstone of Somerset also has a strongly marked cleavage, and was much used in Bristol.[82] On the other hand, these 'slates' were fairly thick, and their weight necessitated substantial rafters to support them. Much superior was 'blue' slate, a metamorphic rock met with only in western Britain, which could be split into very thin and light 'slates'. These true slates were in use in Southampton by 1170,[83] and soon afterwards in Bury St Edmunds, Canterbury, Lincoln and Norwich, as well as in London. Much of the slate used in southern Britain came from coastal quarries in Cornwall and Devon.[84] It was distributed over a wide area by coasting vessel and river craft, and contributed very significantly to the gradual disappearance of thatch from the towns.

Tiles of baked clay were in use in the late twelfth century when roofs in London were ordered to be of slate or tile. Medieval building records often mention the use of *tegulae*, or clay tiles, and these were much used in eastern England, less readily accessible than other parts for true slate.[85] In rural building it was not uncommon to use wooden shingles, or *scindulae*, made by splitting oak. They posed a fire hazard only a degree less serious than straw thatch, and I have found little evidence for their use in towns. It seems probable that by the sixteenth century straw thatch had virtually disappeared from the larger towns, but there is no doubt but that it remained in use in the smaller ones, where, with a less dense housing pattern, the fire risk was diminished.

In most of the larger English towns the main streets had become fully built up by the sixteenth century, though behind the rows of houses and within the blocks formed by intersecting streets there remained extensive open spaces. This is apparent from the late sixteenth-century plans of Braun and Hogenberg and of Speed.[86] By this date houses near the centre customarily reached three storeys, and those of four were not uncommon. The social consequences of this degree of crowding were great. The necessary activities of most householders impinged on their neighbours, who often claimed to have been inconvenienced by them. This led both to brawling and to lawsuits. The cases which came before the courts reveal conditions close to urban anarchy. In this respect London is far better documented than provincial towns. Conditions there may, on account of its very much greater size, have been more acute than elsewhere, but it must be assumed that not dissimilar problems arose in the congested centres of Bristol, Norwich, York and other large towns.

The most frequent source of complaint and of ensuing lawsuits was the placement of toilets and cesspits. The stench which they occasioned must have been a perpetual source of annoyance, yet in this respect complaints before the courts were strangely few. Perhaps it was thought that they were a permanent feature of town life, that everyone was in some measure at fault, and that it was superfluous to protest. Drainage from a cesspit, however, was a different matter. The city area 'was honeycombed with pits, often of considerable size . . . as much as 12 feet across and 12 feet deep',[87] into which went much of the sewage and rubbish generated within the house. A cesspit, if lined with masonry, might approach to within $2\frac{1}{2}$ feet (76 cm) of a neighbour's property, but the cesspit itself discharged nonetheless (Fig. 10.6). One plaintiff complained that 'the sewage penetrates his cellar'[88] from a neighbour's pit, and another that the defendant's privy 'adjoins the earthen wall [*sic*] of his hall too closely'.[89]

A cesspit, probably of thirteenth century date, was discovered on a bombed site in Dover.[90] It consisted of two barrel-vaulted chambers with a connecting opening. The walls were of Kentish 'rag', and the floor was well cemented and probably impermeable. The whole chamber measured 8 feet (2 m) by $8\frac{1}{2}$ feet (2.16 m) and was $7\frac{1}{2}$ feet (19 m) deep. Two chutes discharged into the chamber, and there must have been an overflow for liquids. It is clear that, despite the capacity of the chamber – about 50 cubic feet (about 14 cubic metres) – it must periodically have required cleaning out by hand. Elsewhere the cesspits were lined with basketwork, as in Figure 5.5.

Gutters were constructed to carry away storm water, and were in many cases

10.6 A stone-lined domestic cesspit, excavated in London; after John Schofield, *The Building of London*, British Museum, 1984, 96.

made to run under houses. One defendant had built his privy above his neighbour's gutter in the expectation that the flow of water would carry away its discharge. The opposite happened, and the gutter was choked with consequences that can well be imagined.[91]

A second cause of complaint was the way in which timber-framed buildings would lean to one side or the other. In a rural setting this was of little consequence, but in a town, where plots were small and houses were often built right up to the property line, this became a serious matter. A wall, presumably of a house, was said to overhang another property by $5\frac{3}{4}$ inches (14.6 cm) at one end and by 5 inches (12.7 cm) at the other.[92] A woman in Candlewick street complained that a neighbour's house overhung her land by more than $1\frac{1}{2}$ feet (43 cm) so that she could not build on it.[93] It seems that most of these complaints were made when it was proposed to build another house against one which already existed. The use and misuse of a party wall was a frequent source of dispute. A door was hung on hinges affixed to a neighbour's wall;[94] one defendant had cut holes for joists into the wall of the neighbouring house,[95] and in yet another case a plaintiff was judged to have rights in corbels affixed to a party wall, presumably because they overhung, but not in the wall itself.[96]

Jettied upper floors presented even greater problems. They were often set dangerously low, even after a minimum height of 9 feet (2.75 m) had been set.[97] They often extended not only over the highway but also over a neighbouring plot. This extension into another's 'air-space' was not infrequently followed by a surreptitious attempt to include also some part of the land which lay beneath. Countless cases came before the courts, and it is reasonable to suppose that many more were settled between the parties themselves. There is even a case of a defendant who was ordered to remove 'as much of the solar as overhangs the churchyard',[98] an offence which, it might have been thought, would have been condoned. But we constantly find that the church was more insistent on its rights than ordinary laymen.

Another problem which became increasingly serious as housing became more congested was the blocking of light to the windows of existing houses, and, conversely, the preservation of some degree of privacy. It might be a simple case of a broken fence which allowed neighbours to 'have a view into his courtyard and . . . see his private buisiness',[99] or the construction of a jetty which obstructed the view of the plaintiff,[100] or the removal of a partition protecting a privy 'so that the extremities of those sitting on the seats can be seen, a thing', the document added in an age not noted for its prudery, 'abominable and altogether intolerable'.[101] Another complainant reported that he was overlooked 'by a building with unglazed windows'.[102] Glazed windows, it is to be presumed, given the quality of the glass available, would have been only translucent.

The evidence for housing conditions presented in the preceding pages was mostly taken from the proceedings under the London Assize of Nuisances. A comparable record, some three hundred years later in date, is furnished by the judgments of the 'Viewers', a panel of four, made up of master-masons, carpenters or tilers, and empowered to adjudicate complaints and to order repairs and alterations to be carried out.[103] Viewers continued to operate into the eighteenth century, though their role changed after the Great Fire of 1666. The narrow alleys and ramshackle buildings were swept away in the conflagration, and, even though the ambitious plans for rebuilding were not wholly carried out, there was no return to the disorderly and insanitary conditions which had prevailed before the Plague and Fire.[104]

Even so, the Viewers' certificates of the seventeenth century show a considerable change in urban conditions since the thirteenth. The character of offences was different. Gone are complaints of leaking and offensive cesspits; instead there are disputes about the location of 'privy houses' or 'withdraughts' and the alignment of 'jakes' or masonry conduits leading to cesspits and the obligation to keep them clean. Not all 'jakes', it appears, were of masonry. A case in 1550 mentioned 'a tunnel of boards for a jakes which went through [the defendant's] kitchen'.[105] Indeed, it was not uncommon for the discharge from a privy to be carried under a neighbour's house to join up with a sewer or cesspit. Attempts were even made to contrive *en suite* privies on the upper floors of the better houses. In one instance 'in the wall there come down two tewels [discharge chutes] of two withdraughts which serve the two houses of easement for the houses of both' parties.[106] A comparison of the two sets of documents reveals a small but nevertheless significant improvement in material standards. There were in the sixteenth and later centuries few complaints of filth and garbage in the streets, which were increasingly paved with stone. Indeed, the Viewers in 1551 required one defendant to 'pave the street side before his house', as if it were unusual for it not to have been done.[107]

The type of case that came most frequently before the Viewers related not so much to encroachments as to the angle at which many buildings leaned. This was, of course, a consequence of the increasing age of timber-framed buildings and of the fact that the older and poorer buildings had been erected on wooden sill-plates, which had rotted in the damp soil. At one house the kitchen and entry lacked 'a ground sill to keep it upright and from sinking',[108] and elsewhere 'the ground sills and walls ... are in great ruin and decay and sink to the great hurt of the whole frame' of the house.[109] It is clear from the Viewers' judgments that many houses continued to stand only because they were held up by those on either side.

The tool most frequently used by the Viewers was the plumb-line. They were at pains to define precisely the extent to which the walls of a house inclined from the vertical, even to the nearest half-inch, and were rigorous in demanding that it be rectified: 'if the defendants will not set their house upright ... then it shall be lawful for the plaintif to cut down as much of [it] as overhangs his ground'.[110]

The Great Fire 'spelled the end of medieval London as the viewers and their contemporaries knew it'.[111] A new London emerged from the ashes. Streets were widened, multiple tenancies vanished, and stone and brick very largely replaced timber-framing. Not so, however, in most other large towns. Paris remained largely medieval until the piecemeal rebuilding inspired by Hausmann under the Second Empire. English towns experienced fires, but none were as comprehensive and all-consuming as that of London. Rebuilding was never more than partial, and conditions of congestion and dereliction, less severe no doubt than in London before the fire, survived into the nineteenth century.

Water-supply

Water, in both its provision and its disposal, was a perennial problem in all towns, and the larger the town the more precarious it became. It is probably true to say that most of the urban water-supply was derived from wells, sunk just deep enough to reach the underlying water-table. Urban areas were not notable for their freshwater springs, and drawing water from more distant sources was usually difficult to arrange and costly to implement. Monastic houses needed water on a lavish scale, and usually were able to acquire rights in natural springs.[112] Indeed, they were often able, by a kind of spiritual blackmail, to acquire distant water rights as well as way-leaves to bring it to their houses. One of the earliest of such systems must have been that constructed by Christ Church Priory, Canterbury, to bring water from springs in the chalk to the east of the city.[113] St Peter's Abbey, Gloucester, now Gloucester Cathedral, first obtained water from wells within its precinct, but this source proved to be inadequate, and the monks turned to a small river, the Twyver, which they diverted to serve their needs. This proved to be unsuitable for drinking, and they

369

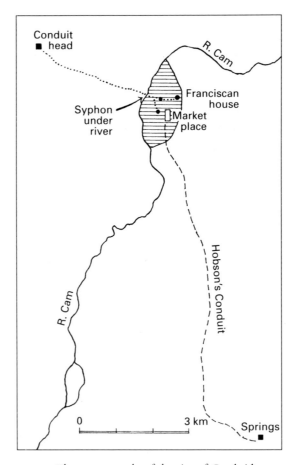

10.7 The water-supply of the city of Cambridge.

then began to use water brought by conduit from Robinswood, 2 miles (3 km) to the east.[114] After the Dissolution this was acquired by the city and became the chief municipal source of supply. A not dissimilar case arose in Cambridge, where the Greyfriars constructed a conduit from a spring 1.5 miles (2.5 km) away at Conduit Head (Fig. 10.7). They had it carried beneath the river Cam by a syphon, consisting of a lead pipe, but in its course it crossed the land of King's Hall – now part of Trinity College. The Fellows tapped into it, at first illicitly, for their own supply. Their tap still remains, its water clearly marked 'Not for drinking'.[115] The town, meanwhile, used wells sunk in the gravels which make up its central area, but later came to depend on a leet, known as Hobson's Conduit, which brought water from springs in the chalk hills to the east to a fountain in the Market Square. The conduit, which still exists in part, was an open watercourse, with a gradient just sufficient to maintain a steady flow.[116]

The water-supply of most British towns had a comparable history, with wells supplemented by attempts, well-meaning but often misguided, to bring water from more distant sources. Urban wells were always suspect. The Assize of Nuisance found a well in London 'for lack of a cover and of cleaning and repair . . . so stopped up with filth that she can get no clean water [*aquam claram*]'.[117] Such cases could be multiplied endlessly. The alternative source, the river, was frequently no less polluted. At Newcastle-upon-Tyne river water was so bad that the citizens were obliged to rely on a spring which the king, doubtless in ignorance of the situation, gave to the local Carmelites.[118] The inhabitants of the small town of Penrith (Cumb.) complained that they had 'no water . . . save a little rivulet', and that the tanners 'come and steep their skins in the rivulet at all times of the year'.[119] A comparable situation arose in York, where the tanners were enjoined to cease their operations.[120]

Little improvement was achieved before the nineteenth century, when cast-iron and glazed ceramic pipes first became available. In the 1830s Edwin Chadwick, Secretary to the Poor Law Commissioners, solicited reports from medical practitioners on the 'sanitary conditions of the labouring poor'.[121] In common with medical opinion of the time, he ascribed infection and disease to exhalations – the *malaria* – arising from putrescent organic matter. His object was to achieve cleanliness rather than a safe water-supply, and, in so far as he called for the latter, it was only in the pursuit of more sanitary living conditions. Nevertheless, many of his informants offered him lurid accounts of the water-supply to small towns as well as large. Until the bacterial origin of disease had been demonstrated, few had reason not to use whatever water was available locally, unless it was positively obnoxious to the taste. In Bath, one of Chadwick's correspondents wrote, 'a man has to fetch water from one of the public pumps, the distance . . . being about a quarter of a mile . . . It is as valuable', he continued, 'as stong beer. We can't use it for cooking, or anything of that sort, but only for drinking and tea.' 'Then where do you get water for cooking and washing?' asked his interrogator. 'Why, from the river. But it is muddy and often stinks bad, because all the filth is carried there.'[122] Inability or unwillingness to carry water from a distance led to the use, even for cooking, of a polluted liquid from the nearby Avon. One must remember, furthermore, that a poor family had little time for water-carrying.

When this conversation was taking place in Bath, there were already five separate water-supply systems, each piping water from small reservoirs set in the surrounding hills.[123] The earliest and most extensive was operated by the city itself, which had obtained a private Act of Parliament authorising it to implement such a plan. But Bath was exceptional. It was at this time a centre of wealth and fashion, and its visitors would have regarded a supply of clean water as a further inducement to visit the city. Furthermore, the configuration of the surrounding hills made it relatively easy to construct holding tanks and to supply water to houses within the city by gravity flow. But only parts of the city, those, one assumes, where the better-off lived, were served; the conversation noted above is witness to the conditions met with on the less privileged periphery. In most English towns – certainly in the larger ones – pump and river continued to serve local needs. This was nearly a century before a contaminated pump led to a cholera epidemic which devastated parts of west London and led to John Snow's empirical conclusions on the source of infection.

Streets and street life

Urban life in the traditional town was lived along its streets. The craftsman worked in or just behind the shop from which his wares were sold. The street itself was used for trading and manufacturing. Not only were market stalls set up along it, but the butcher slaughtered his animals there full in the public view; the smith might establish his forge (p. 361); at Norwich a carpenter dug a sawpit in the middle of the road,[124] and any bulky adjunct to a craft might be set up there.

The maintenance and repair of streets was an obligation which public authorities have always shown a great reluctance to assume. It was probably beyond their capabilities and outside any budgetary provision they could have made. Until well into modern times the streets of most towns were paved at best with coarse stone rubble, and as it was eroded by traffic and potholes appeared in its surface, the remedy was simply to throw down more of the same. The street level thus tended to rise, so that basements which had originally not been significantly below street level, were turned into cellars, reached only by a flight of steps.[125]

Yet attempts were made from a relatively early date to pave the streets. In London there was a gild of paviors, first recognised in 1479, but the poverty and small size of the company – some twenty members with assets of only 30 shillings at the time of Elizabeth – shows that little use was made of its services.[126] The methods adopted by the paviors were not calculated to produce a firm and lasting surface. Their practice, in general, was to spread gravel or sand on the existing surface, to ram it hard, and then to set pebbles or larger stones in it.[127] The level of the road surface was raised by each such repair, despite the injunction not to raise it 'so highe as the grounsells [thresholds] of mens houses'.[128] Usually the road pitched towards the centre, where a channel was sometimes constructed to facilitate the discharge of water. Such pitched roads have survived in some towns into the present century. The alternative pitch was to the sides, leaving a raised crown in the middle and a gutter on each side.[129] Such was the road-building practice of the Romans, but in built-up areas it required raised 'pavements' or 'sidewalks', not only for the convenience of pedestrians but also to keep the discharge from the road surface from flowing into the basements of adjoining houses.[130] This was the method advocated by Palladio and other writers of the Renaissance. It was adopted in France from the seventeenth century, and was eventually copied in Britain.[131] It was also better suited than the alternative method to the wheeled vehicles which were then coming into general use.

In few towns did public authorities assume any responsibility for paving before the eighteenth century. As a general rule they were content to pass the obligation on to those whose houses fronted on the street. Repeatedly the city fathers emphasised that responsibility rested with individual householders, and equally frequently the latter evaded their responsibilities or discharged them in only the most perfunctory manner. Road surfaces were always bad, but the degree of badness varied from one house front to another and was apt to differ on opposite sides of the road.

The maintenance of large open spaces, such as markets, was far beyond the ability of neighbouring householders. This had to be assumed by the town authorities, which sometimes levied a toll on 'foreigners' – that is non-citizens – visiting the market. It was in this way, by raising money and hiring labour, that local governments came to assume responsibility for paving all the main streets. But 'pavage' to cover its cost could not normally be levied at the whim of the town authorities; it had to be authorised by the king, usually by a letter patent. Even so, grants were usually for only a term of years and had to be renewed.

There was neither change nor improvement in ways of constructing and maintaining urban streets before modern times. Change came as a result, in part, of increasing traffic, but also of a growing interest in the roads of classical antiquity.

On the other hand, the wheels of carriages and of other vehicles were modified so that they did less damage to the road surface and springs were improved so that passengers enjoyed a smoother ride. Increasing care was given both to the preparation of a solid road bed and to a smooth and more durable surface. For the latter, pavée, a reticulated pattern of small, square blocks, set usually in sand, gradually came into use. The construction of such roads was beyond the capacity of householders; it required a co-ordinated local authority. The more important streets in the larger towns had some kind of paving by the end of the seventeenth century, and a beginning was made by replacing gutters with shallow channels, covered with stone slabs and set with gratings, through which storm water could disappear. This was assisted from the eighteenth century by the construction of raised 'pavements' defined by 'kerbs' of cut stone, such as are to be found generally today.

Street-cleaning, as anyone walking the streets of London today cannot fail to note, is scarcely less important than the maintenance of the road surface itself. The streets in any traditional town were customarily filthy. The lack of any systematic means of rubbish collection and of sewage disposal meant that much of the domestic waste was merely deposited in the streets, in the hope, rather than the expectation, that it would be redistributed by the rain or removed by the town's 'rakers'. Neither, of course, happened with any regularity, and there was a continuous stream of complaints of the condition of the streets. In 1322, the city authorities at York were instructed 'to cleanse the streets and lanes . . . as the king [who was about to arrive] detested the abominable smell abounding in the said city',[132] and a few years later those at Newcastle upon Tyne were ordered 'to clear away offal and refuse before the castle gate'.[133] Only with the strengthening of town government and the raising of town rates for the purpose could one look for any improvement.[134] The crossing-sweeper, whose task it was to clear a passage through the dirt and debris from the security of one pavement to that on the other side of the road, was still a feature of the London of Charles Dickens and Henry Mayhew.

Religious and public buildings

All older towns were 'overchurched'. Each urban parish had its church. There were more than twenty cathedral towns, and before the Reformation there were countless urban monasteries and friaries. Cathedral and monastic sites were surrounded by a wall, difficult to cross if not actually unscalable, and were entered by a gatehouse calculated more to impress than to deter.[135] Monasteries had from early times tended to cut themselves off from lay society, the extent of their isolation varying from one order to another. But in towns this degree of social distance was not easy to achieve, and the relations of church and laity were often close, but rarely harmonious, and at times even violent and destructive. Urban monasteries, almost all of which belonged to either the Benedictine or Augustinian orders, usually had some parochial function, and the religious commonly assumed some pastoral duties. The local populace was accustomed to attend the monastic church, whose nave was not infrequently given over to their activities. The monks objected to this weekly, even daily, invasion by noisy and often ill-conducted parishioners, but could prevent it only by building a separate church for them on the edge of or beyond their own precinct. Numerous examples survive: Ramsey (Cambs.); Barnwell, Cambridge; Tavistock (Devon.); and, pre-eminently, St Margaret's, Westminster.

The coming of the friars added yet another dimension to the urban scene. There were four major orders, each of which established a 'house' in the chief towns of this country (Fig. 10.8). The number of friaries was a rough measure of the perceived importance of the town and of its need for their services.[136] The friars can be thought of as the 'social workers' of the later Middle Ages, and public attitudes towards them were ambivalent, as they are today towards their modern successors. The parochial clergy disliked them because they competed with parish priests in bestowing pastoral care and collecting alms which the latter thought were rightfully theirs.[137] The laity responded more positively, and it is impossible to exaggerate the monetary bequests that were made to the friars by all levels of society. They made a powerful impact with their preaching and pastoral care, both initiating and responding to a new growth in popular religion.

Somewhat lower in the scale of religious foundations came hospitals and other charitable foundations, established by pious benefactors to provide help and accommodation for specific categories of the aged and infirm. Below these came the numerous chantries and private chapels, many of them short-lived, and all of them terminated and their feeble endowments confiscated at the Dissolution.

The middle years of the sixteenth century saw the end of the monasteries and friaries and also of endowed chantries. Not only was the urban landscape changed profoundly, but the local economy was distorted. Many towns lost sources of employment and also the profits from catering for pilgrims and from the sale of petty objects of spiritual comfort which the latter demanded. On the other hand, church property passed into lay hands, and in the course of time most of the precincts were built over, and the spoil of the monasteries – timber, lead and good ashlar masonry –

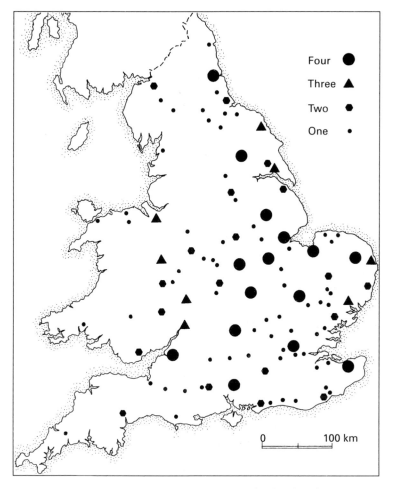

10.8 Map of friaries of the four principal orders in England and Wales. Most towns of importance had houses of at least three orders.

contributed to the expanded building activity of the later sixteenth century and to the replacement of timber-framing with masonry construction. Furthermore, in most of the older towns some of their parishes were merged and unwanted churches destroyed.

Secular public buildings proved to be more lasting than most of the religious ones. Many gilds had some kind of building in which their members met and caroused. The 'gild'-hall was most often a ground-floor or first-floor hall, closely akin to the great hall of a private home, together with kitchen and private rooms. Here the gilds, or at least the more wealthy amongst them, stored their plate, and here they did business and held the feats which, as it were, set a seal on their confraternities. A number of early gildhalls survive, but most were rebuilt in the sixteenth or seventeenth century, and became more secular in design and function.

'Gildhall' and 'townhall' were always very nearly synonymous, because the social groups which provided the gild membership were also those which controlled the destinies of the town. Gildhalls, especially those which adjoined or overlooked the market-place, were adapted in the course of rebuilding to serve the needs of the market itself. Many gildhalls were rebuilt as upper chambers, where the local council met and balls and assemblies were held, with an arcaded shelter beneath, in which stalls could be set up, business transacted, and the 'locals' sit at their ease. At Peterborough, for example, a ground-level market-house was swept away after 1660, and was replaced by one with an arcaded ground floor for market purposes and an assembly room above.[138] Such halls are no longer adequate for the inflated bureaucracy of modern local government, but many survive, serving little economic purpose, but happily protected from misuse or destruction.

Some hundred towns of England and Wales had at one time been surrounded by walls and entered through gates.[139] In most instances this martial display held little significance. No English town was besieged after the early years of the Norman Conquest, though a few were beleaguered during the Civil War. Only in those bordering Wales and the south coast were the burgesses at sufficient risk to justify a heavy expenditure on protecting themselves. Why then did so many towns build walls, gates and towers, which, in general, they failed to maintain and in modern times allowed to fall into ruin? Their purpose was to create a visible divide, a barrier between the incorporated borough and its privileged citizens on the one hand and rural communities on the other. They strengthened the concept which the citizens had of themselves, and for the same reason towns adopted heraldry and heraldic seals, which displayed, as often as not, walls and gates as symbols of their separate status.

A new dimension

The town had few other buildings of a public nature before the seventeenth or eighteenth century. In terms of culture it differed little from the village. Then a fission occurred in the ranks of towns. Some, with little urban pretension and few urban functions, reverted to the role of large, or not so large, villages. Others, mainly the county seats and regional centres, slowly became urban in the modern sense of that term. This 'urban renaissance', as it has been called,[140] consisted primarily in the development of cultural, as distinct from economic, functions and institutions. Borsay has categorised these as the provision of leisure facilities, the development of public entertainment, and the creation of an architectural milieu at once dignified, aesthetic and functional. To a modest degree the gildhalls and town halls of early modern times had served these ends. The gilds themselves had staged plays, but these were generally of a religious nature, were traditional in form, and were put on at regular times in the church's calendar. Of entertainment *per se* there was little evidence.

A change became evident in sixteenth-century London, when, about 1575 the first permanent theatre was established. Others followed, most of them built on a plan which resembled that of an inn. Christopher Wren designed a theatre of more modern plan, which may have been that built in Drury Lane in 1674. It was some time before theatres appeared in the leading provincial towns, but the first in Bath was built about 1705, and by the end of the century a theatre had been established in most towns of any significance. The existence of theatres encouraged, from the age of Shakespeare onwards, the writing of plays for performance and the rise of a class of professional actors. By the mid-eighteenth century the play had become a regular urban entertainment.

Music and the concert developed alongside the theatre, and composers were encouraged to write for public performance. Apart from the cacophony which had accompanied 'carnival' and that which was performed in church, music had been of two kinds, written respectively for the home and the court. It was either madrigal or masque. In the later seventeenth century music for concert performance became more and more common, and opera, an Italian invention, was introduced and eventually written in England. Lastly, the dance moved upmarket from the rowdy, public assemblages in the market-place and on the green to the ballroom.

The growing demand in the eighteenth century for these types of entertainment led to the creation of halls for their performance, more spacious than the cramped and inconvenient facilities afforded by the town hall or tavern. Bath, which was one of the most forward-looking towns after London, had an 'asssembly' room by 1708, and the great structure which survives today was built in 1769–71. No town in the eighteenth century surpassed Bath in its provision for recreation and leisure, but many built more modest 'rooms' and staged less flamboyant entertainments.[141] At the same time, gardens and walks were laid out, like Vauxhall and Ranelagh in London.

The town had always been a focal point for the surrounding countryside. That was its *raison d'être*. The rise of the gentry, their growing wealth, and their increasing participation in public affairs added to the functions of the provincial towns. The assizes became a formal occasion, and to these were added quarter sessions, in which the justices – most of them country gentlemen – participated. The presence of the gentry on a more or less regular basis created the opportunity to meet, to make business arrangements, to arrange marriages, and to turn a judicial occasion into a social event.

At the same time the corporate pride of the provincial town was intensified. Much of the civic ritual which continues to be enacted today was the creation of well-to-do, self-conscious burgesses in the eighteenth and early nineteenth centuries.[142] It is noteworthy that Dr Johnson refused to include the word 'civilisation' in his dictionary, preferring to use the term 'urbanity' for a sophisticated taste and way of living.

The urban landscape was changed not only by the building of theatres and assembly rooms but also by the erection of grander private houses than had been seen there before. These were first built in London,[143] but in provincial towns also houses were erected for the rural aristocracy and gentry, where they could live in some comfort when they came to town for business or pleasure.[144] Such houses departed radically from traditional urban styles. They were great country houses writ small, reduced to fit a good-sized urban plot. All eighteenth-century county towns, and many others, have them. Their classical facades and symmetrical plans, their walled gardens and entrance gates mark them off from all others. They are further evidence of the widening cultural divide between town and village, and, within towns, between the new élite and the mass of the population.

CHAPTER 11

THE FOUNDATIONS OF POPULAR
CULTURE

... the traditional beliefs and customs of the medieval and modern peasant are in nine cases out of ten but the detritus of heathen mythology and heathen worship ... village festivals ... are but fragments of naive cults addressed by a primitive folk to the beneficent deities of field, wood and river.   E. K. Chambers, *The Medieval Stage*

Les fêtes, les jeux, la danse, la musique, le théâtre, les repas de noces ou de funerailles et surtout l'activité rituelle des groupes de la jeunesse locale et des défunts du village ont pour fonction ... de redéfinir fréquemment pour chacun le sens d'appartenance au groupe.   R. Muchembled, *Culture populaire et culture des élites*

In chapter 8 brief mention was made of the games and rituals with which people in a local community enlivened their dull lives and induced a sense, if not of well-being, at least of camaraderie. It is appropriate to examine the assumptions and beliefs, the *mentalité* of ordinary people, which subsumed these activities, and, in so far as this is possible, to trace their origins as far back as practicable. The world-view of traditional peoples was underpinned by the tacit assumption that there were forces external to mankind which could in some way shape human destiny. Both the regularities of nature, the rising and setting of the sun, the phases of the moon, the movements of the planets and the procession of the seasons, no less than its irregularities, like the apparent randomness of weather and the incidence of epidemic disease, called for explanation. Traditional society was pre-scientific, and no explanation that might be termed rational by present-day standards was – or could be – forthcoming. Yet primitive people developed logically from such basic assumptions as they had made. They saw interrelations between natural phenomena and between the latter and the human condition. They had, for example, a profound belief in astrology, in the influence of the heavenly bodies over the lives of people on earth. Astrology has been called 'the most systematic attempt to explain natural phenomena according to rigorous scientific laws'[1] before the modern scientific revolution. Its basic assumptions cannot now be accepted, but the superstructure that was erected upon them in classical and medieval times cannot but command a degree of respect. Some of the supposed links between the physical universe and the

379

human condition have been mentioned earlier. Piers Plowman thought that the ailments of mankind came from 'out of the planets' (p. 237); the doctor in the engraving (Fig. 7.16), instead of attending the woman in labour, was more intent on observing the position of the stars at the moment of the child's birth. Medical education included the study of astrology; the university of Paris ruled that every medical practitioner should have an almanac, telling him the positions of sun, moon and planets at any given time, and its medical faculty bore the name of *Facultas in medicina et astrologia*.[2] The four elements, of which all things on earth were made – fire, air, earth and water – were held to correspond with those which made up the stars as well as with the four 'humours' which composed the human body. Their mutual interactions were taken for granted.

Second only to the belief in astrology was that in witchcraft and the supernatural. This also sprang from the view that all objective phenomena were made up of the same elements, were interrelated and could, if properly manipulated, influence one another. Belief in the existence of 'spirits', in witchcraft, sorcery and demonology lay at the root of popular culture in traditional societies. Two aspects of such popular beliefs are relevant. In the first place, they can change, or be changed only very slowly. It is difficult, if not impossible, to alter opinions which are deeply held and have been built into a system. The human mind cannot readily make such transitions, and modifications in belief can, as a general rule, be made only over generations. For this reason aspects of sorcery and witchcraft continued to be practised in the Age of Enlightenment, when more educated opinion had long rejected them. Secondly, there was always a spectrum of beliefs. For the intellectual élite 'superstition' had a metaphysical foundation; it had been linked in an earlier age with Gnosticism, and at a later with Neoplatonism. The more highly educated might have believed in a 'world soul',[3] an immanent spirit which linked together all aspects of the material universe. To them the influence of the stars was both demonstrable and measurable. Their beliefs formed a system, which yielded only slowly from the later seventeenth century to the rationalism of the Enlightenment. Even so, belief in magic lingered on because it constituted a coherent and satisfying system of thought, and because there was nothing to put in its place. In the sphere of medicine some form of demonology continued to be accepted until the later nineteenth century, when it was at length supplanted by the microbial theory of disease.

Amongst the less educated, popular ideas of magic and sorcery continued to be held, at least superficially, as late as the twentieth century, and there are some to whom they are relevant as the twenty-first approaches. It is difficult to know how deeply they were held, but in gesture (Fig. 11.3) and language they are present still, and belief in astrology, to judge from the space given to it in the popular press, remains as vigorous in some quarters as ever.

It is sometimes said that increasing literacy in the later seventeenth and eighteenth centuries helped to dispel belief in magic, sorcery and demonology. But books could encourage belief in magic as readily as disbelief. The Puritans, who regarded literacy as of the highest importance because it brought the Bible within reach of ordinary people, began to have misgivings when they found that not all popular reading matter was as edifying as they could have wished. Even the Bible itself could be held to support a belief in demonology, and almanacs, which began to proliferate in the seventeenth century, were predicated on a form of magic. The Reformation, instead of leading to a weakening of the belief in magic, probably had the opposite effect. In medieval Christendom the popular view of the priest was of a very special kind of 'cunning man', one who could be called upon to use his magic in the interests of his parishioners. Women in particular often derived support from their priests at a time when familial bonds were weak. At the Reformation the miracle-working priest was replaced by a pastorate which had renounced all such powers. The Puritans claimed no such magic. It was 'never a merry world', wrote John Selden, 'since the parson left conjuring'.[4] There were, nevertheless, clergy of the Anglican communion who continued to practise astrology and magic, but the principal inheritor of the priest's role as 'cunning man' was the astrologer and magician. It was he who undertook to anticipate and avert both accident and evil. The rituals of spring, midsummer and midwinter were, by and large, terminated, but the psychological gap which they left had somehow to be filled. The human mind required no less, and this must be a reason for the proliferation of both witchcraft and astrology during the later sixteenth and the seventeenth centuries and also for it recrudescence today.

Magic and its practitioners

Traditional peoples conceived the world as stable, subject only to the cyclical changes of nature: seedtime and harvest, summer and winter, night and day, birth and death. These all had their established routines and their changes were predictable. But it was a normality that was always liable to be interrupted, and any deviation from the known and expected had always to be attributed to manipulation by outside and generally malign forces. The idea of catastrophe was built into their world-view. Drought might ruin a harvest; flood might prevent winter ploughing; epidemic disease might decimate a community. They were inured to accident and catastrophe, but such events were never seen as arising from natural causes: nature was neutral, and any interruption of its even progress had to be due to supernatural agency. Did not God himself strike the armies of Babylon, turn Lot's wife into a pillar of salt, and calm the storms on the Sea of Galilee? If he could not be blamed for the murrain which afflicted the herds, the hail which flattened the crops, or even the cream which failed to turn to butter in the churn, then there must be other agencies endowed with comparable powers. The traditional world was peopled with opposites. If there was a good spirit, God, then he must be balanced by his opposite, who became personalised as the devil. It was in terms of evil that good was conceptualised and vice versa. The dialectic of extremes is the stuff of which popular culture was woven. The ability to work miracles was not a monopoly of the divinity. Satan himself had been thrown out of heaven, but he had retained his power to interrupt or to distort the order of nature. The world was seen as peopled by spirits

11.1 The motif of St Michael (or St George) overcoming the dragon has always held a great attraction. This twelfth-century sculpture is part of a tympanum of about 1120 in Southwell Minster (Notts.).

which shared this power with Satan. There were good spirits whose aid could be enlisted in time of need, and bad spirits whose evil intentions had continuously to be guarded against. How the existence of spirits, whether good or bad, could be reconciled with the Christian view of an omnipotent and benevolent deity was not a matter with which most people had either the desire or the ability to concern themselves.

The primitive mind thus saw in both the natural world and the world of human activity a kind of dualism. Every phenomenon had its opposite. For every ill there was a remedy, and any condition could be defined in terms of its opposite; evil must exist because without it good would be inconceivable. An agonistic principle was posited; in everything there was struggle between opposites (Fig. 11.1). Witchcraft must be seen in this context. Without the inverted magic of the witch, the magic of God would have been inconceivable. They both belonged to a 'coherent universe of discourse'.[5]

It was thus easy to accept that the world was peopled with spirits. They formed the fundamental premise of the traditional world-view, and, seen in this light, popular culture seemed logical and self-sufficient. There were spirits in the fields and woodlands; spirits entered the home to provoke accidents; they made the milch cows dry up and the crops wither. But spirits were 'to some extent a manageable force',[6] and controlling them was the function of magic. Popular culture cannot be understood apart from magic. Magic could be made to upset the routine of household and farm; it could cause accidents and spread disease; it could wound and kill. But magic could also heal the sick and re-establish the even tenor of domestic or farm life. It could, if handled properly, protect the home from the evil spirits. It

382

could, in short, work miracles. Such views must have been held long before any of them could have been recorded for posterity, and to some extent they are with us still. The anthropologist, Conrad Arensberg, has described how the people of County Clare (Ireland) in the 1930s took the 'good people' for granted, but realised that they were temperamental and unpredictable; they had to be placated and cajoled, 'for fairy faith enforces definite behaviour upon the countryman; it lays down rites and practices which he must perform. If he is to recover his goods that have been taken, restore his threatened animals, friends or children, he must follow a definite course. That course is laid down for him again by his community of belief and habit.'[7]

Keith Thomas has dissected this belief in magic and its consequences for society in such minuteness of detail that one can almost enter the minds of those who practised it or called upon it for help. Any study of popular culture must be overshadowed by his magisterial work.[8] Magic in popular culture, broadly speaking, assumed two forms. There was the magic practised by an individual for good or ill – most often, in the popular mind, for ill, and there was that magic in which the community as a whole participated when it heard mass, went in procession round the church or performed its calendar rituals. Such intercessions had to be unanimous if they were to be effective. Society could not make room for the dissident and the nonconformist; that would impair the magic of its act. The priest had assumed the role of wonderworker *par excellence* on behalf of his community. He could not only achieve the miracle of the mass but also served in other ways as a benevolent and very 'cunning' man. The Book of Common Prayer to this day includes a form of service for exorcism, by which the priest is enabled to rid a place of the spirits that haunted it.

The first of these forms of magic was the domain of the 'cunning' folk, both men and women, who knew how to cast spells, achieve miracles, and in other ways manipulate the spirits which surrounded them. To some extent, also, they could anticipate events and foretell the future. For this they had abundant biblical and classical precedent.[9] Indeed, Christianity had so much in common with popular culture, they borrowed so much from one another, that it was not difficult to conflate the two.[10] The distinction between the 'cunning man' and the local saint was by no means absolute. Both operated, as a general rule, within a very small area, and their reputations were narrowly based. There was a community in southern Italy which claimed that *its* Virgin Mary was more efficacious than that Virgin whose statue stood in the church of a neighbouring parish. The Virgin Mary had no universality. She assumed different forms and possessed different powers in one community from those which she had in another. She was treated as if she were the local 'cunning woman'. 'Cunning' people could act vicariously; they could cast their spells on people and things at a distance, and if this was so, why should they not be able to influence things posthumously, especially if some part of their anatomy or some article closely associated with them when they were alive could be linked with the spell cast in their name? This was the logical basis of the collection of relics and of pilgrimages, since the latter were always made to some place or other associated with a saint. The cult of relics derives directly from the belief in the 'cunning man', and the veneration of relics, it has been said, was the true religion of the Middle Ages.[11] Conversion from animism to Christianity was not a change from magic to belief. It was a transfer of loyalty from one set of spirits which was thought to have failed its clients or devotees to another which was thought of as possessing greater powers, a stronger magic. And this is where the church failed the common people at the time of the Reformation. The priest disclaimed all magical powers; he ceased to celebrate mass; he no longer called upon the saints to protect their people; men and women felt defenceless and turned to those who still claimed some powers of this kind. The astrologer and the 'cunning man', the one able to foresee the coming of evil, the other able to avert it, were the beneficiaries of the desanctification of the Protestant churches.[12]

Saints, like the 'cunning' people, were mercenary, and demanded a reward for their services. The 'cunning man' accepted money or food; the saint expected gifts and votive offerings to be laid at his or her shrine. But 'the faithful and the saint formed a single association ... in order to ensure a saint's "services" for themselves people acquired his relics.'[13] They venerated and showered gifts on *their* saint, but they expected the saint to reciprocate, and, if no miracle followed, they did not hesitate to transfer their veneration and their gifts to another, just as they would abandon the man in their village who had lost his 'cunning' and turn to another if the former's spells failed to work. Late medieval wills occasionally record the bequest of jewellery or other valuables to the *figure* of the saint which stood in the parish church. At Pilton (Som.) in 1499 'a peyr of lanbur [amber] bedys' was left by a certain Margaret Spycer 'to or [our] lady yn the quer [choir]'.[14] And 'or lady' was expected to accede to the donor's wishes: no miracle, no gift. 'The relations between the saint and the faithful were thought of in customary medieval categories of mutual fidelity and aid.'[15] Those of the 'cunning man' and his client were precisely the same: no spell, no payment.

Attitudes to magic and the supernatural changed, though very slowly. Belief in astrology, in the power of celestial bodies to influence human fortunes, reached its peak in the later sixteenth and early seventeenth centuries. Thereafter objections were raised, and during the following century it gradually ceased to commend itself to the more educated and rational. But magic, a naive, crude belief in the power of some individuals to influence or to divert the course of nature, remained active throughout the nineteenth century, though it is likely that the number of those who fully accepted its implications declined.

Calendar customs

The second form assumed by magic in popular culture related to the community rather than to the individual. It was not concerned with what might happen to this person or that, but with matters of general social concern, such as the sequence of the seasons, the quality of the harvest, or the incidence of epidemic disease: indeed, the perpetuation of the community itself. Matters of such moment called for the collective efforts of the *whole* community. The anthropologist Arnold van Gennep has drawn a distinction between calendar customs, related in general to the agricultural year, and cyclical customs, such as saints' days and patronal feasts, in which the relationship to the farming year is less obvious.[16] There was a social compulsion to participate, for to abstain was to weaken the magic of the event. The idea of conformity in this, as in most other aspects of traditional social life, was built into society. Distrust of the nonconformist ran deep, and had its logical basis in the attitudes and beliefs of traditional peoples. Legislation of the sixteenth and seventeenth centuries against nonconformity and recusancy owed its origin basically to the conviction that the magic of an event demanded unanimity.

It would be tedious to catalogue the calendar practices which have been and to a small extent still are practised in this country. They amount to a curious combination of the supplicative and the convenient.[17] The most time-consuming of them come at a time when the agricultural calendar is least crowded, and the most popular of them has always occurred at midwinter, when the fields could be neglected for a while. The midwinter feast was in origin one of the most complex and syncretic, subsuming, as it did, a number of separate strands in popular culture. Foremost was its association with the winter solstice, when days were at their shortest and the sun hung lowest in the sky. 'The Christmas season was more important than Christmas Day.'[18] It was marked by bonfires as was the corresponding midsummer festival, but in winter these were largely indoors, and came ultimately to be restricted to the ritual burning of the 'yule log', the purpose of which seems to have been to avert the spirits that were about at this season of the year.[19]

There were also rituals whose intent was to induce the dormant vegetation to assume a new growth. Wassailing, whatever its inebriated consequences, was an act of drinking to the trees, specifically of cider to the apple trees. Its confusion with that other aspect of popular culture – carnival or 'misrule' – was almost inevitable. The 'twelve days of Christmas', from Christmas Day to Twelfth Night or Epiphany, was marked by a sequence of revels, individually of uncertain origin, but collectively 'the detritus of heathen mythology and heathen worship', all subsumed under and reinforced by the mantle of Christianity.[20]

The coming of spring was similarly marked by a cluster of conflated feasts and rituals, in which the rites of spring, the blessing of the fields at Rogationtide, the Annunciation (Lady Day), and the Passion, Resurrection and Ascension all made their particular contributions.[21] The period of abstinence known as Lent coincided with one of shortages as winter neared its end. Perhaps for this reason those foodstuffs which were still available assumed a greater importance and were consumed with more exaggerated ritual: simnel (*simila* = fine-quality flour) cakes and frumenty (*frumentum* = wheat) on Mothering Sunday, the mid-Sunday of Lent, 'collops' (bacon and eggs) on Shrove Monday and pancakes on Shrove

Tuesday are all relics of this practice. Even the modern Easter cake and hot-cross bun have a respectable ancestry.[22]

A considerable period of time, varying with the date of Easter, separates the calendar customs just mentioned from the celebration of the first of May, or 'Mayday'. The latter was an 'eminently rural custom', marked by the collection of spring flowers and the decoration of homes and churches.[23] It was essentially a ceremony to welcome the coming of spring with song and dance, and such it has remained. The maypole, decked with greenery, is known to have been in use in the fourteenth century and was probably a great deal older. In some degree the Mayday rituals were conflated with those of Whitsun. They were also associated with boisterous activities which included the lighting of bonfires, the playing of rudimentary football games and, locally at least, the rough game of the hobby-horse, from which we derive the concept of 'horse-play'.

The cycle of spring rituals came to an end with the celebration of the summer solstice, after which days began to shorten and the sun to sink lower in the sky. It was at one and the same time a celebration of summer and a propitiatory rite to ensure the return of the sun after the coming winter. It was furthermore conflated with the feast of St John the Baptist, deliberately fixed six months before Christmas. It can hardly be doubted that the bonfires associated with the occasion – St John's fires – are a relic of a primitive cult related to the sun. The day continues to be of ritual significance to some credulous people.

The second half of the year was a barren time. No important celebrations, apart from harvest, Michaelmas and Hallowe'en, marked its course.[24] Even today this long period is interrupted only by the wholly artificial 'late summer holiday' at the end of August. It is not easy to explain the lack of balance between the two halves of the year; perhaps the agricultural routine, with harvest followed quickly by autumn ploughing, was too demanding in the latter half-year for such frivolities to be practicable.

The sequence of feasts and ceremonies which spans the autumn equinox embraces, first and foremost, the rituals of harvest. This was inevitably a period of rejoicing because it inaugurated a period, however short it may sometimes have been, when food was abundant. It was accompanied by propitiatory rites, of which 'crying the neck', still practised in south-western England in recent years, and the 'corn dolly', made from the last straw to be cut, may serve as examples. It is noteworthy that the traditional rites at this season of the year consumed only a very short period of time. The harvest feast, following the intense labour of the harvest itself, calls for no explanation. It is curious, however, that the church itself made no provision for a thanksgiving ritual after harvest. The so-called Harvest Festival is an invention of the Victorians[25] and is nowhere celebrated with greater fervour than by today's urbanised population which has severed all connection with the land.

Rituals marking the onset of winter followed quickly on those of harvest, just as the celebration of summer succeeded the rites of spring. They were gloomy with foreboding as if anticipating the hardships to follow. There was feasting, however, but it was associated more with the slaughter of animals that could not be kept through the winter than with the short-lived abundance following harvest. But Winter's Eve – *Calan gaeaf* or November Day – coming as it did just six months after Mayday, was anticipatory. It was a time when dark spirits were active and when fires were lighted to fend them off. In the western church the rituals of *all* the blessed or All Saints (1 November) and of All Souls (2 November) were set, possibly deliberately, during this season. In parts of Britain, as well as in the United States, Hallowe'en – All Hallows' or All Saints' Eve – remained a time when spirits were supposed to be abroad. The origin of this conflation of Catholic saints with the spirits of evil is obscure. The last day of October marked the end of the Celtic year, and was thus associated with mortality. It consequently became a festival of the dead, a time when their spirits returned to visit or to disturb their descendants. It was an essentially pagan festival until, about 998, Abbot Odilo of Cluny instituted the feast of All Souls. It was at first celebrated only within his own order – the Cluniac – but later spread across the whole of western Christendom. His purpose was to divert the attentions of the faithful from thoughts of evil spirits and of the dead returning to haunt the living, towards the nameless faithful who were making their way to heaven. The feast of All Souls was later moved from the day before to the day after that of All Saints, leaving in its wake the rowdiness and petty crime associated today with Hallowe'en. A further division of the ritual significance of Hallowe'en, at least as far as Great Britain is concerned, has been the removal in the seventeenth century of its bonfire aspect to November 5th.[26] Calendar customs have certain general features in common. They were, in the first place, liable to move within a fairly narrow time band. This is apparent particularly in the rituals of early winter and Christmas. This must derive in part from a very loose concept of time. Another aspect of these customs, not unrelated to their lack of fixity, was their tendency to be conflated, so that a single celebration might serve several different objectives and have significance at various levels. Lastly, there has been a growing tendency 'to manipulate rather than to celebrate folk festivals',[27] to drain them of their folk content, to deck them out with an artificial glitter, and to use them as vehicles of commercial or political exploitation. One particular case is the way in which the spring festival of Mayday has been appropriated by the working-class movement.

'Homo ludens'

All people tend to complicate the conditions of their lives in order to make them more interesting and thus more bearable.[28] This 'superfluous behaviour' sprang, not from some form of naively perceived magic, but from a deep psychological need. Foremost among the forms assumed by superfluous behaviour was 'play'. Life for most people and for most of the time was an interminable and hopeless drudgery. The human mind demands some periodic relaxation, the opportunity for 'a free activity standing quite consciously outside "ordinary" life . . . not serious, but at the same time absorbing the player intensely and utterly. The function of play . . . can largely be derived from two basic aspects under which we meet it: as a contest *for* something or a representation *of* something.' The former thus resolved itself into contests between groups or areas or individuals. Partisanship then developed and gave the contest a sharper edge. City gangs of a medieval city-state or of the modern underworld, the games of primitive football, 'fought' between town and country or between parish and parish, show this play element in culture carried to its violent extreme. That this element of identification and partisanship is with us still is demonstrated by the almost ritual behaviour of football 'fans'.

Not all play is participatory. People can take part by watching, deriving a vicarious pleasure from the fortunes of the contestants. This was so with athletics in classical Greece, with the gladiatorial contests of Rome, the chariot races of Byzantium, tournaments in the Middle Ages and football today. Few watch a game *as a game*; it is almost always seen as a contest with the viewer as a partisan. And, as if simple partisanship were not enough, there has always been the added excitement which arose from betting on the result. This agonistic basis of society must never be underestimated, because there is a constant tendency to derive excitement from the detail of ordinary life by dramatising it, by turning it into a struggle. Even the dull routine of ploughing can on occasion be turned into a ploughing contest, and at the humblest level of everyday life there is an innate urge to emulate one's neighbours.

It is a far cry from screaming football fans to an audience watching a dramatic performance on the stage, but both are witnessing and taking part vicariously in play, and we commonly and correctly subsume both under the mantle of 'play'. Even the miracle and calendar plays of the Middle Ages served the same role, representing 'the change of seasons, the rising and setting of the constellations, the growth and ripening of crops, birth, life and death [in which] archaic man "plays" the order of nature as imprinted on his consciousness'.[29]

The relationship between feasting and playing is close, since both lie outside ordinary life and in both mirth and joy are predominant. In the potlach ceremonies of primitive peoples[30] and the 'church-ales' of the Middle Ages, the elements of feasting and of struggle were always present in the competitive provision of food. Gift-giving has, like the potlach, this element of compulsory and competitive activity.[31] Gifts must be reciprocated, sometimes immediately, sometimes when the appropriate occasion arises, like a birth or a marriage.

The rituals and celebrations which marked the calendar year have thus become inseparable both from play and from feasting. The periodic feast was for most people the only escape they knew from the shortages and, at times, the near-starvation of the real world. Feasts had to be so organised that they fitted into the agricultural surplus to support them. We thus have the regular periods, associated with the harvest, the winter solstice and the spring respectively, when feasting was normal, separated by periods of shortage, institutionalised as Advent and Lent. Feasting was not seen as an imperative, like placating the spirits and ensuring the return of spring, though it could often have strongly religious overtones. It was another form of 'superfluous behaviour', made desirable, if not necessary, by the psychological make-up of the human animal.

Carnival

There were occasions when the human psyche demanded more than vicarious participation in play or the excessive consumption of food and alcohol which marked times of feasting and festival. Escape from reality had to go further, to create 'a second world and a second life outside officialdom, a world in which all medieval people participated more or less, in which they lived during a given time of the year'.[32] This was the world of 'carnival', coarse and irreverent, grotesque and amusing, in which people succeeded in escaping as completely as was possible from the world of reality. Carnival commonly coincided with feasting, as it had to do, since it was in overindulgence that people were released from the mundane in order to participate in the grotesque and irreverent activities of carnival. It was in carnival that the common people thumbed their nose at authority. There was role-reversal, as in the play-acting of the 'boy-bishop' in the weeks before Christmas; there was ridicule and satire. 'It was a prepolitical safety valve for the members of a structured, hierarchical society',[33] and served to loosen its rigours and, temporarily at least, to express the values of egalitarianism. At the same time these activities fitted into the dualism which pervaded social thought. The portrayal of disorder and misrule emphasised the importance of their opposites, order and good government: 'misrule necessarily presupposes the rule that it parodies. Thus the fool could only flourish, in fact or in literary imagination, in societies where the taboos surrounding divine kingship and sacramental worship were especially rigid ... only by exploring this contrary perspective can men make themselves conceptually at home in a world of unchanging polarities ... The things of this world can be truly perceived only by looking at them backwards.'[34]

It is impossible to exaggerate the importance in primitive societies of role-reversal. It was a symbolic overthrow of authority, allowing the underclass momentarily to escape the tyranny of its superiors. It was an essential element in early drama, and it runs through Shakespeare's plays; it is an ingredient of opera and pantomime, which at their very different cultural levels continue the early tradition of escape from reality. Today the officers of certain units in the British Army serve dinner to and wait on their men at Christmas.

Carnival was, furthermore, a communal activity which brought 'coherence to primitive societies; [its] apparent disorder is actually a source of order in societies lacking a contractual relationship'. It contributed to the 'togetherness' of communities which were for much of the time wracked by feuds and dissension. The forms assumed by carnival were diverse, ranging from ball-games to animal contests, from plays and processions to the coarsest buffoonery. But the grotesque was always present. The distortion of reality which it involved was part of the

11.2 Role-reversal was a popular motif; here the hare is seen riding the hound which chases it. From a misericord in Worcester Cathedral.

mocking role of carnival, the coarse language, the degradation, the 'lowering of all that is high, spiritual, ideal, abstract', the free expression of 'the body and bodily functions', the inversion of traditional values (Fig. 11.2). The obscenities of life today derive no less from this urge to express contempt for authority, for education, for culture.[35]

The jester and the clown were expressions of the grotesque because they reduced every high ceremonial gesture or ritual to the lowest material plane. One has only to look to Shakespeare, to the porter in *Macbeth* or to Bottom and his friends in *A Midsummer Night's Dream* to see the liberties which they could take with those in authority by simple parody, imitation and, above all, inversion.

The grotesque is even more readily visible in medieval sculpture and pictorial art. Phallic symbols, exhibitionism, figures known in Irish as *sheela-na-gig*, and other obscenities are not infrequent (Fig. 11.3). Many have been destroyed by those whose sensitivities have been offended, and some survive in the security of museums. The medieval church disapproved of such coarse eroticism, but was obliged to tolerate it in the same way that royalty and aristocracy had to bear with the disrespectful buffoonery of their jesters. Bernard of Clairvaux tried to hide frivolous and obscene sculpture from the eyes of his monks,[36] but there were few monastic churches in which they could not be seen merely by turning up the

11.3 The *sheela-na-gig* at Kilpeck church (Hereford.). It cannot be later than the middle years of the twelfth century.

misericords against which the monks reclined. The latter must have been like the man who today surreptitiously scans *Playboy* on a railway station bookstall.

One tends to look on such eroticism as part and parcel of the grotesqueness of carnival. But it was more than this. It was, on the one hand, the product of an artist giving free rein to his thoughts: 'who can tell what archetypal atavistic symbolism lurks behind the conscious mind of the creative artist?'[37] On the other hand, grotesques may have held a deeper meaning. They may have been seen as fertility symbols, as protectors of the building which they decorated, just as a naked woman was supposed to scare off wrongdoers.

The grotesque was not restricted to art forms. It was apparent in behaviour and in common speech. Coarseness of language, profanity and swearing mark the degradation of speech, an inversion of accepted standards no less than the crudity

11.4 Wooden ceiling boss, Southwark Cathedral.
I will bite my thumb at them; which is a disgrace to them if they bear it.
  Do you bite your thumb at us, sir?
  I do bite my thumb, sir.
    Romeo and Juliet, Act I, scene 1

11.5 The grotesque was an important element in traditional culture. A common motif was the *blemya*, the man whose 'head did grow beneath his shoulders'.

and eroticism of some medieval art and the coarseness of carnival. In all these respects the grotesque in popular culture was a revolt against élite culture. It was a way in which the masses thumbed their noses – itself an obscene gesture of great antiquity (Fig. 11.4) – at their temporal and spiritual masters. It was as if they were saying with Milton 'evil be thou my good'. It may be going too far to see a political statement in the imagery of popular art, but it nevertheless represents a vaguely sensed attitude on the part of the masses towards authority in all its forms.

This apposition of popular and élite culture was expressed in and derived confirmation from the theology of the time. Christianity had early assumed not only a dualism between good and evil but also the physical existence of God and Satan, neither having absolute power over the other. The idea of a superhuman race which in power and influence nevertheless fell considerably short of that of God himself was a widespread element in early popular culture. The apocryphal Book of Enoch[38] tells how the Sons of God, by intercourse with humans, produced a race of giants and fallen angels. The same concept appears in classical mythology as a consequence of the amours of Zeus and, in Norse, of Wotan. Christianity elaborated on this view by claiming that the fallen angels originated in a schism within heaven, the 'fallen' being transformed into devils, continuing their endless struggle with God for men's souls.

Such a *Weltanschauung* had much to recommend it to simple people. It contained an element of contest or struggle; it provided a ready explanation for accident or catastrophe, which could always be ascribed to the machinations of the powerful (but not all-powerful) demons, and it left room for God, his angels and saints, who, by virtue of their superior power, could always be expected to triumph in the end. Lastly, it embodied the grotesque as the normal mode of representing the devil and all his works.

Over the chancel arch in many, perhaps in most, parish churches was a painted Doom, a representation of the Last Judgment. It served to impress or to intimidate the faithful as they stood or knelt irreverently during the 'blessed murmur of the mass', which at best they only half understood. In the midst was God himself, seated imperiously on the rainbow which served in popular mythology as the bridge to heaven.[39] To his right the elect, those whose lives had been judged blameless, were being led upwards by angels. On his left the unjust were being pushed by devils into the jaws of hell. Somewhere on God's right – much depended on the space available to the painter – the Virgin Mary was seen appealing for mercy, and to his left, St Michael, a giant pair of scales in hand, was shown weighing and judging souls, while the devil, just like the merchant in the local market-place, surreptitiously put his finger on the scale to tip the balance in his direction. Devils were always represented as grotesques, fierce, quasi-human figures with grimacing faces, fangs, horns and tails. Sometimes intimate details of hell were presented – it all depended on the space available and the inclinations and skills of the artist. The painting had an earthy, realistic quality, and one can imagine the *frisson* with which the unlettered peasant viewed it; the *Schadenfreude* with which he contemplated the torments of the damned. The function of the Doom was predominantly eschatological. It was to emphasise the metaphysical dualism of good and evil as well as the reality of heaven and hell. It used the grotesque in minatory fashion. It was intended not to scare spirits away but to arouse a profound dread of the consequences of sin. One can only surmise the depth of feeling that the Doom inspired, but did it contribute to better conduct, or did the more sophisticated or cynical dismiss it as grossly overdrawn?

This is not what we are told in one of the fifteenth-century ballades of François Villon:

> within my parish-cloister I behold
> A painted heaven where lutes and harps adore
> And eke an Hell whose damned souls seethe full sore.
> One bringeth fear, the other joy to me.[40]

Man and nature

Judaeo-Christian teaching tended to emphasise also a different kind of dualism, that of mankind against nature, the former made in the image of God, the later created in order to serve his needs. A correspondent in *The Times* of London put the antithesis succinctly: 'mankind and mankind alone is made in the image of the Almighty. Other animal species have been put on this planet to serve mankind.'[41] The writer went on to protest against the assumption that animals have rights. Such a view may be consistent with Christian doctrine; it is not one which this writer can accept.

Early man saw himself as part of nature and closely akin to the wild things around him. In his primitive view he had, as well as his divine soul, a 'bush-soul', incarnate in an animal or a tree, which stood to him as a kind of 'blood brother'.[42] Primitive peoples saw nature as an extension of themselves, rather than as something to be manipulated, used and disposed of.[43] In the Middle Ages, as well as in classical times, the human figure was frequently represented as part-animal.[44] The 'wodewose' or 'wild man', a simple, Papageno-like creature, was a spirit of the wild, generally shown dressed in greenery and sometimes represented as naively innocent, a 'perfect fool' like Parsifal. Other creatures were shown as half-human, half-animal. There were trees that grew human heads, and human figures covered with feathers or furs, their feet with hoofs or claws. They bore a certain similarity to the satyrs and *sileni* of classical mythology and to folkloric denizens of the forest like the Russian *leshiy*.[45] They were generally represented in art as benign or at least neutral spirits. Christianity, ambivalent as always, made great use of animal symbolism. Three of the four evangelists were commonly represented by animals; only St Matthew was shown as a human figure, and Christ himself often appeared in Christian iconography as a lamb – *agnus dei*. An animal disguise was sometimes assumed in carnival. This may have been a conscious role-reversal or an attempt to 'play' the actions of the wild creatures who enjoyed a degree of freedom denied to humans. This does not mean that animals were better treated than might otherwise have been the case. People were cruel to animals, as, indeed, they were to each other, but it is doubtful whether deliberate maltreatment of animals was more common then than now, in our supposedly more humane and enlightened times.

It is possible to discuss only three of the motifs which in their different ways expressed a popular concept of humanity's relationship to nature. All three occur widely in folk art and on occasion also in élite art of the Middle Ages and early modern times: the cult of the head, the green or wild man, and the Tree of Life.

(a)

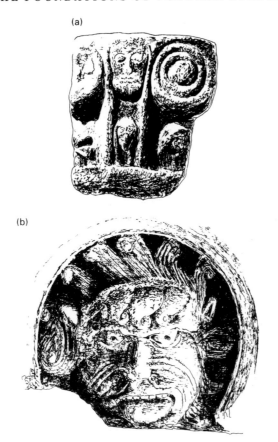

(b)

11.6 The cult of the head has survived from at least the Iron Age (p. 27): (a) a human head between the volutes of a twelfth-century capital; probably from Durham Castle; (b) a head, with protruding tongue (a form of insult or aggression), St Augustine's, Canterbury.

The symbolism of the head

The folk culture of the Middle Ages has left a host of symbols and images in its art or deeply implanted in the popular mind. The serpentine creatures which wind up the shaft of a churchyard cross or decorate the bowl of a twelfth-century font, and the face-masks which adorn capitals or look down from corbel-table or roof-boss all held some meaning for those who created them, though we can only guess what they were intended to convey (Fig. 11.6). Foremost amongst such symbols was the human head or face. We find it everywhere, so stylised in many instances that it cannot have represented any form of portraiture. Pottery face-urns were a feature of the Baltic culture of the early Iron Age.[46] The Romans sometimes used a mould to impress a human face on the damp clay of their pots.[47] During the Middle Ages face-masks were very frequently carved into the corners of baptismal fonts, into the

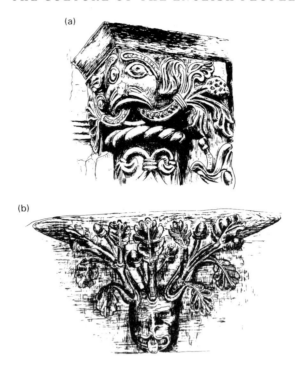

11.7 The foliate head is an aspect of the 'green' or 'wild' man. It is never clear whether he symbolises oneness with nature, as in (a) a capital at Kilpeck (Hereford.), or hostility and aggression, as in (b), a foliate head in a misericord in Exeter Cathedral, with protruding tongue.

corbels which supported the roof trusses, into the label-stops of the dripstones of windows, indeed, everywhere where a rounded surface seemed to invite embellishment. Was it art for art's sake? Was it satirical, or was it minatory or protective? In Celtic folklore – and throughout the whole of Britain there lies a Celtic cultural substratum – the head was an object of particular veneration. The foliate head, with greenery spewing from its mouth (Fig. 11.7), is one of the most widespread representations of the head, and clearly has links with the green man. It lay at 'the core of Celtic religion ... a kind of shorthand symbol for the religious outlook of the pagan Celts'.[48] It was 'the soul, the centre of the emotions as well as of life itself, a symbol of divinity and of the powers of the other world'.[49] This was exemplified in the head-hunting proclivities of the pre-Roman Celts as well as in similar activities among primitive peoples in more recent times. The use of the head was probably thought of as a means of warding off evil, and its benign appearance on baptismal fonts, together with some reptilian creature, may represent the victory of good over evil through the sacrament of baptism, as demonstrated by the carved monsters.

In more recent times the face-mask has reappeared in pottery. In the later Middle Ages jugs with anthropomorphic decoration again spread through parts of eastern

11.8 A Bellarmine jar (a derisive name derived from Cardinal Bellarmine of the late sixteenth century) from Suffolk; after *Proc Suff Inst Arch*, 30 (1967), 88–93.

England.[50] A century or so later the so-called Bellarmine jar (Fig. 11.8)[51] appeared, a tall-necked jar of coarse ware, with a bearded face either imprinted in the clay or as an appliqué affixed like a medallion to it. They are said to have been of Rhenish origin,[52] but were imitated in England. A number of such jugs of seventeenth century date has been reported from Suffolk,[53] and several have been found in the course of excavations in the city of London. The fact that they were called 'witch-bottles' in Suffolk and elsewhere is evidence that they were assumed to have magical powers. In fact, it was held that they could be used to entrap and hold 'familiars' and spirits,[54] and it was presumably for this purpose that they were sometimes buried beneath the threshold of a house. Bellarmine jars passed out of use in the eighteenth century, to be replaced by the 'toby' jug, which continues to have its devotees today, though it is difficult to cite any reason, other than atavism, for its popularity in recent years.

The green man

The green or wild man was a syncretic figure who appeared early in the Middle Ages, and survives today in inn signs and popular folklore. 'Medieval literature and art are shot through with the mythology of the wild man.'[55] He is usually represented as covered with hair and often with animal features such as hoofs and occasionally

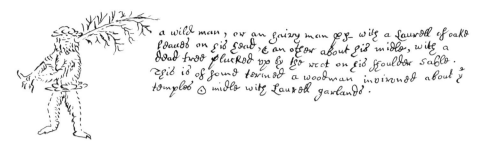

a wild man, or an gairy man or wilg a laurell of oakd leaues on gis head, & an other about gis midle, with a dead tree plucked up by tho root on gis ffoulder sable. This is of some termed a woodman invironed about y temples o midle with laurell garlandd.

11.9 Drawing of a wodewose, of about 1600, copied from BL Harl. 2027.

horns (Fig. 11.9). He is alternately seen as kindly and sinister, as wise and stupid, as an embodiment of freedom and strength and as cowardly and cunning. These contrasts in themselves indicate the breadth of the traditions that have been conflated to produce the syncretic green man. But above all the green man, or 'wodewose' responds 'to a persistent psychological urge . . . to give external expression and symbolically valid form to the impulses of reckless self-assertion which are hidden in all of us . . . projected outward as the image of a man who is as free as the beasts, able and ready to try his strength without regard . . . and therefore able to call up forces which his civilized brother has repressed'.[56] He was both the Tarzan and the Rambo of his times. The poem *Sir Gawayne and the Greene Knight* mentions 'the wodwose that woned [dwelt] in the knarrez [rocks]'. In the Bible wildness, sometimes associated with the accursed, was identified with the wandering life of the hunter, the Nimrod, the outcast, the Ishmaelite.

The green man served yet another purpose, elucidated by Hayden White.[57] He appears to have been used as a negative statement of the values accepted by society. People could not define culture, morality, civilisation, but they could say what it was not. The wild man was thus a figure antithetical to accepted standards, but neverthess one to whom people would on occasion long to revert. He epitomised 'man's uneasiness in his civilization'.[58] It was probably in this sense that the green man became an inn sign. A manuscript of the early eighteenth century spoke of 'woudmen . . . covered with grene boues . . . used as signes by the stillers of strong waters . . . a fit emblem for those that use intosticating lickers which berefts them of their sennes'.[59]

The wodewose appeared prominently in art, especially in East Anglia, where it sometimes served to decorate the stems of late medieval fonts[60] and other places that seemed to call for this kind of adornment.[61] The wodewose, often wielding a cudgel, also appeared in heraldry. Any myth has social importance if it lies at the core of a ritual or cult. In some parts of Europe there was once a ritual hunt for the wild man, sometimes formalised as a dance or 'charivari'. In England the wild man occasionally appeared as a bear or as a dancer in animal disguise. As such the wild man ritual has survived into modern times. At a Twelfth Night entertainment staged for Henry VIII 'eight wyldmen, all apparyled in green mosse with sleved sylke, with ugly weapons and terrible visages ... there foughte with eight knyghtes'.[62] This was perhaps conceived as a contest between good and evil. It is evident that the universality of the green man derives largely from the fact that he can be interpreted at so many levels.

The Tree of Life

The Tree of Life is, as a symbol, probably older and certainly more widespread than the green man. A tree has served as the focus of a cult from the earliest times of which there is record.[63] In the Book of Revelation the Tree of Life grew and bore 'twelve manner of fruits, and yielded her fruits every month, and the leaves of the tree were for the healing of nations'.[64] In the Middle East the symbol of the tree goes very much further back than this. The Jewish *menorah*, or seven-branched candlestick, derived from a tree; a tree in the Garden of Eden bore the fruit of the knowledge of good and evil. And in Norse folklore the cosmic tree marked the point of creation, the ultimate source of reality.[65] The Elder Edda, a Scandinavian poem, probably of the tenth century, tells of the:

> ... nine worlds, nine spheres covered by the tree of the world,
> That tree was set up in wisdom which grows down to the bosom of the earth.
> An Ash I know, Yggdrasil its name,
> With water white is the great tree wet;
> Thence come its dews that fall in the dales,
> Green by Urd's well does it ever grow.[66]

The tree thus lay at the origin of creation, because it was the supreme symbol of life. It put on leaves in spring, a new birth resulting from the marriage – *hieros gamos* – of the Earth Mother with the god of vegetation.[67] In classical Rome the spring festival was marked by the cutting and decoration of a tree. In Britain, a tree, stripped of its branches and adorned with greenery, was set up, while the community, or at least those young and vigorous enough, danced around it. The maypole must be one of the oldest, if not *the* oldest, of all rituals that have survived into modern times. Its significance was wholly antithetical to Christianity, though it was tolerated until after the Reformation.[68] Its revival in Victorian times was merely a piece of antiquarianism, totally devoid of any inner significance. An Elizabethan divine described how the young about the time of Whitsun resorted to the woods, 'where they spend all the night in pleasant pastimes', emerging in the morning with branches, greenery, and, above all, the great maypole: 'this stinkyng ydol', wrote Stubbes, around which they 'fall to daunce ... like as the heathen people did at the dedication of Idols, whereof this is a perfect pattern, or rather the thing itself'.[69] It is, indeed, surprising that the May rituals were able to survive, even in an emasculated form, the attacks made on them by the Puritans.

In medieval iconography the tree is represented as a source of life, whose fruit is able to restore all things (Fig. 11.10).[70] This is in line with the passage from

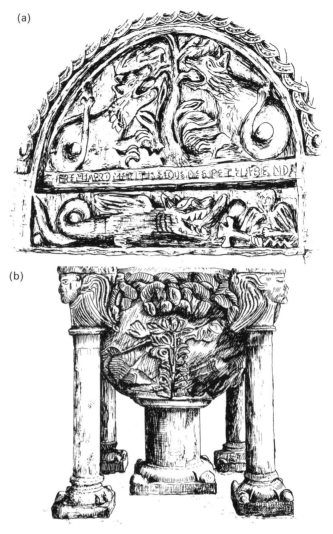

11.10 The Tree of Life, the concept of which long antedates the Book of Revelation. The Tree is sometimes shown guarded by lions. In (a) two animals are shown eating its fruit; below, St Michael is seen overcoming the dragon. In (b) the Tree of Life is carved on the bowl of a baptismal font at Bodmin (Corn.) to represent the new life that is conferred by baptism. The significance of the rope-like figure above is not clear; it is not uncommon on early West Country fonts.

Revelations already quoted, but the tree also appears in the same context in the Edda.[71] In countless churches the Tree of Life stands in low relief, most often above the main entrance. In this location it may be said to symbolise the life-giving powers of the church itself. But, suggestive of its origins in the Cosmic Tree, it is sometimes shown guarded by lions, creatures supposed never to close their eyes, and surrounded by a wall as if in a garden.[72]

400

11.11 The Tree of Jesse, which grew from the body of Jesse and bore, as its fruit, David, Solomon and eventually Christ. Here the 'Tree' is used to decorate the tomb of Bishop Alexander of Lincoln, from an engraving in J. Carter, *Specimens of Ancient Sculpture and Painting*, 1780, pl. 45. The slab still exists, but is too damaged for its detail to be recognisable.

A peculiar aspect of the tree, of Christian origin, though related to the Tree of Life, was the Jesse Tree. It showed the recumbent figure of Jesse with, issuing from it, a tree or vine which bore its fruits in the shape of the descendants of Jesse as far as Christ himself. It lent itself to pictorial representation, and was sometimes shown, as at Dorchester (Oxon.), by a combination of sculpture and stained glass. In one quite exceptional example the tree is depicted on a tomb slab, supposed to be that of Bishop Alexander of Lincoln (d. 1148) (Fig. 11.11).

Related in some way both to the severed head and the Tree of Life and perhaps also to the green man, is the so-called 'foliate' head (Fig. 11.7). A face, sometimes grimacing, usually menacing, is shown with foliage spewing from its mouth.[74] The eyes are usually large, with deep holes for pupils. At Kilpeck (Hereford.), notable for the abundance of its Romanesque sculpture of this kind, two strands of foliage issue from the mouth to terminate in serpents' heads.[75] The 'foliate' head is to be found from the Balkans to Wales, and one might be tempted to suppose that the motif itself had been spread by the Iron Age Celts. It is probably yet another of the many forms assumed by the severed head, while the foliage suggests some form of fertility symbol.

Rites of passage

All societies classify their members according to age and profession. Passage from one to another is accompanied by ceremonies which mark symbolically the change in status. These may be over within a few minutes or they may last for weeks. Some begin with a formal abjuration of the old status and end with the acceptance of the new. For the nobleman assuming the order of knighthood, the layman taking religious orders, the novice entering a monastic community, or the craftsman as he was admitted to his 'mystery', there were appropriate ceremonies. But all such rites paled in importance before the rites of passage by which each individual came into the world and was baptised into the Christian church, was betrothed and married and, in the end, died and was buried. Most such rites had a religious element, since 'to the semi-civilized mind no act is entirely free from the sacred'.[76]

For the lay population of the Christian West three such rites assumed overwhelming importance: baptism, marriage and burial. In the early church baptism followed conversion, and was itself followed immediately by confirmation and communion.[77] As Europe became predominantly Christian and the process of conversion neared its end, so baptism ceased to be an adult ritual and was administered to children and, indeed, to the very young. In the early church it was usually performed at Easter or Whitsun, but the laws of Ine of the West Saxons (c.690) required it to be performed within a month of birth, and this became the normal practice in Britain. The rite of baptism was necessarily detached from those of confirmation and communion, since the child was too young to understand the one or to accept the consecrated elements of the other. Baptism thus became the initial rite of passage by which the child entered the community of Christian souls.

Its performance was mandatory, and was so important that in an emergency it could be performed anywhere and by almost anyone. Baptism by a midwife was specifically authorised. The manual for priests, written by John Mirk in the fifteenth century, described the lengths to which a priest should go to ensure that the child received this prerequisite for salvation (p. 251).

'Every primitive society possesses a consistent body of mythical traditions, a "conception of the world",' wrote Mircea Eliade, 'and it is this conception that is gradually revealed to the novice in the course of his initiation.'[78] The rite of confirmation, or the 'laying on of hands', marked the full admission of a young person to the mysteries of the church. It was the spiritual equivalent of achieving adulthood, even though the age at confirmation might be 10 or even earlier.[79] It must be regarded as a puberty rite, analogous to the Jewish bar mitzvah, and to the more barbarous practices of some primitive peoples today. It was a 'rebirth' by which the novice became a totally different being. For that reason confirmation in Catholic Europe was often accompanied by formal eating and the wearing of ceremonial dress.

Marriage has always been, in its ritual and ceremony, the most lavish of all rites of passage, and has been hemmed in by more restrictions and taboos that almost any other. Its overriding purpose has always been procreation, and the conditions that have surrounded it have been intended to ensure that the children who might be born of a particular marriage would be adequately supported and safeguarded. For this reason extramarital intercourse and prostitution were frowned upon, though both church and society were powerless, and perhaps unwilling, to prohibit them entirely.[80]

In Britain marriage has tended in general to be consensual, that is with both parties freely consenting. It follows that clandestine marriages were acceptable. In fact, the only customary barrier to marriage was consanguinity, and this, as expressed in the later Table of Kindred and Affinity, extended far more widely than strict biological requirements made desirable. It was, for example, wrong for a man to marry his godmother or god-daughter: 'spiritual affinity' it was called. It was never difficult, among the interlocking affinities of a medieval or early modern community, to find grounds for annulling a marriage on grounds of consanguinity. Traditional peoples have always shown a great fear of incest, and folklore contains countless stories of how couples were saved from its dreaded consequences only by the last-minute discovery of a hitherto unknown affinity.[81]

There is no reason to doubt that most marriages, except amongst the landowning classes, were based on mutual attraction and that they were preceded by a more or less long period of courtship, since the man may have had to wait until his apprenticeship was completed or he had inherited or acquired a holding on which to live and support a wife and probable family. Delayed marriage contributed without question to premarital sex and even to illegitimate births, but their frequency is very difficult to quantify before the registration of baptisms and marriages was required in 1538. Analysis of the registers has shown that, although illegitimate births may not have been frequent, the number of bridal pregnancies was very considerable indeed (p. 315).[82]

Both church law and manorial custom frowned on such practices, but were powerless to restrain them. Lust was one of the seven deadly sins represented in painting or sculpture in most parish churches to deter the young,[83] but it was one which the church courts were more likely to condone than any of the others. On many manors it was the custom to exact a fine for premarital sex, if it could be discovered, as well as for illegitimate births, but the irregularity of payments suggests that local 'law' was rarely enforced with any rigour. Indeed, it might be said that premarital sex was condoned, and even encouraged, by village customs. There were even gilds of young men and young women which only 'institutionalized flirtatious behaviour', as at Croscombe (Som.).[84] Young people were frequently 'presented' before the church courts for adultery, but the most severe penalty which they could expect was excommunication. In theory, the 'greater' excommunication meant the loss of civil rights, but this was very rarely enforced. In 1570 the Bishop of St David's complained that two hundred persons had been excommunicated, but that the sheriff had refused to execute the writs against them.[85] At most a culprit might be obliged to do penance by standing in the parish church during service, clad only in a white sheet and reciting his or her sins before the congregation.

The licence which characterised carnival, whether on the occasion of Mayday festivities or harvest or pre-Lent celebrations, frequently encouraged sexual activity. Baptismal registers suggest, if we may assume the lapse of not more than a month between birth and baptism, a relatively large number of conceptions in late spring. It would, however, be rash to associate this too closely with the unbridled licence of carnival.

Free as most young people were to marry whom they wished, there were nevertheless constraints on this liberty. If we ignore the occasional marriage of minors for family or dynastic reasons, we still have evidence for a considerable number of marriages of convenience. We cannot really believe that love played any significant role in the marriage of a young man, barely out of his teens, to an ageing widow, endowed with a substantial holding.[86] The practice of family reconstitution is showing how numerous were second and even third marriages, and in a great many of them the marriage bed must have been baited with a not inconsiderable inheritance.[87]

Marriage itself was normally preceded by betrothal, the latter commonly accompanied by celebration and the exchange of gifts. The period between betrothal and marriage, between the initiation and the completion of this particular rite of passage, might have been of only a few weeks' duration or it could have lasted many months or even years. It was a grey area, and what happened in it was apt to depend on local custom. In some areas the couple would live together, or at least have intercourse. This practice might to some extent be excused by the fact that between the beginning of Advent in late November and Easter there was only a very short period when the church allowed the marriage ceremony to be performed.

Furthermore, in this rough age, when children were a necessity, premarital conception was deliberately intended; the actual marriage was not the shotgun affair that it is often represented to have been.

Marriage, like most other rites of passage, was a very public act, and the church took what steps it could to keep it so. But the fact that it was a consensual act, depending on the consent of the two parties and not on the will of an extended family, meant that it could in fact be clandestine. The church did not altogether approve, but had as a general rule to recognise the validity of such marriages (p. 313). Marriage thus consisted under normal circumstances of two parts, which marked respectively the beginning and the end of this particular rite of passage. Betrothal was a contract, accompanied by the exchange of gifts of which today's engagement ring is almost the sole survival. This contract could be broken, but 'betrothal followed by intercourse became marriage' in the eyes of the church.[88] Custom, however, varied, and the interpretation of canon law by the archdeacon's court was far from consistent.

The wedding itself was preceded by the public announcement of the forthcoming marriage. 'Banns' were called in much the same way as they are today, usually by the parish priest on three successive Sundays. Their purpose was to discover whether there was any impediment to the marriage in canon law. Any objection would have been based, in all probability, on alleged consanguinity or affinity or on some pre-existing marriage contract. The publication of a forthcoming marriage was required by a canon of the Fourth Lateran Council (1216), but it appears to have been practised in Britain before this date. The alternative was marriage by licence of the bishop, but this was expensive and was resorted to only by the rich. That many married or were thought to have married without either banns or licence is apparent from Visitation and Consistory Court records. At Sonning (Berks.) a couple were married 'at night without banns or licence',[89] but it does not appear from the record that anything was or could be done about it. It might have been supposed that in the open society of a medieval village any obstacle to marriage would have been quickly uncovered. On many occasions, however, this was not so, as is demonstrated in the proceedings of the bishop's consistory. Some, who sensed that objections would be raised, might move to another parish where, they hoped, their past would not catch up with them. The proceedings of the bishops' courts are a fertile source of information on breaches of marital custom.

The formal marriage took place at the church door, usually in the shelter of the porch. The couple then publicly accepted each other; the bride was given to her husband usually by her father, and finally the wedding party entered the church for the nuptial mass. The marriage itself was both a civil contract, performed 'at the churchdoor'[90] 'and a sacrament given by the couple to each other', a rite of passage assimilated rather awkwardly into the church's system of ceremonies and sacraments. The couple were then expected to live together, since failure to do so would negate the primary purpose of marriage. The practice was for a parish official, usually a churchwarden, to inform the ecclesiastical authorities of any breach of church discipline in this regard, and the records of the bishops' courts contain not infrequent instances of marriage partners failing to cohabit, and being censured by the church court. In the course of an archdeacon's visitation of Buckinghamshire, then part of the diocese of Lincoln, Elizabeth Burridge and Grace Oviatts were reported for 'absentynge themselves [from church] and not livinge with theire husbandes'. Subsequent enquiry showed that their husbands were day-labourers who worked at a distance and were able to return to their wives only infrequently. The case demonstrates, however, how seriously both church and popular opinion regarded a failure to cohibit.[91] Childbirth was expected to follow marriage within a short period of time, since procreation was its primary purpose. There were few raised eyebrows within the community if the first child came well within nine months of marriage.

Death was the last of the rites of passage, and was for most people preceded by a period when the body was too weak to sustain the rigours of daily labour. All societies have had to face the problem of supporting the aged and sick, whose cost to the community greatly exceeded any input that they might make, and they solved it in many ways. There was no direct provision for the sick and aged before the later Middle Ages, when 'hospitals' for specific categories of people were first established. In traditional societies the aged most often lived with and were dependent upon their children and grandchildren. Manor court rolls and wills are explicit on the ways in which the aged were provided for (p. 323). Loneliness, in consequence, seems to have been much less of a problem in traditional societies than it is today.[92]

Death came from many causes. Accidents were, on the evidence of the coroners' rolls, more frequent than today, and epidemic diseases more common, but most people must have succumbed to lingering illnesses which allowed those whose wealth justified it to make their last will and testament. Death from supposedly 'natural' causes called for no explanation. It was in accordance with the divinely appointed scheme of things, but accidental death lay outside the divine order. Crudely put, it had to be the work of evil forces and had to be dealt with as such. In fact, the practice developed of punishing the instrument of death, which was 'given to God'. The coroners' rolls are full of such cases. The common formula was, after stating the nature of the accident, to put a value on the offending article: ladder, cartwheel, boat, or whatever may have been the cause of death. This sum was then forfeit to the court. The Wiltshire Eyre of 1249 records the payment of no less than twenty-four deodands, but nowhere is there any record of a charitable purpose to which the money might have been put.[93]

Not until wills became numerous in the later fifteenth century and churchwardens began to keep accounts can one be sure of the events which surrounded the last rites of the deceased. Burial was not a sacrament. The last sacrament for the living was extreme unction, which in some form had been authorised from the early days of the church. It marked the beginning of the final rite of passage, which ended with interment, accompanied by the office for the dead or Dirge.[94] The only sacramental element in the burial was the requiem mass which was said after the burial, and generally had to be paid for. One suspects that in the case of the poor it was often omitted. Parish gilds sometimes made financial provision for the last rites of their members. A Suffolk gild, for example, paid 'ffor dyrge and messe ... 4d.'[95] A wealthy Londoner in 1408 required that his funeral be accompanied 'wyth Belle Ryngyng, derge ... & Masse of requiem', but still left only four pence to pay for it.[96] Burial was normally in the consecrated ground of the parochial cemetery. Churches of less than parochial standing were not, as a general rule, accorded rights of burial. In Christian burials feet were placed towards the east, and a lack of regularity in this respect may help to distinguish Christian cemeteries from pagan. The body was placed directly in the soil, covered at most with a winding sheet or shroud, which was required for a period in the seventeenth and eighteenth centuries to be of woollen cloth (p. 225). Most external graves went unmarked before the late seventeenth century, so that those dug later would inevitably cut though earlier burials.[97]

The cost of churchyard burial remained fairly small in traditional societies. Interment within a church was more expensive: deliberately so, because at the parochial level it was a means of raising money. In some churches a chantry chapel, either an adjunct to the church or a screened-off portion of an aisle, served as burial place for members of any pre-eminent local family. They had, however, to pay dearly for the privilege. Less distinguished members of the community might be buried almost anywhere within nave or aisles, the spot being marked by a monumental or inscribed slab.

The last rites did not end with interment. Church doctrine, as it evolved during the Middle Ages, held that the soul required every assistance possible on its path to paradise, and what could serve better than masses sung on its behalf? But masses were expensive: the going rate for a trental – a daily mass for a month – was 10s. and 5s. for a half-trental. The rich made provision for trentals by the score, as well as for 'obits' on the anniversary of their death.[98] How the poor were expected to fare we do not know; they left no wills.

Time and space

Traditional peoples had only a limited perception of time and space. The time with which they were familiar was the present, and their minds reached back only to their childhood. Of the vast span of time that had gone before they had heard only vague rumours, and these they conflated with stories of creation, of giants and of mythical heroes. Their concept of history was of creation by a supernatural being, of the coming of a creative hero, a kind of demiurge. Today most people consider themselves historical beings, the products both physically and culturally of a long evolutionary process which will continue long after they are dead. By contrast, primitive man saw himself as a 'product of a mythical history ... of a series of events that took place *in illo tempore*, at the beginning of Time ... for the man of traditional societies everything [was] significant, that is, everything creative and powerful ...

took place in the beginning, in the Time of Myths.' For him history was closed: 'traditional societies have no historical memory in the strict sense. It took only a few generations ... for a recent innovation to be invested with all the prestige of the primordial revelations.'[99] As it is now, so it has always been, and so it will continue. The painters of the Renaissance portrayed biblical persons and landscapes as they would those they encountered every day in their native Italy, and, despite superficial changes taking place before their eyes, they would have assumed that there would be no fundamental difference until the end of time. The man who required by his will that his family portraits should continue to hang in his hall *for ever* clearly conceived of time and change in this way (p. 327). God created the world, and, in his own judgment of his own handiwork, found that it was good. It would therefore have been an impertinence, if not outright blasphemy, to assume that it could be improved upon, that there could be material progress.

Yet in another sense, traditional people were well aware of time and change. They grew old; buildings decayed; crops were sown, grew and were harvested. And if these changes seemed to them to be immeasurably slow, they had other measures of the passage of time. Time was articulated by the feasts and festivals which punctuated their year and also their lives. Each such event marked the end, the 'death' of one epoch and the 'birth' of another. That was their function, to mark a fresh beginning in the cycle of time.[100] If a person had to answer the question 'when?' he could reply only by reference to one of the 'high' times which had marked the stages in the year or in his own life. Of the progress of sidereal time he could have had little conception, and the succession of the months was made memorable only by the kinds of work that were associated with them. That is why the 'Labours of the Months' came to be represented in almost every art form of the Middle Ages.[101]

There could therefore be no concept of progress, no idea of human betterment or of technological advance. Of course, human beings rose and fell in the scale of status and wealth. The 'wheel of fortune' was one of the commonest moralities to adorn the walls of homes and churches, but changes in fortune had a local and immediate cause, and as one person fell another rose on the wheel as it turned. Change in human attitudes comes very slowly; there has never been a sudden revolution or breakthrough in people's view of the world. And it is this very attitude to change, this denial that there could be an underlying, deep-seated movement towards human betterment, that has helped to obscure the fact that there was indeed such material progress.

But progress was by infinitely small increments, so that people without a sense of history would have been quite unaware of it. In every material sense change came first with the élite and progressed slowly down the social scale. A work like the *Vision of Piers the Plowman* displays no historical sense; everything occurs in the present. The roughly contemporary *Canterbury Tales*, emanating from and appealing to a higher social class, clearly relates to a perceived past, even though historical characters are not wholly divorced from mythical.

A sense of history cannot be separated from literacy, and traditional societies were, by and large, pre-literate. Records in the shape of chronicles and cartularies had been kept from late Saxon times, but these were maintained by the literate for the élite. They would have been inaccessible and unintelligible to the mass of the population. It is a curious fact that, when the latter began to approach the reality of history, they did so through genealogy. Not only did they sense the past through the inferred existence of their ancestors; they relied on genealogy to define their kinship groups. In so far as time was thought of at all, it was conceived in terms of generations. Biblical history is in part a record of generations, of who begot whom, and it is the same with the early Welsh and Irish annals. How ordinary people felt about the past is revealed in the inquests ordered by the king whenever a tenant-in-chief died, leaving an heir who might be under age. If he was, then the king enjoyed the custody and profits of his land until he had attained his majority. A correct historical record was a matter of some pecuniary importance to him. How old was the heir? No one in the community knew for certain, and his age had to be inferred from casual incidents. 'I remember', said one witness, 'seeing him taken out of the font at his baptism; I was then doing this or that,' and so, by the association of ideas and events, an age was arrived at. Even as late as the nineteenth century there were countless people who, like the heir to a lordship, had no precise knowledge of their own age.[102]

Real history, as it filtered down to the illiterate masses by way of legend, hearsay and chapbooks, was merely a compilation of names and heroic deeds, and for all too many even today it is little more. Thomas Hardy's rustics, ruminating on great and imponderable events in their far from remote and backward Wessex, could conflate history, myth and legend with no sense whatever of time.

Conceptions of space were but little more evolved than those of time. Distance is always relative, measured not in miles but in time and difficulty and a vague sense of whether that which lies at the end of the journey is desirable or otherwise. 'These high wild hills and rough uneven ways', wrote Shakespeare of the gentle Cotswolds, 'draws out our miles and makes them wearisome.' How far afield did villagers go for a marriage partner, and in which directions did they look? That they were influenced by their perception of distance and difficulty is apparent. But there was always an element of irrationality, which can be illustrated by an example from France. The inhabitants of Minot, near Châtillon (Côte d'Or) would not have marital dealings any further afield that Moitron 2 miles distant (about 4.5 km): 'from the direction of Moitron came neither good winds [the cold north-easters] nor good people'.[103]

People may have travelled further in traditional societies than is commonly supposed, but their mental horizon was nevertheless narrow. Life centred in their community and parish, and for most people the journey to the nearest market town – probably no more than 10 miles (15 km) distant – was the longest they would be likely to make. People travelled only when they had good reason, and for most people there was little purpose. The upper classes took part in military campaigns and crusades, and went on pilgrimage. But these occupied in the main only those social classes portrayed in Chaucer's *Canterbury Tales*. None of them could be said ever to have ventured into really new and unfamiliar territory, with the exception of the knight, who boasted that:

> At Alisandre he was, whan it was wonne;
> Ful oft tyme he hadde the bord bigonne
> Aboven alle naciouns in Pruce [Prussia].
> In Lettow [Lithuania] hadde he reysed and in Ruce [Russia].[104]

But Chaucer regarded him as far more worldly-wise than the rest of his company, and one can only guess the tales, like those of Sir John Mandeville, that he might have told. There would have been no one to question him. Traditional peoples were familiar only with the 'here and now'. Remote places, like distant times, had no real existence to them. Both were, in a sense, mythical. Their existence was not disputed, but they were peopled with creatures outside their experience. Past times and remote places converged in the unknown lands beyond the horizon.

The mental horizon of all people was being slowly extended during the later Middle Ages and early modern times, in part by the tales of travellers, in part, from the time of the Renaissance onwards, by the appearance of printed books and, above all, of printed maps.[105] As knowledge of the world increased and percolated downwards from the élite to the masses, so the lands inhabited by mythical creatures and people 'whose heads do grow beneath their shoulders' contracted, and popular acceptance of these beasts evaporated for lack of space in which to put them.

There was thus a broadening of conceptual space, of that area of which there was direct or vicarious experience. At the same time there was, in certain respects, a narrowing of the behavioural horizon, of the sphere within which there was social contact and intercourse. This went with a strengthening of what Redford has called the 'little community', and some attempt to sever its links with the 'greater community'.[106] The divisions that arose within a parish may serve as an example. When parishes were first established and their churches built, in the eleventh or twelfth centuries, their parishioners were often obliged to make the sometimes arduous and dangerous journey to the parish church to baptise their infants, bury their dead and discharge their own spiritual obligations. In the course of time many of those who lived a long way from the parish church sought to reduce the burden by petitioning their bishop for permission to have a chapel of their own. The reasons which they advanced, specious though they often were, nevertheless demonstrate a perception of distance, and this perception is related to possessing the means to overcome it (p. 276).[107]

'Culture des élites: culture populaire'[108]

With the withdrawal of Roman authority from Britain, the thin veneer of classical culture was dissipated. It had always been fragile, and below its surface a popular culture had subsisted since the pre-Roman Iron Age. The gods of Rome now disappeared; the cult of the deified emperor vanished, and with it the artificial culture of villa, basilica and forum. Roman material culture was more than a backward economy could support or the Celtic populace felt any need for. The use of the hypocaust of a Roman villa as a ready-made grave for the dead illustrates the reversal of cultural values that took place in the fifth and following centuries. Classical culture, it has been said, yielded to barbarism. It would be truer to say that what remained of the *culture des élites* was overwhelmed by the *culture populaire* of the Celtic Britons and, a century or so later, of the invading Anglo-Saxons.

The expression 'élite culture' is used here for that superficial rationalism which derived from the classical civilisations. It was predicated on the concept of an orderly world, proceeding according to its own 'laws', or at least in known or predictable ways. But its triumph had never been complete, not even in the heartlands of classical civilisations. Human nature, even here, demanded some escape from the real world, like the irrationality of 'carnival'. It showed itself in the Saturnalia, the Lupercalia and the savage spectacles in the arena. Everywhere a popular culture lurked beneath the glitz and gloss of classicism, rising to the surface whenever control was relaxed. In Britain control was not merely relaxed; it disappeared.

Thomas Hobbes has reminded us that the Papacy and the Christian church were but 'the ghost of the deceased Roman Empire, sitting crowned upon the grave thereof'.[109] In Italy the institutions of the Empire, both economic and administrative, survived in some rudimentary form. In particular, there was a general propensity to accept the idea of 'empire', of universal rule, and this assumed institutional form first in the Papacy and later in the Holy Roman Empire. It was the Papacy that recaptured and recolonised western Europe for Rome. It created and diffused a new élite, an élite of priests and monks, of scholars and administrators. The cities of this new culture were the cathedrals and palaces of the bishops, and its villas were monastic cloisters from which its values in increasingly attenuated form reached down to the local level in the ministrations of the parish priest. Of course, the parallel between the culture of the Roman élite and that of the medieval church was never complete, because the circumstances of time and place were different. But it can, at least, be claimed that the Roman church reintroduced to Britain some of the values of the secular civilisation of Rome.

It has always been the role of an élite to set standards in conduct and in art, and in the material things of life, like housing and furnishing, clothing, hygiene and sanitation. This the medieval church succeeeded in doing, but in creating an élite based on religious belief the church came inevitably into contact with the culture of the masses. It was an uneasy relationship. Popular culture could absorb and assimilate some aspects of élite culture, but the popular world-view which emerged 'from the complex and contradictory interaction of the reservoir of traditional culture and Christianity'[110] stood in strong opposition to the official teachings of the church and the attitudes of the élite. In fact, however, their reconciliation was aided by their common acceptance of the dualism of nature and of the supernatural. Evangelisation, furthermore, demanded an effort on the part of the church to understand the language and thought patterns of popular culture. In this way the church succeeded in intruding into the structure of popular culture. [111] In the words of Aelfric (*c.*1000): 'we should not set our hope in medicinal herbs [i.e. as charms or prophylactics], but in the Almighty Creator who has given that virtue to those herbs. No one shall enchant a herb with magic, but with God's word shall bless it, and so eat it.'[112] Aelfric might have drawn a distinction between God's magic and that of men, but to most people they were the same, and acceptance of each was equally easy. The dialectic of the two cultures was worked out over the next thousand years. Despite its reputation for rigidity, the Catholic church showed a marked tendency to compromise: to absorb elements of popular culture, to canonise its heroes and to make use of its motifs and symbols, its carnival and make-believe. The Catholic church of the later Middle Ages thus came to be overlaid with pagan symbolism; its festivals were but a Christian gloss upon pre-Christian rites.[113] Deep-seated human attitudes cannot easily be changed, and the church, in its wisdom, made no sustained effort to do so. We are in fact dealing in the later Middle Ages with a world 'superficiellement christianisée, mais fondamentalement magique'.[114]

A kind of synthesis was thus achieved during the Middle Ages between popular culture and certain elements of the élite culture of the church. But it was far from complete: the church never ceased to denounce many popular customs, though in practice it condoned, through its parochial clergy, their continued use. Most parish priests, it must be remembered, had themselves sprung from the ranks of the peasantry, and would have been not unsympathetic to popular magic and ritual. The gulf was perhaps greater between the secular culture of the aristocracy and gentry on the one hand and of the peasantry on the other. The division was here rather one of wealth, education and upbringing than of tradition and belief, and it related more to material than to non-material culture, to fittings and furnishings, to literature and to the comforts and conveniences of life. Here there was no intellectual gulf that could not have been overcome, and there were few aspects of material culture that the popular classes would not have adopted if they had had the opportunity.

In the course of the sixteenth and following centuries the cultural synthesis which had been achieved was faced with a new challenge. It came both from the Protestant sects and from the reformed and revivified Catholic church that emerged from the long deliberations of the Council of Trent. The new challenge to popular culture was authoritarian and conformist. The Protestant sects were fundamentalist, in so far as their tenets were derived from a text, the Bible, whose literal truth and validity was undisputed. That the Bible became familiar to them was due entirely to the introduction of printing and the increase in literacy; there could be no fundamentalism without the printed word.[115] The newly streamlined Catholic church, for its part, was more rigid in its doctrine than the medieval church had been. It achieved 'a system of parochial conformity similar in character to that which the contemproary Church of England was seeking to impose, though more comprehensive in its detail'.[116] There was no room in either the Protestant or the Catholic scheme of thought for medieval attitudes to kinship groups, family and marriage, nor for the spirit of carnival and play, for the green man, erotic symbolism, and all the calendar customs which had characterised life in pre-Reformation Europe.

It was as if a cloud had descended on the popular culture of Europe, with dogmatism replacing the relative tolerance of the Middle Ages. Authoritarianism in the churches paralleled the concentration of power in the state. The gravest threat to the freedom of the individual and to his right to live his traditional life was the coalescence of spiritual authority with the secular arm of the state, the latter using its coercive power to support and enforce the demands of the former. This is what happened in Spain and in other parts of Catholic Europe. In Germany the adoption in the Treaty of Augsburg, 1555, of the principle that the prince should dictate the religion of his subjects, brought about a not dissimilar situation. And in England and Wales, after the abrupt changes of the middle years of the sixteenth century, the episcopal church became the national church, and the monarch assumed the title of 'Defender of the Faith'. Parliament enacted laws regarding church attendance and the acceptance of the religious beliefs of the established church. There were church courts in every diocese, presided over by the archdeacon or by his deputy, to oversee matters of faith and morals, as well as testamentary affairs. But it is typical of that English ability to compromise, to refrain from pushing matters to an extreme, that the religious courts had no teeth. They could not compel attendance; the most severe penalty they could impose was penance, and above all they found it impossible to turn to the secular arm of the state to enforce their judgments. Nevertheless, there were occasions when lay officials thought it necessary to act with vigour. But these were, in the main, when their pockets and those of their parishioners were touched. They frowned on fornication and adultery and punished severely the parents of an illegitimate child.[117] Bastards, after all, were likely to become a financial liability to the parish.

On the other hand, the Puritans did succeed in eliminating many aspects of popular culture. They put an end to carnival and churchales, and made it difficult to celebrate the coming of May and the lighting of midsummer fires. But what they could not destroy was the *mentalité* which underlay these activities, the urge to escape from reality, to spurn authority, at least temporarily, and to reverse the roles played in ordinary life. For a time these activities had assumed an overtly religious expression. Episcopacy was mimicked and ridiculed; the rich and powerful were, in imagination at least, 'levelled' down to the lowest. 'I am confident', wrote Richard Overton, a Leveller, 'that it must be the poor, the simple and the mean things of this earth that must confound the mighty and strong.'[118] The 'Lord of Misrule' could not have put it more succinctly.

The Restoration of the monarchy in 1660 marked the end of Puritan dominance and the resurgence of the kind of licence that had prevailed under the Tudors. The older institutions did not return, but the attitudes of mind that had given rise to carnival were still present and manifested themselves in masquerade. This was an entertainment in which 'one was obliged to impersonate a being opposite, in some essential feature, to oneself ... women changing into men, and men into women ...

ladies of the night into saints, people of the first quality into beasts or birds, gods or goddesses'.[119] Masquerade reached its apogee in the eighteenth century, and declined during the nineteenth, but never wholly disappeared. It survives in the 'fancy-dress' entertainments of today. The pleasure of the masquerade resulted from 'the experience of doubleness ... [the] fantasy of two bodies simultaneously and thrillingly present, self and other together, the two-in-one',[120] the reconciliation of opposites. The decline of the masquerade after the late eighteenth century may have been due in some measure to the licence, especially sexual, which it encouraged. It was out of tune with the moral concepts of the nineteenth century.

The previous chapters have described a material culture which had developed over the past two thousand years. There was change and improvement in housing, clothing, diet, health and in all the comforts and conveniences of life. These, almost without exception, were first devised or used within the culture of the élite. From the privileged classes they were passed down, like unwanted or worn-out clothes, to the classes below them, while the élite turned their attention to greater comforts and new conveniences as well as to fresh gimmicks and fads. This is no less true of house design than of water-closets and table cutlery. Always we find the culture of the masses limping along in the wake of that of the élite, adopting features of the latter only as they were simplified and, often enough, coarsened to fit their needs and their pockets. It is indeed rare to find any aspect of material culture that has progressed *up* the cultural ladder from the masses to the élite, though it can be claimed that certain foodstuffs have done so.[121]

At the same time there was change in mental attitudes, or *mentalités*, in the world-view held by people both high and low. Here change came more slowly because mental constructs, formed in childhood, are likely to stay with one for the rest of one's life. They are part of the social environment, from which total escape is almost impossible. At most they can be modified only from generation to generation. One tends to regard the peasantry, the principal bearer of popular culture in this sense, as essentially conservative and unwilling to change. In reality, however, culture was never stable; there was always a 'continuous interchange and diffusion of various cultural elements, devices, inventions and even institutions ... The constitutional conservatism of primitive peoples is a fiction.'[122] But change was, nevertheless, very slow. Inertia is a quality of mind rather than of things. But those who first entertained changes in their mental attitudes may not have been the same élite that adopted innovations in material culture. There was an élite of wealth as well as an intellectual élite. The two may have overlapped, but they were not, and never have been, the same. Indeed, there have been times when one almost senses a conflict between them. The mass of the population has always been quicker to adopt advances in the material sphere, since they eased the hardships of life, than to modify its mental constructs. Today, in an age of electronics and nuclear energy, one still reverts instinctively to the thoughts and symbolic acts of generations long past.

CHAPTER 12

CONCLUSION: THE END OF
TRADITIONAL CULTURE

> Modern man's originality, his newness in comparison with traditional societies, lies precisely in his determination to regard himself as a purely historical being, in his wish to live in a basically desacralized cosmos . . . his ideal no longer has anything in common with the Christian message, and ... it is equally foreign to the image of himself conceived by the man of the traditional societies.   Mircea Eliade, *Birth and Rebirth*

Traditional society merged into modern at some indeterminate period in the eighteenth and nineteenth centuries. One cannot be precise to the decade or even the century. It did not result from the Industrial Revolution, though the Industrial Revolution was part of the transition. It did not consist only of material innovations, numerous and important though these were. It was marked by a change in mental attitudes to society and to the world; in short, by cultural change in its most profound sense.[1]

This book has surveyed the ways in which popular culture in Britain has changed and developed during a period of more than two thousand years. This change has arisen from innovations which have been consciously adopted, used and diffused through at least some segment of society. Innovations have, very broadly, been of two kinds. First, there have been those which effected a fundamental change in the ways in which goods were made or people reacted to their environment. Each had long-term consequences, preparing the way for other innovations sometimes in very different fields. The removal of the central fire in the hall to a fireplace built against a wall is an example. So also, within the sphere of traditional culture, were the replacement of round huts by those of rectangular plan, the introduction of a bottom roller in the vertical loom, and the replacement of the distaff and spindle by the spinning-wheel.

The second form of innovation was of the nature of 'superfluous behaviour', discussed earlier (p. 268). It added to the amenities or niceties of life without significantly affecting total production or consumption. In so far as the decoration on a post, a carved jetty or dragon-post, or painted walls gave pleasure they added to the quality of life. They may have been – indeed they often were – ephemeral, and

.

415

were succeeded by other forms of decoration and display. They were not cumulative, like fundamental innovations, representing necessary stages in technological progress. Yet it is, in the main, by such 'superfluous' innovations that cultures can today be distinguished. In the course of time the relative importance of such superfluous things became greater, and their increase formed a significant element in the improvement in the quality of life which has been the dominant feature in the period of history covered by this book.

Innovation took place most often in the upper ranks of society. It involved risk-taking and, as a general rule, expenditure. The higher social classes, by virtue of their greater wealth and security, could afford to innovate; the lower could not. The much-advertised conservatism of the peasant springs largely from his lack of a margin which could allow him to experiment and take risks.

Most of the developments which have shaped material culture in this country have been initiated here. But there have been prominent exceptions. The rapid cultural changes of the Roman period derive from innovations – notably the villa, villa-farming and urban planning and institutions – which had been first adopted in southern Europe. The use of burnt brick in building construction was reintroduced during the twelfth century – probably from the Low Countries – and among minor cultural innovations, table cutlery, especially the fork, came from Italy, and the use of hops in brewing from the nearby continent. Most developments in building construction must be regarded as indigenous, though parallel developments took place in continental Europe. Architectural styles, on the other hand, have been greatly influenced by foreign example. The Perpendicular style, however, appears to have been entirely local.

The indigenous origin of most significant innovations is emphasised by their regional occurrence. Localisms abound, not only in building, but also in decoration, dress, food and in the lesser arts of daily life. In some instances these can be related directly to local environmental factors, like vernacular building in wood or stone or brick, which vary according to physical conditions. On the other hand, there is no such facile explanation for many distribution patterns. Many localisms owe nothing to any environmental imperative. They may have originated with an itinerant craftsman, who spread his ideas and his designs around the countryside, or from the local imitation of one person's ideas. Emulation and imitation have played a very significant role in the growth of material culture.

The process of innovation is one of the least understood of human activities.[2] It is sometimes inferred that it is a communal or social act; that the 'people' in some way create and then value and cherish what they have created. On the contrary, it is the individual who innovates. The society in which he or she lives merely criticises, censors, adopts, rejects. This brings us back to Stuart Piggott's concept of 'innovative' and 'non-innovative' peoples. No less important is what may be termed 'receptive' and 'non-receptive' peoples, predisposed to accept or to reject the products of innovation. A second and no less important aspect of popular culture is that it is never static. It is always in process of slow, outward change and modification. The fact that it was not, like the parallel liturgies of the church, written and recorded facilitated change and adaptation to differing external conditions.

If the externals of traditional activities, which all could observe and compare, were subject to slow change, even more so was their internal content, the meaning and significance of what was made or enacted. The Lenten, Mayday and harvest rituals became shells which people could fill with whatever meaning and significance they chose. It would probably be true to say that in modern times most such rituals have been drained of much of their emotional content, and that their purpose has become mainly social and nostalgic. 'The forests have departed,' wrote Thomas Hardy, of the vale of Blackmore, 'but some old customs of their shades remain. Many ... only in a metamorphosed and disguised form.' The 'club revel', which formed a crucial event in the life of Tess, was but the sanitised survival of Mayday revels, and, in the way that it was practised here, was significant only as a social occasion.[3]

Innovation generates its own progesssive development. Advance in one field of human activity generally facilitates and encourages advance in others: for example, the consequences of innovation in cast-iron technology had ramifications far and wide, in water-supply and sanitation, in cooking and heating, as well as in the provision of countless articles for daily domestic use. Improvements in these fields contributed to manifold other innovations, so that, with increasing opportunities for cross-fertilisation, growth inevitably became exponential. 'The key to cultural development lies precisely in the interconnectedness ... among different activities ... the interdependence of the subsystems of society.' In consequence, 'an innovation in one system tends to favour innovations (and their acceptance) in another.'[4] This is the fundamental reason for the increasingly rapid growth in material comforts, which became conspicuous in the later Middle Ages and accelerated from the sixteenth century onwards.

Innovation and the adoption of new objects of material culture necessitated, as a general rule, the diversion of factors of production – labour, capital, materials – from the creation of more traditional goods, unless total productivity could in some way be increased. In fact, innovations appear to have come in waves, which can generally be associated with periods of greater material production and prosperity. The 'great rebuilding' of the later sixteenth and the seventeenth centuries was such a period, as was the later eighteenth century and at least the earlier part of the nineteenth. Prosperity and depression did not affect all classes equally, and a marginal propensity to adopt new products varied not only through time but also from one social class to another. It must be remembered that the century which saw the greatest prosperity among the aristocracy and gentry and the creation of a large number of the great houses saw also the decay and virtual disappearance of the English peasantry.

One measure of the ability of ordinary people to consume is an index which relates wages to the price of commodities. This has been calculated for building workers between the thirteenth and the twentieth centuries.[5] It shows (Fig. 12.1) a

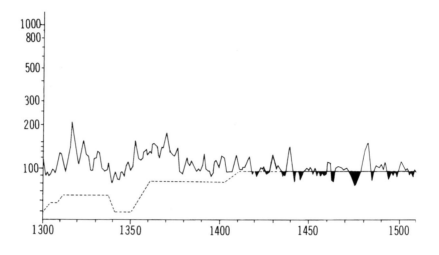

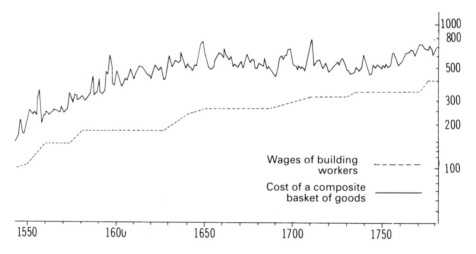

12.1 Graph showing index of the wages of building craftsmen (pecked line) and the price of a composite unit of consumables in southern England; based on E. H. Phelps-Brown and Sheila V. Hopkins, 'Seven centuries of the price of consumables'.

period of prosperity, with low prices for the essential foodstuffs throughout the fifteenth century and at least the first quarter of the sixteenth. Thereafter the ratio remained fairly stable, before declining quite sharply during the seventeenth. There was then no marked increase before the eighteenth, when a significant increase occurred, and a large part of the working population, and not only building workers, began to enjoy a significantly higher standard of material well-being. It was during this latter period that the sharpest increase in the consumption of *things* began.

The growth in privacy

One of the most significant developments in material culture in late medieval and modern times has been the increasing desire for – and provision of – privacy. There was no privacy in early medieval housing conditions, and in Norman times there was little, even in the highest levels of society. Not until life moved out of the castle and into the manor-house could private chambers be built on any considerable scale. The very name given to them – 'solars' – is indicative of the new practice of spending some part of the day *solus* or alone. The increasing provision of chambers, some of them with fireplaces,[6] had become a feature of the sixteenth-century great house, and was beginning to appear in the homes of the yeomen and better-off of the peasantry. By the eighteenth century the two-roomed cottage was something of a rarity.

Privacy conferred benefits beyond mere comfort and convenience. It was a factor in the transformation of family life and the growth of affective relations amongst its members. It encouraged the accumulation of personal possessions beyond the bare necessities for living. Clothing became more abundant. Wills began to record countless small possessions: silver, jewellery, pieces of silk or other fabric and items of sentimental value. A chest in which to store such things became a common piece of bedroom furniture. Privacy also encouraged individual and personal pursuits, including the art of reading. It cannot be said that books figured prominently in probate inventories before the mid-eighteenth century. Nevertheless, there was an increasing demand for the printed word, from religious tracts to chapbooks, and these would most likely have been kept and probably read in a private room.

The accumulation of private possessions, some of them of economic significance, but many of wholly personal or 'sentimental' value, is one of the most conspicuous features of the modern development of popular culture, and led ultimately to the cluttered interior of the Victorian home.[7] It was not that people in earlier times did not treasure personal possessions. They did, but these had to be such as could be worn on the person or carried with them, because there was no safe place in which to keep them. This is why jewellery is so frequently found amongst grave-goods: it was the commonest personal possession. The idea of collecting goods is necessarily modern. It could not develop before the appearance in the sixteenth and seventeenth centuries of the many-roomed houses of the upper classes. It owed much also to the greater privacy and the higher degree of security. People began to acquire items of little practical value but of interest and, often enough, of some aesthetic merit. This acquisitive instinct has probably always been there, but has been shackled by the inability to preserve, display or store things in conditions of relative safety. These were provided as houses became larger and doors and windows more secure. Furthermore, the idea of insurance was extended to cover houses and their contents. The later years of the seventeenth century must be seen as the time when collecting things first became a major interest of those sufficiently well-off to indulge in it.

The end of traditional culture

Every history should have a terminal date, so when did traditional culture die? The answer must be that it has been 'an unconscionable time a-dying', and is not yet truly dead. The downward progression of the material trappings and, to some extent, also of the intellectual furniture of élite culture, has led in large measure to its replacement. But not entirely: relics remain, and have themselves become the objects of élite study, preservation and even revival and imitation. At the same time that peasants 'were beginning to discover the delights of printed cotton curtains and fire-shovels . . . the intellectuals were waxing enthusiastic over home-made furniture and houses without chimneys'.[8] The divergence of élite from mass or popular culture, which started in the early Middle Ages, has led, in the inevitable dialectic of change, to attempts to recover and to save elements of that popular culture. The movement began in the late eighteenth century with the writings of J. G. Herder and his contemporaries and followers, especially in central and eastern Europe.[9] Their work had strong political overtones; it was an attempt to discover the roots of nationalism in order to oppose more effectively the pretensions of the 'empires' which had hitherto controlled the destinies of much of Europe, and in this it met with a measure of success. In Britain there was a similar movement to study, even to resuscitate, elements of popular culture, but here it lacked, except in parts of the 'Celtic fringe', that political edge which made it so powerful a force in central and eastern Europe. Traditional material cultures in Britain have managed to survive in 'folk museums' and at synthetic 'folk festivals'.

Traditional culture was essentially local culture. It belonged to community rather than to country, and could be perpetuated only when a significant proportion of the population continued in the same place from generation to generation. The almost legendary antipathy to 'foreigners' shown by traditional communities must spring from the difficulty in assimilating people with marginally different traditions and practices.

Population has always been to some extent mobile, and many of those who migrated from the countryside have gone to feed the growing urban populations, whose hybrid culture has already been discussed (p. 346). This mobility intensified in early modern times, and culminated during the nineteenth century when little of their original population can have remained in many rural communities. This change would have been most marked in Lowland England, least in those areas of Highland Britain which were not experiencing industrialisation, urban growth and an influx of people from without. The Fox thesis (p. 5) has, by and large, been substantiated in the social history of modern Britain. If the bearers of a culture become diluted by immigrants or weakened by emigration, then that culture must inevitably become attenuated.

The role of the printed word

A second factor in the attrition of popular culture must be the development of printing and the spread of literacy and the printed book. The effect of books, even at the level of the chapbook, was to generalise culture, to produce something that would be recognisable from one end of the country to the other. And in this respect no printed book was more significant than the Bible. One cannot say how many copies in whatever version were turned out by the presses during the first two centuries after the Reformation. It can, however, be said that there was always at least one in every parish in the land, and that, on the evidence of inventories, a great many of the householders above the humblest level also possessed a copy.

Despite differences in theological interpretation, the Protestant Bible spread a kind of cultural unity across the country. Inspired by its word, the reformers attempted – and with a considerable measure of success – to eliminate what had survived of the colourful, rumbustious culture of the later Middle Ages. Of course, there had in time to be a reaction against the extremes of Puritan belief and practice. It came after 1660, but its effect was to affirm the *via media* of the Anglican church, which spread a mantle of uniformity across the land.

From the late seventeenth century revolutions occurred in both technology and intellectual history, the tendency of which was towards levelling the quality of both the artefacts of material life and the *mentalité* of the people. The Industrial Revolution marked the convergence of many lines of innovation and discovery. Its effect was to bring together techniques both of management and of manufacture. It led to a vast increase, achieved over a period of a century and more, in the production of consumer goods. The cotton curtains and iron fire-shovels, mentioned earlier, were the products of mills and workshops radically different from anything that had gone before. Output was increased manyfold, and the cost per item was reduced. A greater volume of goods became available to an ever-increasing number of people. But the goods themselves ceased to be traditional, even though their forms might derive from traditional models. Carried to its extreme in the present century, this became the culture of the mail-order house.

The proliferation of things

The Industrial Revolution entailed immense suffering and degradation for many, as must any revolution which upsets an established social and economic balance, its only justification – if justification it is – the utilitarian claim that it was for 'the greatest happiness of the greatest number'.[10] In the long run, it brought commonplace articles within the reach of almost all; it increased the material content of people's lives and, very slowly and unevenly, it reduced the drudgery.

This proliferation of 'things' reached its apotheosis in the Great Exhibition which was staged in Hyde Park in 1851.[11] Tens of thousands of manufactured, fabricated or processed articles were on show, classified into thirty classes and an infinity of subgroups. Most, whether massive pieces of engineering or humdrum articles of domestic use, had as their objective an increase in production or the betterment of human life. Some were trivial or inconsequential, like the armchair made of papier mâché. Much was ostentatious and over-elaborate, like many new things trying to draw attention to themselves. William Morris condemned the vast collection as 'wonderfully ugly', and devoted much of the remaining years of his life to designing things aesthetically more pleasing. The 'Arts and Crafts' movement and art nouveau were to some extent reactions against what had been exhibited in 1851. Yet, despite the banality of decoration and the ugliness of design, the thousands of exhibits were a monument to human ingenuity and a measure of the material progress that had been achieved in the previous decades. The exhibition demonstrated that British society, despite the manifold survivals, both material and intellectual, in the home, on the farm, in the village, was no longer traditional.

The Great Exhibition was a summation of Britain's achievement in the field of material culture. There was no such milestone in the history of intellectual culture. Change in material things can be observed, dated, measured; above all, copied and diffused. Change in mental attitudes is slow, wavering and uncertain. There is no evidence that actions necessarily mirror beliefs and attitudes. The human body can adapt to new conditions, use new tools, enjoy new physical conditions, but the mind reacts only slowly. As le Goff has remarked: 'matter is often more liable to change than minds ... Motorists use the vocabulary of the horseman ... The history of *mentalité* is the history of the gradual.'[12]

Change in mentalité

In chapter 1 the world-view of traditional peoples was discussed. It was a view which could not conceive of scientific causation, which could see in any departure from a 'natural' course of events only the arbitrary act of some supernatural agency, and which could only appeal to other supernatural forces to bring things back to some vaguely conceived normality. A superficial view of history would appear to suggest that the Reformation of the sixteenth century brought about a change from superstition to a more rational attitude. It did nothing of the kind. It merely substituted a new form of magic for the old. Indeed, it was, along with the Catholic Counter 'Reformation' and the formulation of the proceedings of the Council of Trent, a retrograde step. In place of medieval pluralism and a relative degree of tolerance, they both tended to institutionalise a rigid fundamentalism. They were equally hostile to any attempt to interpret the world along scientific lines. In Britain, carnival, Mayday rites, St John's fires were all suppressed, not because they invoked a kind of magic, but because they smacked of paganism. The Catholic church in continental Europe frowned on them because they were local and not in harmony with the doctrines of the universal church.[13]

The attack on the claims and pretensions of the churches came in the later years of the seventeenth century, gathered pace in the eighteenth, but never before the nineteenth did it even begin to reach the mass of the population. It was an intellectual and élitist movement. In theological terms it was most often deist, with a strong opposition to clericalism and dogma. It laid great stress on careful observation and experiment, and, of course, it rejected magic and all its practitioners. Its appeal was to an educated segment of society, and its impact on popular culture was scarcely felt at all. Its practitioners rejected the superstitions of the lower classes as readily as they did the theology of the churchmen. Nevertheless, the prophets of the Enlightenment did help to mould a climate of opinion, less intolerant and more rational than that which had prevailed before, and more critical of established conventions and beliefs. It is doubtful whether the *philosophes* contributed anything directly to the decline in the belief in magic or in the persecution of witches, but it cannot be assumed that these would have happened in the eighteenth century if a more sceptical attitude had not filtered down to those who managed village and urban affairs and helped to shape opinion. The fact is, as Keith Thomas has emphasised, that 'in England magic lost its appeal before the appropriate technical solutions had been devised to take its place'.[14] The climate of opinion was very slowly changing. This change was part of a wider development induced by the growth of trade, the increase in manufactures and the expansion of urban population. People were learning that success came largely from one's personal efforts, and owed nothing to external forces. Belief in magic was more a rural than an urban phenomenon, because the events with which the countryman had to deal were more varied, more unpredictable, less susceptible to human control. Superstitious beliefs and practices have survived longer in rural than in urban environments,[15] and, within the latter, longer in poor, remote and less accessible regions – in short, 'the dark corners of the land' – than in the more prosperous and open.

As it decayed, popular culture became increasingly depersonalised. No longer was its magic used for personal ends, to injure someone, to retrieve a lost object, or to achieve some particular end. Its purpose became more general, to ensure 'good luck' or to avoid bad. People still, at the end of the twentieth century, 'touch wood' or avoid walking under ladders. But these actions have ceased to be significant, and survive as an almost meaningless ritual. This marks the end of traditional popular culture.

NOTES

INTRODUCTION

1 N. J. G. Pounds, *Hearth and Home*, Bloomington, IN, 1989.
2 Bernard Shaw, *Pygmalion*, Act I.
3 Stuart Clark, 'Inversion, misrule and the meaning of witchcraft', *P & P*, no. 87, May 1980, 98–127; Terry Castle, *Masquerade and Civilization*, London, 1986.
4 Thomas S. Kuhn, *The Structure of Scientific Revolutions*, Chicago, 1962, 2–3.
5 Robert Mandrou, *Introduction à la France moderne (1500–1640): essai de psychologie historique*, Paris, 1961, *passim*.
6 Jacques le Goff, 'Culture clericale et traditions folkloriques dans la civilisation merovingienne', *Ann ESC*, 22 (1967), 780–91.
7 C. G. Jung, ed., *Man and his Symbols*, London, 1964, 107.
8 Sir Cyril Fox, *The Personality of Britain*, National Museum of Wales, Cardiff, 1943.
9 ibid., 88.
10 J. B. Bury, *The Idea of Progress*, London, 1932, 1–36.
11 Colin Renfrew, *Problems in European Prehistory*, Edinburgh, 1979, 18.
12 S. Clark, 'French historians and early modern popular culture', *P & P*, no. 100, Aug. 1983, 62–99.
13 This title derives from Robert Muchembled, *Culture populaire et culture des élites dans la France moderne*, Paris, 1978, a work to which the author is deeply indebted.
14 G. Duby, 'The diffusion of cultural patterns in feudal society', *P & P*, no. 39, April 1968, 3–10.
15 *The Babees Book*, in *Manners and Meals in Olden Time*, ed. F. J. Furnivall, EETS, 1868.
16 Lorna Weatherill, *Consumer Behaviour and Material Culture*, London, 1988, 43–67.

1 THE VIEW FROM DANEBURY

1 This account of Danebury is based on Barry Cunliffe, *Danebury: An Iron Age Hillfort in Hampshire*, CBA RES Rept, 2 vols., 1984; Cuncliffe's reports in *The Antiquaries Journal*, 51 (1971), 240–52; 56 (1977), 198–216; 61 (1981), 238–54; and Barry Cuncliffe, *Danebury: Anatomy of an Iron Age Hillfort*, London, 1983.
2 Barry Cunliffe, 'Pits, perceptions and propitiation in the British Iron Age', *Oxf Jl, Arch*, 11 (1992), 69–83.
3 Caesar, *De Bello Gallico*, VI, 13–14; 17–18.
4 Anne Ross, *Everyday Life of the Pagan Celts*, London, 1970; Miranda Green, *Symbol and Image in Celtic Religious Art*, London, 1989; G. A. Wait, *Ritual and Religion in Iron Age Britain*, BAR, 149, 1985.
5 A. Ross, *Everyday Life of the Pagan Celts*, 154–6.
6 B. Cunliffe, *Iron Age Communities in Britain*, London, 1974.

7 Gerhard Bersu, 'Excavations at Little Woodbury, Wiltshire', *Proc Prehist Soc*, 5 (1940), pt 2, 30–111.
8 Brian T. Perry, 'Iron Age enclosures and settlements on the Hampshire chalklands', *Arch Jl*, 126 (1970), 29–43.
9 B. Cunliffe, *Iron Age Communities*.
10 Arthur Bullied, *The Lake Villages of Somerset*, Glastonbury, 1924.
11 J. M. Coles and B. J. Orme, *Prehistory of the Somerset Levels*, Som Lev Proj, 1982; B. J. Coles, *Sweet Track to Glastonbury*, London, 1986.
12 Jacquetta Hawkes, *A Land*, Harmondsworth, 1959.

2 ROMAN INTERLUDE

1 Graham Webster, *The Roman Invasion of Britain*, London, 1980, 123; Webster, 'The military situation in Britain between AD 43 and 71', *Brit*, 1 (1970), 179–97.
2 P. Salway, *Roman Britain*, Oxford, 1981, 100–23.
3 Tacitus, *Agricola*, 21.
4 Martin Millett, *The Romanization of Britain*, Cambridge, 1990, 74.
5 John Collis, *Oppida: Earliest Towns North of the Alps*, Department of Prehistoric Archaeology, University of Sheffield, 1984.
6 *The Civitas Capitals of Roman Britain*, ed. J. S. Wacher, Leicester, 1966, 101–10.
7 John Percival, *The Roman Villa*, London, 1976, 91–105.
8 M. Millett, *Romanization of Britain*, 98.
9 G. Bersu, 'Excavations at Little Woodbury, Wiltshire'. *Proc Prehist Soc*, 5 (1940), pt 2, 30–111.
10 Dennis Harding, 'Round and rectangular Iron Age houses, British and foreign', *Archaeology into History*, ed. C. and S. Hawkes, London, 1973, 43–59.
11 R. H. Leech, 'Excavation at Catsgore, Somerton, 1971', *Som Arch*, 115 (1971), 57.
12 R. H. Leech, 'Larger agricultural settlements in the West Country', *The Roman West Country*, ed. K. Branigan and P. J. Fowler, Newton Abbot, 1976, 142–61.
13 M. Millett, *Romanization of Britain*, 101.
14 J. Bradford, *Ancient Landscapes: Studies in Field Archaeology*, Bath, 1974.
15 K. D. White, *Agricultural Instruments of the Roman World*, Cambridge, 1967, 16.
16 Sian E. Rees, *Agricultural Implements in Prehistoric and Roman Britain*, BAR, 69, pt 1, 28.
17 Philip Corder, 'Roman spades from Verulamium', *Arch Jl*, 100 (1943), 224–31.
18 S. Applebaum, 'Roman Britain', *The Agrarian History of England and Wales*, vol. I, pt 2, Cambridge, 1972, 108–21; H. Goodwin, *The History of the British Flora*, Cambridge, 1956.
19 S. Applebaum, 'Roman Britain', 119.
20 ibid., 117.
21 D. Williams, 'A consideration of the sub-fossil remains of *Vitis vinifera* L. as evidence for viticulture in Roman Britain', *Brit*, 8 (1977), 327–34; S. Applebaum, 'Roman Britain', 103–4.
22 P. Salway, *The Frontier People of Roman Britain*, Cambridge, 1965.
23 R. G. Goodchild, 'T-shaped corn drying ovens in Roman Britain', *Ant Jl*, 23 (1943), 148–57; J. Liversidge, *Britain in the Roman Empire*, London, 1968, 221–3.
24 J. Liversidge, *Britain in the Roman Empire*, 223
25 A. L. F. Rivet, 'Summing-up: some historical aspects of the *civitates* of Roman Britain', *Civitas Capitals of Roman Britain*, 101–13.
26 Strabo, IV, 1.
27 A. L. F. Rivet, 'Summing-up', 104.
28 M. Millett, *Romanization of Britain*, 74.
29 J. Wacher, *The Towns of Roman Britain*, London, 1974, 22–35.
30 A. Detsicas, *The Cantiaci*, Gloucester, 1983, 39–54.
31 M. Todd, 'The vici of western England', *Roman West Country*, Newton Abbot, 1976, 99–119.

32 *Small Towns of Roman Britain*, ed. Warwick Rodwell and Trevor Rowley, BAR, 15, 1975.

33 S. J. Hallam, 'Villages in Roman Britain: some evidence', *Ant Jl*, 44 (1964), 19–32.

34 D. J. Smith, 'The mosiac pavements', *The Roman Villa in Britain*, ed. A. L. F. Rivet, London, 1969, 71–125.

35 D. J. Smith, 'Mythological figures and scenes in Romano-Britain mosaics', *Roman Art and Life in Britain*, ed. J. Munby and M. Henig, BAR, 41, pt 1 (1977), 105–93.

36 J. Liversidge, 'Furniture and interior decoration', in *The Roman Villa*, 127–72.

37 J. Liverside, 'Recent developments in Romano-British wall painting', *Roman Life and Art in Britain*, pt 1, 75–103.

38 S. S. Frere, *Britannia*, London, 1967, 290.

39 M. S. Briggs, 'Building construction', *Hist Techn*, 2 (1956), 397–448.

40 R. Goodburn, *The Roman Villa Chedworth*, Nat Trust, 1986, 16–21.

41 Quoted in E. J. Phillips, 'The classical tradition in the popular sculpture of Roman Britain', *Roman Life and Art*, 35–49.

42 ibid.

43 Quoted in S. Applebaum, 'Roman Britain', 189–200.

44 H. and T. Miles, 'Trethurgy' *Cur Arch*, 40, (Sept. 1973), 142–7.

45 S. Applebaum, 'Roman Britain', 204–5.

46 J. Liversidge, *Britain in the Roman Empire*, 192.

47 ibid., 158.

48 Sidonius Apollinaris, *Carmina*, XXII, 188ff.

49 G. Webster, 'A note on the use of coal in Roman Britain', *Ant Jl*, 35 (1955), 199–216.

50 G. R. Stephens, 'Civic aqueducts in Britain', *Brit*, 16 (1985), 197–208.

51 F. H. Thompson, 'The Roman aqueduct at Lincoln', *Arch Jl*, 111 (1955), 106–28.

52 J. Liversidge, *Britain in the Roman Empire*, 261–2.

53 John Wacher, *The Towns of Roman Britain*, London, 1974, 388 and *passim*.

54 ibid., 51, 126.

55 G. C. Boon, *Roman Silchester*, London, 1957, 161.

56 J. G. D. Clark and S. Piggott, 'The ages of the British flint mines', *Ant*, 7 (1933), 16–83.

57 R. J. Forbes, *Studies in Ancient Technology*, vol. 6, *Heat and Heating, Refrigeration, Light*, Leiden, 1966, 151–66.

58 J. Liversidge, *Britain in the Roman Empire*, 162–3.

59 J. Liversidge, 'A new year's lamp from Ely', *Cam Ant Soc Proc*, 47 (1954), 40.

60 R. J. Forbes, *Heat and Heating*, 134–42.

61 J. Liversidge, *Britain in the Roman Empire*, 165.

62 ibid., 129–31.

63 *Ebvracum: Roman York*, RCHM, 1962, pl. 54 and 122–4.

64 G. C. Boon, *Roman Silchester*, 124–5.

65 J. Liversidge, *Britain in the Roman Empire*, 424–7.

66 Barry Cunliffe, *Roman Bath*, Rep Res Com Soc Ant, 24 (1969), 4–5.

67 ibid., 151–5; A. Ross, *Pagan Celtic Britain*, London, 1967, 30.

68 J. Liversidge, *Britain in the Roman Empire*, 464–99.

69 E. and J. R. Harris, *The Oriental Cults in Roman Britain*, Leiden, 1965.

70 Charles Thomas, *Christianity in Roman Britain to A.D. 500*, London, 1981.

71 Sir John Lloyd, *A History of Wales*, 1939, vol. I, 102–10.

72 Nora Chadwick, *Celtic Britain*, London, 1963, 143.

3 HOUSE AND HOUSEHOLD

1 Martin Millett, *The Romanization of Britain*, Cambridge, 1990, 212 and *passim*.

2 R. W. Brunskill, *Illustrated Handbook of Vernacular Architecture*, London, 1981, 29.

3 ibid., 27.

4 W. G. Hoskins, 'The rebuilding of rural England, 1570–1640', *P & P*, no. 77 (Nov. 1953), 33–56; Sir Cyril Fox and Lord Raglan, *Monmouthshire Houses*, Cardiff, 1951–4, especially pt 3; R. Machin, 'The great rebuilding: a re-assessment', *P & P*, no. 77 (Nov. 1977), 33–56.

5 Philip Rahtz, 'Building and rural settlement', *The Archaeology of Anglo-Saxon England*, ed. D. M. Wilson, Cambridge, 1976, 49–98.

6 S. E. West, 'The Anglo-Saxon village of West Stowe: an interim report of the excavations 1965–8', *Med Arch*, 13 (1969), 1–20.

7 Helena Hamerow, 'Mucking: the Anglo-Saxon settlement', *Cur Arch*, 10, no. 4 (1988), 128–31.

8 S. E. West, 'The Anglo-Saxon village of West Stowe'.

9 *Kings' Works*, vol. I, 2–5.

10 B. Hope-Taylor, *Yeavering: An Anglo-British Centre of Early Northumbria*, HMSO, 1977; see also review by P. Rahtz in *Med Arch*, 24 (1980), 265–71.

11 P. Rahtz, *The Saxon and Medieval Palaces at Cheddar: Excavations 1960–2*, BAR, 65, 199; *Kings' Works*, I, 5–6.

12 W. A. van Es. 'Friesland in Roman times', *Berich Rijksd Oudhk Bodemdżk*, 15–16 (1965–6), 37–68.

13 *Anglo-Saxon Chronicle*, sub 978.

14 Eric Mercer, *English Vernacular Houses*, RCHM, 1975, 34–44; Maurice Barley, *Houses and History*, London, 1986, 159–61; Iorwerth C. Peate, *The Welsh house*, London, 1940, 62.

15 C. A. Ralegh Radford, 'The Saxon house: a review and some parallels', *Med Arch*, I (1957), 27–38.

16 R. L. S. Bruce-Mitford, 'A Dark Age settlement at Mawgan Porth, Cornwall', *Recent Archaeological Excavations in Britain*, ed. R. L. S. Bruce-Mitford, London, 1956, 167–96.

17 Dorothy Dudley and E. Marie Minter, 'The medieval village at Garrow Tor, Bodmin Moor, Cornwall', *Med Arch*, 6/7 (1962–3), 272–94; E. M. Jope and R. I. Threlfall, 'Excavation of a medieval settlement at Beere, North Tawton, Devon', *Med Arch*, 2 (1958), 112–40,

18 W. Stubbs, *Select Charters*, 9th edn, 1929, 88; F. M. Stenton, 'The thriving of the Anglo-Saxon ceorl', *Preparatory to Anglo-Saxon England*, ed. D. M. Stenton, Oxford, 1970, 383–93.

19 B. K. Davison, 'The origin of the castle in England', *Arch Jl*, 124 (1968), 202–11; Davison, 'Excavations at Sulgrave, Northamptonshire 1960–76', *Five Castle Excavations*, RAI, 1978, 105–14.

20 Maurice Beresford and J. G. Hurst, *Deserted medieval Villages*, 2nd edn, Gloucester, 1989, 76–144; Beresford and Hurst, *Wharram Percy: Deserted Medieval Village*, London, 1990.

21 Chaucer, 'Nonne Preestes Tale', lines 2–13.

22 S. W. Williams, 'An ancient Welsh farmhouse', *Arch Camb*, 5th ser., 16 (1899), 302–5.

23 D. Austin, 'Excavations in Okehampton Park, Devon, 1976–78', *Dev Arch Soc*, 36 (1978), 191–239.

24 Caoimhín O'Danachair, 'The combined byre-and-dwelling in Ireland', *Folk-Life*, 2 (1964), 58–75; Alexander Fenton, 'The longhouse in northern Scotland', *The Shape of the Past*, vol. I, Edinburgh, 1986, 83–95.

25 Quoted in R. K. Field, 'Worcestershire peasant buildings, household goods and farming equipment in the later Middle Ages', *Med Arch*, 9 (1965), 105–45; see also I. C. Peate, 'The longhouse again', *Folk-L*, 2 (1964), 76–9; Guy Beresford, *The Medieval Clay-land Village: Excavations at Goltho and Barton Blount*, Soc Med Arch Mon Ser, 6, 1975, 19–43.

26 *Med Arch*, 10 (1966), 214–16.

27 E. Mercer, *English Vernacular Houses*, 34–44.

28 W. Moffet, *The Irish Hudibras*, 1755, quoted in Caoimhín Ó Danachair, 'The combined byre-and-dwellings in Ireland', *Folk-Lite*, 2 (1964), 58–75.

29 *Shielings and Bastles*, RCHM, 1975; E. Mercer, *English Vernacular Houses*, 44.

30 C. Stell, 'Pennine houses: an introduction', *Folk–L*, 3 (1965), 5–24; E. Mercer, *English*

Vernacular Houses, 45–9; S. O. Addy, *The Evolution of the English House*, revised J. Summerson, London, 1933, 88.

31 F. W. B. Charles, *Medieval Cruck-Building and its Derivatives*, Med Arch Mon Ser, 2, 1967; N. W. Alcock, *Cruck Construction: An Introduction and Catalogue*, CBA Res Rept 42, 1981; L. E. Cave, *The Smaller English House*, London, 1981, 40–53; E. Mercer, *English Vernacular Houses*, 97.

32 F. W. B. Charles, 'The medieval timber-frame tradition', *Scientific Methods in Archaeology*, Berkeley, CA, 1970, 213–37.

33 R. G. Albion, *Forests and Sea Power*, Harvard Economic Series, Cambridge, MA, 1926, 7–10.

34 For documentation, see L. F. Salzman, *Building in England*, Oxford, 1952, 195–209.

35 C. A. Hewitt, *Church Carpentry*, London, 1982, *passim*.

36 John Blair, 'A small fourteenth-century cragloft house at Leatherhead, Surrey', *Ant Jl*, 61 (1981), 328–34.

37 L. F. Salzman, *Building in England*, App. B, no. 98B.

38 William Horman, *Vulgaria*, Roxb C1, 1926, 355.

39 Margaret Wood, *The English Medieval House*, London, 1965, 300–27.

40 *Kings' Works*, I, 45–7; W. R. Lethaby, 'The Palace of Westminster in the eleventh and twelfth centuries', *Arch*, 60, pt 1 (1906), 131–48.

41 *Kings' Works*, II, 854–64.

42 H. M. Colvin, 'Domestic architecture and town planning', *Medieval England*, ed. A. L. Poole, Oxford, 1958, I, 37–97; M. Wood, *English Medieval House*, 35–44; W. Horn, 'The potential and limitations of radiocarbon dating in the Middle Ages: the art historian's view', *Scientific Methods in Medieval Archaeology*, Berkeley, CA, 1970, 23–87; N. W. Alcock and R. J. Buckley, 'Leicester castle: the Great Hall', *Med Arch*, 31 (1987), 73–9.

43 Martin Cherry, 'Nurstead Court, Kent: a reappraisal', *Arch Jl*, 146 (1989), 451–64.

44 H. Hughes, 'Old houses in Llansilin, Denbighshire', *Arch Camb*, 5th ser., 15 (1898), 154–79.

45 Lynn Courtney, 'The Westminster Hall roof and its fourteenth-century sources', *Jl Soc Arch Hist*, 43 (1984), 295–309.

46 Walter Horn and Ernest Born, *The Barns of the Abbey of Beaulieu and its Granges of Great Coxwell and Beaulieu-St Leonards*, Berkeley, CA, 1965.

47 M. Wood, *Christchurch Castle*, HMSO, 1956.

48 *Huntingdonshire*, RCHM, 1926, 135–6.

49 T. D. Atkinson, *An Architectural History of the Benedictine Monastery at Ely*, Cambridge, 1933, 66–9.

50 Robert Willis and John Willis Clark, *The Architectural History of the University of Cambridge*, Cambridge, 1886, vol. II, 120–1.

51 J. R. Kenyon, *Medieval Fortifications*, Leicester, 1990, 97–124.

52 H. M. Colvin, 'Domestic architecture and town planning'.

53 *Piers Plowman*, B Text, X, lines 96–101.

54 Andrew Boorde, *A Dyetary of Helth*, ed. F. J. Furnivall, EETS, 1870, 246.

55 W. G. Hoskins, 'The rebuilding of rural England'.

56 L. F. Salzman, *Building in England*, App. B; see also D. Portman, *Exeter Houses 1400–1700*, Exeter, 1966, 22.

57 *Surveys of the Manors of Philip, Earl of Pembroke and Montgomery 1631–2*, ed. Eric Kerridge, Wilts Arch Soc Rec Br, 9, 1953.

58 J. Chevenix Trench, 'The houses of Coleshill: the social anatomy of a seventeenth century village', *Rec Bucks*, 25 (1983), 61–109.

59 William Harrison, *The Description of England*, Folger Documents of Tudor and Stuart England, Ithaca, NY, 1968, 195.

60 George Owen, *The Description of Pembrokeshire*, ed. H. Owen, Cymm Rec Ser, 1 (1896), pt 1, 76.

61 V. M. and F. J. Chesher, *The Cornishman's House*, Truro, 1968, 14—17.

62 J. Norden, *A Topographical and Historical Description of Cornwall*, London, 1728, 17.

63 M. Laithwaite, 'The building of Burford: a Cotswold town in the fourteenth to nineteenth centuries', *Perspectives in English Urban History*, ed. A. Everitt, London, 1973, 60—90.

64 R. Ross Noble, 'Turf-walled houses of the Central Highlands', *Folk-L*, 22 (1983—4), 68—83.

65 G. Beresford, 'The timber-laced wall in England', *Collectanea Historica: Essays in Memory of Stuart Rigold*, ed. A. Detsicas, Maidstone, 1981, 213—18.

66 E. Estyn Evans, 'A Cardiganshire mud-walled farmhouse', *Folk—L*, 7 (1969), 92—100.

67 J. Samuels, 'Mud-walled buildings at Flintham and Thoroton, Nottinghamshire', Thor Soc, 84 (1980), 44—7.

68 W. Harrison, *Description of England*, 195—7.

69 L. F. Salzman, *Building in England*, 149—53.

70 N. J. G. Pounds, 'Buildings, building stones and building accounts in south-west England', *Stone: Quarrying and Building in England AD 45—1525*, Chichester, 1990, 228—37.

71 W. Harrison, *Description of England*, 256.

72 Jane A. Wright, *Brick Building in England*, London, 1972, 14—16; P. J. Drury, 'The production of brick and tile in medieval England', *Medieval Industry*, ed. D. W. Crossley, CBA Res Rept 40 (1981), 126—42.

73 W. Harrison, *Description of England*, 356.

74 R. W. Brunskill, *Brick Building in Britain*, London, 1990, 21—42.

75 L. F. Salzman, *Building in England*, 140—5.

76 L. S. Harvey, 'A typology of brick: with numerical coding of brick characteristics', *JBAA*, 3rd ser, 37 (1974), 63—87.

77 A. Clifton-Taylor, *The Pattern of English Building*, London, 1972, 210—64.

78 D. Young, 'Brickmaking in Dorset', *Proc Dors NHAS*, 93 (1972), 213—42.

79 D. Smith, 'Some flat-roof thatch survivals', *Folk-L*, 16 (1978), 74—7.

80 E. M. Jope and G. C. Dunning, 'The use of blue slate for roofing in medieval England', *Ant Jl*, 34 (1954), 209—17.

81 The earliest quarries were probably in the sea cliffs; 21 were listed in 1650: *The Parliamentary Survey of the Duchy of Cornwall*, pt 2, ed, N. J. G. Pounds, Dev Cornw Rec Soc, 27 (1984), 183—4.

82 *De Antiquis Legibus: Cronica Maiorum et Vicecomitum Londoniarum*, ed. T. Stapleton, Camd Soc, 34 (1846), 206—11; C. C. Knowles and P. H. Pitts, *The History of Building Regulation in London 1189—1972*, London, 1972, 6—7.

83 L. F. Salzman, *Building in England*, 229—35.

84 P. Smith, 'Some reflections on the development of the centrally-planned house', *Collectanea Historica*, 192—212.

85 P. Smith, *Houses of the Welsh Countryside*, RCAHMW, 1975, 222—63.

86 ibid., 252.

87 ibid., 228.

4 HEAT, LIGHT AND INSECURITY

1 Linda Weatherill, *Consumer Behaviour and Material Culture in Britain 1660—1760*, London, 1988, esp. 25—432; *Deserted Medieval Villages*, ed. M. Beresford and J. G. Hurst, Gloucester, 1989, 98—9.

2 *Libeaus Desconus*, ed. Max Kaluza, *Altenglische Bibliotek*, vol. v, Leipzig, 1890, 186—9.

3 *Deserted Medieval Villages*, 176.

4 *The Portmote or Court Leet Records of Salford*, ed. J. G. de T. Mandley, vol. I, Cheth Soc, 46 (1902), 114.

5 I. C. Peate, *The Welsh House*, London, 1940, 208—9.

6 *Deserted Medieval Villages*, 98—9.

7 *The Portmote or Court Leet Records of Salford*, 114.

8 *Urbanization in History: A Process of Dynamic Interactions*, ed. A. D. van der Woude, A Hayami and J. de Vries, 'Introduction' by the editors, Oxford, 1990, 1–19.

9 *The 1235 Surrey Eyre*, ed. C. A. F. Meekings, Sur Rec Soc, 32 (1983), 431.

10 *Piers Plowman*, C Text, XVI, lines 17–21.

11 Margaret Wood, *The English Medieval Houses*, London, 1965, 261; Lawrence Wright, *Home Fires Burning: The History of Domestic Heating and Cooking*, London, 1964, *passim*; M. W. Barley, *The English Farmhouse and Cottage*, London, 1961, 67–8.

12 D. Hawes Richards, 'The chimney', *JBAA*, 3rd ser., 24 (1961), 67–79.

13 *Essex, North-East*, RCHM, 1922, 51; Sidney Toy, *The Castles of Great Britain*, London, 1963, 161–2.

14 *Essex, North-West*, RCHM, 1922, 55.

15 *Huntingdonshire*, RCHM, 1926, 135–6.

16 Colin Pratt, *Medieval Southampton*, London, 1973, 41–2.

17 M. Wood, *Norman Domestic Architecture*, RAI, 1974, 32–4.

18 ibid., 81–2; M. Wood, *The English Medieval House*, 261–2 and pl. 41.

19 L. A. Shuffrey, *The English Fireplace*, London, 1912, 14ff.

20 G. C. Dunning, 'Medieval chimney-pots', *Studies in Building History*, ed. E. M. Jope, London, 1961, 78–93; D. Hawes Richards, 'The chimney'; M. Wood, *Christchurch Castle, Hampshire*, HMSO, 1956, 2–6.

21 Eurwyn William, 'Yr Aelwyd: the architectural development of the hearth in Wales', *Folk-L*, 16 (1978), 85–100.

22 *English Medieval House*, 263–72.

23 *Bedfordshire Wills Proved in the Prerogative Court of Canterbury 1383–1548*, ed. M. McGregor, Beds Hist Rec Soc, 58 (1959), 48.

24 Maurice Barley, *Houses and History*, London, 1986, 158.

25 R. W. Brunskill, *Illustrated Handbook of Vernacular Architecture*, 3rd edn, 1978, 102–3; E. Mercer, *English Vernacular Houses*, RCHM, 1975, 20–2.

26 Peter Smith, 'Architectural personality of the British Isles', *Arch Camb*, 129 (1980), 1–36.

27 J. Seymour Lindsay, *Iron and Brass Implements of the English House*, London, 1964.

28 Walter Hough, *Fire as an Agent in Human Culture*, Smithsonian Institute Bulletin 139, Washington, DC, 1926, 4.

29 R. Patterson, 'Two hearth-blowers from Henley-on-Thames', *Berks Arch Jl*, 50 (1947), 98–101.

30 *Essex Wills*, vol. I, 1558–65.

31 *Tattershall Castle, Lincolnshire*, Nat Trust, 1974.

32 Andrew Boorde, *A Dyetary of Helth*, ed. F. J. Furnivall, EETS, 1870, 246.

33 N. J. G. Pounds, 'The population of Cornwall before the first census', *Population and Marketing*, Exeter Pap Econ Hist, 11 (1976), 11–30.

34 *Household and Farm Inventories in Oxfordshire, 1550–1590*, ed. M. A. Havinden, HMC, 1965, 21–6.

35 ibid., 'Introduction', 26.

36 W. G. Hoskins, 'An Elizabethan provincial town: Leicester', *Studies in Social History*, ed. J. H. Plump, London, 1955, 33–67; David Crossley, *Post-Medieval Archaeology in Britain*, Leicester, 1990, 226–42.

37 R. J. Charlesworth and L. M. Angus-Butterworth, 'Glass', *A History of Technology*, vol. IIII, Oxford, 1957, 206–44; D. Crossley, *Post-Medieval Archaeology*, 26–42.

38 H. J. Louw, 'The origin of the sash-window', *Archt Hist*, 26 (1983), 49–72.

39 R. J. Forbes, *Studies in Ancient Technology*, vol. VI, *Heat and Heating, Refrigeration, Light*, Leiden, 1966, 126–68.

40 *Medieval Catalogue*, London Museum, HMSO, 1954, 174–6.

41 J. C. Cox, *Churchwardens' Accounts*, London, 1913.

42 William Cobbett, *Cottage Economy*, edn of 1975, Bath, §139.

43 Gilbert White, *The Natural History of Selborne*, London, letter xxvi.

44 O. Curle, 'Domestic candlesticks from the fourteenth to the end of the eighteenth century', *Proc Soc Ant Scot*, 60 (1927), 183–214; H. Swainson Cowper, 'The domestic candlestick of iron in Cumberland, Westmorland, and Furness', *Tr Camb Westm AAS*, 12 (1893), 105–27.

45 J. C. Cox, *English Church Fittings*, London, 1923, 224–30.

46 *Shardeloes Papers of the Seventeenth and Eighteenth Centuries*, ed. G. Eland, Oxford, 1947, 12.

47 E. S. de Beer, 'The early history of London street lighting', *Hist*, 25 (1940–1), 311–24.

48 R. J. Forbes, *Heat and Heating, Refrigeration, Light*, 122–85.

49 *Portmote or Court Leet Records of Salford*, vol. I, 114.

50 Asa Briggs, *Victorian Things*, London, 1988, 187–92.

51 Frederick Pollock and F. W. Maitland, *The History of English Law before the Time of Edward I*, vol. I, London, 1895, 557.

52 H. R. T. Summerson, 'The structure of law enforcement in the thirteenth century', *Am Jl Leg Hist*, 23 (1979), 313–27.

53 *Court Rolls of the Manor of Wakefield*, vol. IV, 1315–17, ed. John Lister, Yks Arch Soc Rec Ser, 78 (1930), 4, 53.

54 ibid., 18.

55 *Crown Pleas of the Devon Eyre of 1238*, ed. H. Summerson, D & C Rec Soc, NS 28 (1985), XXVII-XXXVI.

56 ibid., no. 128, 29.

57 Bracton, *De Legibus*, II, 344.

58 *Crime in East Anglia in the Fourteenth Century: Norfolk Gaol Delivery Rolls, 1307–1316*, ed. Barbara Hanawalt, Norf Rec Soc (1976), nos. 753, 777.

59 B. A. Hanawalt, *Crime and Conflict in English Communities, 1300–1348*, Cambridge, MA, 1979, 66; for types of felony see ibid., 64–5, and F. G. Emmison, *Elizabethan Life: Disorder*, Chelmsford, 1970, 256–79.

60 *Crime in East Anglia in the Fourteenth Century*, no. 222.

61 *Cal Pat R*, 1321–4, 157.

62 *Roll of the Justices in Eyre at Bedford, 122–7*, ed. G. Herbert Fowler, Beds Hist Red Soc, 3 (1916), 1–206 (p. 4).

63 R. R. Davies, 'The survival of the bloodfeud in medieval Wales', *Hist*, 54 (1969), 338–57; Jenny Wormald, 'Bloodfeud, kindred and government in early modern Scotland', *P & P*, no. 87 (May 1980), 54–97; Joel T. Rosenthal, 'Feuds and private peacemaking: a fifteenth century example', *Notts Med St*, 14 (1970), 84–90.

64 Calendar of Coroners' Rolls of the City of London A.D. 1300–1378, ed. R. R. Sharpe, London, 1913, 20.

65 S. Pegge, 'Sketch of the history of asylum or sanctuary', *Arch*, 8 (1787), 1–44.

66 N. J. G. Pounds, 'William Carnsew and his diary', *Jl Roy Inst Cornw*, NS 8 (1978), 14–60.

67 David Cressy, *Literacy and the Social Order*, Cambridge, 1980, 17.

68 Albert A. Hopkins, *The Lure of the Lock*, New York, 1928, 14–21.

69 A. F. Pitt-Rivers, *On the Development and Distribution of Primitive Locks and Keys*, London, 1883, *passim*.

70 *Cal Pat R*, 1385–9, 42.

71 B. Hanawalt, *Crime and Conflict in English Communities*, 82–3.

72 Asa Briggs, *Victorian Things*, 42.

73 A. A. Hopkins, *The Lure of the Lock*, 40–4.

74 A. Briggs, *Victorian Things*, 42.

75 *Piers Plowman*, C Text, IV, lines 104–7.

76 *Court Rolls of the Manor of Acomb*, ed. H. Richardson, vol. I, Yks Arch Soc Rec Ser, 131 (1968), 136.

77 *Portmote or Court Leet Records of Salford*, vol. I, 114.

78 *Court Rolls of the Manor of Acomb*, 70.

79 *Portmote or Court Leet Records of Salford*, vol. I, 114.

80 C. C. Knowles and P. H. Pitt, *The History of Building Regulations in London 1189–1972*, London, 1972, 6–8; also *Cal Letter Books*, C, 1901, 106.

81 *Cal Letter Books*, C, 105.

82 ibid., K, 181.

83 ibid., K, 240.

84 ibid., K, 319.

85 Stephen Porter, 'Fire precautions in early modern Abingdon', *Berks Arch Jl*, 71 (1981–2), 71–7.

86 *Elizabethan Churchwarden's Accounts*, ed. J. E. Farmiloe and Rosita Nixseaman, Beds Hist Rec Soc, 33 (1953), 96.

87 *The Court Rolls of the Lordship of Ruthin or Dyffryn-Clwydd*, ed. R. A. Roberts, Cymm Rec Ser, 2 (1893), 28.

88 T. F. Reddaway, *The Rebuilding of London after the Great Fire*, London, 1940, 26.

89 Statute of Winchester, 1285, *Stubbs' Charters*, 463–9.

90 *Minutes of Proceedings on Quarter Sessions held for the Parts of Kesteven 1674–1695*, ed. S. A. Peyton, vol. I, Lincs Rec Soc, 25 (1910), ix–ixi.

91 N. J. G. Pounds, *Hearth and Home*, Bloomington, IN, 1989, 282–3.

92 *Churchwardens' Accounts of Pittington and other Parishes in the Diocese of Durham*, Surt Soc, 84 (1888).

93 H. A. L. Cockerell and Edwin Green, *The British Insurance Business 1547–1970*, London, 1976, 18–22.

94 P. G. M. Dickson, *The Sun Insurance Office 1710–60*, Oxford, 1960, 62–8.

95 *The Diary of Benjamin Rogers, Rector of Carlton, 1720–71*, ed. C. D. Linnell, Beds Hist Rec Soc, 30 (1949), 49.

96 B. A. Hanawalt, 'Peasant women's contribution to the home economy in late medieval England', *Women and Work in Preindustrial Europe*, ed. Hanawalt, Bloomington, IN, 1986, 3–19.

97 R. F. Hunnicutt, *The Medieval Coroner*, Cambridge, 1961, 9–36.

98 *Select Cases from the Coroners' Rolls AD 1265–1413*, ed. Charles Gross, Seld Soc, 9 (1895), 50.

99 *Bedfordshire Coroners' Rolls*, ed. R. F. Hunnisett, Beds Hist Rec Soc, 41 (1960), 103.

100 *Select Cases from the Coroners' Rolls*, 77.

101 *Cal Pat R*, 1422–29, 47.

5 THE HOUSE FURNISHED

1 E. Phelps Brown and S. V. Hopkins, 'Seven centuries of the price of consumables compared with builders' wages', *Econ*, NS 22 (1956), 296–314.

2 *The Fifty Earliest English Wills in the Court of Probate 1387–1439*, ed. F. J. Furnival, EETS, 1882.

3 Margaret Spufford, *Contrasting Communities*, Cambridge, 1974, 161–4.

4 *Wiltshire Extents for Debts, Edward I – Elizabeth I*, ed. A. Conyers, Wilts Arch Soc Rec Branch, 28 (1972); *Goods and Chattels of our Forefathers*, ed. J. S. Moore, Frampton Cotterell Historical Society, London, 1976.

5 *The Making of King's Lynn: A Documentary Survey*, ed. D. M. Owen, Rec Econ Soc Hist, NS 9 (1984), 235; H. T. Riley, *Memorials of London Life in the XIII, XIV and XV Centuries*, London, 1968, 44.

6 Margaret Spufford, 'The limitations of the probate inventory', *English Rural Society 1500–1800*, ed. J. Chartres and D. Hey, Cambridge, 1990, 139–74.

7 *Household and Farm Inventories in Oxfordshire 1550–1590*, ed. M. A. Havinden, Hist MSS Com, 1965, 6–7.

8 *Elizabethan Life: Wills of Essex Gentry and Merchants*, ed. F. G. Emmison, Chelmsford, 1978, 278.

9 *Bedfordshire Wills Proved in the Prerogative Court of Canterbury*, 125.

10 i.e. 'lame and feeble', *Somerset Medieval Wills (1383–1500)*, ed. F. W. Weaver, Som Rec Soc, 16 (1901), 58, 64, 74 and *passim*.

11 *Household and Farm Inventories in Oxfordshire*, 5–6.

12 Lorna Weatherill, *Consumer Behaviour and Material Culture in Britain 1660–1760*, London, 1988, 212.

13 W. G. Hoskins, 'The rebuilding of rural England', *P & P*, no. 77 (1953), 44–59.

14 Lawrence Stone, 'Social mobility in England, 1500–1700', *P & P*, no. 33 (1966), 16–55.

15 *Household and Farm Inventories in Oxfordshire*, 21.

16 *Essex Wills*, vol. III, 1571–7, ed. F. G. Emmison, New Eng Hist Gen Soc, 1986, xi–xii.

17 *Essex Wills*, vol. I, 1558–65, no. 43, 131.

18 ibid., no. 873.

19 C. E. Freeman, *Elizabethan Inventories*, Beds Hist Rec Soc, 32 (1951), 92–107.

20 *Lancashire and Cheshire Wills and Inventories*, pt 2, ed. G. J. Piccope, Cheth Soc, 51 (1860), 4.

21 *Jacobean Household Inventories*, ed. F. G. Emmison, Beds Hist Rec Soc, 20 (1938), 68.

22 C. E. Freeman, *Elizabethan Inventories*, 92–107.

23 F. A. Page-Turner, 'Bedfordshire wills and administrations proved at Lambeth Palace and in the Archdeaconry of Huntingdon', Beds Hist Rec Soc, 2 (1914), 3–59.

24 *The Making of King's Lynn*, ed. D. M. Owen, 254.

25 William Harrison, *The Description of England*, ed. G. Edelen, Ithaca, NY, 1968, 198–9.

26 W. G. Hoskins, 'An Elizabethan butcher of Leicester', *Essays in Leicestershire History*, Liverpool, 1950, 108–22.

27 *Household and Farm Inventories*, 26.

28 *Essex Wills*, vol. III, no. 534.

29 *Lincolnshire Wills*, vol. II, 23–4.

30 *Essex Wills*, vol. III, 237–8.

31 ibid., no. 416.

32 *Lincolnshire Wills*, vol. III, 96.

33 ibid., 92.

34 *Nottinghamshire Household Inventories*, ed. P. A. Kennedy, Thor Soc Rec Ser, 22 (1963), no. 10.

35 The otherwise well-furnished house of Nicholas Chafyn in Salisbury, 1513, appears not to have had a table (*Wiltshire Extents for Debts*, 47–8), but this was quite exceptional.

36 *Essex Wills*, vol. III, 86.

37 *Wiltshire Extents for Debts*, no. 167.

38 Chaucer, 'Prologue', lines 353–4.

39 *Nottingham Household Inventories*, no. 106.

40 *Elizabethan Inventories*, ed. Freeman, *passim*.

41 Owen Ashmore, 'Household inventories of the Lancashire gentry, 1550–1700', *Tr Hist Soc Lancs Chesh*, 110 (1958), 59–105.

42 *Essex Wills*, vol. III, 77.

43 ibid., 110.

44 *Lancashire and Cheshire Wills and Inventories*, pt 2, Cheth Soc, 51 (1860), 206.

45 *Household Inventories of the Lancashire Gentry*, 66.

46 F. G. Emmison, *Elizabethan Life: Home, Work and Land*, Ess Rec Off Pubns 69 (1976), 12–13.

47 F. A. Page-Turner, 'Bedfordshire wills and administrations', 3–59.

48 E. W. Crossley, 'Two seventeenth-century inventories', *Yks Arch Jl*, 34 (1939), 170–203.

49 F. W. Steer, *Farm and Cottage Inventories of Mid-Essex. 1635–1749*, Ess Rec Off Pubns, 8 (1950), 16–17.

50 W. Harrison, *Description of England*, 201.

51 A hempen cloth imported from Poldavid, in Brittany.

52 *Somerset Medieval Wills*, 2nd series, 1501–30, ed. F. W. Weaver, Som Rec Soc, 19 (1903), 174.

53 *Essex Wills*, vol. III, 63.

54 *London Consistory Court Wills 1492–1547*, ed. Ida Darlington, Lond Rec Soc, 3 (1967) 101–7.

55 Andrew Boorde, *A Compendious Regyment or A Dietary of Helth*, EETS, extra ser., 10 (1870), 236–77.

56 *Essex Wills*, vol. III, 63.

57 *Yorkshire Probate Inventories 1542–1689*, ed. P. C. D. Brears, Yorks Arch Soc Rec Ser, 134 (1972), 141.

58 E. W. Crossley, 'Two seventeenth-century inventories'.

59 *Yorkshire Probate Inventories*, 39.

60 *Essex Wills*, vol. III, xii.

61 A measure of about 9 gallons.

62 *Devon Inventories of the Sixteenth and Seventeenth Centuries*, ed. Margaret Cash, D & C Rec Soc, 11 (1966) no. 1.

63 ibid., no. 12.

64 F. G. Emmison, 'Jacobean household inventories'; J. Seymour Lindsay, *Iron and Brass Implements of the English House*, London. 1964.

65 *Farm and Cottage Inventories of Mid-Essex.* 227.

66 Simon Thurley, 'The sixteenth-century kitchens at Hampton Court', *JBAA*, 143 (1990), 1–28; South Midlands Archaeology, CBA Group 9, Oxford, 1983, 63ff. for reports on medieval kitchens in Oxford colleges.

67 *Lancashire and Cheshire Wills and Inventories*, 108.

68 ibid., 79–81.

69 Quoted in F. G. Emmison, *Elizabethan Life: Home, Work and Land*, 10.

70 A generic term for softwoods imported from the Baltic; see R. G. Albion, *Forests and Sea Power*, Cambridge, MA, 1926, 9–10.

71 G. Montagu Benton, 'Paving-bricks', *Tr Ess Arch Soc*, NS 23 (1942–5), 175–6.

72 *A Calendar of Cornish Glebe Terriers 1673–1735*, ed. Richard Potts, D & C Rec Soc, 19 (1974), 5.

73 O. Ashmore, 'Household inventories of the Lancashire gentry'.

74 *Shardeloes Papers of the Seventeenth and Eighteenth Centuries*, ed. G. Eland, Oxford, 1947, 14.

75 J. Neville Bartlett, *Carpeting the Millions*, Edinburgh, n.d., 1–2.

76 *Wills and Inventories from the Registry at Durham*, ed. H. M. Wood, Surt Soc, 142 (1929), 313.

77 *Elizabethan Life: Wills of Essex Gentry and Yeomen*, ed. F. G. Emmison, Chelmsford, 1980, 63.

78 *Elizabethan Life: Wills of Essex Gentry and Merchants*, 283.

78 *Household and Farm Inventories in Oxfordshire*, 26.

80 *The Making of King's Lynn*, ed. D. M. Owen, 254.

81 F. W. Reader, 'Tudor domestic wall-paintings', *Arch Jl*, 92 (1935), 242–86.

82 E. Clive Rouse, 'Domestic wall-paintings at Chalfont St Peter, Great Pednor and elsewhere', Rec Bucks, 15 (1947–52), 87–96.

83 G. Montagu Benton, 'Some domestic wall-paintings of Essex', *Tr Ess Arch Soc*, 23 (1942–5), 1–17; 24 (1944–9), 132–48.

84 *Wills and Inventories from the Registry at Durham*, 316.

85 Hilary Jenkinson, 'English wall-papers of the sixteenth and seventeenth centuries', *Ant Jl*, 5 (1925), 237–53; Jenkinson, 'A recently discovered wall-paper at Colchester', *Tr Ess Arch Soc*, 19 (1927–39), 225–9.

86 *Yorkshire Probate Inventories*, 1–3; *A Collection of Lancashire and Cheshire Wills, 1301–1752*, ed. W. F. Irvine, Lancs Chesh Rec Soc, 30 (1896), 153.

87 *Devon Inventories*, no. 37.

88 *Yorkshire Probate Inventories*, 134 (1972), 141.

89 R. W. Symonds, *A Book of English Clocks*, London, 1950, 26–30.

90 David S. Landes, *Revolution in Time: Clocks and the Making of the Modern World*, Cambridge, MA, 1983, 83.

91 As in E. G. Norris, 'A seventeenth-century inventory', *Ess Rv*, 15 (1906), 169–75.

92 *Farm and Cottage Inventories of Mid-Essex*, 19–20.

93 *Yorkshire Probate Inventories*, 141.

94 *Jacobean Household Inventories*, 33.

95 L. Weatherill, *Consumer Behaviour and Material Culture*, 40.

96 E. A. Wrigley, 'A simple model of London's importance in changing English society and economy', *P & P*, no. 37 (July, 1967), 44–70.

97 Notably H. J. Perkin, 'The social causes of the British Industrial Revolution', *TrRHS*, 18 (1969), 123–43; A. H. John, 'Agricultural productivity and economic growth in England, 1700–1760', *Jl Ec Hist*, 25 (1965), 19–34.

98 *The Family Papers of the Rev. William Stukeley*, Surt Soc, 73 (1880), 7.

99 For a fuller discussion see L. Weatherill, *Consumer Behaviour*, 43–69; 112–36.

100 *Northern Petitions Illustrative of Life in Berwick, Cumbria and Durham in the Fourteenth Century*, ed. C. M. Fraser, Surt Soc, 194 (1981), 107.

101 *Ancient Petitions Relating to Northumberland*, ed. C. M. Fraser, Surt Soc, 176 (1961), 108–10.

102 *Court Rolls of the Manor of Acomb*, ed. H. Richardson, vol. I, Yks Arch Soc Rec Ser, 131 (1968), 9.

103 A. Boorde, *A Compendyous Regyment*, 256.

104 ibid., 253.

105 *London Assize of Nuisance 1301–1431*, ed. H. M. Chew and W. Kellaway, Lond Rec Soc, 10 (1973), xxv.

106 John Schofield, *The Building of London from the Conquest to the Great Fire*, Brit Mus, 1984, 96; Martin Carver, *Underneath English Towns*, London, 1987, 97–8.

107 E. L. Sabine, 'Latrines and cesspools of mediaeval London', *Spec*, 9 (1934), 303–21.

108 *Wills and Inventories from the Registers of the Commissary of Bury St Edmunds and the Archdeacon of Sudbury*, ed. S. Tymms, Camd Soc, 49 (1850), 20.

109 *The Portmote or Court Leet Records of Salford*, ed. J. G. de T. Mandley, vol. I, Cheth Soc, NS, 46 (1902), 72; 81.

110 A. Boorde, *A Dietary of Helth*, 236.

111 An amusing account of Harington's invention is given in J. Pudney, *The Smallest Room*, London, 1954, 132–50.

112 Asa Briggs, *Victorian Things*, London, 1988, 251–3.

113 *Devon Inventories*, xx.

114 F. W. Steer, 'Smaller houses and their furnishings in the seventeenth and eighteenth centuries', *JBAA*, 3rd ser., 20–1 (1957–8), 140–59,

115 F. Sherwood-Taylor and Charles Singer, 'Pre-scientific chemistry', *Hist Techn*, vol. I, 355–6; F. W. Gibbs, 'Invention in the chemical industries', ibid., vol. III, 676–708.

116 Thomas Coryat, *Coryat's Crudities*, Glasgow, 1905, 98.

117 *Boke of Curtasye*, EETS, 32 (1868), 299–327,

118 Stow's *Survey of London*, London, 1912, 361.

119 Lawrence Wright, *Clean and Decent*, London, 1980, 27–8.

120 *Jacobean Household Inventories*, 12–14, for a discussion of their shortcomings; also Margaret Spufford, 'The limitations of the probate inventory'.

121 Margaret Spufford, 'Peasant inheritance customs'.

122 *Yorkshire Probate Inventories*, 153.

123 N. Z. Davies, 'Printing and the people', *Society and Culture in Early Modern France*, London, 1975, *passim*.

124 John Ashton, *Chapbooks of the Eighteenth Century*, Oxf Rec Sec 1882; Margaret Spufford, *Small Books and Pleasant Histories*, Cambridge, 1985. On literacy see D. Cressy, *Literacy and the Social Order: Reading and Writing in Tudor and Stuart England*, Cambridge, 1980.

125 *Household and Farm Inventories in Oxfordshire*, 10.

126 ibid., 7.

127 Calculated from *Farm and Cottage Inventories of Mid-Essex*, *passim*.

128 J. A. Johnston, 'Worcestershire probate inventories 1699–1716', *Midl Hist*, 4 (1980) 191–211.

129 *Farm and Cottage Inventories of Mid-Essex*, 4–8.

130 *Household and Farm Inventories in Oxfordshire*, 2–4.

131 ibid., 65.

132 L. Weatherill, *Consumer Behaviour and Material Culture*, 160.

133 ibid., 160.

134 Anthony Quiney, *House and Home*, London, 1986, 101–25; John Burnett, *A Social History of Housing 1815–1970*, Newton Abbot, 1970, 54–93; Vanessa Parker, *The English House in the Nineteenth Century*, London, 1970.

6 FOODS, ITS PRODUCTION, PRESERVATION AND PREPARATION

1 William Harrison, *The Description of England*, ed. G. Edelen, Ithaca, NY, 1968, 133.

2 G. Hellman, *Die Entwicklung der meteorologischen Beobachtungen bis zum Ende des XVIII Jahrhunderts*, Abh Preuss Akad Wiss, Phys-Math Klasse, vol. V, 1927.

3 C. Easton, *Les Hivers dans l'Europe Occidentale*, Leyden, 1928; Kurt Weikinn, *Quellentexte zur Witterungsgeschichte Europas von der Zeitwende bis zum Jahre 1850*, 4 vols, Deutsch Akad Wiss Berlin, 1958ff.

4 John Huxham, *Observationes de Aere et Morbis epidemicis ab anno 1728 ad finem anni 1737 Plymuthi factae*, London, 1739. On Boerhaave, see F. H. Garrison, *An Introduction to the History of Medicine*, Philadelphia, PA, 1929, 315ff.

5 'Etude par ordinateur des données météorologiques constituées par les correspondents de la Société Royale de Médicine' in *Médicins, climat et épidemies à la fin du XVIIIe siècle*, Ec Prat Ht Et, Civ et Soc, 29 (Paris, 1972), 23–134.

6 Gordon Manley, *Climate and the British Scene*, London, 1952, 6–23, for a summary of early meteorological investigations; Manley, 'The mean temperature of central England, 1698–1952', *Ou Jl Roy Met Soc*, 79 (1953), 242–61; J. Glasspole, 'Two centuries of rain', *Met Mag*, 63 (1928), 1–6.

7 Luke 12: 54–6.

8 The Book of Enoch, ed. R. H. Charles Oxford, 1912, section IX, pp. 13–15.

9 Quoted in Sir Napier Shaw, *The Drama of Weather*, Cambridge, 1933, 66, and ascribed to Edward Jenner.

10 F. Powicke and Cheney, *Councils and Synods*, Oxford, 1964, vol. II, 1086, no. 27.

11 *Churchwardens' Accounts of Ashburton, 1479–1580*, ed. Alison Hanham, D & C Rec Soc, NS 15 (1970), 42; also xvii.

12 Keith Thomas, *Religion and the Decline of Magic*, London, 1971, 134–6.

13 Aelfric of Eynsham, in A. R. Benham, *English Literature from Widsuth to Chaucer*, New Haven, CT, 1916, 26.

14 Cornw Rec Off, Buller Papers 116; N. J. G. Pounds, 'Barton farming in eighteenth-century Cornwall', *Jl Roy Inst Cornw*, 7, pt I (1973), 55–75.

15 Geoffrey Shepherd, 'Poverty in *Piers Plowman*', *Social Relations and Ideas*, ed. T. H. Aston, P. R. Cross, C. Dyer and J. Thirsk, Cambridge, 1983, 169–89.

16 *Piers Plowman*, C Text, XVI, lines 1–21.

17 E. Le Roy Ladurie, *Histoire du climat depuis l'an mille*, Paris, 1967, 55.

18 H. S. Lucas, 'The great European famine of 1315, 1316, and 1317', *Spec* 5 (1930), 343–77; H. van Werveke, 'La famine de l'an 1316 en Flandre et dans les régions voisines', *Rv Nord*, 41 (1959), 5–1421.

19 Henry and Elizabeth Stommel, 'The year without a summer', *Sci Am*, June 1979.

20 Calculated from B. R. Mitchell, *Abstract of British Historical Statistics*, Cambridge, 1962, 24–7.

21 *Piers Plowman*, C Text, IX, lines 347–9.

22 G. Storms, *Anglo-Saxon Magic*, 177; *Leechdoms, Wortcunning and Starcraft in Early England*, ed. O. Cockayne, RS, 1864–6. vol. I, 402–5.

23 Discussed in ibid., 178–87.

24 A. R. Wright, *British Calendar Customs: England*, ed. T. E. Lones, vol. I, *Movable Festivals*, London, 1936, 182–90.

25 *Class Rv*, 36 (1992), 129–60; A. R. Wright, *British Calendar Customs*, vol. I, 129–60.

26 *Oxford Dictionary of the Christian Church*, *sub* 'Rogation Days'.

27 Aron Gurevich, *Medieval Popular Culture: Problems of Belief and Perceptions*, Cambridge, 1988, 81.

28 R. W. Ambler, 'The transformation of harvest celebrations in nineteenth-century Lincolnshire', *Midl Hist*, 3 (1976), 298–306. The revival of harvest celebrations is commonly attributed to Stephen Hawker of Morwenstow (Corn.); it was certainly a West Country phenomenon.

29 A. R. Wright, *British Calendar Customs*, vol. II, *Fixed Festivals*, London, 1938, 50–60.

30 R. U. Sayce, 'Seasonal bonfires', *Montg Collns*, 50 (1948), 77–91, 189–208; N. J. G. Pounds, *Hearth and Home*, Bloomington, IN, 1989, 6–7.

31 *Piers Plowman*, C Text, VII, lines 267–71.

32 *Lathe Court Rolls and Views of Frankpledge in the Rape of Hastings, 1387–1474*, ed. E. J. Courthope and B. E. R. Formoy, Suss Rec Soc, 37 (1931), 23.

33 *Court Rolls of the Manor of Acomb*, ed. H. Richardson, vol. I, Yks Arch Soc Rec Ser, 131 (1968), 135.

34 *Court Rolls of the Manor of Wakefield*, vol. I, 1274–97, ed. W. P. Baildon, Yks Arch Soc Rec Ser, 29 (1900), 246.

35 ibid., 113.

36 *Crown Pleas of the Wiltshire Eyre, 1249*, ed. C. A. F. Meekings, Wilts Arch Soc Rec Br, 16 (1960), no. 172, p. 186.

37 *Roll of the Justices in Eyre at Bedford, 1227*, ed. G. H. Fowler, Beds Hist Rec Soc, 3 (1916), 1–206 (pp. 189–90).

38 Thomas Tusser, *Five Hundred Pointes of Good Husbandrie*, ed. W. Payne and S. J. Herrtage, Eng Dial Soc, 1878, 144.

39 H. J. Habakkuk, 'La disparition du paysan anglais', *Ann ESC*, 20 (1965), 649–63.

40 G. C. Homans, *English Villagers of the Thirteenth Century*, New York, 1960, 309–27.

41 Alan Macfarlane, *The Origins of English Individualism*, Oxford, 1978, 19–23.

42 ibid., 32. The Macfarlane thesis has prompted a vigorous debate on the relations of family, kinship and land. See: R. M. Smith, 'Kin and neighbours in a thirteenth-century Suffolk community', *Jl Fam Hist*, 4 (1979), 219–56; Miranda Chaytor, 'Household and kinship: Ryton in the late sixteenth and early seventeenth centuries', *Hist Wkshp*, no. 10 (1980), 25–60; K. Wrightson, 'Household and kinship in sixteenth-century England', ibid., no. 12 (1981), 151–8; Zvi Razi, 'The erosion of the family–land bond in the late fourteenth and fifteenth centuries: a methodological note', *Land, Kinship and Life-Cycle*, ed. R. M. Smith, Cambridge, 1984, 292–304; C. Dyer, 'Changes in the link between families and land in the west Midlands in the

fourteenth and fifteenth centuries', ibid., 305–11; K. Wrightson, 'Kinship in an English village: Terling, Essex 1500–1700', ibid., 313–32; A Macfarlane, 'The myth of the peasantry: family and economy in a northern parish', ibid., 333–49.

43 Mildred Campbell, *The English Yeoman under Elizabeth and the early Stuarts*, New Haven, CT, 1942, 7–20.

44 H. J. Habakkuk, 'La disparition du paysan anglais'.

45 H. S. A. Fox, 'The alleged transformation from two-field to three-field systems in medieval England', *EcHR*, 39 (1986), 526–48.

46 A. G. Little 'Corrodies at the Carmelite friary of Lynn', *Jl Eccles Hist*, 9 (1958), 8–29.

47 William Harrison, *The Description of England*, ed. G. Edelen, Ithaca, NY, 1968, 134–5.

48 Quoted in N. J. G. Pounds, *An Economic History of Medieval Europe*, London, 1974, 191.

49 William Ashley, 'The place of rye in the history of English food', *Ec Jl*, 31 (1921), 285–308; A. G. L. Rogers, 'Was rye ever the ordinary food of the English?', *Ec Jl*, 32 (1922), 119–24.

50 *The Compotus of the Manor of Kettering, for 1292*, ed. Charles Wise, Kettering, 1899, 49–57. The term 'dredge' is still used in Cornwall for mixed grains.

51 *Robert Loders Farm Accounts 1610–1620*, ed. G. E. Russell, Camd Soc, 3rd ser., 53 (1936), xiii–xxv, for evidence of departures from the regular cropping system.

52 Sir William Ashley, *The Bread of our Forefathers*, Oxford, 1928, 14; E. J. T. Collins, 'Dietary change and cereal consumption in Britain in the nineteenth century', *Agr Hist Rv*, 23 (1975), 97–115.

53 Richard Carew of Anthony, *The Survey of Cornwall*, ed. F. E. Halliday, London, 1953, 102.

54 C. Dyer, 'English diet in the later Middle Ages', *Social Relations and Ideas*, Cambridge, 1983, 191–216.

55 'Collops', a Middle English word denoting 'egg and bacon'.

56 *Piers Plowman*, B Text, VI, lines 281–5.

57 Andrew Boorde, *A Compendyous Regyment or A Dietary of Helth*, EETS, extra ser., 10 (1870), 222–303 (p. 259).

58 *Northern Petitions Illustrative of Life in Berwick, Cumbria and Durham in the Fourteenth Century*, ed. C. M. Fraser, Surt Soc, 194 (1981), 107.

59 David J. Eveleigh, *Firegrates and Kitchen Ranges*, Aylesbury, 1983, 15–23.

60 Quoted in H. E. Hallam, 'The life of the people', *The Agrarian History of England and Wales*, 2 (1988), 818–53.

61 After H. E. Hallam, and based on *The Compotus of the Manor of Kettering*, ed. C. Wise.

62 *Piers Plowman*, B Text, VI, lines 281–94.

63 ibid., 303–6, Lammas was traditionally 1 August. Here it means harvest-time.

64 Dorothea Oschinsky, *Walter of Henley and Other Treatises on Estate Management*, Oxford, 1971, cap. 47, p. 321.

65 Supported by the manorial accounts of the Bishopric of Winchester; J. Titow, 'Evidence of weather in the Account Rolls of the Bishopric of Winchester', *EcHR*, 12 (1959–60), 360–407.

66 C. Dyer, *Standards of Living in the later Middle Ages*, Cambridge, 1989, 261ff.

67 J. Titow, 'Evidence of weather in the Account Rolls of the Bishopric of Winchester'.

68 W. G. Hoskins, 'Harvest fluctuations and English economic history, 1480–1619', *Agr Hist Rv*, 2 (1953–4), 28–46.

69 G. Shepherd, 'Poverty in *Piers Plowman*'.

70 John Gardener, MS of *c*.1440, quoted in Evelyn Cecil, *A History of Gardening in England*, London, 1910, 45. This book has a valuable section on the kitchen garden.

71 Chaucer, The Clerkes Tale, 224–6.

72 *Piers Plowman*, B Text, VI, line 282.

73 W. Harrison, *Description of England*.

74 J. H. Harvey, 'Vegetables in the Middle Ages', *Gdn Hist*, 12 (1984), 89–99.

75 J. C. Drummond and Anne Wilbraham, *The Englishman's Food*, London, 1958, 20–3; 29–31.

76 A. Boorde, *A Dietary of Helth*, 278–9.

77 Chaucer, 'Prologue', line 634.

78 R. N. Salaman, *The History and Social Influence of the Potato*, Cambridge, 1949, 424–33.

79 A. P. Phillips, 'The diet of the Savile household in the seventeenth century', Thor Soc, 63 (1959), 57–70.

80 H. E. Hallam, 'Southern England', *Agrarian History of England and Wales*, 2 (1988), 341–68.

81 I. Kershaw, *Bolton Priory, the Economy of a Northern Monastery, 1286–1325*, Oxford, 1973.

82 Kate Mason, 'Yorkshire cheese-making', *Folk-L*, 6 (1968), 7–17.

83 E. Miller, 'Northern England', *Agrarian History of England and Wales*, 3 (1991), 399–411.

84 H. E. Hallam, 'England before the Norman Conquest', *Agrarian History of England and Wales*, 2 (1988), 1–44; E. Ekwall, *The Chief Elements used in English Place-Names*, Eng P-N Soc, 1, pt 2, Cambridge, 1922, 12, 16.

85 Cornw Rec Off, Trebartha MSS, *The Spoure Book*.

86 A. Boorde, *A Dyetary of Helth*, 252–3.

87 H. A. Monckton, *A History of English Ale and Beer*, London, 1966.

88 R. J. Forbes, 'Food and drink', *A History of Technology*, 2 (1956), 103–46.

89 *Court Rolls of the Borough of Colchester*, vol. II, (1353–67), trans I. H. Jeayes, Colchester, 1938, 37–9.

90 *Farm and Cottage Inventories of Mid-Essex, 1635–1749*, ed. F. W. Steer, Chelmsford, 1950, 32–6.

91 Peter Clark, *The English Alehouse: A Social History*. London, 1983, 99ff.

92 Printed in Paul Slack, *Poverty in Early-Stuart Salisbury*, Wilts Rec Soc, 31 (1975), 109–34.

93 *West Riding Sessions Records*, vol. II, ed. John Lister, Yks Arch Soc Rec Ser, 53 (1915), xxxvi–xxxvii.

94 *Lancashire and Cheshire Wills and Inventories*, pt 2, Cheth Soc, 51 (1860), 277ff.

95 C. Dyer, *Standards of Living in the Later Middle Ages*, 58.

96 Author's calculation from C. Dyer's statistics of land use and cropping at Bishop's Cleeve (Glos), *Standards of Living*, 113.

97 *VCH, Sussex*, vol. II, 261.

98 H. A. Monckton, *A History of English Ale and Beer*, 77.

99 A. Boorde, *A Dietary of Helth*, 256.

100 Quoted in *Tudor Economic Documents*, vol. III, ed. R. H. Tawney and E. Power, London, 1924, 1–11.

101 P. Clark, *The English Alehouse*, 14.

102 Quoted in P. Clark, *The English Alehouse*, 14.

103 ibid., 211; *The English Glass Bottle through the Ages*, exhibition catalogue, County Museum, Truro, 1976, 'Introduction'.

104 R. J. Forbes, *Short History of the Art of Distillation*, Leiden, 1948, 89–97; John Philipson, 'The distillation of spirits in the eighteenth and early nineteenth centuries', *Arch Ael*, 4th ser., 36 (1958), 47–54.

105 J. C. Drummond and Anne Wilbraham, *The Englishman's Food*, London, 1959, 115–16.

106 In French *genièvre*; hence 'genever' and 'gin'.

107 Charles Wilson, *England's Apprenticeship, 1603–1763*; London, 1965, 307–9.

108 R. J. Forbes, 'The rise of food technology (1500–1900)', *Janus*, 47 (1958), 101–27, 139–55.

109 P. Clark, *The English Alehouse*, 214.

110 R. J. Forbes, 'Chemical, culinary and cosmetic arts', *A History of Technology*, vol. I, 238–98; J. Drummond and A. Wilbraham, *The Englishman's Food*, 313–26.

111 Sir Lindsay Scott, 'Corn-drying kilns', *Ant*, 25 (1951), 196–208: Gavin Bowie, 'Corn-drying kilns, meal milling and flour in Ireland', *Folk-L*, 17 (1979), 5–13.

112 R. J. Forbes, *Studies in Ancient Technology*, vol. III.

113 J. Drummond and A. Wilbraham, *The Englishman's Food*, 194–5.

114 R. J. Forbes, 'Chemical, culinary and cosmetic arts'.
115 *Diana Astry's Recipe Book*, ed. Bette Stitt, Beds Hist Rec Soc, 37 (1956), 83—168, no. 166.
116 W. D. Rasmussen, 'Food technology', *Tech & Cult*, 1 (1959—60), 376—81.
117 J. Storck and W. D. Teague, *Flour for Man's Bread: A History of Milling*, Minneapolis, MN, 1952.
118 Richard Bennett and John Elton, *History of Corn Milling*, vol. 1, *Handstones, Slave and Cattle Mills*, London, 1898.
119 V. G. Childe, 'Rotary querns on the continent and in the Mediterranean Basin', *Ant*, 17 (1943), 19—26.
120 E. C. Curwen, 'Querns', *Ant*, 11 (1937), 133—51; Curwen, 'More about querns', *Ant*, 15 (1941), 15—32.
121 R. Bennett and J. Elton, *History of Corn Milling*, vol. III, *Feudal Laws and Customs*, 1900.
122 M. T. Hodgen, 'Domesday water mills', *Ant*, 13 (1939), 261—79.
123 H. C. Darby, *Domesday England*, Cambridge, 1977, 270—5.
124 R. Wailes, *The English Windmill*, London, 1954.
125 John Salmon, 'A note on early tower windmills', *JBAA*, 3rd ser., 29 (1966), 75.
126 'Mills grinding exceeding far', *The Times*, 5 August, 1988.
127 O. G. S. Crawford and J. Roder, 'The quern-quarries of Mayen in the Eifel', *Ant*, 29 (1955), 68—76.
128 J. Radley, 'Peak millstones and Hallamshire grindstones', *Tr Newc Soc.* 36 (1963—4), 165—73.
129 J. Radley 'A millstone maker's smithy on Gardom's Edge', *Derb Arch Jl*, 84 (1964), 123—7; R. Meredith, 'Millstone making at Yarncliff in the reign of Edward IV', *Derb Arch Jl*, 101 (1981), 102—6.
130 J. Storck and W. D. Teague, *Flour for Man's Bread*, 197, 226.
131 Quoted in N. A. Bringeus, 'Man, food and milieu', *Folk-L*, 8 (1970), 45—56.
132 ibid.
133 James Woodforde, *The Diary of a Country Parson*, Oxford, World's Classics edn of 1949, 393; the date was 14 February 1791.
134 William Edward Mead, *The English Medieval Feast*, London, 1931, esp, 109ff.; *Two Fifteenth-Century Cookbooks*, ed. Thomas Austin, EETS, 1888, 91.
135 R. N. K. Rees and Charles Fenby, 'Meals and meal-times', *Englishmen at Rest and Play*, ed. R. Lennard, Oxford, 1931, 205—34.
136 *Manners and Meals in Olden Time*, ed. F. J. Furnivall, EETS, 1868, 5.
137 William Vaughan, *Naturall & Artificial Directions for Health*, 1602, printed in *Manners and Meals in Older Time*, ed. F. J. Furnivall, EETS, 1868, 249—53.
138 *The Household Book of Dame Alice de Bryene*, ed. V. B. Redstone, Suff Inst Arch, 1931.
139 'The household accounts of Elizabeth Berkeley, Countess of Warwick, 1420—1', ed. C. D. Ross, *Tr B & G Arch Soc*, 70 (1951), 81—105.
140 *Diana Astry's Recipe Book*.
141 B. K. Wheaton, *Savouring the Past: The French Table and Kitchen from 1300 to 1789*, London, 1983, 27—31.
142 From the German *Buchweizen* (='beech-wheat', from the shape of its seeds). It was a herbaceous plant, not a cereal.
143 Gunther Wiegelmann, 'Innovation in food and meals', *Folk-L*, 12 (1974), 20—30.
144 F. A. Filby, *A History of Food Adulteration and Analysis*, London, 1934.
145 J. Drummond and A. Wilbraham, *The Englishman's Food*, 186—90.

7 IN SICKNESS AND IN DEATH

1 J. Huizinga, *The Waning of the Middle Ages*, London, 1924, edn of 1954, esp. 29—31 and ch. 2; Jean Delumeau, *La Peur en occident (XIVe—XVIIIe siècles)*, Paris, 1978, 19—21, 211—43.

2 E. Clive Rouse, *Discovering Wall Paintings*, Princes Risborough, 1980, 40–1.

3 T. S. R. Boase, *Death in the Middle Ages*, London, 1972, 97ff.

4 *English Wills, 1498–1526*, ed. A. F. Cirket, Beds Hist Rec Soc, 37 (1956), 1–82.

5 *Somerset Medieval Wills (1383–1500)*, ed. F. W. Weaver, Som Rec Soc, 16 (1901), 80.

6 R. Burn, *Ecclesiastical Law*, vol. IV, London, 1775, 41–56.

7 G. Montagu Benton, 'Fingringhoe wills, A.D. 1400 to A.D. 1550', *Tr Ess Arch Soc*, NS 20 (1933), 51–728. For example *Lincoln Wills*, vol. II, Lincs Rec Soc, 22–3.

8 *English Wills 1498–1526*, 2–4.

9 Hen VIII, c. 5.

10 1 Vict, c. 26, sect. 9.

11 Margaret Spufford, 'The scribes of villagers' wills in the sixteenth and seventeenth centuries and their influence', *Loc Pop St*, 7 (1971), 28–43.

12 R. C. Richardson, 'Wills and will-makers in the sixteenth and seventeenth centuries: some Lancashire evidence', *Loc Pop St*, 9 (1972), 33–42.

13 For example the will of Henry de Colebi, 1271, *Lincoln Wills*, vol. II, 215–17.

14 *Lincoln Wills*, vol. II, xvii.

15 On probate formalities see *Lincoln Wills registered in the District Probate Registry at Lincoln*, vol. II, Lincs Rec Soc, 10 (1918), x–xxv; R. Burn, *Ecclesiastical Law*, vol. IV, London, edn of 1763, 176–214.

16 D. M. Owen, *The Records of the Established Church*, Brit Rec Assn, 1970, 44–5, 47–8.

17 *Before the Baudy Court*, ed. P. Hain, London, 1972, *passim*,

18 20/21 Vict, c. 77.

19 *The Ipswich Probate Inventories 1583–1631*, ed. Michael Reed, Suff Rec Soc, 22 (1981).

20 *Lincoln Wills*, vol. II, 23–4, 91; vol. III, 92.

21 *Lincoln Wills*, vol. III, 96.

22 *Lincoln Wills*, vol. II, 101–2.

23 J. M. C. Toynbee, *Death and Burial in the Roman World*, London, 1971, 43–63.

24 A. G. Langdon, *Old Cornish Crosses*, Truro, 1896.

25 H. W. Macklin, *The Brasses of England*, London, 1907; Muriel Clayton, *Catalogue of Rubbings of Brasses and Incised Slabs*, Victoria and Albert Museum, HMSO, 1968.

26 B. Kemp, *English Church Monuments*, London, 1980.

27 Katherine A. Esdaile, *English Church Monuments 1510–1840*, London,, 1946.

28 Quoted in F. Burgess, *English Churchyard Monuments*, London, 1963, 20.

29 *Lincoln Wills*, vol. II, 2.

30 *Somerset Medieval Wills*, 2nd ser, 1501–30, ed. F. W.Weaver, Som Rec Soc, 19 (1903), 211.

31 *Somerset Medieval Wills*, (1383–1500), Som Rec Soc, 16 (1901), 401.

32 Quoted in F. Burgess, *English Churchyard Memorials*, London, 1963, 25.

33 Warwick Rodwell, *The Archaeology of the English Church*, London, 1981, 134–66.

34 *The Yorkshire Diaries*, ed. C. E. Whiting, Yks Arch Soc Rec Ser, 117 (1951), 127.

35 *Lincoln Wills*, vol. III, 186.

36 F. Burgess, *English Churchyard Monuments*, 116–18.

37 H. Leslie White, *Monuments and their Inscriptions: A Practical Guide*, Soc Geneal, 1978; J. L. Rayment, *Notes on the Recording of Monumental Inscriptions*, Fed Fam Hist Soc, Plymouth, 1978.

38 From Old English *lic*, meaning corpse; cf German *Leiche*.

39 The Book of Common Prayer of the Anglican church contains a somewhat simplified version of the Latin liturgy.

40 Charles-Edward Amory Winslow, *The Conquest of Epidemic Disease*, Princeton, NJ, 1943, 3–52.

41 ibid., 236–66.

42 J. C. Cox, *The Parish Registers of England*, London, 1910.

43 J. T. Krause, 'The changing adequacy of English registration, 1690−1837', *Population in History*, ed. D. V. Glass and D. E. C. Eversley, London, 1965, 379−93.

44 E. A. Wrigley and R. S. Schofield, *The Population History of England 1541−1871*, London, 1981.

45 Most medieval tax records give only a parochial assessment. The Poll Tax of 1381 gives the numbers of the taxable population for each parish. The Poll Tax of 1661 and also the Hearth Taxes list tax-payers by name for each parish. Not all the parochial returns, however, have survived.

46 Jean Pierre Peter, 'Une enquête de la Société Royal de Médicine: malades et maladies à la fin du XVIIIe siècle', *Ann ESC*, 22 (1967), 711−51, trans. in *Biology of Man in History*, ed. Robert Forster and Orest Ranum, Baltimore, MD, 1975, 81−124.

47 Chaucer, *Canterbury Tales*, 'Prologue', lines 443−4.

48 *Leechdoms, Wortcunning and Starcraft of Early England*, ed. O. Cockayne, *RS*, 3 vols., 1864−6, esp. vol. I, 385−405. For the *Herbarium* of Dioscorides see vol. I. Vol. II contains the collection of leechdoms, or folk remedies.

49 Charles Singer, 'Early English magic and medicine', *Proc Brit Acad*, 1919−20, 341−74; G. Storms, *Anglo-Saxon Magic*, The Hague, 1948, 114−17.

50 SATOR = sower, i.e. creator.

51 G. Storms, *Anglo-Saxon Magic*, 281.

52 S. Rubin, *Medieval English Medicine*, Newton Abbot, 1974, 97−9; C. H. Talbot, *Medicine in Medieval England*, London, 1967, *passim*.

53 Theodor Puschmann, *A History of Medical Education, 1891*, edn of 1966, New York, 410ff.; R. S. Roberts, 'The personnel and practice of medicine in Tudor and Stuart England', *Med Hist*, 6 (1962), 363−82; 8 (1964), 217−34.

54 Quoted in F. N. L. Poynter and W. J. Bishop, 'A seventeenth-century doctor and his patients, 1592−1662', Beds Hist Red Soc, 31 (1950), 25−6.

55 R. S. Roberts, 'The personnel and practice of medicine in Tudor and Stuart England'.

56 PRO, SP/46/71, printed in N. J. G. Pounds, 'William Carnsew of Bokelly and his diary, 1576−7', *Jl Roy Inst Cornw*, 8, pt 1 (1978), 14−60.

57 Antimony trisulphide, which had been much used as an emetic.

58 *The Diary of Ralph Josselin 1616−1683*, ed. Alan Macfarlane, Rec Econ Soc Hist, NS 3, Oxford, 1976, 281.

59 See also *The Diary of Benjamin Rogers, Rector of Carlton. 1720−71*, Beds Hist Rec Soc, 30 (1949), 62.

60 N. J. G. Pounds, 'John Huxham's medical diary 1728−1752', *Loc Pop Stud*, no. 12 (1974), 34−7; reprinted in *Dev Hist*, no. 10, April 1975, 17−21.

61 J. Huxham, *Observations on the Air and Epidemic Disease*, London, 1759.

62 *Piers Plowman*, B, Text, XX, lines 81−7.

63 Robert Creswell, '*Une communauté rurale de l'Irelande*', Trav Mem Inst Eth, 74 (1969), 206−11.

65 A. Garfield Tourney, 'The physician and witchcraft in Restoration England', *Met Hist*, 16 (1972), 143−55.

65 Keith Thomas, *Religion and the Decline of Magic*, London, 1971; Penguin edn of 1973, 224. It is impossible to exaggerate the importance of this work.

66 Robert Burton, *The Anatomy of Melancholy*, vol. I, 256.

67 Thomas Hobbes, *Leviathan*, ed. M. Oakeshott, London, 1946, 12.

68 J. F. D. Shrewsbury, *A History of the Bubonic Plague in the British Isles*, Cambridge, 1971, 7−16; L. F. Hurst, *The Conquest of Plague*, Oxford, 1953.

69 G. Melvyn Howe, *Man, Environment and Disease in Britain*, Harmondsworth, 1972, 180−8.

70 P. E. Razzell, 'Population change in eighteenth-century England: a reinterpretation', *EcHR*, 18 (1965), 312−32; L. Clarkson, *Death, Disease and Famine in Pre-Industrial England*, Dublin, 1975, 54−6.

71 E. A. Wrigley and R. S. Schofield, *The Population History of England 1541–1871*, 390–1.

72 W. G. Hoskins, 'Harvest fluctuations and English economic history', *Agr Hist Rv*, 2 (1953–4) 28–46; E. Le Roy Ladurie, *Time of Feast, Time of Famine: A History of Climate since the Year 1000*, New York, 1971, *passim*.

73 The data are mainly for isolated records of seed used and of harvest gathered; see Slicher van Bath, 'Yield ratios', *AAG Bijd*, 10 (1963), *passim*.

74 A. B. Appleby, *Famine in Tudor and Stuart England*, Liverpool, 1978, 7.

75 E. Le Roy Ladurie, 'Famine amenorrhoea', *Biology of Man in History*, 163–78.

76 S. C. Watkins and E. van de Walle, 'Nutrition, mortality and population: Malthus' court of last resort', *Jl Interdisc Hist*, 14 (1983–4), 205–26.

77 K. F. Helleiner, 'The population of Europe from the Black Death to the eve of the vital revolution', *Camb Econ Hist Eur*, 4 (1967), 1–95; Helleiner, 'The vital revolution reconsidered', in *Population in History*, 79–86.

78 Thomas McKeown, *The Modern Rise of Population*, London, 1976, *passim*.

79 A. B. Appleby, 'Nutrition and disease: the case of London, 1550–1750', *Jl Interdisc Hist*, 6 (1975–6), 1–22.

80 MacArthur, 'Old-time typhus in Britain', *Tr Roy Soc Trop Med*, 20 (1926–7), 487–503.

81 Massimo Livi-Bacci, 'The nutrition–mortality link in past times', *Jl Interdisc Hist*, 14 (1983–4), 293–8.

82 G. E. Rothenberg, 'The Austrian sanitary cordon and the control of the bubonic plague 1710–1871', *Jl Hist Med Sci*, 28 (1973), 15–23.

83 P. Razzell, 'Population change in eighteenth-century England: a reinterpretation'.

84 L. Bradley, *Smallpox Innoculation: An Eighteenth-Century Mathematical Controversy*, Nottingham, 1971.

85 Cornw Rec Off, Parish Register, Wendron.

86 G. Talbot Griffith, *Population Problems of the Age of Malthus*, Cambridge, 1926, 250–1.

87 T. McKeown, *The Modern Rise of Population*, 108–9.

88 D. E. C. Eversley, 'Mortality in Britain in the eighteenth century', *Actes Coll Int Dem Hist*, Liège, n.d.

89 J. Stevenson, 'Food riots in England, 1792–1818', *Popular Protest and Public Order*, ed. R. Quinault and J. Stevenson, London, 1974, 33–74.

90 Based on W. G. Hoskins, 'Harvest fluctuations and English economic history'.

91 Quoted in W. S. C. Copeman, *Doctors and Disease in Tudor Times*, London, 1960, 157.

92 ibid.

93 Magnus Pike, *Success in Nutrition*, London, 1975 for a summary of dietary requirements.

94 *London Assize of Nuisance 1301–1431*, ed. H. M. Chew and W. Kellaway, Lond Rec Soc, 10 (1973), xxv.

95 C. M. Cipolla, *Cristofano and the Plague*, London, 1973, 24ff.

96 Philip Ziegler, *The Black Death*, London, 1969, esp. 259–79; Johannes Nohl, *The Black Death*, London, 1961, 134–44.

97 P. Ziegler, *The Black Death*, 270.

98 L. F. Hurst, *The Conquest of Plague*, 29ff.

99 W. S. C. Copeman, *Doctors and Disease in Tudor Times*, 127–31.

100 N. J. G. Pounds, 'John Huxham and his diary'.

101 W. H. McNeil, *Plagues and Peoples*, New York, 1976, 262–4. John Huxham recorded Asian cholera in Plymouth. If correct the infection must have been brought in by ship. Evidently it was contained.

102 *Snow on Cholera, being a Reprint of Two Papers by John Snow, MD*, New York, 1936.

103 G. R. Batho, 'The plague of Eyam: a tercentenary evaluation', *Derb Arch Jl*, 84 (1964), 81–91.

104 William H. McNeil, *Plagues and Peoples*, New York, 1976.

105 John Hatcher, *Plague, Population and the English Economy 1348–1530*, London, 1977; E. A. Wrigley and R. S. Schofield, *The Population History of England*.

106 E. A. Wrigley, 'Family limitation in pre-industrial England', *EcHR*, 19 (1966), 82–109.

107 The term 'birth-rate' is used for convenience; what the registers show is, of course, the baptismal rate.

108 E. A. Wrigley, 'Mortality in pre-industrial England: the example of Colyton, Devon, over three centuries', *Population and Social Change*, ed. D. V. Glass and R. Revelle, London, 1972, 243–73.

109 J. D. Post, *The Last Great Subsistence Crisis in the Western World*, Baltimore, MD, 1977; Henry and Elizabeth Stommel, 'The year without a summer', *Sci Am*, June 1979, 134–40.

110 E. A. Wrigley, 'Family limitation in pre-industrial England'.

111 'Infant' is generally taken to be up to one year; 'child' from one to the early 'teens; see L. Bradley, *A Glossary for Local Population Studies*, Nottingham, 1971.

112 T. H. Hollingsworth, 'The importance of the quality of data in historical demography', *Population and Social Change*, 71–86.

113 U. M. Cowgill, 'Life and death in the sixteenth century in the city of York', *Pop St*, 21 (1967), 53–62.

114 D. E. C. Eversley, 'A survey of population in an area of Worcestershire from 1660 to 1850 on the basis of parish registers', *Population in History*, 394–419.

115 Roger Schofield, 'An anatomy of an epidemic', *The Plague Reconsidered*, Cambridge, 1977, 95–126.

116 E. A. Wrigley and R. S. Schofield, *The Population History of England*, 389–91.

117 *The Autobiography of Mrs Alice Thornton*, Surt Soc, 62 (1873), 95.

118 ibid., 49, 139–41.

119 John Mirk, *Instructions for Parish Priests*, ed. Edward Peacock, London, 1868, lines 91–4.

120 R. Burn, *Ecclesiastical Law*, vol. I, 105–7.

121 *The Journal of Nicholas Assheton of Downham*, ed. F. R. Raines, Cheth Soc, 14 (1848), 81.

122 Quoted in T. R. Forbes, in *Med Hist*, 8 (1964), 235–44.

123 *The Autobiography of Mrs Alice Thornton*, 144–5.

124 *The Autobiography of Sir John Bramston*, Camd Soc, 1845, 111.

125 T. R. Forbes, 'The regulation of English midwives in the sixteenth and seventeenth centuries', *Med Hist*, 8 (1964), 235–44.

126 F. H. Garrison, *An Introduction to the History of Medicine*, Philadelphia, PA, 1929.

127 T. McKeown, *The Modern Rise of Population*, 105–6.

128 E. M. Halcrow, 'The charity for the relief of poor women lying-in at their own homes', *Arch Ael*, 4th ser., 34 (1956), 110–29.

129 C. White, *A Treatise on the Management of Pregnant and Lying-in Women*, London, 1773, *passim*.

8 THE COMMUNITY OF PARISH AND VILLAGE

1 For a collection of such 'laws' see *The Book of John Rowe*, ed. W. H. Godfrey, Suss Rec Soc, 34 (1928), *passim*.

2 A. Macfarlane, 'History, anthropology and the study of communities', *Soc Hist*, no. 5 (1977), 631–52.

3 The chief works are: A. Macfarlane, 'History, anthropology and the study of communities'; Lawrence Stone, *The Family, Sex and Marriage 1500–1800*, London, 1977; John Bossy, 'Blood and baptism: kinship, community and Christianity in western Europe from the fourteenth to the seventeenth centuries', *Sanctity and Secularity: The Church and the World*, ed. D. Baker, Studies in Church History, 10 (1973), 129–43.

4 Lawrence Stone, *The Family, Sex and Marriage*, 98.

5 Keith Thomas, *Religion and the Decline of Magic*, Harmondsworth, 1973, 669–80; Keith Wrightson, 'Aspects of social differentiation in rural England', *Jl Peas St*, 5 (1977–8), 33–47.

6 J. A. Sharpe, 'Such disagreement between neighbours: litigation and human relations in early modern England', in *Disputes and Settlements: Law and Human Relations in the West*, ed. J. Bossy, Cambridge, 1983, 167–87.

7 J. Bossy, 'Holiness and society', *P & P*, no. 75 (1977), 119–37.

8 ibid.

9 J. Bossy, 'Blood and baptism'.

10 ibid.

11 *Piers Plowman*, B Text, XVIII, line 378.

12 J. Bossy, 'Blood and baptism'.

13 *Norwich Consistory Court Depositions, 1499–1512*, ed. E. D. Stone and B. Cozens-Hardy, Norf Rec Soc, 10 (1938), no. 57. For an early instance of the merging of parishes see *The Register of William Wickwane, Lord Archbishop of York 1279–1285*, Surt Soc, 114 (1907), 21.

14 The Church of Wales was disestablished and was separated from the Church of England in 1920.

15 C. Hill, *Society and Puritanism in Pre-Revolutionary England*, London, 1964, 420–42.

16 There are instances of the burial of baptismal fonts that have been abandoned for regular use beneath the floor of the chancel.

17 A particularly detailed account of the parochial participation in the building of the local parish church is J. J. Wilkinson, 'Receipts and expenses in the building of Bodmin Church, 1469, to 1472', *Camd Misc 7*, Camd Soc, ser. 2, 14 (1875).

18 *Visitations in the Diocese of Lincoln 1517–1531*, ed. A. Hamilton Thompson, Lincs Rec Soc, 33 (1940), editor's introduction, xxv–xxxvii.

19 ibid., xxvi.

20 *Miscellany Accounts of the Diocese of Carlisle with Terriers*, ed. R. S. Ferguson, *Tr Cumb Westm AAS* (1877), 93.

21 J. W. Goering, 'The changing face of the village parish II: the thirteenth century', *Pathways to Medieval Peasants*, 323–33.

22 A. F. Johnston, 'Parish entertainments in Berkshire', *Pathways to Medieval Peasants*, ed. J. A. Raftis, Toronto, 1981, 335–8.

23 James Obelkevich, *Religion and Rural Society: South Lindsey 1825–1875*, Oxford, 1976, 281.

24 William A. Chaney, 'Paganism to Christianity in Anglo-Saxon England', *Harv Theol Rv*, 53 (1960), 197–217.

25 J. Obelkevich, *Religion and the People 800–1700*, Chapel Hill, NC, 1979, 5.

26 J. Bossy, 'The Counter-Reformation and the people of Catholic Europe', *P & P*, no. 47 (1970), 51–70.

27 C. G. Jung, *Man and His Symbols*, London, 1964, especially 'Ancient myths and modern man', 104–57.

28 Robert Redfield, *Peasant Society and Culture*, Chicago, 1956, 71–2; also Jean Delumeau, *Le Catholicisme entre Luther et Voltaire*, Paris, 1977, 236–7.

29 Thomas Hobbes, *Leviathan*, xiii.

30 C. von Sydow, *Selected Papers on Folklore*, Copenhagen, 1948, 11ff., 16ff.

31 Tina Solas and Franꝗise Zonabend, 'Tillers of the fields and woodspeople', *Rural Society in France*, ed. R. Forster and O. Ranum, Baltimore, MD, 1977, 126–51.

32 K. Thomas, 'Work and leisure in pre-industrial society', *P & P*, no. 29 (1964), 50–66.

33 Johann Huizinga, *Homo Ludens: A Study of the Play Element in Culture*, London, 1970, 34.

34 ibid., 205.

35 G. C. Homans, quoted in Trefor Owen, *Welsh Folk Customs*, Nat Mus Wales, 1974, 20.

36 Trefor M. Owen, *Welsh Folk Customs*, 20–1.

37 *Encycl Brit*, 1962 edn, *sub* 'Dance'.

38 The dance performed at the 'disco' today seems to this non-participant to be returning to its primitive and uncoordinated roots.

39 *Lambeth Churchwardens' Accounts, 1504–1645 and Vestry Book 1610*, ed. C. Drew, Surr Rec Soc, 18 (1941), 82.

40 *Tudor Churchwardens' Accounts*, ed. A. Palmer, Herts Rec Soc, 1 (1985), 66.

41 *Churchwardens' Accounts of Croscombe, Pilton, Yatton, Tintinhull Morebath and St Michael's Bath*, ed. Bishop Hobhouse, Som Rec Soc, 4 (1890), 4.

42 Bob Scribner, 'Reformation, carnival and the world turned upside-down', *Soc Hist*, 3 (1978), 303–29.

43 Thomas G. Barnes, 'County politics and a Puritan *cause célèbre*: Somerset churchales, 1633', *TrRHS*, 5th ser., 9 (1959), 103–22.

44 A. Swinburne, 'Persephone'.

45 G. R. Owst, *Literature and Pulpit in Medieval England*, Oxford. 1961, 37.

46 Anthony Weir and James Jerman, *Images of Lust: Sexual Carvings on Medieval Churches*, London, 1986, 11–22.

47 M. A. Murray, 'Female fertility figures', *Jl Roy Anthr Inst*, 64 (1934), 93–100.

48 Illustrated in G. R. Lewis, *Illustrations of Kilpeck Church, Hertefordshire*, London, 1842. The drawing of the *sheela* is noticeably bowdlerised. It appears also in A. Weir and J. Jerman, *Images of Lust*, 16.

49 Aron Gurevich, *Medieval Popular Culture: Problems of Belief and Perceptions*, Cambridge, 1988, xviii.

50 J. Delumeau, *Le Catholicisme entre Luther et Voltaire*, 160.

51 ibid., 78–98.

52 ibid., 96.

53 J. W. Goering, 'The changing face of the village parish'.

54 J. Bossy, 'The Counter-Reformation and the people of Catholic Europe'.

55 A. Hamilton Thompson, *The English Clergy and their Organization in the later Middle Ages*, Oxford, 1947, esp. 115–17.

56 Robert Muchembled, *Culture populaire et culture des élites dans la France moderne (xve–xviiie siècles)*, Paris, 1978, 50–61.

57 The term 'beating' is synonymous with walking; cf the policeman's 'beat'.

58 Helen Cam, *Law-finders and Law-makers*, London, 1963, 12.

59 *Ledger-Book of Vale Royal Abbey*, ed. J. Brownbill, Lancs Chesh Rec Soc, 68 (1914), 31.

60 *Select Pleas in Manorial and Other Seigneurial Courts*, vol. I, ed. F. W. Maitland, Seld Soc, 2 (1988), 'Introduction'.

61 W. A. Morris, *View of Frankpledge*, Cambridge, 1910. For a detailed consideration of the system at a local level, P. A. S. Pool, 'The tithings of Cornwall', *Jl Roy Inst Cornw*, NS (1981), 275–337.

62 *Piers Plowman*, C Text, VIII, lines 30–4.

63 Mary C. Hill, 'Dowdeswell Court Book, 1577–1673', *Tr B & G Arch Soc*, 67 (1946–8), 119–216.

64 R. H. Hilton, *A Medieval Society*, London, 1966, 149.

65 *The Register of Edmund Stafford (1395–1419)*, ed. F. C. Hingeston-Randolf, London, 1886, 239–40.

66 J. H. Matthews, *History of St Ives, Towednack, Zennor*, London, 182, 54–8, 98–9.

67 *Magnum Registrum Album*, ed. H. E. Savage, Collns Hist Staffs (1924), 40.

68 J. A. Raftis, *Tenure and Mobility*, Pont Inst Med St, Toronto (1964), 133–8, 268–70.

69 J. A. Raftis, *Tenure and Mobility*, 139–52.

70 W. E. Tate, *The Parish Chest*, Cambridge, 3rd edn, 1969, 43–83.

71 J. C. Cox, *Churchwardens' Accounts*, London, 1913.

72 Elsbeth Philipps, 'A list of printed churchwardens' accounts', *EHR*, 15 (1900), 335–41.

73 *Elizabethan Churchwardens' Accounts*, ed. J. E. Farmiloe and R. Nixseaman, Beds Hist Rec Soc, 33 (1953), xi–xvi.

74 ibid., xxix.

75 Christopher Hill, 'The secularization of the parish', *Society and Puritanism in Pre-Revolutionary England*, London, 1964, 420–42.

76 Thomas L. Tudor, 'Notes on an old churchwardens' account book (1598–1718) concerning the church and parish of St Werburgh in Derby', *Jl Derb Arch Soc*, 39 (1917), 192–223; 40 (1918), 214–37; 41 (1919), 38–51.

77 *Lambeth Churchwardens' Accounts*, xi–xiv.

78 J. C. Cox, *Bench Ends in English Churches*, Oxford, 1916, 1–10.

79 *Tudor Parish Documents of the Diocese of York*, ed. J. S. Purvis, Cambridge, 1948, 61; the floor was likely to have been of beaten earth.

80 Quoted in J. C. Cox, *Bench Ends in English Churches*, 4–6.

81 F. G. Emmison, *Elizabethan Life: Morals and the Church Courts*, Chelmsford, 1973, 131.

82 *The Archdeacon's Court: Liber Actorum, 1584*, vol. II, ed. E. R. Brinkworth, Oxf Rec Soc, 24 (1942), 171.

83 *The Churchwardens' Presentments in the Oxfordshire Peculiars of Dorchester, Thame and Banbury*, ed. S. A. Peyton, Oxf Rec Soc, 10 (1928), xxxii.

84 *Lambeth Churchwardens' Accounts*, liii–liv.

85 *Churchwardens' Accounts of Ashburton, 1479–1580*, ed. Alison Hanham, D & C Rec Soc, 15 (1970), 41.

86 Sir John Maclean, 'Notes on the accounts of the procurators, or churchwardens, of the parish of St Ewen's, Bristol', *Tr B & G Arch Soc*, 15 (1890–1). 139–82.

87 *Churchwardens' Accounts of the Town of Ludlow*, ed. Thomas Wright, Camd Soc, 102 (1869).

88 *The Rector's Book, Clayworth, Notts*, ed. H. Gill and E. L. Guilford, Nottingham, 1910, 26.

89 Cornw Rec Off, P128/6/2.

90 Richard Gough, *The History of Myddle*, edn of 1981, Harmondsworth; the seating plan is shown on pp. 80–3; see also David G. Hey, *An English Rural Community: Myddle under the Tudors and Stuarts*, Leicester, 1974.

91 J. B. Black, *The Reign of Elizabeth 1558–1603*, Oxford, 1959, 170.

92 As shown in many churchwardens' accounts. Most early pulpits are of Elizabethan date.

93 The disabilities of nonconformists continued until, in 1871, they were admitted to the older universities.

94 S. A. Peyton, 'The religious census of 1676', *EHR*, 48 (1933), 99–104; Thomas Richards, 'The religious census of 1676', *Tr Cymm*, suppl. vol., 1927.

95 *Visitations in the Diocese of Lincoln 1517–1531*, xxv–xxvii.

96 *Tudor Parish Documents of the Diocese of York*, 181; the patron who was so obdurate was Queen Elizabeth I.

97 *Miscellany Accounts of the Diocese of Carlisle*, 26.

98 A. Betterton and D. Dymond, *Lavenham, Industrial Town*, Lavenham, 1989, 12.

99 *Tudor Parish Documents of the Diocese of York*, 54.

100 Cornw Rec Off, P132/8/1.

101 *Elizabethan Churchwardens' Accounts*, 33.

102 *Churchwardens' Accounts of Croscombe*, etc., 221–2.

103 *Miscellany Accounts of the Diocese of Carlisle*, 42.

104 *Churchwardens' Accounts of Croscombe*, etc., 209.

105 C. B. Firth, 'Village gilds of Norfolk in the fifteenth century', *Norf Arch*, 18 (1914), 161–203; J. C. S. Stevenson, 'A Dorset parish guild', *Proc Dors NHAS*, 61 (1939), 86–8; F. E. Warren, 'Gild of S. Peter in Bradwell', *Proc Suff Inst Arch*, 11 (1903), 81–145.

106 The archers were linked with the names of Robin Hood and Little John, suggesting that their activities were mainly convivial. The 'hogglers' could possibly have been labourers; see *Churchwardens' Accounts of Croscombe*, etc., 251–3.

107 R. B. Dobson, 'The foundation of perpetual chantries by the citizens of medieval York', *Studies in Church History*, 4, *The Province of York*, Leiden, 1967, 22–38; A. Hamilton Thompson, 'The chantry certificates for Northamptonshire', *Ass Arch Soc, Repts Pap*, 31 (1911–12), 87–178.

108 *The Account Books of the Gilds of St George and of St Mary in the Church of St Peter, Nottingham*, Thor Soc Rec Ser, 7 (1939), 34.

109 ibid., 43.

110 ibid., 69ff.

111 The Poor Law of 1598 in fact codified and systematised a vast amount of national legislation and local practice.

112 *Elizabethan Churchwardens' Accounts*, 96.

113 *South Newington Churchwardens' Accounts*, 36.

114 *The Rector's Book, Clayworth*, 24.

115 *Visitations of the Diocese of Lincoln*, lii.

116 *Boxford Churchwardens' Accounts 1530–1561*, ed. Peter Northeast, Suff Rec Soc, 23 (1982), 42.

117 *South Newington Churchwardens' Accounts, 1553–1684*, ed. E. R. C. Brinkworth, Banb Hist Soc, 6 (1964), 16.

118 *Tudor Parish Documents*, 178.

119 *The Archdeacon's Court: Liber Actorum*, 43.

120 *Tudor Parish Documents*, 56; other instances of the profanation of both church and churchyard are cited.

121 'Episcopal visitations in the diocese of Durham 1662–1671', *Arch Ael*, 34 (1956), 92–109.

122 *Churchwardens' Accounts of Ashburton*, 82–3.

123 *Elizabethan Churchwardens' Accounts*, 8.

124 ibid., 10.

125 ibid., xxxix.

126 *Before the Bawdy Court*, no. 99, p. 64; also *The Archdeacon's Court: Liber Actorum*, 4.

127 *Boxford Churchwardens' Accounts*, xiii.

128 *Churchwardens' Presentments in the Oxfordshire Peculiars*, liv–lv.

129 *South Newington Churchwardens' Accounts*, vii.

130 *Elizabethan Churchwardens' Accounts*, 6–7.

131 *Churchwardens' Accounts of Marston, Spelsbury, Pyrton*, ed. F. W. Weaver and G. N. Clark, Oxf Rec Soc, 6 (1925), 13.

132 *Churchwardens' Accounts of the Parish of South Littleton, Worcestershire, 1548–1571*, ed. E. A. B. Barnard, Tr Worcs Arch Soc, 3 (1925–6), 60–106.

133 *Churchwardens' Accounts of Croscombe*, etc., 80.

134 *The Churchwardens' Accounts of St Nicholas, Strood*, ed. H. R. Plomer, Kent Rec Soc, 5 (1927), xxxi.

135 W. E. Tate, *The Parish Chest*, 94; the act in question was 31 and 32 Vict, c. 109 (1867–8).

136 Peter Mews *Ex-aletation of Ale*, 1671.

137 W. E. Tate, *The Parish Chest*, 87–90.

138 *Lambeth Churchwardens' Accounts*, vol. I, li–liv; this is a very good survey of parochial income and expenditure.

139 *Calendar of Coroners' Rolls of the City of London 1300–1378*, ed. R. R. Sharpe, London, 1913, Roll A, no. 21.

140 This must have been akin to traditional Cornish 'wrestling', in which the contestants held one another by their coats.

141 *West Riding Sessions Records*, vol. II, ed. John Lister, Yks Arch Soc Rec Ser, 52 (1915), 8.

142 J. Huizinga, *Homo Ludens*, 205.

143 R. W. Malcolmson, *Popular Recreations in English Society, 1700–1850*, Cambridge, 197?, 75.

144 J. Huizinga, *Homo Ludens*, 78–9.

145 C. Daryll Forde, *Habitat, Economy and Society*, London, 1934, 88–90.

146 C. O'Rahilly, *Tain Bo Cualnge*, Dublin, 1967, 158–9.

147 I. J. Stewart and M. J. Watkins, 'An 11th-century bone *tabula* set from Gloucester', *Med Arch*, 28 (1984), 185–90; I. J. Stewart, 'Note on the *tabula*, 1983–84', *Med Arch*, 32 (1988), 31–5.

148 BL, Add MS 4230, fo. 76v.

149 *Before the Bawdy Court*, no. 17, p. 38.

150 E. Clive Rouse, *Discovering Wall Paintings*, Shire Publications, 1991, 42.

151 A stick-and-ball game was frequently mentioned in early Irish writings, and was the forerunner of both hurling and hockey; *Encycl Brit*, *sub* 'Hockey', 'Hurling'.

152 C. O'Rahilly, *Tain*, 159.

153 Anne Ross, *The Pagan Celts*, London, 1986, 79.

154 *Foedera*, vol. III, pt 2, 704; on objections to games see Dennis Brailsford, *Sport and Society: Elizabeth to Anne*, London, 1969.

155 *Blundell's Diary*, ed. T. Ellison Gibson, Liverpool, 1895, 160 and *passim*.

156 Philippe Ariès, *Centuries of Childhood*, London, 1962, 70.

157 *South Newington Churchwardens' Accounts*, 52.

158 Notably in *Episcopal Visitations in the Diocese of Durham 1662–1671*, ed. J. Rogan, *Arch Ael*, 34 (1956), 92–109.

159 *The Constitutional Documents of the Puritan Revolution 1625–1660*, ed. S. R. Gardiner, Oxford, 1906, 99–103.

160 'Churchwardens' accounts of All Saints' Church Walsall 1462–1531', ed. G. P. Mander, *Collns Hist Staffs* (1928), 173–267.

161 *Churchwardens' Accounts of Croscombe*, etc., 13.

162 *Elizabethan Churchwardens' Accounts*, xxiv.

163 *Churchwardens' Accounts of Ashburton*, 53.

164 *Boxford Churchwardens' Accounts*, 2.

165 J. J. Raven, *Church Bells*, London, Antiquaries' Library; *Elizabethan Churchwardens' Accounts*, xxiff.

166 *Before the Bawdy Court*, 81.

167 *Churchwardens' Accounts of St Nicholas, Strood*, 24, 27.

9 THE FAMILY

1 *The Rector's Book, Clayworth, Nottinghamshire*, ed. H. Gill and E. L. Guilford, Nottingham, 1910, 19.

2 ibid., 83–8.

3 For an analysis of this document see Peter Laslett, 'Clayworth and Cogenhoe', *Family Life and Illicit Love in Earlier Generations*, Cambridge, 1977, 50–101.

4 A woman's previous marriage would have been noted only if there had been children by it.

5 Margaret Spufford, *Contrasting Communities: English Villagers in the Sixteenth and Seventeenth Centuries*, Cambridge, 1974, xxii and *passim*.

6 M. Spufford, 'Peasant inheritance customs and land distribution in Cambridgeshire from the sixteenth to the eighteenth centuries', *Family and Inheritance*, ed. J. Goody, J. Thirsk and E. Thompson, Cambridge, 1976, 156–76.

7 R. H. Hilton, 'A crisis of feudalism', *P & P*, no. 80 (1978), 3–19.

8 F. M. Stenton, 'The free peasantry of the northern Danelaw', *Bul Roy Soc Lund*, 1925–6, 79; H. C. Darby, *Domesday England*, Cambridge, 1977, 57–87.

9 Robert Redfield, *Peasant Society and Culture*, Chicago, 1956, 27–8.

10 G. R. J. Jones, 'Post-Roman Wales', *The Agrarian History of England and Wales*, vol. I, pt 2, 283–382.

11 Cicely Howell, 'Peasant inheritance customs in the Midlands, 1200–1700', *Family and Inheritance*, 112–55.

12 Alan Macfarlane, *The Origins of English Individualism*, Oxford, 1978, 19.

13 A. Macfarlane, 'The myth of the peasantry: family and economy in a northern parish', *Land, Kinship and Life-Cycle*, ed. R. M. Smith, Cambridge, 1984, 333–491.

14 Bracton, *De Legibus Angliae*, RS, vol. I, 2–4.

15 *Carte Nativorum*, ed. C. N. L. Brooke and M. M. Poston, Northants Rec Soc, 20 (1960), xxxi.

16 G. R. J. Jones, 'Post-Roman Wales', 283–382.

17 R. R. Davies, 'The survival of the blood-feud in medieval Wales', *Hist*, 54 (1969), 338–57. See also ch. 4, n. 63.

18 R. M. Smith, 'Kin and neighbours in a thirteenth-century Suffolk community', *Jl Fam Hist*, 4 (1979), 219–56.

19 Miranda Chaytor, 'Household and kinship: Ryton in the late 16th and early 17th centuries', *Hist Wkshp*, 10 (1980), 25–60.

20 Keith Wrightson, 'Household and kinship in sixteenth-century England', *Hist Wkshp*, 12 (1981), 151–8.

21 *The Diary of Ralph Josselin, 1616–1683*, ed. A. Macfarlane, Rec Econ Soc Hist, NS 3 (1976).

22 K. Wrightson, 'Kinship in an English village: Terling, Essex, 1500–1700', *Land, Kinship and Life-Cycle*, 313–32.

23 Lawrence Stone, 'The rise of the nuclear family in early modern England: the patriarchal stage', *The Family in History*, ed. C. E. Rosenberg, Philadelphia, PA, 1975, 13–57.

24 Richard Wall, 'The household: demographic and economic change in England, 1650–1870', *Family Forms in Historic Europe*, ed. R. Wall, J. Robin and P. Laslett, Cambridge, 1983, 493–512.

25 Philip E. Mosely, 'The distribution of the Zadruga within southeastern Europe', *The Joshua Starr Memorial Volume, Jew Soc St*, 5 (1953), 219–30.

26 T. H. Hollingsworth, *The Demography of the British Peerage*, Pop St, Supplementary vol., 1964.

27 T. H. Hollingsworth, *Historical Demography*, London, 1969, 139–45; W. E. Tate, *The Parish Chest*, 3rd edn, 1969, 43–83.

28 The Cambridge Group for the History of Population and Social Structure has promoted the analysis of a large number of registers.

29 P. Laslett, *The World We Have Lost*, 2nd edn, Cambridge, 1971, 84–92.

30 F. G. Emmison, *Elizabethan Life: Morals and the Church Courts*, Chelmsford, 1973, 164.

31 ibid., 158; *Act Book of the Archdeacon of Taunton*, ed. J. Jenkins, Collectanea II, Som Rec Soc, 43 (1928), 30; *Norwich Consistory Court Depositions, 1499–1512 and 1518–1530*, ed. E. D. Stone and B. Cozens-Hardy, Norf Rec Soc, 10 (1938), no. 90.

32 J. Bossy, 'Blood and baptism: kinship community and Christianity in western Europe from the fourteenth to the seventeenth centuries', *Sanctity and Secularity: The Church and the World*, ed. D. Baker, Studies in Church History, 10 (1973), 129–43.

33 *Piers Plowman*, B Text, IX, lines 113–17.

34 *Before the Bawdy Court*, ed. P. Hair, London, 1972, 239–40.

35 ibid., 147.

36 ibid., 25; P. E. H. Hair, 'Bridal pregnancy in earlier rural England', *Pop St*, 24 (1970), 59–70; Hair, 'Bridal pregnancy in earlier rural England further examined', *Pop St*, 24 (1970), 59–70.

37 In conversation with the author.

38 *Before the Bawdy Court*, no. 59.

39 ibid., nos. 84, 244.

40 F. G. Emmison, *Elizabethan Life*, 36–7.

41 P. Laslett, 'Long-term trends in bastardy in England', *Family Life and Illicit Love in Earlier Generations*, Cambridge, 1977, 102–59.

42 *Before the Bawdy Court*, no. 101.

43 *Churchwardens' Presentations*, pt 1, ed. Hilda Johnstone, Suss Rec Soc, 49 (1947–8), 8.

44 M. Chaytor, 'Household and kinship'; K. Wrightson, 'Household and kinship in sixteenth-century England'.

45 *Oxford Dictionary of the Christian Church*, Oxford, 1958, *sub* 'Matrimony'.

46 Chaucer, 'Prologue', line, 460.

47 John R. Gillis, 'Conjugal settlements: resort to clandestine and common law marriage in England and Wales, 1650–1850', *Disputes and Settlements; Law and Human Relations in the West*, ed. J. Bossy, Cambridge, 1983, 261–86.

48 Facsimile of records in P. Laslett, *Family Life and Illicit Love*, 121.

49 Olive Anderson 'The incidence of civil marriage in Victorian England and Wales', *P & P*, no. 69 (1975), 550–87.

50 P. Laslett, 'Long-term trends in bastardy'.

51 A Hanseatic seaman. Sailors at loose in a foreign port would then, as now, have been particularly vulnerable to the operations of a pimp.

52 *Before the Bawdy Court*, no. 533.

53 ibid., no. 507; F. G. Emmison, *Elizabethan Life*, 31ff.

54 Added by Cranmer: L. Stone, 'The rise of the nuclear family in early modern England: the patriarchal stage', *The Family in History*, ed. C. E. Rosenberg, Philadelphia, PA, 1975, 13–57.

55 *Before the Bawdy Court*, no. 99; in other dioceses the midwife's oath was broadly similar.

56 ibid., nos. 212, 322.

57 David Clark, Dissertation, History Department, Indiana University.

58 Lawrence Stone, *The Family, Sex and Marriage in England, 1500–1800*, London, 1977, 107–8.

59 *The Oxford Dictionary of the Christian Church*, Oxford, 1958, *sub* 'Baptism'.

60 F. G. Emmison, *Elizabethan Life*, 140.

61 B. Midi Berry, 'Age at baptism in pre-industrial England', *Pop St*, 25 (1971), 453–63; Stephen Porter, 'Age at baptism in Gloucester in the mid-seventeenth century', *Tr B & G Arch Soc*, 98 (1980), 131–4.

62 P. Laslett, 'Mean household size in England since the sixteenth century', *Household and Family in Past Time*, Cambridge, 1972, 125–58, a revised version of 'Size and structure of the household in England over three centuries', *Pop St*, 23 (1969), 199–223. But see also Nigel Goose, 'Household size and structure in early Stuart Cambridge', *Soc Hist*, 5 (1980), 347–85.

63 Infant mortality was that occurring during the first year of life; childhood mortality is taken as that from 1 to about 14 years.

64 E. A. Wrigley, 'Mortality in pre-industrial England: the example of Colyton, Devon, over three centuries', *Daed*, (Spring 1968), 546–80.

65 Philippe Ariès, *Centuries of Childhood*, London, 1962, 62–99.

66 ibid., 70.

67 *Journal de Jean Héroard*, ed. E. Soulie and E. de Bartelemy, Paris, 1868, 2 vols; also Ariès, *Centuries of Childhood*, London, 1962, *passim*.

68 On the sexual education of the young, see L. Stone, *The Family, Sex and Marriage*, 507–18.

69 Arnold van Gennep, *Rites of Passage*, London, 1960, 65–115.

70 *Oxford Dictionary of the Christian Church*, *sub* 'Confirmation'.

71 *Calendar of the Bristol Apprentice Books*, pt 1, ed. D. Hillis, Brist Rec Soc, 14 (1949); ibid., pt 2, ed. E. R. and N. M. Hardwick, Brist Rec Soc, 23 (1980); Anne Yarbrough, 'Geographical and social origins of Bristol apprentices 1542–1565', *Tr B & G Arch Soc*, 98 (1980), 113–29.

72 *The Babees Book*, ed. F. J. Furnivall, EETS, 32 (1868), 13ff.

73 P. Laslett, 'Mean household size in England'; the period covered was 1574–1821.

74 P. Laslett, 'Clayworth and Cogenhoe'.

75 P. Laslett, 'Mean household size in England'.

76 J. Hajnal, 'European marriage patterns in perspective', *Population in History*, ed. D. V. Glass and D. E. C. Eversley, 1965, 101–43.

77 J. Hajnal, 'Age at marriage and proportions marrying', *Pop St*, 7 (1953), 111–36.

78 J. Hajnal, 'European marriage patterns'.

79 J. B. Post, 'Ages at menarche and menopause: some medieval authorities', *Pop St*, 35 (1971), 83–7.

80 P. Laslett, 'Ages at sexual maturity in Europe since the Middle Ages', *Family Life and Illicit Love*, 214–32.

81 P. Laslett, 'Long-term trends in bastardy in England'.

82 Keith Thomas, *Religion and the Decline of Magic*, Harmondsworth, 1973, 223.

83 H. G. Dick, 'Students of physic and astrology', *Jnl Hist Med*, 1 (1946), 300–15, 419–33.

84 E. A. Wrigley, 'Family limitation in pre-industrial England', *EcHR*, 19 (1966), 82–109.

85 Confirmed from other sources, including L. Henry, *Anciennes familles genevoises*, Paris, 1956.

86 *Before the Bawdy Court*, no. 400.

87 E. A. Wrigley, *Population and History*, London, 1969, 87.

88 P. Laslett, 'Parental deprivation in the past', *Family Life and Illicit Love*, 106–73.

89 But see P. Laslett, 'The history of aging and the aged', *Family Life and Illicit Love*, 174–213.

90 'Elderly' is taken to imply those over 60; 'aged' those over 65.

91 W. K. Jordan, *Philanthropy in England 1480–1660*, London, 1959.

92 W. K. Jordan, *The Charities of Rural England 1480–1660*, London, 1961, 25–6.

93 *Essex Wills*, vol. III, 1571–7, ed. F. G. Emmison, New Eng Hist Gen Soc (1986), x.

94 *Lincoln Wills Registered in the District Probate Registry at Lincoln*, vol. II, 1505–30, ed. C. W. Foster, Lincs Rec Soc, 10 (1914), 101–2.

95 *Lincoln Wills*, vol. III, Lincs Rec Soc, 24 (1930), 79.

96 Barbara Todd, 'Freebench and free enterprise: widows and their property in two Berkshire villages', *English Rural Society*, ed. J. Chartres and D. Hey, Cambridge, 1990, 175–200; B. A. Holderness, 'Widows in pre-industrial society: an essay upon their economic functions', *Land, Kinship and Life-Cycle*, ed. R. M. Smith, Cambridge, 1984, 423–42.

97 B. A. Holderness, 'Widows in pre-industrial society'.

98 F. G. Emmison, *Elizabethan Life: Wills of Essex Gentry and Yeomen*, Chelmsford, 1980.

99 *Lincoln Wills*, vol. II, Lincs Rec Soc, 10 (1914), 149.

100 ibid., 171.

101 *Essex Wills*, vol. I, 1558–65, no. 745.

102 ibid., no. 790.

103 *Elizabethan Wills of South-west Essex*, 102.

104 *Essex Wills*, vol. I, nos. 131, 873.

105 *Essex Wills*, vol. III, no. 318.

106 *Lincoln Wills*, vol. II, 102–3.

107 *Lincoln Wills*, vol. III, 146.

108 *Somerset Medieval Wills, 1501–1530*, ed. F. W. Weaver, Som Rec Soc, 19 (1903), 87.

109 *A Collection of Lancashire and Cheshire Wills, 1301–1752*, ed. W. Fergusson Irvine, Lancs Chesh Rec Soc, 30 (1896), 29.

110 *Somerset Medieval Wills, 1383–1500*, Som Rec Soc, 16 (1901), 250.

111 ibid., 401.

112 ibid., 148.

113 A trental was one mass per day for thirty days.

114 *Somerset Medieval Wills, 1383–1500*, 15.

115 ibid., 128.

116 *Lincoln Wills*, vol. II, 89.

117 *London Consistory Court Wills 1492–1547*, ed. Ida Darlington, Lond Rec Soc, 3 (1967), 31.

118 *Somerset Medieval Wills 1383–1500*, 145.

119 *Collection of Lancashire and Cheshire Wills 1301–1752*, 153.

120 *Essex Wills*, vol. III, 276.

121 A. Macfarlane, *Origins of English Individualism*, 19.

122 ibid., 80.

123 ibid., 163.

124 *Carte Nativorum*, Northants Rec Soc, 20 (1960).

125 Anne De Windt, 'A peasant land market and its participants: King's Ripton 1280–1400', *Midl Hist*, 4 (1977–80), 142–59.

126 Eugen Weber, *Peasants into Frenchmen*, London, 1979, *passim*.

127 F. Pollock and F. W. Maitland, *The History of English Law*, Cambridge, 1895, vol. I, 351–8.

128 On copyhold see Lord Ernle, *English Farming Past and Present*, London, edn of 1961, 69–70; F. Pollock and F. W. Maitland, *The History of English Law*, vol. I, 351–2.

129 F. W. Maitland, *Constitutional History of England*, Cambridge, 1908, 204–5.

130 J. Ambrose Raftis, *Tenure and Mobility*, Toronto, 1964, 202.

131 H. J. Habakkuk, 'La disparition du paysan anglais', *Ann ESC*, 20 (1965), 649–63.

132 Midland Campbell, *The English Yeoman*, New Haven, CT, 1942, 105–55.

133 A. Macfarlane, *The Family Life of Ralph Josselin*, Cambridge, 1970, 54 and *passim*.

134 M. Spufford, 'Peasant inheritance customs'.

135 M. Spufford, *Contrasting Communities*.

136 M. Spufford, 'Peasant inheritance customs'.

137 The death of the last 'life' constituted the pivotal event in Thomas Hardy's *The Woodlanders*.

138 *Progress Notes of Warden Woodward for the Wiltshire Estates of New College, Oxford*, ed. R. L. Rickard, Wilts Rec Soc, 13 (1957), 18, 39.

139 F. Pollock and F. W. Maitland, *History of English Law*, vol. I, 252–82.

140 J. Goody, 'Introduction', *Family and Inheritance: Rural Society in Western Europe, 1200–1800*, ed. J. Goody, J. Thirsk and E. P. Thompson, Cambridge, 1976, 1–9.

141 Joan Thirsk, 'Industry in the countryside', *Essays in the Economic and Social History of Tudor and Stuart England*, ed. F. J. Fisher, Cambridge, 1961, 70–88.

142 H. E. Hallam, 'The new lands of Elloe', Occ Pap Loc Hist 6, Leicester, 1954, 39–42.

143 J. Thirsk, 'The farming regions of England', *Agr Hist Eng Wales*, vol. IV, 1500–1640, Cambridge, 1967, 1–112 (p. 11).

144 M. Spufford, 'Peasant inheritance customs'.

145 ibid., 159.

146 Bracton, *De Legibus*, RS, 221.

147 Inheritance by a single member of the family, not necessarily the eldest son.

148 C. C. Homans, 'The rural sociology of medieval England', *P & P*, no. 4 (1953), 32–43.

149 J. Thirsk, 'The farming regions of England', 11, 71.

150 G. H. Rendall, *Denham in History*, Colchester 1937, 33–6.

151 Conrad M. Arensberg and S. T. Kimball, *Family and Community in Ireland*, 2nd edn, Cambridge, MA, 1968, 1968, 77–86.

152 J. Thirsk, 'The family', *P & P*, no. 27 (1964), 116–22.

153 Georges Duby, *La Société aux XIe et XIIe siècles dans la région Maconnais*, Paris, 1953, *passim*.

154 K. Thomas, *Religion and the Decline of Magic*, 222–3.

155 *Oxfordshire Archaeological Society Report*, 70 (1925), 95.

156 Barbara A. Kellum, 'Infanticide in England in the later Middle Ages', *Hist Childh Qu*, 1 (1973–4), 367–88.

157 P. Ariès, *Centuries of Childhood*, London, 1962–71.

158 N. J. G. Pounds, 'Barton farming in eighteenth-century Cornwall', *Jl Roy Hist Cornw*, 71 pt 1 (1973), 55–75.

159 P. Ariès, *Centuries of Childhood*, 340–43.

160 J. H. Plumb, 'The new world of children in eighteenth-century England', *P & P*, no. 67 (1975), 64–93.

161 The author found a poor law document of about 1800 in the Lostwithiel parish records authenticated by the local schoolmaster with his mark.

162 *Blundell's Diary*, ed. T. Ellison Gibson, Liverpool, 1895, 199.

163 E. P. Thompson, '"Rough music": le charivari anglais', *Ann ESC*, 27 (1972), 285–315; the skimmington ride also figures prominently in Thomas Hardy's *The Mayor of Casterbridge*.

164 *The Autobiography of Sir John Bramston*, Camd Soc (1845), 111.

165 J. Thirsk, 'The family'.

166 Robert Mandrou, *Introduction à la France moderne*, Paris, 1961, 42.

167 Natalie Zemon Davis, 'Printing and the people', *Society and Culture in Early Modern France*, London, 1975, 189–226; also 'Proverbial wisdom and popular errors', ibid., 227–67.

168 Quoted in Lawrence Stone, *The Family, Sex and Marriage in England 1500–1800*.

10 THE CULTURE OF CITIES

1 Susan Reynolds, *An Introduction to the History of English Medieval Towns*, Oxford, 1977, esp. chapters 1 and 2.

2 Maurice Beresford, *New Towns of the Middle Ages*, London, 1967; Alan Everitt, 'The Banburys of England', *Urb Hist Ybk* 1974, 28–38.

3 ibid., 116, 244.

4 W. G. Hoskins, *Devon: A New Survey of England*, London, 1954, 58–9.

5 W. G. Hoskins, 'The wealth of medieval Devon', *Devonshire Studies*, ed. W. G. Hoskins and H. P. R. Finberg, London, 1952, 212–49; also in Hoskins, *Old Devon*, Newton Abbot, 1966, 159–94.

6 John Alexander, 'The basic–nonbasic concept of urban economic functions', *Econ Geog*, 30 (1954), 246–61.

7 H. C. Darby, *Domesday England*, Cambridge, 1977, 289–95.

8 ibid., Appendix 16. The size of London must remain problematic.

9 Based on J. C. Russell, *British Medieval Population*, Albuquerque, NM, 1948, 140–6.

10 R. B. Dobson, 'Urban decline in late medieval England', *Tr RHS*, 5th ser., 27 (1977), 1–22; *Crisis and Order in English Towns 1500–1700*, ed. P. Clark and P. Slack, London, 1972, esp. editors' 'Introduction', 1–56.

11 The recorded population of England and Wales in 1801 was 8,893,000. That of Scotland was 1,608,000. No census was held in Ireland until 1821.

12 N. J. G. Pounds, 'The social structure of Lostwithiel in the early nineteenth century', *Reactions to Social and Economic Change 1750–1939*, ed. W. Minchinton, Ex Pap Econ Hist, 12 (1979), 30–48.

13 Anne Yarborough, 'Geographical and social origins of Bristol apprentices 1542–1565', *Tr B & G Arch Soc*, 98 (1980), 113–29; *Calendar of the Bristol Apprentice Book 1532–1565*, pt 1, ed. D. Hollis, Brist Rec Soc, 14 (1949); pt 2, ed. Elizabeth Ralph and Nora M. Hardwick, Brist Rec Soc, 33 (1980).

14 Louis Wirth, 'The urban society and civilization', *Am Jl Soc*, 45 (1940), 743–55. But see also Peter Burke, 'Some reflections on the pre-industrial city', *Urb Hist Ybk*, 1975, 13–21.

15 Mack Walker, *The German Home Towns: Community, State and General Estate*, Ithaca, NY, 1971, *passim*.

16 Rhoads Murphey, 'The city as a center of change', *Ann Ass Am Geog*, 44 (1954), 349–62.

17 *Ramsey Abbey Cartulary*, RS, 1, 145; 2, 264; F. W. Maitland, *Township and Borough*, Cambridge, 1868, 174.

18 RCHM, *City of Cambridge*, HMSO, 1959, vol. II, 255–7.

19 For example, St Mary's, Tanner Street, Winchester; see M. Biddle, 'Excavations at Winchester, 1971: tenth and final interim report', *Ant Jl*, 55 (1975), 295–337; Derek Keene, *Survey of Medieval Winchester*, Winchester Studies, vol. II, pt 1, Oxford, 1985.

20 Susan Brigden, 'Tithe controversy in Reformation London', *Jl Eccles Hist*, 32 (1981), 285–301.

21 Norman P. Tanner, *The Church in Late Medieval Norwich 1370–1532*, Pontifical Institute of Medieval Studies, Toronto, Studies and Texts, 66, 1984; C. N. L. Brooke and Gillian Keir, *London 800–1216: The Shaping of a City*, London, 1975.

22 D. Keene, *Survey of Medieval Winchester*, vol. II, pt 1, Oxford, 1985, 23.

23 *York Civic Records*, vol. II, ed. Angelo Raine, Yks Arch Soc Rec Ser, 103 (1941), 130–1.

24 H. C. Coote, 'The English gild of knights and their socn', *Tr L & M Arch Soc*, 5 (1881), 477–93.

25 C. Gross, *The Guild Merchant*, London, 1890.

26 *Liber Custumarum*, ed. H. T. Riley, 1860.

27 E. Lipson, *The Economic History of England: The Middle Ages*, London, 1959, 267ff.

28 ibid., 266.

29 *English Gilds: Original Ordinances of more than One Hundred Early English Gilds*, ed. Toulmin Smith, EETS 1870; esp. 'Introduction' by Lujo Brentano.

30 G. Unwin, *The Gilds and Companies of London*, London, 1908, Appendix A, 370–1.

31 ibid., 371.

32 *Réglemens sur les arts et métiers de Paris rédigés au XIIIe siècle et connus sous le nom du Livre d'Étienne Boileau*, ed. G.-B. Depping, Col docts Inéd, 1837.

33 *English Gilds*, lxxxvi.

34 ibid., xc.

35 Robert Redfield, *The Little Community*, Chicago, 1955.

36 A. de Tocqueville, *Democracy in America*, ed. H. Commager, Oxford, 1946, 56.

37 Louis Chevalier, *Labouring Classes and Dangerous Classes*, London, 1973.

38 P. Clark and P. Slack, *Crisis and Order in English Towns*, 6.

39 A. D. Dyer, *The City of Worcester in the Sixteenth Century*, Leicester, 1973.

40 For the economic consequences of a *crise de subsistence* see H. van Werveke, 'La famine de l'an 1316 en Flandres et les régions voisines', *Rv Nord*, 41 (1959), 5–14.

41 Aristophanes, *Acharnians*, lines 33–7.

42 This is the title – *Ziemia Obiecana* – of a novel by the Polish author, Władisław Reymont, showing how impoverished peasants migrated to Łódź.

43 Gideon Sjoberg, *The Preindustrial City Past and Present*, New York, 1960, 109.

44 ibid., 133–77. The author is here looking for a term which would be equally applicable to the non-western city.

45 PRO, SC 12/2/27; a different list is printed in *The Caption of Seisin of the Duchy of Cornwall (1337)*, ed. P. L. Hull, *D & C Rec Soc*, 17 (1971), 36–8.

46 Sir Frances Hill, *Medieval Lincoln*, Cambridge, 1948, 295.

47 G. Unwin, *Gilds and Companies of London*, 72–81.

48 ibid., 85–7.

49 *Coventry Apprentices and their Masters 1781–1806*, ed. Joan Lane, Pub Dugd Soc, 33 (1983), xi.

50 E. Martin, 'La population de Vannes au début et à la fin du XVIIIe siècle', *Ann Bret*, 35 (1921–3), 610–26; also O. H. Hufton, *Bayeux in the Late Eighteenth Century*, Oxford, 1967, 58.

51 Parl Pap, 1842, reprinted as *Report on the Sanitary Conditions of the Labouring Poor by Edwin Chadwick, 1842*, ed. M. W. Flinn, Edinburgh, 1965.

52 J. C. Russell, *British Medieval Population*, 283–306.

53 ibid., 142–3.

54 Roger Finlay and Beatrice Shearer, 'Population growth and suburban expansion', *London 1500–1700*, ed. A. L. Beier and Roger Finlay, London, 1986, 37–59.

55 E. A. Wrigley, 'A simple model of London's importance in changing English society and economy 1650–1750', *P & P*, no. 37 (1967), 44–70.

56 P. Clark and P. Slack, *English Towns in Transition 1500–1700*, Oxford, 1976, 82–96.

57 B. R. Mitchell, *Abstract of British Statistics*, Cambridge, 1962, 24–7.

58 *Yorkshire Inquisitions*, vol. II, ed. William Brown, Yks Arch Soc Rec Ser, 23 (1897), no. 10, 9–11.

59 D. J. Keene, 'Suburban growth', *The Plans and Topography of Medieval Towns in England and Wales*, ed. M. W. Barley, CBA Res Rept, 14 (1976), 71–82.

60 *London Assize of Nuisance, 1301–1431*, ed. H. M. Chew and William Kellaway, Lond Rec Soc, 10 (1973), nos. 2, 19, 26, 183; *The London Eyre of 1244*, ed. H. M. Chew and M. Weinbaum, Lond Rec Soc, 6 (1970), no. 418.

61 *London Assize of Nuisance*, nos. 206, 234.

62 *London Eyre of 1234*, nos. 362, 364, 413, 445, 480.

63 R. Hunnisett, *The Medieval Coroner*, Cambridge, 1961.

64 C. C. Knowles and P. H. Pitt, *The History of Building Regulation in London 1189–1972*, London, 1972, 66–7.

65 *Select Rentals and Accounts of Medieval Hull, 1293–1528*, ed. Rosemary Horrox, Yks Arch Soc Rec Ser, 141 (1981), 11.

66 E. and P. Rutledge, 'King's Lynn and Great Yarmouth: two thirteenth-century surveys', *Norf Arch*, 37 (1978), 92–114.

67 *London Assize of Nuisance*, nos. 483, 547.

68 ibid., no. 617.

69 ibid., Introduction, xx–xxi.

70 Anthony Quiney, *The Traditional Buildings of England*, London, 1990, 127–32.

71 *London Assize of Nuisance*, no. 617.

72 D. Portman, *Exeter Houses 1400–1700*, Exeter, 1966, 4.

73 ibid., 2–5.

74 D. Portman, *Exeter Houses*, Exeter, 1966, 3.

75 H. M. Colvin, 'Domestic architecture and town planning', *Medieval England*, ed. A. L. Poole, Oxford, 1958, vol. I, 37–97.

76 F. Barlow, M. Biddle *et al.*, *Winchester in the Early Middle Ages*, Winch St, 1, (1976), 345.

77 L. F. Salzman, *Building in England*, Oxford, 1952, 75.

78 R. H. Gretton, *The Burford Records: A Study in Minor Town Government*, Oxford, 1920, 171–2.

79 F. Barlow *et al.*, *Winchester in the Early Middle Ages*, 345.

80 *London Viewers and their Certificates 1508–1558*, ed. J. S. Loengard, Lond Rec Soc, 26 (1989), no. 390. This would probably have been Reigate stone, obtained from the Greensand to the south of London.

81 A. Clifton-Taylor, *The Pattern of English Building*, London, 1972, 103–5.

82 E. M. Jope and G. C. Dunning, 'The use of blue slate for roofing in medieval England', *Ant Jl* 34 (1954), 209–17.

83 Colin Platt and R. Coleman-Smith, *Excavations in Medieval Southampton 1953–1969*, Leicester, 1975, vol. I, 25.

84 E. M. Jope and G. C. Dunning, 'The use of blue slate'.

85 J. A. Wright, *Brick Building in England*, London, 1972, 27.

86 R. A. Skelton, 'Tudor plans in John Speed's theatre', *Arch Jl*, 108 (1951), 109–20.

87 *London Assize of Nuisance*, xxiv–xxv.

88 ibid., no. 2, p. 1.

89 ibid., no. 183, p. 38.

90 M. M. Rix and G. C. Dunning, 'Excavation of a medieval garderobe in Snargate Street, Dover, in 1945', *Arch Ael*, 69 (1955), 132–58.

91 *London Assize of Nuisance*, no. 214, p. 45.

92 ibid., no. 304, p. 70.

93 ibid., no. 31.

94 ibid., no. 204.

95 ibid., no. 581.

96 ibid., no. 92.

97 *De Antiquis Legibus Liber*, ed. T. Stapleton, Camd Soc, 34 (1846), 206–11.

98 *London Assize of Nuisance*, no. 502.

99 ibid., no. 30.

100 ibid., no. 77.

101 ibid., no. 325.

102 ibid., no. 340.

103 *London Viewers and their Certificates*, xi–xxi.

104 T. W. Reddaway, *The Rebuilding of London after the Great Fire*, London, 1940, 31–9.

105 *London Viewers and their Certificates*, 288.

106 ibid., 190.

107 ibid., 310.

108 ibid., 114.

109 ibid., 114.

110 ibid., 181.

111 ibid., lix.

112 Lawrence Wright, *Clean and Decent: The History of the Bath and Loo*, London, 1980, 18–24.

113 L. F. Salzman, *Building in England*, 268–72.

114 L. E. W. O. Fullbrook-Leggatt, 'Water supplies of the Abbey of St Peter and the Priory [sic] of the Greyfriars, Gloucester, from Robinswood Hill', *Tr B & G Arch Soc*, 87 (1968), 111–18.

115 R. Willis and J. W. Clark, *The Architectural History of the University of Cambridge*, Cambridge, 1886, vol. II, 427–30.

116 Arthur Gray, *The Town of Cambridge: A History*, Cambridge, 1925, 75.

117 *Assize of Nuisance*, no. 633.

118 *Ancient Petitions relating to Northumberland*, ed. C. M. Fraser, Surt Soc, 176 (1961), 108–10.

119 *Northern Petitions Illustrative of Life in Berwick, Cumbria and Durham in the Fourteenth Century*, ed. C. M. Fraser, Surt Soc, 194 (1981), 107.

120 *York Memorandum Book*, pt 2 (1388–1493), ed. Maud Sellers, Surt Soc, 125 (1914), 247.

121 *The Sanitary Condition of the Labouring Poor*, Parl Pap 1842; reprinted (ed. M. W. Feinn), Edinburgh, 1965, 141–2.

122 ibid., 146.

123 *John Snow on Cholera, Being a Reprint of Two Papers by John Snow, M.D.* New York edn, 1936, esp. p. 45.

124 *Records of the City of Norwich*, ed. W. Hudson and J. C. Tingey, London, 1906, vol. I, 386.

125 G. T. Salusbury-Jones, *Street Life in Medieval England*, Oxford, 1938, 35.

126 G. Unwin, *The Gilds and Companies of London*, 342.

127 R. J. Forbes, 'Roads, to *c.* 1900', *Hist Tech*, 4 (1958), 520–47.

128 Rupert H. Morris, *Chester in the Plantagenet and Tudor Reigns*, printed privately, n.d.; London Letter Books, D, 17.

129 C. Welch, *History of the Worshipful Company of Paviors of the City of London*, London, 1909; Calendar of London Letter Books, D, 17127; G. T. Salusbury-Jones, *Street Life in Medieval England*, 19.

130 *Cal Pat R*, 1284; *Public Works in Medieval Law*, ed. C. T. Flower, Seld Soc, 2 vols., 1915, 1923.

131 R. J. Forbes, 'Roads to *c.* 1900'.

132 *Cal Close R*, 1330–3, 610.

133 *Cal Close R*, 1334–7, 697.

134 E. T. Meyer, 'Boroughs', *The English Government at Work, 1327–1336*, ed. J. F. Willard, W. A. Morris and W. H. Dunham, vol. III, Med Acad Am, 1950, 105–411.

135 Charles Coulson, 'Hierarchism in conventional architecture', *Med Arch*, 26 (1982), 69–100.

136 Jacques le Goff, 'Ordres mendiants et urbanisation dans la France médiévale', *Ann ESC*, 25 (1970), 924–46.

137 William Langland, who appears to have been a priest, cherished an intense dislike of the friars.

138 *Peterborough Local Administration: Churchwardens' Accounts*, ed. W. T. Mellows, Northants Rec Soc, 9 (1937), xcviii.

139 Hilary L. Turner, *Town Defences in England and Wales*, London, 1970.

140 Peter Borsay, 'The English urban renaissance: the development of provincial urban culture', *Soc Hist*, no. 5 (1977), 581–603.

141 Penelope Corfield, 'A provincial capital in the late seventeenth century: the case of Norwich', *Crisis and Order in English Towns*, 263–310.

142 David Cannadine, 'The transformation of civic ritual in modern Britain: the Colchester oyster feast', *P & P*, no. 94 (1982), 107–30.

143 Alan Everitt, 'Country, county and town: patterns of regional evolution in England', *Tr RHS*, 5th ser., 29 (1979), 79–108: Thomas Burke, *The English Townsman as He Was and Is*, London, 1946, 62–71.

144 Christopher Simon Sykes, *Private Palaces: Life in the Great London Houses*, London, 1985, 18–59; Lawrence Stone, 'The residential development of the west end of London in the seventeenth century', *After the Reformation: Essays in Honour of J. H. Hexter*, ed. B. C. Malament, Manchester, 1980, 167–212.

11 THE FOUNDATIONS OF POPULAR CULTURE

1 Bernard Capp, *English Almanacs 1500–1800*, Ithaca, NY, 1979, 15.

2 Quoted in B. Capp, *English Almanacs*, 17.

3 Charles-Edward Amory Winslow, *The Conquest of Epidemic Disease: A Chapter in the History of Ideas*, Princeton, NJ, 1943.

4 John Selden, *Table Talk*, ed. S. H. Reynolds, Oxford, 1892, 130.

5 Stuart Clark, 'Inversion, misrule and the meaning of witchcraft', *P & P*, no. 87 (May 1980), 98–127.

6 Carolly Erickson, *The Medieval Vision: Essays in History and Perception*, New York, 1976, 27ff.

7 Conrad Arensberg, *The Irish Countryman*, Am Mus Nat Hist, New York, 1968, 174.

8 Keith Thomas, *Religion and the Decline of Magic*, London, 1971.

9 ibid., ch. 8; K. C. White, 'The wise man and his community', *Folk-L*, 15 (1977), 24–35.

10 C. Grant Loomis, *White Magic: An Introduction to the Folklore of Christian Legend*, Med Acad Am, 1948, esp. 3–7.

11 Ronald C. Finucane, *Miracles and Pilgrims: Popular Beliefs in Medieval England*, London, 1977, 25.

12 B. Capp, *English Almanacs*, 20–113.

13 Aron Gurevich, *Medieval Popular Culture: Problems of Belief and Perception*, Cambridge, 1988, 40.

14 *Churchwardens' Accounts of Croscombe, Pilton, Yatton, Tintinhull, Morebath and St Michael's Bath*, ed. Bishop Hobhouse, Som Rec Soc, 4 (1890), 65.

15 A. Gurevich, *Medieval Popular Culture*, 41.

16 Arnold van Gennep, *Manual de folklore français contemporain*, Paris, 1937– , vol. I, pt 3, 833.

17 E. Durkheim, *The Elementary Forms of Religious Life*, tr. J. W. Swan, New York, 1961, 21; E. P. Thompson, 'Patrician society, plebeian culture', *Jl Soc Hist*, 7 (1974), 382–405.

18 A. R. Wright, *British Calendar Customs*, ed. T. E. Lones, Folk Soc, 1938.

19 T. M. Owen, *Welsh Folk Customs*, Welsh Folk Museum, 1974, 28.

20 R. U. Sayce, 'Seasonal bonfires', *Montg Collns*, 50 (1948), 77–91 and 189–208.

21 N. Z. Davies, 'The reason of misrule', *Society and Culture in Early Modern France*, London, 1975, 97–123.

22 T. M. Owen, *Welsh Folk Customs*, 72–87; A. R. Wright, *British Calendar Customs*, vol. I, 70–6.

23 A. R. Wright, *British Calendar Customs*, vol. II, 195–236.

24 C. Pythian-Adams 'Ceremony and the citizen: the communal year at Coventry 1450–1550', *Crisis and Order in English Towns*, ed. P. Clark and P. Slack, London, 1972, 57–85.

25 R. W. Ambler, 'The transformation of harvest celebrations in nineteenth-century Lincolnshire', *Midl Hist*, 3 (1976), 298–306.

26 *Oxford Dictionary of the Christian Church*, *sub* 'All Saints'.

27 *Encycl Brit*, 1962, *sub* 'Hallowe'en'.

28 G. C. Homans, as quoted in T. M. Owen, *Welsh Folk Customs*, 20; Keith Thomas, 'The place of laughter in Tudor and Stuart England', *TLS*, 21 Jan. 1977.

29 John Huizinga, *Homo Ludens: A Study of the Play Element in Culture*, London, 1970, 32.

30 C. Daryll Forde, *Habitat, Economy and Society*, London, 1934, 89–90.

31 Marcel Mauss, *The Gift*, London, 1966, 33–7.

32 Mikhail Bakhtin, *Rabelais and his World*, Cambridge, MA, 1968, 6.

33 N. Z. Davies, 'The reasons of misrule'.

34 S. Clark, 'Inversion, misrule and the meaning of witchcraft'. See also Orrin E. Klapp, 'The fool as a social type', *Am Jl Soc*, 55 (1949–50), 157–62; Enid Welsford, *The Fool: His Literary and Social History*, London, 1935.

35 M. Bakhtin, *Rabelais and his World*, 8–20.

36 Anthony Weir and James Jarman, *Images of Lust*, London, 1986, 10; Ruth Mellinkoff, *The Horned Moses in Medieval Art and Thought*, Berkeley, CA, 1970, esp. 19–27.

37 Robert Muchembled, *Culture populaire et culture des élites dans la France moderne*, Paris, 1978, 117–40.

38 The Book of Enoch, ed. R. H. Charles, Oxford, 1912, caps. civ–cv.

39 Compare Wagner's use of the 'rainbow bridge' at the end of *Das Rheingold*.

40 Quoted in E. Clive Rouse, *Discovering Wall Paintings*, 4th edn. Shire Publications, 1991, 58.

41 *The Times of London*, 19 Sept. 1989.

42 C. G. Jung, 'Approaching the Unconscious', *Man and his Symbols*, ed. C. G. Jung, London, 1964, 18–103.

43 A. J. Gurevich, *Categories of Medieval Culture*, London, 1985, 44–6.

44 Zofia Ameisenowa, 'Animal-headed gods, evangelists, saints and righteous men', *Jl Wbg/Court Inst*, 12 (1949), 21–45; Miranda Green, 'Theriomorphism and the role of divine animals in Romano-British cult art', BAR, 41, pt 2 (1977), 297–326.

45 A. J. Gurevich, *Categories of Medieval Culture*, 53.

46 Marija Gimbutas, *The Balts*, London, 1963, 74–9.

47 N. Smedley and E. Owles, 'A face-mould from the Romano-British kiln site at Homersfield', *Proc Suff Inst Arch*, 30 (1964–6), 210–12.

48 A. Ross, *The Pagan Celts*, London, 1986, 121–2.

49 J. V. S. Megaw, *Art of the European Iron Age*, Bath, 1970, 20.

50 H. E. Jean le Patourel, 'Hallgate, Doncaster, and the incidence of face-jugs with beards', *Med Arch*, 10 (1966), 160–4.

51 It derived its name from the late sixteenth-century Cardinal Bellarmine, who became a figure of fun in Protestant England.

52 M. R. Holmes, 'The so-called "Bellarmine" mask on imported Rhenish stoneware', *Ant Jl*, 31 (1951), 173–9. art in Antiquity, 1989.

53 N. Smedley and E. Owles, 'More Suffolk witch bottles', *Proc Suff Inst Arch*, 30 (1967), 88–93.

54 Ralph Merrifield, *The Archaeology of Ritual and Magic*, London, 1987, 159–75.

55 Richard Bernheimer, *Wild Men in the Middle Ages*, Cambridge, MA, 1952, 2; G. C. Druce, 'Some abnormal and composite human forms in English church architecture', *Arch Jl*, 72 (1915), 135–86; Ronald Sheridan and Anne Ross, *Grotesques and Gargoyles: Paganism in the Medieval Church*, Newton Abbot, 1975, 31–6; H. D. Ellis, 'The wodewose in East Anglian church decoration', *Proc Suff Inst Arch*, 14 (1912), 287–93.

56 R. Bernheimer, *Wild Men in the Middle Ages*, 3–4.

57 Hayden White, 'The wild man within', *Forms of Wildness*, ed. E. Dudley and M. E. Novak, Pittsburgh, PA, 1972, 2–38 (excellent on the philosophical concepts involved).

58 R. Bernheimer, *Wild Men in the Middle Ages*, 102–4.

59 For an exhaustive study of the wodewose see William Anderson, *Green Man: The Archetype of our Oneness with the Earth*, London, 1990.

60 Francis Bond, *Fonts and Font Covers*, London, 1908, 255.

61 H. D. Ellis, 'The wodewose in East Anglian church decoration'.

62 Quoted in R. Bernheimer, *Wild Men in the Middle Ages*, 71.

63 Miranda Green, *Symbol and Image in Celtic Religous Art*, London, 1989, 152–3.

64 Revelations of St John the Divine 22: 1–2.

65 Roger Cook, *The Tree of Life*, London, 1974, 9.

66 A. Bellows, *The Poetic Edda*, Wotan's staff, in *The Ring*, it will be remembered, was hewn from the 'World Ash Tree'.

67 R. Cook, *The Tree of Life*, 13.

68 For a collection of tree rituals, see Sir James Frazer, *The Golden Bough*, abridged edn, London, 1932, 120–35.

69 Philip Stubbes, *Anatomie of Abuses*, London, 1583.

70 In *The Ring*, Freia tends the apple-tree whose lifegiving fruit sustains the gods.

71 M. R. Bennet, 'The legend of the green tree and the dry', *Arch Jl*, 83 (1926), 21–32.

72 Ellen Ettlinger, 'Folklore in Oxfordshire churches', *Folk-L*, 73 (1962), 160–77.

73 G. Zarnecki, *Romanesque Lincoln: The Sculpture of the Cathedral*, Lincoln, 1988, 93–6. The slab lies under the easternmost arch of the north nave arcade; see J. Carter, *Specimens of Ancient Sculpture and Painting*, London, 1784.

74 R. Sheridan and A. Ross, *Grotesques and Gargoyles*, 39–43.

75 G. R. Lewis, *Illustrations of Kilpeck Church*, London, 1842; A. Weir and J. Jerman, *Images of Lust*, London, 1986, 124.

76 Arnold van Gennep, *The Rites of Passage*, London, 1970, 3.

77 J. D. C. Fisher, *Christian Initiation: Baptism in the Medieval West*, Alc Club Collns, 47, 1965.

78 Mircea Eliade, *Birth and Rebirth*, New York, 1958, ix–xii.

79 *Oxford Dictionary of the Christian Church*, *sub* 'Confirmation'.

80 Barbara Hanawalt, *The Ties that Bound*, Oxford, 1986, 197.

81 Edward Shorter, *The Making of the Modern Family*, New York, 1975.

82 P. E. H. Hair, 'Bridal pregnancy in earlier rural England further examined', *Pop St*, 24 (1970), 59–70.

83 B. Hanawalt, *The Ties that Bound*, 193.

84 *Churchwardens' Accounts of Croscombe*, etc.

85 Christopher Hill, 'The rusty sword of the church', *Society and Puritanism in Pre-Revolutionary England*, London, 1964, 354–81.

86 Peter Laslett, 'Clayworth and Cogenhoe', *Family Life and Illicit Love in Earlier Generations*, Cambridge, 1977, 50–101.

87 P. E. H. Hair, 'Bridal pregnancy in earlier rural England further examined'.

88 M. M. Sheehan, 'The formation and stability of marriage in fourteenth-century England: evidence of an Ely register', *Med St*, 33 (1971), 228–63.

89 *The Register of John Chandler Dean of Salisbury, 1404–17*, ed. T. C. B. Timmins, Wilts Arch Soc Rec Br, 39 (1983), 94.

90 Chaucer, *Canterbury Tales*, 'Prologue', line 460.

90 *Episcopal Visitation Book for the Archdeaconry of Buckingham, 1662*, ed. E. R. C. Brinkworth, Bucks Rec, 7 (1947), 10.

92 Peter Laslett, 'The history of aging and the aged', *Family Life and Illicit Love*, 174–213.

93 *Crown Pleas of the Wiltshire Eyre, 1249*, ed. C. A. F. Meekings, Wilts Arch Soc Rec Br, (1960), 150.

94 So called from its opening words *Dirige Dominus Deus meus in conspectu tuo viam meam.*

95 F. E. Warren, 'Gild of S. Peter in Bardwell', *Proc Suff Inst Arch*, 11 (1903), 81–133.

96 *The Fifty Earliest English Wills in the Court of Probate 1387–1439*, ed. F. J. Furnivall, EETS, 1882, 15.

97 P. A. Rahtz, 'The archaeology of the churchyard', *The Archaeological Study of Churches*, ed. P. Addyman and R. Morris, CBA Res Rept 13, 1976.

98 *The Fifty Earliest English Wills in the Court of Probate 1387–1439*, 14–16.

99 M. Eliade, *Birth and Rebirth*, x–xii.

100 E. R. Leach, *Rethinking Anthropology*, LSE Mon Soc Anthr, 22, 1961, 133–6.

101 James Carson Webster, *The Labors of the Months in Antique and Medieval Art*, Princeton, NJ, 1938.

102 The Census of 1841 asked only for age within ten years. When in 1851 the precise age was asked, the answer was not infrequently prefaced with 'about'.

103 Tina Jolas and Françoise Zonabend, 'Tillers of the fields and woodspeople', *Rural Society in France*, ed. R. Forster and O. Ranum, Baltimore, MD, 1977, 126–51; trans from *Ann ESC*, 28 (1973), 285–305.

104 Chaucer, *Canterbury Tales*, 'Prologue', lines 51–4.

105 E. L. Eisenstein, *The Printing Revolution in Early Modern Europe*, Cambridge, 1983, 6ff.

106 Robert Redford, *The Little Community*, Chicago, 1955, 3–20; Redford, *Peasant Society and Culture*, Chicago, 1956, 71–2.

107 Christopher Kitching, 'Church and chapelry in sixteenth-century England', *The Church in Town and Countryside*, ed. D. Baker, St Ch Hist, 16 (1979), 279–90.

108 The title is derived from R. Muchembled, *Culture populaire et culture des élites dans la France moderne*. See also *Kultura elitarna a kultura masowa w Polsce późnego Średniowiecza*, ed. Bronisław Geremek, Warsaw, 1978.

109 T. Hobbes, *Leviathan*, IV, 47.

110 A. Gurevich, *Medieval Popular Culture*, xv.

111 Jacques le Goff, 'Culture cléricale et traditions folkloriques dans la civilisation mérovingiennne, *Ann ESC*, 22 (1967), 780–91.

112 Quoted in Wilfred Bonser, 'Survivals of paganism in Anglo-Saxon England', *Tr Birm Ach Soc*, 56 (1932), 37–70.

113 Peter Burke, *Popular Culture in Early Modern Europe*, London, 1978, 3–32.

114 R. Muchembled, *Culture populaire et culture des élites*, 117.

115 David Cressy, *Literacy and the Social Order: Reading and Writing in Tudor and Stuart England*, Cambridge, 1980, 3–6.

116 John Bossy, 'The Counter-Reformation and the people of Catholic Europe', *P & P*, no. 47 (1970), 51–70; B. Baranowski, 'Les caractères spécifiques de la civilisation populaire polonaise des XVIIe–XVIIIe siècles', *Eth Slav*, 8–9 (1976–7), 37–44.

117 *West Riding Sessions Records*, vol. II, ed. John Lister, Yks Arch Soc Rec Ser, 53 (1915), xviff.

118 Christopher Hill, *The World Turned Upside-Down*, London, 1972, 31; this book is invaluable on Puritan *mentalité* during this period.

119 Terry Castle, *Masquerade and Civilization*, London, 1986, 5–6.
120 ibid., 4.
121 J. Obrebski and B. and J. Halpern, *The Changing Peasantry of Eastern Europe*, Cambridge, MA, 1976, 27.
122 G. Duby, 'The diffusion of cultural patterns in feudal society', *P & P*, no. 39 (April 1968), 3–10.

12 CONCLUSION: THE END OF TRADITIONAL CULTURE

1 J. H. Plumb, 'The acceptance of modernity', *The Birth of a Consumer Society*, ed. N. McKendrick, J. Brewer and J. H. Plumb, London, 1983, 316–34.
2 Colin Renfrew, *Approaches to Social Archaeology*, Edinburgh, 1984, 274.
3 Thomas Hardy, *Tess of the Durbervilles*, chapter 2.
4 Peter Burke, *Popular Culture in Early Modern Europe*, London, 1978, 1–22; see also N. McKendrick, J. Brewer and J. H. Plumb, *The Birth of a Consumer Society*, London, 1983, 1–13.
5 E. H. Phelps-Brown and Sheila V. Hopkins, 'Seven centuries of consumables, compared with builders' wage-rates', *Econ*, 23 (1955), 296–314.
6 Andrew Boorde, *A Dyetary of Helth*, ed. F. J. Furnivall, EETS 1870, 246–7.
7 Asa Briggs, *Victorian Things*, London, 1988.
8 Peter Burke, 'The "discovery" of popular culture', *People's History and Socialist Theory*, ed. Raphael Samuel, Hist Wkshp Ser, London, 1981, 216–26.
9 P. Burke, *Popular Culture in Early Modern Europe*, 1–22.
10 Jeremy Bentham, 'Utilitarianism', *Collected Works of Jeremy Bentham*, ed. A. Goldworth, vol. III, London, 198, 285–318, esp.§6.
11 Asa Briggs, *Victorian Things*, 53–79.
12 Quoted in M. A. Gismondi, 'The gift of theory: a critique of the *Histoire des mentalités*', *Soc Hist*, 10 (1985), 211–30.
13 James Obelkevich, *Religion and the People 800–1700*, Chapel Hill, NC, 1979, 5–6.
14 Keith Thomas, *Religion and the Decline of Magic*, London, 1971, 786.
15 J. Obelkevich, *Religion and Rural Society: South Lindsey 1825–1875*, Oxford, 1976, 280–95 and 307–11.

INDEX